Write Source
Teacher's Edition
Grade 4

Dave Kemper, Patrick Sebranek,
and Verne Meyer

WRITE SOURCE®

GREAT SOURCE EDUCATION GROUP
a division of Houghton Mifflin Company
Wilmington, Massachusetts

Reviewers

Editorial: **Bev Jessen, Michele Order Litant, Patricia Moore**

Production: **Compset**

Technology Connection for *Write Source*

Visit our Web site for additional student models, writing prompts, updates for citing sources, multimedia reports, information about submitting your writing, and more.

The Write Source Web site . . . . thewritesource.com

Introduction

The Writing Process

contents

The Forms of Writing

PARAGRAPH WRITING

DESCRIPTIVE WRITING

NARRATIVE WRITING

Speaking and Writing to Learn

SPEAKING TO LEARN

WRITING TO LEARN

The Basic Elements of Writing

WORKING WITH WORDS

BUILDING EFFECTIVE SENTENCES

A Writer's Resource

Selecting Ideas

Improving Organization

PERMISSION SLIP

Proofreader's Guide

Teacher Resources

An Overview

With the help and feedback of teachers from all over the country, we've taken some of the things you and your students have always loved about *Writer's Express* and made them even better. We've included a variety of new features to help students improve writing and learning skills across the curriculum and on state writing assessments, plus we've added materials to help teachers help all their students become better writers, thinkers, and learners.

Comprehensive

The new *Write Source* provides even more information on the writing process and forms of writing, including

- **integrated six-traits instruction in every writing unit;**
- detailed **coverage of all the key forms of writing,** complete with student notes;
- a wide variety of activities in the pupil edition that **support active instruction and immediate application of writing forms** and related grammar skills;
- guidelines in the Teacher's Edition for **differentiated instruction** to help teachers **meet the needs of English language learners, struggling, and advanced students.**

Student-friendly

The new pupil editions maintain the same personal, reassuring, voice unique to all the *Write Source* materials, plus new features that will truly make it students' favorite writing resource.

- The **friendly voice, colorful artwork,** and **humorous illustrations** capture student interest.
- **Student models** help students understand what is expected in each lesson while color coding and graphic organizers help students understand and remember key points.
- **Integrated writing activities and prompts** help students apply to their writing what they have learned in the lesson.
- **Six-trait checklists in every unit** serve as handy references.

Easy to Implement

Flexible enough to serve as the foundation for a writing-based language arts program or as a supplement to any literature program, *Write Source* offers

- a **clear, logical sequence for instruction,** beginning with the writing process and the six traits and then applying this information to specific genres;
- a **grade-specific pupil edition for every grade**;
- a **wraparound Teacher's Edition** with pupil edition facsimiles, step-by-step lesson plans, assessment information, and support for six-trait instruction.

Strategies for Writing Across the Curriculum

Write Source helps students improve their writing and learning skills in all subject areas with

- **guidelines for cross-curricular writing forms** to build students' writing skills for social studies, science, and math classes;
- information on **important classroom skills including listening, giving oral presentations, taking notes, completing assignments, and taking tests.**

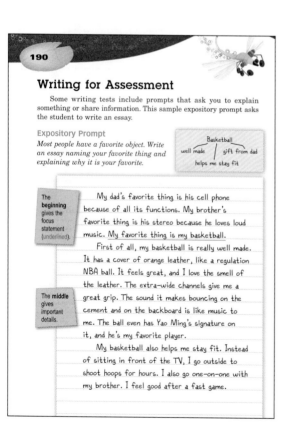

Integrated Grammar Instruction

A variety of **activities for building mechanics, usage, and grammar skills** are included in every unit in the pupil edition as well as in the **Proofreader's Guide, Working with Words,** and **Writing Effective Sentences sections** of the pupil edition. Additional grammar activities are also available in the *SkillsBook, Interactive Writing Skills CD-ROM,* and *Daily Language Workouts.*

Six-Trait Instruction and Test Preparation

Write Source integrates the six traits of effective writing into each lesson and provides benchmark papers and guidelines for helping students perform well on writing assessments. See next page for details.

Six Traits, Assessment, and Test Preparation in *Write Source*

The new *Write Source* program provides detailed guidelines to help students become better writers and revisers using the six traits of effective writing along with a variety of lessons, activities, and guidelines to prepare students for high-stakes writing assessments.

Connections to the Six Traits of Effective Writing

Write Source now incorporates the six traits of writing into the writing process. Each core writing unit integrates six-trait rubrics into the lesson so students have a reference for

- **reviewing the expectations,**
- **assessing their work throughout the writing process,**
- **revising and editing their work.**

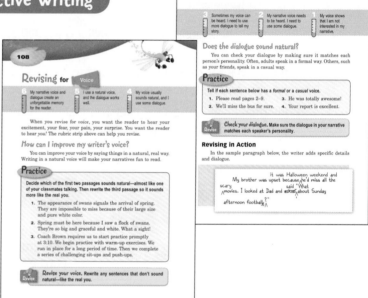

Assessment and Test Preparation

Ideal to prepare students for state assessments, the *Write Source* program

- offers **writing and mechanics, usage, and grammar pretests, post-tests, and quarterly tests** modeled after state assessments;

- focuses on the **core forms of writing most commonly included on writing assessments;**

- includes **writing for tests guidelines** and prompts in each unit;

- provides **genre-specific writing prompts, rubrics, and benchmark papers** for every core form of writing.

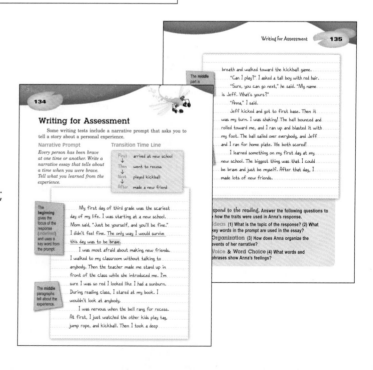

Write Source Research Base

Feature from *Write Source*	Research Base/Citation
Students need frequent writing opportunities to become strong writers. *Write Source* provides daily scaffolded writing activities in every lesson that help students learn to apply writing strategies, write to learn, and prepare for writing assessments.	National Reading Panel (2000). *Teaching children to read: An evidence-based assessment of the scientific research literature on reading and its implications for reading instruction.* Washington, D.C.: National Institute of Child Health and Human Development. U.S. Department of Education Office of the Secretary (2001). *Back to school, moving forward: What No Child Left Behind means for America's communities.* Washington, D.C.
Teaching writing as a process enables students to gain control over the complex task of writing. Furthermore, research suggests that when writing is taught as a process, student achievement increases (e.g., Hillocks, 1986; Holdzkom, Reed, Porter, & Rubin, 1982; Keech & Thomas, 1979).	Hillocks, G., Jr. (1986). Research on written composition: New directions for teaching, Urbana, IL. *ERIC Clearinghouse on Reading and Communication Skills.* Holdzkom, D., Reed, L., Porter, H.J, & Rubin, D.L. (1982). *Research within reach: Oral and written communication.* St. Louis: Cemrel, Inc. Keech, C., & Thomas, S (1979). *Compendium of promising practices in composition instruction. Evaluation of the Bay Area Writing Project.* Berkeley, CA: California University School of Education.
Mastery of the mechanics of writing—punctuation, spelling, and correct usage—is important to becoming an effective writer whose writing is understood and taken seriously (Graves, 1994; Spandel, 2001). In *Write Source,* skills lessons are introduced when they are meaningful in the context of students' writing. Opportunities for extensive skills practice are found in the pupil edition, *SkillsBook, Interactive Writing Skills CD-ROM,* and *Daily Language Workouts.*	Graves, D. H. (1994). *A fresh look at writing.* Portsmouth, NH: Heinemann. Spandel, V. (2001). *Creating writers through 6-trait writing assessment and instruction.* (3rd ed.) Boston: Addison Wesley Longman.
Writing across the curriculum lessons for every form of writing help students connect writing in the same mode to different content areas and helps them use writing as a tool for thinking and learning (Perkins, 1992; Vacca & Vacca, 2002).	Perkins, D. (1992). *Smart schools: Better thinking and learning for every child.* New York: The Free Press. Vacca, R. T., & Vacca, J. L. (2002). Content area reading: Literacy and learning across the curriculum (7th ed.). Boston: Allyn & Bacon.
Understanding the six traits of effective writing and how to revise effectively is essential to becoming a skillful, independent writer (Spandel, 2001). Six-trait writing instruction has also been shown to improve student writing test scores (Jarner, Kozol, Nelson, & Salsberry, 2000).	Jarner, D., Kozol, M., Nelson, S., & Salsberry, T. (Fall/Winter 2000). Six-trait writing model improves scores at Jennie Wilson Elementary. *Journal of School Improvement.* www.ncacasi.org/jsi/2000vli2/six_trait_model.adp. Spandel, V. (2001). *Creating writers through 6-trait writing assessment and instruction.* (3rd ed.) Boston: Addison Wesley Longman.

Program Resources

Pupil Edition

The *Write Source* pupil edition reflects the latest and best research on writing and learning and provides everything a student needs to become a better writer, thinker, and learner, including

- **clear coverage of the writing process and the six traits of writing within every unit** to help students become focused writers and revisers;

- **a friendly, reassuring voice, colorful artwork,** and **humorous illustrations** that speak to students;

- **integrated mechanics, usage, and grammar activities** so students improve key skills through every writing unit;

- **student models for every form of writing** to motivate students and help them understand what is expected of them in each lesson;

- **guidelines for cross-curricular writing forms** to build writing skills in other content areas, including social studies, science, and math;

- **strategies for developing other useful classroom skills** including listening, making oral presentations, note taking, and taking tests.

Grade 4 Pupil Edition shown.

Teacher's Edition

The *Write Source Teacher's Edition* makes implementing the new program a breeze for all teachers—including new teachers and those not specifically trained in writing instruction. Clear and easy-to-follow, this resource includes

- **a wraparound format** with reduced pupil edition pages and step-by-step **teacher notes correlated to national standards;**

- additional **information on the writing process and six traits** (as well as alternative 4- and 5-point rubrics) for teachers new to these topics;

- **differentiated instruction** for English language learners, struggling, and advanced students as well as **support for cross-curricular writing instruction** in science, social studies, and math;

- **an emphasis on core forms of writing commonly included on state writing assessments,** genre-specific writing prompts, benchmark papers, and tests to assess students' understanding of mechanics, usage, and grammar skills.

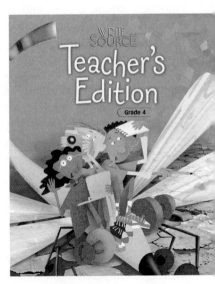

Grade 4 Teacher's Edition shown.

Teacher's Resource Pack

The **Teacher's Resource Pack** provides a variety of additional resources to help teachers get the most out of the *Write Source* program—

SkillsBook

Designed to help students practice and improve their essential grammar, mechanics, and usage skills, the *SkillsBook* addresses the basic writing and language skills covered in the pupil edition "Proofreader's Guide" with

- **more than 90 editing and proofreading activities**,
- **clear and easy-to-follow activities**,
- additional "Next Step" **follow-up or enrichment activities**.

SkillsBook Teacher's Edition is also included.

Assessment Book

This convenient teacher resource provides **copy masters for a pretest, interim tests,** and a **posttest** to help teachers monitor students' progress.

Overhead Transparencies

Convenient overhead transparencies feature graphic organizers and benchmark papers for whole-class instruction.

Write Source Interactive Writing Skills CD-ROM

Packed with interactive activities that support six language skill areas, including punctuation, mechanics, spelling, usage, understanding sentences, and parts of speech, this student-friendly CD-ROM provides

- **animated lessons that explain a key grammar concept**,
- **engaging, interactive activities**,
- **printable and e-mailable reports** for students' scores on each activity.

Daily Language Workouts

This flexible teacher's resource builds students' editing and proofreading skills through **5- to 10-minute language activities**.

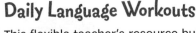

Grade 4 Teacher's Resource Pack components shown.

A Closer Look at the Teacher's Edition

Teacher's Edition lessons provide explicit instruction presented in a wraparound format that shows reduced pupil edition pages accompanied by background notes, lesson plans, guidelines for differentiated instruction, assessment guidelines, and copy masters for a variety of writing tools and strategies.

Writing Standards addressed within each unit are listed at the beginning of each unit overview. The writing standards covered within the program are based on a blend of selected state and NCTE standards.

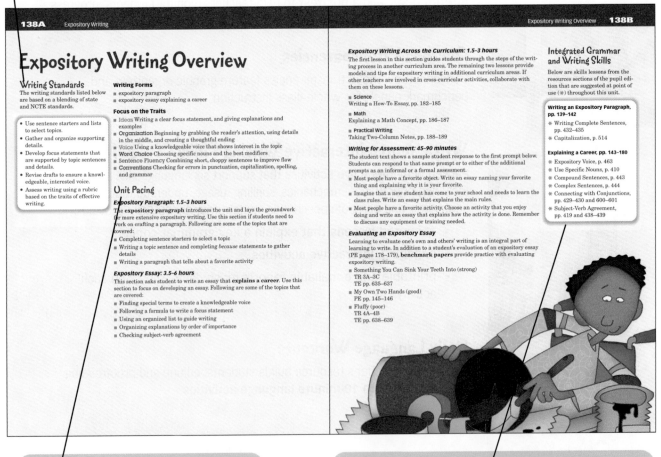

138A Expository Writing

Expository Writing Overview

Writing Standards
The writing standards listed below are based on a blending of state and NCTE standards.

- Use sentence starters and lists to select topics.
- Gather and organize supporting details.
- Develop focus statements that are supported by topic sentences and details.
- Revise drafts to ensure a knowledgeable, interested voice.
- Assess writing using a rubric based on the traits of effective writing.

Writing Forms
- expository paragraph
- expository essay explaining a career

Focus on the Traits
- **Ideas** Writing a clear focus statement, and giving explanations and examples
- **Organization** Beginning by grabbing the reader's attention, using details in the middle, and creating a thoughtful ending
- **Voice** Using a knowledgeable voice that shows interest in the topic
- **Word Choice** Choosing specific nouns and the best modifiers
- **Sentence Fluency** Combining short, choppy sentences to improve flow
- **Conventions** Checking for errors in punctuation, capitalization, spelling, and grammar

Unit Pacing

Expository Paragraph: 1.5–3 hours
The **expository paragraph** introduces the unit and lays the groundwork for more extensive expository writing. Use this section if students need to work on crafting a paragraph. Following are some of the topics that are covered:
- Completing sentence starters to select a topic
- Writing a topic sentence and completing *because* statements to gather details
- Writing a paragraph that tells about a favorite activity

Expository Essay: 3.5–6 hours
This section asks student to write an essay that **explains a career**. Use this section to focus on developing an essay. Following are some of the topics that are covered:
- Finding special terms to create a knowledgeable voice
- Following a formula to write a focus statement
- Using an organized list to guide writing
- Organizing explanations by order of importance
- Checking subject-verb agreement

Expository Writing Overview **138B**

Expository Writing Across the Curriculum: 1.5–3 hours
The first lesson in this section guides students through the steps of the writing process in another curriculum area. The remaining two lessons provide models and tips for expository writing in additional curriculum areas. If other teachers are involved in cross-curricular activities, collaborate with them on these lessons.
- **Science**
Writing a How-To Essay, pp. 182–185
- **Math**
Explaining a Math Concept, pp. 186–187
- **Practical Writing**
Taking Two-Column Notes, pp. 188–189

Writing for Assessment: 45–90 minutes
The student text shows a sample student response to the first prompt below. Students can respond to that same prompt or to either of the additional prompts as an informal or a formal assessment.
- Most people have a favorite object. Write an essay naming your favorite thing and explaining why it is your favorite.
- Imagine that a new student has come to your school and needs to learn the class rules. Write an essay that explains the main rules.
- Most people have a favorite activity. Choose an activity that you enjoy doing and write an essay that explains how the activity is done. Remember to discuss any equipment or training needed.

Evaluating an Expository Essay
Learning to evaluate one's own and others' writing is an integral part of learning to write. In addition to a student's evaluation of an expository essay (PE pages 178–179), **benchmark papers** provide practice with evaluating expository writing.
- Something You Can Sink Your Teeth Into (strong)
TR 3A–3C
TE pp. 635–637
- My Own Two Hands (good)
PE pp. 145–146
- Fluffy (poor)
TR 4A–4B
TE pp. 638–639

Integrated Grammar and Writing Skills
Below are skills lessons from the resources sections of the pupil edition that are suggested at point of use (✳) throughout this unit.

Writing an Expository Paragraph, pp. 139–142
- ✳ Writing Complete Sentences, pp. 432–435
- ✳ Capitalization, p. 514

Explaining a Career, pp. 143–180
- ✳ Expository Voice, p. 463
- ✳ Use Specific Nouns, p. 410
- ✳ Compound Sentences, p. 443
- ✳ Complex Sentences, p. 444
- ✳ Connecting with Conjunctions, pp. 429–430 and 600–601
- ✳ Subject-Verb Agreement, pp. 419 and 438–439

Unit Pacing details the key topics and approximate length of each lesson.

Integrated Grammar and Writing Skills lists pupil edition skills lessons that are suggested for the unit. These lessons are indicated with the (✳) symbol at point of use within each lesson.

The **Additional Grammar Skills** section of the unit overview suggests additional relevant skills lessons found in other program components including the *SkillsBook, Interactive Writing Skills CD-ROM,* and *Daily Language Workouts.*

Objectives for the lesson are listed at the beginning of each lesson.

Family Connection Letters to be sent home at the start of each unit are available as copy masters in both English and Spanish.

Materials are listed at the beginning of each section of the unit. TE page numbers indicate where the materials will be used.

Across the curriculum activities in the writing units provide opportunities for students to apply specific writing forms to different content areas including
- social studies,
- math,
- science,
- assessment.

A Closer Look at the Teacher's Edition, continued

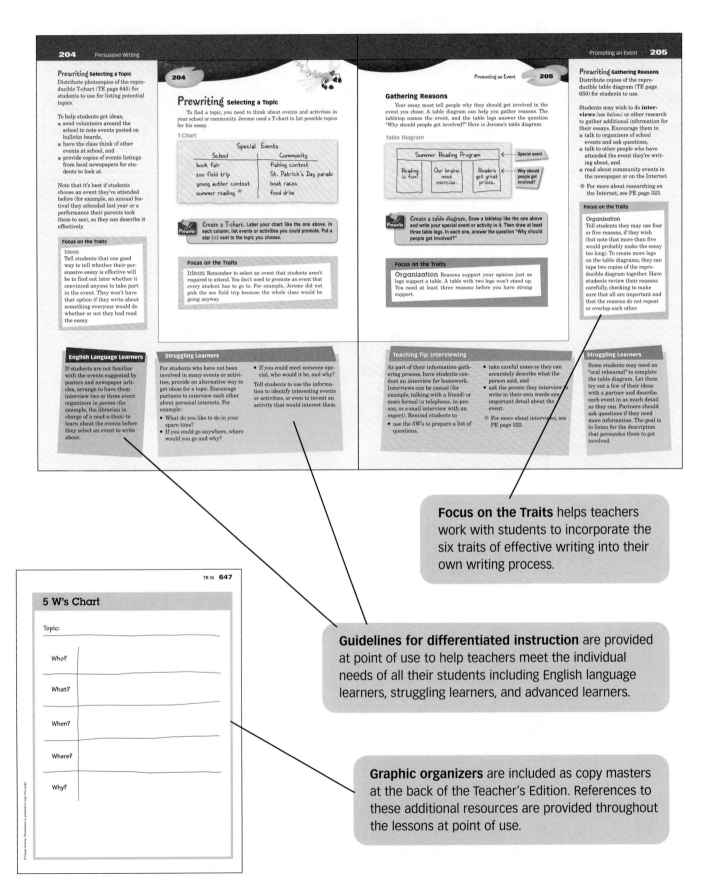

Focus on the Traits helps teachers work with students to incorporate the six traits of effective writing into their own writing process.

Guidelines for differentiated instruction are provided at point of use to help teachers meet the individual needs of all their students including English language learners, struggling learners, and advanced learners.

Graphic organizers are included as copy masters at the back of the Teacher's Edition. References to these additional resources are provided throughout the lessons at point of use.

Student Self-Assessments in each core unit provide opportunities for students to evaluate and score their own work based on the six traits of effective writing.

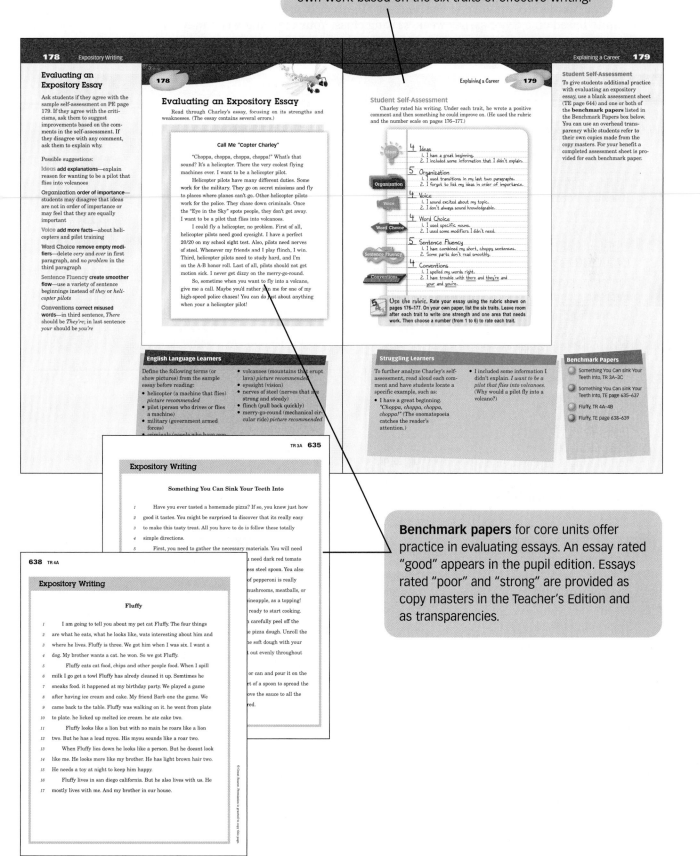

Benchmark papers for core units offer practice in evaluating essays. An essay rated "good" appears in the pupil edition. Essays rated "poor" and "strong" are provided as copy masters in the Teacher's Edition and as transparencies.

Yearlong Timetable

The suggested Yearlong Timetable is just that—suggested. It presents a sequence of writing units based on a five-day-per-week writing class. Your teaching week may offer fewer hours for teaching writing. That's why the Teacher's Edition provides guidelines to help you customize the timetable and the sequence of units to meet your particular needs.

First Quarter

Wk	Writing Lesson	Student Book
1	Getting Started	TE pages 668–670
2	Understanding the Writing Process Keeping Journals and Learning Logs	3–8 379–386
3	One Writer's Process Using a Rubric One Writer's Process (cont.)	9–18 31–38 19–20
	Listening and Speaking Peer Responding	368–372 39–42
4	Understanding the Traits of Writing Writing Paragraphs	21–30 50–57
5	Writing Paragraphs (cont.) Writing a Descriptive Paragraph	58–61 62–64
6	Writing a Descriptive Paragraph (cont.) Describing a Place	65–66 67–71
7	Describing a Place Publishing and Portfolios	72–74 43–49
8	Writing for Assessment Taking Classroom Tests	80–81 399–405
9	Writing a Narrative Paragraph	82–86

Second Quarter

Wk	Writing Lesson	Student Book
1	Sharing an Experience	87–96
2	Sharing an Experience (cont.)	97–107
3	Sharing an Experience (cont.)	108–119
4	Sharing an Experience (cont.) Writing for Assessment	120–124 134–137
5	Writing an Expository Paragraph Explaining a Career	138–142 143–146
6	Explaining a Career (cont.)	147–152
7	Explaining a Career (cont.)	153–163
8	Explaining a Career (cont.)	164–175
9	Explaining a Career (cont.) Writing for Assessment Portfolio Review	176–180 190–193

Third Quarter

Wk	Writing Lesson	Student Book
1	Writing a Persuasive Paragraph Improving Viewing Skills	194–198 393–398
2	Promoting an Event	199–208
3	Promoting an Event (cont.)	209–219
4	Promoting an Event (cont.) Giving Speeches	220–231 373–378
5	Promoting an Event (cont.) Writing for Assessment Portfolio Review	232–236 248–251
6	Writing a Response Paragraph Writing a Book Review	252–256 257–260
7	Writing a Book Review (cont.)	261–266
8	Writing a Book Review (cont.) Other Forms of Responding	267–272 273–279
9	Other Forms of Responding (cont.)	280–297

Fourth Quarter

Wk	Writing Lesson	Student Book
1	Writing Stories	298–303
2	Writing Stories (cont.)	304–310
3	Writing Poems	311–315
4	Writing Poems (cont.) Taking Notes	316–319 387–392
5	Building Skills	320–332
6	Writing a Summary Paragraph	333–336
7	Writing a Research Report	337–344
8	Writing a Research Report (cont.)	345–354
9	Writing a Research Report (cont.)	355–362
	Developing Multimedia Presentations	363–367

Lesson Planning Guidelines

The authors of the *Write Source* program understand that teachers of writing need a wealth of resources that can be used flexibly. The guidelines here will assist you in using the *Write Source* program to best advantage for you and your students.

Determining Priorities

The first step in planning is to determine the priorities for the year. What must you accomplish with your students by the end of the year? To establish your priorities, you will need to

- become familiar with state and local curriculum requirements for the grade you teach;
- understand the content of any state or standardized tests that your students will take; and
- evaluate the writing experience and ability of your students by examining their records and portfolios from previous years, administering a classroom writing test (including the Pretest in the *Write Source* Assessment Book, available in the Teacher's Resource Pack), and/or observing samples of students' writing early in the year.

Once you have determined the major focus of instruction for the year, you will need to consider other factors, such as how much time you have to spend on writing instruction and practice, in what order you will address the priorities, and other topics you want to include to round out your writing plan.

Time Allotment

The time allotted for writing instruction will vary according to school and classroom schedules. To help you make the most of the time you have, each Unit Overview provides the following information about the upcoming unit:

- the objectives and content of the unit,
- a range of times that could be spent on the unit subsections, and
- related *Write Source* materials that can be used to supplement instruction.

With this information, you can begin to sketch out your schedule, balancing instruction with time available for writing.

Yearly Planning

The priorities you have established form the basis for your yearly plan. Once you know what students must accomplish, then you can begin to determine what you need to teach, when to teach it, and how long you will spend teaching it. To plan a year-long writing curriculum,

- list the priorities for the year,
- determine the *Write Source* units that support your priorities,
- lay out a sequence of units, and
- determine how long to devote to particular units according to student need.

Re-evaluate your overall plan several times during the year to make adjustments.

Sequencing the Units

The *Write Source* pupil edition is divided into six sections: The Writing Process, The Forms of Writing, Speaking and Writing to Learn, The Basic Elements of Writing, A Writer's Resource, and Proofreader's Guide. Familiarity with these sections will help you in your planning (see below and the table of contents).

The authors of the *Write Source* program recommend that before you begin formal writing instruction you spend some class time helping students become familiar with the book so that they can get the most out of it. Getting Started activities (see TE pages xlv–xlvi and 668–670) will help you ensure that your students know the extent of the resources available to them and can use them to become better writers, thinkers, and learners in all their classes. The next step is to move to the first section of the book, The Writing Process. These chapters will provide a common foundation of writing knowledge for your students about the writing process and the traits of effective writing.

There is no specific order for teaching the forms of writing. Plans for teaching the major writing units will depend on state, district, or school curriculum; the state test; and specific classroom assignments. Address the following considerations to make your planning decisions:

- Take into account the timing of state or standardized writing tests.

- Coordinate with schoolwide or content-area assignments. (For example, if the whole grade studies biography, then you will want to address that form in a timely way. If the social studies teacher assigns a research report, then support your colleague and students by providing instruction in how to do a research report.)

- Use Descriptive Writing as a way to observe students' writing abilities. It is a shorter unit than the full-blown core writing units (Narrative Writing, Expository Writing, Persuasive Writing, and Response to Literature) and description is a feature of all genres.

The final sections of *Write Source*—The Basic Elements of Writing, A Writer's Resource, and Proofreader's Guide—can be used as resource sections for your student writers when they have questions about writing skills and strategies. They are integrated into the Forms of Writing chapters so that each form is well supported by appropriate writing skills and strategies (see Unit Planning below). However, students can access these sections at any time to answer their questions about sentences, paragraphs, parts of speech, punctuation, and so forth.

Unit Planning

As you plan each writing unit, there are a number of choices that you will make to best meet the needs of your students and the curriculum. The units purposely have an abundance of information to accommodate the writing needs of many students, so you will want to choose the parts of each unit that help you achieve your priorities. Use the information below and in each Unit Overview in conjunction with the Unit Planning Worksheet (TE pages 671–672) to begin to make appropriate choices for your students.

How much of the unit should I cover?

Each of the four core writing units (Narrative Writing, Expository Writing, Persuasive Writing, and Response to Literature) and Research Writing have multiple sections. Students have the opportunity to write a paragraph, a full-blown essay, a second essay, across-the-curriculum forms, and a response to a writing prompt. You may decide to use all or most of the writing opportunities for a form of writing that is very important in your curriculum. On the other hand, you may decide that your students can already write well-constructed paragraphs and only need to work on the full-blown essay or the second essay.

How do I select the best supporting skills and resources?

Each Unit Overview offers a list of skills and strategies available in other parts of the pupil edition and in other program components that support the writing form. Use your knowledge of your students, based on assessments and observation, to help you decide which integrated skills and strategies to use. Multiple opportunities exist for some skills, and you will want to decide how much is enough for your students.

What sections should I focus on within the writing process?

The pupil edition takes students through the writing process for each form of writing. Consider your students' familiarity with the steps of the writing process and how much time you should devote to each. The section on revising offers you the opportunity to teach each of the six traits; however, as you probably know, it is best to focus on only one or two traits at a time. At the beginning of the year, concentrate on ideas or organization. Later in the year, work on voice, word choice, and sentence fluency. Conventions will be present throughout the year in the section on editing.

Do I need to cover all the activities in Writing Across the Curriculum?

The Writing Across the Curriculum activities are included to illustrate how the various writing forms can be woven throughout the whole curriculum. An effective use of these activities is to share them with the content-area teachers, who may decide to integrate them into their classes. Students can study the sample passages as examples of the genres, and they can write their own if they need further practice in a genre.

Scope and Sequence

FORMS OF WRITING	Grade 3	Grade 4	Grade 5
Narrative Writing			
important person essay	✔		
narrative prompts	✔	✔	✔
paragraph	✔	✔	✔
personal experience		✔	✔
Expository Writing			
explaining a career essay		✔	
explaining a process essay			✔
expository prompts	✔	✔	✔
paragraph	✔	✔	✔
why something is important essay	✔		
Persuasive Writing			
expressing an opinion essay			✔
paragraph	✔	✔	✔
persuasive letter	✔		
persuasive prompts	✔	✔	✔
promoting an event essay		✔	
Response to Literature			
book review	✔	✔	✔
paragraph		✔	✔
response journal		✔	✔
response prompts	✔	✔	✔
Descriptive Writing			
descriptive prompts	✔	✔	✔
paragraph	✔	✔	✔
person			✔
place		✔	
special object	✔		
Creative Writing			
alphabet poem	✔		
clerihew	✔		
diamante			✔
fantasy story		✔	
five W's poem	✔		
free-verse poem		✔	✔

	Grade 3	Grade 4	Grade 5
historical fiction short story			✔
imaginative story	✔		
limerick	✔		
list poem			✔
play		✔	✔
realistic fiction story		✔	
rhyming poem	✔		
split couplet		✔	
tall tale			✔
tercet			✔
"Where I'm From" poem		✔	

Research Writing

	Grade 3	Grade 4	Grade 5
famous person report			✔
interesting invention report		✔	
multimedia presentation	✔	✔	✔
summary paragraph	✔	✔	✔
topic of interest report	✔		

Speaking and Writing to Learn

	Grade 3	Grade 4	Grade 5
giving speeches	✔	✔	✔
improving viewing skills	✔	✔	✔
journal writing	✔	✔	✔
learning logs	✔	✔	✔
listening in class	✔	✔	✔
note taking	✔	✔	✔
taking classroom tests	✔	✔	✔

THE WRITING PROCESS

Prewriting

Selecting a Topic

	Grade 3	Grade 4	Grade 5
brainstorm		✔	✔
character chart		✔	✔
chart	✔	✔	✔
choose an article	✔	✔	✔
cluster	✔	✔	✔
focus statement			✔
freewrite		✔	✔
gathering wheel	✔		
grid		✔	

	Grade 3	Grade 4	Grade 5
line diagram			✔
list	✔	✔	✔
select a book	✔	✔	✔
sentence starters		✔	✔
topic sentence			✔
Gathering Details			
amazing details			✔
answer questions	✔	✔	✔
avoid plagiarism		✔	✔
beginning-middle-ending map		✔	
cluster		✔	✔
collection sheet		✔	✔
details chart		✔	✔
fact sheet		✔	
five Ws and H	✔		✔
freewrite	✔		✔
gathering grid	✔	✔	✔
HOW questions		✔	
interview	✔		
KWL chart			✔
list details	✔	✔	✔
media grid	✔		
picture diagram	✔	✔	
planning chart			✔
read articles		✔	✔
selecting main reasons	✔	✔	✔
sensory chart	✔	✔	✔
sentence starters		✔	✔
special terms		✔	
story map	✔		
T-chart	✔	✔	✔
table diagram		✔	✔
theme chart			✔
three-two-one chart	✔		
time line	✔	✔	✔
tracking sources		✔	✔
underline details	✔	✔	✔
Venn diagram		✔	

	Grade 3	Grade 4	Grade 5
Organizing Details			
call to action		✔	
figures of speech		✔	✔
focus statement	✔	✔	✔
gathering grid	✔	✔	✔
line breaks		✔	
line diagram		✔	
list	✔	✔	✔
main idea	✔	✔	
note cards	✔	✔	✔
opinion statement	✔	✔	✔
order of importance		✔	✔
order of location		✔	
organized list		✔	✔
outline ideas	✔	✔	✔
plot chart	✔	✔	✔
poetry techniques	✔	✔	✔
repetition		✔	
table diagram		✔	✔
thesis statement		✔	✔
time line	✔	✔	✔
time order		✔	✔
topic sentence	✔	✔	✔
traits chart		✔	
Venn diagram	✔		
Sizing Up Your Topic			
answer questions	✔	✔	
five W's memory chart		✔	
list questions	✔		✔

Writing

	Grade 3	Grade 4	Grade 5
Beginning Paragraph			
ask a question	✔	✔	✔
be creative	✔	✔	✔
clever comparison	✔		
connect with reader	✔	✔	✔
create a picture	✔		✔
familiar saying			✔
focus statement	✔	✔	✔

	Grade 3	Grade 4	Grade 5
important facts	✔		
interesting fact/details		✔	✔
introduce topic/main idea	✔	✔	✔
middle of action	✔	✔	✔
opening sentence		✔	✔
opinion statement	✔	✔	✔
quotation		✔	
refer to an expert			✔
start with dialogue	✔	✔	✔
surprising information		✔	✔
tell an anecdote	✔	✔	✔
thesis statement		✔	✔
time and place			✔
topic sentence	✔	✔	
Middle Paragraphs			
action words	✔		✔
answer questions	✔	✔	
build to high point		✔	✔
comparisons	✔	✔	✔
dialogue	✔	✔	✔
direct quotations	✔	✔	✔
explain terms		✔	✔
explain theme		✔	✔
facts	✔	✔	✔
focus on one scene	✔		
important ideas	✔	✔	
key event		✔	✔
personal feelings	✔	✔	✔
reasons	✔	✔	
repeated words			✔
sensory details	✔	✔	✔
specific details		✔	
supporting details	✔	✔	✔
topic sentences	✔	✔	✔
transitions		✔	✔
Ending Paragraph			
ask a question		✔	
call to action	✔	✔	✔
closing sentences	✔	✔	✔

	Grade 3	Grade 4	Grade 5
connect with reader	✔	✔	✔
connect subject to life	✔		
create a list		✔	
explain theme	✔	✔	✔
final comment/interesting thought		✔	✔
final surprising detail		✔	✔
how you changed		✔	✔
how you felt		✔	✔
interesting fact	✔	✔	✔
refer back to beginning	✔	✔	✔
respond to main idea		✔	
restate main idea	✔		
restate opinion/thesis		✔	✔
share an experience			✔
share feelings	✔	✔	
summarize		✔	✔
what you learned		✔	✔
what you wonder	✔		

Revising

Ideas

	Grade 3	Grade 4	Grade 5
anecdote		✔	
answer the 5 W's		✔	
clear message			✔
dialogue	✔		✔
explanations		✔	
examples		✔	
factual statements	✔		✔
focus statement		✔	
important/interesting details	✔	✔	✔
main events		✔	✔
main idea		✔	✔
quotations		✔	
reasons	✔		
sensory details	✔	✔	✔
"show, don't tell"	✔	✔	✔
supporting details		✔	✔
theme			✔
topic sentence	✔	✔	✔
unnecessary details	✔	✔	✔

	Grade 3	Grade 4	Grade 5
Organization			
beginning captures reader's interest	✔	✔	✔
check overall organization	✔	✔	✔
clear beginning	✔	✔	✔
ending asks reader to do something	✔	✔	
ending comes after most important part			✔
ending gives reader something to think about			✔
logical order	✔	✔	✔
order of ideas/details	✔	✔	✔
order of importance		✔	✔
order of location		✔	✔
time order	✔	✔	✔
topic sentences	✔		✔
transition words		✔	✔
Voice			
bandwagoning		✔	
caring/concerned		✔	✔
convincing	✔	✔	
dialogue			✔
entertaining			✔
exaggerating		✔	
excited	✔		✔
fits audience		✔	✔
formal		✔	✔
fuzzy thinking		✔	
informal		✔	✔
informative		✔	✔
interested	✔	✔	✔
knowledgeable		✔	✔
natural	✔	✔	✔
original		✔	✔
serious			✔
Word Choice			
action verbs	✔	✔	
active verbs		✔	

	Grade 3	Grade 4	Grade 5
colorful adjectives			✔
connotation		✔	✔
define unfamiliar words		✔	✔
descriptive words			✔
helping verbs	✔		
loaded words			✔
modifiers		✔	
onomatopoeia			✔
present-tense verbs		✔	✔
repeated words		✔	
sensory words		✔	
simile			✔
specialized words			✔
specific adjectives		✔	
specific action verbs		✔	✔
specific nouns	✔	✔	✔
synonyms		✔	
vivid verbs			✔
wordiness			✔
Sentence Fluency			
choppy sentences	✔	✔	✔
combining sentences	✔		
complete sentences	✔	✔	✔
complex sentences		✔	
compound sentences	✔	✔	
different kinds of sentences			✔
expanded sentences		✔	✔
fragments		✔	✔
rambling sentences		✔	
run-on sentences	✔		✔
short sentences	✔	✔	✔
smooth flow		✔	✔
variety of beginnings		✔	✔
variety of lengths	✔	✔	✔
variety of types		✔	

	Grade 3	Grade 4	Grade 5
Editing			
Capitalization			
beginning of sentences	✔	✔	✔
proper nouns	✔	✔	✔
Grammar			
correct forms of verbs	✔	✔	✔
correct verb tenses		✔	
homophones	✔	✔	✔
person of subject pronouns		✔	
possessive pronouns		✔	
pronoun agreement			✔
subject-verb agreement	✔	✔	✔
using the right words	✔	✔	✔
Punctuation			
apostrophes in contractions	✔		
apostrophes to show possession		✔	
commas after introductory word groups		✔	✔
commas between items in a series	✔	✔	✔
commas in compound sentences		✔	✔
commas in dates and addresses	✔		
commas to set off speaker's words		✔	✔
end punctuation	✔	✔	✔
punctuating dialogue	✔	✔	✔
punctuating titles	✔	✔	✔
punctuating works-cited page		✔	
quotation marks around direct quotations			✔
Spelling			
commonly misused words		✔	✔
double-checking words	✔	✔	✔

WRITING ACROSS THE CURRICULUM	Grade 3	Grade 4	Grade 5
Narrative Writing			
biographical narrative	✔		
e-mail message		✔	✔
friendly letter	✔		
historical moment			✔
math personal experience			✔
observation report		✔	
story problems		✔	
Expository Writing			
comparison-contrast essay			✔
how-to essay	✔	✔	
math concept		✔	✔
news report	✔		
two-column notes		✔	✔
Persuasive Writing			
brochure			✔
business letter	✔	✔	✔
editorial			✔
e-mail message	✔		
persuasive letter		✔	✔
poster	✔		
problem-solution essay		✔	
thermometer graph		✔	
Response to Literature			
anecdote			✔
comparing a fiction and a nonfiction book	✔		
nonfiction article		✔	✔
nonfiction book	✔	✔	
poem	✔	✔	✔
quotation			✔
tall tale		✔	
Descriptive Writing			
chemical change			✔
historical landmark		✔	
person from history			✔
plant description		✔	

GRAMMAR	Grade 3	Grade 4	Grade 5
Understanding Sentences			
clauses		✔	✔
complete predicates	✔	✔	✔
complete subjects	✔	✔	✔
compound predicates	✔	✔	✔
compound subjects	✔	✔	✔
dependent clauses		✔	✔
independent clauses		✔	✔
modifiers		✔	✔
phrases		✔	✔
predicates		✔	✔
simple predicates	✔	✔	✔
simple subjects	✔	✔	✔
subjects		✔	✔
types of phrases		✔	✔
Using the Parts of Speech			
Adjectives			
articles	✔	✔	✔
common adjectives		✔	✔
comparative adjectives	✔	✔	✔
compound adjectives	✔	✔	✔
demonstrative adjectives		✔	✔
indefinite adjectives		✔	✔
irregular forms	✔	✔	✔
positive adjectives	✔	✔	✔
predicate adjectives		✔	✔
proper adjectives	✔	✔	✔
superlative adjectives	✔	✔	✔
Adverbs			
adverbs of degree		✔	✔
adverbs of manner	✔	✔	✔
adverbs of place	✔	✔	✔
adverbs of time	✔	✔	✔
comparative adverbs		✔	✔
irregular forms		✔	✔
positive adverbs		✔	✔
superlative adverbs		✔	✔

	Grade 3	Grade 4	Grade 5
Conjunctions			
coordinating conjunctions	✔	✔	✔
correlative conjunctions		✔	✔
subordinating conjunctions	✔	✔	✔
Interjections	✔	✔	✔
Nouns			
abstract nouns		✔	✔
collective nouns		✔	✔
common nouns	✔	✔	✔
compound nouns		✔	✔
concrete nouns		✔	✔
noun gender		✔	✔
object nouns		✔	✔
plural nouns	✔	✔	✔
possessive nouns	✔	✔	✔
predicate nouns		✔	✔
proper nouns	✔	✔	✔
singular nouns	✔	✔	✔
subject nouns		✔	✔
Prepositions			
prepositional phrases	✔	✔	✔
Pronouns			
antecedents		✔	✔
demonstrative pronouns		✔	✔
first person pronouns		✔	✔
indefinite pronouns		✔	✔
intensive pronouns		✔	✔
interrogative pronouns		✔	✔
object pronouns		✔	✔
personal pronouns	✔	✔	✔
possessive pronouns	✔	✔	✔
reflexive pronouns		✔	✔
relative pronouns		✔	✔
second person pronouns		✔	✔
singular and plural pronouns		✔	✔
subject pronouns		✔	✔
third person pronouns		✔	✔
Verbs			
action verbs	✔	✔	✔

	Grade 3	Grade 4	Grade 5
active and passive verbs		✔	✔
future perfect tense verbs		✔	✔
future tense verbs	✔	✔	✔
helping verbs	✔	✔	✔
intransitive verbs		✔	✔
irregular verbs	✔	✔	✔
linking verbs	✔	✔	✔
past perfect tense verbs		✔	✔
past tense verbs	✔	✔	✔
present perfect tense verbs		✔	✔
present tense verbs	✔	✔	✔
singular and plural verbs	✔	✔	✔
transitive verbs		✔	✔
transitive or intransitive verbs			✔

Mechanics

Abbreviations

	Grade 3	Grade 4	Grade 5
acronyms	✔	✔	✔
address abbreviations	✔	✔	✔
common abbreviations	✔	✔	✔
initialisms	✔	✔	✔

Capitalization

	Grade 3	Grade 4	Grade 5
abbreviations	✔	✔	✔
days, months, holidays	✔	✔	✔
first words	✔	✔	✔
geographic names	✔	✔	✔
historical events		✔	✔
names of people	✔	✔	✔
official names		✔	✔
organizations		✔	✔
particular sections of the country	✔	✔	✔
proper nouns and adjectives	✔	✔	✔
races, languages, nationalities, religions		✔	✔
titles	✔	✔	✔
titles used with names	✔	✔	✔
words used as names	✔	✔	✔

Numbers

	Grade 3	Grade 4	Grade 5
numbers under 10	✔	✔	✔
numerals only	✔	✔	✔

	Grade 3	Grade 4	Grade 5
sentence beginnings	✔	✔	✔
very large numbers	✔	✔	✔
Plurals			
adding an 's		✔	✔
compound nouns		✔	✔
irregular spelling	✔	✔	✔
most nouns	✔	✔	✔
nouns ending in *ch*, *sh*, *s*, *x*, and *z*	✔	✔	✔
nouns ending in *f* or *fe*		✔	✔
nouns ending in *ful*		✔	✔
nouns ending in *o*		✔	✔
nouns ending in *y*	✔	✔	✔
Punctuation			
Apostrophes			
in contractions	✔	✔	✔
in place of omitted letters or numbers		✔	✔
to form plural possessives	✔	✔	✔
to form possessives with indefinite pronouns		✔	✔
to form singular possessives	✔	✔	✔
to form some plurals		✔	✔
to show shared possession		✔	✔
Colons			
after salutations	✔	✔	✔
as a formal introduction		✔	✔
between numbers in time	✔		✔
to introduce lists	✔	✔	✔
Commas			
between items in a series	✔	✔	✔
in compound sentences	✔	✔	✔
in dates and addresses	✔	✔	✔
in direct address		✔	✔
in letter writing	✔	✔	✔
to keep numbers clear	✔	✔	✔
to separate equal adjectives	✔	✔	✔
to separate introductory clauses and phrases	✔	✔	✔
to set off appositives			✔

	Grade 3	Grade 4	Grade 5
to set off dialogue	✔	✔	✔
to set off explanatory phrases		✔	✔
to set off interjections		✔	✔
to set off interruptions		✔	✔
Dashes			
for emphasis		✔	✔
to indicate interrupted speech		✔	✔
to indicate a sudden break		✔	✔
Ellipses			
to show omitted words		✔	✔
to show pauses		✔	✔
Exclamation Points			
to express strong feelings	✔	✔	✔
Hyphens			
between numbers in a fraction		✔	✔
in compound words		✔	✔
to create new words		✔	✔
to divide words	✔	✔	✔
to join letters to words		✔	✔
Italics and Underlining			
for names of aircraft and ships	✔		
for scientific and foreign words		✔	✔
for special uses		✔	✔
in titles	✔	✔	✔
Parentheses			
to add information	✔	✔	✔
Periods			
in abbreviations	✔	✔	✔
after initials	✔	✔	✔
as decimal points	✔	✔	✔
at end of sentences	✔	✔	✔
Question Marks			
at end of direct questions	✔	✔	✔
tag questions		✔	✔
to show doubt		✔	✔
Quotation Marks			
for special words		✔	✔
placement of punctuation		✔	✔

	Grade 3	Grade 4	Grade 5
to punctuate titles	✔	✔	✔
to set off a speaker's exact words	✔	✔	✔
Semicolons			
to join two independent clauses		✔	✔
to separate groups that contain commas		✔	✔
Usage			
Spelling			
consonant endings	✔	✔	✔
i before *e*	✔	✔	✔
silent *e*	✔	✔	✔
words ending in *y*	✔	✔	✔
Using the right word	✔	✔	✔

Getting Started Activities

The *Write Source* pupil edition is full of helpful resources that students can access throughout the year while they are developing their writing skills. Getting Started activities are provided as copy masters on TE pages 668–670. They will

- help students discover the kinds of information available in different sections of the book,

- teach students how to access that information,

- familiarize students with the layout of the book.

The more familiar students are with the text, the more proficient they will be in using its resources. (The answer key for the activities is on the next page.)

Scavenger Hunts

Students enjoy using scavenger hunts to become familiar with a book. The scavenger hunts we provide can be done in small groups or as a class. They are designed for oral answers, but you may want to photocopy the pages for students to write on. Also, you may want to vary the procedure, first having students take turns finding the items and then, on the next scavenger hunt, challenging students to "race" for the answers.

After your students have done each scavenger hunt, you can challenge them to create their own versions. For example, small groups can work together to create "Find the Fours" or "Search for Sixes" scavenger hunts and then exchange their "hunts" with other groups.

Special Challenge: Develop questions that teams of students try to answer using the book. Pattern this activity after a popular game show.

Other Activities

- Give students the following assignment: Across the top of a sheet of paper, write down three things you find difficult about school (e.g., taking notes, taking tests, writing essays, spelling, using commas). Then explore your book to find chapters, sections, examples, and so on, that might help you with your problem area. Under each problem, write the titles or headings and the page numbers where you can find help. Keep this sheet to use throughout the year.

- A variation on the above activity is to have students write down all the subject areas they study and list under each heading the parts of the book that might help them in that subject.

- Have students write a thought-trap poem: After reviewing the book, close it. The first line of your poem will be the title of the book. Then list thoughts and feelings about the book, line by line. When you have listed everything you want to say, "trap" your thoughts by repeating the title.

- Have pairs of students create poster-size advertisements for the book. Each ad should have a headline, list important features (what is in the book) and benefits (whom it can help and how), show an example of illustrations (made by tracing), and urge readers of the ad to get their books now!

- Have students imagine that they are each going to send a copy of *Write Source* to a pen pal in another state. Have each student write a letter to send along with it to tell the pen pal about the book.

Getting Started Activity Answers

Scavenger Hunt 1: Find the Threes

1. create a list, sum up the reasons, ask a question
2. diagrams, graphs, pictures
3. ask questions, review, study
4. keep reading, make writing fun, play with words
5. show something about a speaker's personality, add details, keep the action moving
6. coordinating, subordinating, correlative
7. know your purpose for listening, take notes, ask questions
8. start with an interesting fact, ask a question, tell how you became interested in the job

Scavenger Hunt 2: What Is It?

1. a graphic organizer that helps you put story events in time order (page 261)
2. a way to organize paragraphs by giving details in the order in which they happened (page 56)
3. a poem that does not follow a rhyming pattern (page 312)
4. an incomplete sentence that is missing a subject, a predicate, or both (page 436)
5. qualities of writing: ideas, organization, voice, word choice, sentence fluency, conventions (page 22)
6. a figure of speech that compares two different things using *like* or *as* (page 318)
7. the noun that a pronoun refers to or replaces (page 576.1)
8. the words that are defined on a dictionary page (page 330)

Getting to Know *Write Source*

1. 318
2. 52–53
3. 441
4. 307
5. 472
6. 232–233
7. 274–295
8. 536–559
9. 453–477
10. 293, 457

Why Write?

You may think of writing simply as an assignment. But there are many other ways to look at writing.

Writing can . . .

- **exercise your brain.** Essays and learning logs can give you a deeper understanding of the things you are learning in school.

- **guide your life.** Personal journals can help you sort out your thoughts and feelings about the things that happen around you.

- **connect you with friends.** Letters and e-mail messages help you communicate with people you care about.

- **rocket you through time and space.** Poems, stories, and plays can carry you away to any places that you can dream of.

Remember . . .

To be a writer, all you have to do is write. Some people seem to be born writers. Others become successful writers thanks to practice and determination. Spend a little time writing every day, and you're on your way to becoming a terrific writer.

Why Write?

Before introducing students to this section, have them evaluate their current attitudes toward writing. Do not discourage humorous or negative responses, as the goal here is to get students to explore their feelings and attitudes toward writing, and to give you a general sense of the enthusiasm and interest of the class at this point.

- Ask students to complete this sentence starter: *I write because . . .*
- Invite volunteers to read aloud their completed sentence.
- Have students save the completed sentences in their writing folders or notebooks. From time to time during the year, have students read their sentence again and re-evaluate their reasons for writing. While currently they may write because they have to, as their skills improve and they become more comfortable as writers, students may discover that they are writing for a variety of reasons, and that they actually want to write.

English Language Learners

If possible, meet individually with students to confer about what they think their strengths and weaknesses are in English writing.

- For each weakness (keep the list short), help students write a short goal for themselves on how to progress in English writing.

- Make sure that each goal is simply stated and attainable within a reasonable period of time.

Goals may include ideas such as

- using correct tenses,
- learning and using certain spelling rules,
- being very specific, such as using the words *in* and *on* correctly.

The Writing Process Overview

Writing Standards

The writing standards listed below are based on a blending of state and NCTE standards.

- Learn about the steps in the writing process.
- Understand the six traits of effective writing.
- Learn to use rubrics and the six traits of writing to assess one's own and others' writing.
- Learn to respond constructively to others' writing.
- Learn about ways to publish writing and prepare portfolios.

Writing Process

- **Prewriting** Select a topic, and gather and organize details.
- **Writing** Create a first draft, getting all the ideas on paper.
- **Revising** Review the first draft and make improvements by adding new details, deleting ideas that don't belong, and changing parts that aren't clear.
- **Editing** Check revised writing for errors, write a final copy, and proofread the final copy.
- **Publishing** Share final copy with others.

Focus on the Traits

- **Ideas** Focusing on a specific topic and including ideas and details that support it
- **Organization** Forming a clear beginning, middle, and ending
- **Voice** Using an appealing voice that shares ideas and feelings
- **Word Choice** Choosing specific nouns, strong verbs, and colorful adjectives to add meaning and feeling
- **Sentence Fluency** Varying sentence beginnings and lengths to create a smooth flow
- **Conventions** Checking for errors in punctuation, capitalization, spelling, and grammar

Unit Pacing

Understanding the Writing Process: 1–1.5 hours

This section introduces the five steps of the **writing process**. Use this section if students are not familiar with the process or if you want to provide a refresher. Following are some of the topics that are covered:

- Learning good writing habits
- Seeing the writing process in action
- Working with the traits

One Writer's Process: 1.75–2.5 hours

In this section, students follow one writer's process from prewriting through publishing. Use this section to demonstrate each step of the writing process in action. Following are some of the topics that are covered:

- Setting writing goals
- Listing to select a topic
- Creating a time line to gather and organize details
- Using a peer response to revise
- Reflecting on the process

Understanding the Traits of Writing: 2–3 hours

In this section, students learn how the six traits of effective writing guide the writing process. Use this section to lay the groundwork for all future writing assignments. Following is the topic that is covered:

- Understanding the six traits of effective writing

Using a Rubric: *1.5–2.25 hours*

This section focuses on using a rubric to guide students' writing and to assess finished work. Use this section to teach students how to revise and edit with a rubric, and how to assess with a rubric. Following are some of the topics that are covered:

- Understanding rubrics
- Reading a rubric
- Assessing with a rubric

Peer Responding: *1–1.5 hours*

In this section, students learn how to engage in peer-responding sessions. Use this section to teach students how to give specific, constructive feedback to peers. Following are some of the topics that are covered:

- Understanding the roles of writer and responder
- Making helpful responses
- Completing a peer response sheet

Publishing and Portfolios: *1.5–2.25 hours*

This section offers basic design guidelines and describes different types of portfolios. Use this section to teach students how to prepare their writing for publication, and how to create a portfolio and select work to include in it. Following are some of the topics that are covered:

- Designing a piece of writing
- Types of portfolios
- Parts of a portfolio
- Portfolio reflections

Integrated Grammar and Writing Skills

Below are skills lessons from the resources sections of the pupil edition that are suggested at point of use (✳) throughout this unit.

Understanding the Writing Process, pp. 3–8

- ✳ Increase Vocabulary Skills, pp. 466–469
- ✳ Writing Terms, p. 465
- ✳ Collect Details, pp. 456–457

One Writer's Process, pp. 9–20

- ✳ Time Line, p. 457
- ✳ Proofreader's Guide, pp. 478–605

Understanding the Traits of Writing, pp. 21–30

- ✳ Find a Topic, pp. 454–455
- ✳ Describing with Adverbs, pp. 426–427
- ✳ Combine Short Sentences, pp. 445–447

Publishing and Portfolios, pp. 43–49

- ✳ Add Diagrams, Graphs, and Pictures, pp. 474–475

Additional Grammar Skills

Below are skills lessons from other components that you can weave into your unit instruction.

Understanding the Writing Process

Daily Language Workouts

Week 1: The End of the Line, p. 4–5
Week 1: California's Name, p. 78

One Writer's Process

SkillsBook

Colons 1 and 2, p. 29
Semicolons, p. 31
Punctuation Review 2, p. 39

Daily Language Workouts

Week 2: Get in Line, pp. 6–7
Week 2: If You're an Anteater, p. 79

Understanding the Traits of Writing

SkillsBook

Commas to Set Off Appositives, p. 13
Key Words, p. 105
Phrases, p. 107
Compound Subjects and Predicates, p. 109
Sentence-Combining Review 1 and 2, p. 111
Adverbs, p. 171
Types of Adverbs, p. 172
Forms of Adverbs, p. 173

Interactive Writing Skills CD-ROM

Parts of Speech 2: Adverbs—Types and Comparative

Using the Writing Process

Understanding the Writing Process

Olympic athletes train for years. They exercise, lift weights, eat special foods, and practice their sports. The training process helps everyday athletes become world-class competitors.

Writers follow a process, too. They read a lot, keep a personal journal, and follow the steps in the writing process. If you "train" in the same way, you can become a world-class writer!

Mini Index

- **Becoming a Writer**
- **The Steps in the Writing Process**
- **The Process in Action**
- **Working with the Traits**

Understanding the Writing Process

Objectives

- build good writing habits
- understand the five steps in the writing process
- learn the six traits of effective writing

Point out to students that Olympic athletes set goals as they train. In the beginning, their goals might be modest. For example, a young Olympic swimmer might be happy to beat her own personal best record. As that swimmer becomes more skilled and more relaxed in competition, her goal may be to win a gold, silver, or bronze medal, or break the world record.

Encourage students to set their own personal goals as they "train" to become world-class writers. They can continue to set new goals as they become more skilled and more comfortable writers. If they are keeping a writing portfolio (PE pages 43–49) suggest that they write down their writing goals and keep them in their portfolio.

Family Connection Letters

As you begin this unit, send home the Writing Process Family Connection letter, which describes what students will be learning.

- Letter in English (TE p. 652)
- Letter in Spanish (TE p. 660)

Materials

Posterboard (TE pp. 4, 5)

Writing samples (TE pp. 5, 7)

Copy Masters/ Transparencies

Graphic organizers (TE p. 6)

Becoming a Writer

Students might not yet be sophisticated enough readers or writers to make the connection between reading and writing. Point out the benefits of reading that will help make students better writers.

- They will become more aware of how writers put words and sentences together to express ideas.
- They will begin to notice that different forms of writing follow different patterns.
- They will also begin to build a bigger vocabulary.

Have students read aloud the quotation from *Wind in the Willows* several times to hear the effect of the playful language. Explain that in order to be able to play with words this way, a writer has to have a good vocabulary.

✳ To help students play with words, refer them to Increase Vocabulary Skills on PE pages 466–469.

Becoming a Writer

The following tips can help you become a good writer.

Keep Reading!

One of the best ways to learn about writing is to read.

> "I love reading, so naturally I like to write."
>
> —Beverly Cleary

Make Writing Fun.

At home, write in a journal about anything and everything. Try writing poems, stories, or even a TV script. Find a pen pal!

> "I keep the stories enjoyable for my readers by keeping them enjoyable for me."
>
> —Gordon Korman

Play with Words.

English overflows with dazzling words. Enjoy them!

> "All was a-shake and a-shiver—glints and gleams and sparkles, rustle and swirl, chatter and bubble."
>
> —from *Wind in the Willows* by Kenneth Grahame

 Write about a quotation. Write nonstop for 3 to 5 minutes about one of the quotations on this page. Tell what it means to you.

English Language Learners

Provide writing practice by beginning a dialogue journal with each student. Give students topics only if necessary, and continue journal dialoguing throughout the year. Do not overtly correct this writing, but model correct English by restating students' most common errors in correct form.

Advanced Learners

Ask students to collect additional quotations about writing from various authors' Web sites, such as this one from Betsy Byars: "When I was your age, I was like you—I read all the time. That was one of the main reasons I succeeded as a writer—I had developed an ease with words. That's my first tip—READ!" (www.betsybyars.com)

Depending on how many students collect quotations, encourage them to share them with the class by

- creating a poster for each quotation, or
- typing each quotation in an attractive font on a separate page and compiling them into a classroom notebook.

The Steps in the Writing Process

Some writers try to do everything all at once. However, it's much better to work on your writing one step at a time.

The Steps in the Writing Process

Prewrite At the beginning of the process, the writer chooses a topic, gathers details about it, and makes a plan to organize the details.

Write Creating the first draft is the exciting step of getting all the ideas on paper.

Revise After reviewing the first draft, the writer can add new details, delete ideas that don't belong, and change parts that aren't clear.

Edit Next, the writer looks over the revised writing for mistakes in capitalization, punctuation, spelling, and grammar.

Publish In the end, the writer shares the final copy with a parent, some classmates, or the world!

Think about writing. Look at the steps above. What part is the hardest for you to do? What part is the easiest? Why?

The Steps in the Writing Process

After you discuss the steps in the writing process, extend the Think about writing questions. Read the description of the steps below, pausing after each one to ask: What tips could you give someone who finds this step difficult?

■ **Prewriting**—This is the step where writers explore a topic. Many writers use graphic organizers to collect their ideas on several topics before choosing one.

■ **Writing**—In this step writers see where their ideas about a topic will take them. They decide how to "speak" to the reader and what details they will use to support their topic.

■ **Revising**—In this step, writers look for ways to improve their writing. It's another chance to make it better.

■ **Editing**—Do I capitalize this noun? Should I use *has* or *have*? Did I spell all of my words correctly? A writer can answer these questions in the editing step.

■ **Publishing**—Writers like to share their ideas with others. Publishing is sharing.

✳ To make sure that students are familiar with terms for important parts of the writing process, review Writing Terms on PE page 465.

English Language Learners

Make a poster that shows the steps in the writing process and hang it in the classroom. For each step, attach a sample piece of writing that shows an assignment at that stage of the process. Highlight important elements of each step in the writing samples for students to refer to when they write their own pieces.

Struggling Learners

To reinforce the importance of the prewriting stage, help students brainstorm examples of life situations that correspond to it, such as:

● A chef chooses a recipe, ingredients, and utensils before preparing a meal.

● A singer selects the right combination of music and lines up musicians before practicing for a concert.

● A horseback rider plans a route; packs supplies; and brushes, saddles, and bridles the horse before going on a trail ride.

The Process in Action

Prewriting Selecting a Topic

One of the most common refrains among student writers is, "I can't think of anything to write about." Point out that once in a while, a good writing idea will just pop into their heads. The rest of the time, they have to work at coming up with an idea. Assure students that throughout this book, they will learn and practice a variety of techniques for selecting topics.

Prewriting Gathering Details

Display and discuss several kinds of graphic organizers that are suitable for gathering details for a variety of different writing assignments and forms of writing.

＊ For examples of graphic organizers students can use to Collect Details, see PE pages 456–457 and TE pages 645–651.

Writing
Developing the First Draft

This is a good opportunity to remind students who plan to write on a computer to save their work frequently and to make a back-up copy or printout of their work at the end of each writing session.

The Process in Action

Using the writing process is like following a recipe. The next two pages will tell you what to do during each step of the process.

 tip The graphic below shows how writing can move forward *and* backward. Collecting more details after writing a first draft is an example of moving backward.

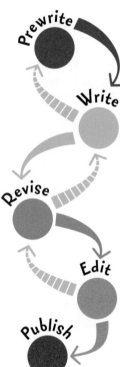

Prewriting
Selecting a Topic

- Think about your assignment: What do you want your writing to do? Who is your audience? What form of writing are you using?
- Choose a topic that really interests you.

Gathering Details

- Search for interesting details about your topic and take notes.
- Find a focus for your writing—what you want to emphasize about your topic.
- Organize your details.

Writing
Developing the First Draft

- Write freely to get your ideas on paper (or on your computer screen).
- Use your prewriting notes as you write.
- Include a beginning, a middle, and an ending.

Struggling Learners

Whenever possible, allow students to use computers or laptop word processors as they write. The ease with which text can be added, deleted, changed, and moved on the page frees reluctant writers to concentrate on their ideas during the drafting stage rather than on the physical act of writing.

Revising Improving Your Writing

- Read your writing out loud. Then read it silently.
- Ask a classmate, family member, or teacher to read your work.
- Use these questions to guide your changes:
  1. **Does the beginning grab the reader's attention?**
  2. **Do the details in the middle support my focus?**
  3. **Does the ending say something important about the topic?**
  4. **Do I sound interested in the topic?**
  5. **Do I use specific nouns and verbs?**
  6. **Are my sentences and ideas connected?**
- Improve your writing by adding, cutting, moving, or rewriting parts.

Editing Checking for Conventions

- Correct errors in capitalization, punctuation, spelling, and grammar.
- Ask another person to help you check your writing for errors.
- Write a neat final copy and proofread it.

Publishing Sharing Your Writing

- Share your finished writing.
- Put your best pieces of writing in a portfolio.

 Study the process. Pick one step in the writing process. Write down at least two reasons why the step is important.

The Writing Process
Writing is a step-by-step process.

Revising Improving Your Writing

To help students appreciate the advantage that revising offers them, use the following comparison:

- What if, as you were about to hand in a test, you were told that you could look in your textbook to make sure that all your answers were correct? Wouldn't you want that second chance to get all the answers right and improve your grade? (Students are certain to answer yes.)
- The revising step of the writing process is your second chance to get it right before you turn in your work.

Editing Checking for Conventions

Review the Editing and Proofreading Marks on the inside back cover of the pupil edition. Tell students to use these marks for the editing step of the writing process.

Publishing Sharing Your Writing

Encourage students to start thinking of different ways they can share their writing throughout the year. For example, they may enjoy publishing a monthly collection of their best writing in a class journal.

Working with the Traits

Emphasize the idea that the step-by-step design of the writing process helps writers slow down so that they can give each trait and each writing step the right amount of attention.

Help students connect the traits to the writing process. Explain that just as they will work on their writing one step-of-the-process at a time, they will also use a few traits at each step:

- Prewriting—Ideas and Organization
- Writing—Voice, Word Choice, and Sentence Fluency
- Revising—Organization, Voice, Word Choice, and Sentence Fluency
- Editing—Conventions

 Use the Process

Answers

1. D
2. A
3. C
4. E
5. B

8

Working with the Traits

Writers have to answer many questions about the traits of writing.

Ideas

Organization

Voice

Word Choice

Sentence Fluency

Conventions

What main ideas should I write about?
How should I organize my details?
How can I make my writing voice stronger?
What are the best words to use?
Are my sentences easy to read?
Have I checked for errors?

The writing process helps writers focus on each question at the proper time. For example, **ideas** are important in the beginning of a writing project, while **word choice** becomes more important later on.

The Writing Process in Review

 Use the process. Colin wrote an essay about dolphins. On your own paper, match Colin's activities with the correct step of the writing process.

___ **1.** Fix a spelling mistake—"dollphin."

___ **2.** Research dolphins at the library.

___ **3.** Add drawings to the final draft.

___ **4.** Ask Josh to read the finished essay.

___ **5.** Create a first draft.

A. Prewriting

B. Writing

C. Revising

D. Editing

E. Publishing

Struggling Learners

Discuss how voice and word choice change depending on the audience. Give the following examples:

- An email to a friend might end with *Write back soon!*
- A business letter might end with *I look forward to hearing back from you at your earliest convenience.*

Write the two sentences on the board. Point out the differences in word choice and end punctuation in each sentence and discuss how that changes the tone (voice) of the sentence.

One Writer's Process

Producing a piece of pottery involves several steps. The potter must prepare the clay, shape the pot, fire it in a kiln, and glaze it. Each step affects the quality of the final piece.

Writing also involves several steps. The steps in the writing process include *prewriting, writing, revising, editing,* and *publishing.* This chapter shows how Fumi used the writing process to create an essay about an activity she enjoys—making pottery!

Mini Index

- Previewing the Goals
- Prewriting
- Writing
- Revising
- Editing
- Assessing the Final Copy
- Reflecting on Your Writing

One Writer's Process

Objectives

- examine the goals for expository writing
- evaluate one writer's work step-by-step through the writing process
- review one writer's final essay and assessment

Write the following sentences on chart paper and post them in the classroom writing center:

- Write what you know.
- Write about something you enjoy.
- Write about something that interests you.

Have students read aloud the sentences. Point out that these three sentences are often given as advice to new writers. Ask students why they think this is good advice.

Students will probably recognize that when writers care about their topics, the writing process is more enjoyable, and the writing reflects their interest and enjoyment.

Materials

Chart paper (TE p. 9)

Previewing the Goals

After discussing the goals of an expository (how-to) essay, focus on sentence fluency. Point out that students can learn a lot about sentence fluency from their favorite writers. As they read and come across sentences that they like, they can practice **sentence modeling** (see below) to write sentences that follow the same pattern.

Answers

Possible answers:

1. Fumi should select a topic about a favorite activity that she knows how to do well and can explain to others.
2. Her essay will be easy to follow from beginning to end.
3. Her voice should show that she is interested in her topic.

Previewing the Goals

For a class assignment, Fumi needed to write a how-to essay about an activity she enjoyed. Before she started writing, she studied the goals for the assignment.

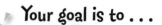

Your goal is to . . .

Ideas   Select a favorite activity you know how to do and can explain to others.

Organization   Make sure your essay is easy to follow from beginning to ending.

Voice   Let your reader know that you are interested in the topic.

Word Choice   Use specific nouns and verbs.

Sentence Fluency   Write sentences that flow smoothly and clearly.

Conventions   Follow the rules for punctuation, capitalization, spelling, and grammar.

 Answer the following questions about Fumi's assignment.

1 What type of topic should Fumi select?

2 How will she know if her work is well organized?

3 How should her writing voice sound in the essay?

Teaching Tip: Sentence Modeling

Explain to students that studying and copying the pattern of sentences by other writers is called sentence modeling. When they use professional models, they can learn a great deal about writing fluent sentences.

- Ask students to find a well-constructed sentence or short passage by one of their favorite writers.

- Tell them to copy the sentence or passage on their paper.
- Then have them practice writing sentences that follow the same patterns as the professional models, using a topic of their choice.
- Suggest that they focus on one part of a sentence at a time.
- When they have finished, invite students to share their new sentences with classmates.

✳ For more about sentence modeling, see PE page 449.

This activity provides an opportunity to reinforce the idea that one of the best ways to learn about writing is to read.

Prewriting Selecting a Topic

Fumi was given the following assignment: *Write an expository essay that explains how to do an activity you enjoy.* To think of topics, Fumi created a list.

List

> ### Activities I Enjoy
>
> playing soccer   making sushi
> painting   camping
> making pottery   swimming

Fumi decided to write about making pottery. She knew the process had clear steps that she could explain.

Gathering and Organizing Details

Now that she had a topic, Fumi needed to gather and organize details about her topic. She used a time line to list the main steps in the process of making pottery.

Time Line

> ### Making Pottery
>
> | First | Prepare the clay. |
> | Next | Shape the pot. |
> | Then | Bake the pot in a kiln. |
> | Then | Glaze the pot. |
> | Last | Bake the pot in the kiln again. |

Prewriting Selecting a Topic

Give students a few minutes to create a list of topics about activities they enjoy. Then ask them which item on their list they would select as a topic for a how-to essay and have them explain why they would choose to write about this topic.

If time is available, encourage students to use the topic they selected to practice the different stages of the writing process explained in this section.

Prewriting
Gathering and Organizing Details

Ask students to suggest ways that the completed time line will help Fumi write her essay. Students should recognize that the time line can work as a mini outline for Fumi. It shows the order in which she should present ideas. After she writes, she can use her time line to check that she hasn't left out any important details in the process.

✱ For more information about using a Time Line, see PE page 457.

English Language Learners

Many students who are learning English may feel overwhelmed by trying to choose writing topics because they do not believe they have enough English vocabulary to develop their topics. Often, help is needed to even begin generating a topics list.

- If possible, converse individually with each student about his or her interests and help them to generate a list of at least three possible topics. Then allow them to choose their favorite.
- Once they have chosen a topic, help each student to make a list of important vocabulary that they will need for the topic to describe it adequately.

Struggling Learners

As students select an item on their list for a topic, help them determine whether an activity is too simple or too complex to cover in a how-to essay. For example:

- Making toast could be explained in a single paragraph.
- Telling how to win a game of chess would take several pages.

Writing
Completing Your First Draft

To avoid having students become distracted by unfamiliar terms as they read the sample essay, review the meaning of *focus statement* and *transitions,* which appear in the callouts.

- A *focus statement* is a sentence that tells the specific part of the topic that the writer is going to focus on, or develop, in the rest of the essay. Fumi's focus statement is the last sentence in the first paragraph.
- *Transitions* are words and phrases that connect ideas in sentences and paragraphs. Transitions that show time order are words like *first, next, then,* and *last.*

Assure students that they will learn more about these terms later.

Suggest that students read the essay through once for meaning. Then ask them to read it a second time, looking back at the time line on PE page 11 to see how Fumi used the details in her draft. This will help students see how useful it is to gather and organize details before they write.

12

Writing Completing Your First Draft

When Fumi wrote her first draft, she tried to get all of her thoughts down on paper. She used her time line (page 11) as a basic guide. (There are some errors in Fumi's first draft.)

> The beginning paragraph includes a focus statement (underlined).

Did you ever think pinching is fun? I did when I learned how to make a pinch pot. <u>There are four steps to making a pinch pot.</u>

> Fumi writes about the steps in middle paragraphs.

Start by preparing the clay. Bubbles can make the clay explode when it's heated in the kiln. SLAM the clay on the table a couple of times. This is the lowdest part of the proces! If there's a whole group making pinch pots, it's one huge slamma-ramma! Next, shape the pinch

> Transitions help to show time order and connect details.

pot. Roll out a ball of clay. Push you're thumb into the center. Keep pinching and turning the clay. When your pinch pot looks right, flatten the bottom on a table.

English Language Learners

Define the following words before students read the passage:

- pinching (squeezing between fingers)
- pot (small bowl or dish)
- clay (soft, sticky earth)
- slam (throw down hard)
- firing (heating and drying, like cooking)
- glaze (shiny paint)

If possible, show students pictures of this process or show them a ceramic pot so that they better understand the topic before reading.

Advanced Learners

The errors in the sample drafts throughout the book might distract students who strive to do everything perfectly every time. Reassure them that part of the satisfaction of the writing process is having the freedom to try different techniques and put creativity in command during the writing stage because errors can be fixed during the revising and editing stages.

One Writer's Process **13**

Get an adult to put your pinch pot in a kiln. A kiln is an oven that fires the clay. The clay hardens in the kiln. After firing, the pot comes out pale white. It is ready for glazing.

Glaze is a wierd paint. It looks gray when you put it on your pot. Have the adult put the pinch pot in the kiln again. The glaze will come out smooth like glass. A completely new color!

I love seeing a finished pot. It's almost as good as making it. When I'm done, all I want to do is start pinching again!

Unfamiliar terms are defined.

Fumi tells why she enjoys the activity.

Practice

Review the goals for ideas, organization, and voice on page 10. Does Fumi reach those goals in her first draft? Explain.

Have students work in small groups to complete the **Practice** activity. Suggest that students elect one member of the group to lead the discussion and jot down the conclusions of the group during the discussion. After students have completed the activity, have group leaders share the responses of their group.

Practice Answers

Answers will vary. Possible answers:

Fumi reaches her goals for a first draft.

■ She explains how to make a pinch pot, which she really enjoys doing.
■ She presents the steps for making a pinch pot in the order in which she listed them in her time line. The steps are easy to follow from beginning to end.
■ She gives specific, interesting details about preparing the clay, shaping the pot, and firing the pot to show how much she knows about the topic and how interested she is in it. She ends by saying that she loves seeing a finished pot and that she can't wait to start pinching again.

English Language Learners

Before beginning the assignment, review the meaning of ideas, organization, and voice on PE page 10. Allow students to work in groups with English-proficient students who can help them understand by pointing out specific examples from the text of how the sample writing reaches its goals.

Advanced Learners

Focus attention on how Fumi defines *glaze* in her essay. Challenge students to find examples from their recent reading in which the author makes the meaning clearer by directly defining unfamiliar terms. Point out that authors may also

● describe the word;
● provide examples; or

● directly link the word to synonyms, antonyms, or other clues to its meaning.

Revising Improving Your Writing

Some students may feel that the detail that Fumi removed (*one huge slamma ramma*) was one of the most appealing details in her essay. It's fun and colorful, and exactly the kind of detail young writers tend to include. Remind students that in a how-to essay, all the details should help explain the process. Since this detail does not help explain how to make a pinch pot, Fumi's decision to remove it was correct.

Practice Answers

Answers will vary. Possible responses:

- The definition of a pinch pot makes the topic clearer for readers.
- The explanation of why you slam the clay connects ideas between sentences.
- The *slamma ramma* detail is distracting and doesn't belong.
- The new paragraph signals a new step in the process. When following the steps in a process, readers like to read small chunks of text.
- Adding the detail about forming the sides of the bowl makes the process clearer.

14

Revising Improving Your Writing

After Fumi reviewed her first draft, she made the following changes.

> Did you ever think pinching is fun? I did
> when I learned how to make a pinch pot. There
> _{a small bowl called}
> are four steps to making a pinch pot.
>
> Start by preparing the clay. Bubbles can
> make the clay explode when it's heated in the
> kiln. SLAM the clay on the table a couple of
> _{To get rid of bubbles,}
> times. This is the lowdest part of the proces!
> ~~If there's a whole group making pinch pots, it's~~
> ~~one huge slamma ramma~~ Next, shape the pinch
> pot. Roll out a ball of clay. Push you're thumb
> into the center. Keep pinching and turning the
> clay. When your pinch pot looks right, flatten the
> _{to form the sides of the bowl}
> bottom on a table.

An idea is made clearer.

An explanation is added.

An unneeded detail is removed.

A new paragraph is started for the second step.

An important detail is added.

Practice

Review Fumi's changes. Which change seems most important to you? Explain your choice.

Struggling Learners

Focus attention on the creation of a new paragraph in Fumi's draft. Explain that making new paragraphs cuts text up into smaller chunks. This appeals to many readers because

- the white space makes the page look more inviting (they can easily find each step in the process), and

- the frequent breaks help readers find their places after looking up (they can re-read each step for understanding).

Have students examine pages in their textbooks with long, medium, and short paragraphs and discuss which they find easier and more enjoyable to read.

Revising Using a Peer Response

Fumi asked a classmate to comment on her essay. Then she made more changes to improve her work.

What are the four steps?

What does it mean to prepare the clay?

Why flatten the bottom on the table?

Did you ever think pinching is fun? I did when

I learned how to make a small bowl called a pinch
                    preparing, shaping, firing, and glazing.
pot. There are four steps to making a pinch pot.
          this means getting rid of bubbles.
Start by preparing the clay. Bubbles can

make the clay explode when it's heated in the

kiln. To get rid of bubbles, SLAM the clay on the

table a couple of times. This is the lowdest part of

the proces!

    Next, shape the pinch pot. Roll out a ball of

clay. Push you're thumb into the center. Keep

pinching and turning the clay to form the sides of

the bowl. When your pinch pot looks right, flatten
              Then your pot will sit level.
the bottom on a table.

Practice

Answer the following questions: How did peer responding help Fumi? What do you think is the most helpful comment above? Why?

Revising Using a Peer Response

Ask students to think about the times readers have responded to their first drafts.

- What kinds of responses were most helpful to them?
- What kinds of responses were least helpful?

Remind students that when they respond to a classmate's writing, they should be polite, positive, and specific.

Emphasize that as writers, students make the final decision about what to change, add, or cut in their writing. However, they should think carefully about comments from a peer responder. If the changes will improve the meaning, flow, and sound of their writing, then they probably should make those changes.

Practice Answers

Answers will vary. Possible answers:
- Peer responding helped Fumi see where she needed to explain things in more detail.
- The most helpful comment is probably the one about the four steps. Naming the four steps adds specific details and prepares readers for what they are going to learn about making a pinch pot.

English Language Learners

Remind students that when they are revising, both individually and with a peer, they should focus on content and not on editing for punctuation, spelling, and grammar errors. If students are writing about a topic that is unfamiliar to classmates, pair them with a peer who can help them to define important terms.

Struggling Learners

Point out that Fumi's classmate asks her to tell what the four steps are. Ask students why they think the classmate wants to know. (It gives the reader a clearer idea of what the essay is about.) Help students understand how helpful this can be by discussing other situations in which previews help us organize our thoughts:

- A teacher posts a daily agenda on the chalkboard each morning.
- A parent gives a child a specific list of chores to complete on a Saturday morning.
- A student looks at the table of contents to see what he'll be reading about in a science textbook.

Editing Checking for Conventions

Give students a few minutes to look at the editing and proofreading marks on the inside back cover of their book. Then ask volunteers to tell what each of the marks Fumi made in her essay means.

If students have been practicing the steps of the writing process using a topic they selected earlier (TE page 11), suggest that they use editing marks (see inside back cover) as they check their writing for punctuation, capitalization, spelling, and grammar errors.

✱ Preview the Proofreader's Guide on PE pages 478–605 with students, and encourage them to refer to it whenever they are editing their writing.

16

Editing Checking for Conventions

Before writing a final copy, Fumi checked her essay for punctuation, capitalization, spelling, and grammar errors. (See the inside back cover of this book for a list of editing and proofreading marks.)

A verb tense is corrected.	Did you ever think pinching ~~is~~ was fun? I did when I learned how to make a small bowl called a pinch
Punctuation errors are corrected.	pot. There are four steps to making a pinch pot: preparing, shaping, firing, and glazing.
Capitalization errors are corrected.	Start by preparing the clay. ~~t~~This means getting rid of bubbles. Bubbles can make the clay explode when it's heated in the kiln. To get rid of bubbles, ~~slam~~ SLAM the clay on the table a couple of times. This is the ~~lowdest~~ loudest part of the ~~proces~~ process!
Misspellings and a misused word are fixed.	Next, shape the pinch pot. Roll out a ball of clay. Push ~~you're~~ your thumb into the center. Keep pinching and turning the clay to form the

Practice

Review Fumi's editing. Do you make some of the same types of errors? How do you use editing marks in your writing?

English Language Learners

If students are new to English, give them only one or two specific conventions to check. For example, ask students to check for correct use of

- words like *on* and *in*, or
- third person singular verbs in the present tense (add an *s*).

Fumi's Final Copy

Fumi felt proud of her final essay. It clearly described each step in the process of making pottery.

Fumi Akimoto

Pinching for Fun

Did you ever think pinching was fun? I did when I learned how to make a small bowl called a pinch pot. There are four steps to making a pinch pot: preparing, shaping, firing, and glazing.

Start by preparing the clay. This means getting rid of bubbles. Bubbles can make the clay explode when it's heated in the kiln. To get rid of bubbles, slam the clay on the table a couple of times. This is the loudest part of the process!

Next, shape the pinch pot. Roll out a ball of clay. Push your thumb into the center. Keep pinching and turning the clay to form the sides of the bowl. When your pinch pot looks right, flatten the bottom on a table. Then your pot will sit level.

Fumi's Final Copy

Working as a class, use the goals on PE page 10 and the rubric on PE pages 176–177 to identify elements of Fumi's final copy that make it a good example of an expository essay.

Ideas
The writer explains how to do an activity she enjoys.

Organization
- The beginning of the essay grabs the reader's attention and makes the reader want to learn more.
- The steps are presented clearly and in the correct order.
- The essay flows easily from beginning to end.

Voice
The writer uses specific details that show her knowledge and interest in the topic.

Ask students to suggest ways that Fumi could publish her essay to make it even more interesting, informative, and fun.

Possible ideas include the following:
- add photographs of pinch pots Fumi has made
- add a series of numbered drawings that show each step in the process, perhaps in cartoon style
- give an oral reading followed by a live demonstration of how to make a pinch pot

This activity will help students realize the many different and creative ways there are to approach the final step in the writing process.

Akimoto 2

Afterward, get an adult to put your pinch pot in a kiln. A kiln is an oven that fires, or bakes, the clay. The clay hardens in the kiln. After firing, the pot comes out pale white. It is ready for glazing.

Glazing is the last step. Glaze is a weird paint that looks gray when you paint it onto your pot. To set the glaze, have the adult put the pinch pot in the kiln for one more firing. The glaze will come out smooth like glass. It will be a completely new color!

It's exciting to look at the finished pot. It's almost as much fun as making the pot. In fact, when I'm done, all I want to do is start pinching again!

English Language Learners

When students have their final copies written, invite them to read their writing aloud to a small group of students. This should be to celebrate their success with writing in English, not to critique their work. Some students may want to practice their pronunciation first. Provide time for them to practice with you.

Advanced Learners

Invite small groups of students to rewrite Fumi's essay in a new genre and then rehearse and present it to the class. For example, they might create

- a television commercial,
- a Reader's Theater script, or
- an interview.

Assessing the Final Copy

The teacher used the rubric on pages 176–177 to assess Fumi's final copy. A six is the very best score a writer can receive for each trait. The teacher also included helpful comments under each trait.

5 Ideas
I like your topic and the details you include.

6 Organization
You give a clear description of each part of the process, and you use transitions very well.

5 Voice
I can tell you really enjoy working on pottery.

5 Word Choice
You've chosen some strong verbs, such as "slam," "roll," "push," and "flatten."

4 Sentence Fluency
You have too many short sentences.

6 Conventions
You did an excellent job of editing.

 Discuss the assessment. Do you agree with Fumi's teacher? Why or why not? What parts of the essay do you like? Would you have written any part in a different way?

Assessing the Final Copy

Ask students to put themselves in Fumi's place as they read this assessment.

- What would their overall feeling be after reading the comments?
- Do they understand the comment about sentence fluency and can they suggest ways to fix this to improve the rating?
- What questions would they have for the teacher?

Tell students that whenever they receive an assessment that they don't agree with or that they have questions about, they should ask for a **writing conference** (see below) with you.

Teaching Tip: Writing Conferences

Brief, one-on-one discussions can help some students gain the confidence they need to ask questions about an assessment or to even challenge the validity or accuracy of an assessment.

- Assure students that you value their opinion, and that you are willing to change or modify an evaluation if the student makes a valid point. Emphasize that

your primary goal is to help them grow as writers.

- Ask students to jot down questions and notes about the assessment ahead of time. This will help them stay focused during the conference, especially if they suddenly feel self-conscious for questioning your comments.
- Arrange to meet with students in a relaxed setting, away from the busyness of the classroom.

English Language Learners

Make sure that students are only assessed on the conventions that they practiced for this writing assignment or have thoroughly studied. If they have not had an in-depth exposure to all of the traits, only focus on the ones they have used.

Reflecting on Your Writing

Explain to students that reflecting on your writing simply means taking another look at a piece of writing, and thinking about what they learned and how they can use what they learned the next time they write. In this way, reflecting can help make them better writers.

Reflecting is not an easy task for young writers. Most students will need a great deal of guidance and encouragement to complete a reflection sheet like this, especially if they have never practiced doing this before.

Explain that when they reflect on a piece of writing, they should consider any comments they have received from you or from their peers. For example, if they look back at the peer responses on PE page 15 and the teacher comments on PE page 19, they can see how Fumi arrived at her ideas for items 1, 2, and 3 on her reflection sheet.

Reflecting on Your Writing

Once the process was finished, Fumi filled out a reflection sheet. This helped her think about how she would do her next writing assignment.

> Thinking about your writing helps you find ways to improve as a writer.

Fumi Akimoto

My Expository Essay

1. The best part of my essay is . . .
   how I describe each step of making pottery.

2. The part that still needs work is . . .
   the lengths of my sentences.

3. The main thing I learned about writing an expository essay is . . .
   you have to use specific terms. Words like "fire," "kiln," and "glaze" are important for the reader to understand.

4. The next time I write an expository essay, I would like to . . .
   explain how to make sushi.

5. Here is one question I still have about expository writing.
   What other kinds of expository essays are there?

Struggling Learners

After following Fumi through the process of writing her essay, use the questions on her reflection sheet to determine what students have learned and what they might need help with on the essay they wrote (if they did so, that is). Have them share and discuss their own responses to the following two points from the reflection sheet:

- the main thing I learned about writing an expository essay
- one question I still have about expository writing

Understanding the
Traits of Writing

Picture a friend of yours. How tall is your friend? What does he or she like to wear? What makes your friend laugh? You can describe people by sharing both physical and personality traits about them.

Now think about an essay or a story you have written. What is the main **idea**? How is your writing **organized**? Does the writing have **voice**? You can describe your work by talking about the traits of writing. This chapter will show you how.

Mini Index

- **Introducing the Traits**
- **Understanding the Traits**

Understanding the
Traits of Writing

Objectives

- understand each of the six traits of effective writing
- apply the concepts of the traits to writing

If possible, have students apply the three questions in the second paragraph, which focus on the first three traits of writing, to a piece of their own writing. If they have not produced a story or an essay yet, have them use Fumi's essay on PE pages 17–18.

- What is the main idea? (how to make a pinch pot)
- How is your writing organized? (in order of the four steps for making a pinch pot)
- Does the writing have a voice? (Yes. The specific word choice shows her knowledge and interest.)

Materials

Books that illustrate the traits (TE p. 22)

Magazines (TE p. 26)

Copy Masters/ Transparencies

Graphic organizers (TE p. 24)

Introducing the Traits

Students may feel overwhelmed by the idea that they have to follow all six traits as they write. To ease their anxiety, remind students that the steps of the writing process are designed so that they only have to focus on a few traits at a time.

- During prewriting, they focus on ideas and organization.
- During writing, they focus on voice and word choice.
- During revising, they focus on sentence fluency and review each trait separately to see if they have achieved their goals.
- During editing, they focus on conventions.

Assure students that the more they practice writing, the more natural it will be for them to apply these six traits.

22

Introducing the Traits

Writing has six main traits, or qualities. Knowing about these traits will help you become a better writer.

 Ideas The best writing focuses on a specific topic and includes specific ideas and details to support that topic.

 **Organization** Good writing has a clear beginning, middle, and ending. It is easy to follow.

 Voice The best writing has an appealing voice. Voice is the special way a writer shares ideas and feelings.

 **Word Choice** Good writing uses specific nouns (*zebra*, *plum*, *canoe*), strong verbs (*squish*, *pounce*, *ooze*), and colorful adjectives (*soggy*, *crooked*, *delicate*).

 **Sentence Fluency** Strong writing flows smoothly. Sentences begin in different ways and have different lengths.

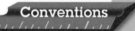 **Conventions** Good writing has correct punctuation, capitalization, spelling, and grammar.

 tip Don't forget **presentation!** The final copy of the writing should look neat and follow guidelines for margins, spacing, and design. (See pages **44–46**.)

English Language Learners

Students need to see many examples of good writing in English that exemplify the six traits. Before students write, share excerpts from published works that use each trait. For example:

- **Ideas:** *The Mysteries of Harris Burdick* by Chris Van Allsburg
- **Organization:** *Seedfolks* by Paul Fleischman
- **Voice:** *Desert Voices* by Byrd Baylor
- **Word Choice:** *Brave Irene* by William Steig
- **Sentence Fluency:** *The House on Mango Street* by Sandra Cisneros
- **Conventions:** *Your Move* by Eve Bunting

For more examples, see the book *Books, Lessons, Ideas for Teaching the Six Traits* by Vicki Spandel (Great Source Education Group, 2001).

Advanced Learners

Invite students to create a bulletin board depicting good examples of each of the six traits. Tell them they can create brief writing samples from their favorite books or pull them from newspapers, magazines, and junk mail.

Understanding Ideas

Good writing starts with quality ideas. Author Jane Yolen gives this advice: "Think of an idea or topic that is so strong within you that it's going to come out passionately as you write about it."

How can I select a topic that fits my purpose?

Make sure that you understand the purpose of the assignment before you select a topic. The lists below will help you select the best topics for different kinds of assignments.

- **For Descriptive Writing**

    Purpose: To show what a topic looks like, sounds like, and so on

    Reminder: Choose people, places, or things that you know well.

    Example Topic: Describing your favorite aunt or uncle

- **For Narrative Writing**

    Purpose: To share an experience

    Reminder: Choose experiences that you clearly remember.

    Example Topic: Telling about a bicycle adventure or accident

- **For Expository Writing**

    Purpose: To share information, to explain

    Reminder: Select topics that truly interest you.

    Example Topic: Sharing information about tarantulas or iguanas

- **For Persuasive Writing**

    Purpose: To convince someone to agree with you

    Reminder: Select topics that you have strong feelings about.

    Example Topic: Persuading someone to read a book or see a movie

Practice

On your own paper, list two possible writing topics for each type of writing listed above.

Understanding Ideas

Make sure students understand Jane Yolen's quotation at the top of the page.

- First, invite volunteers to express the quotation in their own words.
- Then, ask students to write down on a piece of paper an idea or a topic that they would like to write about more than anything else.
- Next, have them read through the different kinds of writing assignments, and jot down the kind of writing their topic fits.
- Suggest that they put this idea or topic in their writing portfolio. Then when they are assigned that kind of writing, they will have an opportunity to write about something that truly interests them.

Consider doing the **Practice** activity as a whole class activity. Post the list of topics in the classroom for students to refer to when it's time to select a topic for various writing assignments.

✱ For more information about how to Find a Topic, see PE pages 454–455.

Advanced Learners

Challenge students to go to the school library and locate examples of descriptive, narrative, expository, and persuasive writing to check out and share with the class. Suggest that they look for examples in books for young children. Ask them to briefly explain how each one fits the designated genre.

Review the strategies for gathering details. Point out that there are two important things students should keep in mind as they gather details for a writing assignment:

- Purpose—this is their reason or goal for the different types of writing assignments. For example, the pupil edition is expository writing, and its purpose is to help students learn about writing (page iii).
- Audience—usually they will write for other students and teachers.

Ask students why they think it is important to keep purpose and audience in mind when gathering details. (So that the details they select will help them achieve their purpose and so that their audience can relate to and understand the details.)

What details should I gather about a topic?

The details you collect will depend on your writing assignment.

- **For Descriptive Writing**
  1. List everything that you remember.
  2. Observe your topic, if possible, to gather even more details.
  3. Complete a sensory chart. (See page **71** for an example.)

- **For Narrative Writing**
  1. Write down what you remember about the experience.
  2. Ask other people what they remember.
  3. Complete a 5 W's chart. (See page **93** for an example.)

- **For Expository Writing**
  1. List what you already know and questions that you have.
  2. Research your topic. (See pages **342–345**.)
  3. Complete a cluster or web if you are sharing information. (See page **456** for an example.) Complete a time line if you are explaining steps. (See page **457** for an example.)

- **For Persuasive Writing**
  1. Write down your thoughts and feelings (an opinion) about the topic.
  2. Research the facts about your topic.
  3. Complete a table diagram. (See page **205** for an example.)

Practice

Gather details for one of the descriptive or narrative topics that you listed for page 23.

English Language Learners

Allow students to gather details in their first language so that they are not weighed down in translations while they are brainstorming. Then, depending on the topic and the audience for their writing, ask students to translate important ideas, or leave important terms in their first language and define the terms in English.

Struggling Learners

Explore the sensory chart (PE page 71), 5 W's chart (PE page 93), cluster or web (PE pages 456–457), time line (PE page 457), and table diagram (PE page 205), and discuss why each one is appropriate for the form of writing under which it is listed. Then ask students to share other graphic organizers they like to use while gathering details.

Provide photocopies of the reproducible sensory chart, 5 W's chart, time line, and table diagram (TE pages 646–650), and help students choose one to use for gathering details for their topic for the **Practice** activity.

Understanding Organization

Writer Joan Lowery Nixon understands the importance of organization right from the beginning: "Work extra hard on the beginning of your story, so it snares readers instantly."

Why is the beginning important?

The beginning gets the reader's attention and gives the focus.

Beginning Paragraph

> **Interesting opening**
>
> **Focus (underlined)**
>
> My backyard has an enormous oak tree. A family of squirrels lives in the tree. To them, the tree is a home, a playground, and a grocery store! An oak tree has everything a squirrel needs.

What should I include in the middle?

The middle part of your writing should include specific details that support your focus. Here are some ways to do this.

Explain: Share information about your topic.

Define: Tell what important terms mean.

Describe: Give sensory details.

Compare: Show how two things are alike.

Middle Paragraph

> **Shared information**
>
> All year, the squirrels spend their time in our oak tree. In the fall, squirrels collect the tree's acorns and bury them. They also build leaf nests in the tree's top branches. During the winter, these nests are cozy sleeping places. Once spring comes, the squirrels hop along the ground and dig up their acorns.

Understanding

Organization

Focus students' attention on the word *snares* in Joan Lowery Nixon's quotation at the top of the page. To make sure students understand the meaning of that word here, have them generate a list of appropriate synonyms. For example, students might suggest *grabs, hooks, captures,* and *catches.*

To help students understand what makes the sample beginning paragraph interesting, read aloud the paragraph once as it is written, and once without the third sentence. Point out that the third sentence is both playful and surprising. It creates a strong image that makes readers say to themselves, "I want to keep reading to find out how the tree is a home, a playground, and a grocery store for squirrels."

Struggling Learners

Students will benefit from reading examples of how an author "snares" readers at the beginning of the story. Invite students to share the opening paragraphs of their current library books. Then discuss each author's technique for "snaring" readers. Some possible techniques are the following:

- ask a question
- use exaggeration
- use an exclamation
- describe a setting
- set up a conflict

Encourage students to copy an example of a technique they like and keep it in their writing folder. They can use it as a model the next time they write.

Tell students that writers often think of an ending as they are writing their beginning or middle paragraphs. Suggest that if a good idea for an ending comes to them while they are working on the beginning or middle of a piece of writing, they should jot down their ideas so that they don't forget them.

If students have trouble thinking of an ending, encourage them to try these strategies:

- Put your writing aside for a while. Then read it over from the beginning. A good idea for an ending may come to you then.
- Ask a friend to read what you have written, and suggest ideas for an ending.
- Try restating an idea from your beginning paragraph in different words.

Practice   **Answers**

Answers will vary.

Invite students to share their new endings with classmates. Have classmates try to identify the technique that the writer used in the ending.

26

Why is the ending important?

The ending is the last part of your writing. An ending works well when it does one or more of these things:

- reminds the reader about your topic.
- reviews the important points.
- stresses one main point.
- answers any last questions.
- gives the reader something to think about.

Ending Paragraph

Something to think about

The oak tree helps the squirrels in many ways. Squirrels help the oak tree, too. They love to bury acorns, but sometimes they forget where they buried them. Some of the acorns grow into new oak trees! I wonder what forgetful squirrel planted the tree in my backyard. I'd like to thank him.

End strong! Give yourself plenty of time to create a powerful finish to your writing.

Practice

Write a new ending to the squirrel essay, using one of the other techniques mentioned above.

Advanced Learners

Have students look through grade-appropriate magazines for stories and nonfiction articles with satisfying endings. Then challenge them to find endings that are too abrupt and leave them hanging or, conversely, examples of endings that never seem to end. Invite students to share their findings with the class. Encourage all students to discuss what makes each ending satisfying or frustrating.

Understanding Voice

Writing that has "voice" sounds as exciting as a real conversation. As writer Peter Elbow says, "Writing with *real voice* has the power to make you pay attention."

Why is voice so important?

Voice is what makes you want to read every book that your favorite author wrote.

WRITING THAT LACKS VOICE

I saw a deer on a path. It came close to me. It was neat.

WRITING THAT HAS VOICE

Crash! A huge buck came leaping out of the woods. Instantly, he stopped just a few feet away from me. My heart felt like it would pop out of my chest. Then, before I knew it, the deer disappeared back into the woods.

How can I write with voice?

You can practice **freewriting**. It is one of the best ways to discover your writing voice. Read these steps before you freewrite.

1 Think about something that recently happened to you.

2 Write nonstop about this experience for 3 to 5 minutes.

3 After you finish, read your writing out loud. Does it sound as if you were talking to a friend?

4 Practice freewriting every day, and you'll begin to unlock your personal writing voice.

Practice

Write for 3 to 5 minutes nonstop on the following topic: *a time I remember.* Afterward, underline two or three ideas that sound like the real you.

Understanding Voice

Emphasize that a writer's voice should say the following things to readers:

- I am interested in my ideas or topic.
- I know a lot about my topic.
- I care about my topic.
- I want you to care about my topic as much as I do.

Ask students to prepare a reading of a passage that they especially like from a book by their favorite author, one that they think captures the voice of the author. Then give students the opportunity to share their reading in class. It may be helpful to review a few **tips for speaking in class** (see below) with students first.

After each student presents a passage, ask listeners to try to describe the writer's voice, using terms, such as excited, interested, enthusiastic, thoughtful, serious, funny, and so on. This will help simplify the concept of voice, which is often difficult for students to grasp.

Teaching Tip:
Tips for Speaking in Class

Briefly discuss these guidelines for becoming a better speaker:

- Look up from your paper from time to time. Try to make eye contact with the audience.
- Stand up straight and don't fidget.
- Speak loudly, clearly, and slowly.
- ✳ For more on speaking and listening, see PE pages 369–378.

English Language Learners

To demonstrate what voice is, read a phrase to students, such as *I got a B on my essay.* Stand with your back to students so they can't see your facial expressions.

- Read the phrase several times, using a different tone of voice each time to express frustration, pride, boredom, questioning, and other emotions.

- Ask students if they can tell the difference in your voice each time you read the phrase. How do they interpret those differences?

- Then ask students to write phrases that could describe the sentence each time it expresses a different feeling. Discuss what words work best to express each tone of voice.

Understanding
Word Choice

Have students create a word wall of general and specific nouns and verbs that they can refer to when they write. They can start by writing and adding to the nouns and verbs on this page (building/post office, rock/granite, insect/ladybug, step/pounce) Encourage students to add to their word wall on a regular basis. Each week, invite a different pair of students to be in charge of collecting and adding words to the word wall.

Young writers tend to overuse modifiers, thinking more is better. For example, instead of writing *Todd looked nervously around the class-room*, they are more apt to write, *Todd looked carefully, quickly, and nervously around the classroom.*

Emphasize that they should use adjectives or adverbs sparingly. Similar to deciding which colors to use when painting a picture, choosing the right modifiers will make the writer's ideas clear and focused.

✱ For information about Describing with Adverbs, see PE pages 426–427.

Understanding Word Choice

Working with words is fun. As author Paul Fleischman says, "We grew up knowing that words felt good in the ears and on the tongue, that they were as much fun to play with as toys."

How can I choose the best words?

Look for words that add meaning and feeling to your writing.

Choose Specific Nouns

General nouns like *building, rock,* and *insect* give the reader a general picture. Specific nouns like *post office, granite,* and *ladybug* give a clearer, more detailed picture.

Use Strong Action Verbs

Specific action verbs add energy to your writing. A statement like "The cat *pounced* on the string" is much more interesting than "The cat *stepped* on the string."

Select Effective Modifiers

The right **adjectives** paint clear word pictures. "Roscoe is a *playful* dalmatian" says much more than "Roscoe is a dalmatian."

The right **adverbs** make action more specific. The sentence "Todd looked *nervously* around the classroom" is clearer than "Todd looked around the classroom."

Practice

Read over the last story you wrote. Replace at least one noun and one verb with more specific words. Also add an adjective or an adverb to make an idea clearer.

English Language Learners

Help students find interesting verbs and descriptive words that could be used to express different emotions, such as anger, fear, excitement, happiness. Add words from these lists to a word wall and have students refer to them for use when they need to express an emotion about a topic. Lists could also be put in their writing notebooks for easy access.

These lists of words can also be used to review correct use of English grammar; for example, *nervous* is an adjective used to describe a noun, while *nervously* is an adverb and describes how an action is done.

Struggling Learners

Explain that when choosing a specific verb, you must choose just the right one. To demonstrate this, have students use a thesaurus to list synonyms for an overused verb, such as *talk*, and then rate them according to strength and voice. For example:

1–whisper	4–yell
2–mumble	5–scream
3–say	

Understanding Sentence Fluency

Smooth-reading sentences help the reader follow your ideas. As writer Russ Freedman says, "You want the reader to feel swept along, as if on a kind of trip, from sentence to sentence."

How can I make my sentences flow smoothly?

Vary Your Sentence Lengths. If your sentences are all the same length, your writing will sound choppy. (See pages **445–447**.)

TOO MANY SENTENCES ABOUT THE SAME LENGTH

My neighbor Betty is my friend. She is old enough to be my grandmother. Sometimes we just chat. She tells me stories about when she was a girl. She remembers a lot.

VARIED SENTENCE LENGTHS

My neighbor Betty is my friend, yet she's old enough to be my grandmother. Sometimes we just chat, and she tells me stories about when she was a girl. She remembers a lot.

SHORT, CHOPPY SENTENCES

Betty loves hats. She wears wooly hats. She also has floppy hats and sun hats. She has plastic rain hats. She also collects baseball caps. My favorite hat is her blue hat. It is straw.

COMBINED SENTENCES

Betty loves hats. She wears wooly hats, floppy hats, sun hats, plastic rain hats, and even baseball caps. My favorite one is her blue straw hat.

Practice

Review a paragraph or story you have written. Try to improve one or two sentences to make your writing easier to read. Use the information above as a guide.

Understanding

Sentence Fluency

Students may recall that when they were tracking Fumi's writing process earlier in the unit, her teacher thought she had too many short sentences in her final copy (PE page 19). After reading and discussing the information on this page, have partners work together to review "Pinching for Fun" (PE pages 17–18) for sentence fluency.

- Tell students to find places where Fumi's writing sounds choppy. If they have trouble, suggest that they take turns reading the paragraphs to each other to listen for short, choppy sentences.
- Have students combine these sentences to create a smoother flow.
- Invite students to share their revisions with the class.

✱ Encourage students to Combine Short Sentences (see PE pages 445–447) for practice in writing sentences that flow smoothly.

Struggling Learners

Review how to use commas in a series when combining short, choppy sentences. To demonstrate how comma placement can affect meaning, write the following sentence on the board, leaving out the commas:

You'll need paper bags glue sticks colored yarn and scissors.

Guide students in adding punctuation. Ask: Is it paper *and* bags or paper bags? Glue *and* sticks or glue sticks?

Understanding
Conventions

Provide these additional tips for checking for mistakes in punctuation, capitalization, spelling, and grammar.

- Read a piece of writing backward, from the end to the beginning. Then you won't be distracted by the meaning of the words.
- Read a piece of writing through four times, each time looking for a different kind of mistake (punctuation, capitalization, spelling, grammar).
- Check your last two or three pieces of writing to see if you repeated any kinds of mistakes. For example, did you often misuse or misspell the homonyms *they're, their,* and *there*? Look for those same kinds of mistakes in the writing you are currently checking. (Refer students to the Proofreader's Guide, PE pages 479–605.)

30

Understanding Conventions

Conventions cover the rules of punctuation, capitalization, spelling, and grammar. When you follow these rules, your writing will be clear and easy to understand.

How can I make sure my writing follows the rules?

A conventions checklist like the one below will guide you as you edit and proofread your writing. When you are not sure about a rule, check the "Proofreader's Guide." (See pages 478–605.)

Conventions

PUNCTUATION
_____ 1. Do I use correct end punctuation after every sentence?
_____ 2. Do I use commas in compound sentences?
_____ 3. Do I use apostrophes correctly to show possession *(the dog's bed)*?

CAPITALIZATION
_____ 4. Do I start every sentence with a capital letter?
_____ 5. Do I capitalize the names of people and places?

SPELLING
_____ 6. Have I checked my spelling?

GRAMMAR
_____ 7. Do my subjects and verbs agree *(she walks,* not *she walk)*?
_____ 8. Do I use the right words *(to, too, two)*?

Always have at least one other person check your writing for conventions. Ask a classmate, a teacher, or a family member for help.

Using a Rubric

During checkups, doctors listen to your breathing, check your pulse, look in your ears, tap your knees, and take a blood sample to be tested in the lab. Checking these things tells a doctor about your general health.

As a writer, you can use a rubric to check the "health" of your stories and essays. A **rubric** is a chart that lists the traits or characteristics for a specific form of writing. Once you learn to use a rubric, you'll understand the importance of traits like effective ideas, word choice, and sentences in your writing.

Mini Index

- **Understanding Rubrics**
- **Reading a Rubric**
- **Assessing with a Rubric**
- **Reviewing an Assessment**
- **Assessing a Narrative**

Using a Rubric

Objectives
- understand the rating scale on a rubric
- learn how to read a rubric
- use a rubric to assess writing

Rubrics, which appear in the revising and editing sections of the core units in the pupil edition (narrative, expository, and persuasive), can be used throughout the writing process. Point out to students that as they become more familiar with the layout and language used in the rubrics, they will discover that rubrics can

- help them prepare at the beginning of a project,
- provide guidance as they develop their first draft,
- help in the revising and editing processes, and
- provide a way to evaluate, or judge, their overall final copy.

Materials

Personal narrative (TE p. 34)

Copy Masters/ Transparencies

Assessment sheet and 4-point rubric (TE p. 34)

Understanding Rubrics

The **tip** at the top of the page explains how the rubrics in this book are arranged. To give students an even clearer understanding of this arrangement, have them look at the rubric for one of the core units, for example the narrative rubric on PE pages 120–121.

Rating Guide

Explain to students that unless they totally ignore all the help that they are offered as they complete an assignment, you don't expect to see many 1 or 2 ratings. On the other hand, there probably won't be many 6 ratings either, at least at first.

Tell students to expect most of their ratings to fall within the 3–5 range. However, if they feel that they are making improvements in certain traits but their ratings do not go up, then they should not hesitate to come to you to discuss their progress.

32

Understanding Rubrics

Teachers often use rubrics to rate writing. The rubrics in this book use a 6-point scale.

6	5	4	3	2	1
Amazing	Strong	Good	Okay	Poor	Incomplete

tip The rubrics are arranged according to the main traits of writing—*ideas, organization, voice, word choice, sentence fluency,* and *conventions.*

Rating Guide

This guide will help you understand the rating scale.

A **6** means that the writing is truly **amazing**. It far exceeds the main requirements for a trait.

A **5** means that the writing is very **strong**. It meets the main requirements for a trait.

A **4** means that the writing is **good**. It meets most of the requirements for a trait.

A **3** means that the writing is **okay**. It needs work to meet the main requirements for a trait.

A **2** means that the writing is **poor**. It needs a lot of work.

A **1** means that the writing is **incomplete**. It is not yet ready to assess for a trait.

Advanced Learners

Ask students to look for examples of other kinds of ratings that are arranged in various ways. Suggest that they look for ratings by movie critics, sports analysts, booksellers, and others in newspapers and magazines.

Have students bring examples to class and then discuss how the ratings are arranged:

- Are they in order?
- Are they numbered?
- Are they marked with stars or other graphics?

Reading a Rubric

For the rubrics in this book, each trait has its own color bar (green for *ideas,* pink for *organization,* and so on). Descriptions for each rating help you evaluate the quality of a certain trait.

Rubric for Narrative Writing

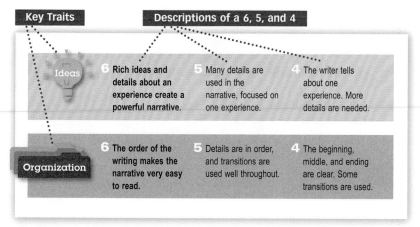

Key Traits

Descriptions of a 6, 5, and 4

Ideas

6 Rich ideas and details about an experience create a powerful narrative.

5 Many details are used in the narrative, focused on one experience.

4 The writer tells about one experience. More details are needed.

Organization

6 The order of the writing makes the narrative very easy to read.

5 Details are in order, and transitions are used well throughout.

4 The beginning, middle, and ending are clear. Some transitions are used.

A Closer Look

When you read a rubric to judge a trait, follow these steps:

1 First read the 5 descriptions. *(A 5 is very strong writing that meets the main requirements for that trait.)*

2 Decide if your writing should get a 5 for that specific trait.

3 If not, read 6, 4, 3, and 2 until you find the rating that best fits your paper.

4 If you are still revising and your rating is 4 or lower, make the necessary changes to improve the rating for that trait.

Review the complete narrative rubric. Look at the rubric on pages 120–121. For which traits will it be hard for you to achieve a 5 or 6 rating? For which will it be easy? Explain.

Reading a Rubric

The colors associated with each trait can also be used during revising and editing. For example, when students are checking for ideas, they could use a green colored pencil. When students are checking for organization, they could use a pink colored pencil, and so on.

A Closer Look

Make sure students understand that they are to read the level 5 descriptions for all six traits.

Most students will have a difficult time giving themselves a low rating for two reasons:

- First, they are still trying to understand the traits so they may or may not recognize that they have not achieved their goals for that trait.
- Second, most students won't want to admit that their work deserves a lower rating.

Therefore, try to allow time for writing conferences to evaluate their writing. Students can then compare those ratings with their own to arrive at a more balanced, honest evaluation.

Assessing with a Rubric

Review the process for using an assessment sheet. Rather than having students make their own assessment sheet each time they complete a piece of writing, you can provide photocopies of the reproducible assessment sheet on TE page 644.

If this is students' first experience with using an assessment sheet or if they have not written **personal narratives** (see below), consider filling in an assessment sheet together for a sample personal narrative (see PE page 89–90), or perhaps one written by an anonymous student.

- Distribute copies of the narrative, and give students time to read it through.
- Divide students into six groups. Assign each group a trait, and have them evaluate the narrative for that particular trait.
- Use an overhead projector to display a blank assessment sheet (TR 7).
- Work together to complete the assessment sheet based on the evaluations of each group.
- Assure them that as they practice with rubrics, they will be able to score all the traits.

34

Assessing with a Rubric

Follow the steps below when you use a rubric like the one on page 35 to assess a piece of writing.

1 Make an assessment sheet. Create a sheet like the one on this page.

2 Read the final copy. Get an overall feeling for the writing before you evaluate it.

3 Assess the writing. Find the rating on the rubric that best fits each trait in the writing. Write that number on your assessment sheet.

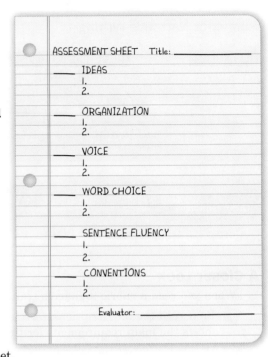

ASSESSMENT SHEET   Title: _____

____ IDEAS
 1.
 2.

____ ORGANIZATION
 1.
 2.

____ VOICE
 1.
 2.

____ WORD CHOICE
 1.
 2.

____ SENTENCE FLUENCY
 1.
 2.

____ CONVENTIONS
 1.
 2.

Evaluator: _____

4 Make comments under each trait.
(Your teacher may or may not ask you to do so.)

Make an assessment sheet. Make an assessment sheet like the one above. Then evaluate one of your personal narratives using the rubric on pages 120–121. For each trait, write something you did well and something you'd like to do better. (See the sample on page 37.)

Teaching Tip: Personal Narrative

Students may benefit from a reminder of what a personal narrative is before they attempt to complete an assessment sheet for a personal narrative. Provide this brief definition:

- A personal narrative (see PE pages 87–124) shares a true story from the writer's life.
- A strong, natural storytelling voice, sensory details, and lively

dialogue show the reader what happened and make the writer's story come to life so that readers truly care about what happened to the writer.

English Language Learners

Asking students who are still in the early stages of learning to evaluate their writing by first reading the 5 description in each trait may be unreasonable at the beginning. So that they do not get frustrated, tell students to first read the 3 descriptions.

- Provide a 4-point rubric (TE page 624) on which the 3 rating is second highest.

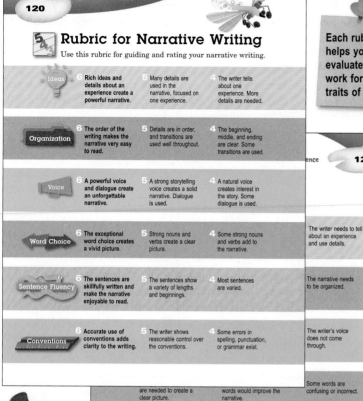

Using a Rubric **35**

120

Rubric for Narrative Writing

Use this rubric for guiding and rating your narrative writing.

Ideas
6 Rich ideas and details about an experience create a powerful narrative.
5 Many details are used in the narrative, focused on one experience.
4 The writer tells about one experience. More details are needed.

Organization
6 The order of the writing makes the narrative very easy to read.
5 Details are in order, and transitions are used well throughout.
4 The beginning, middle, and ending are clear. Some transitions are used.

Voice
6 A powerful voice and dialogue create an unforgettable narrative.
5 A strong storytelling voice creates a solid narrative. Dialogue is used.
4 A natural voice creates interest in the story. Some dialogue is used.

Word Choice
6 The exceptional word choice creates a vivid picture.
5 Strong nouns and verbs create a clear picture.
4 Some strong nouns and verbs add to the narrative.

Sentence Fluency
6 The sentences are skillfully written and make the narrative enjoyable to read.
5 The sentences show a variety of lengths and beginnings.
4 Most sentences are varied.

Conventions
6 Accurate use of conventions adds clarity to the writing.
5 The writer shows reasonable control over the conventions.
4 Some errors in spelling, punctuation, or grammar exist.

121

The writer needs to tell about an experience and use details.

The narrative needs to be organized.

The writer's voice does not come through.

Some words are confusing or incorrect.

3 are needed to create a clear picture.
2 words would improve the narrative.

3 A better variety of sentence lengths and beginnings is needed.
2 Many sentences are the same length or begin the same way.
1 Too many sentences sound the same.

3 A number of errors could confuse the reader.
2 Many errors make the narrative hard to read.
1 Help is needed to make corrections.

The rubrics are based on a six-point rating scale. A 6 is the highest rating, and a 1 is the lowest rating.

Each rubric helps you evaluate your work for the traits of writing.

Use the following questions to guide a final review of the arrangement of a rubric.

- What is the purpose of the colored strips? (They identify each of the traits.)
- How many colored strips are there? (There are six, one for each of the traits: ideas, organization, voice, word choice, sentence fluency, and conventions.)
- How do you read the rubric? (You find the heading for a trait in the left column, then you read across the strip.)
- What do the numbers stand for? (They are the ratings. A score of 6 means the writing is "powerful;" a score of 1 means the writing is "incomplete.")
- How can you use the descriptions in each strip? (You can use the descriptions to judge the writing and figure out how to make it better.)

* The complete six-point rubric for narrative writing is found on PE pages 120–121. Four- and five-point rubrics are available on TE pages 624 and 627.

Reviewing an Assessment

Read the essay together as a class. Then have students work with partners to read the essay again and to use the rubric for narrative writing on PE pages 120–121 to jot down notes about the strengths and weaknesses of the essay. The following questions, which are based on that rubric, can provide additional help in identifying the strengths and weaknesses.

- What experience is the essay mostly about?
- Which details does the writer use to describe that experience?
- Does the writer provide enough details so that you really understand how he felt during that experience?
- Are you able to follow the writer's ideas easily? Why or why not?
- Which details show the writer's feelings and level of interest in the story?
- Are the sentences different lengths? Do the sentences have different beginnings?
- Are there mistakes in spelling, grammar, and punctuation?

Reviewing an Assessment

These two pages show how one student used a rubric to evaluate his writing.

Personal Narrative

The following narrative deals with a painful experience for the writer. As you read this essay, pay special attention to its strong points and weak points.

Left Behind

It was really quiet at home. Everyone was at the hospital with my little brother José. José had hurt his wrist while playing baseball with our cousins. My dad's family was visiting, because it was a family reunion.

I had come inside to get a drink of lemonade when José got hurt. I heard lots of shouting. Mom was really worried. Dad ran out front. He started the minivan. Everyone jumped into cars and headed to the hospital. No one realized that I had been left behind.

After a while, the phone rang. My dad said he'd be home soon. The dog herd the cars before I did. He started barking and jumping. Before long the house was full of noisey family. José came running up to me. I felt worried when I saw his arm in a sling. He said it was really cool how the doctor took care of his wrist. Then he ran out.

I watched everyone head back outside. Grandpa said, "Sorry we rushed off without you." He bent down and wrapped me in a really big hug. I hugged him back. He stood up, "Now let's go play some ball, eh?"

English Language Learners

To make connections to the situation before reading the narrative, ask students if they or someone they know has hurt themselves playing baseball.

To make the details clear to students, define the following words before reading the passage:

- wrist (the joint close to the hand that allows it to bend)

- reunion (a party given to get together people who have been apart for a while)
- minivan (a large car that has two or three rows of seats)
- sling (a cloth used to hold an arm still)
- wrapped (surrounded)

Sample Self-Assessment

The student who wrote "Left Behind" used the rubric on pages 120–121 to evaluate his narrative. Beneath each trait, he named one strength (1) and one weakness (2) in his writing.

ASSESSMENT SHEET   Title: <u>Left Behind</u>

4   IDEAS
1. My background details are clear.
2. I need more details about what I did while I was alone.

4   ORGANIZATION
1. The beginning names my topic.
2. I could have used more transitions.

4   VOICE
1. I sound interested.
2. I should have shared more of my feelings.

5   WORD CHOICE
1. My words are clear.
2. I could have used more feeling words.

4   SENTENCE FLUENCY
1. The sentences are easy to read.
2. I have too many short, choppy sentences in the second paragraph.

4   CONVENTIONS
1. I used correct punctuation.
2. I need to double-check my spelling.

Evaluator: <u>Pablo Sanchez</u>

Review the self-assessment. Read through the assessment sheet. Then list one strength and one weakness (for any trait) that the writer may have missed.

Sample Self-Assessment

Have students look at the notes they jotted down earlier about "Left Behind" (TE page 36) to find one strength and one weakness that the writer may have missed in his self-assessment. Invite volunteers to share their ideas with the class.

Encourage students to tell which rating in the self-assessment that they most agree with, and which they most disagree with, and to explain why. Remind students that their judgments should be based on the rubric for narrative writing on PE pages 120–121.

Struggling Learners

Explain that Pablo can use his self-assessment of his essay to set goals for himself on his next writing project. Focus attention on each weakness (item 2 under each trait) Pablo listed, and discuss what goal he might set for each one. Answers might include the following:

- gather more details before beginning to write
- use more transition words and phrases
- be more open about my feelings
- use sentences of different lengths
- keep a dictionary and my spelling journal nearby

Assessing a Narrative

It may be helpful if you **analyze the personal narrative** (*see below*) together, before you ask students to assess it.

NOTE: In each core unit (narrative, expository, and persuasive) there are two additional writing samples that teachers can use with students for further assessment practice (TE pages 630–643). The writing samples are provided in transparency form so that you can work together as a group. (A copy master version is available for students.) A reproducible assessment sheet, based on the traits of writing, allows you and students to rate the writing samples. Finally, a completed assessment sheet is provided to guide teachers through the assessment.

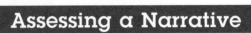

Assessing a Narrative

Read the personal narrative below and pay attention to the strengths and weaknesses in the writing. Then follow the directions at the bottom of the page.

Rainy Day

I stared out the window. "Why does it have to rain today?" I asked my dad. We were supposed to go camping. Rotten rain.

"Guess we'll have to camp right here in the living room," Dad said. I turned around. He was unrolling the sleeping bags. He put them in front of the fireplace. Then he pulled out the little camping table. He set that in the corner. It wasn't the same as camping outside, but it still looked fun.

Later we were sitting by a roaring fire. Dad ran outside in the rain for some more wood. We roasted hot dogs and marshmallows. I drank hot cider that Mom had put in a thermos. We turned out all of the lights. Dad read a book by the firelight. I was starting to like camping indoors.

Later that night I curled up in my sleeping bag. I watched the hot coals glowing in the fireplace. I listened to the rain outside. I whispered in the dark, "Dad? Can we go camping again next weekend?"

Use a narrative rubric. Assess the narrative you have just read using the rubric on pages 120–121 as a guide. Before you get started, create an assessment sheet like the one on page 34.

Teaching Tip: Analyze the Narrative

Work with students to analyze the elements that make "Rainy Day" a good personal narrative. Focus on the three traits that relate to the development of content and form.

Ideas—The writer tells about one experience, a rainy day indoor camping experience. The writer provides specific, sensory details so that readers can picture the experience. (rotten rain, unrolling the sleeping bags, camping table, roaring fire, roasted hot dogs and marshmallows, read a book by firelight, listened to the rain)

Organization—The order of events is easy to follow from beginning to end. The transition *later* helps show time order.

Voice—The writer uses natural sounding language (rotten rain) and dialogue to reveal the character's personalities and feelings.

Peer Responding

Have you ever made chili and asked someone to try it? The person's response will tell you if the chili is as good as you hoped it would be. Having people "try" your writing is helpful, too.

Your classmates can read your writing and tell you what works well and what could work even better. This chapter explains the process of sharing writing in peer-response conferences.

Mini Index

- Peer-Responding Guidelines
- Making Helpful Responses
- Peer Response Sheet

Objectives

- understand the role of the author and the role of the responder in peer responding
- learn how to give helpful responses
- practice using a peer response sheet

At first, students may be uncomfortable with the idea of peer responding. Point out that even professional writers wouldn't think of publishing a piece of writing without asking for opinions and suggestions from trusted friends and family, people the writers know will give them honest and valuable advice for improving their work. Even when a professional writer doesn't have friends or family members read a piece of writing, the writer's editor spends a lot of time working with the writer so that the final work is as close to perfect as it can be. When students share their writing with a peer responder, they show that they are willing to do whatever is necessary to make their writing the best it can be.

Materials

Index cards (TE p. 40)

Peer Responding Guidelines

Students generally don't like to hurt each other's feelings, and no matter how much you emphasize that they are evaluating the work and not the person, most students are going to be hesitant to say anything negative. On the other hand, there may be some students who relish the opportunity to be critical. Finding the balance here can be a challenge.

At this point, probably the best way to ensure that students follow the guidelines for writers and responders is to closely monitor their peer-responding sessions.

Remind students that editors do not expect the work of a professional author to be perfect the first time around. Peer responders do not expect the writing they are reviewing to be perfect either. Like editors, peer responders are trying to help writers figure out how to make their writing better.

Peer-Responding Guidelines

Peer responding takes teamwork. The writer has one job, and the responder has a different job.

The Writer's Job

As the writer, you need to present a piece of your writing. Try to have a copy for each responder. Then follow these guidelines:

- **Introduce your writing,** but don't say too much.
- **Read your work aloud,** or let the responders read it silently.
- **Ask for comments.** Listen carefully.
- **Write down** the suggestions to help you remember them.
- **Ask for advice** about any specific trouble spots.

The Responder's Job

As a responder, be kind, respectful, and helpful. Follow these guidelines:

- **Listen (or read) carefully.** Take some notes.
- **Mention what you like** about the writing. Be specific. *(Sample responses: I like the way you explain new words. Your characters seem so real.)*
- **Ask questions** if you are unsure about something or have an idea about what could be improved.

 tip Get to the point. "Nice job!" sounds encouraging, but it won't help the writer discover ways to make the paper better.

Struggling Learners

Students may be overwhelmed by learning the responsibilities of both the writer and the responder. Have them make a note card they can refer to during the peer responding process.

- Give each student an index card.
- Have them copy the "Writer's Job" bold-faced guidelines on one side of the card.

- Have them copy the "Responder's Job" bold-faced guidelines on the other side of the card.

Tell students to keep their note card handy when assuming either role during a peer responding session. Not only will it remind them of what to do for each role, but it will also help them stay on track.

Making Helpful Responses

The best responders ask questions that will help the writer discover ways to improve the writing.

Ask Specific Questions

Avoid asking questions that can be answered yes or no. Instead, ask questions that really help the writer think about the writing.

- How did you get interested in this topic?
- Which detail is your favorite?
- What one idea do you want the reader to remember?

Ask Positive Questions

Negative questions don't help the writer very much.

NEGATIVE QUESTIONS:	POSITIVE QUESTIONS:
✗ Why didn't you tell more about your lighthouse?	✔ How big is the lighthouse light?
✗ Why are your verbs so dull?	✔ What exciting verbs could you use?
✗ Where's your ending?	✔ What new idea could you include in your ending?

Practice

As a class, discuss the types of comments that are most helpful to writers during peer-responding sessions. Make a chart of helpful comments to post in the classroom.

Making Helpful Responses

Emphasize that the best responders always begin a response with a positive comment, such as, "The sensory details you use really create a picture in my mind."

Ask Specific Questions

Point out that students can make the questions shown on the page even more specific. For example, instead of asking, "How did you get interested in this topic?" they might ask, "How did you get interested in pottery?"

Ask Positive Questions

To help students understand the effect of negative and positive questions on a writer, alternate reading the negative and positive questions shown on the page, and add additional questions of your own. After you read each question, have students write down one or two words that describe how that question would make them feel as a writer.

Students may enjoy creating a cartoon of a class writing mascot that they can name and include on their chart of helpful comments and on other writing materials posted in the classroom.

Peer Response Sheet

If you plan to use a different type of response sheet than the one shown here, take time to familiarize students with the format now.

Remind students that any questions that they ask should be related to the topic of the essay and should help the writer improve the ideas, organization, voice, and fluency of the piece of writing.

Peer Response Sheet

A sheet like the one below can guide your peer response. Tasha filled in this sheet for Tristan's expository essay about lighthouses.

Peer Response Sheet

Writer: .....Tristan Jones.....   Responder: .....Tasha Kirk.....

Title: ....."The Lighthouse, A Ship's Best Friend".....

What I liked about your writing:

*I like how you began the essay with a line about lighthouses from a sailor song.

*I didn't know lighthouses are so important.

*I like the quotation from the lighthouse keeper.

Questions I have . . .

*How many lighthouses in the United States still have keepers?

*What kind of fuel did old-time lighthouses use?

Practice

Now it's your turn! Exchange a piece of writing with a classmate. Read the writing and then fill out a response sheet like the one above.

Struggling Learners

Some students might choose less effective responses simply because they get discouraged writing long sentences on the Peer Response Sheet. In this case, suggest that the responder respond orally to the writer, who can record the responder's ideas on the response sheet.

Publishing and Portfolios

Once you complete a writing assignment, it's time to publish it! Dress up your work to make it look its very best. You can also put it in a portfolio, something like a photo album for writing. Each essay or story in your portfolio shows something important about your writing. This chapter will explain publishing and different kinds of portfolios.

Mini Index

- **Designing Your Writing**
- **Types of Portfolios**
- **Parts of a Portfolio**
- **Portfolio Reflections**

Publishing and Portfolios

Objectives
- learn how to format and design writing for publication
- understand types of portfolios
- understand parts of portfolios

Ask students what they think of when they hear the word *publishing*. (Most students probably think of printed books or magazines.)

Pass around several books and magazines for students to examine. Explain to students that when they look at a book or a magazine, they are seeing the final result of a great many decisions. Ask students what kinds of decisions they think have to be made before a book or magazine is published. (Possible responses: page size and length, what pictures to use, cover art, page layouts, size of the type)

Explain to students that in this section, they are going to learn how to make some of those decisions for publishing their own writing.

Materials

Books and magazines (TE pp. 43, 44)

Portfolio examples (TE p. 47)

Designing Your Writing

Encourage students to choose fonts for their papers that are clear and easy to read. If necessary, provide additional guidelines for **choosing suitable fonts** *(see below)*.

Tell students that generally you will not ask them to illustrate a piece of writing. However, some graphic elements, like lists, can be used to make specific ideas stand out, and some graphic elements, like diagrams, graphs, and pictures, can be used to make their ideas clearer.

✱ For information about how to Add Diagrams, Graphs, and Pictures, see PE pages 474–475.

44

Designing Your Writing

A computer can help you make your paper look great. The following guidelines tell you how to design the final look of your paper.

Typography—the style or appearance of letters

- Use a simple font for most of your paper.
- Use a bold font for headings.
- Keep the title and headings short.

Spacing and Margins—the white space on a page

- Leave one-inch margins on all four sides.
- Double-space your writing.
- Indent the first line of every paragraph.
- Don't leave a heading or the first line of a paragraph at the bottom of a page. Put it at the top of a new page instead.

Graphics—lists, pictures, and charts

- Use lists to highlight important points.
- Include a picture or chart if it will make an idea clearer. Add a label if necessary.

Practice

Look through this book to find a page that looks good to you. Discuss the page with your classmates and point out at least three design details that you like.

Teaching Tip: Choosing Suitable Fonts

Students who are using a computer will have a multitude of fonts to choose from. Some students may be tempted to choose a font that is decorative, ornate, or whimsical. Point out that most of the time, these fonts are not suitable for preparing a final piece of writing to share because they can be difficult to read.

Discuss when decorative fonts are appropriate, for example in advertisements, cartoons, or posters.

If necessary, select four or five standard acceptable fonts and tell students to choose from among these fonts. Suggest that students use 12-point type size for body text, and a slightly larger type size for headline text.

Advanced Learners

Ask students to look through magazines and newspapers to find examples of headlines and paragraphs in the different types of acceptable fonts you've chosen for classroom use. Invite students to create a wall display of the examples they find to help writers make a selection during the publishing stage.

Great-Looking Design in Action

Aaron Olson

Seeing the Windy City

Do you enjoy dolphins, stars, dinosaurs, or sports? Then Chicago has something for you! This amazing city is located in the northeastern part of Illinois, along Lake Michigan.

The font is easy to read.

Sharks, Stars, and Dinosaurs

Chicago, often called the Windy City, has many great attractions.

- **Shedd Aquarium:** The entrance has a gigantic circular tank filled with fish, sea turtles, and stingrays. Other underwater viewing areas let visitors watch otters, penguins, and dolphins.
- **Adler Planetarium and Astronomy Museum:** The planetarium has a constellation show that makes visitors feel like they are sitting under a night sky. The guide tells what ancient cultures thought about the stars.
- **Field Museum of Natural History:** This place has the biggest T. rex skeleton ever found. With exhibits about dinosaurs, animals, gemstones, and even Native American traditions, this museum is an adventure!

A list helps organize the essay.

Great-Looking Design in Action

Encourage students to point out the design elements of Aaron's paper that make it a great looking paper.

- the use of a bold font for the headings
- the clear and easy-to read font for the body text
- the short but informative headings that tell exactly what a section is going to be about
- the bulleted list that calls out the three attractions and the numbered list for four ways to reach Chicago (PE page 46)
- the short blocks of text that make it inviting to read

Be sure students are aware of any conventions that you require for submission of final copies. For example, some teachers require the students' name, teacher and grade, and class designation at the top of each page.

Point out to students that while white space makes an essay easy to read, leaving too much white space may indicate to you that a student hasn't completed the assignment.

46

Olson 2

Batter Up!

Chicago is famous for its baseball teams. The Chicago Cubs play at Wrigley Field, one of the most historic baseball parks. It was built in 1914. The White Sox play at U.S. Cellular Field, one of the most high-tech baseball parks! FUNdamentals is a baseball-skills area in the park for kids.

Map Out an Adventure

For people who would like to spend time in the Windy City, there are four ways to reach Chicago.

1. Ride into the city on a train.
2. Drive into Chicago on one of the freeways.
3. Fly into O'Hare or Midway Airport.
4. Sail into Chicago on Lake Michigan or on the Chicago River.

Thousands of people visit Chicago every year. They enjoy parks, concerts, festivals, shops, and food. Don't just dream about it. Plan a visit to the Windy City soon!

> White space makes the page look better.

> A numbered list makes the essay easy to read.

Struggling Learners

Some students who struggle with reading and writing may excel at computer skills. Invite students well-versed in computer graphics to present mini-lesson demonstrations to the class on skills such as creating bulleted and numbered lists and adding headings.

Types of Portfolios

A portfolio is a group of writing samples collected for a special purpose. Here are four basic types.

Showcase Portfolio

A showcase portfolio features samples of your very best writing. Teachers use these portfolios to evaluate your work. (See page 48.)

Personal Portfolio

A personal portfolio holds writing that is important to you, your friends, and your family. It is a great place to keep ideas, poems, letters, journal pages, and other finished writing.

Growth Portfolio

A growth portfolio shows how your writing has improved over time. You can see your growth as a writer throughout the year as you compare different essays and stories.

Electronic Portfolio

An electronic portfolio is posted on a Web site or saved on a disk or hard drive. It includes writing, graphics, and sometimes even sounds and animation. Electronic portfolios let you share your work with many people.

Practice

Pick a type of portfolio that appeals to you. Think of two or three pieces of writing you would like to include in a portfolio of this type. Explain why you chose each piece.

Types of Portfolios

If students are going to be keeping different types of portfolios, suggest that they use different color folders for each type.

Since some pieces of writing will overlap into different portfolios, encourage students to print out multiple copies of their final drafts for these works to put into appropriate portfolios, rather then have them shift pieces of writing back and forth between portfolios.

English Language Learners

Show students examples of each kind of portfolio so they can better understand what each term means. You might use the following:

- Showcase Portfolio: a collection of a student's best writing
- Personal Portfolio: a classroom or family photograph album
- Growth Portfolio: a student's writing folder

- Electronic Portfolio: the school's Web site, or a Web site for a popular author

Point out how the contents differ according to each portfolio's function.

Advanced Learners

Many students like to write at home as well as at school. Encourage them to create separate portfolios to keep at home for independent projects.

Parts of a Portfolio

If you ask students to keep a Show-case Portfolio, establish a schedule for reviewing individual portfolios on a regular basis and post the schedule in the classroom. This will prevent you from having to review all the portfolios at once, and it will encourage students to keep their portfolios up-to-date.

Gathering Tips

Remind students that a Showcase Portfolio features samples of their very best work. When it comes time to choose a piece for their portfolio, they should think about

- the feelings and level of interest they had when they wrote it,
- how the piece of writing makes them feel when they reread it,
- how others responded to the piece of writing,
- what they learned as they wrote it, and
- what it shows about their writing abilities.

Parts of a Portfolio

You may be asked to keep a showcase portfolio. It should include the following parts.

- A **table of contents** lists the writing samples you have included in your portfolio.
- An **introduction** (either a paragraph, a short essay, or a letter) tells how you created the portfolio and what it means to you.
- The **writing samples** show off your best writing. Your teacher may want to see each step for some pieces (planning, research notes, drafts, revising, editing, final draft).
- **Reflection sheets** or **checklists** show what you have learned during each project.
- A **creative cover** uses drawings, special lettering, and perhaps a poem to express your unique personality.

GATHERING TIPS

- **Save all of your work.** Keep prewriting notes, first drafts, and revisions. Make sure everything is dated.
- **Store your writing in a pocket folder.** It's easier to create a portfolio if your work is organized in one place.
- **Be proud of your work.** You want your portfolio to show your best writing skills.

Practice

Plan a unique cover for a showcase portfolio. Include your name, a title, and drawings or graphic elements.

Struggling Learners

Many students need help organizing their work on a daily basis. Create a checklist for them to use at the end of the day (or the end of the writing period) to ensure that the right papers are stored in the right folders.

Publishing and Portfolios **49**

Sample Portfolio Reflections

For each essay or story in your portfolio, write a reflection. See the samples below.

Student Reflections

After writing my essay "Pinching for Fun," I realized how much more I have to learn about pottery. During my research, I read about all sorts of ways to decorate pottery, like soda and salt glazes. I can't wait to ask my grandpa about these things.

—Fumi Akimoto

I wrote "Seeing the Windy City" because I had a great time in Chicago with my family. I didn't know what to write about, so I looked through our photo album. I took notes as I flipped through the pages. My notes were about different places, so that's what I wrote about. When I read it, I feel like I am back in Chicago.

—Aaron Olson

Professional Reflections

Thurber did not write the way a surgeon operates; he wrote the way a child skips rope, the way a mouse waltzes.
—E. B. White

In beginning to write *The Giver*, I created—as I always do, in every book—a world that existed only in my imagination—the world of "only us, only now."
—Lois Lowry

Sample Portfolio Reflections

Point out to students that writing a reflection for an essay or a story can help them see what they learned about the topic and about writing.

Have students read aloud the student reflections and suggest what the writers learned from the assignment and how it might help them in the future.

- Fumi discovered that she has a lot to learn about pottery. Maybe she can use decorating pottery as a topic for another expository essay.
- Aaron had trouble thinking of a topic, so he looked through his personal photo album to find an idea. In the future, when he has trouble coming up with a topic, he will probably look in his photo album or his personal journal, if he keeps one.

Struggling Learners

Together, compare Fumi's reflection form on PE page 20 with the one on this page. Point out that each type of reflection has a different purpose as well as a different format.

Paragraph Writing Overview

Writing Standards

The writing standards listed below are based on a blending of state and NCTE standards.

- Understand the structure of a paragraph.
- Learn to develop a topic sentence.
- Use different kinds of supporting details.
- Understand and use different patterns of organization.
- Write a summary paragraph as testing practice.

Unit Pacing

The Parts of a Paragraph: 25–45 minutes

This section introduces the **main parts of a paragraph**. Following are some of the topics that are covered:

- Writing a topic sentence that names the topic and shares an important idea or feeling about it
- Using specific details in the body
- Summing up the paragraph's message with a closing sentence

Writing Strong Topic Sentences: 15–20 minutes

This section describes strategies students can use to write a strong topic sentence. Following are some of the topics that are covered:

- Making a list
- Using a number
- Using word pairs

Using Details: 20–30 minutes

In this section, students learn how to use three kinds of details in the body of a paragraph. Following are some of the topics that are covered:

- Adding information with facts
- Answering *why* with reasons
- Showing something with explanations

Organizing Your Paragraph: 45–60 minutes

This section describes some common organization patterns that can be used for paragraph writing. Following are some of the topics that are covered:

- Using time order to organize details in the order in which they happened
- Using order of location to describe the topic from top to bottom, left to right, and so on
- Using order of importance to show the most important detail first or last
- Using logical order to organize details in a way that makes the best sense

Writing Guidelines: 45–90 minutes

In this section, students plan and write a paragraph. Following are some of the topics that are covered:

- Selecting a specific topic from a general topic
- Using a graphic organizer to collect and organize details
- Writing a topic sentence, supporting sentences in the body, and a closing sentence
- Revising to improve the first draft
- Editing for conventions

Test Prep for Paragraphs: 45–90 minutes

This section offers tips and practice for writing a paragraph that summarizes a reading selection. Following are some of the topics that are covered:

- Planning the paragraph
- Using your own words to summarize
- Reviewing work to make changes and corrections

Integrated Grammar and Writing Skills

Below are skills lessons from the resources sections of the pupil edition that are suggested at point of use (✳) throughout this unit.

Writing Paragraphs, pp. 51–61

- ✳ Topic Sentences, p. 460
- ✳ Using the Right Word, pp. 536–559

Additional Grammar Skills

Below are skills lessons from other components that you can weave into your unit instruction.

Writing Paragraphs

SkillsBook

Interactive Writing Skills CD-ROM

Mechanics: Abbreviations

Punctuation: Commas 4—Letter Writing

Daily Language Workouts

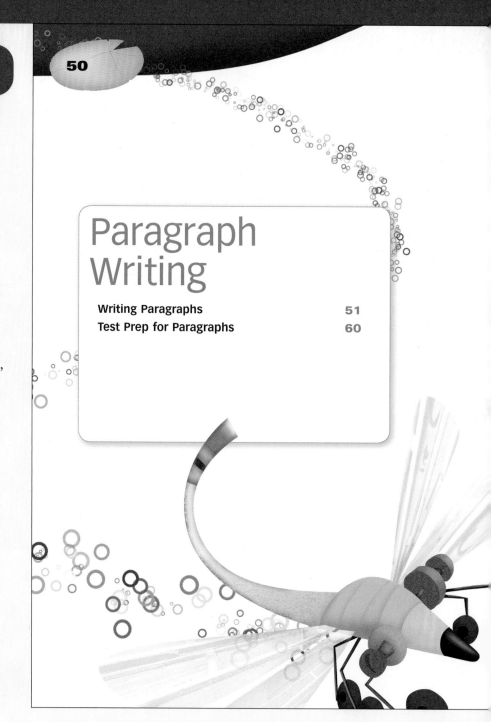

50

Paragraph Writing

Writing Paragraphs

A paragraph is a group of sentences that tell about one topic. The first sentence usually identifies the topic or main idea. The other sentences give details and facts about it.

Here are the four main reasons to write a paragraph.

1. **Describe** a person, place, or thing.
2. **Tell a story** about an event or an experience.
3. **Explain** or give information about a topic.
4. **Share** your opinion about something.

Mini Index

- **The Parts of a Paragraph**
- **Writing Strong Topic Sentences**
- **Using Details**
- **Organizing Your Paragraph**
- **Writing Guidelines**
- **Test Prep for Paragraphs**

Objectives

- understand the parts of a paragraph
- plan, draft, revise and edit a paragraph about something in the news
- use writing tips to practice writing for assessment

Remind students that a **paragraph** is a group of sentences that focus on a specific topic. Usually several paragraphs are put together to create a longer work on a topic. In this unit, students will practice writing informative paragraphs that stand alone.

Review the names of the four different types of writing represented by the list of reasons given for writing a paragraph:
1. descriptive writing
2. narrative writing
3. expository writing
4. persuasive writing

Explain that students will work through units devoted to each of these four types of writing as the year progresses. (If you will not be covering all four types of writing, encourage students to consult the units on their own whenever they need more information.)

Materials

Books and magazines (TE pp. 52, 54)

Newspaper articles (TE p. 60)

Copy Masters/ Transparencies

5 W's chart (TE p. 55)

Graphic organizers (TE pp. 53, 58)

The Parts of a Paragraph

Have students look in books and magazines and try to find paragraphs with topic, body, and closing sentences. Explain that they'll find paragraphs that don't have all three parts. For example:

- In dialogue, each time the speaker changes, the paragraph does, too.
- In longer writing, not every paragraph has a conclusion. The main thing is to support the topic of the whole piece.
- In longer narratives, paragraphs might not have topic sentences. They might just tell what happened next.

 Respond to the reading.

Answers

1. Scientists want to know what happened to King Tut.
2. Answers will vary. Possible answers:
   - Tut died in his teens.
   - Scientists made a CT scan of his body.
   - He had a broken leg.
   - They found no clues about how he died.
3. There's something unknown about King Tut.

The Parts of a Paragraph

A paragraph has three main parts. (1) It begins with a **topic sentence** that states the main idea. (2) The **body** contains sentences that share details about the main idea. (3) The **closing sentence** sums up the paragraph's message.

Topic sentence ....

Body

Closing sentence ....

The Mystery of King Tut

Scientists are still trying to solve the mystery of what happened to King Tut. He became an Egyptian king when he was only eight years old, and he died when he was just a teenager. For years, scientists have wondered how he died. Recently, they looked at King Tut's mummy using a special X-ray called a CT scan. Scientists took more than 1,700 pictures of the mummy's bones and organs. They hoped that these special pictures would show what happened to the young king. The X-rays showed that King Tut had a broken leg, but there were no clues about how he might have died. Now, the mystery of what happened to the king may never be solved.

 Respond to the reading. (1) What is the main idea of this paragraph? (2) Which details do you feel are most important? (3) What does the title tell you about the paragraph?

English Language Learners

Some students will find it more helpful to look for examples of paragraphs in text they have previously read and understood. Locate good examples of paragraphs that include all three parts in familiar text and direct students to read pre-selected pages to find paragraphs with topic, body and closing sentences.

Struggling Learners

To help students remember the parts of a paragraph, have them visualize a cheeseburger:

- The topic sentence is the top bun.
- The body is the meat, cheese, garnishes, and condiments in the middle.
- The closing sentence is the bottom bun.

Explain that the bread at the top and bottom, like the topic and closing sentences of a paragraph, hold everything together, and the ingredients in the middle, like good detail sentences in a paragraph, make an interesting sandwich.

Writing Paragraphs 53

A Closer Look at the Parts

The Topic Sentence

The **topic sentence** tells the reader what the paragraph is about. A good topic sentence (1) names the topic and (2) shares an important idea or feeling about it.

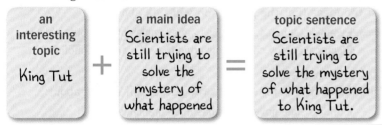

The Body

The **body** sentences share details about the topic.

- **Use specific details.** Details are highlighted (in blue) below:

  He became an Egyptian king when he was only eight years old, and he died when he was just a teenager. For years, scientists have wondered how he died. Recently, they looked at King Tut's mummy using a special X-ray called a CT scan. Scientists took more than 1,700 pictures of the mummy's bones and organs.

- **Organize the sentences.** Put your sentences in the best possible order *(time order, order of location, order of importance,* or *logical order).* (See pages 56–57.) Transition words are highlighted (in blue) below:

  For years, scientists have wondered how he died. Recently, they looked at King Tut's mummy using a special X-ray called a CT scan.

The Closing Sentence

The **closing sentence** sums up the paragraph's message.

Now, the mystery of what happened to the king may never be solved.

A Closer Look at the Parts

The Topic Sentence

Tell students that the best topic sentences make the reader want to know more. Ask why the sample topic sentence works (mentioning a mystery gets readers curious). If they don't think it works, have them explain, and challenge them to create a better one.

✶ For more information about writing Topic Sentences, see PE page 460.

The Body

Explain that although deciding the order for presenting details may seem complicated, sometimes the kinds of details students find may help them decide which order to use for organizing their sentences.

The Closing Sentence

Use the sample to point out that both the topic and the closing sentence make the same statement of fact. For this paragraph, it makes sense for the writer to remind the reader of the unsolved mystery in the closing sentence.

English Language Learners

The demands of thinking and writing in a second language can interfere with some students' ability to conceptualize organization. As you discuss the second bullet (Organize the sentences), show the transparencies for various graphic organizers (TE pages 645–651) and explain that students will be using these different organizers to help them plan their paragraph.

Writing Strong Topic Sentences

Ask students to focus on the sample topic sentences and to tell what the body of each of these paragraphs will contain.

- What geometric objects are
- How heat, light, and motion are produced by electrical energy
- What the three branches of Florida's government are
- At least three ways to improve eating habits (It is best to use *several* to mean "more than two.")
- What makes a bicycle safe and how the rider can behave to avoid accidents

Point out that, depending on the strategy used, details must be provided about each item listed, each item included in a number, or both items in a word pair.

Tell students that for the **Practice** activity, they can either write their sentences about three different topics or use the three strategies to write three sentences on the same topic.

Practice Answers

Answers will vary.

54

Writing Strong Topic Sentences

A good paragraph begins with a strong topic sentence. Here are some ideas that might help you write a strong topic sentence. (For more strategies, see page 460.)

Make a List:
List the ideas that the paragraph will talk about.

- Pyramids, spheres, **and** cubes **are examples of geometric objects.**
- **Electrical energy can be converted to** heat, light, **and** motion.

Use a Number:
Use number words to tell what the paragraph will be about.

- **Florida's state government has** three **branches.**
- **There are** several **ways to solve the problem of poor eating habits.**

Use Word Pairs:
Use pairs of conjunctions to connect ideas.

- Both **a safe bicycle** and **a careful rider are necessary to avoid accidents.**

Word Pairs

either . . . or
not only . . . but also
whether . . . or
both . . . and

Practice

Reread the information above. Then write three topic sentences, using each of the ideas listed.

English Language Learners

Some students have difficulty understanding written directions. Have students read the **Practice** directions and tell in their own words what they are to do. Modify the task as necessary:

- Assign a general topic such as "safety on the playground" to help students focus on writing topic sentences.
- Have students choose one of the strategies listed.

Advanced Learners

Ask students to reexamine the paragraphs they found in books and magazines (TE page 52) to see if any of the topic sentences include a list, a number, or a word pair. If other techniques are discovered, have students name them and present the examples to the class as alternative strategies for writing topic sentences.

Using Details

The sentences in the body (middle) of a paragraph include different kinds of specific details about the topic—facts, reasons, and explanations. Examples are often added to make the ideas clear.

Facts add information.

> **Topic sentence:** Yesterday, our class had a special visitor.
>
> **Facts:** His name is Charles Hoover. He was born in 1925, and he is 81 years old.

Reasons answer the question *why?*

> **Reason:** He came to explain what life was like here in Montgomery, Alabama, more than 75 years ago.
>
> **Examples:** He told us about old-time cars, Negro baseball leagues, and games he played as a boy.

Explanations show something.

> **Reason:** He could tell us a lot about the history of our state.
>
> **Explanation:** That's what we have been studying this month.
>
> **Example:** Mr. Hoover was part of the Selma-to-Montgomery civil rights march in 1965.

 tip Match the colors for facts, reasons, examples, and explanations to see how details are arranged in the paragraph below.

Yesterday, our class had a special visitor. His name is Charles Hoover. He was born in 1925, and he is 81 years old. He came to explain what life was like here in Montgomery, Alabama, more than 75 years ago. He talked about old-time cars, Negro baseball leagues, and games he played as a boy. He could tell us a lot about the history of our state. That's what we have been studying this month. Mr. Hoover was part of the Selma-to-Montgomery civil rights march in 1965.

Using Details

Explain that the best way to choose good information for a paragraph is to include several different kinds of details and to make sure every detail answers a 5 W question.

To demonstrate how the sample details apply to the 5 W's, use the 5 W's transparency (TR 10) and work with students to list the details in the appropriate columns. For example:

- Who: a special visitor; Charles Hoover
- What: his life; old cars; Negro baseball leagues; games; state history; the Selma-to-Montgomery march
- When: yesterday (the visit); 1925 (Mr. Hoover's birth year); 75 years ago (the time he talked about); 1965 (the civil rights march)
- Where: in class (the visit); Montgomery (their town)
- Why: to talk about what life in Montgomery used to be like; to help students learn about Alabama's history

Organizing Your Paragraph

On the board, write the 5 W words: *who, what, when, where, why*. Ask students which W words are best applied to the first three patterns of organization.

- Time order tells *when* things happened or *when* they should be done.
- Order of location tells *where* things are.
- Order of importance tells *why* about the topic sentence or the opinion statement.

To help students practice using these ideas, divide the class into groups of three. Under the appropriate 5 W words on the board, write prompts that make use of the three organizational patterns. For example:

- Under *when*: Describe the most exciting part of your favorite action movie. (time order)
- Under *where*: Describe the layout of your bedroom. (order of location)
- Under *why*: What are your three most favorite activities—and why? (order of importance)

Have group members choose a different prompt and share their response with the group.

56

Organizing Your Paragraph

The sentences in a paragraph should be put in order so that the reader can easily follow the ideas. Here are four ways to organize paragraphs.

Time Order . . .

Time order gives details in the order in which they happened. Transition words like *first, next,* and *then* are used.

First, read the directions for the recipe carefully. **Next,** gather all the ingredients. **Then** get a large bowl and the measuring spoons and cup you'll need. **Finally,** begin mixing the best trail mix you'll ever eat.

- Time order works well with narrative and expository paragraphs.

Order of Location . . .

Order of location describes a topic from top to bottom, left to right, near to far, or in some other order. Transition words and phrases like *on top of, next to,* and *underneath* are used.

In the picture, a team of oxen stands **in front of** a tall prairie schooner wagon. **Above** the wagon, the white cover looks like a giant sail. The wagon box **below** the canvas is made of thick, gray wood. Four big wheels are attached to **the bottom** of the box **at the corners.**

- Order of location works well for descriptive paragraphs.

Order of Importance . . .

Order of importance tells the most important detail first or last. Transition words and phrases like *first of all, also,* and *most importantly* are used.

> **Every family should have a fire-escape plan. For one reason, a plan makes sure that everyone knows where to go in case there is a fire. In addition, practicing the plan will make you less afraid if there is a real fire. Most importantly, an escape plan can save your life.**

■ Order of importance works well with persuasive and expository paragraphs.

Logical Order . . .

Logical order means that you organize details in a way that makes the best sense. Transition words like *in fact, for example,* and *also* are used.

> **Trees are a very important form of plant life. Trees add beauty to the landscape and give shelter to wildlife. Because of their deep root system, trees also prevent soil erosion and help store water. In addition, some types of trees supply lumber for building houses and furniture. Other trees provide food and medicines . . .**

■ Use a logical order in expository paragraphs.

Practice

Find a paragraph in one of your school texts that uses one of the organizational patterns shown on these two pages.

Focus on the idea of logical order. Point out that whatever order best suits a topic could be considered the logical one. But the term is used here especially for details and facts that aren't organized by time, location, or importance—or that use a combination of strategies.

■ Sometimes, as in the sample paragraph, the writer might be explaining *why* something is true but the details are all about equally important, so order of importance doesn't work.

■ Or the writer could be describing *what* something is, as in the first paragraph of the article on PE page 61. The writer explains Earth Day by telling the different things people do to celebrate, and the details are all about equally important.

Provide several examples from novels and textbooks. Point out that storywriters usually use time order and, sometimes, order of location to tell their stories. Nonfiction writers generally use order of importance or logical order to organize information for the reader.

English Language Learners

Students' written English may be influenced by the way they think and organize ideas in their first language, so the "logical order" pattern common to English can be especially difficult. Have students create class lists of the transition words associated with each organizational pattern. Help students look for transition words in their reading and add them to their lists.

Advanced Learners

Point out that when arranging details in order of importance, personal opinion can make a difference. Have students discuss how they would arrange the following details in a persuasive paragraph from least to most important or from most to least and why.

I'd like to go to the movie because:

- I just got my allowance so I can pay my own way.
- I haven't been to a movie in a long time.
- My best friend is going.
- I could compare the movie to the book for a writing project at school.
- My brother (or other family member) said he could take me the night the movie opens.

Writing Guidelines

Prewriting Selecting a Topic

If you do not plan to coordinate the paragraph with something students are studying, suggest that they consider writing about something in the news, as suggested in the **Practice** activity on PE page 59.

If students are having difficulty in **choosing a topic** *(see below)*, work together as a class to brainstorm topic ideas. If students make their own choices, confirm that the topic they're considering isn't too broad (or narrow), and that they have correctly identified the paragraph writing form that best suits their topic.

Review the use of graphic organizers and distribute copies of the reproducible sensory chart, 5W's chart, time line, and Venn diagram (TE pages 646–648 and 651).

As students begin working on their topic sentences, suggest that they write down the topic and main idea as an addition problem (see PE page 53), then think of ways of making them into one sentence. Remind them to try to write a couple of topic sentences before choosing one (see PE page 54).

58

Writing Guidelines

Prewriting Selecting a Topic

The instructions below and on the next page can be used to write a paragraph. Your teacher may give you a general subject, and you will need to select a specific topic to write about. (See page **455**.)

1 Choose a topic that interests you.

2 Make sure that your topic is the right size.

> Too big: My whole school year
> Too small: A few minutes early this morning
> Just right: My first week in fourth grade

3 Collect your details.

For descriptive paragraphs,	*collect*	sights, sounds, smells, and tastes.
For narrative or story paragraphs,	*answer*	who? what? when? where? and why?
For expository (factual) paragraphs,	*gather*	important facts and examples.
For persuasive paragraphs,	*list*	reasons that explain your opinions.

4 Use graphic organizers.

Choose a cluster, time line, sensory chart, 5-W's chart, or story map to help you organize your details. (See pages **456–457**.)

5 Write a topic sentence.

Once you have gathered your details, try writing a topic sentence that states the main idea of your paragraph. Then, think about the best way to organize your details.

Teaching Tip: Choosing a Topic

Some students may be daunted by the prospect of choosing a topic, making sure it is the right size, and deciding which form of writing it takes. As students brainstorm topic ideas, list them on one side of the board. On the other side of the board, write the headings *Too Big, Too Small,* and *Just Right*.

- Guide students in determining under which heading to write each of their suggested topic ideas.
- For each topic listed under *Just Right*, guide students in determining which paragraph writing form (descriptive, narrative or story, expository, persuasive) they should use, and write the first letter for the form next to the topic.

English Language Learners

Just as some students may be daunted by the task of choosing a topic, many students are daunted by the prospect of sharing ideas orally in a large group. To make sure students participate in the class brainstorm activity, have them first share their ideas with a partner. Practicing one-on-one helps students gain confidence in their speaking skills and with sharing their ideas.

Writing Paragraphs **59**

Writing Creating Your First Draft

When you write your first draft, your goal is to get all of your ideas on paper. Begin with your topic sentence. Then add supporting details (facts, reasons, examples, and explanations) in the body sentences. End with a closing sentence that sums up the message of your paragraph.

Revising Improving Your Paragraph

Ask yourself the following questions. Then make changes to your paragraph.

1. Is my topic sentence clear?
2. Have I included all of the important details in the best order?
3. Do I sound interested in my topic?
4. Do I use specific nouns and action verbs?
5. Do I use a variety of sentence lengths?
6. Do my sentences read smoothly?

Editing Checking for Conventions

Carefully check your revised paragraph for punctuation, capitalization, spelling, and grammar errors.

1. Do I use correct punctuation and capitalization?
2. Do I use the right words (*too, to, two*)?
3. Do I spell words correctly? Have I used my spell-checker?

Practice

Plan and write a paragraph about something in the news. Review the sample paragraph on page 52 and the guidelines on pages 58–59.

Writing Creating Your First Draft

Ask students to check off each detail in their notes or on their graphic organizer as they mention it in the draft. That way they won't forget to include anything, and they'll follow their organizational plan more closely.

Encourage students to concentrate on just getting all of their ideas down on paper. They don't have to worry about perfect sentences or mistakes—they can fix those during revising and editing.

Revising
Improving Your Paragraph

If possible, have students revise on a different day than the day they write. This is a good way of getting around a writer's resistance to revising—it's easier to evaluate your work with fresh eyes.

Editing Checking for Conventions

Have students trade papers with a partner and check each other's work. Remind them to be on the lookout for correctly spelled words that have been misused. These tricky words cannot be found by computer spell-checkers.

✳ For information about Using the Right Word, see PE pages 536–559.

English Language Learners

Some students may have difficulty writing their first draft.

- Before asking them to write, provide time for an "oral rehearsal." Have them tell you their story as they share their graphic organizers.

- Encourage students who are not sure of the English word they want to write to mark the space with a blank line and continue writing. Remind them they can return and make changes during revising.

Test Prep for Paragraphs

Remind students that a summary paragraph is a paragraph that restates the main ideas from a larger piece of writing, using your own words.

Writing Tips

Discuss each of the tips on the page, asking students why they think each is important. For example, it is important to

- read the selection twice to make sure that you don't overlook important details;
- budget your time (and keep the topic specific and the paragraph short) because tests limit the amount of time you have to work in; and
- use your own words, both because the whole point of a summary is to talk about a subject in your own words and because using other people's words without crediting them is **plagiarism** *(see below)*.

60

Test Prep for Paragraphs

On a writing test, you may be asked to write a paragraph summarizing a reading selection. Use the tips below.

WRITING TIPS

Before you write . . .

- **Read the selection twice.** Read it once for the general meaning. Read it again to understand all the details.
- **Plan your paragraph.** Write a topic sentence that sums up the main idea of the selection. Decide which details to use in the middle of the paragraph.
- **Use your time wisely.** Spend a few minutes planning what you will write.

During your writing . . .

- **Keep it short.** A summary paragraph for a short reading selection should be about six to eight sentences long.
- **Use your own words.** Include words from the selection only when you are sharing basic facts.

After you write . . .

- **Reread your summary paragraph.** Change any ideas that are unclear or incorrect.

Practice

Find an informational section in a science or history text. (Your teacher may assign one.) Write a short summary of the reading. Follow the tips above and look at the sample summary on the next page before you begin.

Teaching Tip: Plagiarism

It may take some time for students to understand that plagiarism is wrong and how careful they need to be to avoid it. Some students have a hard time putting what they read on the page into their own words. To help them avoid plagiarizing, suggest that they

- close their eyes after reading each paragraph,
- think about what they read,

- record each piece of information on a graphic organizer in no more than two or three words, and then
- write their summary using the details on their graphic organizer.

After writing their first draft, students can look back at the original text to make sure they've included the most important points.

Struggling Learners

Before asking hesitant writers to write a summary on their own, do a Think-Aloud to model the process, using a short, interesting newspaper article. Next, share a similar article with students and discuss possible topic sentences, details to highlight, and closing sentences. Finally, write a summary paragraph together.

Writing Paragraphs **61**

Original Reading Selection

Still Celebrating Earth Day

Earth Day is celebrated on April 22. It is a special day when people take care of the earth and sponsor environmental cleanups. On this day, people all around the world find special ways to improve the earth where they live. Some walk or bike to work instead of driving their cars. Many people plant flowers and trees.

The first Earth Day was held on April 22, 1970. A senator from Wisconsin named Gaylord Nelson created it. He worried that the world was becoming polluted. On that day, he asked everyone to do something to make our earth a better place for all.

Today, people all over the world know that the earth needs help. There is still much to be done. Some people argue that it is not enough to have one special day to remember the earth. They think that every day should be Earth Day.

Sample Summary

Topic sentence

Body

Closing sentence

Earth Day Anniversary

Earth Day is a special day when people help the earth to be a better place. Some people walk to work instead of drive. Others have cleanup projects and plant trees. The first Earth Day was April 22, 1970. Senator Gaylord Nelson from Wisconsin created it. He wanted the earth to be a better place for everyone. People still celebrate Earth Day on April 22. Some of them believe that Earth Day should be every day.

Tell students that, whenever possible, it's a good idea to underline the important details in the article itself as part of their prewriting. Suggest that they make a habit of first reading the entire article without underlining, so they know what the whole thing says. The second time through, they should underline.

Before students look at the sample summary paragraph, have them read the article and write down the details they think are most important.

Ask students to read the summary and compare it to the details they wrote down. Did they agree with the writer about what was most important? What improvements can they suggest for the sample summary? Responses include:

- Some of the wording is close to the original. For example, the sentences *The first Earth Day was April 22, 1970* and *Senator Gaylord Nelson from Wisconsin created it* are facts from the original version.
- The writer omitted details about Earth's ongoing environmental problems. This makes the last sentence of the summary paragraph less clear.

English Language Learners

Some students may not yet have the language proficiency to read and respond to the selection and sample summary. Have proficient readers read the selections aloud. As students suggest ways to improve the sample summary, rephrase and record their ideas in simple language on a poster titled, "How To Write a Good Summary." For example, *the wording is close to the original* could be written as: *Use your own words.*

Descriptive Writing Overview

Writing Standards

The writing standards listed below are based on a blending of state and NCTE standards.

- Use freewriting and a list to explore possible topics.
- Use sensory charts, drawings, and lists to gather and organize details.
- Draft an essay that has a clear beginning, middle, and ending.
- Revise drafts to make ideas clearer and sensory details more vivid.
- Edit drafts to ensure correct use of conventions.

Writing Forms

- descriptive paragraph
- descriptive essay that describes a place

Focus on the Traits

- **Ideas** Including sensory details
- **Organization** Using an organized list and transitions to write a clear beginning, middle, and ending
- **Voice** Showing knowledge and enthusiasm about the subject
- **Word Choice** Using sensory details and specific, descriptive words
- **Sentence Fluency** Writing complete sentences that read smoothly
- **Conventions** Checking for errors in punctuation, capitalization, spelling, and grammar

Unit Pacing

Descriptive Paragraph: 1.5–3 hours

The **descriptive paragraph** introduces the unit and lays the groundwork for more extensive descriptive writing. Use this section if students need to work on crafting a paragraph. Following are some of the topics that are covered:

- Freewriting to select a topic
- Using a sensory chart to gather details
- Using transition words and phrases to connect details

Descriptive Essay: 3.5–6 hours

This section asks students to describe **their favorite room**. Use this section to focus on developing an essay. Following are some of the topics that are covered:

- Creating a topics list
- Drawing a floor plan
- Making a sensory chart to gather details
- Using an organized list to plan writing
- Creating an ending that tells why the room is special

Descriptive Writing Across the Curriculum: 1.5–3 hours

This section provides models and tips for descriptive writing in various curriculum areas. If other teachers are involved in cross-curricular activities, collaborate with them on these lessons.

■ **Social Studies**

Describing a Historical Landmark, pp. 76–77

■ **Science**

Describing a Plant, pp. 78–79

Writing for Assessment: 45–90 minutes

The student text shows a sample student response to the first prompt below. Students can respond to that same prompt or to the additional prompt as an informal or a formal assessment.

■ Imagine a place you have visited. Write a paragraph that describes it using sensory details. Paint a vivid picture with your words.

■ Think of a place where you had fun. Write a paragraph that describes that place and tells why it's special to you.

Integrated Grammar and Writing Skills

Below are skills lessons from the resources sections of the pupil edition that are suggested at point of use (✱) throughout this unit.

Writing a Descriptive Paragraph, pp. 63–66

✱ Freewriting, p. 454

✱ Sentence Variety, pp. 440–449

Describing a Place, pp. 67–74

✱ Descriptive Voice, p. 462

✱ Order of Location, pp. 56 and 458

✱ Commas in Compound Sentences, p. 482

Additional Grammar Skills

Below are skills lessons from other components that you can weave into your unit instruction.

Writing a Descriptive Paragraph

SkillsBook

Double Negatives, p. 95
Kinds of Sentences, p. 115
Sentence Variety Review, p. 129

Daily Language Workouts

Week 4: A Number of Interruptions,
   pp. 10–11
Week 4: Rain, Rain, Go Away, p. 81

Describing a Place

SkillsBook

Commas in Compound Sentences,
   p. 7
Hyphens 1 and 2, p. 27

Interactive Writing Skills CD-ROM

Punctuation: Commas 1—
   Compound Sentences and in a
   Series

Daily Language Workouts

Week 5: Pause for a Clause, pp.
   12–13
Week 5: Mt. McKinley First, p. 82

Writing Across the Curriculum

Daily Language Workouts

Week 6: Hyperlinks, pp. 14–15
Week 6: Football Fans, p. 83

Descriptive Writing

Descriptive Writing

Descriptive Paragraph

What is your favorite place? The school gym or your bedroom at home? A busy street or a quiet backyard? The local zoo or a giant shopping mall?

In this chapter, you'll learn how to use sensory details to describe a favorite place. Your goal is to use sights, sounds, smells, and other senses to take your classmates on a tour of that special spot.

Writing Guidelines

Subject: A favorite place
Form: Descriptive paragraph
Purpose: To describe a place you know well
Audience: Classmates

Descriptive Paragraph

Objectives
- understand the content and structure of a descriptive paragraph
- choose a topic (a favorite place) to develop with sensory details
- plan, draft, revise, and edit a descriptive paragraph

A **descriptive paragraph** uses sensory details to create a clear mental image of a person, a place, a thing, or an event. A paragraph has a topic sentence, a body, and a closing sentence.

✳ For information about Paragraph Writing, see PE pages 50–61.

Ask students to imagine that the alien in the drawing lands its ship in the schoolyard and asks for a tour. The alien's eyes do not see, but instead work as sensors. The alien's brain, however, is capable of producing mental photographs when it is fed sensory details. Have students work together to generate a list of details that appeal to the senses (seeing, hearing, smelling, tasting, and feeling or touching) that will help the alien create a mental photograph of the schoolyard and the school.

Family Connection Letters

As you begin this unit, send home the Descriptive Writing Family Connection letter, which describes what students will be learning.

 Letter in English (TE p. 653)

 Letter in Spanish (TE p. 661)

Materials

Pictures (TE p. 64)

Copy Masters/ Transparencies

Sensory chart (TE, p. 65)

Descriptive Paragraph

Explain to students that in a descriptive paragraph, a writer uses certain words and phrases called **transitions** *(see below)* to organize the details, much in the same way that a filmmaker uses a camera to pan, or move around, a space so that the audience can see where things are in that space.

 Respond to the reading.

Answers

Ideas 1. lilac bush, tangerine halves, sweet juice, crabapple tree, narrow cloth bag, thistle seeds, green metal bird feeder, sunflower seeds, seeds fallen on the ground

Organization 2. by the kitchen window, (stuck) on it, next to the lilacs, on the bag, on the other side of the tree, below the squirrel, on the ground

Voice & Word Choice 3. love to eat, sweet juice, slams shut, chatters and scolds, my favorite place to visit

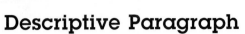

64

Descriptive Paragraph

Your descriptive paragraph will use sensory details to create a clear picture of a place. The **topic sentence** should name your favorite place, and the **body sentences** should include specific details. The **closing sentence** ends the description. In the following paragraph, Joe describes his backyard and its bird feeders.

 Topic sentence

 Body

Closing sentence

Backyard Buffet

Our backyard is a restaurant for birds. The lilac bush by the kitchen window has tangerine halves stuck on it. Orange and black orioles love to eat the fruit and drink the sweet juice. Next to the lilacs, a crabapple tree holds a narrow cloth bag. Goldfinches hang on the bag and pluck thistle seeds out of tiny holes. On the other side of the tree, a green metal bird feeder stands on a pole. A squirrel leaps onto it, but it slams shut! The squirrel chatters and scolds because he can't get at the sunflower seeds. Below the squirrel, cardinals and blue jays find the seeds that have fallen on the ground. If I were a bird, our backyard buffet would be my favorite place to visit.

Respond to the reading. On your own paper, answer the questions below.

- **Ideas** (1) What details help the reader see the backyard buffet?
- **Organization** (2) What transition words and phrases help you picture the location of each detail?
- **Voice & Word Choice** (3) What specific words make the writer's voice sound excited about the topic?

Writing a Descriptive Paragraph ⟨ **65**

Prewriting Selecting a Topic

Think about a few of your favorite places. Freewriting can help you choose a place to write about. Here is some of Joe's freewriting.

Freewriting

> What places do I know? Bob's bike shop is cool, but I guess I don't know it that well. What about the mall? That's too big. Is there a small place that I know? I've got a very small backyard. It's just a bunch of bird feeders. Birds and squirrels that come there are fun to watch. . . .

Select a topic. Freewrite for 3 to 5 minutes to find a place you know well enough to describe in a paragraph.

Gathering Details

A strong description contains sensory details. They help the reader experience the place. Joe used a sensory chart to gather his details.

Sensory Chart

See	Hear	Smell	Taste	Touch
purple lilacs cardinals blue jays goldfinches	scolding chattering slam	lilacs tangerines	tangerines sunflower seeds sweet juice	smooth metal

Make a sensory chart. Write *See, Hear, Smell, Taste,* and *Touch* on the top. List details about your topic for each sense.

Prewriting Selecting a Topic

To help students explore suitable places for a topic during freewriting, ask them to think about places where they

- play alone or with friends,
- visit with relatives,
- eat, or
- relax and think.

✱ For more information about freewriting, see PE page 454.

Before students select a topic, suggest that they look at the sensory chart at the bottom of the page. Will they be able to list at least one detail about their favorite place for each column? If not, perhaps they should select a different place to write about.

Prewriting Gathering Details

Explain to students that sensory details will help them **show, not tell** *(see below)* the reader what the place they are describing looks like.

Provide photocopies of the reproducible sensory chart (TE page 646) for students to use to gather details for their paragraphs.

Teaching Tip: Show, Not Tell

While students are frequently advised to "show, not tell," most students will not fully comprehend the distinction between showing and telling without further explanation and examples.

Read aloud the descriptions below. After you read each description, ask students to draw a quick sketch of what you have described.

- The whole wall was covered with stuff.
- The far end of the long, red brick wall was covered with bright, colorful circus posters. In the middle of the wall, someone had spray-painted the words *We love summer!* in giant letters. Help Wanted ads and Lost and Found flyers had been pasted over the rest of the wall.

Have students compare drawings. Students should realize that the first sentence "told" them about the wall. It did not provide enough specific details for them to see the wall in their mind. The second sentence "showed" them the wall so that they could picture exactly what it looked like.

Writing Creating Your First Draft

Remind students to refer to the sensory chart that they filled in during prewriting. Tell them to be sure to include any new images that come into their heads as they write their draft, too.

Remind students to avoid writing cliché or boring beginning and ending sentences, such as "My favorite place is" and "That's why this is my favorite place." Encourage them to try to use a **simile or a metaphor** (*see below*) to make their descriptive writing more colorful and interesting.

Revising
Improving Your Paragraph

Suggest that students read aloud their paragraph to a partner who can listen for complete sentences that flow smoothly.

✱ Discuss how students can write smooth-flowing sentences by using Sentence Variety (PE pages 432–435).

Editing Checking for Conventions

Provide time for students to share their edited paragraphs with the class.

66

Writing Creating Your First Draft

In your first draft, you want to get your ideas on paper. Your topic sentence should introduce the place. Write body sentences that include sensory details. Use transition words and phrases to connect the details. End with a closing sentence that shares a final thought.

Write your first draft. Be sure to include sensory details to help the reader experience your place.

Revising Improving Your Paragraph

When you revise your paragraph, you make changes to improve your work. You may add, rearrange, and cut details.

Improve your paragraph. Use the following questions.
1. Does my topic sentence tell which place I will describe?
2. Do I use transition words and phrases?
3. Do I sound like I know the place I am describing?
4. Have I used sensory words to describe the place?
5. Have I used complete sentences that flow smoothly?

Editing Checking for Conventions

After you have revised your paragraph, check the punctuation, capitalization, spelling, and grammar. Correct any errors you find.

Check for conventions. The questions below will help.
1. Are my punctuation and capitalization correct?
2. Have I spelled words correctly?
3. Have I used the right words (*too, to, two*)?

Teaching Tip: Similes and Metaphors

Make sure that students understand the difference between a simile and a metaphor.

- A simile compares two different things using *like* or *as*.
- A metaphor compares two different things without using *like* or *as*.

Ask students to point out and explain the metaphors at the beginning and end of the sample paragraph on PE page 64. (*Our backyard is a restaurant for birds* and *our backyard buffet . . .*) These metaphors compare the backyard to eating places. Discuss how they make the paragraph more interesting.

✱ For more information about using figures of speech, see PE pages 318 and 464.

Struggling Learners

To help students develop confidence using similes, read aloud the following "simile starters" and ask for original endings:

- as old as
- laughs like
- as light as
- sings like
- as hungry as
- fits like

Descriptive Writing
Describing a Place

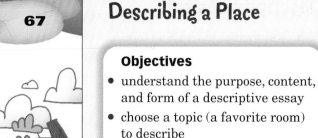

67

Everyone has a favorite room. Maybe you like the art room at school because of its sunrise mural and the mobiles that dangle from the ceiling. Maybe you like your uncle's workshop because of the smell of sawdust, the buzz of the saws, the tap-tap-tap of the hammers, and the sight of the beautiful things he makes out of wood.

Whatever room is your favorite, a descriptive essay can let you explore it. This chapter will help you write your descriptive essay. When you are finished, your reader can "take the tour" of your favorite room!

Writing Guidelines

Subject: A favorite room
Form: Descriptive essay
Purpose: To describe a place
Audience: Classmates

Describing a Place

Objectives
- understand the purpose, content, and form of a descriptive essay
- choose a topic (a favorite room) to describe
- plan, draft, revise, and edit a descriptive essay

A **descriptive essay** presents a vivid, detailed picture of a person, a place, a thing, or an event. In a descriptive essay about a place, the writer
- provides an overall description of the place,
- presents details in order of location,
- focuses on one special feature of the place, and
- explains why the place is special.

Encourage students to start thinking about rooms that feel special to them.

Materials

Drawing paper (TE pp. 68, 70)

Pictures and objects (TE p. 68)

Graph paper (TE p. 70)

Writing sample (TE p. 74)

Copy Masters/ Transparencies

Sensory chart (TE pp. 69, 71)

Descriptive Essay

To help students understand how to develop the body of an effective descriptive essay, discuss the purpose of each middle paragraph of the model essay (overall description, details by order of location, and focus on one special part).

While students may appreciate the overall description, it may benefit them to see exactly how the writer uses sensory details and transitions to create a vivid mental picture of the cabin in their minds. If there is time, have students work with a partner or in a small group to discuss the details and to create a sketch of the cabin, based on their interpretation of the details. Then have students compare pictures and discuss the reasons for the differences in their drawings.

68

Descriptive Essay

In the following essay, Jack describes his favorite room. The side notes will help you understand the different parts of his essay.

Little Cabin in the Woods

BEGINNING
The writer introduces the room he will describe.

You might think that staying in a one-room log cabin would be rough. I did, too, until I went to a summer camp on Norton's Lake. At first, the little cabin seemed kind of unfinished, but now it is one of my favorite places!

MIDDLE
The first middle paragraph gives an overall description.

The cabin is one big room. The walls are real logs that someone notched and put together without nails. The edges of the logs have rough ax marks on them, but the wood floor feels smooth from camper's feet. Because of all that wood, the cabin smells of pine. Only the dusty stone fireplace isn't made of wood, but it smells like wood ashes!

The second middle paragraph describes details by order of location.

The cabin has old furniture in it. Metal bunk beds stand along the walls near the fireplace. They have musty mattresses on plywood boards. On the wall across from the fireplace, there's a window and a white rusty sink. A pump sticks out the top, and it's fun

English Language Learners

Before reading, use pictures and objects to help students understand the concepts of some of the vocabulary used in the passage.

- Show a picture of a one-room log cabin, and point out which parts are the logs and even how they are notched. Explain that these cabins used to be quite common in the US, although are not as popular for everyday living now.

- Try to provide a piece of pine or something that is pine-scented for students to smell.
- Show or draw a picture of bunk beds, a pump sink, a fold-up table, and an outhouse.

Try to not give definitions for these words; objects and visuals are more effective in this case.

Describing a Place **69**

to pump it to get water. The cabin has no bathroom, but there's an outhouse down the hill!

The best part about the cabin is the fold-up table. It's next to the sink, and it lifts up to attach to the wall. Whenever the table's down, campers pull up the split-log benches and play board games. When the table is up, campers sit on the benches for cabin meetings or for evening storytelling times.

The counselors call the cabin "rustic." At first, I thought that word meant "junky." Now I know it means everything you really need and nothing you don't need. Whenever I smell wood smoke or pine trees, it always makes me want to be back in the cabin in the woods.

The third middle paragraph focuses on one special part.

ENDING
The writer tells why the room is special to him.

 Respond to the reading. Answer the following questions about the essay.

- **Ideas** (1) What details help you see, hear, feel, or smell things in the cabin?
- **Organization** (2) What words and phrases tell you where each part of the cabin is?
- **Voice & Word Choice** (3) What words show how the writer feels about the cabin?

Respond to the reading.

Answers

Ideas **1.** Possible choices:

(see)
- little cabin
- one big room
- walls are real logs
- logs that someone notched
- edges have rough ax marks
- wood floor
- dusty stone fireplace
- metal bunk beds
- plywood boards
- white rusty sink
- fold up table
- split-log benches

(smell)
- pine
- wood ashes
- musty

(touch or feel)
- rough
- smooth
- dusty
- rusty

Organization 2. Possible choices:
- along the walls
- across from the fireplace
- sticks out the top
- next to the sink

Voice & Word Choice 3.
- one of my favorite places
- fun to pump
- best part
- want to be back

Prewriting Selecting a Topic

Suggest that students look back at the prewriting they did for their descriptive paragraph (PE page 65). Ask them if they mentioned a room in their freewriting that they didn't choose to write about then, but that they might like to write about now.

Circulate among students as they create their topic list to make sure they are selecting an appropriate room for a topic. For example, a train depot (shown in the Topic List) in a small town is a reasonable topic for an essay. However, Grand Central Station in New York City is not suitable because it is huge and would take too long to describe.

Prewriting Drawing the Room

Emphasize that students do not have to create a work of art here. If they are not comfortable drawing realistic objects, like the couch or duck basket, suggest that they just draw simple, representative shapes, like squares, rectangles, circles, and ovals. They should, however, take the time to label each object accurately.

If possible, have students bring in photographs of their favorite room to recall details for their floor plan.

70

Prewriting Selecting a Topic

A topic list can help you select a favorite room to describe in your essay.

Topic List

Everyday Rooms	Fun Rooms
bedroom	train depot
school auditorium	ice-cream shop
Grandma's living room ✳	

 Make a topic list. Use the sample above as a guide. Put a star (✳) next to the room you want to write about.

Drawing the Room

You can draw a floor plan to show a top-down view of your room.

Floor Plan

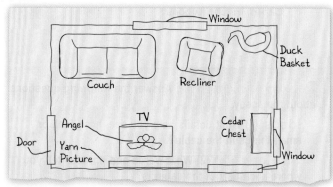

 Draw a floor plan. Create a picture of your room seen from above. Label the parts of your picture.

As students make their drawings, help them to label each piece of furniture or area of interest so that they have the necessary vocabulary for writing their first drafts. You may even want to prepare them further by having them include now one or two adjectives for each item to incorporate later into their first drafts.

Invite students who desire more detailed prewriting graphic organizers to

- measure the actual objects in their chosen room (or estimate the measurements) and
- then create scale-size diagrams on graph paper.

Describing a Place **71**

Making a Sensory Chart

Once you draw your floor plan, you need to gather sensory details about the room. A sensory chart like the one below can help you.

Sensory Chart

See	Hear	Smell	Feel	Taste
windows	jazz CD	pinecones, oranges	yarn picture	
couch	meowing	cinnamon sticks	knitting	
basket		scented apples		

 Prewrite **Create a sensory chart.** Make a sensory chart like the one above to gather details about the room you will describe.

Creating an Organized List

Look at your floor plan and make a list like the one below to help you organize your details.

Directions	Organized List
	Grandma's living room
Name your place.	
Describe the room overall.	1. little room, wide windows, sunshine
Describe details by order of location.	2. couch, recliner, duck-shaped basket, TV, angel
Describe a special feature.	3. cedar chest where the puzzles are and where the cat sits

 Prewrite **Create an organized list.** Follow the directions above to write your own organized list.

Prewriting
Making a Sensory Chart

Point out that in the sample sensory chart, the writer has nothing listed under *Taste*. Tell students that it's possible that they will not be able to list a sensory detail under every heading in the chart. However, if they discover that all of their details are listed under one heading, for example, *See*, then they may want to return to their Topic List to select a different topic for which they can generate a variety of sensory details. This will help make their essays more interesting and vivid.

Provide photocopies of the reproducible sensory chart (TE page 646) for students to use to gather details for their essay.

Prewriting
Creating an Organized List

Have students notice that the details in the sample list are described starting with the couch, at the top left corner of the sample floor plan on PE page 70, and then they are listed in spatial order, moving clockwise around the room. The special feature, the cedar chest, is listed separately. Suggest that students follow this same order to create their own organized list.

Advanced Learners

Invite students to choose other interesting, logical ways to organize their details (besides clockwise around the room), such as the following:

- ceilings, walls, and floors
- large furniture, medium accessories, and small decorative items
- color scheme, such as red, black, and yellow items
- materials, such as metal, wood, and fabric items

Writing **Starting Your Essay**

Tell students to write on every other line to leave room for revisions. If they are using a computer, they can double space.

Encourage students to write two beginnings, using the methods shown. Students can then

- read aloud both beginnings to a partner for feedback and
- decide which one to use, based on the feedback as well as their own preferences.

Focus on the Traits

Voice

Remind students that voice is how your writing sounds to a reader. To achieve a natural, enthusiastic voice, they should ask themselves the following questions:

- Is this what I would say if I were talking to a friend?
- Does this word or phrase help me show my real feelings about the room?

* For information about writing in a Descriptive Voice, see PE page 462.

72

Writing **Starting Your Essay**

Your beginning paragraph should get the reader's attention and introduce the room you will describe. Here are two ways to begin your description.

> Beginning
> Middle
> Ending

Beginning Paragraph

- **Ask the reader a question.**

> What's the coziest place you know of? The coziest place I know is my grandma's house. I go there for holidays and during the summer. The best room in the house is Gram's living room.

- **Begin with a surprising fact.**

> My grandma was born in the house where she lives. No wonder she loves it so much. I just visit her, but I love it, too. My favorite place in her house is the living room.

 Write your beginning paragraph. You can use one of the ideas above to get started, or use one of your own. If your first version doesn't work well, try another one.

Focus on the Traits

Voice Your own special way of expressing yourself is called your *writing voice*. The words you choose, the details you include, and the ways you connect those details all help to shape your writing voice.

English Language Learners

To help students write a captivating beginning, allow them to use a phrase from their first language if the place they are describing has to do with their culture, so that they and their readers can better identify with the place. For example,

- if they are describing a place where they meditate, they may begin with a sound word like *Ohm*; or

- if the place is a social spot, they might start with *¡Qué viva la fiesta!*

Have students translate their phrases into English as a second sentence to further draw in English-speaking readers.

Advanced Learners

Invite students to conduct a classroom poll to obtain a "surprising fact" with which to begin their essays. For example, if they're describing a bedroom:

- What percentage of students have their own bedroom?
- What's the most popular wall color used in bedrooms for boys? For girls?
- How many students make their bed every day?

Developing the Middle Part

The middle paragraphs share the details you included in your organized list. The side notes below tell what goes in each paragraph.

Describing a Place   **73**

Beginning

Middle

Ending

Middle Paragraphs

First, the writer gives an overall description of the room.

The living room is small, but it has big windows on three sides. Grandma calls this room her jewel box because it glows with sunlight. The windows are as tall as doors. Sun catchers hang in the windows and make rainbows on the yellow walls and the green carpet.

Then she tells about details by order of location.

The furniture is old but comfortable. Grandma has a big couch with a flowery cover on it. I sit there, but Grandma likes her recliner next to the couch. By the recliner, she has a duck-shaped basket. It holds pinecones, dried oranges, cinnamon sticks, and scented wooden apples. Across the room, Grandma has her big, old TV with a blue glass angel on top. Above the TV hangs a yarn picture of frogs, cattails, and dragonflies.

Last, she describes her favorite part of the room.

The best part of the room is the cedar chest. It sits below the biggest window. The chest has puzzles in it, which is why I like it. Grandma's cat, Merlin, sits on the chest so he can watch the birds and squirrels at the feeder outside. Sometimes he also curls up in Grandma's knitting if she leaves it on top of the chest.

Create your middle paragraphs. Use your organized list (from page 71) to help you write each paragraph.

Writing

Developing the Middle Part

Make sure students notice that the order of the middle paragraphs follows the order of items 1 through 3 in the organized list on PE page 71:

- overall description
- details by order of location
- favorite part (special feature)

Read the middle paragraphs with students and have them find the prepositional phrases that are used as transitions. They help to organize or locate each item in the room in relation to the others (*by* the recliner, *across* the room, *on* top, *above* the TV, *below* the biggest window, *on* the chest).

✶ For information about describing details by Order of Location, see PE pages 56 and 458.

English Language Learners

Many students may have difficulty finding just the right words to convey the mood or feeling they have in their room. After students include the details from their organized list in their paragraphs, have them work with an English-proficient partner or a thesaurus to find specific descriptive words for those details.

Struggling Learners

Because students often feel anxiety over the number of sentences they should write, if possible, have them write their paragraphs on a computer. Their paragraphs will look more developed, even if their sentences are fewer and shorter than the model.

Writing Ending Your Essay

Remind students that the ending is the last thing a reader reads and so it should be at least as strong and effective as the beginning and middle paragraphs. Tell students that a good ending for their essay can impress the reader in a variety of ways.

- It can leave the reader with a mental picture of the room and the writer.
- It can offer the reader descriptive details to remember.
- It can offer the reader an idea to think about.

Discuss the sample ending and ask students what impression they think the writer was trying to achieve.

Revising and Editing

Remind students that one way to achieve sentence fluency is to use a variety of sentence patterns, including compound sentences. If necessary, remind students that a compound sentence is made up of two or more simple sentences joined together with a conjunction.

✱ Before students use the Conventions checklist on PE page 30, review using Commas in Compound Sentences on PE page 482.

74

Writing **Ending Your Essay**

Your ending paragraph should tell how you feel about the place you are describing.

Beginning
Middle
▶ Ending

Ending Paragraph

The writer tells how she feels about the room.

Grandma's living room might be small, but the sunlight makes it feel big. I like to sit on the couch and read or sit by the cedar chest and pet Merlin. In fact, I like being in Grandma's living room better than almost anywhere else.

 Create your ending. Tell the reader why this room is so special to you.

Revising **and Editing**

 Improve your description. Use the questions below as a guide when you make changes to your essay.

- **Ideas** Do I include enough sensory details?
- **Organization** Do my beginning, middle, and ending parts work together?
- **Voice** Do I show the reader how much I like the room?
- **Word Choice** Do I use specific descriptive words?
- **Sentence Fluency** Do my sentences read smoothly?

 Check your description. Use the checklist on page 30 as a guide to edit your work. Then prepare a neat final copy and have a classmate or parent help you proofread it.

English Language Learners

Depending on students' English levels, you may want them to focus revising on only a few of the traits listed. Model for students that they should read their essay several times, each time looking for only one trait to improve.

- Read through a sample writing and revise it just for the Ideas question, then

- read it another time revising just for the Organization question, and so on.

Struggling Learners

Make sure students understand what a compound sentence is. Have them locate and read aloud some compound sentences in the model essay. For example: *The living room is small, but it has big windows on three sides.*

Then have students locate short, choppy sentences in their own essay and combine them into compound sentences.

Descriptive Writing
Across the Curriculum

"What did you do during vacation?" Friends and family naturally want to know about things you've seen and done. What does the world look like, sound like, and feel like to you? To help them understand, it's important to be able to describe things well.

Descriptive writing is often required for school assignments. In social studies, you may describe a historical place; in science, you may describe a plant or an animal. This chapter will help you write descriptions that capture the world around you.

Mini Index

- **Social Studies:** Describing a Historical Landmark
- **Science:** Describing a Plant
- **Assessment:** Writing for Assessment

75

Across the Curriculum

Objectives
- apply what has been learned about descriptive writing to other curriculum areas
- practice writing for assessment

The lessons on the following pages provide samples of descriptive writing students might do in different content areas.

Assigning these forms of writing will depend on
- the skill level of your students,
- the subject matter they are studying in different content areas, and
- the writing goals of your school, district, or state.

Materials

Photograph of Plymouth Rock (TE p. 76)

Landmark brochures (TE p. 77)

Plant books, botanical calendars, garden center catalogue, and live plants (TE p. 79)

Copy Masters/ Transparencies

Sensory chart (TE p. 77)

Social Studies: Describing a Historical Landmark

Use the call-out labels to discuss the organization of the sample social studies essay.

Discuss how the model compares to the descriptive paragraph and the essay that students wrote.

Similar:
- It describes a place.
- It uses order of location to organize ideas.
- It uses sensory details.
- It shares the writer's feelings.

Different:
- It contains dates and facts.
- It describes a public place that anyone can go to see.

76

Social Studies: Describing a Historical Landmark

Your teacher may ask you to write about a landmark from history. Notice how descriptive writing is used in the essay below.

The **beginning** names the landmark.

The **middle** describes the landmark and what makes it interesting.

The **ending** shares a final thought about the landmark.

Plymouth Rock

Everybody has heard of Plymouth Rock, and people may have a picture of it in their heads. Actually seeing it, though, is very surprising.

The rock is surrounded by a special monument. It looks like a rectangular Greek temple with tall, white stone columns and a roof to protect visitors. The top level inside is a balcony. From there, people can look down on the rock. Plymouth Rock rests on beach sand at the bottom level of the monument. The walls near the rock have fenced openings to let in the ocean tides. Twice a day the sea surrounds the rock, just like when the Pilgrims first landed. The whole place smells like salt water, and seagull calls echo through the air.

I thought that Plymouth Rock would be as big as a car, but it's only half the size of my bed. The rock used to be much larger. Long ago, people chipped pieces off for souvenirs. The rock is gray and smooth and has the date 1620 carved into it. That's the year the Pilgrims landed in Plymouth.

So, Plymouth Rock isn't what I thought it would be. However, it was awesome to see a place that marks the early beginnings of our country.

English Language Learners

Many students may not know what Plymouth Rock is. Show them a photograph of Plymouth Rock from a library book or the Internet as a reference, and describe why it has historical value.

While looking at the picture, have students tell what things the writer of the sample essay does well to describe the landmark.

Then compare the essay and the photograph. Ask:
- Is the author accurate?
- What other details could have been included?
- What details did the author add from personal experience?

Writing in Social Studies **77**

WRITING TIPS

Before you write . . .

- **Choose a historical landmark.**
  Select a place you have been to or studied in school.
- **Do your research.**
  Find information about the place and look at pictures. What makes the place important in history?
- **Take notes.**
  Focus on the physical details that make the place unique and interesting.

During your writing . . .

- **Organize your details.**
  Introduce your topic in the beginning, give details in the middle, and end with a final thought.
- **Show, don't tell.**
  Use descriptive details that help the reader "see" the place.
- **Sound excited.**
  Use specific words that show you know the place well.

Plan and write an essay.
Choose a historical landmark and write a detailed description of the place following these writing tips.

After you've written a first draft . . .

- **Check for completeness.**
  Make sure to include enough details to give a clear picture of the place.
- **Check for correctness.**
  Proofread your essay for errors in punctuation, capitalization, spelling, and grammar.

Writing Tips

Help students choose a topic to write about. Make a three-column chart on the board with the following headings: *Family Vacations, School Field Trips, Places I've Read About* (in school or on their own). Then have students brainstorm historical landmarks for each heading.

As students do their research, they are probably going to come across a lot of historical information related to their topic. Although they may have to provide readers with some background information, their goal is not to give the history of the place. Their goal is to describe it. So they should concentrate on gathering facts and details that will help readers picture the place in their mind. Students can look back at the sample essay on PE page 76 to see how the writer incorporated just one or two historical facts into the description.

English Language Learners

Ask a travel agent for brochures of historical landmarks with pictures to help students learn about the popularity of the site that they will describe. First, have them brainstorm details from the pictures they see, and then assist them in reading the brochures or other information to make sure that they understand new vocabulary.

Struggling Learners

Invite students to work in small groups to research a landmark and discuss their findings.

- First, have them list the details they find on a sensory chart (TE page 646).
- Then have them use the chart to write their own essay.

Afterward, have the same group do a "round robin" peer review of each other's work to check for accuracy of facts and details.

Science: Describing a Plant

Use the sample essay to point out that the main difference between this plant description and the description of a favorite place relates mostly to voice.

- In a description of a favorite place, the voice is enthusiastic and emotional. The writer shares personal feelings about the place. Students can look at the earlier samples and at their own favorite place paragraph and room essay for examples.

- In this description of the Texas bluebonnet, the voice is factual and informative. The writer describes the plant in detail, but does not share personal feelings about the plant.

Science: Describing a Plant

Scientists called botanists study and describe the many types of plants in the world. Describing a particular plant helps you to understand it better.

The Texas State Flower

The beginning introduces the plant and its scientific name.

The Texas bluebonnet is the state flower of Texas. Its scientific name is <u>Lupinus texensis</u> (loo-PIE-nus teck-SEN-sis). Bluebonnets grow beside many highways in the state. These flowers can survive in the dry soil of the Texas prairie.

From the ground, the bluebonnet's round, velvety stem grows 12 to 24 inches high. The leaves sprout along the stem in bunches, and each bunch fans out from a leaf stem. The leaves are thin and have round tips. They look like tiny green bunny ears!

The middle describes the plant and its parts.

At the top of the plant is a stalk of small, sweet-smelling flowers. Each one is bright bluish purple with a white center. These tiny blossoms give the bluebonnet its name because each little flower looks like an old-fashioned bonnet.

The ending includes a final thought about the topic.

So, when you're in Texas, and you see huge fields of blue flowers, you'll know what they are. They're Texas bluebonnets, the state flower.

flower

stem

leaf bunch

Struggling Learners

Discuss the text features the sample writer uses to clarify factual information, such as the following:

- a specific title
- a scientific name
- a respelling to help pronunciation
- a diagram

Then encourage students to use these techniques in their own science essays.

Writing in Science **79**

WRITING TIPS

Before you write . . .

- **Choose a topic that interests you.**
  Select a plant that you have studied or one you know from everyday life.
- **Research the plant.**
  Look up the scientific name and other details. Include a pronunciation guide for hard words.
- **List the main ideas you want to include.**
  Describe the plant and any of its special features.

During your writing . . .

- **Write a clear beginning, middle, and ending.**
  Introduce the plant in the beginning, describe it in the middle, and end with a summary or personal comment.
- **Organize your details.**
  Describe your plant from bottom to top or from top to bottom.
- **Use specific words.**
  Select words that give the reader a clear picture of the plant.

After you've written a first draft . . .

- **Check for completeness.**
  Add details to make your topic clearer.
- **Check for correctness.**
  Proofread your description for errors in punctuation, capitalization, spelling, and grammar.

Describe a plant. Use these tips to guide your writing.

Writing Tips

Reassure students that the task of writing a description of a plant will not be any more difficult than the task of writing a description of a place. Explain that they will follow the same process they followed to write a descriptive paragraph and an essay:

- They will choose a topic (a plant) that interests them.
- They will describe the plant using sensory details that will help the reader form a clear mental picture.
- They will arrange details by order of location.

To help students choose a plant to write about, have them look through botanical calendars, garden center catalogues, and plant books.

English Language Learners

As a group, describe a plant that is easily found in your area. If possible, bring in a plant for students to describe. Model the use of sensory words that describe and transition words that organize the kinds of details you want students to develop. Come up with a list of descriptors that students can use as a reference to describe their plant.

Advanced Learners

To extend the project, invite students to compile the class essays into a booklet, a computer display using presentation software, or a hall display with illustrations to share with other members of the school community.

Writing for Assessment

If your students must take school, district, or state assessments this year, focus on the writing form on which they will be tested.

Explain to students that whenever they have to respond to a writing prompt, they should take time to highlight or underline the key words in the prompt that explain what to do. Then ask them what words they would highlight in the sample prompt (place you have visited, paragraph that describes, sensory details, vivid picture).

 Respond to the reading.

Answers

Ideas 1. Possible responses: concrete platform; strange, cool wind; wide yellow lines; deep trenches; disappear into blackness; oily, old garage; ground shakes; cars roar; wheels screech; monster breathing

Organization 2. by location from the doorway into the station, down the stairs, to the platform, down onto the tracks and along the tracks into the darkness

Voice & Word Choice 3. underground world, science-fiction adventure

---

80

Writing for Assessment

Some writing tests include a descriptive writing prompt. Read the following prompt and the student's response.

Descriptive Prompt

Think of a place you have visited. Write a paragraph that describes it using sensory details. Paint a vivid picture with your words.

The **topic sentence** (underlined) paints a vivid picture.

Descriptive details fill the **body** sentences.

The **closing sentence** makes a personal comment about the subject.

> The subway station is a doorway to an underground world. Stairs lead down, down to the concrete platform. A strange, cool wind always seems to be blowing. Wide yellow lines warn people to stand away from the deep trenches where tracks disappear into blackness in both directions. The air smells like an oily, old garage. When the train light appears, the ground shakes as the subway cars roar into the station. As the wheels screech to a stop, all the opening and closing doors sound like a monster breathing. My stepdad and I often ride the subway, and it always seems like a science-fiction adventure to me.

 Respond to the reading. Answer the following questions about the response paragraph.

- **Ideas (1)** What sensory details stand out? Name two.
- **Organization (2)** How did the writer organize the details in the body of the paragraph?
- **Voice & Word Choice (3)** What words show that the writer cares about the topic?

Writing for Assessment   **81**

WRITING TIPS

Before you write . . .

- **Understand the prompt.**
  Be sure you understand what you need to describe.
- **Use your time wisely.**
  Take a few minutes to plan and make some notes.

During your writing . . .

- **Write an effective topic sentence.**
  Use words related to the prompt to introduce your subject and form a topic sentence.
- **Be selective.**
  Choose sensory details that describe your topic.
- **End in a meaningful way.**
  Close with a personal comment about the topic.

After you've written a first draft . . .

- **Check for completeness and correctness.**
  Make sure your ideas make sense and correct any errors.

Descriptive Prompt

■ Think of a place where you had fun. Write a paragraph that describes that place and tells why it's special to you.

 Plan and write a response. Respond to the "descriptive prompt" above. Finish your writing in the amount of time your teacher gives you. Afterward, underline something that you like and something that could be better in your response.

Writing Tips

Point out that students must approach writing-on-demand assignments differently from open-ended writing assignments and that timed writing creates pressures for everyone.

Descriptive Prompt

To teach students who must take timed assessments how to approach their writing, allow them the same amount of time to write their response essay as they will be allotted on school, district, or state assessments. Break down each part of the process into clear chunks of time. For example, you might give students

- 15 minutes for note taking and planning,
- 20 minutes for writing, and
- 10 minutes for editing and proofreading.

Tell students when time is up for each section. Start the assignment at the top of the hour or at the half-hour to make it easier for students to keep track of the time.

If your state, district, or school requires students to use and submit a graphic organizer as part of their assessment, provide a copy of one of the reproducible charts (TE pages 645–651) or refer students to PE pages 456–457.

English Language Learners

Ask each student individually to repeat back to you the directions they are to follow in their own words so that you can check for correct comprehension. Make sure that they know the difference between describing

- a *place where* they had fun and
- a *time when* they had fun.

A short brainstorming conversation with you may help them to develop ideas and write a better essay than if they are left to do the planning (or, prewriting) on their own.

Narrative Writing Overview

Writing Standards

The writing standards listed below are based on a blending of state and NCTE standards.

- Use charts, clusters, lists, and time lines to gather and organize information that supports a central idea.
- Expand the central idea using sensory details and dialogue.
- Revise drafts to ensure a strong beginning, middle, and ending; to use active verbs; and to improve sentence variety.
- Edit a final draft to ensure correct use of pronouns and verb tenses and to check punctuation and spelling.
- Assess writing using a rubric based on the traits of effective writing.

Writing Forms

- narrative paragraph
- narrative essay about sharing an experience

Focus on the Traits

- **Ideas** Including sensory details that help the reader clearly imagine the events in the story
- **Organization** Creating a beginning that grabs the reader's interest, a middle that is organized in time order, and an ending that brings the narrative together
- **Voice** Using dialogue that sounds natural and shows the personality of each character
- **Word Choice** Choosing active verbs and words with the right feeling
- **Sentence Fluency** Varying sentence beginnings and sentence lengths to keep the narrative moving smoothly
- **Conventions** Checking for errors in punctuation, capitalization, spelling, and grammar

Unit Pacing

Narrative Paragraph: 1.5–3 hours

The **narrative paragraph** introduces the unit and lays the groundwork for more extensive narrative writing. Use this section if students need to work on crafting a paragraph. Following are some of the topics that are covered:

- Creating a web to select a topic
- Using a details chart to collect details
- Writing a paragraph with a natural voice

Narrative Essay: 3.5–6 hours

This section asks students to **share an unforgettable experience.** Use this section to focus on developing an essay. Following are some of the topics that are covered:

- Freewriting a list to brainstorm for topics
- Making a 5 W's memory chart to size up the topic
- Creating a transition time line to organize events
- Developing the middle part with sensory details and dialogue
- Using verb tenses correctly

Narrative Writing Across the Curriculum: 1.5–3 hours

The first lesson in this section guides students through the steps of the writing process in another curriculum area. The remaining two lessons provide models and tips for narrative writing in additional curriculum areas. If other teachers are involved in cross-curricular activities, collaborate with them on these lessons.

■ **Math**
Creating a Story Problem, pp. 126–129

■ **Science**
Writing an Observation Report, pp. 130–131

■ **Practical Writing**
Writing to an E-Pal, pp. 132–133

Writing for Assessment: 45–90 minutes

The student text shows a sample student response to the first prompt below. Students can respond to that same prompt or to either of the additional prompts as an informal or a formal assessment.

■ Every person has been brave at one time or another. Write a narrative essay that tells about a time when you were brave. Tell what you learned from the experience.

■ Who is the most unforgettable person you have ever met? Show what this person did to make himself or herself unforgettable.

■ Write a letter to a friend and tell about a memorable experience during your first day of a new school year.

Evaluating a Narrative Essay

Learning to evaluate one's own and others' writing is an integral part of learning to write. In addition to a student's evaluation of a narrative essay (PE pages 122–123), **benchmark papers** in transparency and copy master form provide practice with evaluating narrative writing.

■ El Niño at Its Best (strong)
TR 1A–1C
TE pp. 630–632

■ Out of Gas (good)
PE pp. 122–123

■ Las Vegas (poor)
TR 2A–2B
TE pp. 633–634

Integrated Grammar and Writing Skills

Below are skills lessons from the resources sections of the pupil edition that are suggested at point of use (✳) throughout this unit.

Writing a Narrative Paragraph, pp. 83–86

✳ Web Organizer, p. 456
✳ Choosing Verbs, p. 416

Sharing an Experience, pp. 87–124

✳ Narrative Voice, p. 462
✳ Share the Right Feeling, p. 422
✳ Commas to Separate Introductory Phrases and Clauses, p. 484
✳ Expand Sentences with Prepositional Phrases, p. 448
✳ Tenses of Verbs, p. 418

Additional Grammar Skills

Below are skills lessons from other components that you can weave into your unit instruction.

Writing a Narrative Paragraph

SkillsBook

Types of Verbs 1 and 2, p. 157
Parts of Speech Review 1, 2, and 3, p. 184

Interactive Writing Skills CD-ROM

Parts of Speech: Verbs 1—Action and Linking Verbs

Daily Language Workouts

Week 7: It's All Yours, pp. 16–17
Week 7: Good Books, p. 84
Week 8: And I Quote . . ., pp. 18–19
Week 8: Girl with the Crooked Hair, p. 85

Sharing an Experience

SkillsBook

Commas to Set Off Introductory Phrases and Clauses, p. 8
Prepositional Phrases, p. 83
Expanding Sentences with Prepositional Phrases, p. 127
Simple Verb Tenses, p. 159
Prepositional Phrases 1 and 2, p. 175

Interactive Writing Skills CD-ROM

Punctuation: Commas 2— Introductory Phrases and Clauses
Sentences: Parts of a Sentence 3— Phrases and Clauses
Parts of Speech 1: Verbs 2—Tenses
Parts of Speech 2: Prepositions

Daily Language Workouts

Week 9: Capital Idea! pp. 20–21
Week 9: The Real McCoy, p. 86
Week 10: Geographically Speaking, pp. 22–23
Week 10: The Perfect Vacation, p. 87

82

Narrative Writing

Writing Across the Curriculum

Daily Language Workouts

Week 11: One Is a Lonely Number, pp. 24–25
Week 11: Looking at Art, p. 88
Week 12: One Potato, Two Potato, Three Potato, Four, pp. 26–27
Week 12: The First Americans, p. 89

Narrative Writing

Narrative Paragraph

What makes you laugh? What funny experiences have you had with your family or friends? If you think about it, you probably have many humorous stories to tell. And sharing these stories can be a lot of fun.

Writing about personal experiences is a form of narrative writing. The best narrative writing makes an experience come alive for the reader. On the following pages you will learn to write a narrative paragraph about something funny that happened to you.

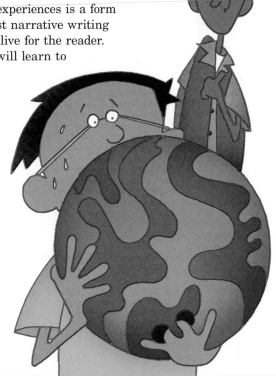

Writing Guidelines

Subject:	A funny experience
Form:	Narrative paragraph
Purpose:	To entertain
Audience:	Classmates

Narrative Paragraph

Objectives

- demonstrate an understanding of the content and structure of a narrative paragraph
- choose a topic (a funny experience) to write about
- plan, draft, revise, and edit a narrative paragraph

A **narrative paragraph** tells a brief story. Ask students to name the parts of a paragraph (topic sentence, body, and closing sentence).

※ For information about writing paragraphs, see PE pages 50–61.

Ask students what makes a story funny. Possible answers:

- The characters get into trouble in funny ways.
- The characters tell jokes or say other funny things.
- The characters play tricks on each other.
- One or more of the characters do really silly things.

Ask students to give examples from stories they know and encourage the class to keep these ideas in mind as they think about funny topics for their paragraphs.

Family Connection Letters

As you begin this unit, send home the Narrative Writing Family Connection letter, which describes what students will be learning.

○ Letter in English (TE p. 654)

○ Letter in Spanish (TE p. 662)

Materials

Sample paragraph with editing errors, blank overhead transparency (TE p. 86)

Narrative Paragraph

After students have read the paragraph, ask them to think about how the paragraph might sound when it is read aloud. Invite a volunteer to read it to classmates.

Talk about students' responses. Ask those who laughed out loud to explain why they laughed. Ask the others for their responses. Possible responses:

- The way the writer said things was funny—for example, "Pow!" is like a comic book.
- The writing created funny images, such as the ball stopping in the middle of the alley.

Respond to the reading.

Answers

Ideas 1. An embarrassing first bowling experience

Organization 2. Time order

Voice & Word Choice 3. Answers will vary. Possible choices:

- . . . like he was putting on his old baseball glove . . .
- . . . watched the ball sail down the alley.
- All ten pins went flying.
- . . . rolling very, very slowly
- But it stopped dead.
- Everybody was pointing and laughing.

84

Narrative Paragraph

Funny things can happen almost anywhere. In this story, Jason shares a humorous memory about the first time he went bowling.

Topic sentence

Body

Closing sentence

Crash Landing

Now I'm a great bowler, but I remember the very first time I went bowling with my dad. I was only five years old. His fingers fit into the ball like he was putting on his old baseball glove. I saw Dad's mighty swing and watched the ball sail down the alley. Pow! All ten pins went flying. Then it was my turn. The ball was so heavy, but I held on. Taking a deep breath, I aimed for the pins. "Come on, strike," I said as I ran a few steps and swung the ball hard. It crashed down and started rolling very, very slowly. I kept saying, "Go, go." But it stopped dead. Everybody was pointing and laughing. Dad had to call the manager to push my ball into the gutter. It was one of the most embarrassing and funny moments of my life.

Respond to the reading. **Answer the following questions on your own paper.**

- **Ideas** **(1) What is the topic of this paragraph?**
- **Organization (2) Does Jason organize the details by time order or by order of location?**
- **Word Choice (3) What words and phrases create pictures in your mind? Name two.**

English Language Learners

Students who have not bowled may not fully appreciate the humor in the model paragraph. Before asking a student to read the paragraph aloud, survey the class to discover if there are students who have not bowled. Ask students who have bowled to draw a diagram and pantomime as they describe the game.

Writing a Narrative Paragraph **85**

Prewriting Selecting a Topic

The writer of "Crash Landing" used a web to help him remember some of his funny experiences.

Web

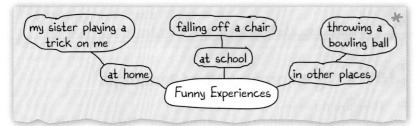

 Create a web like the one above. Include your own funny experiences at home, at school, and in other places. Put a star (✱) next to the experience you want to write about.

Gathering Details

Asking questions is a good way to gather and organize details. Jason used a chart to collect details for his paragraph.

Details Chart

How does the story start?	What events lead up to the funniest moment?	What is the funniest moment in the story?
I went bowling with my dad.	My dad got a strike. I didn't throw the ball hard enough.	The ball crashed, rolled slowly, and stopped. The manager had to come.

 Collect details. Make a chart like the one above. Fill it in with details about your experience.

Prewriting Selecting a Topic

For those who have trouble **choosing a topic** *(see below)*, provide enough time to brainstorm.

- Draw a large web on the board and suggest several funny experiences that are easy to visualize, such as learning to roller skate or attempting to juggle, whistle, or use chopsticks.
- Assure students that sharing their funny stories will connect them to other people who have had similar experiences.

✱ For information about using a web organizer, see PE page 456.

Prewriting Gathering Details

Have students copy the column headings onto their own charts and ask them to respond to the questions. Encourage them to add additional columns for other questions to consider while planning their paragraph:

- When did I begin to laugh about the experience?
- Who helped make the experience funnier?

Teaching Tip: Choosing a Topic

Students may worry that other people won't think their topic is funny. Engage the class in a discussion of different kinds of humor; for example, slapstick, stand-up comedy, and situational humor. Some stories make people laugh out loud, while others make people smile or chuckle quietly to themselves. Reassure students that if they found their experience funny, others will, too.

English Language Learners

Students may need additional help with the vocabulary needed to share their story in English. Have students make a storyboard to gather and organize details. Before asking them to write, allow them to sketch their story with a cooperative partner. This will give them an opportunity to "rehearse" the story orally and receive help with the vocabulary.

Writing
Developing the First Draft

Before students begin to write, ask them to close their eyes and think about the story they're about to tell. Encourage them to picture each detail as vividly as possible.

Remind students to
- begin with a topic sentence that introduces the story in an interesting way,
- create a detailed picture of events in time order, and
- end with a final thought about what happened.

Revising
Improving Your Paragraph

Have students use the tips to revise their drafts. Ask students to circle all the verbs in their paragraph. Can the verbs be improved to show more action? Ask students to replace two verbs. Point out that this may involve rewriting some sentences.

✱ For more about choosing action verbs, see PE page 416.

Editing Checking for Conventions

Write a sample paragraph with editing errors in it on an overhead transparency. Demonstrate for students how to check for errors and how to mark errors.

86

Writing Developing the First Draft

In your narrative paragraph, your topic sentence introduces your story. The body sentences contain details about what happened to you. The closing sentence sums up your experience.

 Write your first draft. Write with a natural writing voice as if you were telling a friend about your funny experience.

Revising Improving Your Paragraph

Here are three helpful revising tips.
- **Show, don't tell.** Instead of writing "Dad got a strike," write "I saw Dad's mighty swing and watched the ball sail down the alley. Pow! All ten pins went flying."
- **Check your organization.** Tell the events in the order in which they happened.
- **Check words and sentences.** Use specific nouns (*baseball glove*) and action verbs (*crashed*). Make your sentences flow.

 Revise your paragraph. Use the tips above as you make changes to improve the first draft of your narrative paragraph.

Editing Checking for Conventions

After revising your first draft, you must correct any punctuation, capitalization, spelling, or grammar errors in your paragraph.

 Edit and proofread your work. Use the following questions to check and correct your narrative paragraph.

1. Have I ended each sentence with a punctuation mark?
2. Are my capitalization and spelling correct?

English Language Learners

Do a Think-Aloud to model for students what to do if they cannot think of a word when they are writing. Possible strategies:

- Draw a line for the missing word and continue writing.
- Circle a word they want to question during the revision stage.
- Use a word from their first language.

Struggling Learners

To practice showing instead of telling, have students work in groups to revise simple declarative sentences orally. For example: *I forgot my homework* can be restated as *I wildly dug through my backpack, pulling out books, papers, and pens, but I couldn't find my math homework. Then I remembered—I'd left it on the kitchen table the night before.*

Other possible sentences are the following:

- My suitcase was full.
- The electricity went out.
- The mattress was hard.
- My little brother gets into my stuff.
- The lemonade tasted really strange.

Narrative Writing
Sharing an Experience

Everyone has had unforgettable experiences. Some of these memories may be happy or exciting. Others may be sad or even scary. You can write about these times in personal narratives. A **personal narrative** is a form of writing that sheds light on a true story from your life.

In this chapter, you will write a personal narrative about an unforgettable experience. Your goal is to make your story as fresh and vivid for your reader as it actually was for you.

Writing Guidelines

Subject:	An unforgettable experience
Form:	Personal narrative
Purpose:	To share a true story
Audience:	Classmates

Sharing an Experience

Objectives
- demonstrate an understanding of the purpose, content, and form of a personal narrative
- choose a topic (an unforgettable experience) to write about
- plan, draft, revise, edit, and publish a personal narrative

Explain that a **personal narrative** is an account of an event the writer experienced. Point out that *unforgettable* can be used to describe anything they'll never forget, whether it is a happy, sad, funny, or scary experience.

To prompt students to think in terms of memorable topics,
- ask students to brainstorm forgettable, everyday events (like putting on their socks or brushing their teeth);
- write the ideas on the board as students call them out; and
- when you have a good list, invite students to think of ways to turn these common events into unforgettable ones. Encourage students to be imaginative. (For example, while putting on a sock they find a moth in the toe.)

Materials

It Looked Like Spilt Milk by Charles G. Shaw (Harper Trophy, 1988) (TE p. 90)

Samples of dialogue (TE p. 109)

Sample dialogue, blank overhead transparency (TE p. 118)

Sentences that contain commonly confused words (TE p. 118)

Examples of movie and book posters, drawing supplies, and poster board (TE p. 119)

Copy Masters/ Transparencies

5W's chart (TE p. 93)

Time line (TE p. 94)

Sensory chart (TE p. 95)

Benchmark Papers

El Niño at Its Best (strong)
- TR 1A–1C
- TE pp. 630–632

Las Vegas (poor)
- TR 2A–2B
- TE pp. 633–634

Understanding Your Goal

Three traits relate to the development of the content and the form. They provide a focus during prewriting, drafting, and revising.

- Ideas
- Organization
- Voice

The other three traits relate more to form. Checking them is part of the revising and editing processes.

- **Word Choice**
- **Sentence Fluency**
- **Conventions**

✳ The six-point rubric on PE pages 120–121 is based on these traits. Four- and five-point rubrics are available on TE pages 624 and 627.

Review the narrative rubric (pages 120–121) as a class, comparing it with the goals. Can students find details in one list that aren't in the other? Possible answers:

- Ideas goal says to make the reader want to know what happens next.
- Organization goal specifies to use time order.
- Voice goal says to show the personality of each person.
- Sentence Fluency goal is to vary sentence length to create flow.

88

Understanding Your Goal

Your goal in this chapter is to write a personal narrative about an unforgettable experience. The traits listed in the chart below will help you meet that goal.

Your goal is to . . .

Ideas
Use specific details to show what happens. Make the reader want to know what happens next.

Organization
Grab the reader's interest in the beginning. Organize your ideas using time order. Bring your narrative together in the ending.

Voice
Use a strong storytelling voice. Show the personality of each person in your narrative.

Word Choice
Use specific nouns and verbs.

Sentence Fluency
Write sentences that flow smoothly from one to the next and keep the narrative moving.

Conventions
Be sure that the punctuation, capitalization, spelling, and grammar are correct.

 Get the big picture. Review the rubric on pages 120–121. It will help you check your progress as you write your narrative.

English Language Learners

Some students may be confused by the subjective vocabulary (for example, *many, some*) used in the rubric on pages 120–121. Explain that you will hold conferences with them to clarify the rubric and help them identify what they need to do to improve their writing throughout the year.

Personal Narrative

In this personal narrative, Shana shares an unforgettable memory of a scary storm.

Sharing an Experience **89**

The Green, Howling Day

BEGINNING
The beginning catches the reader's interest.

One day, I was looking out my bedroom window when the sky began to turn a weird shade of green! Just then, I heard our city's emergency siren start wailing. That meant trouble.

Danika, my four-year-old sister, was in the hallway. She was crying, flapping her arms, and jumping up and down. That's what she does when she's scared. Mom came running upstairs to get us. She grabbed Danika and carried her down the steps. "Get to the basement!" she ordered.

MIDDLE
The middle is organized in chronological (time) order.

By the time we reached the kitchen, the wind was howling like a wolf. I saw rain whizzing sideways past the window and trees bending over. It was like we were in the middle of the twister in The Wizard of Oz. As soon as we got to the basement steps, the sky turned as black as night. My sister screamed as the lights flickered and went out.

Suddenly the basement felt cold and damp. It smelled like laundry soap and bleach. Mom snapped on a flashlight and led us to a safe place. Then she tried to calm Danika. Finally, she turned on our portable radio. "A tornado is

---

Personal Narrative

Work through this sample essay with the class, pointing out the elements that make it a good personal narrative.

Ideas
- The narrative focuses on one unforgettable experience.
- The writer uses specific details.

Organization
- The opening makes you want to know what will happen next.
- The details are in time order.
- The ending tells how it turned out and how the writer felt.

Voice & Word Choice
- The writer uses a natural voice.
- The writer describes characters' actions in a way that establishes strong personalities (the writer, Danika, Mom).
- The writer uses active verbs and specific nouns.

Ask students where the topic is revealed (end of paragraph 4). Acknowledge that students have learned to put the topic in the first paragraph. Explain that the writer didn't follow convention because she wanted to create suspense. Tell students that they may break the "rules" if they have a good reason.

English Language Learners

Students may have difficulty comprehending figurative language, and they may not comprehend the model essay well enough to understand the elements that make the essay a good example. To make sure students participate in the discussion, use these strategies:

- Have volunteers read each paragraph aloud.

- Ask students to predict what might happen next.
- Model how to ask questions about vocabulary and figurative language and encourage students to ask their own questions.

Tell students that one technique used very effectively in the essay is comparison. The writer uses a kind of comparison called simile, which describes something by using the word *like* or *as* and giving an example. Ask students to look for examples of simile in the essay.

- ... howling like a wolf.
- It was like we were in ... *The Wizard of Oz.*
- ... the sky turned as black as night.
- It smelled like laundry soap ...
- ... it sounded like a train ...

✳ For more about similes, see PE page 411.

Respond to the reading.

Answers

Ideas 1. A scary tornado

Organization 2. Time order

Voice & Word Choice 3. Answers will vary but should demonstrate casual voice or strong word choice.

- ... the sky began to turn a weird shade of green!
- ... rain whizzing sideways ...
- ... huddled against the cold concrete blocks ...
- What damage had the tornado done?

90

MIDDLE
The middle includes strong details.

moving through this area," the weather reporter said. "Seek shelter immediately."

We huddled against the cold concrete blocks, far away from the windows. Mom sang lullabies for my little sister and squeezed us close. She tried to sound strong, but her voice was shaky. The wind rumbled and growled outside. It grew louder and louder until it sounded like a train roaring over our heads. Lightning flashes exploded and lit the room with a weird glow. Then everything was still.

ENDING
The closing tells how the experience ended.

We didn't know what we'd see when we went upstairs. What damage had the tornado done? Our house was fine, but tree branches and junk had blown all over the place. Danika crawled through the branches of the tree that had fallen across the driveway. Mom and Danika were afraid of the tornado, but I wasn't. Still, I was glad it was over and that we were all safe.

Respond to the reading.

- **Ideas (1)** What unforgettable experience does Shana share?
- **Organization (2)** How does Shana organize the events in her story?
- **Voice & Word Choice (3)** What words and phrases help you share in her experience? Name two.

English Language Learners

If students have difficulty finding the examples of simile or understanding the examples, share the book *It Looked Like Spilt Milk* by Charles G. Shaw. Have students create their own similes for some of the pictures to reinforce the concept and language of similes.

Struggling Learners

Help students locate the powerful verbs in Shana's essay and discuss how they emphasize the actions and emotions by creating "mind movies."

- wailing
- flapping
- grabbed
- ordered
- howling
- whizzing
- screamed
- snapped
- huddled
- squeezed
- rumbled
- growled
- roaring
- exploded

Prewriting

First you need to choose an unforgettable experience to write about. Then you will gather details you remember.

Keys to Prewriting

1. **Think** of unforgettable experiences in your life.

2. **Choose** one experience to write about.

3. **Use** a time line to organize your story.

4. **Gather** sensory details to help the reader share your experience.

Prewriting Keys to Prewriting

Remind students of the purpose of the prewriting stage in the writing process: It is when the writer selects a topic, gathers details, and decides how to organize those details.

The Keys to Prewriting list lays out the process students will be guided through on PE pages 92–96.

Remind them that the writing process is broken down into stages (like prewriting), with steps they can follow in each stage (like the Keys to Prewriting). This helps writers to take each step as they prepare to write. Gradually, one step leads to another until they have built the whole piece of writing. It is similar to the way all of the many separate parts of a house, such as wooden beams and bricks and roof shingles, can be put together to build a house.

Prewriting Selecting a Topic

After students have read through Tyrone's list of ideas, point out that, with the exception of the bike accident, the topics are pretty much about simple, normal activities. Explain that although students might have something very dramatic to write about—something that's the absolute best or worst or scariest—**everyday topics** *(see below)* can be just as interesting.

Suggest that students who are having trouble thinking of topics begin by borrowing ideas from Tyrone's list. Do they remember the following?

- being in a play
- something funny their pet has done
- a stormy day

Starting their freewriting with these ideas will help other ideas begin to flow.

92

Prewriting Selecting a Topic

Tyrone found ideas for his personal narrative by making an "I remember when . . ." list like the one below.

List

> I remember when . . .
>
> I was a toad in our first-grade play.
>
> my teacher retired, and I read her a poem.
>
> my family went without TV for a whole weekend.
>
> my guinea pig sneaked onto the school bus.
>
> we had a snow day, and I built a snow fort.
>
> I helped plant a memory tree in front of our school.
>
> my wrist got broken when I fell off my bike.

Some of your best stories come from your memories.

 Brainstorm for topics. On your own paper, make an *I remember when . . .* list using the model above. Keep these things in mind:

1 Freewrite your list. Keep writing until you can't think of any more ideas.

2 Read your ideas and circle the one that you think will make the best story.

Teaching Tip: Interesting Everyday Topics

To reinforce the idea that everyday topics can be interesting, encourage students to think about books they have read and liked.

- Did some of the books include parts about everyday events like eating, going to sleep, being bored?
- Invite students to mention the book titles and briefly describe the topic or the scene they have in mind.

Remind students that it can be fun to hear friends' or relatives' accounts of everyday events.

English Language Learners

Allow students to use drawings, single words and/or phrases instead of complete sentences to make their own "*I remember when . . .*" list.

If students have trouble deciding which idea will make the best story, have them share their ideas with a partner to find out which story the partner wants to know more about.

Sharing an Experience 93

Sizing Up Your Topic Idea

A good story includes plenty of details. How much do you remember about your experience? Who was there? What happened? When, where, and why did it happen? What did people say? Making a 5 W's memory chart will help you remember.

Do you remember enough interesting details about your experience?

5 W's Memory Chart

Who?	me, my brother, Dad, Mom
What?	My brother was upset. Dad built a campfire. Mom read a story. We ate pizza, played games, and carved pumpkins.
When?	Halloween time
Where?	the backyard, the kitchen table, our living room
Why?	no television for a whole weekend

 Prewrite

Make a memory chart. Make a chart like the one above. Write down as much as you can about your experience.

Sizing Up Your Topic Idea

Provide copies of the reproducible 5 W's chart (TE page 647) for students to fill out as they size up their topic.

Consider assigning this stage of the process as homework. If you do, encourage students to go home and ask family members or friends who were also involved in the event what they remember about it. This can help students fill in missing details. If students ask others to help confirm their memories, remind them to

- describe the event the way they remember it and ask if the person remembers it the same way;
- ask about specific details they know they've forgotten; and
- listen carefully to the answers they receive, jotting down notes.

English Language Learners

Students may come from homes where the family members involved in the event do not speak English. Encourage them to use their first language to discuss the event and to use drawings or words from their first language to add details to their 5 W's chart. Provide time for students to share their 5 W's chart with a proficient bilingual or cooperative classmate to help them clarify or develop vocabulary in English.

Struggling Learners

To help students become more skilled with the 5 W's, use the chart to analyze a class read-aloud. For example:

- **Who:** Maya Lin
- **What:** Designed the Viet Nam Veteran's Memorial
- **When:** During college
- **Where:** Washington, D.C.
- **Why:** Won a design contest

Prewriting
Putting Events in Order

Distribute photocopies of the reproducible time line (TE page 648) for students to use as an alternative to the transition time line in the sample.

Whichever style of time line students use, tell them to leave at least one line space between each item. That way, if they realize they've forgotten an important detail, there will be space to go back and insert it.

Focus on the Traits

Organization
To help students get the chain of events straight in their minds,

- have partners take turns telling each other their stories;
- have the listener take notes, recording the events in order on a time line; and
- have the listener give the storyteller the notes to refer to while planning.

Have students trade roles and repeat the process.

94

Prewriting Putting Events in Order

Narratives are usually organized in chronological (time) order. Transition words and phrases (*first, second, after that, then, before long*) can help you put your events in order. See Tyrone's list below.

Transition Time Line

First . . .	my parents decided we wouldn't watch TV for a whole weekend.
Next . . .	we ate supper, and it got dark outside.
After that . . .	we made a campfire in the backyard.
Then . . .	we went inside and carved pumpkins.
Before bed . . .	we played a board game.
Finally . . .	my family decided to turn off the TV every Tuesday night and have fun together.

Prewrite **Create your time list.** On your own paper, make a list like the one above. Use transitions to help you list important details in the order in which they happened.

Focus on the Traits

Organization A good story has an easy, natural order. Think of stories you've read or heard from your teacher, family, or friends. They often sound like someone is "telling" it just the way it happened.

English Language Learners

Note taking can be difficult because of the time it takes students to listen for familiar words, process what they hear, and write in a second language. To help students focus on the order of events, pair English language learners, and provide each with a graphic organizer such as a blank storyboard. Have students number the boxes before they listen to their partner and ask them to use drawings and/or words to record the events.

Advanced Learners

Point out that writers sometimes start in the present and then back up to tell their stories in time order. For example, on PE page 84, Jason writes, *"Now I'm a great bowler, but I remember . . ."* Invite students to try this technique in their own writing.

Sharing an Experience 95

Gathering Sensory Details

A good narrative includes sights, sounds, smells, tastes, and even details about how things feel. These kinds of details make the story real for the reader. Your choice of details gives the narrative your voice. You can gather sensory details in a chart like the one below.

Sensory Chart

Sights	Sounds	Smells	Tastes	Touch
sparks flying	doorbell ringing	wood burning	s'mores	warm jackets
glowing pumpkin faces	fire crackling	fresh air	pumpkin seeds	cool air
orange flames	Mom reading a story	pumpkin candles	pizza	gooey pumpkin seeds
starry sky				huddling together near the fire

Prewrite Create a sensory chart. Think about your story. Then list sensory words and phrases that will help the reader share your memorable experience.

Gathering Sensory Details

Discuss why including details about the five senses helps to make writing seem more real. (In the real world we experience things through the five senses, so writing that includes these details helps the reader experience the event.)

Give students photocopies of the reproducible sensory chart (TE page 646) and encourage them to brainstorm as many sensory details about their topic as they can. Note that they may think of more sensory details than they actually need to use in the essay. Their work is not wasted, however—the more time they spend working on their memories of the events, the more details they'll have to choose from when they are writing and revising the draft.

Prewriting
Thinking About Dialogue

Ask students what they would say if they were responding to the statement "You will have to get along without TV."

Ask students to try to come up with realistic-sounding dialogue to express their response. Possible examples:

- "Um . . . I don't know what I'll do without TV . . ."
- "Argh! We have to have a television! We have to!"
- "Are you sure it's a good idea to get rid of the TV?"

Point out how different the responses are and note that students should try to capture that variation in their stories by choosing words and ways of speaking that suit each speaker.

Focus on the Traits

Voice
Point out that different kinds of writing require different kinds of voices. The style of the writing (which depends on topic, audience, and purpose) may call for a more formal, authoritative, or moderate voice at times.

* For more about writing in a narrative voice, see PE page 462.

96

Prewriting Thinking About Dialogue

Dialogue makes an experience come alive for the reader. The chart below shows the three main things that dialogue can do.

		Without dialogue	With dialogue
1	Show something about a speaker's personality.	I was mad. How could I get along without TV?	"What?" I said. "No television! I don't think I can survive without it."
2	Add details.	I knew I'd miss Sunday afternoon football.	I looked at Dad and said, "What about Sunday afternoon football?"
3	Keep the action moving.	We went back in the house.	Once we got back in the house, Dad said, "I have a surprise."

Prewrite **Plan some dialogue.** Think about what the people in your story said to each other. Make your dialogue sound real.

Focus on the Traits

Voice Your writing voice is like your fingerprint. It belongs to only you. When you write with your natural voice, your story will be interesting and believable.

English Language Learners

Embedded dialogue in text may be a challenge for some students. On the board, record students' responses to the statement, "You will have to get along without TV." Use a two-column graphic organizer to identify each speaker and what the speaker said. Model using quotation marks, capitalization, and appropriate end punctuation. Have students use a two-column organizer to plan what the characters in their story might say to each other.

Struggling Learners

For additional practice with dialogue, have student partners create oral or written conversations for the following scenarios:

- My grandparents are coming for the weekend.
- I'm hungry.
- I want to go to the movie with my sister.

Sharing an Experience 97

Writing

Now that you have collected and organized the details for your narrative, you are ready to write your first draft. Your goal is to put all your thoughts about your experience on paper.

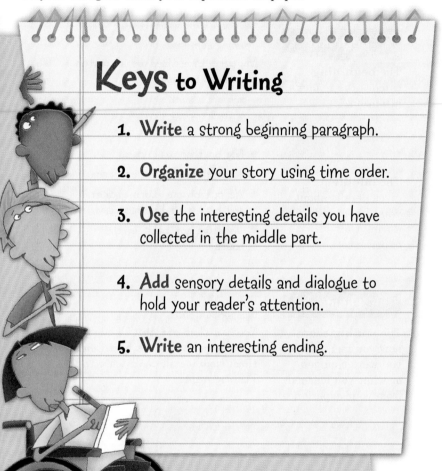

Keys to Writing

1. **Write** a strong beginning paragraph.

2. **Organize** your story using time order.

3. **Use** the interesting details you have collected in the middle part.

4. **Add** sensory details and dialogue to hold your reader's attention.

5. **Write** an interesting ending.

Writing Keys to Writing

Remind students that the writing stage is when they get to write, or draft, their ideas on paper.

The Keys to Writing list lays out the process students will be guided through on PE pages 98–102.

After reading through the steps with the class, explain that for this first essay they will work through each item on the list in order. Later, when they get more familiar with the process, they might choose to do the steps in a different order. For example:

- After they have gathered and organized details, they might decide to get the middle paragraphs down first, while the information is still fresh in their minds.
- Or they might get sudden inspiration about their closing paragraph just as they begin working on the draft, so they might stop and write that down first.

Point out that, in any case, steps 3 and 4 on the list can't really be addressed in order—they have to be sprinkled throughout the whole draft.

English Language Learners

Some students may be so concerned about neatness, the accuracy of word choice, or trying to remember the rules of English that they are not able to focus on the message. Remind them that they do not need to worry about recalling every word in English in their first draft because they will have time to make changes when they revise and edit their writing.

Writing Getting the Big Picture

Explain that the following pages will guide students through the process of creating each of these three parts of an essay.

Have students turn to PE page 84 and review the parts of a narrative paragraph. Do they see similarities between the structure of a paragraph and the structure of an essay? (Yes. Each has a beginning, middle, and ending—for a paragraph they're called the topic sentence, body, and closing sentence.)

Focus briefly on how to decide when enough details have been collected and it is time to begin writing the story. Explain that this can be difficult to decide, especially if students are very interested in their topic and have a lot to say. Suggest that students consider

- how long the essay is supposed to be,
- whether they have enough details to cover each part of the story, and
- whether they have gathered different kinds of details—such as details relating to three or four different senses.

98

Writing Getting the Big Picture

The chart below shows how the parts of a personal narrative fit together. (The examples are from the narrative on pages 99–102.) You're ready to write your essay once you have . . .

- gathered enough details to tell your story, and
- put the events of your story in time order.

Beginning	**Opening Sentence**
The **beginning** catches the reader's attention.	My parents decided we all watch too much television.

Middle	
The **middle** part gives details about what happened during the experience.	• My brother was upset . . . • Just then, the doorbell rang. • We put on our warm jackets and headed to the backyard. • Once we got back in the house, . . .

Ending	**Closing Sentences**
The **ending** shows how you feel, how you were changed, or what you learned from your experience.	Now we shut off the TV every Tuesday night, and we have family time. Now we all can't wait for Tuesday night.

English Language Learners

Have students prepare their storyboard to write their draft (see English Language Learners on TE page 94). Provide students with a different color highlighter for each part of their essay. Ask them to highlight any dialogue with the color assigned to the appropriate part so they will know where it belongs.

Starting Your Personal Narrative

In the first paragraph, you should get the reader's attention and introduce your personal experience. Here are three ways to begin your paragraph.

- **Start by using dialogue.**

  "What?" I said. "No television! I don't think I can survive without it."

- **Begin with an interesting statement or fact.**

  My parents decided we all watch too much television. So they made a rule that no one would watch TV for one whole weekend.

- **Put yourself in the middle of the action.**

  When my parents said no one could watch television all weekend, I was so mad! I couldn't imagine Saturday without cartoons.

Beginning Paragraph

The writer begins with an interesting statement and includes dialogue.

> My parents decided we all watch too much television. So they made a rule that no one would watch TV for one whole weekend. "What?" I said. "No television! I don't think I can survive without it."

You should write on every other line as you write your first draft.

 Write your beginning. Try at least two ways to begin your paragraph. Then choose the way you like best and finish your beginning paragraph.

Starting Your Personal Narrative

Have students look at the dialogue they wrote while working on PE page 96 to see if part of it would make a good opener.

Point out that after the writer of the sample essay chose his opening sentence (My parents decided . . .), he was able to use one of his other ideas to finish the paragraph ("What? I said . . ."). Encourage students to keep the lists of ideas they brainstorm and to refer to them as they work on their drafts. An idea that doesn't work in one place might fit nicely into another.

Advanced Learners

Point out that instead of *telling* his parents how he felt, Tyrone might have reacted with *inner thoughts*.

- Have students look for examples of this technique in books or magazines. Note that inner thoughts are sometimes shown in regular type and sometimes they are italicized.

- Suggest that students experiment with both inner and spoken dialogue in their narratives.

Writing
Developing the Middle Part

Have students arrange the notes they made during prewriting so they can see them as they work.

Remind students that they'll be going back to make improvements to the draft later.

- Explain that their main goal at this point is to write down everything that happened. Encourage them to check off items on the time line as they put them into the draft so that they don't forget anything.
- Remind students to try to use dialogue, sensory details, and feelings to show what happened.
- Tell students that they don't have to use all the details from their 5 W's and sensory charts. Those notes are a little like a box of paints—students may decide to use just a few of the colorful details for the part of the picture they're working on.
- Assure students that it's fine to add any new dialogue or ideas they think of as they write.

100

Writing **Developing the Middle Part**

The middle part of your narrative shares your story. Choose details carefully to *show* the reader what happened.

Beginning
Middle
Ending

- **Use sensory details** to help the reader share your experience.
- **Use dialogue** to reveal the personalities of the people in your story.
- **Share your feelings** so the reader will care about what happened to you.

Middle Paragraphs

> **Dialogue shows the speaker's personality.**
>
> My brother was upset because it was Halloween weekend, and he'd miss all the scary movies. I looked at Dad and said, "What about Sunday afternoon football?" Just then, the doorbell rang. It was the pizza guy delivering our supper. Instead of comparing who had the most pepperoni on a slice, we ate without saying much. Mom told us to finish up because it was getting dark outside. Who cared?
>
> **Transition words (blue) help connect the ideas.**
>
> After we ate, we grabbed our jackets and headed out to the backyard. Dad had built a roaring campfire. Then Mom brought out a dusty, old book. She began reading a scary ghost story out loud. I huddled closer to Dad

Sharing an Experience **101**

Strong sensory details help the reader "see" and "feel" what happened.

and the fire. The fire crackled, and sparks shot up to the stars. Even when it got too cool to stay outside, I didn't want to go in.

Once we got back in the house, Dad said, "I have a surprise." Two huge pumpkins sat on newspapers on the kitchen table. We drew faces on them, pulled out all their gooey seeds, carved them, and lit them with candles. Meanwhile, Mom washed, salted, and roasted the pumpkin seeds. Then we ate them while we played a board game together.

Write freely, put your ideas on paper, and have fun!

Write your middle paragraphs. Before you begin, read through your memory chart, time list, and sensory chart from pages 93–95. Use your best details.

To discuss how the writer uses details to show what happened instead of just telling, have students complete this sentence starter: You can tell that . . .

- . . . the brothers are upset because they don't compare pepperoni slices at dinner.
- . . . the storyteller is changing his mind about being upset because he enjoys the campfire (the story is scary, he huddles near his dad, watches the fire).
- . . . the family is having fun together because they eat pumpkin seeds and play a game.

Have students point out sensory details. Possible answers:
- the doorbell rang (sound)
- pepperoni pizza (taste/smell)
- roaring campfire (sound/sight)
- fire crackled (sound)
- sparks shot up (sight)
- two huge pumpkins (sight)
- gooey seeds (touch)
- salted, roasted pumpkin seeds (taste)

Writing
Ending Your Personal Narrative

To help students begin thinking about their endings, suggest that they ask themselves "Why did I decide to tell this story?" (Note that *why* is one of the 5 W's.) The response they come up with should help focus their ideas.

For those who have difficulty deciding how to proceed, hold a brief writer's conference. Ask the student to read his or her unfinished draft out loud. Formulate two or three sentence starters to provide momentum.

■ In the end, I felt . . .
■ Afterward, things were different for me because . . .
■ It all made me realize that . . .

Tell students they are welcome to use the wording in the starter, but encourage them to try to rephrase the same idea in their own words, remembering to show, with details and examples, rather than tell.

102

Writing Ending Your Personal Narrative

The last paragraph should bring your narrative to a close. Here are three possible ways to end your story.

Beginning
Middle
Ending

■ **Tell how the experience made you feel.**
  Going without television wasn't so bad after all.

■ **Explain how the experience changed you.**
  Going without TV changed my family. Now we shut off the TV every Tuesday night.

■ **Share what you learned from the experience.**
  I learned that it can really be fun to do things with my parents and my brother.

Ending Paragraph

The writer tells how the experience changed the whole family.

Going without TV changed my family. We had so much fun that whole weekend that we didn't even think about television. Now we shut off the TV every Tuesday night, and we have family time. Now we all can't wait for Tuesday night.

Write your ending. Try one of the three ways listed above to end your narrative. If you don't like how it sounds, try another of the ways or an idea of your own.

Struggling Learners

Explain that the way the ending is handled determines how memorable the narrative will be to readers. Without evidence of emotion or impact on the writer's life, the memory will seem like a normal, everyday event rather than an "unforgettable experience."

Sharing an Experience **103**

Revising

Revising your narrative is a very important step in the writing process. When you revise, you change and improve the ideas in your narrative.

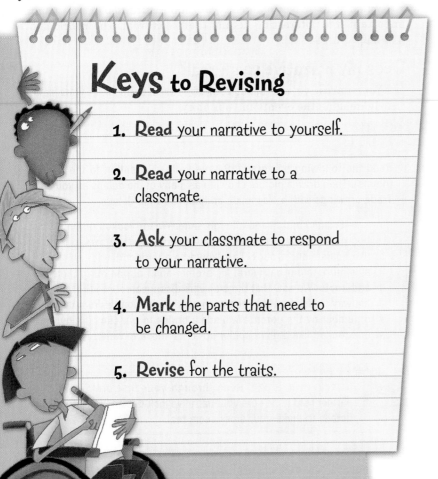

Keys to Revising

1. **Read** your narrative to yourself.

2. **Read** your narrative to a classmate.

3. **Ask** your classmate to respond to your narrative.

4. **Mark** the parts that need to be changed.

5. **Revise** for the traits.

Revising Keys to Revising

Remind students that the revising stage is when writers have an opportunity to make improvements to their first drafts. At this stage they can think about refinements they might not have considered when they were drafting.

The Keys to Revising list lays out the process students will be guided through on PE pages 104–114.

Have students turn back to PE page 88 and review the goals for each trait.

Explain that during the revising process they will work through all the traits except conventions, which is addressed during the next stage (Editing).

Reassure students that they will focus on the traits one at a time. With practice, the process will become almost second nature.

Consider having students share their drafts with partners throughout the revising process, so that they can help each other evaluate the drafts in detail.

English Language Learners

The cognitive demands of reading aloud may make it difficult for some students to read their narratives to classmates.

- Instead of having students read their essays for Step 2, ask cooperative peers to read the narratives aloud to the writer.

- Instruct English learners to ask specific questions (for example, *What question(s) do you have?"* *"Is this the right word?"*) to prompt focused responses that will help them make specific revisions.

Revising for Ideas

The rubric strips that run across all of the revising pages (104–113) are provided to help students focus their revising and are related to the full rubric on pages 120–121.

Focus on the question *Does my narrative seem real?* Invite a volunteer to read the **Practice** paragraph aloud and note that the images are vivid, fun to imagine, and realistic.

Practice Answers

Answers will vary. Invite students to make drawings in the form of a comic strip, if they would like to show several images.

104

Revising for Ideas

6 My details focus on one experience and make my narrative come alive.

5 My narrative tells about one experience. I use effective sensory details.

4 My narrative tells about one experience. More details would make it better.

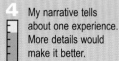

When you revise for *ideas,* you make sure you have included important and interesting details that seem real. The rubric above will help you.

Does my narrative seem real?

Your narrative will seem real if your details help your reader clearly imagine the events in your story.

Practice

Read the following paragraph. Pay very close attention to the details (nouns). Then draw a picture showing as many of the details as you can. Trade drawings with a classmate and compare the details.

1 It rained and rained all night long. When I looked out my
2 bedroom window, I saw waves in the street. Parked cars looked
3 like boats along a dock. This would be a perfect day for an
4 adventure in our backyard. My brother and I put on our jackets
5 and boots. We saw that the sidewalk disappeared into the water
6 halfway to the garage. Then we hauled some boards from the pile
7 of lumber by the porch. We made a bridge to our climbing gym
8 that looked like a giant spider up to its knees in water.

 Revise **Check your ideas.** Read through your first draft or have a partner read it. Be sure your narrative includes enough interesting details to make your story seem real.

English Language Learners

Restate the question *Does my narrative seem real* before discussing the practice paragraph:

- Does the narrative seem true?
- Will the reader believe this really happened?

Sharing an Experience **105**

3 I need to focus on one experience. Some of my details don't relate to the topic.

2 I have more than one focus sometimes, and I need to add details about the topic.

1 My topic is still unclear.

Have I included the important details?

If you have answered the 5 W's (*who, what, when, where,* and *why*), your narrative should have the important details it needs.

Practice

Read the paragraph below. Tell which of the 5 W's still need to be answered to make this paragraph clear.

1   I was in an important school event. When I went out there, I
2   looked straight ahead of me. I got scared. I was supposed to say
3   one sentence, but I couldn't. Someone whispered something to
4   me, and I knew what I had to do. I bravely stood up and said it.

 Revise

Review your details. Check to make sure you have included important details that answer the 5 W's.

Revising in Action

Below, the writer adds details to make the experience more real.

After we ate, we ⌃ headed out to the backyard. Dad
         grabbed our jackets and
had built a roaring campfire. Then Mom ⌃ ~~came outside.~~
                              brought out a dusty old book.
She began reading ⌃.
       a scary ghost story

Invite volunteers to read the writer's original sentences (leaving out the revisions) and the revised version. What does each of the changes accomplish?

- *grabbed our jackets*: Adds a realistic detail.
- *brought out a dusty old book:* Includes a visual detail.
- *a scary ghost story:* Gives more information about what Mom was reading.

Practice Answers

Answers will vary, but examples of all the 5 W's could be addressed. Be sure students are aware of this. Questions may include the following:

- What kind of event is it?
- When was the event?
- Where was the event?
- Why was storyteller scared?
- What was storyteller supposed to say?
- Who whispered to storyteller?
- What did storyteller end up saying?

Revising for Organization

After students have finished the **Practice** exercise, point out that it was possible to tell what order the sentences should be in, even though they didn't contain any transition words. What words provided the clues about time order? Possible answers:

- *woke up*: Before starting their activity, they had to get out of bed.
- *noon* and *lunch*: Lunch is usually around noon, so it makes sense that they would hike until then before stopping to eat.
- *sore feet*: They wouldn't have sore feet until they had been hiking for a while.

Encourage students to use clue words like these, as well as transition words, to show time order.

Practice Answers

3. We woke up . . .
2. We hiked until noon.
1. We enjoyed lunch . . .

106

Revising for Organization

| **6** The way I order events makes my narrative enjoyable and easy to read. | **5** My events are in time order. I have a strong beginning, middle, and ending. | **4** My events are in time order. I have a beginning, a middle, and an ending. |

When you revise for *organization,* you check that your narrative has a strong beginning, middle, and ending.

How do I know if my beginning works well?

Your beginning works well if it interests the reader and introduces the story. Have a partner read your beginning and answer these questions.

1. What grabs my interest?
2. What makes me want to keep reading?
3. What is this story about?

 Revise **Review your beginning.** Reread your beginning. Will it catch your reader's interest? If not, write a new beginning.

How do I check the middle?

The events in the middle of your story should be in time order.

Practice

Put these three sentences in time order.
1. We enjoyed lunch and rested our sore feet.
2. We hiked until noon.
3. We woke up, packed our backpacks, and hiked up the trail.

 Revise **Check the middle part.** Make sure the events of your story are organized in time order.

English Language Learners

Some students may not be familiar with the expression, *grabs my interest.* Have students review the characteristics of an effective beginning on PE pages 89 and 99 or remind them that the best way to begin a story (narrative) is to write sentences that make the reader excited and want to read the story to learn more about the topic.

Sharing an Experience **107**

 3 Some of my events are out of order. My beginning or ending is weak.

2 I need to use time order. My beginning, middle, and ending all run together.

1 My writing is confusing. I need to put my events in time order.

How do I know if my ending is strong?

You know your ending is strong if it . . .
- explains how you feel,
- tells how the experience changed you, or
- shares what you learned from the experience.

 Check your ending. Did you end your narrative in one of the ways listed above? If not, try writing another ending.

Revising in Action

Below, the writer moves a sentence to put ideas in a clear order.

> Now we shut off the TV every Tuesday night, and we have family time. We had so much fun that whole weekend that we didn't even think about television. Going without TV changed my family. Now we all can't wait for Tuesday night.

Challenge students to improve the sample ending by adding a piece of dialogue, adding a sensory detail, or by **varying sentence types** *(see below)*. Suggested changes might include the following:

- Add dialogue: Change the last sentence to *Now every Monday night somebody asks, "So, what are we going to do tomorrow?"*
- Add a sensory detail: Change the third sentence to *Now—click!— we turn off the TV every Tuesday night . . .*
- Vary sentence types: Change the second sentence to *Who can think about television when they're having so much fun?*

Have students make a similar adjustment to their own closing paragraph and then read both versions to a partner. Which one works better?

Teaching Tip: Varying Sentence Types

Remind students that one way to draw readers in is to involve the reader personally. Most of their sentences will be statements, but

- the enthusiasm expressed in an *exclamation* can be infectious;
- a *command* tells readers to do something; and
- a *question* addressed to readers gets them thinking.

In addition, varying sentence types helps sentence fluency, another trait of good writing. Point out, though, that overusing these special sentence types can make them less effective.

✳ For more about different sentence types, see PE page 441.

English Language Learners

Some students may be confused by the different sentence types. Model them for students by reading a sentence out loud, changing the intonation, depending on which end punctuation is used. Challenge students to create an example for each of the three sentence types.

Revising for Voice

Play "Guess the Writer," using the **Practice** activity:

- When students finish rewriting the third passage, ask them to copy it onto a clean sheet of paper and not to sign it.
- Students will try to guess whose paper is whose, so they may want to disguise their handwriting.
- Number the papers and post them on a bulletin board or pass them around the class.
- Give students time to read each one and jot down who they think wrote it.
- Call out each number and have students say who they think is the writer. Did any of them guess the same person? Ask the writer of the paragraph to stand.

Practice Answers

Answers will vary. Possible answers:

1. Sentence 2 is conversational in tone. Most students sound more like this.
2. Wording should be different for each student.

108

Revising for Voice

6 My narrative voice and dialogue create an unforgettable memory for the reader.

5 I use a natural voice, and the dialogue works well.

4 My voice usually sounds natural, and I use some dialogue.

When you revise for *voice*, you want the reader to hear your excitement, your fear, your pain, your surprise. You want the reader to hear *you!* The rubric strip above can help you revise.

How can I improve my writer's voice?

You can improve your voice by saying things in a natural, real way. Writing in a natural voice will make your narratives fun to read.

Practice

Decide which of the first two passages sounds natural—almost like one of your classmates talking. Then rewrite the third passage so it sounds more like the real you.

1. The appearance of swans signals the arrival of spring. They are impossible to miss because of their large size and pure white color.

2. Spring must be here because I saw a flock of swans. They're so big and graceful and white. What a sight!

3. Coach Brown requires us to start practice promptly at 3:10. We begin practice with warm-up exercises. We run in place for a long period of time. Then we complete a series of challenging sit-ups and push-ups.

 Revise your voice. Rewrite any sentences that don't sound natural—like the real you.

English Language Learners

Some students may have distinctive language acquisition errors in word order and word choice that will make it easy for others to identify them as the authors of the third-passage rewrites. Instead of posting all of the "Guess the Writer" papers, read samples to the class. As students tell why they think a specific student wrote each piece, record the descriptions that speak to the writers' "voice." Reassure any English learners who are concerned that their English is not "perfect" that they have already become better speakers, readers, and writers and the more they write, the more they will improve their English.

Advanced Learners

Invite students to experiment with voice by writing three or four sentences about the following scenarios from the perspective of a preschooler, a fourth grader, and an adult "expert" such as a tour guide, scientist, or college professor:

- visiting the Grand Canyon
- seeing a rainbow
- watching a dinosaur movie

Sharing an Experience **109**

3 Sometimes my voice can be heard. I need to use more dialogue to tell my story.

2 My narrative voice needs to be heard. I need to use some dialogue.

1 My voice shows that I am not interested in my narrative.

Does the dialogue sound natural?

You can check your dialogue by making sure it matches each person's personality. Often, adults speak in a formal way. Others, such as your friends, speak in a casual way.

Practice

Tell if each sentence below has a *formal* or a *casual* voice.

1. Please read pages 2–9.
2. We'll miss the bus for sure.
3. He was totally awesome!
4. Your report is excellent.

 Check your dialogue. Make sure the dialogue in your narrative matches each speaker's personality.

Revising in Action

In the sample paragraph below, the writer adds specific details and dialogue.

> My brother was upset because it was Halloween weekend and he'd miss all the scary movies. I looked at Dad and said "What asked about Sunday afternoon football?"

Work through the sample revision with students, asking them to tell why they think each change was made. Possible answers:

■ The detail about Halloween weekend answers the question *when?*
■ The adjective *scary* makes the word *movies* more specific.
■ Rewording the sentence as dialogue gives information by showing, not telling.

Focus on matching dialogue to the **different personalities** (see below) of the characters. Bring in books with samples of dialogue between two people who have different ways of speaking. Have students choose roles and read the dialogue aloud.

Practice Answers

1. Formal
2. Casual
3. Casual
4. Answers may vary, since *excellent* can be used in a formal or a casual sense. Ask students to explain their answers and have them read the sentence aloud to show how they imagine it.

Teaching Tip: Different Dialogue for Different People

The popular *Star Wars* movies provide vivid illustrations of different characters' dialogue. Invite students to talk about the ways the characters speak. Remind them that accents can often be expressed in writing.

- Yoda uses word order that is different from usual English (*Powerful you have become*).

- Darth Vader breathes heavily and usually gives commands when he speaks.
- C-3PO speaks very formally, with a British accent.

If students are not familiar with the *Star Wars* characters, encourage them to identify and mimic familiar cartoon characters that have distinctive ways of speaking.

Revising for Word Choice

Help students use active verbs in their narrative. Have them do the following:

- Revise all sentences written in the passive voice. For example, change *Our dessert is eaten after dinner* to *We eat dessert after dinner.*
- Write auxiliary verb phrases in the active voice, as in this example: *We are eating dessert after dinner.*
- Substitute a main verb for a linking verb. For example, revise *We are ready for dessert* to *We want dessert.*

If you have time, provide additional examples of sentences that use auxiliary and linking verbs, and revise for a strong, active voice. Point out that usually the revision is shorter than the original.

✳ For more about types of verbs, see PE page 582.

Practice   Answers

1. Mia won the race.
2. Lightning struck the tree.

110

Revising for ⟨ Word Choice ⟩

| **6** My original word choice creates a true-to-life picture for the reader. | **5** I create a clear picture by using active verbs and words with the right feeling. | **4** Most of my verbs are active, and most of my words have the feeling I want to express. |

When you revise for *word choice,* check to see if you've used active verbs and words with the right feeling (connotation). The rubric strip above can guide you.

Have I used active verbs?

You have used an **active verb** if the subject of the sentence is doing the action:

Active Verb: The dog ate the hamburger.

You have used a **passive verb** if the subject is receiving the action:

Passive Verb: The hamburger was eaten by the dog.

The best way to replace a passive verb is to change the sentence so that the new subject is doing the action. Look at the verb and ask, "Who or what is doing the action?"

Practice

Rewrite each sentence, changing the passive verbs to active verbs.

- I *was scared* by a cat's cry.
  A cat's cry scared me.

1. The race *was won* by Mia.
2. The tree *was struck* by lightning.

 Revise   **Check your verbs.** Underline the verbs in your narrative. The subject should be doing the action in most of the sentences.

Sharing an Experience   **111**

3 I need to use more active verbs and words with the right feeling.

2 I need to replace many passive verbs with active verbs.

1 I am unsure about how to use words.

Do my words have the right feeling (connotation)?

You can tell if your words have the right feeling by reading your narrative aloud. It should sound like you are experiencing the event again.

Practice

Read the following sentences. Then choose the word in parentheses that would give this mystery story the right feeling.

1. I *(went / crept)* toward the creepy, dark barn.
2. I carefully opened the *(squeaky / big)* wooden door.
3. Then I saw a pair of *(pretty / glaring)* eyes.

Revise — **Check your words.** How do you want the reader to feel? Use words that will make that feeling strong.

Revising in Action

In the sample below, the writer makes a passive verb active and adds words that give the right feeling.

> Mom told us
> ~~We were told by Mom~~ to finish up because it
> Who cared?
> was getting dark outside.∧

Use the discussion of choosing words with the right connotation to talk about using a thesaurus.

Remind students that a thesaurus is a collection of synonyms, or words with similar meaning. It can help them find a specific word to replace a more general one.

Remind students that two words rarely mean *exactly* the same thing. The synonyms listed can be very different. For example, the synonyms *gobble* and *nibble* would both be listed under the entry word *eat*.

Encourage students to replace a couple of words in their essay, using a thesaurus to find synonyms that have the connotation they want.

✳ To discuss using verbs that share the right feeling, refer students to PE page 422.

Practice   Answers

1. Answers may vary. The verb *crept* is more vivid but may be too similar to the related adjective, *creepy.* Have students substitute another adjective for *creepy,* for example, *eerie,* and defend their choice of verb.
2. *Squeaky* adds a sensory detail.
3. The best answer for a mystery story is *glaring.*

English Language Learners

Not all thesauruses provide enough context to be helpful resources for English language learners. Encourage students to ask cooperative classmates or classroom assistants to use possible synonyms in sentences before they choose to include the synonyms in their revisions.

Advanced Learners

Have students create word choice lists by "ranking" synonyms for common verbs and adjectives according to strength. Then have them act out each word, illustrate it, or use it in a sentence to demonstrate its connotation. For example:

- walk—shuffle, tiptoe, amble, saunter, stroll, hike, march, stride, jog, race
- happy—content, pleased, cheerful, jovial, joyful, excited, delighted, ecstatic

Revising for Sentence Fluency

Tell students they can also use introductory clauses to begin sentences. Remind them that

- both phrases and clauses are groups of related words;
- a phrase doesn't have a subject and a verb; but
- a clause has both a subject and a verb.

Explain that there's usually a comma between an introductory phrase or clause and the rest of the sentence.

Challenge students to redo the **Practice** exercise, adding introductory clauses such as

1. When I saw that, I nearly . . .
2. As far as I was concerned, the dinosaurs . . .
3. As I stood there, I felt . . .
4. Before I was ready, Julius . . .
5. After he said that, we . . .

✱ For more on using commas to separate introductory phrases and clauses, see PE page 484.

Practice Answers

Possible answers:
1. Surprised, I nearly . . .
2. Wow, the dinosaurs . . .
3. For a few seconds, I felt . . .
4. Finally, Julius told us . . .
5. Carefully, we backed away . . .

112

Revising for Sentence Fluency

| **6** My sentences are skillfully written and keep the reader's interest from start to finish. | **5** I use a variety of sentence lengths, and I vary my sentence beginnings. | **4** I include a variety of sentence lengths, but I need to vary my sentence beginnings. |

When you revise for *sentence fluency*, make sure you have varied your sentence beginnings and lengths. The rubric strip will guide you.

How can I vary my sentence beginnings?

You can vary your sentence beginnings by starting with an introductory word or phrase instead of the subject.

1. Use an introductory word.

First, Julius led us to the dinosaur exhibit.

Suddenly, we stood in front of a huge torosaurus skeleton.

2. Begin with an introductory phrase.

A little later, we entered an eerie cave.

Around another corner, a gigantic T. rex was fighting a triceratops!

Practice

Add an introductory word or phrase to each sentence below.

1. I nearly jumped out of my skin.
2. The dinosaurs looked real.
3. I felt as if I were back in the Cretaceous period.
4. Julius told us it was time to move on.
5. We backed away from the terrible T. rex.

 Revise Check your sentence beginnings. Make sure you have started some sentences with introductory words or phrases.

English Language Learners

Because some students' spoken and written language will reflect their internalized sense of how English works, requests to review their own writing to make sure they have used a variety of sentence beginnings and lengths may be frustrating. Provide students with multiple opportunities to work with English proficient students in small groups to complete all **Practice** exercises. Encourage the groups to discuss unfamiliar words and phrases as well as to complete the exercises.

Struggling Learners

Point out that using introductory words and phrases in *too many* sentences defeats the goal of sentence fluency. For example:

Before long, my alarm went off. *Suddenly,* I heard it ringing. *Jumping out of bed,* I rushed to turn it off. *Climbing back in,* I hoped Mom would let me sleep awhile longer. *Luckily,* she did.

Sharing an Experience **113**

3 A few of my sentences need to be varied in length and in the way they begin.

2 I need to use different kinds of sentences and vary their beginnings.

1 Most of my sentences start the same way. I need to vary their beginnings.

How can I vary my sentence lengths?

You can vary your sentence lengths by expanding short, choppy sentences. Add details that answer *who, what, when, where,* or *why.* (See pages **445-448** for more information.)

SHORT SENTENCE

Julius took us.

EXPANDED SENTENCE

Last Saturday, Julius took us to the public museum
<u>When?</u>   <u>Where?</u>
to see the new dinosaur exhibit.
              <u>Why?</u>

Expand short, choppy sentences. Expand your short, choppy sentences by adding details that tell *who, what, when, where,* or *why.*

Revising in Action

In the example below, the writer varies a sentence beginning with an introductory phrase and expands another sentence.

> On the way to the house,
> ∧Dad said, "I have a surprise." Two huge pumpkins
> on newspapers on the kitchen table.
> sat/~~there~~ We drew faces on them, pulled out all . . .

Have students circle all sentences in their draft with fewer than six words. Should the sentences be expanded?

- Tell students they don't need to expand *every* short sentence. A short sentence here and there adds variety.
- If short sentences are close together in the paragraph, one or more should be revised. Suggest that students read the passage aloud to see if it sounds choppy.
- Students should expand sentences that are too general or lacking in detail.
- They should expand any sentence that provides a good opportunity to add an interesting detail.

Have students consult the 5 W's memory chart they made during prewriting to see if it contains details they'd like to use to expand their sentences.

* For information about how to expand sentences with prepositional phrases, see PE page 448. (Note, however, if students ask, that the second *to* in the expanded sentence is not a preposition; it is part of the infinitive verb *to see.*)

Revising Using a Checklist

Ask students to copy the checklist onto their own paper. If they have a concern that isn't mentioned on the list, invite them to add it to the checklist. Additional ideas might include the following:

- **Ideas:** Do I answer all the 5 W questions?
- **Ideas:** Do all the details relate to the topic?
- **Organization:** Does my opening sentence make my reader want to know more?
- **Word choice:** Have I used specific nouns?

Suggest that students photocopy their blank checklists so they can use them anytime they write a narrative essay and so they'll have enough to give copies to family members or friends who read and respond to their essays.

114

Revising Using a Checklist

Check your revising. Number your paper from 1 to 10. Read each question and put a check mark after the number if the answer to a question is "yes." Otherwise, continue to work with that part of your essay.

Ideas

____ **1.** Do I tell about one unforgettable experience?
____ **2.** Do I include sensory details?

Organization

____ **3.** Do my beginning, middle, and ending work well?
____ **4.** Have I reordered parts that were out of place?

Voice

____ **5.** Does my voice sound natural?
____ **6.** Does the dialogue fit the speakers' personalities?

Word Choice

____ **7.** Have I used active verbs?
____ **8.** Have I used words with the right feeling?

Sentence Fluency

____ **9.** Have I varied my sentence beginnings?
____ **10.** Have I varied the lengths of my sentences?

Make a clean copy. After revising your narrative, make a clean copy for editing.

English Language Learners

Students who are still in the process of acquiring English may be overwhelmed by the request to evaluate all their essays for all traits at the same time. Modify the assignment by having a conference with students instead of having them complete the checklist.

- Ask students to identify the traits they thought were the easiest and the most difficult to work on. Have students rate only those two traits.
- Suggest other questions that will help students improve their evaluation of those two traits.
- Focus on those traits in all writing until new goals are established in a subsequent conference.

Editing

Sharing an Experience **115**

Prewrite   Revise   Publish
Write   Edit

Editing is the next step in the writing process. When you edit, you make sure that you have followed the rules for capitalization, punctuation, spelling, and grammar. These rules are called the "conventions" of writing.

Keys to Editing

1. **Use** a dictionary, a thesaurus, and the "Proofreader's Guide" in the back of this book for help.

2. **Edit** on a printed copy if you use a computer. Then make your changes on the computer.

3. **Use** the editing marks shown inside the back cover of this book.

4. **Ask** someone else to check your writing for errors, too.

Editing Keys to Editing

Remind students that during the editing stage, they have a chance to find and correct errors in
- punctuation,
- capitalization,
- spelling, and
- grammar.

The Keys to Editing list lays out the process students will be guided through on PE pages 116–118.

Suggest that students try the following hints when they edit their papers:
- Take a break. If possible, put the essay down for a whole day—or at least a night—before starting to edit.
- Use a different colored pencil or pen to mark editing changes, so the changes will stand out and so there's no danger they'll be overlooked when recopying the essay.
- Ask a friend to read the paper. Someone who's not already familiar with it may have an easier time spotting mistakes.

English Language Learners

Some students' errors in language conventions may be related to the effort it takes to write in a new language, not to carelessness. Students may go through prolonged stages of over generalizing newly-learned conventions. Use your knowledge of each student's needs to help them edit for specific conventions.

Struggling Learners

Remind students that reading the essay aloud one last time is an effective way to check for editing conventions. For example:
- When pausing at the end of a sentence, check for a period, question mark, or exclamation point and make sure the next sentence begins with a capital letter.

- When reading dialogue, check to make sure it's enclosed in quotation marks.
- If a proper noun is used, be sure it's capitalized.

Listen for grammar that doesn't sound right, such as *The student write a letter.*

Editing for Conventions

Remind students that a pronoun is a short word that's used in place of a noun, and a subject pronoun is a pronoun that serves as the subject of a sentence. It's important that readers always know what noun a pronoun is replacing (which is called its antecedent). Write the subject pronouns on the board:

I	we
you	they
he	
she	
it	

Have students circle all the subject pronouns they find in their essay and draw an arrow pointing to the antecedent.

Practice Answers

1. Sam started the lawn tractor near the truck. The lawn tractor had just returned from the shop. It ran smoothly.
2. Mara pulled a banana out of her lunch bag. The banana felt mushy.

116

Editing for Conventions

6 I accurately use conventions, which makes my writing clear and trustworthy.

5 I have a few minor errors in punctuation, capitalization, spelling, or grammar.

4 I need to correct some errors in punctuation, capitalization, spelling, or grammar.

When you edit for *conventions,* you check your writing for errors. The rubric above will help you edit your work.

Are all my subject pronouns clear?

Your subject pronouns are clear when the reader understands which word or words each pronoun replaces. You often find an unclear subject pronoun in a sentence when the pronoun's antecedent is in a previous sentence. (See pages **412–415**.)

Mary and Eva **sprinted to the soccer field.** She **tripped and fell.** She **skinned her knee.** (It is not clear who fell.)

Mary and Eva **sprinted to the soccer field.** Mary **tripped and fell.** She **skinned her knee.**

Practice

Rewrite each sentence, making any unclear subject pronouns clear.

1. Sam started the lawn tractor near the truck. It had just returned from the shop. It ran smoothly.
2. Mara pulled a banana out of her lunch bag. It felt mushy.

 Edit

Check your use of pronouns. Read the examples above to make sure that you used pronouns correctly in your story. If you need more help, see pages **412–415**.

English Language Learners

Number and gender of nouns and pronouns are not universal concepts. Errors in pronoun usage are common. Have students use sticky notes to tab PE pages 412–415 and encourage them to use and return to the reference section as they edit their writing.

Sharing an Experience **117**

3 Some errors may distract the reader. I need to punctuate my dialogue correctly.

2 Many errors make my narrative and dialogue hard to read. I need to correct them.

1 I need to correct numerous errors in my writing.

Have I used verb tenses correctly?

You have used verb tenses correctly if you have stated an action that . . .

- is happening now (or regularly) in **present tense**.

    I walk to school. We play soccer every day.

- already happened in the **past tense**.

    Shondra performed in the show. She sang well.

- will take place in the **future tense**.

    I will study Spanish. We will buy a piñata for my birthday party.

 Edit verb tenses. Make sure you have used verb tenses correctly in your narrative. For help, see pages 418 and 584.

Editing in Action

Below, the writer corrects both a subject-pronoun problem and an incorrect verb tense.

> My parents ~~decide~~ <u>decided</u> we all watch too much television. So ~~you~~ <u>they</u> made a rule that no one would watch
>
> TV for one whole weekend. "What?" I said.

To help students practice using different verb tenses, call out a verb and invite volunteers to make up sentences that demonstrate its use in the present, past, and future tenses. Be sure to include some irregular verbs such as the following:

- eat (ate, will eat),
- drink (drank, will drink),
- see (saw, will see), and
- go (went, will go).

Encourage students to keep a list of irregular verbs that give them trouble and to study it from time to time. They can refer to the list whenever they want to use irregular verbs.

✱ To review tenses of verbs, see PE page 418.

English Language Learners

During a writing conference, help each student select the one or two conventions that most interfere with a reader's ability to concentrate on the writer's message. Modify the Editing Checklist to help the student focus on improving those areas until sufficient improvement is noted and new goals are established in a subsequent conference.

Struggling Learners

Have students check their work for subject-verb agreement. Write the following sentences on the board and invite volunteers to correct the verbs:

- He type his science report for school. (types, is typing)
- They talks to their friends on the phone. (talk, are talking)

Editing **Using a Checklist**

Give students a few moments to look over the Proofreader's Guide (PE pages 478–605). Throughout the year, they can refer to the instruction, rules, and examples to clarify any checklist items or to resolve questions about their own writing.

Review items students may not have focused on recently, such as proper nouns or using a **spell checker** *(see below)*. Go over the rules for punctuating dialogue. Write out sample dialogue on the board or on a blank overhead transparency. Make sure to cover the following rules:

- Put double quotation marks around the words spoken.
- Usually separate a speaker's words from the rest of the sentence with commas.
- If the speech ends with an exclamation point or a question mark, no comma is needed.
- Start a new paragraph every time the speaker changes.

Adding a Title

Reassure students that it may take time to decide on a title and suggest that they jot down title ideas throughout the writing process. Later they can check to see if they like an idea on their list.

118

Editing **Using a Checklist**

Edit **Check your editing.** On a piece of paper, write the numbers 1 to 10. If you can answer "yes" to a question, put a check mark after that number. If not, continue to edit your writing for that convention.

Conventions

PUNCTUATION

_____ 1. Do I use end punctuation after all my sentences?
_____ 2. Do I punctuate my dialogue correctly?

CAPITALIZATION

_____ 3. Do I start all my sentences with capital letters?
_____ 4. Do I capitalize all proper nouns?

SPELLING

_____ 5. Have I spelled all my words correctly?
_____ 6. Have I double-checked the words my spell-checker may have missed?

GRAMMAR

_____ 7. Do my subjects and verbs agree in number? (She and I *were* going, not She and I *was* going.)
_____ 8. Do all my subject pronouns have clear antecedents?
_____ 9. Do I state all actions in the correct tense?
_____ 10. Do I use the right words *(their, there,* and *they're)*?

Adding a Title

- Use strong, colorful words: **A Scary Weekend Without TV**
- Give the words rhythm: **My Shocking Surprise**
- Be imaginative: **I Survived Being Unplugged**

Teaching Tip: Spell Checkers

Remind students that they cannot assume the spell checker will catch all spelling mistakes.

- Explain that a computer cannot evaluate words in *context,* that is, as they are being used in the sentence. Therefore, it will overlook homophones (words that sound the same but are spelled differently) and other correctly spelled words that are used in the wrong context.

- Encourage students to write down and study homophones and tricky words.
- Hold a spelling-bee style competition in which you read sentences with tricky words and have students spell the words.

✴ For more on using the right words, see PE pages 536–559.

Struggling Learners

Tell students that two other popular options for titles are to use a word or phrase from the essay itself or to use alliteration—words that begin with the same sound. Have students brainstorm related ideas for Tyrone's essay, such as *Too Much Television* (phrase from the essay) or *Weird Weekend* (alliteration).

Publishing

When you're done editing your story, make a neat final copy to share. You may also decide to share your story as a picture book, as a Web page, or in your classroom library. (See the suggestions below.)

Presentation

- Use blue or black ink and write neatly.
- Write your name in the upper left corner of page 1.
- Skip a line and center your title; skip another line and start writing.
- Indent every paragraph and leave a one-inch margin on all sides.
- Write your last name and the page number in the upper right corner of every page after the first one.

Make a Picture Book

Illustrate your story and make it into a book. Share your book with younger children, especially your younger brothers and sisters.

Upload It

If your class has a Web page, you can publish your narrative there.

Add It to a Classroom Collection

Create a cover for your narrative and add it to the class library or writing corner for your classmates to enjoy.

 Make a final copy. Follow your teacher's instructions or use the guidelines above. (If you are using a computer, see pages 43–46.) Write a clean final copy of your essay.

Publishing

Before students share their essays (in whatever way you choose), have them make a "promotional poster" for their stories.

- Show pictures of book and movie posters. (Many Web sites, such as teachers' resource sites, have posters available to look at. Preview the sites and bookmark good examples.)
- Can students think of a slogan or "teaser" line to promote the story?
- What scene will be on the poster? Suggest that students hint at a surprise in the story, being careful not to give it away.
- Have students think of a fancy way to write the title on the poster. Show students several posters, noting how prominent the titles are.
- Remind students to include their name—tell them to be as bold as they like (*By the acclaimed author of . . .*).

Distribute poster board and drawing supplies and have students create their posters. Display the finished works in the classroom.

Rubric for Narrative Writing

Remind students that a rubric is a chart that helps you evaluate your writing.

- The rubrics in this book are based on a six-point scale, in which a score of 6 indicates an amazing piece of writing and a score of 1 means the writing is incomplete and not ready to be assessed.

- Explain that the purpose of the rubric is to help students break down the assessment process by evaluating each of the six traits individually—ideas, organization, voice, word choice, sentence fluency, and conventions.

- Point out that rubrics are also helpful during the writing process. They can guide you whenever you write because they tell you what elements to include in your writing and how to present them.

- Explain that students will most likely have different ratings for the traits. For example, they may give themselves a 5 for ideas but a 4 for organization.

* Four- and five-point rubrics for narrative writing can be found on TE pages 624 and 627.

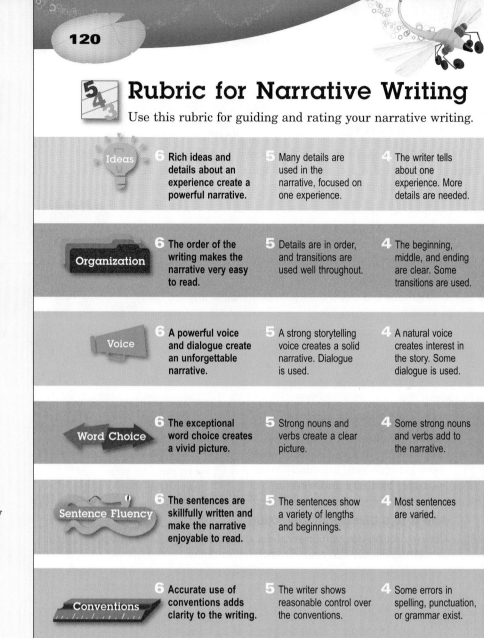

120

Rubric for Narrative Writing

Use this rubric for guiding and rating your narrative writing.

Ideas
- **6** Rich ideas and details about an experience create a powerful narrative.
- **5** Many details are used in the narrative, focused on one experience.
- **4** The writer tells about one experience. More details are needed.

Organization
- **6** The order of the writing makes the narrative very easy to read.
- **5** Details are in order, and transitions are used well throughout.
- **4** The beginning, middle, and ending are clear. Some transitions are used.

Voice
- **6** A powerful voice and dialogue create an unforgettable narrative.
- **5** A strong storytelling voice creates a solid narrative. Dialogue is used.
- **4** A natural voice creates interest in the story. Some dialogue is used.

Word Choice
- **6** The exceptional word choice creates a vivid picture.
- **5** Strong nouns and verbs create a clear picture.
- **4** Some strong nouns and verbs add to the narrative.

Sentence Fluency
- **6** The sentences are skillfully written and make the narrative enjoyable to read.
- **5** The sentences show a variety of lengths and beginnings.
- **4** Most sentences are varied.

Conventions
- **6** Accurate use of conventions adds clarity to the writing.
- **5** The writer shows reasonable control over the conventions.
- **4** Some errors in spelling, punctuation, or grammar exist.

3 The writer needs to focus on one experience. Some details do not relate to the story.

2 The writer needs to focus on one experience. Details are needed.

1 The writer needs to tell about an experience and use details.

3 Most details are in order. Transitions are needed.

2 The beginning, middle, or ending parts need to be clearer.

1 The narrative needs to be organized.

3 Sometimes a voice can be heard. More dialogue is needed.

2 The voice needs to be stronger. Dialogue is missing.

1 The writer's voice does not come through.

3 Strong nouns and verbs are needed to create a clear picture.

2 Fewer general and overused words would improve the narrative.

1 Some words are confusing or incorrect.

3 A better variety of sentence lengths and beginnings is needed.

2 Many sentences are the same length or begin the same way.

1 Too many sentences sound the same.

3 A number of errors could confuse the reader.

2 Many errors make the narrative hard to read.

1 Help is needed to make corrections.

Evaluating a Narrative

Ask students if they agree with the sample self-assessment on PE page 123. If they agree with the criticisms, ask them to suggest improvements based on the comments in the self-assessment. If they disagree with any comment, ask them to explain why.

Possible suggestions:

Ideas **tell more about Gramps—** Gramps wasn't scared at all. He just kept talking about this time he ran out of gas when he was a kid.

Organization **ending—**Walking on that dark . . . done. In a way, it was kind of fun, too, like listening to a good ghost story. I still made Gramps promise to get a cell phone, though!

Voice **add dialogue—**Then I remembered how Gramps would always say, "Cell phones! Bah! I wouldn't carry one if you paid me."

Word Choice **more specific words—** *keychain flashlight, rough wool jacket,* give name of city

Sentence Fluency **combine short sentences—**It was a lonely night and so dark I could hardly see . . .

Conventions **correct spelling errors—**capitalize *Gramps, Gramps's, flashlight, held on to, shiny, waddled, farmhouse*

122

Evaluating a Narrative

As you read Jonathan's narrative on this page, focus on its strengths and weaknesses. (The essay contains some errors.) Then read the student self-evaluation on page 123.

Out of Gas

One night, Gramps and I were driving in the country when his car died. Chug-a-chug, sput, sput, stop. We were out of gas!

At first, I wasn't worried. We would just use a cell phone to get help. Then I remembered that Gramps doesn't like cell phones. We were stuck without a phone!

"Let's walk, Jonathan," Gramps said. It was a dark, lonely night. I could hardly see two feet in front of me. A tiny beam from gramps flash light hardly cut through the blackness. I held onto Grandpa's jacket. Shinny, little eyes peeked out at me from the woods. I heard strange noises. A small animal wadled across the road in front of me. I didn't like this at all.

We walked forever before we saw a farm house with its lights on. It was the house of some of Gramps friends. We went to the door, and they let us in. Lucky gramps has lived around here forever! The farmer filled a red can with gas, and he drove us back to our car. Soon, we were safe and headed back to the city.

I made Gramps promise to get a cell phone. Walking on that dark road was the scariest thing I have ever done. It's a good thing Gramps had friends nearby. Otherwise, we might have had to walk all night.

Sharing an Experience **123**

Student Self-Assessment

Jonathan used the rubric and number scale on pages 120–121. He made two comments under each trait. First, he wrote something he did well. Then he wrote about something he could have done better.

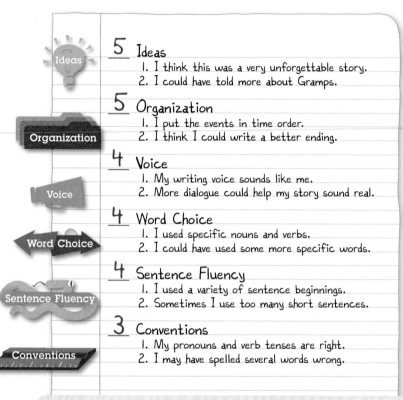

5 Ideas
1. I think this was a very unforgettable story.
2. I could have told more about Gramps.

5 Organization
1. I put the events in time order.
2. I think I could write a better ending.

4 Voice
1. My writing voice sounds like me.
2. More dialogue could help my story sound real.

4 Word Choice
1. I used specific nouns and verbs.
2. I could have used some more specific words.

4 Sentence Fluency
1. I used a variety of sentence beginnings.
2. Sometimes I use too many short sentences.

3 Conventions
1. My pronouns and verb tenses are right.
2. I may have spelled several words wrong.

Use the rubric. Assess your narrative using the rubric on pages 120–121. On your own paper, list the six traits. Write one strength and one weakness for each trait. Number each trait from 1 to 6 to show how well you used it.

Student Self-Assessment

If students determine that the sentence fluency problems in the essay are caused more by lack of variation in sentence beginnings than by choppy, short sentences, invite students to suggest changes.

- To keep from getting lost, I held on to . . .
- Suddenly, a small animal waddled across . . .
- After walking forever, we finally saw a farmhouse . . .

To give students additional practice with evaluating a narrative essay, use a reproducible assessment sheet (TE page 644) and one or both of the **benchmark papers** listed in the Benchmark Papers box below. You can use an overhead transparency while students refer to their own copies made from the copy masters. For your benefit, a completed assessment sheet is provided for each benchmark paper.

English Language Learners

Tell students to focus on the traits they previously identified as the easiest and most difficult for them (see TE page 114). If they finish evaluating their targeted traits before the students who are rating all six traits, invite them to choose another one or two traits to evaluate. Use these selections to identify goals for future conferences.

Advanced Learners

To provide additional effective models for the class to read, invite students to rewrite Jonathan's essay, incorporating the six suggestions on his self-assessment sheet.

Benchmark Papers

El Niño at Its Best (strong)
- TR 1A–1C
- TE pp. 630–632

Las Vegas (poor)
- TR 2A–2B
- TE pp. 633–634

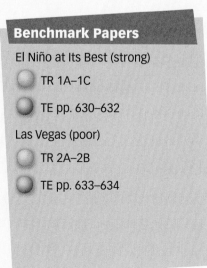

Reflecting on Your Writing

Have students put the date on their reflections and save them, along with their planning notes and final version of the essay, in their writing portfolio.

For students who keep journals, suggest that they make a habit of including reflections about their writing in journal entries.

✻ For more about portfolios and journals, see PE pages 47–49 and 380–382.

Encourage students to look back at their reflections occasionally—a particularly good time is when they are starting a new project. This will help them to

- see how much progress they have made as a writer,
- identify areas they need to work more on, and
- remember interesting ideas they had that they might be able to use for their next essay.

124

Reflecting on Your Writing

You've put a lot of time and effort into writing an interesting and entertaining personal narrative. Now take some time to think about your writing. On your own paper, finish each sentence starter below.

When you think about your writing, you will see how you are growing as a writer.

My Narrative Essay

1. The best part of my narrative is . . .

2. The part that still needs work is . . .

3. The main thing I learned about writing a personal narrative is . . .

4. In my next narrative, I would like to . . .

Advanced Learners

More confident students may be willing to share their reflections with the class. Invite those who are willing, to

- read their recorded thoughts aloud,
- facilitate a brief discussion, and
- answer questions about their ideas.

125

Across the Curriculum

Narrative Writing
Across the Curriculum

Narrative writing is useful in many classes. In math, you may have to write a story problem about dividing up a pizza. In science, you may be assigned an observation report about hatching chicks. You can also write an e-mail message to a friend about something interesting that happened to you.

In this section, you'll practice narrative writing and also learn how to respond to a narrative prompt on a writing test.

Mini Index

- **Math:** Creating a Story Problem
- **Science:** Writing an Observation Report
- **Practical Writing:** Writing to an E-Pal
- **Assessment:** Writing for Assessment

Objectives
- apply what has been learned about narrative writing to other curriculum areas
- practice writing for assessment

The lessons on the following pages provide samples of narrative writing students might do in different content areas. The first lesson guides students through the steps of the writing process in math. The second and third lessons provide models and writing tips for narrative writing in science and when corresponding with an e-pal.

Assigning these forms of writing will depend on
- the skill level of your students,
- the subject matter they are studying in different content areas, and
- the writing goals of your school, district, or state.

Students who write e-mail or use instant messaging may already have discovered how helpful their new narrative writing skills can be. Explain that in this section students will apply their skills to subjects that they may not have considered a form of narrative writing.

Copy Masters/ Transparencies

Time line (TE p. 130)

Math: Creating a Story Problem

Note that if Amelia had chosen to include more details that answered 5 W's questions—who, what, when, where, and why—she might have presented her math problem in a more story-like form. Challenge students to rewrite the beginning paragraph so it's more entertaining. Remind them that they must keep all the details of the math problem. For example:

Sammy's [*who*] favorite food was Simply Sunshine [*what*] orange drink. He just couldn't get enough of it—especially since his mom thought it should be only a special-occasion treat. "Mom, it's good for me!" he said one Saturday morning [*when*] at the breakfast table [*where*].

"Really? How good for you?" she responded.

"I bet it's got lots of vitamin C."

Sammy and his mom looked at the nutrition label on the back of the carton.

"Well, Sammy," she said, "if you drink one cup of this, you'll get twenty percent of the vitamin C you need. Do you realize how many cups you'd have to drink to get one hundred percent of the recommended daily requirement?"

Sammy got to work to figure it out. [*why*]

126

Math: Creating a Story Problem

In one math class, students wrote story problems based on nutrition labels. Amelia developed her problem based on an orange-drink label.

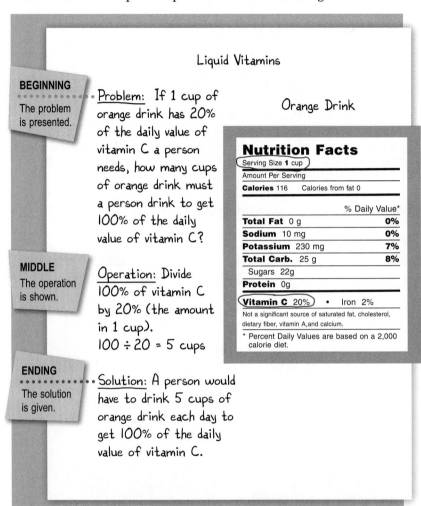

Liquid Vitamins

BEGINNING
The problem is presented.

Problem: If 1 cup of orange drink has 20% of the daily value of vitamin C a person needs, how many cups of orange drink must a person drink to get 100% of the daily value of vitamin C?

Orange Drink

Nutrition Facts
Serving Size **1** cup

Amount Per Serving

Calories 116   Calories from fat 0

% Daily Value*

Total Fat 0 g	**0%**
Sodium 10 mg	**0%**
Potassium 230 mg	**7%**
Total Carb. 25 g	**8%**
Sugars 22g	
Protein 0g	

Vitamin C 20% • Iron 2%

Not a significant source of saturated fat, cholesterol, dietary fiber, vitamin A, and calcium.

* Percent Daily Values are based on a 2,000 calorie diet.

MIDDLE
The operation is shown.

Operation: Divide 100% of vitamin C by 20% (the amount in 1 cup).
100 ÷ 20 = 5 cups

ENDING
The solution is given.

Solution: A person would have to drink 5 cups of orange drink each day to get 100% of the daily value of vitamin C.

Writing in Math **127**

Prewriting Selecting a Topic

To select a topic for her story problem, Amelia made a "favorite foods" list like the one below.

Ideas List

Favorite Foods

-macaroni and cheese   -eggs

-green beans   -milk ✳

List favorite foods. Make a list of foods you enjoy that come in a package that shows nutritional information. Put a star (✳) beside the food you choose to write about.

Finding Facts on the Food Label

Next, you'll need to study the facts on the label of your favorite food.

Fact Sheet

Food: 2% milk
Serving Size: 1 cup
Nutrient: Calcium
Percentage (or amount): 30%

2% Milk

Nutrition Facts		
Serving Size **1** cup (236ml)		
Servings Per Container 1		
Amount Per Serving		
Calories 120	Calories from fat 45	
		% Daily Value*
Total Fat 5 g		
Saturated Fat 3g		
Trans fat 0g		
Cholesterol 20 mg		**7%**
Sodium 120 mg		**5%**
Total Carbohydrate 11 g		**4%**
Dietary Fiber 0g		
Sugars 11g		
Protein 9g		
Vitamin A 10%	• Vitamin C 4%	
Calcium 30%	• Vitamin D 25%	
* Percent Daily Values are based on a 2,000 calorie diet. Your daily values may be higher or lower depending on your calorie needs.		

Create a fact sheet. List the facts you want to use in your story problem. Include the food, the serving size, one nutrient, and its percentage.

Prewriting Selecting a Topic

Before students begin their own work, collaborate with the class to create a story problem based on Amelia's notes about the calcium in 2% milk. Write the problem on the board as students call out ideas.

Consider using the story problems as the basis for a class project about the nutritional values of foods. Have students brainstorm food ideas, and then coordinate their choice of topics so that all of the food groups—milk, meat and beans, vegetables, fruits, and grains—are represented.

Prewriting

Finding Facts on the Food Label

Food labels for many kinds of foods, even different brands, are available online at www.nutritiondata.com. If a computer is available, bookmark the site and allow students to search for their chosen food in the database.

Writing
Creating Your Story Problem

Circulate as students work on their problems, helping them to decide what to focus on and how to articulate the "if-how" statement.

For a class nutrition project, provide some guidance about what nutritional information to focus on. For example, if the topic is avocados, it may be more informative to focus on the nutrients provided (such as iron, vitamins C or A, calcium, or protein), rather than the fat or calorie content.

Some students may find it easier to write out their problem as an equation first and *then* translate it into a sentence or sentences. Tell them to feel free to do so.

128

Writing Creating Your Story Problem

Your fact sheet will help you to write your story problem. Also use the tips below.

■ **State the Problem**

First, set up the problem by asking a question. Begin with an "if-how" statement.

- **Write *if*** and include the information from your fact sheet:
  If 1 cup of reduced-fat milk has 30% of the calcium a person needs each day, . . .

- **Write *how*** and end with the question you want to ask:
  How much calcium will a person get from 4 cups of milk?

■ **Show the Operation**

Next, write the operation. **Begin with the operation word** *add, subtract, multiply,* or *divide.*

- Then finish writing the problem.
  Multiply the 30% of the daily value of calcium found in 1 cup of milk by 4 cups.

- Write the math problem as an equation.
  30 X 4 = 120

■ **Write the Solution**

Write your solution in a complete sentence.
  A person will get 120% of the daily value of calcium each day by drinking 4 cups of milk.

Create your story problem. Use the directions and examples above to create your own nutritional story problem.

Struggling Learners

To provide additional support, allow students to work in small groups and

- use the same food, serving size, nutrient, and percentage;
- write their own if-how statements, operations, and solutions;
- compare results; and

- help each other with any obvious errors before proceeding to the revision and editing stages.

Writing in Math **129**

Revising Improving Your Writing

After you've written the first draft of your story problem, you'll need to revise it. The following questions can help you revise.

- **Ideas** Do I include the information I need from my fact sheet?

- **Organization** Do I present a problem, an operation, and a solution? Are the facts and the answer correct?

- **Voice** Do I state everything clearly?

- **Word Choice** Do I include specific words such as *percent, milligram,* or *cup?*

- **Sentence Fluency** Do I use complete sentences for each part of my story problem?

Improve your writing. Use the questions above to review your story problem. Also ask a classmate to look over your problem and solve it. Then make any needed changes in your writing.

Editing Checking for Conventions

When you have finished revising, it's time to edit for conventions. The following questions can help you.

- **Conventions** Have I checked for errors in punctuation, capitalization, spelling, and grammar? Have I checked all the numbers in my story problem?

Check your work. Write a neat final copy and proofread it before you hand it in.

Revising
Improving Your Writing

Ask students to choose partners to check each other's math problems:

- Have them trade only the first section of the essays, the description of the problem.

- Have readers ask questions if they don't understand the problem. Tell the writers that they may want to consider clarifying their sentences if their reader has trouble with the problem.

- Have readers circle any words that could be made more specific.

- After readers have solved the problem, the writers can check their partners' work against the operation and solution sections of the story problem.

Editing
Checking for Conventions

Emphasize that the most important goals in a math story problem are clearly stating the problem and providing the correct solution. Have students check their math again on their own and then trade papers with another partner to check it one more time.

Science: Writing an Observation Report

If possible, coordinate the observation report with students' work in science class.

Note that according to the date at the top of the sample page, the report was begun on November 5. The writer then added observations directly to the report on November 15 and 16.

Another, perhaps more common, way of writing this kind of report would be to jot down observations as notes and then recopy them into a final version. This will make it easier to create a neat-looking report. Often teachers prefer that students write the completion date at the top of the page. Any important starting dates should be mentioned in the purpose section—for example, *On November 5, Ms. Webber brought an egg incubator to class.*

Distribute photocopies of the reproducible time line (TE page 648) for students to use for jotting down their observations as notes.

130

Science: Writing an Observation Report

When you write a science-class observation report, you will use narrative writing to tell what happened. Justin wrote a report about baby chicks hatching in his classroom.

Nov. 5

Baby Chicks Break Out

The **beginning** introduces the project.

PURPOSE:
Ms. Webber brought an egg incubator to class. She carefully put three chicken eggs inside it. Ms. Webber says the eggs are 20 days old. Eggs usually hatch after 30 days. Our class is going to observe how chicks hatch.

OBSERVATIONS:

The **middle** gives dates and records what happened.

November 15
9:30 The chicks have started hatching! I see a few tiny cracks in the eggshells.
11:23 The eggshells are covered with cracks. Bits of shell are starting to break off. I can see the beaks of two chicks breaking out.
2:30 All three chicks are climbing out of their shells. They look slimy. The chicks are weak and clumsy.
November 16
9:30 The chicks' feathers have dried. They are balls of fluffy yellow. Now they can walk without wobbling.
10:25 The chicks are eating food and drinking water on their own.

The **ending** summarizes what was learned.

CONCLUSIONS: I learned chicks have to work hard to break out of their shells. I also learned that at first they are slimy and ugly. Most important, I learned that after chicks hatch, it doesn't take long for them to be ready to live on their own.

Writing in Science   **131**

WRITING TIPS

Before you write . . .

- **Make careful observations.**
  Pay attention to any changes that take place.
- **Take notes.**
  Write down dates and times of each observation. Use specific words to describe shape, size, color, texture, movement, and behavior.

During your writing . . .

- **Write the purpose.**
  In the opening paragraph, tell the reason for the observation report. Include details by answering the 5 W questions.
- **Record your observations.**
  Include the dates and times of important events. List details in the order they happened.
- **Write your conclusions.**
  Tell what you have learned.

After you've written a first draft . . .

- **Revise your writing.**
  Make sure the events are in correct time order.
- **Edit for conventions.**
  Correct any errors in punctuation, capitalization, spelling, and grammar.

> Write an observation report. Choose a topic you are presently studying in science class.

Writing Tips

Ask students to identify the 5 W's in the purpose section of the sample report:

- **Who**: Ms. Webber
- **What:** three chicken eggs
- **When:** after 30 days (10 days from the date of the report)
- **Where:** in an incubator in the classroom
- **Why:** to observe chicks hatching

If there are students in the class keeping learning logs for science, note that the observation report format can be a great way to write log entries.

✳ For more about learning logs, see PE pages 383–386.

Practical Writing:
Writing to an E-Pal

To arrange for students to correspond with an e-mail pen pal, check for approved Web sites for student pen pals.

Talk with the class about corresponding by letter or e-mail:

- Note that before students used e-mail, they wrote paper letters to pen pals in foreign countries or other parts of the United States. Have any students had a pen pal or e-pal before? Do they still have one?
- How many students have written letters or e-mails to friends and family?
- Invite students to talk about the people they write to and what kinds of things they write about.
- What do they like most about the letters or e-mail they have received back?

132

Practical Writing: Writing to an E-Pal

E-mail connects friends across town or across the world. In this e-mail message, Sal shares a fishing story with his e-pal.

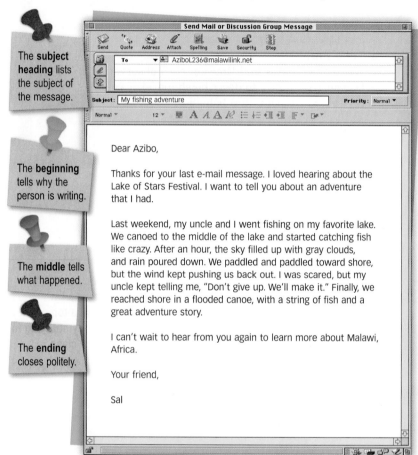

The **subject heading** lists the subject of the message.

The **beginning** tells why the person is writing.

The **middle** tells what happened.

The **ending** closes politely.

Send Mail or Discussion Group Message

Send   Quote   Address   Attach   Spelling   Save   Security   Stop

To ▼ | AziboL236@malawilink.net

Subject: | My fishing adventure | Priority: Normal ▼

Normal ▼   12 ▼

Dear Azibo,

Thanks for your last e-mail message. I loved hearing about the Lake of Stars Festival. I want to tell you about an adventure that I had.

Last weekend, my uncle and I went fishing on my favorite lake. We canoed to the middle of the lake and started catching fish like crazy. After an hour, the sky filled up with gray clouds, and rain poured down. We paddled and paddled toward shore, but the wind kept pushing us back out. I was scared, but my uncle kept telling me, "Don't give up. We'll make it." Finally, we reached shore in a flooded canoe, with a string of fish and a great adventure story.

I can't wait to hear from you again to learn more about Malawi, Africa.

Your friend,

Sal

Advanced Learners

To emphasize the topic possibilities of e-mail, have students compose several imaginary communications between two people or story book characters, such as the President of the United States and a student in the fourth grade, or Jack and the giant at the top of Jack's beanstalk.

Practical Writing **133**

WRITING TIPS

Before you write . . .

- **Choose a topic.**
  Select an interesting event that you would like to share.
- **Remember details.**
  Jot down some notes about what you saw, heard, smelled, tasted, and felt.

During your writing . . .

- **Fill in the heading.**
  Double-check the address and write a clear subject line.
- **Connect with your e-pal.**
  Comment on your e-pal's last message before telling your news.
- **Focus on the details.**
  Share interesting details about the event.
  Use words that your reader will understand.
- **Use a friendly voice.**
  Write as if you were talking to your e-pal.

After you've written a first draft . . .

- **Edit for correctness.**
  Read your whole message to catch any errors before hitting *Send*.

Write an e-mail to a friend. Tell him or her about an exciting experience you recently had.

Writing Tips

Explain that people may write drafts of important business letters and then revise and recopy them, but most of the time people don't do a full revision of a friendly letter. One advantage of e-mail over hand-written letters is that you can easily go back and fix mistakes before sending the message. But one disadvantage of e-mail is that you can easily send a message before catching your errors.

Focus on a few of the tips. For example:

- Students can type their notes about what they might want to say straight into the e-mail—but they must remember to delete them before they send the message.
- Always double-check the address before you press *send*. Some e-mail programs automatically fill in addresses as the user types in letters. If you stop typing too early and don't notice, the wrong e-mail address might be entered. It would be embarrassing to send e-mail to the wrong person.
- In addition to commenting on their e-pal's last message, students should be sure to answer all the pal's questions.

Writing for Assessment

If your students must take school, district or state assessments this year, focus on the writing form on which they will be tested.

Review test-taking tips such as the following:

- Always read the prompt twice before getting to work.
- Decide ahead of time how long to spend on planning, writing, and revising.
- Keep your topic specific.
- Use a graphic organizer for your notes.
- Bring extra pencils, in case your pencil breaks.

✳ For more about responding to prompts, see PE pages 404–405.

Ask students to pick out the two key ideas in the sample prompt.
1. Tell about a time when you were brave.
2. Tell what you learned from the experience.

Point out that this prompt solves a potential writer's problem. It tells students what to write about in the ending (tell what you learned). Tell students to be alert for such directions whenever they read a prompt.

134

Writing for Assessment

Some writing tests include a narrative prompt that asks you to tell a story about a personal experience.

Narrative Prompt

Every person has been brave at one time or another. Write a narrative essay that tells about a time when you were brave. Tell what you learned from the experience.

Transition Time Line

First	arrived at new school
↓ Then	went to recess
↓ Next	played kickball
↓ After	made a new friend

The beginning gives the focus of the response (underlined) and uses a key word from the prompt.

> My first day of third grade was the scariest day of my life. I was starting at a new school. Mom said, "Just be yourself, and you'll be fine." I didn't feel fine. <u>The only way I would survive this day was to be brave.</u>

The middle paragraphs tell about the experience.

> I was most afraid about making new friends. I walked to my classroom without talking to anybody. Then the teacher made me stand up in front of the class while she introduced me. I'm sure I was so red I looked like I had a sunburn. During reading class, I stared at my book. I wouldn't look at anybody.
>
> I was nervous when the bell rang for recess. At first, I just watched the other kids play tag, jump rope, and kickball. Then I took a deep

The **middle** part is organized by time.

breath and walked toward the kickball game.

"Can I play?" I asked a tall boy with red hair.

"Sure, you can go next," he said. "My name is Jeff. What's yours?"

"Anna," I said.

Jeff kicked and got to first base. Then it was my turn. I was shaking! The ball bounced and rolled toward me, and I ran up and blasted it with my foot. The ball sailed over everybody, and Jeff and I ran for home plate. We both scored!

The **ending** tells what the writer learned.

I learned something on my first day at my new school. The biggest thing was that I could be brave and just be myself. After that day, I made lots of new friends.

Respond to the reading. Answer the following questions to see how the traits were used in Anna's response.

- **Ideas** (1) What is the topic of the response? (2) What key words in the prompt are used in the essay?
- **Organization** (3) How does Anna organize the events of her narrative?
- **Voice & Word Choice** (4) What words and phrases show Anna's feelings?

Ask students' opinions of the sample. Have them explain what they think is good or could be improved about the essay. Possible answers:

- The topic is very focused.
- The topic is one that everybody can relate to.
- The writer could have done more showing. Some phrases, like *I was most afraid* and *I was nervous,* tell more than they show.
- The writer could have used more specific words (for example, give the teacher's name).

 Respond to the reading.

Answers

Ideas 1. Anna's first day of third grade
2. brave, learned

Organization 3. time order

Voice & Word Choice 4. Answers will vary. Possible answers:
- scariest day of my life
- I didn't feel fine.
- the only way I would survive
- I was most afraid about . . .
- I'm sure I was so red . . .
- I was nervous
- took a deep breath
- I was shaking!
- We both scored!

Struggling Learners

To provide additional practice in narration, have students jot down beginning, middle, and ending notes about their own experiences of being brave and then have them orally share their stories with partners or in small groups.

Writing Tips

Point out that students must approach writing-on-demand assignments differently from open-ended writing assignments and that timed writing creates pressures for everyone.

Narrative Prompts

To teach students who must take timed assessments how to approach their writing, allow them the same amount of time to write their response essay as they will be allotted on school, district, or state assessments. Break down each part of the process into clear chunks of time. For example, you might give students

- 15 minutes for note taking and planning,
- 20 minutes for writing, and
- 10 minutes for editing and proofreading.

Tell students when time is up for each section. Start the assignment at the top of the hour or at the half-hour to make it easier for students to keep track of the time.

If your state, district, or school requires students to use and submit a graphic organizer as part of their assessment, provide a copy of one of the reproducible charts (TE pages 645–651) or refer students to PE pages 456–457.

136

WRITING TIPS

Before you write . . .

- **Understand the prompt.**
  Make sure you understand what you are being asked to write.
- **Plan your narrative.**
  Jot down a time line of events.

Time Line

> Event
> First–
> Then–
> Next–
> Finally–

During your writing . . .

- **Decide on a focus.**
  Use key words from the prompt in your focus statement.
- **Choose carefully.**
  Make sure your details keep your story going.
- **End in a meaningful way.**
  Connect the experience to the prompt or tell why it was important.

After you've written a first draft . . .

- **Check the prompt and your narrative.**
  Make sure you have done what the prompt asks.
- **Check for conventions.**
  Correct any errors you find.

Narrative Prompts

- Who is the most unforgettable person you have ever met? Show what this person did to make him or her so unforgettable.
- Write a letter to a friend and tell about a memorable experience during your first day of the school year.

Plan and write a response. Respond to one of the narrative prompts above within the amount of time your teacher gives you.

Narrative Writing Checklist **137**

Narrative Writing in Review

In narrative writing, you tell a story about something that has happened. You may write about your own personal experiences.

Select a topic from your life experiences. (See page 92.)

Gather important details. Use a graphic organizer to list details for your narrative. (See pages 93–95.)

In the beginning, introduce your story and grab the reader's attention. (See page 99.)

In the middle, tell the events of your story in time order. Use your own words and show your feelings. Use sensory details and dialogue. (See pages 100–101.)

In the ending, tell why the experience was important and what you learned from it. (See page 102.)

First, review your ideas, organization, and **voice.** Then check for **word choice** and **sentence fluency.** (See pages 104–114.)

Check for conventions. Look for punctuation, capitalization, spelling, and grammar mistakes. Also ask a friend to edit your writing. (See pages 116–118.)

Make a final copy and proofread it before sharing it with other people. (See page 119.)

Use the narrative rubric to assess your finished narrative. (See pages 120–121.)

Narrative Writing in Review

Go over the information on the page, inviting students to talk about their experiences with each step of the process.

- What was most difficult for them?
- What taught them the most?
- What did they like best?

Have students mark the page with a sticky note or paperclip, so that they can easily refer to it when they are working on a narrative essay.

Expository Writing Overview

Writing Standards

The writing standards listed below are based on a blending of state and NCTE standards.

- Use sentence starters and lists to select topics.
- Gather and organize supporting details.
- Develop focus statements that are supported by topic sentences and details.
- Revise drafts to ensure a knowledgeable, interested voice.
- Assess writing using a rubric based on the traits of effective writing.

Writing Forms

- expository paragraph
- expository essay explaining a career

Focus on the Traits

- **Ideas** Writing a clear focus statement, and giving explanations and examples
- **Organization** Beginning by grabbing the reader's attention, using details in the middle, and creating a thoughtful ending
- **Voice** Using a knowledgeable voice that shows interest in the topic
- **Word Choice** Choosing specific nouns and the best modifiers
- **Sentence Fluency** Combining short, choppy sentences to improve flow
- **Conventions** Checking for errors in punctuation, capitalization, spelling, and grammar

Unit Pacing

Expository Paragraph: 1.5–3 hours

The **expository paragraph** introduces the unit and lays the groundwork for more extensive expository writing. Use this section if students need to work on crafting a paragraph. Following are some of the topics that are covered:

- Completing sentence starters to select a topic
- Writing a topic sentence and completing *because* statements to gather details
- Writing a paragraph that tells about a favorite activity

Expository Essay: 3.5–6 hours

This section asks student to write an essay that **explains a career**. Use this section to focus on developing an essay. Following are some of the topics that are covered:

- Finding special terms to create a knowledgeable voice
- Following a formula to write a focus statement
- Using an organized list to guide writing
- Organizing explanations by order of importance
- Checking subject-verb agreement

Expository Writing Across the Curriculum: 1.5–3 hours

The first lesson in this section guides students through the steps of the writing process in another curriculum area. The remaining two lessons provide models and tips for expository writing in additional curriculum areas. If other teachers are involved in cross-curricular activities, collaborate with them on these lessons.

■ **Science**

Writing a How-To Essay, pp. 182–185

■ **Math**

Explaining a Math Concept, pp. 186–187

■ **Practical Writing**

Taking Two-Column Notes, pp. 188–189

Writing for Assessment: 45–90 minutes

The student text shows a sample student response to the first prompt below. Students can respond to that same prompt or to either of the additional prompts as an informal or a formal assessment.

■ Most people have a favorite object. Write an essay naming your favorite thing and explaining why it is your favorite.

■ Imagine that a new student has come to your school and needs to learn the class rules. Write an essay that explains the main rules.

■ Most people have a favorite activity. Choose an activity that you enjoy doing and write an essay that explains how the activity is done. Remember to discuss any equipment or training needed.

Evaluating an Expository Essay

Learning to evaluate one's own and others' writing is an integral part of learning to write. In addition to a student's evaluation of an expository essay (PE pages 178–179), **benchmark papers** provide practice with evaluating expository writing.

■ Something You Can Sink Your Teeth Into (strong)
TR 3A–3C
TE pp. 635–637

■ My Own Two Hands (good)
PE pp. 145–146

■ Fluffy (poor)
TR 4A–4B
TE pp. 638–639

Integrated Grammar and Writing Skills

Below are skills lessons from the resources sections of the pupil edition that are suggested at point of use (✳) throughout this unit.

Writing an Expository Paragraph, pp. 139–142

✳ Writing Complete Sentences, pp. 432–435

✳ Capitalization, p. 514

Explaining a Career, pp. 143–180

✳ Expository Voice, p. 463

✳ Use Specific Nouns, p. 410

✳ Compound Sentences, p. 443

✳ Complex Sentences, p. 444

✳ Connecting with Conjunctions, pp. 429–430 and 600–601

✳ Subject-Verb Agreement, pp. 419 and 438–439

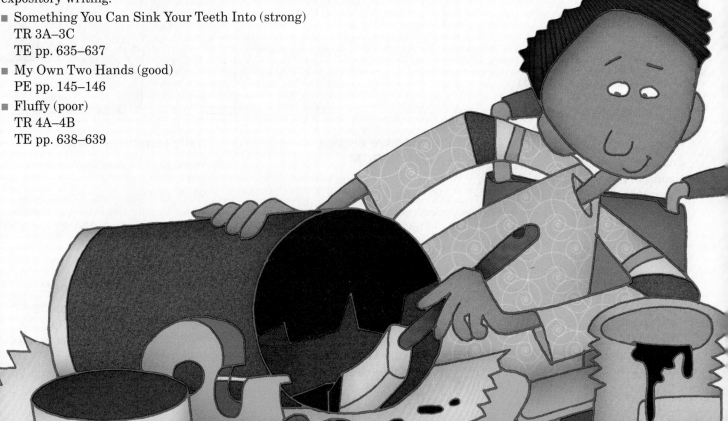

Additional Grammar Skills

Below are skills lessons from other components that you can weave into your unit instruction.

Writing an Expository Paragraph

SkillsBook

Interactive Writing Skills CD-ROM

Daily Language Workouts

Explaining a Career

SkillsBook

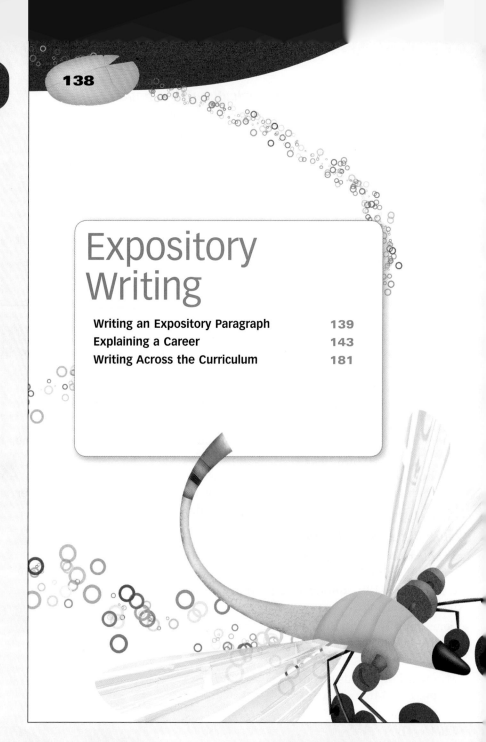

Expository Writing

Interactive Writing Skills CD-ROM

Daily Language Workouts

Writing Across the Curriculum

Daily Language Workouts

Expository Writing

Expository Paragraph

What do you enjoy doing? Some people may love to paint pictures. Other people may love to watch birds or build forts. People enjoy different activities. If you write to explain how to do something or to share information about an activity, that's expository writing.

In this chapter, you will have a chance to write an expository paragraph. You'll tell about a favorite activity and explain why you enjoy it. The next best thing to doing your favorite activity is writing about it!

Writing Guidelines

Subject: A favorite activity
Form: Expository paragraph
Purpose: To explain
Audience: Classmates

Expository Paragraph

Objectives

- demonstrate an understanding of the content and structure of an expository paragraph
- choose a topic (a favorite activity) to write about
- plan, draft, revise, and edit an expository paragraph

An **expository paragraph** explains a topic by clearly telling what something is, how something works, or how to do something. An expository paragraph contains a topic sentence, body sentences, and a closing sentence.

✱ For information about Paragraph Writing, see PE pages 50–61.

Ask students to draw a quick sketch that shows them doing an activity that they truly enjoy. Then invite volunteers to share their drawings and tell why they enjoy this activity. Point out that when people enjoy something, they usually have no trouble talking about it. Explain that if students can talk about a favorite activity, they can write about it, too.

Suggest that students save their drawings as a possible source for a topic idea.

Family Connection Letters

As you begin this unit, send home the Expository Writing Family Connection letter, which describes what students will be learning.

- Letter in English (TE p. 655)
- Letter in Spanish (TE p. 663)

Materials

Drawing paper (TE p. 139)

Sample topic sentences and sentence starter template (TE p. 141)

Expository Paragraph

Thinking about an expository paragraph from the reader's point of view can help students decide what kinds of details to include when it's time to write their paragraph. Ask students why they might want to read about someone else's favorite activity. They may suggest that it's a good way

- to learn what other students their age enjoy,
- to learn why an activity is enjoyable, or
- to find out if the activity is something they would like to try.

 Respond to the reading.

Answers

Ideas 1. Drawing sets Rosa's imagination free. She enjoys drawing her dreams, grown-ups as kids, and places she'd like to see.

Organization 2. Rosa ends with her strongest detail about drawing Paris from the Eiffel Tower.

Voice & Word Choice 3. The words make Rosa sound knowledgeable and enthusiastic, and as if she truly enjoys drawing.

Expository Paragraph

An expository paragraph starts with a **topic sentence**, which tells what the topic is. The sentences in the **body** support the topic sentence, and the **closing sentence** completes the explanation. In the following paragraph, Rosa tells about her favorite activity.

Topic sentence

Body sentences

Closing sentence

Drawing

    Drawing sets my imagination in motion. Sometimes I draw things from my dreams, like a picture of me flying with an eagle. Other times, I imagine grown-ups as kids. It's fun to draw my teacher or my coach as a little kid. My favorite drawings are places I'd like to see someday. I drew Paris with the Eiffel Tower and Notre Dame Cathedral. Maybe someday I'll draw Paris from the top of the Eiffel Tower. For me to be happy, all I need is a pencil, some paper, and my never-ending imagination.

 Respond to the reading. On your own paper, answer each of the following questions.

- **Ideas** (1) Why does Rosa like drawing? Find three details that help explain her topic sentence.
- **Organization** (2) Does Rosa start with her strongest detail or lead up to it near the end?
- **Voice & Word Choice** (3) Find the following words in Rosa's essay: *favorite, imagination, dreams, fun, happy*. How do these words make Rosa's voice sound?

Writing an Expository Paragraph **141**

Prewriting Selecting a Topic

You can find a topic by completing some sentence starters. Here are Rosa's completed sentences.

Sentence Starters

> <u>When I'm inside, I enjoy</u> . . . playing the piano.
> <u>When I'm outside, I enjoy</u> . . . hiking in the woods.
> <u>When I'm alone, I enjoy</u> . . . drawing in my sketchbook. *
> <u>When I'm with friends, I enjoy</u> . . . going to the skate park.

Complete sentences. On your own paper, write the underlined sentence starters above. Complete each one. Put a star (*) next to the activity you want to write about.

Gathering Details

Rosa wrote a topic sentence that tells why she enjoys drawing. To gather specific details, she completed three *because* statements.

"Because" Completions

> <u>Drawing sets my imagination in motion.</u>
> <u>because</u> . . . I draw things from my dreams.
> <u>because</u> . . . I imagine how grown-ups looked as kids.
> <u>because</u> . . . I draw pictures of places I'd like to see.

Do some "because" completions. Write your topic sentence that tells why you enjoy your activity. Under it, write *because* three times. Write three completions.

Prewriting Selecting a Topic

Provide these additional sentence starters to spark more topic ideas.

- When I'm on vacation, I enjoy . . .
- When I'm with my (aunt, grandmother, sister), I enjoy . . .
- When I'm at the (gym, track, park), I enjoy . . .

If students created drawings of themselves enjoying a favorite activity (TE page 139), remind them to look at their drawings now for another topic idea.

Prewriting Gathering Details

Use Rosa's topic sentence as an example of an interesting and effective topic sentence. Encourage students to create strong and effective **topic sentences** (*see below*) for their paragraphs.

Make sure students understand that the *because* statements are the reasons that they will use to explain why they enjoy the activity. If students seem confused, suggest that instead of writing *because* in a column, as shown, they write out their topic sentence three times followed by *because* and the reason.

Drawing sets my imagination in motion <u>because I draw things from my dreams</u>.

Teaching Tip: Strong and Effective Topic Sentences

Whenever students are asked to write about a favorite activity, they inevitably write a topic sentence that starts with "My favorite activity is . . ." Provide guidance for creating interesting and effective topic sentences.

- Remind students that a strong topic sentence identifies the topic and shares an important idea or feeling about it.

- Read a variety of effective topic sentences from expository writing assignments, books, or sample paragraphs you've saved as examples, and discuss what makes them interesting and effective.

* For more on writing strong topic sentences, see PE page 54 and 460.

Struggling Learners

Some students may become so focused on writing the sentence starters, they have trouble focusing on ideas for completions. Provide a fill-in-the-blank template with the suggested sentence starters for each writer to complete during the topic selection step.

Writing Creating Your First Draft

Before students begin their drafts, have them organize their *because* statements (TE page 141).

- Have them number their *because* statements 1, 2, and 3, with 1 being the least important reason, and 3 being the most important reason.
- Direct them to present their reasons in order, starting with the least important.
- Encourage them to add one example for each reason. Point out how Rosa presented her *because* statements as reasons (PE page 140), and then gave at least one example for each reason (see Struggling Learners below).

Revising
Improving Your Paragraph

Remind students to check that every sentence has a subject and verb.

✳ For information about Writing Complete Sentences, see PE pages 432–435.

Editing Checking for Conventions

Have partners make sure that every sentence begins with a capital letter and ends with the correct punctuation.

✳ For information about Capitalization, see PE page 514.

Writing Creating Your First Draft

The first draft of your paragraph should start with a **topic sentence** that tells what you especially like about your activity. The **body sentences** will include supporting details and examples. Finally, a **closing sentence** will complete your explanation.

 Write your first draft. Begin with a topic sentence, include supporting ideas, and end with a thoughtful closing sentence.

Revising Improving Your Paragraph

To decide what to change in your paragraph, check for *ideas, organization, voice, word choice,* and *sentence fluency.*

 Revise your paragraph. Use these questions as a guide.

1. Does my topic sentence name a favorite activity and what I like about it?
2. Do the body sentences include details and examples?
3. Does my writing voice show I'm interested in my topic?
4. Do specific words make my topic clear?
5. Do I use complete sentences?

Editing Checking for Conventions

To edit your paragraph, you correct any errors in *conventions.*

 Edit your work. Ask yourself the questions below.

1. Does each sentence begin with a capital letter and end with punctuation?
2. Have I checked my spelling?
3. Have I used words correctly *(to, too, two)*?

English Language Learners

If students are unable to revise their own work adequately, allow them to work with an English-proficient partner to help them. Encourage students to focus only on writing clear sentences and including details if some traits, such as voice and word choice, are too advanced for students' English levels.

Struggling Learners

To help students understand how examples support the reasons, have them turn back to PE pages 140–141. Point out that the "because" sentences at the bottom of PE page 141 became the writer's reasons.

- Have students find the reasons in the model essay on PE page 140.
- Have students find an example for each.

Reason: I draw things from my dreams.
Example: . . . a picture of me flying with an eagle.
Reason: I imagine grown-ups as kids.
Example: . . . my teacher or my coach as a little kid.
Reason: . . . places I'd like to see someday.
Example: Paris with the Eiffel Tower and Notre Dame.

Expository Writing
Explaining a Career

What do you want to be when you grow up? You've probably heard that question hundreds of times, and you may hear it hundreds more!

In this chapter, you'll write an expository essay that explains the work you want to do when you grow up. Dream big—you might be a jet pilot, a computer-game designer, or even president of the United States!

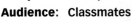

Writing Guidelines

Subject:	A future career
Form:	Expository essay
Purpose:	To explain
Audience:	Classmates

Explaining a Career

Objectives
- understand the purpose, content, and form of an expository essay
- choose a topic (a future career) to write about
- plan, draft, revise, and edit an expository essay

An **expository essay** explains a topic, using explanations and examples that illustrate the writer's knowledge and interest in the topic.

Invite students to share what they learned about expository writing when they wrote their expository paragraph earlier. Possible responses:

- Write a clear topic sentence that identifies the topic and tells why it is important to the writer.
- Use supporting details and examples that show knowledge and interest in the topic.

Explain to students that now they can use what they learned about expository writing as they write an expository essay.

Materials

Magazine articles (TE p. 144)

Assorted pictures to clarify vocabulary (TE pp. 145, 178)

Books about careers (TE p. 147)

Index cards (TE p. 149)

Examples of transitions in paragraphs (TE p. 156)

Chart paper (TE p. 159)

Blank overhead transparency (TE p. 167)

Writing samples, newspaper articles, magazines (TE p. 169)

Alphabet samples (TE p. 171)

Sample résumés (TE p. 175)

Benchmark Papers

Something You Can Sink Your Teeth Into (strong)
- TR 3A–3C
- TE p. 635–637

Fluffy (poor)
- TR 4A–4B
- TE pp. 638–639

Understanding Your Goal

Three traits relate to the development of the content and the form. They provide a focus during prewriting, drafting, and revising.

- Ideas
- Organization
- Voice

The other three traits relate more to form. Checking them is part of the revising and editing processes.

- **Word Choice**
- Sentence Fluency
- **Conventions**

✱ The six-point rubric on PE pages 176–177 is based on these traits. Four- and five-point rubrics are available on TE pages 625 and 628.

Understanding Your Goal

Your goal in this chapter is to write an expository essay that explains a job you would enjoy doing as a grown-up. The traits listed in the chart below will help you reach your goal.

Your goal is to . . .

 **Ideas** — Select an interesting career (job), write a clear focus statement, and give explanations and examples.

 Organization — Begin by grabbing the reader's attention. In the middle, explain the career with details. Write a thoughtful ending.

 **Voice** — Use a writing voice that is knowledgeable and shows your interest in the topic.

 **Word Choice** — Choose words that make every part of your explanation clear.

 **Sentence Fluency** — Write clear, complete sentences, including some compound and complex sentences.

Conventions — Create an essay that has correct punctuation, capitalization, spelling, and grammar.

 Get the big picture. Review the rubric on pages 176–177. This rubric can help you measure your progress as you write.

Expository Essay

In the following expository essay, David explains why carpentry is the right job for him.

Expository Essay

Work through this sample essay with the class, pointing out the elements that make it a good expository essay.

BEGINNING
The beginning gets the reader's attention and gives the focus statement (underlined).

MIDDLE
The first middle paragraph explains the job.

My Own Two Hands

My dad is a carpenter, and I want to be one, too. I grew up around hammers and saws. When I was five, Dad and I built a doghouse. <u>Someday, I'll be a carpenter and make things with my own two hands.</u>

Carpenters build all kinds of things with wood. Carpenters like my dad mostly frame houses, hang drywall, and nail moldings. That's the kind of carpenter I want to be! Other carpenters build furniture. My dad does that, too. He even made my bunk bed.

I believe that I would be a good carpenter. The most important thing a carpenter needs is experience. I'm

Ideas
- The focus statement identifies the topic and shares a strong feeling about it.
- The beginning gets the reader's attention.
- The writer explains the career and uses examples to show why it is a good choice.

Organization
- The opening identifies the career and tells why the writer is interested in it.
- The middle uses details to explain the career.
- The ending leaves the reader with a final thought.

Voice & Word Choice
- The writer uses an interested, knowledgeable voice.
- The special terms show that the writer understands the career.
- The vocabulary inspires confidence in the writer's knowledge about the topic.

English Language Learners

Before reading the model essay, review the following terms with students:

- carpenter (a person who builds things from wood)
- frame houses (build the wooden "skeleton" of houses)
- drywall (material used for making walls inside a building)
- moldings (decorative frames around doors and windows)
- bunk bed (two beds stacked one on top of the other)
- apprentice (a person who is learning a skill from another experienced person)
- boards (flat pieces of wood)

Provide picture support for the above-mentioned words, if possible.

Students are going to learn about using special terms during Prewriting. To preview this skill and help them appreciate the effect of special terms on the writing voice, ask them to point out terms in the sample essay that make David sound like he knows all about being a carpenter. (Possible responses: hammers, saws, frame houses, hang drywall, moldings, tenpenny nail, sawdust, boards)

 Respond to the reading.

Answers

Ideas 1. Possible responses:

- He grew up around hammers and saws.
- He and his dad built a doghouse.
- He's already an apprentice carpenter.
- He and his dad built a closet.
- He can pound a tenpenny nail in four hits.
- He has sawdust in his blood.

Organization 2. Possible responses:

- when
- someday
- most important
- finally

Voice & Word Choice 3. David means that he loves doing carpentry work and that it's part of his nature to be a carpenter, just like his dad.

MIDDLE
The second middle paragraph explains why the writer would do the job well.

already an apprentice carpenter since I help Dad with all of his home projects. We built a new closet in my sister's bedroom. Carpenters also need to be strong. I can already pound in a big tenpenny nail in four hits. Finally, carpenters need to love their work. Dad says instead of iron in my blood, I must have sawdust!

ENDING
The ending leaves the reader with a final thought.

I want to make things with my hands. Carpenters can take a pile of boards and make something great. If somebody can dream it, my dad can build it. Someday, I want people to say the same thing about me.

 Respond to the reading. On your own paper, answer the following questions about the sample essay.

- **Ideas** (1) What three details show that David would make a good carpenter?
- **Organization** (2) What transition words and phrases help connect the ideas?
- **Voice & Word Choice** (3) What does David mean about having "sawdust" in his blood?

English Language Learners

Students may have difficulty understanding English expressions, such as the one used in question 3. Explain that David doesn't mean that he actually has sawdust in his blood. Point out the following line in the essay:

Dad says instead of iron in my blood, I must have sawdust!

- Explain that iron is a mineral that is actually in our blood.

- Explain that sawdust is the shavings and dust created when wood is cut, and is *not* actually in our blood.

Explain that the saying that something (like sawdust) is in a person's blood means that it is so important to them, it's part of who they are, just as blood is part of who they are. Discuss how this is an effective description in the essay because it makes a point without being too obvious.

Prewriting

Prewriting is the first step in the writing process. Prewriting helps you decide what to write about and prepares you to write your first draft.

Keys to Prewriting

1. **Select** a career (job) to explain.

2. **Gather** facts and details about the career.

3. **Find** special terms that describe the job.

4. **Write** a focus statement and topic sentences.

5. **Create** an organized list of your facts and details.

Prewriting Keys to Prewriting

Remind students of the purpose of the prewriting stage in the writing process: It is when the writer selects a topic, gathers details, and decides how to organize those details.

The Keys to Prewriting list lays out the process students will be guided through on PE pages 148–152.

Focus attention on item 1. This is a good opportunity to encourage students who may not receive support and encouragement outside of school to dare to dream big about the future.

■ When it is time to list possible careers, make sure that students don't eliminate careers because their current life situation makes the idea seem impossible.

■ Encourage students to think about their future as a blank page. Since they are the authors of their future, they can write anything they want on that page.

English Language Learners

Students may have a difficult time selecting an interesting career depending on their knowledge of career choices and their correct titles.

- Make a list of interesting and exciting careers so that students can match their interests to one of the careers.
- Provide a selection of books about each career so that students can have a reference to

terms and concepts that relate to the career that they choose. Ask the librarian for books written for younger children.

This will enable students to write more freely about the topic without getting stuck on vocabulary.

Prewriting Selecting a Topic

Help students generate good ideas for their jobs list. Suggest that they think about the jobs and careers of the following people:

- family, friends, and neighbors
- celebrities (for example, athletes, performing artists, political figures)
- people they have read about in books or learned about through a television documentary or the news
- people they have met on vacation and in their travels within and outside of the community

Focus on the Traits

Ideas

Be sure students read **Focus on the Traits** before they choose a topic.

- Before students star a topic, suggest that they rate each topic on their list, using their own dream scale ratings. Tell them to use ratings of 1 to 5, with 1 being "Just Okay," and 5 being "Dream Job."
- Tell students to quickly jot down two or three words about each job on their list. This will help them determine if they have enough interest in the topic to write about it.

Prewriting Selecting a Topic

First, you need to choose a job or career that you would enjoy doing. Sumie made a list of jobs she would like to do.

Ideas List

> ### Jobs I Would Like
>
> | | |
> |---|---|
> | sea captain | vet |
> | forest ranger | farmer |
> | firefighter | lion tamer |
> | singer | dolphin trainer* |

 Prewrite — **Create an ideas list.** Write "Jobs I Would Like" at the top of a piece of paper. Then list jobs underneath. Put a star (*) next to the job you would like to write about.

Focus on the Traits

Ideas Your topic is the "big idea" of your writing. Choose your topic carefully. If it interests you, it will probably also interest your reader as well. Also, if you like your topic, you will enjoy gathering details about it.

Struggling Learners

Some students may still have difficulty committing to a topic. Assure them that if during detail gathering they find that the career they've chosen isn't so interesting to them after all, they can return to their ideas list and choose a new one.

Finding Details

Now it's time to gather details about the job you have chosen. Sumie used some questions to help her gather details. She checked articles in encyclopedias and on Web sites to find answers.

Questions and Answers

What job would I like? dolphin trainer

Why am I interested in this job? I would like to swim with and work with these amazing animals. I saw how much fun the trainer was having at a dolphin water show.

What are three main duties for this job?

1. A dolphin trainer feeds and cares for the dolphins.
2. The trainer must teach the dolphins tricks.
3. Trainers need to clean the dolphin tank.

Why would I be good at this job?

1. I love dolphins.
2. I am patient.
3. I work hard.

Prewrite

Gather details. Copy and answer each of the underlined questions above. Try to find at least three answers for each of the last two questions.

Prewriting Finding Details

Suggest that students **use note cards to take notes** *(see below)* as they do research for their essay.

Provide students with the necessary information for accessing online encyclopedias, which are constantly updated and therefore more accurate than old editions of print encyclopedias.

Review the guidelines for using the Internet in the classroom. If students will be doing their research at home, tell them to make sure that they follow their family's established guidelines for using the Internet.

Teaching Tip: Using Note Cards to Take Notes

Students should apply good note-taking techniques whenever they take notes. First, help students set up their note cards. Tell them to

- use a separate note card for each question,
- number each note card, and
- write the question at the top of the card and their answers under the question.

Then provide students with a few tips for taking good notes for their essay.

- Skim a reading to see what it is about and if it will help them explain the career.
- Look for specific details about the duties, responsibilities, and education or training requirements for the job.
- Write only important ideas.

- Jot down the name of the source and the page number or Web address in case they want to find it again.

* For more on taking reading notes, see PE page 390.

Prewriting Finding Special Words

Remind students that in the sample expository essay on PE pages 145–146, David's use of carpentry terms, such as *frame houses, hang drywall, nail moldings,* and *ten-penny nail,* adds interest to his essay, and also makes readers believe that David knows a lot about carpentry.

Practice Answers

Possible responses:
- veterinarians
- dorsal fins
- flippers
- tail flukes

Focus on the Traits

Voice

Encourage students to develop a list of special terms for their essay.
- Have them draw a cluster diagram with their topic (job or career) in the center oval.
- Tell them to surround the topic with as many special terms that relate to their topic as they can.
- Invite classmates to suggest other special terms for students' diagrams.

Prewriting Finding Special Words

In an expository essay, you can show your knowledge of a topic by using special words, or terms, that are related to it. You can find these terms in the articles you read.

Practice

Read the following article about dolphin trainers. Then write down at least three special terms that Sumie could use in her essay.

Trainers Teach Tricks for Health

Dolphin tricks aren't just showstoppers. Trainers teach some behaviors that help veterinarians keep the animals healthy. For example, dolphins need to learn to open their mouths for a dental checkup. They also must learn how to show their dorsal fin, flippers, and tail flukes for inspection. As with any animal, dolphins that are familiar with people are easier to check for injury or disease. This is important because by instinct dolphins hide any illness or disease so that they don't look like easy prey.

 Find special words. Read about your topic and write down special terms that you could use in your essay.

Focus on the Traits

Voice When you use special terms, the reader feels confident that you know your subject well.

English Language Learners

If their topics are related to careers from their cultures, encourage students to interview family and friends from their culture to learn about specific terms for their careers. Make sure that students understand special terms from whatever career they chose by asking them for simple definitions of words that they use.

Struggling Learners

To provide support for using specialized vocabulary, have all students brainstorm words related to the following careers:

- mail carrier
- teacher
- photographer
- restaurant manager
- dentist
- astronaut

Create a chart for students to refer to as they write.

Writing a Focus Statement

Your focus statement should name the job you chose and tell why you are interested in it.

name the job	tell why you are interested in it	a strong focus statement
dolphin trainer	**+** I'd like to swim with dolphins, keep them healthy, and teach them tricks.	**=** I want to be a dolphin trainer so that I can swim with dolphins, keep them healthy, and teach them tricks.

 Prewrite **Write your focus statement.** Follow the formula above to write your own focus statement. You may need to try it a few times before you find the one that works for you.

Writing Topic Sentences

Your essay will have two middle paragraphs, and each will start with a topic sentence. Here are the topic sentences Sumie wrote.

Topic Sentence 1: Write a sentence about the main duties of the job.

A dolphin trainer has many duties.

Topic Sentence 2: Write a sentence about why you would be good at the job.

I have the right personality to be a dolphin trainer.

 Prewrite **Write your topic sentences.** Use Sumie's sentences as models for your own topic sentences.

Prewriting Organizing Your Ideas

Explain to students that once they have made their organized list, they will have created an easy-to-follow blueprint, or framework for their essay. So before they make their list, they should make sure to

- look over all of their prewriting materials,
- decide if they are satisfied with their focus statement and topic sentences, and
- check that they have at least three details to support each of their topic sentences.

Focus on the Traits

Organization

When it is time to write and revise their essay, students will be asked to check that each middle paragraph contains explanations and examples, and that the explanations are presented in order of importance (see TE pages 156–157 and PE pages 160–161).

Encourage students to take time now to put their explanations and examples in order of importance, from most important to least important, or from least important to most important. Even if students decide to reorder their ideas later, they will still have a good working plan to begin writing.

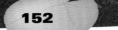

152

Prewriting Organizing Your Ideas

Your focus statement, topic sentences, and details can be put into an organized list that will guide your writing.

Organized List

Focus statement	I want to be a dolphin trainer so that I can swim with dolphins, keep them healthy, and teach them tricks.
First topic sentence	1. A dolphin trainer has many duties.
Details	– keep dolphins healthy – teach tricks – clean the tanks
Second topic sentence	2. I have the right personality to be a dolphin trainer.
Details	– love dolphins – patient – work hard

Prewrite **Organize your essay.** Follow the model above to make your own organized list. (Refer to your work from pages 149–151.)

Focus on the Traits

Organization Your organized list shows you what you should include in each part of your essay.

English Language Learners

If students have gathered details on note cards (TE page 149), give them time to organize their cards into different categories of information. Help students color-code their cards; for example:

- all of the cards about the responsibilities of the job have a blue dot, and
- all of the cards about the personality of the professionals have a red dot.

Then have students set out all of their blue-dot cards together on a table to decide in what order the information should be presented. Have them repeat this with the red-dot cards.

With these visual clues, students should have an easier time writing their organized lists and outlines.

Explaining a Career   **153**

Writing

Now that you've selected a career, gathered details, and made an organized list, you are ready to create a first draft. This is your chance to put all your ideas on paper or in a computer file.

Keys to Writing

1. **Write** a strong beginning paragraph that ends with your focus statement.

2. **Start** each middle paragraph with a topic sentence.

3. **Include** explanations and examples in your middle paragraphs to support each topic sentence.

4. **Write** a thoughtful ending paragraph.

English Language Learners

As students begin to write, monitor their work to make sure that they do not begin too many sentences in a similar way, which many second-language learners have the tendency to do. If more than two sentences per paragraph begin in the same way, help students to vary their wording.

Writing Keys to Writing

Remind students that the writing stage is when they get to write, or draft, their ideas on paper.

The Keys to Writing list lays out the process students will be guided through on PE pages 154–158.

Tell students to keep their organized list in sight for easy reference as they write their draft. Suggest that they cross out or put a red check mark next to each idea in the organized list once they use it in their essay. Then when they have finished their draft, they can skim their organized list to make sure that they didn't leave out any important ideas.

Writing Getting the Big Picture

Assure students that they are now ready to write their draft. If students are concerned that they have not yet explored ideas for their ending, assure them that writers may develop ideas for an ending of an expository essay when they first decide on a topic, as they gather details, when they create their organized list, or after they have written their beginning and middle.

- If students already have an idea for an ending in mind, suggest that they quickly draft a closing sentence and add it to the bottom of their organized list now to use later.
- If students do not have an idea for their ending yet, but would like to take a few minutes to review their prewriting materials to see if they can come up with an idea for a thoughtful ending paragraph, provide time for them to do so now.
- If students want to wait until after they have drafted their beginning and middle paragraphs, tell them that that is acceptable, too.

Writing Getting the Big Picture

The chart below shows how the parts of an expository essay fit together. (The examples are from the sample essay on pages 155–158.) You are ready to write your essay when you have . . .

- gathered details and special terms,
- written your focus statement and topic sentences, and
- created an organized list.

Beginning	Focus Statement
The **beginning** gets the reader's attention and gives the focus statement.	I want to be a dolphin trainer so that I can swim with them, keep them healthy, and teach them tricks.
Middle	Topic Sentences
Each **middle** paragraph explains a different part of the focus.	• A dolphin trainer has many duties. • I have the right personality to be a dolphin trainer.
Ending	Closing Sentence
The **ending** leaves the reader with a final thought.	Maybe, if I become a trainer, dolphins will dream about swimming with me.

Struggling Learners

To emphasize the importance of all three parts of an expository essay, put students in groups of three and have each person describe what would happen at the beginning, middle, or end of the following:

- a baseball game (gather on the field, play the game, record the final score)
- a recipe (gather the ingredients, follow the recipe, eat)
- a concert (appear in the auditorium, perform, receive applause)
- a joke (find an audience, start the story, say the punch line)
- a computer set-up (read the manual, follow the directions, try it out)

Explaining a Career **155**

Starting Your Essay

Your beginning paragraph should catch the reader's attention. Here are some ways to do that.

| Beginning |
| Middle |
| Ending |

- **Start with an interesting fact.**
  Dolphins have bigger brains than humans do.

- **Ask a question.**
  Have you ever trained an animal?

- **Tell how you became interested in the job.**
  Last year, I saw a dolphin show on television.

Beginning Paragraph

Sumie used the third strategy to start her beginning paragraph.

The last sentence is the focus statement (underlined).

Last year, I saw a dolphin show on television. The dolphins jumped so high! It was exciting, and I learned a lot about dolphins. They are amazing animals. <u>I want to be a dolphin trainer so that I can swim with them, keep them healthy, and teach them tricks.</u>

Write your beginning paragraph. Try one of the ideas at the top of this page to get started. Then lead into your focus statement.

Writing
Developing the Middle Part

Use the sample middle paragraphs to model how to present explanations and examples (supporting details).

- Topic sentence 1 (a dolphin trainer has many duties) tells the main point of the paragraph.
- The first explanation sentence (The most important duty . . .) helps explain the main point presented in the topic sentence of the paragraph.
- The example sentence (That means feeding them . . .) immediately follows, and makes the explanation clearer.

Help students find the two other explanations and any examples in the paragraph. Then have students find the topic sentence, explanations, and examples in the paragraph on PE page 157. For more about using explanations and examples, see PE pages 160–161.

Writing Using Transitions

Remind students that transitions should be used to connect ideas between sentences within paragraphs, and to connect ideas from one paragraph to the next.

✱ Encourage students to use some of the transitions on PE page 473 for emphasizing a point and adding information.

Writing Developing the Middle Part

Each middle paragraph in your essay begins with one of your topic sentences (page 151). The body sentences should contain supporting details and terms (pages 149–150).

Beginning		
Middle		
Ending		

Using Transitions

Make sure to connect your ideas with transition words and phrases like those shown below. They make your ideas easy to follow.

The most important . . .	To start,	To begin with,
Secondly,	Also,	In addition,
The third thing . . .	Finally,	In conclusion,

Middle Paragraphs

Topic sentence 1

What are the three main duties?

Transitions are underlined.

A dolphin trainer has many duties. <u>The most important</u> duty is to take care of the dolphins. That means feeding them and making sure they don't get sick. <u>Secondly,</u> trainers teach dolphins tricks. Tricks are used in shows, but some tricks actually help veterinarians keep the dolphins healthy. Tricks also keep dolphins from being bored. <u>The third thing</u> trainers do is clean the tanks. It's hard work, but it's important!

English Language Learners

Point out that some of the transition words are synonyms, such as:

- *To start* and *To begin with*
- *Also* and *In addition*
- *Finally* and *In conclusion*

If possible, show students an example of how each one is used correctly in a paragraph. Limit students to using only a few transition words at first, so that they can incorporate them well and master their usefulness before going on to other words.

Advanced Learners

Challenge students to find newspaper and magazine articles with examples of transition words and phrases. Have them highlight the transitions, bring the articles to class, and create a bulletin board display to serve as a classroom writing resource.

Topic
sentence 2

Why would
you be good
at this job?

Transitions are
underlined.

I have the right personality to be a dolphin trainer. <u>To begin with,</u> I love dolphins. As a trainer, I could help other people love and protect dolphins. I am <u>also</u> patient. I have two little brothers, and I've helped them learn to swim and taught them how to do special dives and somersaults! <u>Finally,</u> I work hard and get along with others. Trainers have to work long days with each other and the public.

Write your middle paragraphs. Use your organized list from page 152. Include one topic sentence and its supporting details in each paragraph. Connect your ideas with transitions.

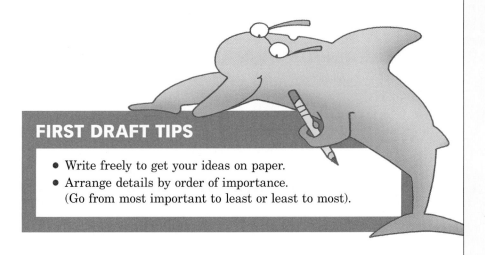

FIRST DRAFT TIPS

- Write freely to get your ideas on paper.
- Arrange details by order of importance.
  (Go from most important to least or least to most).

English Language Learners

When writing freely to get their ideas on paper, allow students to add words from their first language if they do not know the words in English so that they are not slowed down by having to use a dictionary too much. Make sure that they do most of their writing in English, and that any important terms about the career from their first language are explained in English.

Some students will find it more natural to arrange details from most important to least important. Others will prefer to go from least important to most important. Point out to students that writers may choose the latter (least important to most important) because they think that building up to an idea is more effective and interesting for readers. It gives them something to anticipate, or to look forward to. However either pattern of organization is acceptable.

Students may be confused by the first set of directions telling them to use their organized list to write their middle paragraphs and the second set telling them to write freely to get their ideas on paper. Explain that they should use their organized list as a guide so that they do not get off track as they write. However, if a good idea comes into their head that isn't spelled out on their organized list, they should include it in their draft. When they revise, they can check to make sure the idea belongs in the essay.

Writing Ending Your Essay

Writing Ending Your Essay

Encourage students to stay away from the "And that's why I want to be a _____" type of ending.

Have students write two different endings, using two of the four ways shown. Suggest that they read over their essay first with one ending and then with the other ending. If they still can't decide which ending to use, have them ask a partner to read the essay and the endings and answer these questions:

- Which ending wraps up my ideas best?
- Which ending do you think most readers will remember?
- Which ending do you like best?

Partners should be ready to give reasons for their choices.

Your ending paragraph gives you one last chance to speak to the reader. Here are some ways to write a strong ending.

- **Connect the end to the beginning.**
  Someday people may see me on a dolphin TV show!

- **Give the reader a final thought.**
  If a dog is our best friend on land, a dolphin is our best friend in the sea.

- **Connect with the reader.**
  Everybody has a dream, and my dream is to swim with dolphins.

- **End with a surprise.**
  Maybe, if I become a trainer, dolphins will dream about swimming with me.

Ending Paragraph

The writer ends with a surprise.

> Dolphins are our water friends. Training dolphins is an important job. It's one way to encourage people to enjoy and protect these amazing animals. At night, I even dream about swimming with dolphins. Maybe, if I become a trainer, dolphins will dream about swimming with me.

Write your ending. Use one of the four ways above to give your essay a strong ending.

Form a complete first draft. Write a complete copy of your essay on every other line to make room for your revising changes.

Revising

Once you have completed your first draft, you are ready to make changes to improve your writing. When you revise, you check your essay for *ideas, organization, voice, word choice,* and *sentence fluency.*

Keys to Revising

1. **Read** your essay out loud once to see how you feel about it.

2. **Review** each part: the beginning, the middle, and the ending.

3. **Ask** a classmate to read your first draft, too.

4. **Change** any parts that need to be improved.

Revising Keys to Revising

Remind students that the revising stage is when writers have an opportunity to make improvements to their first drafts. At this stage they can think about refinements they might not have considered when they were drafting.

The Keys to Revising list lays out the process students will be guided through on PE pages 160–180.

Have students expand the Keys to Revising list. Suggest that they review the goals on PE page 144 to get ideas of what to add to the list. Have students jot down all their ideas and then work together to select the best ones to add to the expanded Keys to Revising list. Invite volunteers to write the expanded list on chart paper, and display it in the classroom to use as a quick reference during revising. Besides the four ideas listed here, the expanded Keys to Revising list might include the following tips:

■ Check that the focus statement clearly states the topic.
■ Make sure explanations and examples are in the right order.
■ Look to see if you need to add more special terms to make you sound confident.

Revising for Ideas

The rubric strips that run across all of the revising pages (160–169) are provided to help students focus their revising and are related to the full rubric on pages 176–177.

Make sure students are aware that the two questions (What are the three main duties for this job? Why would I be good at this job?) are rewordings of the directions for writing Topic Sentences 1 and 2 on PE page 151.

When students developed their organized list (PE page 152) and wrote their draft, it is possible that they discovered that the job or career they chose does not have three main duties. Perhaps it has two or four. Assure students that it is far more important to explain the actual duties clearly than to have precisely three duties to explain.

Practice Answers

- Sentences 1, 3, and 5 explain the topic sentence.
- Sentences 2, 4, and 6 do not explain the topic sentence.

Have a volunteer read aloud the **Practice** paragraph without sentences 2, 4, and 6 so that students understand how much more focused the paragraph is without them.

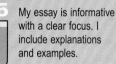

Revising for Ideas

| **6** My topic, focus, explanations, and examples make my essay truly memorable. | **5** My essay is informative with a clear focus. I include explanations and examples. | **4** My essay has a clear focus. I need more explanations or examples. |

When you revise for *ideas,* you make sure your paragraphs include explanations and examples. The rubric above can help you revise.

How can I use explanations in a paragraph?

You can use explanations to support your topic sentence, which focuses on the question for that paragraph. (See page 55.)

Middle Paragraph 1: What are three main duties for this job?
Middle Paragraph 2: Why would I be good at this job?

Practice

Read the following middle paragraph. Find three sentences that explain the topic sentence (in black). Find three sentences that do not do this.

Movie actors have three main duties. (1) Most importantly, actors have to learn their lines. (2) It's really hard work to be an actor. (3) Secondly, actors need to say their lines and move like their character would. (4) They get to wear different costumes as well. (5) Lastly, actors must listen to the director. (6) After shooting a movie, an actor can celebrate with a party.

Check your explanations. In each middle paragraph, make sure your sentences explain the topic sentence. Cross out any sentences that do not explain the topic sentence.

English Language Learners

Make sure that students understand that their middle paragraphs should not have only three sentences that list the duties of their jobs. They may try to do this due to limited language skills. If so, make sure that at least for some explanations they use details to support their ideas. Give this example for the **Practice** paragraph:

After sentence 1, the writer could add, *They may need to practice on their own for several hours.*

This detail supports the idea and makes the paragraph more interesting, although it is not complicated English.

Advanced Learners

Have students determine which sentence in the **Practice** paragraph is an opinion rather than a fact (#2). Emphasize that facts are the basis of powerful expository writing and that any opinions stated must be backed up by proof in the form of facts or real-life examples. Have students check their explanations to see if they included any opinions instead of facts.

Explaining a Career **161**

3 My focus needs to be clear, and I need more explanations and examples.

2 I need a focus and more details.

1 My topic is unclear.

How can I use examples to explain my topic?

You can use an example to give the reader a clearer picture. An example is something that has happened or could happen.

Topic Sentence: I could be a good movie actor.

Explanation: For one thing, I have a terrific memory.

Example 1: Some actors must memorize very long parts.

Example 2: I had the lead in our class play and remembered all of my lines!

Add examples. Read your essay and check your explanations. Try to add an example or two to make each explanation clearer.

Revising in Action

The writer adds an example to make the explanation clearer.

> A dolphin trainer has many duties. The most
> important duty is to take care of the dolphins. ∧
>
> ^That means feeding them and making sure they don't get sick.
>
> Secondly, trainers teach dolphins tricks. . . .

Suggest that students use red, green, and blue colored pencils to check their middle paragraphs for topic sentences, explanations, and examples. Tell them to underline
- the topic sentence in each paragraph in red,
- the explanations in green, and
- the examples in blue.

By looking at the pattern of colored lines (for example, red, green, blue; green, blue, blue; green, blue), they can make sure that the explanations follow the topic sentence, and that examples immediately follow each explanation.

Revising for Organization

Items 1, 2, and 3 of the Scavenger Hunt are objective, while item four (strong ending paragraph) is more subjective and therefore more difficult for students to assess.

Remind students that their ending paragraph is the last thing that their readers will read. A strong ending paragraph, therefore, needs to make an impression on readers. To help students determine if they have a strong ending paragraph, tell them to ask themselves these questions, which are based on the suggestions for writing a strong ending on PE page 158:

- Does my ending connect to the beginning?
- Will the reader be left with one final thought to remember and thing about?
- Does the ending connect with the reader?
- Will the ending surprise the reader?

Tell students that if they can honestly answer yes to one or more of these questions, then they can give themselves a star.

162

Revising for Organization

6 My essay is clear and easy to read, with every part in just the right place.

5 I have a strong beginning, middle, and ending, and my explanations are in order.

4 My essay has a clear beginning, middle, and ending, but I need to reorder one explanation.

When you revise for *organization,* you make sure each part of your essay is in the right spot and does its job. Make sure your explanations appear in the best order, too. The rubric strip above can help you revise your writing.

How can I check my organization?

You can check the overall organization of your essay by doing the following scavenger hunt.

Organization Scavenger Hunt

1. Place a ⁋ beside each paragraph indent.
2. If your focus statement is in your beginning paragraph, put a ✳ next to it.
3. If a middle paragraph starts with a topic sentence and has three more sentences with explanations or examples, put a ☺ next to it.
4. Add another ✳ if you have a strong ending paragraph.

Revise

Do the scavenger hunt. Mark your own essay or exchange papers with a partner. Then, add up how many marks you have made (⁋ , ✳ , ☺). You should have 8 points. If you don't, go back and make changes until you do.

| 3 | One part of my essay is weak. I need to put my explanations in order. | 2 | I need to put my beginning, middle, and ending into paragraphs. | 1 | I need to completely reorganize my essay. |

How should I organize my explanations?

You should organize your explanations by putting your most important explanation first (or last).

Practice

Which explanation below is most important for the topic sentence "I want to work on fishing boats? Tell why.

1. I love riding in boats.　　**3.** I want to travel around the world.

2. Waves don't bother me.　　**4.** I have always liked fishing.

 Revise　**Check the organization of your explanations.** Make sure you have put your strongest explanation first (or last).

Revising in Action

The writer moves an explanation to a better place.

> To begin with, I am ∧also patient. I have two little
>
> brothers, and I've helped them learn to swim.
>
> ~~Also,~~ I love dolphins. As a trainer, I could help
>
> other people love and protect dolphins.

Have students exchange papers with a partner and read each other's work to
- make sure the strongest explanation is first (or last) and the other explanations follow this order, and
- decide if the writer's ideas would be more effective and interesting if the order of the explanations was changed, for example, by putting the most important explanation last (or first).

Practice **Answers**

Possible answers: 1, 3, and 4. Discuss with students that one person's most important reason may differ from another person's reason. Some students may say that item 3 (I want to travel around the world) is the best choice because it is more interesting than the other choices, and it would capture the reader's interest. In that case, items 1 and 4 may be used as explanations in a paragraph about why the writer would be good at this job.

Review the use of proofreading marks as shown in the revised passage at the bottom of the page and on the inside back cover of the pupil edition.

Revising for Voice

Help students check their essay for a strong, knowledgeable voice.

- In a column on the left side of a piece of paper, have students write all of the adjectives used to describe voice in the first two descriptions of the rubric strip—*strong, lively, knowledgeable, enthusiastic, well informed,* and *interested*. Tell students to skip a line between each word.
- Then have students look for facts and details in their essay that fit one or more of the adjectives. Tell students to make a hash mark (/) next to an adjective on their list for every fact or detail that fits its description.
- After, have them count hash marks. A good number of hash marks (six to eight, perhaps) suggests a knowledgeable voice. Only one or two hash marks suggests that they need to add more facts to their essay.

✱ For information about writing in an Expository Voice, see PE page 463.

Practice Answers

1, 3, 5

Revising for Voice

6 My voice is strong and lively. I sound knowledgeable and enthusiastic.	**5** I sound well informed and interested.	**4** I sound well informed and interested most of the time.

When you revise for *voice,* make sure you sound knowledgeable and interested. The rubric strip above can help you.

How can I make my voice sound knowledgeable?

Your voice will sound knowledgeable if you include interesting facts about your topic.

Practice

Read the following job facts about firefighters. Which three facts could a writer include to sound more knowledgeable?

1. Firefighters open high-pressure hydrants, attach hoses, and turn on the water.
2. They fight fires that are caused by many different things.
3. It takes several firefighters to handle a hose since a person can be knocked down by the water pressure.
4. Firefighters use water.
5. Firefighters must sometimes climb tall ladders or enter burning buildings.

 Revise **Check your facts.** Make sure you include some facts that the reader might not know. Add more facts to your essay if necessary.

English Language Learners

Expressing voice in English may be a difficult trait for students to accomplish alone. Invite students to hold a conference with you or other students to gather ideas about how to show interest in their topic.

Generate lists of words that students could use in their writing that illustrate the adjectives used in the rubric. For example, come up with words and phrases that show *enthusiastic* voice in a piece of writing, such as:

- I can't wait to . . .
- I still jump up and down when . . .
- There's nothing in the world I'd rather do than . . .

Struggling Learners

To help students understand why two of the **Practice** facts do not sound knowledgeable, point out that:

- Sentence 2 is too general. The reader will want to know *what kinds* of things cause the fires.
- Sentence 4 doesn't offer any new information. Everyone already knows that firefighters use water.

Explaining a Career **165**

3 Sometimes I sound unsure of my topic.

2 I sound unsure of my topic.

1 I need help understanding what my writing voice is.

How can I make my voice sound more interested?

Your voice will sound interested if you care about your topic.

Practice

Read the following paragraph about firefighters. Write down three words or phrases that show how the writer feels.

I would make a good firefighter for many reasons. Most importantly, I like to help people. When my neighbor broke his leg, I walked his dog every day. Also, firefighters need to be in great shape. I love sports, and I lift weights three times a week. Finally, a firefighter has to work well under pressure. When the kids play football in my neighborhood, I love being in the middle of a blitz.

 Revise | **Review your voice.** Look for words or phrases that show that you care about your topic. Add a few more if you can.

Revising in Action

The writer adds a sentence to show that she cares about the topic.

Tricks also keep dolphins from being bored. The third
It's hard work, but it's important!
thing trainers do is clean the tanks./

Point out to students that at this stage in the revising process, their goal is not to figure out how much they care about their topic. They chose their topic because it does interest them and because they do care about it. However, unless they have used words and phrases that show their interest, readers aren't going to believe that they care about their topic. This may be a good opportunity for students to participate in **peer responding** *(see below)* to get a better idea of how well they are conveying their level of interest to readers.

Practice Answers

- I like (to help people.)
- I love (sports.)
- I love (being in the middle of a blitz.)

Teaching Tip: Peer Responding

Before students participate in a peer responding session to evaluate the interest level of their writing voice, take time to review the basic guidelines for peer responding. Remind students that peer responding takes teamwork, and that both the writer and the responder have responsibilities.

For this session, the writer's job is to

- present the piece of writing,
- ask for comments and advice, and
- write down ideas that will help improve the voice of the essay.

The responder's job is to

- listen or read carefully,
- point out favorite parts of the writing, and

- ask questions that will help the writer improve the voice of the essay.

✳ Additional guidelines for peer responding can be found on PE pages 40–42.

Revising for Word Choice

Suggest that students add or set aside a section in their writing journal or portfolio for specific words. Tell them to provide at least one page each for nouns, verbs, adjectives, and adverbs and to create charts like the one shown here for each part of speech. Suggest that they set up the charts in two columns so that they can continually add to each chart as their writing experience and vocabulary increase.

✳ For more information about how to Use Specific Nouns, see PE page 410.

Practice Answers

1. guitarist
2. songs
3. trumpets
4. the drums
5. souvenirs

Point out that good writers always choose specific nouns, verbs, adjectives, and adverbs over general words because they know that specific language creates more vivid pictures in the reader's mind. To demonstrate this, ask students to read sentence 3 in the **Practice,** first with *horns* and then with *trumpets.* If they were asked to draw this sentence, which noun would help them draw the most accurate picture? (*trumpet*)

Revising for Word Choice

6 The words I use make my essay very clear, informative, and fun to read.

5 I use specific nouns and only the best modifiers.

4 I use specific nouns, but I should cut a few extra modifiers.

When you revise for *word choice,* you make sure you use specific nouns and modifiers (adjectives and adverbs). The rubric strip above will help you revise.

How can I use specific nouns?

You can replace general nouns with specific nouns to make your writing more informative. (Also see page 410.)

GENERAL NOUNS	singer	music	place	people
SPECIFIC NOUNS	soprano	jazz	concert hall	fans

Practice

For each sentence below, decide which noun in parentheses is more specific.

1. A rock band always has a lead (*musician, guitarist*).
2. Pop bands can play different (*things, songs*).
3. Some band members play (*horns, trumpets*).
4. If I were in a band, I would play (*an instrument, the drums*).
5. A band can sell (*stuff, souvenirs*) to the fans.

 Revise

Replace general nouns. Read your essay and look for nouns that are too general. Replace them to make your writing more informative.

Advanced Learners

Point out the general nouns *things* and *stuff* in the **Practice** sentences and emphasize that careful writers try not to use these particular words. To demonstrate their ineffectiveness, have students

• brainstorm equally vague synonyms for *things* and *stuff,* such as *objects, items, articles,* and *gadgets;* and

• create and perform a brief, humorous skit using all of these words in as many ways as possible.

3 I need to replace some general nouns and choose better modifiers.

2 Most of my nouns are general, and my modifiers are not well chosen.

1 I need help with my word choice.

How can I use the best modifiers?

The best modifiers (adjectives and adverbs) make your ideas clearer. Words like *really, very,* or *totally* are empty modifiers. If an idea is clear without the modifying word, remove the modifier.

Practice

Rewrite the following sentences, removing any empty modifiers.

1. I would be very excellent as a pop music performer.
2. I really have a lot of talent and am totally terrific on stage.
3. A pop star needs a very lovely voice and a really trendy look.
4. I totally imagine myself as a world-famous singer.

 Check your modifiers. Read your work and look for empty modifiers. Remove any that you find.

Revising in Action

The writer replaces a general noun and cuts an empty modifier.

> personality
> I have the right ~~stuff~~ to be a dolphin trainer. To
> begin with, I ~~totally~~ love dolphins. As a trainer, . . .

Wordiness is a common problem among young writers. However, most writers get extremely attached to their words and have a difficult time cutting anything. Provide additional guidance for eliminating wordiness. For example, besides looking for empty modifiers, suggest that they also look for other kinds of **unnecessary modifiers** *(see below)* in their essays as well.

Practice Answers

1. I would be excellent as a pop music performer.
2. I have a lot of talent and am terrific on stage.
3. A pop star needs a lovely voice and a trendy look.
4. I imagine myself as a world-famous singer.

Empty modifiers are often words like *totally*, a legitimate word when used correctly, that becomes an empty modifier when young people make it part of their vernacular and give it a new slang meaning. Many of these words fade in and out of fashion. If you are aware of other empty modifiers that have crept into your students' vocabulary, advise them to be on the lookout for these words as they revise.

Teaching Tip: Unnecessary Modifiers

Explain that the use of empty, unnecessary modifiers creates wordiness, which can bore the reader. Wordiness can make the reader think that the writer has nothing important to say and so is using a lot of unnecessary words just to fill the space. As students check to make sure that they have used the best modifiers, have them also check to make sure that they have not used the following kinds of unnecessary modifiers:

- Long strings of adjectives when one or two adjectives will do (I want to build the *best, most unique, most beautiful, biggest* houses.)
- Unnecessary adjectives that say what other words already say. (I'd like to stand at the top of a *tall* skyscraper.)

Advanced Learners

Challenge students to write on a blank overhead transparency sentences that have unnecessary adjectives, such as:

- She <u>whispered quietly</u> to her friend.
- Let's have an <u>afternoon</u> meeting at <u>2:00 p.m.</u>
- <u>Quickly</u>, he <u>raced</u> across the room.

Use the transparency to illustrate the second bullet in the Teaching Tip.

Revising for Sentence Fluency

Remind students that

- a simple sentence contains a subject and a predicate, and expresses a complete thought;
- a compound sentence is made up of two or more simple sentences joined by a comma and a coordinating conjunction; and
- in a compound sentence, the comma comes after the first main clause (or simple sentence) and before the coordinating conjunction, as shown in the sample.

✳ For more information about Compound Sentences, see PE page 443.

Practice Answers

Students may use different conjunctions.

1. Hot-air balloons are huge, <u>and</u> the baskets can carry 10 people.
2. The pilot controls altitude, <u>but</u> direction depends on the wind.
3. The pilot can make the balloon rise with heat, <u>or</u> he can release weights.
4. People like the gentle ride, <u>for</u> balloon rides are very quiet.

168

Revising for Sentence Fluency

6 My sentences are well written and flow smoothly. People will enjoy reading them.

5 My sentences flow smoothly, and I use compound and complex sentences.

4 Most of my sentences flow well, but I need to combine a few more short sentences.

When you revise for *sentence fluency,* you combine short, choppy sentences into compound or complex sentences. The rubric strip above can help you.

How can I write compound sentences?

You can write a compound sentence by joining two choppy sentences using a comma and a coordinating conjunction. (See page 443.)

Coordinating Conjunctions   and, but, or, nor, for, so, yet

SHORT, CHOPPY SENTENCES
  I like hot-air balloons. Someday I'll fly one.

COMPOUND SENTENCE
  I like hot-air balloons, and someday I'll fly one.

Practice

Combine each set of sentences using a comma and a coordinating conjunction: *and, but, or, nor, for, so,* or *yet.*

1. Hot-air balloons are huge. The baskets can carry 10 people.
2. The pilot controls altitude. Direction depends on the wind.
3. The pilot can make the balloon rise with heat. He can release weights.
4. People like the gentle ride. Balloon rides are very quiet.

 Revise   **Combine short, choppy sentences.** Look for short, choppy sentences and combine them into compound sentences.

3 Many of my sentences are short. I need to combine them.

2 All of my sentences are short. I need to combine most of them.

1 I need to use complete sentences.

How can I write complex sentences?

Another way to combine short, choppy sentences is to write a complex sentence. You can do this by adding a subordinating conjunction to one sentence. Use a comma after the clause with the conjunction if it begins the new sentence. (See page **444**.)

Some Subordinating Conjunctions after, although, because, before, if, since, though, unless, until, when, while

SHORT, CHOPPY SENTENCES
Hot-air balloon pilots enter festivals. They fly with many balloons.

COMPLEX SENTENCES
When hot-air balloon pilots enter festivals, they fly with many balloons.
Hot-air balloon pilots fly with many balloons when they enter festivals.

 Revise · **Write complex sentences.** Look for two short, choppy sentences to combine into a complex sentence.

Revising in Action

The writer makes a compound sentence from two sentences.

> but
> Tricks are used in shows. ⁀Some tricks actually help
> veterinarians keep the dolphins healthy. Tricks also . . .

When students are encouraged to combine short sentences into compound or complex sentences, they may become overzealous and combine ideas that aren't related and that should not be joined. Point out to students that sometimes it won't make sense to combine two short sentences. To see if two sentences should be joined into a complex sentence, suggest that they ask themselves these questions:

■ Are these two sentences about the same idea?

■ Does the idea in one sentence depend or rely on the idea in the other sentence?

■ Does the combined sentence make sense?

■ Does the combined sentence flow better than the two separate sentences?

✳ For more information about Complex Sentences, see PE page 444; and for information about Connecting with Conjunctions, see PE pages 429–430 and 600–601.

English Language Learners

Many students may be more familiar with coordinating conjunctions than with the subordinating conjunctions listed. Give students examples by

● sharing several writing samples that show how each subordinating conjunction is used correctly, and

● having students look for their use in other language activities during their day, such as in textbooks or independent reading books.

Have students use only the subordinating conjunctions that they thoroughly understand and can consistently use correctly.

Struggling Learners

To provide additional practice with compound and complex sentences, have students work with partners or in small groups to highlight examples in newspaper articles or grade-appropriate magazines. When finished, have each student read aloud one example and ask listeners to classify it as compound or complex.

Revising Using a Checklist

Revising checklists follow all of the major writing assignments in this book. If you haven't already done so, establish a process for using the revising checklist to ensure that students benefit from its use, and to avoid having them automatically check off each item without thought.

- Have students use the checklist only after they have addressed all of the issues for each of the traits.
- Have students exchange revised essays in groups. Assign each member of the group a different trait, and have them check the essay for their assigned trait, offering useful comments for improvement.
- Have partners ask the questions on the checklist to the writer. If the writer responds "yes," the writer also has to provide examples from the essay that support the response.

Revising Using a Checklist

Revise

Check your revising. Number a piece of paper from 1 to 10. If you can answer "yes" to a question, put a check mark after that number. If not, continue to work with that part of your essay.

Ideas

_____ **1.** Do I have a clear focus statement?

_____ **2.** Do I include topic sentences in my middle paragraphs?

_____ **3.** Do I use explanations and examples?

Organization

_____ **4.** Have I checked my overall organization?

_____ **5.** Do I put my most important explanation first (or last)?

Voice

_____ **6.** Does my voice sound knowledgeable and interested?

Word Choice

_____ **7.** Have I used specific nouns?

_____ **8.** Have I chosen the best adjectives and adverbs?

Sentence Fluency

_____ **9.** Have I included some compound sentences?

_____ **10.** Have I included some complex sentences?

Revise

Make a clean copy. When you finish making changes to your essay, make a clean copy for editing.

Editing

Once you have revised your essay, editing is the next step in the writing process. When you edit, you check to make sure you have followed the rules of English. These rules are called "conventions."

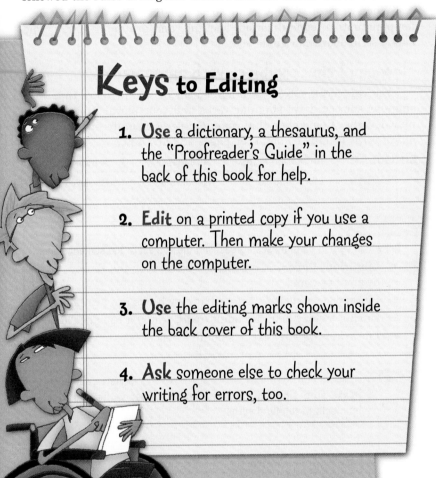

Keys to Editing

1. **Use** a dictionary, a thesaurus, and the "Proofreader's Guide" in the back of this book for help.

2. **Edit** on a printed copy if you use a computer. Then make your changes on the computer.

3. **Use** the editing marks shown inside the back cover of this book.

4. **Ask** someone else to check your writing for errors, too.

Editing **Keys to Editing**

Remind students that during the editing stage, they have a chance to find and correct errors in

■ punctuation,
■ capitalization,
■ spelling, and
■ grammar.

The Keys to Editing list lays out the process students will be guided through on PE pages 172–174.

Share editing tricks you use to make sure you don't miss any mistakes. Then invite students to share their own tricks for editing. Ideas that may be shared include the following:

■ using a frame (a narrow rectangle cut-out on a piece of stiff paper) to pass over each word to check for spelling
■ looking for each type of mistake, one at a time (such as going through the whole essay to check that every sentence begins with a capital letter and ends with punctuation)
■ marking different kinds of mistakes in different colors to find them easily
■ reading the essay backward so that the meaning of the sentences is not a distraction

English Language Learners

If students are accustomed to another alphabet, give them a copy of the English alphabet (a desk sticker, for example) to aid them when using a dictionary or thesaurus. Ensure that all students are able to look up words in a dictionary before beginning to edit. Try looking up several words as a group for practice.

Editing for Conventions

Check that students understand the difference between singular and plural subjects and verbs by asking them to point out examples in their essays. If there is any confusion, provide additional instruction on subject-verb agreement and more examples before assigning the **Practice** activity.

✳ For more information about Subject-Verb Agreement, see PE pages 419 and 438–439.

Practice Answers

1. organize
2. tell
3. reads
4. are

Have students share their answers and explain how they knew the correct answer.

172

Editing for Conventions

| **6** I accurately use conventions that make my writing exact and clear. | **5** I have few errors in punctuation, spelling, or grammar. | **4** I have several errors in punctuation, spelling, or grammar. |

When you edit your writing for *conventions,* you need to check for punctuation, capitalization, spelling, and grammar errors. The rubric strip above can guide you.

How can I check subject-verb agreement?

You can check subject-verb agreement by making sure that your singular subjects have singular verbs and your plural subjects have plural verbs. Remember that *singular verbs* usually end in *s,* but *plural verbs* usually do not. (See pages **438** and **439**.)

| SINGULAR | A librarian helps. | A reader asks. | A book informs. |
| PLURAL | Librarians help. | Readers ask. | Books inform. |

Practice

Tell which verb in parentheses agrees with the subject of the sentence.

1. Librarians *(organize, organizes)* books using the Dewey decimal system.
2. Library journals *(tell, tells)* what new books are available.
3. During a story hour, an adult *(read, reads)* a book out loud.
4. Librarians *(is, are)* experts on all kinds of books.

 Edit **Check your subject-verb agreement.** Review your essay. Make sure singular subjects have singular verbs and plural subjects have plural verbs.

English Language Learners

Subject-verb agreement is often a difficult concept for non-native English speakers. Teach a mini lesson to students with difficulty in this area, not just about the third-person subject, but also for first person singular and plural (I, we) and second person (you). Have students work in pairs to edit for subject-verb agreement in their writing.

Struggling Learners

Explain that two words commonly confused in subject-verb agreement are *everyone* and *everybody.* Although the words refer to more than one person, they are considered singular subjects. For example:

- <u>Everyone reads</u> for twenty minutes after school.
- <u>Everybody is coming</u> on the field trip.

Explaining a Career **173**

| **3** My errors may confuse the reader. I need to fix them. | **2** Many errors make my essay hard to read. I need to correct them. | **1** I need to correct numerous errors in my writing. |

How can I be sure my verb tenses are correct?

Check your verbs to make sure you don't change tenses accidentally. There are three basic tenses. Most of your essay should be written in the present tense. However, if you give examples that happened in the past, past tense is correct. Also, when you talk about something that hasn't happened yet, you will use future tense. (See page 418.)

Present	*Past*	*Future*
carry	carried	will carry

Practice

Rewrite each sentence below, first in the past tense and then in the future tense.

1. Librarians sort books and place them on the shelves.
2. People with overdue books pay fines.
3. Libraries organize fiction books by the author's last name.
4. Reference librarians help students find articles.

Editing in Action

The writer fixes subject-verb agreement and verb tense errors.

> Training dolphins ~~are~~ *is* an important job. . . . At night,
> I even ~~dreamed~~ *dream* about swimming with dolphins. . . .

Remind students that tense tells when an action takes place.

■ Present tense: the action is happening now.
■ Past tense: the action already happened.
■ Future tense: the action is going to happen. The action has not happened yet.

Review how to **form the past tense** *(see below)* and future tense of most regular verbs.

Practice Answers

1. Librarians sorted books and placed them on the shelves. Librarians will sort books and (will) place them on the shelves.
2. People with overdue books paid fines. People with overdue books will pay fines.
3. Libraries organized fiction books by the author's last name. Libraries will organize fiction books by the author's last name.
4. Reference librarians helped students find articles. Reference librarians will help students find articles.

Teaching Tip: Forming Past Tense

Students may benefit from a refresher on forming the past tense of verbs before they complete the **Practice** activity.

● Remind students that most regular verbs form the past tense by adding -d or –ed to the present tense. Invite volunteers to write the past tense of the following regular verbs on the board or on chart paper: *walk, play, dance, learn, look, need, talk.*

● Remind students that some verbs are irregular. They use different words to form the past tense. Invite volunteers to write the past tense of the following irregular verbs: *write, know, say, make, drink, sing.*

✱ Students can use a dictionary or the list of common irregular verbs on PE page 588 to check the past tense form of irregular verbs.

English Language Learners

Discriminating different tenses may be a challenge to some students. Review the rules of when each tense is used and provide more practice with changing sentences from one tense to another, as in the **Practice** activity. Also have students read several passages from books and decide what tense is used each sentence.

Editing Using a Checklist

Give students a few moments to look over the Proofreader's Guide (PE pages 478–605). Throughout the year, they can refer to the instruction, rules, and examples to clarify any checklist items or to resolve questions about their own writing.

Remind students that a computer spell-checker will not catch words that are typed incorrectly but that form actual words, such as *sons* instead of *songs*, or are actual words that are used incorrectly, such as *to* instead of *too* or *two*.

Adding a Title

Ask students what they think a good title should do (grab the reader's attention and suggest what the essay is about).

Point out to students that some writers use a working title as they write. Others think of a title as they are writing and revising. Still others wait until they are done writing to think of a title. If students don't already have a title in mind, encourage them to try all three suggestions for creating a title (name the topic, use an expression, repeat a sound) before deciding on one.

Editing Using a Checklist

Edit

Check your editing. Number a piece of paper from 1 to 10. If you can answer "yes" to a question, put a check mark after that number. If not, continue to edit for that convention.

Conventions

PUNCTUATION

_____ **1.** Do I use end punctuation after all my sentences?

_____ **2.** Do I use commas after introductory word groups?

_____ **3.** Do I use commas in all my compound sentences?

CAPITALIZATION

_____ **4.** Do I start all my sentences with capital letters?

_____ **5.** Do I capitalize all names (proper nouns)?

SPELLING

_____ **6.** Have I spelled all my words correctly?

_____ **7.** Have I checked for words my spell-checker might miss?

GRAMMAR

_____ **8.** Do all my subjects and verbs agree?

_____ **9.** Are my verb tenses correct?

_____ **10.** Do I use the right word *(to, too, two)*?

Adding a Title

Here are some suggestions for writing a title.

- Name the topic: **Being a Dolphin Trainer**
- Use an expression: **Jumping Through Hoops**
- Repeat a sound: **Dreaming About Dolphins**

Publishing

It's time to proofread your essay and make a neat final copy to share. You can also turn your writing into a résumé, a skit, or a poster. (See the suggestions below.)

Presentation

- Use blue or black ink and write neatly.
- Write your name in the upper left corner of page 1.
- Skip a line and center your title; skip another line and start writing.
- Indent every paragraph and leave a one-inch margin on all sides.
- Write your last name and the page number in the upper right corner of every page after the first one.

Create a Résumé

Pretend you are applying for the job you chose. Write your name and address and then list the skills you have that make you right for the job.

Perform a Skit

Team up with a partner and act out a skit about the jobs you chose.

Make a Poster

Create an informative poster about the career you chose. Make sure to include the main duties of the job.

Make a final copy. Follow your teacher's instructions or use the guidelines above to format your essay. (If you are using a computer, see pages 44–46.) Create a clean final copy of your essay and carefully proofread it.

Publishing

Another idea for publishing is to have students present their essays as part of a Career Week event. If possible, students can extend invitations to the people who inspired their career or job choice to come and speak about actual job experiences.

For students who choose to create a résumé, provide samples of simple résumés for them to use as models.

Rubric for Expository Writing

Remind students that a rubric is a chart that helps you evaluate your writing.

- The rubrics in this book are based on a six-point scale, in which a score of 6 indicates an amazing piece of writing and a score of 1 means the writing is incomplete and not ready to be assessed.

- Explain that the purpose of the rubric is to help students break down the assessment process by evaluating each of the six traits individually—ideas, organization, voice, word choice, sentence fluency, and conventions.

- Point out that rubrics are also helpful during the writing process. They can guide you whenever you write because they tell you what elements to include in your writing and how to present them.

- Explain to students that they will most likely have different ratings for the traits. For example, they may give themselves a 5 for ideas but a 4 for organization.

✻ Four- and five-point rubrics for expository writing can be found on TE pages 625 and 628.

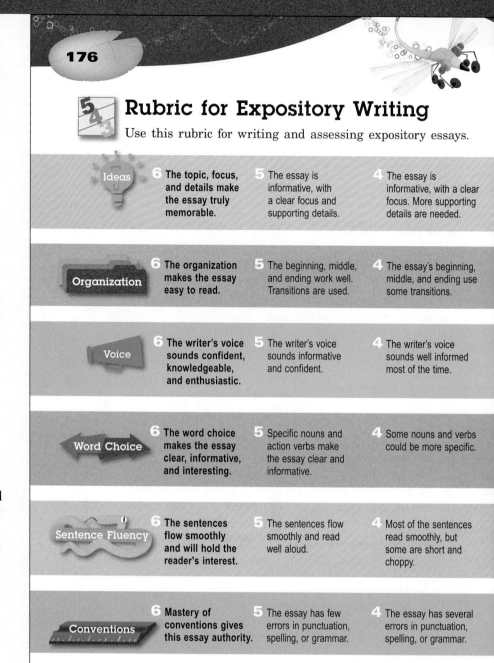

176

Rubric for Expository Writing

Use this rubric for writing and assessing expository essays.

Ideas	**6** The topic, focus, and details make the essay truly memorable.	**5** The essay is informative, with a clear focus and supporting details.	**4** The essay is informative, with a clear focus. More supporting details are needed.
Organization	**6** The organization makes the essay easy to read.	**5** The beginning, middle, and ending work well. Transitions are used.	**4** The essay's beginning, middle, and ending use some transitions.
Voice	**6** The writer's voice sounds confident, knowledgeable, and enthusiastic.	**5** The writer's voice sounds informative and confident.	**4** The writer's voice sounds well informed most of the time.
Word Choice	**6** The word choice makes the essay clear, informative, and interesting.	**5** Specific nouns and action verbs make the essay clear and informative.	**4** Some nouns and verbs could be more specific.
Sentence Fluency	**6** The sentences flow smoothly and will hold the reader's interest.	**5** The sentences flow smoothly and read well aloud.	**4** Most of the sentences read smoothly, but some are short and choppy.
Conventions	**6** Mastery of conventions gives this essay authority.	**5** The essay has few errors in punctuation, spelling, or grammar.	**4** The essay has several errors in punctuation, spelling, or grammar.

English Language Learners

Help students to avoid getting discouraged if their final scores are not as high as those of some of their English-proficient peers. Remind them that by using a rubric on all of their assignments for the year, they will be able to track their progress not only in writing but in their English acquisition.

Explaining a Career **177**

3 The focus of the essay needs to be clearer, and more supporting details are needed.

2 The topic needs to be narrowed or expanded. Many more supporting details are needed.

1 The topic has been chosen but needs to be developed.

3 The middle needs transitions and a paragraph for each main point.

2 The beginning, middle, and ending all run together. Paragraphs are needed.

1 The essay is hard to follow.

3 The writer sometimes sounds unsure.

2 The writer sounds unsure in many parts.

1 The writer needs to sound much more confident.

3 Too many general words are used. Specific nouns and verbs are needed.

2 General or missing words make this essay hard to understand.

1 The writer needs help finding specific words.

3 Many short, choppy sentences need to be rewritten to make the essay read smoothly.

2 Many sentences are choppy or incomplete.

1 Many sentences are difficult to follow.

3 Some errors confuse the reader.

2 Many errors make the essay confusing and hard to read.

1 Help is needed to make corrections.

Evaluating an Expository Essay

Ask students if they agree with the sample self-assessment on PE page 179. If they agree with the criticisms, ask them to suggest improvements based on the comments in the self-assessment. If they disagree with any comment, ask them to explain why.

Possible suggestions:

Ideas add explanations—explain reason for wanting to be a pilot that flies into volcanoes

Organization order of importance—students may disagree that ideas are not in order of importance or may feel that they are equally important

Voice add more facts—about helicopters and pilot training

Word Choice remove empty modifiers—delete *very* and *ever* in first paragraph, and *no problem* in the third paragraph

Sentence Fluency create smoother flow—use a variety of sentence beginnings instead of *they* or *helicopter pilots*

Conventions correct misused words—in third sentence, *There* should be *They're*; in last sentence *your* should be *you're*

Evaluating an Expository Essay

Read through Charley's essay, focusing on its strengths and weaknesses. (The essay contains several errors.)

Call Me "Copter Charley"

"Choppa, choppa, choppa, choppa!" What's that sound? It's a helicopter. There the very coolest flying machines ever. I want to be a helicopter pilot.

Helicopter pilots have many different duties. Some work for the military. They go on secret missions and fly to places where planes can't go. Other helicopter pilots work for the police. They chase down criminals. Once the "Eye in the Sky" spots people, they don't get away. I want to be a pilot that flies into volcanoes.

I could fly a helicopter, no problem. First of all, helicopter pilots need good eyesight. I have a perfect 20/20 on my school sight test. Also, pilots need nerves of steel. Whenever my friends and I play flinch, I win. Third, helicopter pilots need to study hard, and I'm on the A-B honor roll. Last of all, pilots should not get motion sick. I never get dizzy on the merry-go-round.

So, sometime when you want to fly into a volcano, give me a call. Maybe you'd rather join me for one of my high-speed police chases! You can do just about anything when your a helicopter pilot!

English Language Learners

Define the following terms (or show pictures) from the sample essay before reading:

- helicopter (a machine that flies) *picture recommended*
- pilot (person who drives or flies a machine)
- military (government armed forces)
- criminals (people who have committed a crime)

- volcanoes (mountains that erupt lava) *picture recommended*
- eyesight (vision)
- nerves of steel (nerves that are strong and steady)
- flinch (pull back quickly)
- merry-go-round (mechanical circular ride) *picture recommended*

Explaining a Career **179**

Student Self-Assessment

Charley rated his writing. Under each trait, he wrote a positive comment and then something he could improve on. (He used the rubric and the number scale on pages 176–177.)

Ideas

4 Ideas
1. I have a great beginning.
2. I included some information that I didn't explain.

Organization

5 Organization
1. I used transitions in my last two paragraphs.
2. I forgot to list my ideas in order of importance.

Voice

4 Voice
1. I sound excited about my topic.
2. I don't always sound knowledgeable.

Word Choice

4 Word Choice
1. I used specific nouns.
2. I used some modifiers I didn't need.

Sentence Fluency

5 Sentence Fluency
1. I have combined my short, choppy sentences.
2. Some parts don't read smoothly.

Conventions

4 Conventions
1. I spelled my words right.
2. I have trouble with there and they're and your and you're.

Use the rubric. Rate your essay using the rubric shown on pages 176–177. On your own paper, list the six traits. Leave room after each trait to write one strength and one area that needs work. Then choose a number (from 1 to 6) to rate each trait.

Student Self-Assessment

To give students additional practice with evaluating an expository essay, use a blank assessment sheet (TE page 644) and one or both of the **benchmark papers** listed in the Benchmark Papers box below. You can use an overhead transparency while students refer to their own copies made from the copy masters. For your benefit a completed assessment sheet is provided for each benchmark paper.

Struggling Learners

To further analyze Charley's self-assessment, read aloud each comment and have students locate a specific example, such as:

- I have a great beginning. *"Choppa, choppa, choppa, choppa!"* (The onomatopoeia catches the reader's attention.)

- I included some information I didn't explain. *I want to be a pilot that flies into volcanoes.* (Why would a pilot fly into a volcano?)

Benchmark Papers

- Something You Can sink Your Teeth Into, TR 3A–3C

- Something You Can sink Your Teeth Into, TE page 635–637

- Fluffy, TR 4A–4B

- Fluffy, TE page 638–639

Reflecting on Your Writing

Students should use comments you've written on their final essay to answer questions 1 and 2 with more validity.

Have students date their reflection sheet and save it in their writing portfolio with other reflections they have completed this year. Encourage students to look back on them from time to time to check their progress as writers.

Point out that some writers find it helpful to look at past reflections when beginning a new writing assignment. Since reflections often include specific remarks about areas that need improvement, writers know to pay special attention to that particular area as they write.

Reflecting on Your Writing

Now that you've finished your expository essay, take a moment to reflect on the job you have done. On your own paper, complete each sentence starter below.

> Take a moment to reflect on the essay you wrote!

My Expository Essay

1. The best part of my essay is . . .

2. The part that still needs work is . . .

3. The main thing I learned about expository writing is . . .

4. Next time I write an expository essay, I would like to . . .

Expository Writing
Across the Curriculum

Sometimes expository writing answers the question "Can you explain that?" For example, your science book might explain how to make a pinhole camera. Your math book might explain what division is. Those are both forms of expository writing.

Throughout your school day, textbooks give you the explanations you need. With practice, you can develop your expository writing skill . . . and explain things yourself!

Mini Index

- **Science:** Writing a How-To Essay
- **Math:** Explaining a Math Concept
- **Practical Writing:** Taking Two-Column Notes
- **Assessment:** Writing for Assessment

Across the Curriculum

Objectives
- apply what has been learned about expository writing to other curriculum areas
- practice writing for assessment

The lessons on the following pages provide samples of expository writing students might do in different content areas. The first lesson guides students through the steps of the writing process in science. The second and third lessons provide models and writing tips for expository writing in math and in taking notes.

Assigning these forms of writing will depend on
- the skill level of your students,
- the subject matter they are studying in different content areas, and
- the writing goals of your school, district, or state.

Materials

Social studies article or text (TE p. 189)

Copy Masters/ Transparencies

Time line (TE p. 184)

Science:
Writing a How-To Essay

Have students read the sample essay and tell how it is like the expository essay they wrote about a career, and how it is different. This will help ease any anxiety they may have about writing a how-to essay while preparing them for the task.

Ways it is alike:
- It has a clear focus statement that shows the writer is interested and cares about the topic.
- It uses special terms and specific nouns to help the reader understand the topic.
- Its purpose is to explain.
- It has a strong ending.
- It contains only details that help explain the topic.

Ways it is different:
- It lists materials and tools.
- It organizes steps in sequence, in the order they should be followed.
- It does not use extra examples.
- It uses the second person pronouns *you* and *your* instead of first person pronouns *I* and *me*.
- Most of the sentences are imperative sentences (commands).

Science:
Writing a How-To Essay

A how-to essay explains how to do something. In this essay, a student gives step-by-step instructions for making a pinhole camera.

BEGINNING

The beginning gives the focus statement (underlined).

How to Make a Pinhole Camera

If you like taking pictures, you might like making a pinhole camera. You need just a few supplies and some patience. <u>Making a pinhole camera is easy and fun for camera lovers.</u>

Start by gathering your supplies. You need a round oatmeal carton, black spray paint, black paper, tape, scissors, and a needle. You also need film paper from a camera store.

MIDDLE

The middle lists materials and leads the reader through each step.

Next, get your oatmeal carton ready. Spray-paint it black, inside and out. Then poke the needle through the middle of the bottom. This hole is your "lens." Cut out a small piece of black paper and tape it over the lens so it can flip up. This is your "shutter." Last, go into a dark room and tape your film paper inside the box top. Seal the box tight.

Now you can take a picture! Go outside on a sunny day and prop up your camera to take a picture. Open the shutter for two seconds (count 1,000-one, 1,000-two) and close it again. Then take your camera to the camera store to develop your film or learn to develop your own film.

ENDING

The ending leaves the reader with a final thought.

Experiment with your camera. See what great pictures you can take. The only thing more fun than making a pinhole camera is using it!

Prewriting **Choosing a Topic**

First, you need to pick a topic for your explanation, or how-to essay. A cluster can help you think about things you know how to do.

Cluster

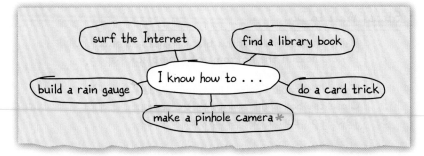

surf the Internet
find a library book
I know how to . . .
build a rain gauge
do a card trick
make a pinhole camera *

Create a cluster. Write *I know how to . . .* and circle it. Then write things you know how to do. Choose a topic that has steps.

Listing Materials and Tools

Now you should list the necessary materials and tools.

List

Materials	Tools
oatmeal carton	scissors
black spray paint	sewing needle
black paper	
film paper	
tape	

Create a list. Write *Materials* and *Tools* at the top of a piece of paper. Under them, list materials that are needed.

Prewriting **Choosing a Topic**

Making a pinhole camera is a unique and fun idea. Most students are going to want to write about equally interesting and fun ideas, and, as a result, may be tempted to choose a topic that they have only a vague understanding of and that is beyond their ability to explain.

Encourage students to write only things in their cluster that they know how to do because they have done them, and that they are certain they will be able to explain.

Prewriting
List Materials and Tools

Tell students to list as many of the necessary materials and tools that they can think of now. It's possible, that when they start planning the steps of their how-to, they will realize that they have left out one or two materials, which they can then add to the list.

Prewriting **Organizing Your Steps**

Distribute photocopies of the reproducible time line (TE page 648) and have students use it to organize their steps.

To make sure students understand how to use a time line and how to add in forgotten steps, model the process, using the time line transparency (TR 10) and an overhead projector. Use a simple topic that most students will know, such as making a sandwich, and organize the steps. Be sure to "forget" one of the steps so that you can show students how to add it to the time line later.

Prewriting
Writing a Focus Statement

Students' focus statements probably won't vary that much in style from the sample focus statement. In fact, if students wish they can use the sample focus statement and **sentence modeling** (*see below*) to create their focus statement.

Prewriting **Organizing Your Steps**

Next, write down the steps (include at least three) in the order you do them. A time line can help you organize your steps.

Time Line

Steps	What to Do
1	Paint the oatmeal carton black inside and out.
2	Poke a hole in the bottom and tape black paper over it.
3	Tape film paper inside the top (in a dark room).
4	Close the box tight and keep it closed.
5	Take a picture (two-second exposure).

 Prewrite **Create a time line.** Write *Steps* and *What to Do* on a piece of paper. Then list each step in order. If you forget a step, write it beside the others and draw a line to show where it goes.

Prewriting **Writing a Focus Statement**

Your focus statement names your topic and gives the reader a reason to try it. Here is a formula for writing your focus statement.

topic		reason to try it		a strong focus statement
how to make a pinhole camera	+	easy and fun for camera lovers	=	Making a pinhole camera is easy and fun for camera lovers.

 Prewrite **Write your focus statement.** Use the formula above. Write several versions until you have a good focus statement.

Teaching Tip: Sentence Modeling

Explain to students that copying the pattern of sentences by other writers is called sentence modeling, and that it's a good way to learn about writing sentences. Have students copy the sample focus statement in a single line across their paper. They may have to turn their paper sideways to accommodate the text. Then have them divide the sample sentence into chunks as shown here:

Making a pinhole camera | is easy and fun | for camera lovers.

Have students write their focus statement underneath the sample focus statement. Tell them to write the following:

- a phrase about your topic that matches *Making a pinhole camera*, for example, *Doing a card trick*
- adjectives for the topic to replace *is easy and fun,* for example, *is simple and entertaining*
- a phrase for the audience to match *for camera lovers,* for example, *for magic lovers*

You now have a complete focus statement.

Writing in Science   185

Writing Creating Your First Draft

The main parts of your first draft should do these things:

- **Beginning:** Introduce your topic and state your focus.
- **Middle:** Describe materials and explain each step.
- **Ending:** Encourage the reader to try the process.

Write your first draft. Use your list and time line from pages 183 and 184 to guide your writing.

Revising Improving Your Writing

Next, you'll probably need to make some changes.

- **Ideas** Is my focus clear? Have I listed materials and all the steps?
- **Organization** Are my steps in the right order?
- **Voice** Do I sound interested?
- **Word Choice** Do I use specific nouns and active verbs?
- **Sentence Fluency** Do my sentences read smoothly?

Revise your work. Use the questions above to make changes in your first draft. Then make a clean copy for editing.

Editing Checking for Conventions

It's also important to follow the rules of English.

- **Conventions** Have I checked for punctuation, capitalization, spelling, and grammar errors?

Edit your work. Edit your essay using the question above. Then make a clean final copy and proofread it.

Writing Creating Your First Draft

Suggest that students cross off items in their materials list and time line as they use them in their draft. This will make it easy for them to see if they have left out any important details from their explanations.

Have students look back at the sample essay on PE page 182 to refresh their memory about the use of commands (Cut out a small piece. . . Go outside. . .) and the second person pronouns *you* and *your* to explain the process.

Revising Improving Your Writing

Students may assume readers have as much knowledge as they have, and so they don't have to explain every little step in the process. As a result, students may omit details readers need to understand the process. To make sure all of the steps are clear and complete, have students exchange papers with partners who can identify places where details are missing.

Editing Checking for Conventions

Tell students to pay particular attention to the spelling of special terms, and if they are unsure of a word's spelling, to check it in the dictionary.

Struggling Learners

Remind students to use transition words when writing a how-to essay so that readers can easily move from step to step. For example, in *How to Make a Pinhole Camera*, the writer prefaces instructions with words such as *start, next, now, then, last,* and *also.*

Math: Explaining a Math Concept

Ask students to point out two places in Josie's explanation where she connects division to her everyday life (dividing her room, cutting up pizza). Point out to students that by including these kinds of details, Josie adds interest to her math explanation. She also shows that she understands math is not just a subject she studies in school. Math is a real part of her everyday life.

Have students point out the sentences in the explanation that the drawing clarifies (If you divide them into 2 equal groups . . ., If you divide the 24 lines into 4 equal groups . . .)

Math: Explaining a Math Concept

Writing about a concept you learn in math class can often help you understand it better. In this example, Josie explained division.

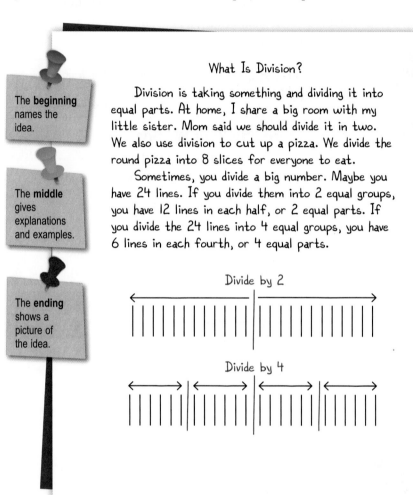

The **beginning** names the idea.

The **middle** gives explanations and examples.

The **ending** shows a picture of the idea.

What Is Division?

Division is taking something and dividing it into equal parts. At home, I share a big room with my little sister. Mom said we should divide it in two. We also use division to cut up a pizza. We divide the round pizza into 8 slices for everyone to eat.

Sometimes, you divide a big number. Maybe you have 24 lines. If you divide them into 2 equal groups, you have 12 lines in each half, or 2 equal parts. If you divide the 24 lines into 4 equal groups, you have 6 lines in each fourth, or 4 equal parts.

Divide by 2

Divide by 4

Writing in Math **187**

WRITING TIPS

Before you write . . .

- **Choose a math concept.**
  Use a math concept or process you've studied or the concept your teacher gives you.
- **Talk about the concept.**
  List the steps you need to explain and then explain them to a partner. Jot down some of the thoughts from your discussion.

During your writing . . .

- **Define the concept or process.**
  Write an opening sentence that defines the concept.
- **Share examples.**
  Tell how the concept or process can be used in daily life. Use examples to help the reader understand the concept.
- **Make a math picture.**
  Give another example and use a math picture to explain it.

After you've written a first draft . . .

- **Edit your work.**
  Check for errors in punctuation, capitalization, spelling, and grammar.

> Explain a math concept or process. Follow the tips above and remember to include a drawing.

Writing Tips

Choose a math concept for students to explain. Give students the option of selecting this concept as a topic, or of choosing a concept of their own. They can look in their math book or at past math tests to find a concept that they are certain they understand.

Emphasize that any drawings students include in their math explanation must help to make an idea clearer for the reader. Students should not include drawings that are just for decoration.

English Language Learners

Allow students to write about the math concept of their choice so that they can focus only on their language and writing skills and not on their math knowledge as well. This assignment may be very difficult if students have limited math knowledge and limited vocabulary about a topic. In that case, you will need to provide both math concept support and a list of well-defined vocabulary in order for students to be able to describe the topic well.

Struggling Learners

To help students choose a topic, make a chart together that shows various math concepts and two examples of how each one can be used in daily life. For example:

- perimeter – choosing a rug size, sectioning off a vegetable garden
- decimals – adding money, recording body temperature

Practical Writing:
Taking Two-Column Notes

Explain that two-column notes can help students in a variety of ways. For example, they can help students

■ remember important facts and details for a test,

■ organize ideas for an expository essay, and

■ break down difficult or challenging information into an easy-to-read format, which makes it easier to understand.

Remind students that the main idea is what a piece of writing is mostly about. To find the main idea of a passage, they should check to see what all or most of the sentences in the passage are about. They can also look for a topic sentence that directly states the main idea.

188

Practical Writing:
Taking Two-Column Notes

Being able to take notes will help you in your classes. In the sample below, Mark took notes while studying a book about his state's history.

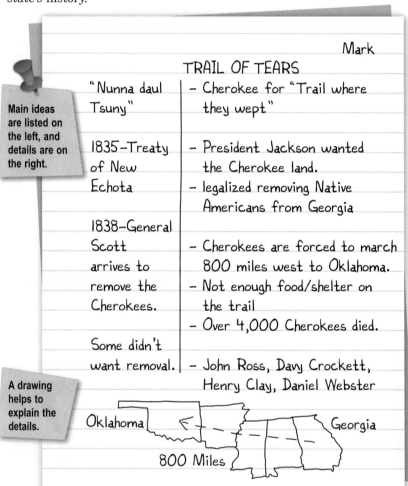

Mark

TRAIL OF TEARS

Main ideas are listed on the left, and details are on the right.

"Nunna daul Tsuny"	– Cherokee for "Trail where they wept"
1835–Treaty of New Echota	– President Jackson wanted the Cherokee land. – legalized removing Native Americans from Georgia
1838–General Scott arrives to remove the Cherokees.	– Cherokees are forced to march 800 miles west to Oklahoma. – Not enough food/shelter on the trail – Over 4,000 Cherokees died.
Some didn't want removal.	– John Ross, Davy Crockett, Henry Clay, Daniel Webster

A drawing helps to explain the details.

Oklahoma — 800 Miles — Georgia

English Language Learners

In order for students to understand the examples of two-column notes, you may need to give some background about the Trail of Tears if students have not studied it. Explain that it was when the U.S. government ordered a nation of Native Americans to move from their homeland. They were forced to walk many miles across the country, and many of the people died along the way.

Practical Writing **189**

WRITING TIPS

Before you write . . .

- **Create a heading.**
  Write your topic heading at the top of your paper.
- **Divide your paper into two columns.**
  Create a narrower column on the left.
- **Write neatly.** You must be able to read your notes later.

During your writing . . .

- **Write the main ideas on the left side.**
  Leave room between each main idea so that you have plenty of room to fit the details on the right side.
- **Write the details on the right side.**
  Use words and phrases instead of complete sentences.
- **Use drawings.**
  Add pictures to your notes to make information clear.

After you've written . . .

- **Review your facts.**
  Be sure the facts are correct and complete.
- **Write any questions you still have.**
  Jot down questions in your notes. Then check your book or ask your teacher for help to find the answers.
- **Use your notes to help you study.**
  Read over your notes before a test. Have a friend or family member ask you questions from your notes.

Take notes. Use the tips above as you take notes in your classes.

Writing Tips

Have students take two-column notes as part of a social studies class assignment or in preparation for a social studies test.

- Divide students into groups.
- Assign the same section of a social studies text to each group, or distribute a social studies article to each group.
- Have students work together to discuss the reading and to create their two-column notes.
- Encourage students to add drawings to their notes. Remind them to include only drawings that make ideas clearer, and not to include any decorative art. Examples of useful drawings would be maps, charts, and diagrams.
- Display the completed notes in the classroom so students can compare notes.

Writing for Assessment

If your students must take school, district, or state assessments this year, focus on the writing form on which they will be tested.

Help students recall the goals for writing an expository essay (PE page 144). Then suggest that they look to see if the writer of the sample essay achieved these goals:

- a clear focus statement
- a beginning that grabs the reader's attention
- middle paragraphs that explain the topic with explanations and examples
- a strong, thoughtful ending
- an interested, knowledgeable voice
- the use of specific nouns and special terms

Writing for Assessment

Some writing tests include prompts that ask you to explain something or share information. This sample expository prompt asks the student to write an essay.

Expository Prompt

Most people have a favorite object. Write an essay naming your favorite thing and explaining why it is your favorite.

> Basketball
> well made | gift from dad
> helps me stay fit

The beginning gives the focus statement (underlined).

My dad's favorite thing is his cell phone because of all its functions. My brother's favorite thing is his stereo because he loves loud music. <u>My favorite thing is my basketball.</u>

First of all, my basketball is really well made. It has a cover of orange leather, like a regulation NBA ball. It feels great, and I love the smell of the leather. The extra-wide channels give me a great grip. The sound it makes bouncing on the cement and on the backboard is like music to me. The ball even has Yao Ming's signature on it, and he's my favorite player.

The middle gives important details.

My basketball also helps me stay fit. Instead of sitting in front of the TV, I go outside to shoot hoops for hours. I also go one-on-one with my brother. I feel good after a fast game.

Still, the best thing about my basketball is that my dad gave it to me. We play together whenever I spend a weekend with him. The rest of the time, that basketball makes me feel like he's still with me. Dad says if I keep studying and practicing, I might get a college scholarship just like he did.

The **ending** wraps up the explanation.

My basketball is my favorite thing for a lot of reasons. It's well made, it helps me stay in shape, and it's from my dad. When I feel that leather and hear that special bounce sound, I start dreaming about making three-pointers as my dad shouts from the bleachers.

Respond to the reading. Answer the questions below about the response you just read.

- **Ideas** (1) What is the focus of the writer's response? (2) What details support the focus?

- **Organization** (3) How does the writer introduce the topic? (4) How does he restate the topic in the ending?

- **Voice & Word Choice** (5) What sentences show the writer's strong feelings? (6) What key words from the prompt also appear in the essay?

Respond to the reading.

Answers

Ideas **1.** The writer's focus is about his favorite thing, his basketball.
2. He likes his basketball because it is well made, it helps him stay fit, and it was a gift from his father.

Organization 3. He begins by talking about his father's favorite thing and his brother's favorite thing, which leads to his favorite thing, his basketball.
4. He restates his focus statement, and then he sums up the three reasons he likes his basketball, which he explains in greater detail in the middle paragraphs.

Voice & Word Choice 5. Possible responses:

- It feels great, and I love the smell of the leather.
- The extra-wide channels give me a great grip.
- The sound it makes bouncing . . . like music to me.
- That basketball makes me feel like he's still with me.

6. favorite thing

Advanced Learners

Challenge students to respond to the sample prompt from the point of view of a fairy tale character. For example, they can write about

- Red Riding Hood's cape,
- the golden goose Jack acquired from the top of the beanstalk, or
- Cinderella's glass slipper.

Invite students to illustrate and compile their essays into a book to keep in the classroom or school library for students to enjoy.

Writing Tips

Point out that students must approach writing-on-demand assignments differently from open-ended writing assignments and that timed writing creates pressures for everyone.

Expository Prompts

To teach students who must take timed assessments how to approach their writing, allow them the same amount of time to write their response essay as they will be allotted on school, district, or state assessments. Break down each part of the process into clear chunks of time. For example, you might give students

- 15 minutes for note taking and planning,
- 20 minutes for writing, and
- 10 minutes for editing and proof-reading.

Tell students when time is up for each section. Start the assignment at the top of the hour or at the half-hour to make it easier for students to keep track of the time.

If your state, district, or school requires students to use and submit a graphic organizer as part of their assessment, provide a copy of one of the reproducible charts (TE pages 645–651) or refer students to PE pages 456–457.

192

WRITING TIPS

Planning your response . . .
- **Understand the prompt.**
  Read the prompt carefully and look for key words.
- **Gather your ideas.**
  Make a list or fill in a simple graphic organizer.
- **Form a focus statement.**
  Write your main point in a single sentence.
- **Use your time wisely.**
  Save a few minutes at the end to check your work.

Writing your response . . .
- **Begin with a strong opening paragraph.**
  Clearly state your main idea.
- **Organize your details.**
  Divide your details into two or three well-organized paragraphs.
- **End effectively.**
  Leave the reader with something to think about.

Checking your response . . .
- **Check for correctness.**
  Rewrite any confusing parts and correct any errors.

Expository Prompts

- Imagine that a new student has come to your school and needs to learn the class rules. Write an essay that explains the main rules.
- Most people have a favorite activity. Choose an activity that you enjoy doing and write an essay that explains how the activity is done. Remember to discuss any equipment or training needed.

 Respond to an expository prompt. Write a response to one of the prompts above. Finish within the time your teacher gives you.

English Language Learners

If students write about the first prompt given on the page, encourage them to imagine that the student is coming from their culture or language background. Tell them to be sure to describe for the new student the extra challenges he or she may face in the school. This may allow students to express themselves more enthusiastically and therefore write with voice.

Expository Writing in Review

In expository writing, you explain something to a reader.

Select a topic that truly interests you and will also interest your reader. (See page 148.)

Gather and organize details about your topic using a graphic organizer. (See pages 149–150.)

Write a focus (thesis) statement, naming your topic and a special part of it that you plan to cover. (See page 151.)

In the beginning, introduce your topic and state your focus. (See page 155.)

In the middle, give the details that explain or support the focus. (See pages 156–157.)

In the ending, summarize your main points and make a final comment about the topic. (See page 158.)

Review the ideas, organization, and voice of your writing first. Then review for **word choice** and **sentence fluency**. Make changes to improve your first draft. (See pages 160–170.)

Check your writing for conventions. Also have a trusted classmate edit your writing. (See pages 172–174.)

Make a final copy and proofread it for errors before sharing it. (See page 175.)

Use the expository rubric to assess your finished writing. (See pages 176–177.)

Expository Writing in Review

Encourage students to refer to this page whenever they have to write an expository paragraph or essay. Suggest that they create a bookmark out of stiff construction paper and use it to mark the page.

Explain to students that this list of guidelines, along with the specific page references, is like a roadmap. If students follow this roadmap, they will end up with a well-constructed, interesting essay. And just as drivers do not have to look at a map after they have traveled the same route several times, eventually students will not have to refer to this page to develop successful expository paragraphs and essays.

Persuasive Writing Overview

Writing Standards

The writing standards listed below are based on a blending of state and NCTE standards.

- Use lists, charts, and diagrams to select a topic and gather details.
- Write a clear opinion statement.
- Use order of importance and a strong call to action to convince readers to participate.
- Assess writing using a rubric based on the traits of effective writing.
- Share finished pieces with classmates and others.

Writing Forms

- persuasive paragraph
- persuasive essay promoting an event

Focus on the Traits:

- **Ideas** Gathering strong reasons that persuade readers to participate
- **Organization** Creating an opinion statement (beginning) and a call to action (ending) that work together, and a middle that leads up to the most important reason
- **Voice** Using a clear, convincing voice that avoids bandwagon thinking and exaggerations
- **Word Choice** Choosing persuasive words that strengthen the call to action
- **Sentence Fluency** Writing complete sentences that flow smoothly
- **Conventions** Checking for errors in punctuation, capitalization, spelling, and grammar

Unit Pacing

Persuasive Paragraph: 1.5–3 hours

The **persuasive paragraph** introduces the unit and lays the groundwork for more extensive persuasive writing. Use this section if students need to work on crafting this type of paragraph. Following are some of the topics that are covered:

- Creating a quick list to select a topic on a special event at school
- Completing sentence starters to gather reasons
- Writing an ending sentence that restates the opinion

Persuasive Essay: 3.5–6 hours

This section asks students to **promote an event**. Use this section to focus on developing an essay. Following are some of the topics that are covered:

- Using graphic organizers to select a topic and gather details
- Writing topic sentences that use transition words to connect ideas
- Creating a call to action
- Arranging middle paragraphs by order of importance
- Using apostrophes after nouns to show possession

Persuasive Writing Across the Curriculum: 1.5–3 hours

The first lesson in this section guides students through the steps of the writing process in another curriculum area. The remaining two lessons provide models and tips for persuasive writing in additional curriculum areas. If other teachers are involved in cross-curricular activities, collaborate with them on these lessons.

■ **Science**
Writing a Problem-Solution Essay, pp. 238–241

■ **Math**
Creating a Thermometer Graph, pp. 242–243

■ **Practical Writing**
Drafting a Letter of Request, pp. 244–247

Writing for Assessment: 45–90 minutes

The student text shows a sample student response to the first prompt below. Students can respond to that same prompt or to the additional prompt as an informal or a formal assessment.

■ To save money, your principal wants to cancel all field trips for the rest of the year. Write a letter to the principal to express your opinion about canceling field trips. Support your opinion with reasons.

■ Your school is going to start requiring two hours of homework every night. Write a persuasive essay to let the school board know your opinion of this idea. Give reasons to support your opinion.

Evaluating a Persuasive Essay

Learning to evaluate one's own and others' writing is an integral part of learning to write. In addition to a student's evaluation of a persuasive essay (PE pages 234–235), **benchmark papers** provide practice with evaluating persuasive writing.

■ Help Save Our Manatees (strong)
TR 5A–5B
TE pp. 640–641

■ Walk for a Cure! (good)
PE pp. 234–235

■ Why Smog Is Bad (poor)
TR 6A–6B
TE pp. 642–643

Integrated Grammar and Writing Skills

Below are skills lessons from the resources sections of the pupil edition that are suggested at point of use (✳) throughout this unit.

Writing a Persuasive Paragraph, pp. 195–198

✳ Order of Importance, pp. 57 and 458

✳ End Punctuation, pp. 479–481

Promoting an Event, pp. 199–236

✳ Use Transitions, pp. 472–473

✳ Persuasive Voice, p. 463

✳ Fixing Fragments, p. 436

✳ Apostrophes, pp. 490–493

✳ Possessive Pronouns, p. 413

Additional Grammar Skills

Below are skills lessons from other components that you can weave into your unit instruction.

Writing a Persuasive Paragraph

SkillsBook

End Punctuation 1 and 2, p. 3
End Punctuation and Comma
  Review, p. 17

Interactive Writing Skills CD-ROM

Punctuation: End Punctuation

Daily Language Workouts

Week 19: History of Language,
  pp. 40–41
Week 19: Fingers Do the Talking,
  p. 96
Week 20: The English Language,
  pp. 42–43
Week 20: Spelling Challenge, p. 97

Promoting an Event

SkillsBook

Apostrophes 1, 2, and 3, p. 19
Fragments 1 and 2, p. 85
Rambling Sentences, p. 93
Sentence Problems Review 1 and 2,
  p. 96
Person of a Pronoun, p. 143
Number of a Pronoun 1 and 2,
  p. 145
Subject and Object Pronouns, p. 147
Possessive Pronouns, p. 151
Indefinite Pronouns, p. 153
Demonstrative Pronouns, p. 154
Pronoun-Antecedent Agreement,
  p. 155

Interactive Writing Skills CD-ROM

Punctuation: Apostrophes 1—
  Contractions
Punctuation: Apostrophes 2—
  Singular and Plural Possessives

Parts of Speech 1: Pronouns 1—
  Antecedent Agreement
Parts of Speech 1: Pronouns 2—
  Uses

Daily Language Workouts

Week 21: Something Fishy,
  pp. 44–45
Week 21: Fishy Facts, p. 98
Week 22: Animals on Parade,
  pp. 46–47
Week 22: Good Dog, p. 99

Persuasive Writing

Writing Across the Curriculum

Daily Language Workouts

Week 23: Maps, Maps, Maps,
  pp. 48–49
Week 23: The Gulf Stream,
  p. 100
Week 24: On a Map . . . pp. 50–51
Week 24: Look at Minnesota,
  p. 101

Persuasive Writing
Persuasive Paragraph

How would you complete the next sentence? "The best event at school is . . . . " Would you say hat day, grandparents' day, the school carnival? A special event can make a whole week, or even a whole year, more fun.

In this chapter, you'll write a paragraph that uses reasons to convince others to agree with your opinion about a special school event.

Writing Guidelines

Subject: A special event at school

Form: Persuasive paragraph

Purpose: To persuade (convince the reader to do something)

Audience: Parents and students

Persuasive Paragraph

Objectives

- demonstrate an understanding of the content and structure of a persuasive paragraph
- choose a topic (a special school event) to write about
- plan, draft, revise, and edit a persuasive paragraph

Persuasive writing expresses the opinion of the writer. A writer uses reasons, examples, and other details to try to convince—or *persuade*—the reader to agree with that opinion. A **persuasive paragraph** has a topic sentence that states the opinion, body sentences that give reasons for agreeing with the opinion, and a closing sentence that sums up the argument.

✳ For more about writing paragraphs, see PE pages 51–60.

Point out that people try to persuade one another about things all the time. Invite students to tell about a time they tried to get someone to agree with them. Then have them brainstorm examples of other occasions when persuasive language is used. These may include advertising, editorials in newspapers, presidential debates, and arguing cases in court.

Family Connection Letters

As you begin this unit, send home the Persuasive Writing Family Connection letter, which describes what students will be learning.

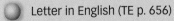 Letter in English (TE p. 656)

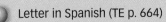 Letter in Spanish (TE p. 664)

Persuasive Paragraph

After students read the paragraph, but before they answer the **Respond to the reading** questions, ask them to

- identify the writer's opinion (everyone should attend the school carnival);
- point out the three main reasons why people should go to the carnival (activities, prizes, clown contest);
- say what clue words help them to find the three main reasons (*first, secondly,* and *the best part*); and
- tell how Willis sums up his paragraph (he restates the beginning as a command).

 Respond to the reading.

Answers

Ideas 1. Answers may vary from the general (having summer fun in January, creating an activity) to the specific (shoe scrambles, relay races, and clown contest).

Organization 2. "The best part" signals the writer's most important reason, the clown contest.

Voice & Word Choice 3. Possible answers: special event, I like, the best part, pretty funny, laugh and laugh.

 196

Persuasive Paragraph

A persuasive paragraph starts with a **topic sentence**, which states an opinion about something. The **body** sentences give reasons that support the opinion, and the **closing sentence** may state the opinion in a new way. In the following paragraph, Willis tells about a favorite school event and gives reasons why everyone should attend.

Topic sentence

Body

Closing sentence

Have Some Summer Fun!

Our school carnival is a special event everyone should attend. One Friday night in January, our whole school becomes a summer carnival. Each classroom has a game or an activity. Students help in their own rooms and then visit the other rooms. First of all, there are activities for everyone. This year our room had a fishpond for the little kids. Another room painted a clown with a huge mouth for a beanbag toss. I like the shoe scrambles and relay races. Secondly, each room gives prizes like yo-yos, bug-eye glasses, and light-up pens. The best part is the clown contest. Old clothes, face paint, wigs, big clunky shoes, and wild ties make it pretty funny. Adults and kids laugh and laugh. For a little summer fun in January, come to our school carnival.

 Respond to the reading.
On your own paper, answer each of the following questions.

- **Ideas** (1) What does Willis like about the school carnival?
- **Organization** (2) What reason is most important to him?
- **Voice & Word Choice** (3) What words or phrases show excitement about the topic?

English Language Learners

Some students may come from cultures that do not encourage children to express their opinions. Before introducing the paragraph, have students respond to a comment such as, "We should have pizza for lunch twice a week." Emphasize that there is no "correct" response, because students should state what they believe. Those who do not like pizza should not agree. Restate each response to reinforce the concept: "Maria's opinion is that we should not have pizza twice a week."

Prewriting Selecting a Topic

Think of events you enjoy at school. Making a quick list will help you find an idea for your persuasive paragraph.

Quick List

Create a quick list. List events at your school. Star (✻) the one you choose.

- field day
- school carnival ✻
- Arbor Day tree planting
- student-teacher basketball game

Writing an Opinion

Next, form your opinion. An opinion is something you believe.

Formula: A specific subject (our school carnival)
  + your opinion (is a special event everyone should attend)
  = a good opinion statement

Write your opinion statement. Use the formula above to write your own opinion statement.

Gathering Reasons

You'll need to give good reasons to support your opinion.

First of all, there are activities for everyone.
Secondly, each room gives prizes.
The best part is the clown contest.

Complete sentence starters. Copy and complete the underlined sentence starters above to find three reasons that support your opinion.

Prewriting Selecting a Topic

Have the class work together to brainstorm a list of all the special events that happen at the school. Write the list on the board as students call out ideas.

There may be new students in the class who haven't experienced special events yet. Encourage them to write about an event they experienced at their old school. Suggest that they may want to persuade their new principal to add that event to the calendar.

Prewriting Gathering Reasons

Tell students they should put their least important reason first, their second-most important reason next, and their most important reason last. Organizing their ideas in this way will help them support their opinion effectively.

✻ For more about listing details in order of importance, see PE pages 57 and 458.

Students may wish to give more than three reasons to support their opinions. The paragraph format will accommodate four reasons, but encourage students not to use more than four.

English Language Learners

Students benefit from repeated presentations of new information in a consistent format. Rewrite the opinion statement formula as a math sentence: *A specific subject + your opinion = a good opinion statement.* This formula is consistent with the Prewriting formats used on pages 206 and 240.

Writing Creating Your First Draft

Point out that students' prewriting notes give them a big head start on their paragraph. All they have to do to complete the first draft is

- state their opinion,
- choose the best three supporting reasons, filling in a specific example or two after each reason; and
- think of a good way to restate their opinion.

Revising
Improving Your Paragraph

Ask students to begin revising by reading the draft aloud to a partner. How do students feel and sound when they read? Do the words they chose help them use a persuasive tone of voice?

Editing Checking for Conventions

Talk students through the process of editing their paragraphs. Have them go sentence-by-sentence to

- check the end punctuation,
- confirm that the first letter of the next sentence is capitalized, and
- circle any words they're not absolutely sure about.

✱ For information about punctuation, see PE pages 479–481.

198

Writing Creating Your First Draft

The first draft of your paragraph should start with your topic sentence, which states your opinion about a special school event. The body sentences should give your reasons along with details and examples. The closing sentence can restate your opinion.

Write your first draft. Follow the suggestions above. Remember that your audience includes adults and students. Use your topic sentence and reasons from page 197.

Revising Improving Your Paragraph

When you revise, check your paragraph for *ideas, organization, voice, word choice,* and *sentence fluency.*

Revise your paragraph. Use these questions as a guide.
1. Does my topic sentence give an event and my opinion about it?
2. Do my body sentences give reasons for my opinion?
3. Is my writing voice convincing?
4. Do I use specific nouns and strong verbs?
5. Do I use complete sentences?

Editing Checking for Conventions

Editing means looking for errors in *conventions.*

Edit your work. Ask yourself the following questions.
1. Does each sentence end with punctuation?
2. Have I checked my spelling?
3. Have I used the right words *(threw, through)*?

Persuasive Writing
Promoting an Event

When a circus comes to town, performers try to convince people to come see the show. They parade elephants down Main Street, put up posters, and appear on TV. There are many ways to promote a circus.

You can promote an event by writing a persuasive essay. In the essay, you name the event or activity and give the reader reasons to become involved. This chapter will help you write an essay that will make an event a big success!

Writing Guidelines

Subject:	An event or activity
Form:	Persuasive essay
Purpose:	To promote an event
Audience:	Classmates

Promoting an Event

Objectives
- demonstrate an understanding of the purpose, content, and form of a persuasive essay
- choose a topic (an event or activity) to write about
- plan, draft, revise, edit, and publish a persuasive essay

A **persuasive essay** is a piece of writing that
- gives an opinion,
- provides reasons, supported by examples, for agreeing with the opinion, and
- calls on readers to act.

Tell students that two ways events are promoted in writing are
- press releases—essays the company that created the event sends to news organizations to persuade them to report on it, and
- reviews—articles describing the event and urging people to go see it (or not!).

Read examples of reviews and press releases for movies, performances (theater, music, dance), and special events (circus, antique auto show, flower show).

Materials

Sample reviews, press releases, and newspaper listings for events (TE pp. 199, 202, and 204)

Posterboard (TE p. 202)

Colored index cards (TE pp. 206, 208)

Out-of-focus picture (TE p. 220)

Picture of bandwagon (TE p. 220)

Sample essay for transparency (TE p. 227)

Paper and drawing supplies (TE pp. 230, 231)

Copy Masters/ Transparencies

T-chart (TE p. 204)

Table diagram (TE p. 205)

Benchmark Papers

Help Save Our Manatees (strong)

◯ TR 5A–5B

◯ TE pp. 640–641

Why Smog Is Bad (poor)

◯ TR 6A–6B

◯ TE pp. 642–643

Understanding Your Goal

Three traits relate to the development of the content and the form. They provide a focus during prewriting, drafting, and revising.

- Ideas
- Organization
- Voice

The other three traits relate more to form. Checking these is part of the process of revising and editing.

- Word Choice
- Sentence Fluency
- Conventions

To give students more detailed information about the goals, preview the rubric for persuasive writing on PE pages 232–233 and review the procedure for using a rubric (see PE pages 31–38). Note that if students successfully meet all the goals, they will have written an excellent essay that would score a 5 or higher for each of the traits.

✳ The six-point rubric on PE pages 232–233 is based on these traits. Four- and five-point rubrics are available on TE pages 626 and 629.

200

Understanding Your Goal

Your goal in this chapter is to write a persuasive essay that promotes an event or activity. The traits listed in the chart below will help you reach your goal.

Your goal is to . . .

Ideas — Select an event or activity and gather strong reasons for people to become involved in it.

Organization — Create a clear beginning, middle, and ending, and lead up to your most important reason.

Voice — Use a writing voice that sounds clear and convincing.

Word Choice — Choose words that make your writing persuasive.

Sentence Fluency — Write complete sentences that flow smoothly from one to another.

Conventions — Check your essay for correct punctuation, capitalization, spelling, and grammar.

 Get the big picture. Look at the rubric on pages 232–233. It can help you measure your progress as you write.

Persuasive Essay

Promoting an Event **201**

In the following persuasive essay, Desirée promotes a contest at her school. The side notes tell what each part of the essay does.

Help Make History

Sometimes at recess, I stand by the mural wall. I like the people painted there. One girl is my favorite because my mom painted her 20 years ago. Now, the old mural has to go. The paint is all faded and flaking off. Jones Elementary is having a new mural contest, and every student should get involved.

The first reason kids should help out is that the mural represents Jones Elementary. Students will decide what kind of picture they want. Then they can draw pictures and enter them in the contest. The artist hired by the school will choose pictures that tell the city something about us.

Also, kids need to help because the new mural is going to take a lot of work. The artist can't do it all alone. She needs a whole crew of kids to help paint the new mural. Some kids can help during recess. Other kids can help on

---

BEGINNING

The beginning gets the reader's attention and gives the opinion statement (underlined).

MIDDLE

Each middle paragraph gives reasons to support the opinion.

Persuasive Essay

Work through this sample essay with the class, pointing out the elements that make it a good persuasive essay.

Ideas
- The opinion statement tells what the writer thinks.
- The beginning tells why the writer likes the mural.
- The writer gives convincing reasons and supports them with details.

Organization
- The opening paragraph explains the writer's feelings about the old mural; then it makes a good transition to talking about the new mural.
- The reasons are given in order of increasing importance.
- The ending restates the opinion and uses an exclamatory command for the call to action.

Voice & Word Choice
- The writer uses a casual voice.
- The writer uses transition words to move smoothly from one reason to the next.
- The writer uses persuasive words *(should, reason, need to, can, get ready, help)*.

English Language Learners

Students may have difficulty understanding that words can have multiple meanings. Some may only understand *promote* to mean "pass on to the next grade." Explain that *promote* also means to "support" or "advertise." Provide an example, such as noting that a popular sports figure promotes drug-free schools, a soft drink, or exercise, and ask students to suggest other examples.

Ask students if they can suggest ways to improve the essay. Possible responses:

1. Use more specifics. For example,
   - tell what the people in the old mural are doing,
   - briefly describe the "girl" the writer's mother painted, or
   - give the name of the artist.
2. Strengthen the first sentence of the last paragraph. Readers are less likely to disagree with a sentence such as *The mural represents everybody at Jones Elementary, so . . .*

 Respond to the reading.

Answers

Ideas 1. The mural represents the school; the artist needs help; it's going to be around for 20 years.

Organization 2. *The first reason; Also;* and *The most important reason*

Voice & Word Choice 3. Answers will vary. Possible answers:

- persuasive verbs such as *should, need, help, get involved, start dreaming*
- active verbs such as *stand, like, decide, painted, grab*
- Note that using the future tense (verbs with *will*) adds certainty and authority.

202

MIDDLE
Transition words and phrases help show which reason is most important.

ENDING
The ending asks the reader to do something (a call to action).

Saturdays. If we all help, the mural will get done quickly.

The most important reason to get involved is that this mural is going to be around for 20 years. When we are grown up, we will want to point to the wall and tell which parts we painted. As Mom says, "The mural is part of our history and part of our future."

The mural wall is important to everybody at Jones Elementary, so everybody should help with the mural contest. Start dreaming of a new mural, draw your best ideas, and send them in. Then get ready to put on a painting shirt, grab a paintbrush, and help make history!

 Respond to the reading. On your own paper, answer the following questions about the sample essay.

- **Ideas** (1) What reasons does Desirée use to promote the mural contest?
- **Organization** (2) What transition words or phrases does Desirée use to connect her middle paragraphs?
- **Voice & Word Choice** (3) What verbs does Desirée use to make her voice sound convincing?

English Language Learners

Many students may not yet be using the verbs associated with persuasive speech. Have students do Think-Pair-Share to respond to the reading. Record responses to question 3 on a poster of persuasive words writers use. Continue to add words to the poster throughout the unit.

Advanced Learners

For additional writing practice, tell students to imagine they are newspaper reporters. Their job is to write an article that describes the mural contest event and persuades the public to see the mural.

Students will need to visualize and describe the pictures and convey the excitement of painting the mural with the artists. Remind students to use specific examples to help readers visualize the mural.

Provide newspaper articles about events for students to use as models.

Prewriting

Promoting an Event **203**

The writing process starts with prewriting. During this step, you decide on a topic and get ready to write your first draft.

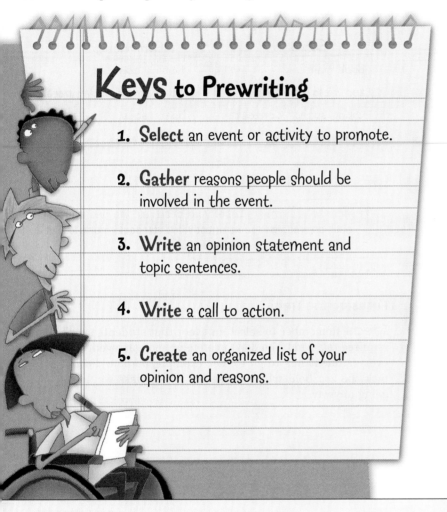

Keys to Prewriting

1. **Select** an event or activity to promote.

2. **Gather** reasons people should be involved in the event.

3. **Write** an opinion statement and topic sentences.

4. **Write** a call to action.

5. **Create** an organized list of your opinion and reasons.

Prewriting Keys to Prewriting

Remind students of the purpose of the prewriting stage in the writing process: It is when the writer selects a topic, gathers details, and decides how to organize those details.

The Keys to Prewriting list lays out the process students will be guided through on PE pages 204–208.

Remind students that persuasive writing is based primarily on their own ideas, thoughts, and experiences. Because of this, they'll have an easier time writing their essay if they choose a topic that is something they care about and something they can support with good reasons.

Prewriting Selecting a Topic

Distribute photocopies of the reproducible T-chart (TE page 645) for students to use for listing potential topics.

To help students get ideas,

- send volunteers around the school to note events posted on bulletin boards,
- have the class think of other events at school, and
- provide copies of events listings from local newspapers for students to look at.

Note that it's best if students choose an event they've attended before (for example, an annual festival they attended last year or a performance their parents took them to see), so they can describe it effectively.

Focus on the Traits

Ideas
Tell students that one good way to tell whether their persuasive essay is effective will be to find out later whether it convinced anyone to take part in the event. They won't have that option if they write about something everyone would do whether or not they had read the essay.

204

Prewriting Selecting a Topic

To find a topic, you need to think about events and activities in your school or community. Jerome used a T-chart to list possible topics for his essay.

T-Chart

Special Events	
School	Community
book fair	fishing contest
zoo field trip	St. Patrick's Day parade
young author contest	boat races
summer reading *	food drive

Prewrite

Create a T-chart. Label your chart like the one above. In each column, list events or activities you could promote. Put a star (✳) next to the topic you choose.

Focus on the Traits

Ideas Remember to select an event that students aren't required to attend. You don't need to promote an event that every student has to go to. For example, Jerome did not pick the zoo field trip because the whole class would be going anyway.

English Language Learners

If students are not familiar with the events suggested by posters and newspaper articles, arrange to have them interview two or three event organizers in person (for example, the librarian in charge of a read-a-thon) to learn about the events before they select an event to write about.

Struggling Learners

For students who have not been involved in many events or activities, provide an alternative way to get ideas for a topic. Encourage partners to interview each other about personal interests. For example:

- What do you like to do in your spare time?
- If you could go anywhere, where would you go and why?

- If you could meet someone special, who would it be, and why?

Tell students to use the information to identify interesting events or activities, or even to invent an activity that would interest them.

Promoting an Event **205**

Gathering Reasons

Your essay must tell people why they should get involved in the event you chose. A table diagram can help you gather reasons. The tabletop names the event, and the table legs answer the question "Why should people get involved?" Here is Jerome's table diagram.

Table Diagram

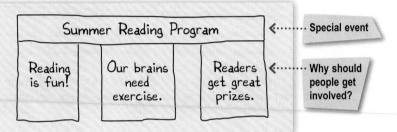

Prewrite

Create a table diagram. Draw a tabletop like the one above and write your special event or activity in it. Then draw at least three table legs. In each one, answer the question "Why should people get involved?"

Focus on the Traits

Organization Reasons support your opinion just as legs support a table. A table with two legs won't stand up. You need at least three reasons before you have strong support.

Prewriting Gathering Reasons

Distribute copies of the reproducible table diagram (TE page 650) for students to use.

Students may wish to do **interviews** *(see below)* or other research to gather additional information for their essays. Encourage them to
■ talk to organizers of school events and ask questions,
■ talk to other people who have attended the event they're writing about, and
■ read about community events in the newspaper or on the Internet.

✷ For more about researching on the Internet, see PE page 323.

Focus on the Traits

Organization
Tell students they may use four or five reasons, if they wish (but note that more than five would probably make the essay too long). To create more legs on the table diagrams, they can tape two copies of the reproducible diagram together. Have students review their reasons carefully, checking to make sure that all are important and that the reasons do not repeat or overlap each other.

Teaching Tip: Interviewing

As part of their information-gathering process, have students conduct an interview for homework. Interviews can be casual (for example, talking with a friend) or more formal (a telephone, in-person, or e-mail interview with an expert). Remind students to
● use the 5W's to prepare a list of questions,

● take careful notes so they can accurately describe what the person said, and
● ask the person they interview to write in their own words one important detail about the event.

✷ For more about interviews, see PE page 322.

Struggling Learners

Some students may need an "oral rehearsal" to complete the table diagram. Let them try out a few of their ideas with a partner and describe each event in as much detail as they can. Partners should ask questions if they need more information. The goal is to listen for the description that persuades them to get involved.

Prewriting
Writing an Opinion Statement

Remind students that the purpose of the essay is to persuade people to attend an event or participate in an activity. To write an opinion statement, they just need to come up with an interesting way of expressing a **should** statement *(see below)*: *You should go to* _____ *or You should participate in* _____.

Prewriting
Writing Topic Sentences

Remind students to arrange their topic sentences in order, from least important to most important.

Suggest that they try out the transition words shown (or similar transition words), but note that the transition words don't always have to appear at the beginning of the sentence. Give examples and challenge students to think of additional examples. These might include:

- Reading is fun, for one thing.
- The summer reading program also gives out great prizes.

＊ For information about how to use transitions, see PE pages 472–473.

Prewriting Writing an Opinion Statement

Your opinion statement should name the event and tell people to get involved. Use the word *should* to make a strong opinion statement.

name the event		tell how people should get involved		a strong opinion statement
Befford reading program	**+**	students should sign up for summer reading	**=**	Students at Befford School should sign up for summer reading.

 Write your opinion statement. Follow the formula above to write your own opinion statement. Try a few different versions.

Writing Topic Sentences

Each of your topic sentences will be about one of the reasons in your table diagram from page 205. The sentences will begin the three middle paragraphs of your essay. Here are Jerome's topic sentences.

1. To start with, reading is fun.
2. Also, the summer reading program gives out great prizes.
3. The best reason is that the summer reading program keeps your brain strong.

 Write your topic sentences. Include one reason from your table diagram in each topic sentence. Use transition words and phrases to connect your ideas.

First of all,	The first reason	To start with,
In addition,	Another reason	Also,
Most importantly,	The biggest reason	The best reason

Teaching Tip: *Should*

Focus on the use of *should* as an auxiliary, or helping, verb. Explain that when *should* is paired with another verb, it adds the meaning of being obligated to take the action expressed. (Encourage interested students to consult a dictionary to investigate other meanings of *should*.)

Should is not the only way to express strong need or obligation.

Challenge students to think of alternatives. Examples may include

- using *ought, need,* or *must*: You *ought to / need to / must* work hard at school.
- using adjectives: It's *important / imperative / crucial* that you work hard at school.

English Language Learners

To help students focus on organization, have them

- write their topic sentences without transition words on different colored index cards,
- rearrange the cards until they are satisfied with the order, and then
- add transition words and phrases.

Promoting an Event   **207**

Creating a Call to Action

Persuasive writing tries to convince the reader to do something. A **call to action** is usually written as a command, with the understood subject, *you*, referring to the reader. Jerome wrote this call to action in his essay.

(You) Go to the library, sign up, and start reading!

Practice

Change the following statements into commands (remove the subject and helping verb). Begin your command with the main verb.

1. Students should come to band information night.
2. People should bring canned food for the local food pantry.
3. Students should volunteer for the school cleanup day.
4. Everyone should donate money to the Arbor Day fund.
5. Kids should get pledges for the jump rope fund-raiser.
6. Students should take part in the reading challenge.

Prewrite

Write a call to action. Write a command sentence about your event that tells the reader what to do. Make sure to start your sentence with a verb.

Focus on the Traits

Voice Writing your call to action as a command makes your voice more persuasive. A command tells the reader how to respond to your idea—with action.

Prewriting

Creating a Call to Action

Explain that commands can end with a period or an exclamation point. Exclamation points add emphasis, but point out that using too many exclamation points can make the writer sound surprised instead of well informed.

Practice Answers

1. Come to band . . .
2. Bring canned food for . . .
3. Volunteer for the school . . .
4. Donate money to . . . .
5. Get pledges for . . .
6. Take part in . . .

Focus on the Traits

Voice

Discuss other reasons it is a good idea to use a command for the call to action.

- It creates variety by adding a different kind of sentence (chances are, the essay uses mostly statements).
- It ends an essay with a bang.

* For information about writing in a persuasive voice and using different kinds of sentences, see PE pages 463 and 441.

English Language Learners

Students may not be familiar with the meaning of the word *command*. Explain that a command tells people what to do. Before introducing the practice exercise, have groups of students think of commands they hear every day (for example, "Put your books away") and share their examples with the class.

Prewriting Organizing Your Ideas

Have students take out a blank sheet of paper, their completed table diagram (see PE page 205), and all their other notes, including any notes from their research. Ask them to write on the sheet of paper

- their opinion statement,
- three (or more) topic sentences in order from least important to most important, and
- a call to action.

Have students leave space after each topic sentence so they can add notes about supporting details.

Encourage students to consult their notes often to make sure they don't forget any important details.

- Remind students that each detail should relate to its topic sentence.
- Ask them to think of two or three details for each topic sentence.
- Explain that the notes they make now can just be brief reminders of what they want to mention in the draft; they don't have to write full sentences.

 208

Prewriting Organizing Your Ideas

An organized list of your ideas gives you a final plan for writing your essay. The list contains your opinion statement, topic sentences with details, and a call to action.

Organized List

Opinion statement	Students at Befford School should sign up for summer reading.

First topic sentence **List of details**	1. To start with, reading is fun.
	   – amazing books
	   – lots of titles to choose from

Second topic sentence **List of details**	2. Also, the summer reading program gives out great prizes.
	   – pizza
	   – mini-golf and go-carts
	   – Adventure Island

Third topic sentence **List of details**	3. The best reason is that the summer reading program keeps your brain strong.
	   – exercises your brain
	   – helps you succeed next year

Call to action	Go to the library, sign up, and start reading!

 Organize your essay. Make your own organized list, using the example above as a guide.

English Language Learners

Students may need more time to accomplish writing tasks. Reduce the amount of required writing by having students reuse their topic sentence index cards (see TE page 206) and write details for each topic sentence on additional color-coded index cards. Have students write their opinion statement on a piece of paper, paste their index cards on the paper in order, then write their call to action at the end to create their organized list. For students who really struggle with getting their ideas on paper, modify the assignment further by requiring only one or two middle paragraphs.

Writing

Promoting an Event **209**

Now that you've completed your prewriting, you are ready to write your first draft. Your main job is to put all your ideas on paper or in a computer file.

Keys to Writing

1. **Write** a strong beginning paragraph that includes your opinion statement.

2. **Start** each middle paragraph with a topic sentence that gives one reason.

3. **Include** details in each paragraph to support the topic sentence.

4. **Write** an ending paragraph that includes your call to action.

Writing Keys to Writing

Remind students that the writing stage is when they get to write, or draft, their ideas on paper.

The Keys to Writing list lays out the process students will be guided through on PE pages 210–214.

Point out to students that they made a detailed organized list—or outline—during the prewriting stage. Explain that the main thing they have to do to create a first draft is connect all the pieces.

At the same time, they shouldn't let themselves feel trapped by the outline. If students discover they want to do something differently from how they had originally planned, they should feel free to make the necessary changes.

Remind students that a first draft is only a test version of the final paper. It doesn't need to be perfect, because they'll be going back over it to make improvements and fix mistakes. Tell students to be sure to double space their drafts so there will be room for them to write corrections during the revising stage.

Writing Getting the Big Picture

Note that the three-part format of an essay should be familiar to students because all the kinds of essays they've learned about are divided into a beginning, a middle, and an ending. Paragraphs, also, are divided into three parts that correspond to beginning, middle, and ending (see PE page 196)—topic sentence, body sentences, and closing sentence.

Point out that persuasive essays have specific vocabulary associated with them that isn't used for other kinds of writing.

- The opinion statement is often called the focus statement in other kinds of essays. In a persuasive essay the focus of the essay is the writer's *opinion*.
- The call to action is called the closing sentence in other kinds of writing.

✻ For more about the parts of narrative and expository essays, see PE pages 98 and 154.

Have students label the corresponding parts of their organized list as the *beginning, middle,* and *ending*.

210

Writing Getting the Big Picture

The chart below shows how the parts of a persuasive essay fit together. (The examples are from the sample essay on pages 211–214.) You are ready to write your essay when you have . . .

- written your opinion statement and topic sentences,
- written a call to action, and
- created an organized list.

Beginning

The **beginning** gets the reader's attention and gives the opinion statement.

Opinion Statement
Students at Befford School should sign up for summer reading.

Middle

Each **middle** paragraph starts with a topic sentence that gives one reason for the opinion. The body sentences provide details.

Topic Sentences
To start with, reading is fun.

Also, the summer reading program gives out great prizes.

The best reason is that the summer reading program keeps your brain strong.

Ending

The **ending** tells the reader to do something (call to action).

Call to Action
Go to the library, sign up, and start reading!

Promoting an Event **211**

Starting Your Essay

Your first paragraph should get the reader's attention and provide your opinion statement. Here are several ways to get your reader's attention:

> Beginning
>
> Middle
>
> Ending

- ■ **Start with a question.**
  Where did you go on your last summer vacation?

- ■ **Surprise your reader.**
  Last summer, I traveled to faraway Treasure Island!

- ■ **Be creative.**
  Books invite you into a time machine.

- ■ **Use a quotation.**
  "Sign up for summer reading!" shouts the poster in the library.

Beginning Paragraph

The first sentence catches the reader's attention.	"Sign up for summer reading!" shouts the poster in the library. I can just imagine my friends saying that summer is for being outside! I agree with both. Summer is for exercising your body, but it's also for exercising your brain. <u>Students at Befford School should sign up for summer reading.</u>
The last sentence includes the opinion statement (underlined).	

 Write your beginning paragraph. Try one of the strategies above to get your reader's attention. End your paragraph with your opinion statement.

Writing Starting Your Essay

Some students tend to always start their essays the same way. To help them break away from that habit, have students write two opening opinion statements, using different starting strategies.

Divide the class into groups of three or four and have students take turns reading their two openers to the group. Which one works best? Why? Do all the listeners agree in their preferences? To help students keep their discussions on track, circulate among the groups as students talk.

Remind students that when they are responding to a peer's writing they should always
- ■ listen carefully,
- ■ be polite and helpful, and
- ■ make their comments specific.

✶ For more about peer responding, see PE pages 39–42.

English Language Learners

Modify the assignment so that students do not need to write two different opinion statements. Help students select two of the strategies for starting their essay. Have them rehearse their opening statements orally with you or with a considerate, cooperative partner before writing the beginning paragraph they prefer.

Struggling Learners

To help students think of ideas for the first paragraph, suggest that they use the 5 W questions. Ask students to provide examples for the summer reading program at Befford. For example:

- ● What can you do on a rainy day in summer?
- ● Where can you go to have fun in the summer?

Advanced Learners

Remind students that using similes is a creative and snappy way to catch the reader's attention. For example:

- ● Reading a book is like traveling in a time machine.
- ● Reading a book is like going away on a vacation.

Encourage students to begin their paragraph with a simile.

Writing
Developing the Middle Part

Tell students that the process of creating the middle part of their essay is similar to writing three separate persuasive paragraphs. Note that there are a couple of differences:

- Students should use transitions so that one paragraph leads to the next, and all are connected to the topic.
- It isn't necessary to restate the topic sentence at the close of each paragraph.

Writing Understanding
Order of Importance

Explain that one way to arrange information in order of importance is to mention the most important idea first and the least important idea last. However, in persuasive writing it's best to end with the most important reason. Ask students to speculate about why that is true. (When you're trying to persuade someone to agree with you, you don't want to use up your best reason first. You want start with a good reason, then follow with better and better reasons, so your argument gets stronger as you go along.)

212

Writing Developing the Middle Part

In your first paragraph, you got the reader's attention and led up to your opinion statement. Each of your middle paragraphs should focus on one reason people should get involved with your event, arranged by order of importance. Write at least three body paragraphs that begin with a topic sentence. Use your organized list as a guide.

> Beginning
>
> Middle
>
> Ending

Understanding Order of Importance

Order of importance simply means that you share ideas from most to least important or from least to most important. The transition words and phrases you use with each topic sentence help to show this order of importance.

Middle Paragraphs

> **Topic sentence 1**
> Details support the first reason.

> **Topic sentence 2**
> Details support the second reason.

To start with, reading is fun. Sure, it's great to play basketball and soccer with friends. It's also great to dig a tunnel to the center of the earth and fly to Jupiter. Books let you do things like that. When the weather's nice, go out and ride your bike. When it's too hot or rainy, stay in and take a trip in a rocket!

Also, the summer reading program gives out great prizes. The prize for reading 5 books is a free pizza. Just think of every chapter as a small slice! The prize for reading 10 books is a free ticket for mini-golf and go-carts. If you read 20 books, you get to go to Adventure

---

Advanced Learners

To focus students' attention on topic development, invite them to reread the first two middle paragraphs to see how they work. (Though the purpose is to entice the audience to read, the writer has anticipated excuses others may have, such as going out to play. He explains that reading is a worthwhile alternative.)

Encourage students to think about their audience. How can they tempt those who may not be interested in their event? Have students try out their ideas in their writing.

Promoting an Event   **213**

Island for free! Last summer, I got to go to Adventure Island.

    The best reason is that the summer reading program keeps your brain strong. The poster in the library says, "Brains need exercise!" If you keep reading all summer, you'll put thousands of miles on your imagination. Your brain will also be geared up for heading back to school in the fall.

Topic sentence 3
Details support the third reason.

Arrange your paragraphs by order of importance, ending with the most important reason.

Write your middle paragraphs. Use your organized list from page 208.

Ask students to compare the middle paragraphs to the organized list on PE page 208 and talk about what they notice. Possible responses:

Topic sentence 1:
- The writer's notes are very general and aren't mentioned in the paragraph. Instead, he talks more about how you can play outside *and* read during vacation.
- He implies that there are lots of good titles to choose from by giving examples of interesting book subjects such as flying to Jupiter. (Note that it might have been a good idea to mention specific book titles, too.)

Topic sentence 2:
- The writer mentions all three details and adds specific information about how to win the prizes.

Topic sentence 3:
- The writer supports his most important reason about exercising the brain by quoting a poster.
- He implies that reading can help you succeed next year by saying that it will help you get ready for school.

English Language Learners

To provide students with time to focus on writing details that support their topic sentences, have them use the topic sentences and transition words they recorded on index cards for the organized lists they created on PE page 208.

Struggling Learners

After students have compared the sample paragraphs to the organized list (PE page 208), have them write their own middle paragraphs. Then invite them to examine their work to decide whether they have added examples and explanations. Have them

- underline text that is the same in red, and
- underline new text in blue.

Have partners work together to clarify or add more interesting information.

Writing Ending Your Essay

After students have reviewed the page, point out the following:

- It's possible to combine two ending strategies into one. For example, the suggestions for summing up reasons and asking a question both contain the same information (reading is fun, and it exercises your brain).

- The writer saved an important piece of information for the last paragraph. Challenge students to identify the new information. (It doesn't cost anything to participate in the reading program.) This is a good idea, because it lets the writer slip in one very convincing reason for readers to agree with him.

Encourage students to think of ways to combine ending strategies and to come up with a new piece of information to put in the closing paragraph.

Writing Ending Your Essay

The last paragraph should review your reasons and give your call to action. Here are three ways to review your reasons.

> Beginning
> Middle
> ► Ending

- **Create a list.**
  If you want to have fun, win prizes, and develop a first-class brain, you should join the Befford summer reading program.

- **Sum up the reasons.**
  Summer reading is fun and keeps your mind in shape.

- **Ask a question.**
  Are you looking for a way to have fun and give your brain a good summer workout?

Ending Paragraph

> The writer ends with a call to action.
>
> If you want to have fun, win prizes, and develop a first-class brain, you should join the Befford summer reading program. It's free, and so are the library books. Go to the library, sign up, and start reading!

Write your ending. Use one of the strategies above to give your essay a strong ending. Remember to include your call to action.

Form a complete first draft. Write a complete copy of your essay. Write on every other line to make room for changes when revising.

English Language Learners

Because students learned on PE page 207 to write command sentences to create a closing call to action, they may be confused about using a question in their ending. Explain that the three examples are different *opening sentences* for the final paragraph of the essay. Read aloud each opening sentence and pair it with the call to action. Help students distinguish the opening sentences from the call-to-action.

Revising

After completing your first draft, it's time to revise your work using the steps below. When you revise, you check your essay for *ideas, organization, voice, word choice,* and *sentence fluency.*

Keys to Revising

1. **Read** your essay once to see how you feel about it.

2. **Review** each part: the beginning, the middle, and the ending.

3. **Ask** a classmate to read your first draft and respond to it.

4. **Change** any parts that need to be improved.

Revising Keys to Revising

Remind students that the revising stage is when writers have an opportunity to make improvements to their first drafts. They can think about refinements they might not have considered when they were drafting.

The Keys to Revising list lays out the process students will be guided through on PE pages 216–236.

Point out that the first step in the revision process is reading the draft all the way through to see how they feel about it.

■ Have students read the draft this first time without stopping to make any corrections. This will help them get a feel for the piece as a whole.
■ Suggest that students first read their essay out loud. It can be very helpful to hear the words spoken.

Explain that the second step in the list calls for students to read through their essay more slowly, concentrating on each part and taking time to make changes.

Before students begin actively revising, have them review the goals on PE page 200 and the rubric on PE pages 232–233.

English Language Learners

The internalized patterns of speech of students' first language and their oral English proficiency influence their writing. Some may find it easier to recognize errors in their draft if they hear a proficient English speaker read it out loud. Modify the first step of the checklist by substituting a statement such as, "Listen to a partner read my first draft out loud so I can listen to what I wrote."

Revising for Ideas

The rubric strips that run across all of the revising pages (PE pages 216–225) are provided to help students focus their revising and are related to the full rubric on PE pages 232–233.

Explain that an anecdote is a brief story that can be used in writing to give an example or provide a transition to an idea. For example, below is an anecdote that could be used to introduce the information that the writer has decided to join a band:

Two years ago, I heard my brother play in the fourth-grade band. It was so different from the times my parents nagged him to get out his French horn and practice! In the band, he was really having fun. That's when I decided I'd like to try playing an instrument too.

Challenge students to add one anecdote to their essays.

Practice   Answers

Items number 1, 3, and 4 are anecdotes. Invite volunteers to make up a complete two- or three-sentence story using one of those choices to start off.

216

Revising for Ideas

6 My essay strongly promotes my topic. I use many convincing details.

5 I convince the reader by using different kinds of details.

4 My essay is somewhat convincing, but adding an anecdote or a quotation would make it stronger.

When you revise for *ideas,* you check the kinds of details (including anecdotes and quotations) you have used. The rubric above can help you revise.

How can I use an anecdote in my essay?

You can use an anecdote to gain your reader's interest or to support a reason. An anecdote is a little story that makes an idea clearer.

To capture the reader's interest in the beginning . . .
Two years ago, I heard my brother play in the fourth-grade band.

To support one of your reasons in a paragraph . . .
When I first tried the trombone, I couldn't believe how loud it was.

Practice

Find three anecdotes for an essay about joining the band.

1. When my brother joined the band, he didn't know how to read music, but now he plays saxophone like a pro.
2. I started school a week late because I had the flu.
3. Last Fourth of July, I heard the band play in the park.
4. When I went to band information night, the school stage had stands with flutes, clarinets, trumpets, and drums.
5. Most parades have marching bands.

 Revise

Think of anecdotes. List brief stories that are related to the event or activity you are writing about. Add one to your beginning or to support a reason.

English Language Learners

If students remember anecdotes in their first language, they may have difficulty retelling the stories in English. Have them use a storyboard to depict their anecdotes and ask them to describe their illustrations to a cooperative partner. This will help them to rehearse the story orally and receive help with vocabulary before they begin writing.

Struggling Learners

Use the following prompts with students who are having difficulty adding an anecdote to their essay:

- Tell me about your event.
- Why did you want to go?
- How did you know about it?

Help students identify information that can be used as an anecdote, and help them locate an appropriate place to insert the story into their essay.

Promoting an Event   **217**

| 3 My essay is not very convincing. I need to add more kinds of details. | 2 My essay needs many more details to be convincing. | 1 My essay and details are confusing. |

How can I use a quotation in my essay?

Quotations from experts can be very convincing. You can find quotations in books, in magazines, and on Web sites, or by interviewing people around you.

Practice

Read the following quotations. Choose the best one for an essay about joining the band. Tell why you think it is best.

1. Once I heard a high school student say, "I like band."
2. Ray Charles said, "I was born with music inside me."
3. Our band teacher, Mrs. Jensen, says, "Learning music makes kids better students."

Search for quotations. Look for a quotation about your topic. Choose one that will make your essay clearer or more convincing.

Revising in Action

The writer adds a quotation to make the essay more convincing.

The best reason is that the summer reading program
The poster in the library says, "Brains need exercise!"
keeps your brain strong.∧If you keep reading . . .

Remind writers that when they use a quotation they should always
■ provide information about the source, and
■ be careful to get the wording right—the quotation must match exactly what the person said or what is in the printed source.

✱ For more about citing sources, see PE page 346.

Practice   Answers

Answers will vary. Possible answers:
1. This could be the best choice if the writer goes on to say that the high school student was someone he particularly admired and whose opinion he trusted.
2. This could be best for a writer who admires Ray Charles and wants to be a professional musician.
3. This could be best for a writer who wants to do well in school.

Revising for Organization

Have students write out their opinion statement followed by their call to action on a slip of paper and pass the slip of paper to the student sitting to their right. Do the sentences work well as a team? Remind students to

■ look for the word *should* (or an equivalent word, like *ought*) in the opinion statement and
■ check that the call to action restates the opinion as a command.

Have students give each other brief feedback as they return the slips of paper to one another.

Practice   Answers

Explanations will vary. Possible responses:

1. Does not work as a team. *Don't litter in the park* is not a good call to action because it tells people what *not* to do rather than what to do. It doesn't restate the opinion as a command.
2. Works well as a team.
3. Does not work as a team. The call to action does not refer back to the opinion statement.

218

Revising for Organization

6 My organization makes my essay logical and very convincing.

5 My beginning and ending work together, and I use order of importance for my reasons.

4 My beginning and ending work well, but I need to use order of importance for my reasons.

When you revise for *organization,* you make sure your beginning and ending work together. You also check the order of your reasons. The rubric strip above can help you revise.

How can I check my beginning and ending?

You can check your beginning and ending by making sure your opinion statement and your call to action work as a team.

Opinion statement: Says what the reader should do
Call to action: Tells the reader to do it

Practice

Read the following pairs of sentences. Which pair works as a team? Tell why the other pairs do not work together.

1. Opinion statement: Students should join the cleanup crew.
   Call to action: Don't litter in the park.
2. Opinion statement: Kids should donate to the coat drive.
   Call to action: Bring in a coat you've outgrown and warm up someone's life.
3. Opinion statement: Students should try out for the musical.
   Call to action: Have fun!

 Revise

Check your beginning and ending. Find out if your opinion statement and your call to action work as a team. Change them until they do work well together.

Promoting an Event **219**

3 My beginning or ending is weak, and I need to use order of importance for my reasons.

2 My essay runs together, and I need to put my reasons in a clear order.

1 I need help understanding the parts of my essay.

How can I check order of importance?

You can check order of importance by deciding which reason is the most convincing. Put that reason last. (See also page 57.)

Practice

Read the opinion statement. Then decide which reason is most convincing. Tell why you think so.

Opinion statement: Kids should donate to the coat drive.
Reason A: If a coat doesn't fit, you may as well donate it.
Reason B: Many kids need coats to stay healthy this winter.
Reason C: It's easy to drop off coats in the school office.

 Revise   **Check order of importance.** Make sure your most convincing reason comes last.

Revising in Action

The writer changes the call to action to better match the opinion statement. (See page 211.)

If you want to have fun, win prizes, and develop a
first-class brain, you should join the summer reading
Go to the library, sign up, and start reading!
program. ~~Try it, you'll like it!~~

Work through the **Practice** exercise as a class, encouraging students to explain their answers. Note that although order of importance in a persuasive essay can be a matter of opinion, there are some reasons that most people would agree are more important than others. Focus on two of the items in the Practice:

- Reason A: Remind students that many people have younger siblings to hand their old coats down to. This reason may not be convincing to them.
- Reason C: While this is worth mentioning, most people would say that it's better to do something because it will help people than because it is easy.

Practice Answers

Explanations will vary. Possible response:

Students will probably pick B. Most will agree that helping people stay healthy is a better reason to do something than because it is easy.

Have students tell a partner their opinion and the reasons for it, in order. Does the partner agree with the order they chose? If not, why?

Revising for Voice

Discuss the terms *fuzzy thinking* and *bandwagon thinking.*

- Fuzzy thinking is unfocused (the way a picture that is out of focus looks fuzzy). It means drawing conclusions without having good reasons for doing so.
- Accepting an opinion just because lots of people have that opinion is bandwagon thinking. The term comes from the word for the wagon that carries a band during a parade—it has lots of people riding it. A common expression, *to jump on the bandwagon,* means "to join the crowd." Bandwagon thinking is one kind of fuzzy thinking.

Remind students that something isn't necessarily true just because a lot of people believe it's true—more evidence is needed.

Practice   Answers

Sentences 2 and 4.

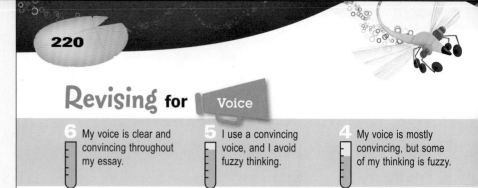

220

Revising for Voice

| **6** My voice is clear and convincing throughout my essay. | **5** I use a convincing voice, and I avoid fuzzy thinking. | **4** My voice is mostly convincing, but some of my thinking is fuzzy. |

When you revise for *voice,* you watch out for fuzzy thinking like exaggeration and bandwagon thinking. The rubric strip above can help you avoid these problems.

How can I spot and fix bandwagon thinking?

Bandwagon thinking is trying to convince the reader to do something by saying, "Everybody else is doing it." Bandwagon thinking is not convincing.

Everybody goes to open swim night, so you should, too!

Avoid bandwagon words:	all	everyone	everybody		no one
Choose qualifying words:	some	most	many	few	several

Practice

Which of the following sentences are examples of bandwagon thinking?

1. Open swim night has activities for all ages.
2. Every fourth grader loves open swim night.
3. The lifeguards are friendly and helpful.
4. Nobody wants to miss out on open swim night.

 Revise

Watch for bandwagon thinking. Read your essay and look for bandwagon ideas. Remove them.

English Language Learners

To help students learn meanings of new words, pair the words with concrete examples or visuals whenever possible. Use an out-of-focus picture on the overhead to demonstrate *fuzzy / out of focus.* Show a picture of a wagon full of people that is labeled *opinion* to illustrate that *bandwagon thinking* means "lots of people having the same opinion."

Promoting an Event **221**

3 I need to remove fuzzy thinking, which makes my essay less convincing.

2 My thinking is confusing and unconvincing.

1 My opinion and reasons are unclear.

How can I recognize exaggerations?

Exaggerations stretch the truth. They make your writing less convincing. (See page 464.)

Practice

Read the following paragraph. Tell which sentence is an exaggeration.

The best reason to come to open swim night is to use the diving boards. The low board is three feet off the water and has great spring. The high board must be 100 feet high. Some kids who go to open swim night learn how to do tricks off the diving boards.

 Revise **Watch for exaggerations.** Read your essay to find places where you may have stretched the truth. Rewrite those parts.

Revising in Action

The writer rewrites an exaggeration to make the essay more convincing.

> Also, the summer reading program gives out great
> The prize for reading 5 books is a free pizza.
> prizes. ~~One kid won a thousand pizzas.~~ Just think of
> each chapter as a small slice! The prize for . . .

Practice Answer

The high board must be 100 feet high.

Point out that sometimes it's okay to use exaggeration. If it's clear that the writer is using exaggeration on purpose, it can create a comic effect or help express how something feels. For example, in the **Practice** paragraph the writer could have said: *Standing with your toes hanging over the edge of the high board, you'll feel 100 feet tall, even though the board's only 15 feet high.*

Have students exchange papers with a partner and read through each other's drafts, looking for unsupported statements.

- Are any of the unsupported statements examples of bandwagon thinking or exaggeration?
- If students can explain the statements, have them insert the supporting details.
- If they cannot explain the statements, ask students to rewrite or replace them.

Note that exaggerations are a kind of fuzzy thinking. When exaggerations are used to try to support an argument, as in the examples, they ask readers to believe something that just isn't true.

English Language Learners

Students may be unfamiliar with the expression, *stretch the truth.* Explain that exaggerations are statements that are not true. There may be an element of truth in what is said, but the statement goes beyond what is real. Before introducing the **Practice** exercise, use concrete examples to help demonstrate that exaggerations are statements that are not true. For example, tell students a large and heavy book you are holding weighs a ton. Ask volunteers to describe other common classroom items using exaggerations. Have groups restate the descriptions to eliminate the exaggerations.

Revising for Word Choice

Before students complete the **Practice** exercise, tell them that they can do more than simply replace the overused words with synonyms. They can make the following kinds of changes:

- Use pronouns to replace overused nouns. For example, in *He eats pretzels every afternoon because he loves pretzels,* the second *pretzels* could be replaced with the pronoun *them.*
- Delete the second mention if the meaning is clear without it. For example, *A few of the students had read the book, but the rest of the students had not* could be changed to *A few of the students had read the book, but the rest had not.*

✻ For more about pronouns, see PE pages 576–581.

Remind students who use a thesaurus for the **Practice** exercise that they must choose synonyms that match the **tone** *(see below).* Slang words like *dough, moolah,* and *bread* won't fit the context of the paragraph.

Practice Answers

Money is overused. Synonyms may include *cash, funds, profit, income.*

222

Revising for Word Choice

6 The words I use in my essay are strong and convince the reader.

5 I use synonyms and modifiers to make my writing persuasive.

4 My essay is persuasive, but more synonyms or modifiers would help.

When you revise for *word choice,* you use synonyms and modifiers to make your essay more persuasive. The rubric strip above will help you revise.

How can synonyms improve my writing?

Synonyms can help you avoid using the same word again and again. A synonym is a word that has the same meaning (or nearly the same meaning) as another word. A thesaurus can help you find synonyms. (See page 332.)

Practice

Read the following paragraph. Decide which word is being used too often. Then find two synonyms for the word. Use a thesaurus if you need help.

Most importantly, kids should work at the rummage sale because the money helps the fourth-grade classes. Some of the money pays for field trips. The rest of the money pays for the classroom supplies and room decorations. Last year's sale made so much money that some of the money paid for snacks for this year!

Revise

Replace overused words. Read your essay. Watch for words that you use again and again. Replace some of them with synonyms.

Teaching Tip: Tone

Explain that sometimes the casual voice students are trying to establish in their writing can become *too* casual. Point out that while students should try to sound friendly and conversational, they also need to sound knowledgeable and polite. Using slang or making silly jokes can work against them by giving the impression that they don't take their topic seriously.

Suggest that students imagine their audience as someone friendly and older, whose respect they want to win. Then they can adjust their tone accordingly.

English Language Learners

Students' limited vocabularies may make it difficult for them to think of synonyms independently and to select appropriate synonyms from a thesaurus. Before students choose to use an unfamiliar word from a thesaurus, encourage them to ask you or a classmate to use the word in a sentence to help clarify the meaning.

Promoting an Event **223**

3 I need more synonyms and modifiers to be persuasive.

2 I need to replace many repeated or confusing words.

1 My word choice does not fit a persuasive essay.

How can I write strong statements?

You can write strong statements by using persuasive words that send a clear message to the reader.

Weak Statements (weak words are underlined):

It would probably be a good idea to have a collection for the community food pantry. I think every student could bring one food item.

Strong Statements (persuasive words are underlined):

We need to have a collection for the community food pantry. Every student should bring one food item.

 Revise Review your sentences. Make sure you have used persuasive words that make strong statements.

Revising in Action

The writer cuts weak words to make the call to action stronger.

> ~~If you want to take part in~~ summer reading, ~~you could~~
> go to the library, sign up, and start reading.

Expand on the information about strong sentences by offering additional hints about how students can improve their sentences.

- Remember to choose active verbs and specific nouns whenever possible.
- Consider cutting any words that don't play a real part in the sentence. For example, in *Birds flock to the feeder that is in our backyard,* the words *that is* can be cut without changing the meaning at all.
- It is rarely necessary to say *I think* in writing—it's already understood that an essay (especially a persuasive essay) is saying what the writer thinks.
- Intensifiers like *very, really,* and *extremely* seem as if they'll make what you say stronger, but often they just take up space. Try cutting them. Chances are, the sentence will sound better without them.

Revising for Sentence Fluency

Explain that sentence fragments often occur when a writer intends to use a comma but uses end punctuation instead. Suggest that students look for fragments by reading sentences one by one, starting at the end of the essay. This can help them evaluate each sentence on its own terms.

＊ For more information about fixing fragments, see PE page 436.

Note that some kinds of fragments can be used on purpose. Have students point out the two fragments in the following: *My brother said he was too busy to help me rake the yard. Busy doing what? Playing video games, of course!* Why are the fragments effective? (They add to the conversational voice.)

Practice Answers

Answers will vary. Possible answers:

1. For our projects, we choose topics from the science textbook.
2. I'm going to make a diorama of the earth's layers.
3 & 4. When all the projects have been judged, the teachers will award ribbons for each project in the fair.
5. After the science fair, my parents always take me out for pizza.

224

Revising for Sentence Fluency

6 My sentences read smoothly. They are complete, correct, and enjoyable to read.

5 My sentences read smoothly and are well written.

4 Most of my sentences are easy to read.

When you revise for *sentence fluency,* you fix sentence errors such as fragments and rambling sentences. Use the rubric strip above as a guide.

How can I fix sentence fragments?

You can fix fragments by making sure that each sentence has a subject and a predicate and expresses a complete thought. (See page 436.) Here are some sentence fragments:

Often work hard on a science-fair project. (missing a subject)
Milo and his whole class. (missing a predicate)
Because they have done research. (not a complete thought)

Practice

Change each sentence fragment into a complete sentence. Use your own words and ideas to add whatever is missing.

1. Topics from the science textbook.
2. A diorama of the earth's layers.
3. When all of the projects have been judged.
4. Ribbons for each project in the fair.
5. After the science fair.

 Revise

Check for sentence fragments. Make sure each of your sentences has a subject and a predicate and expresses a complete thought. Revise to fix any fragments you find.

Struggling Learners

Meet with students who have difficulty identifying sentence fragments in their own work. Copy some of their sentences on the board. Do a Think-Aloud to model how to identify the subject and predicate. Note whether each is a complete thought. Continue the activity, inviting student participation. Transfer the task to partners who can work together to complete the revision assignment.

Promoting an Event **225**

3 I need to correct a few sentence errors that may confuse the reader.

2 Many sentence errors will confuse the reader. I need to correct my sentences.

1 My essay is hard to read. I need to rewrite most of my sentences.

How can I fix rambling sentences?

You can fix rambling sentences by splitting them into smaller sentences. Rambling sentences are often connected with words such as *or, but, and,* or *so.* Remove the extra conjunctions and add end punctuation and capital letters as needed.

Practice

> **Rewrite this rambling sentence as three sentences.**
>
> Kids should enter the science fair because it lets them learn about a science topic and students get to learn about other people's projects by looking at the exhibits and it is also great to get a ribbon!

 Fix rambling sentences. Look for sentences that ramble on and on. Fix them by breaking them up into shorter sentences.

Revising in Action

The writer splits a rambling sentence into three sentences.

> Sure, it's great to play games with friends, but it's also
> great to dig a tunnel to the center of the earth and
> fly to Jupiter. and books let you do things like that.

Explain to students that rambling sentences usually happen when a writer has lots of ideas and strings together too many into one sentence. Point out that it's great to have so many ideas! All they have to do to fix the problem is break the rambling sentence into smaller pieces.

Sometimes, as in the Revising in Action example, it's possible to fix a rambling sentence, or a related problem sentence, the run-on, by substituting periods for the conjunctions. Remind students that they can also consider adding transition words to create smoothly flowing sentences.

✽ For more about run-on sentences, see PE page 437.

Practice Answers

Answers may vary. Possible answer:

Kids should enter the science fair because it lets them learn about a science topic. They'll also get to learn about other people's projects by looking at the exhibits. Plus, it's great to get a ribbon!

English Language Learners

Students create rambling sentences because overuse of conjunctions is common when they have not yet acquired an internalized sense of how English works. Some may find it easier to recognize and revise the rambling sentences if you do the following with each student:

- Read one of the student's own rambling sentences aloud in one breath, rushing through the last words to demonstrate how difficult it is to read the entire sentence.
- Have the student attempt to read the sentence in one breath.
- Demonstrate how to create shorter sentences; then read the revised sentences with the student.
- Encourage students to use the one-breath technique as they read aloud other sentences.

Revising Using a Checklist

Note that students have addressed each of the items on the checklist as they worked through the revising section. Encourage them to consult the corresponding pages if they need a reminder of what to look for.

Have students copy out a blank revising checklist. For homework (perhaps over a weekend), ask students to

- give the checklist, along with their draft, to a parent or friend outside class, so that person can read and evaluate their work;
- incorporate into their draft any changes suggested during that final review; and
- make a clean copy to bring to the next class.

226

Revising Using a Checklist

Revise **Check your revising.** Number a piece of paper from 1 to 10. If you can answer "yes" to a question, put a check mark after that number. If not, continue working on that part of your essay.

Ideas

_____ **1.** Do I have a clear opinion statement?

_____ **2.** Do my middle paragraphs have topic sentences?

_____ **3.** Do I use different kinds of details (such as anecdotes and quotations) to help persuade the reader?

Organization

_____ **4.** Do my opinion statement and call to action work together?

_____ **5.** Do I have my reasons in order of importance?

Voice

_____ **6.** Have I avoided bandwagon thinking and exaggeration?

Word Choice

_____ **7.** Have I replaced repeated words with synonyms?

_____ **8.** Have I used persuasive words?

Sentence Fluency

_____ **9.** Have I fixed fragments?

_____ **10.** Have I fixed rambling sentences?

Revise **Make a clean copy.** When you've finished revising your essay, make a clean copy for editing.

Editing

Promoting an Event **227**

The next step in writing your essay is editing. When you edit, you make sure you have used the rules of English, called "conventions," correctly.

Keys to Editing

1. **Use** a dictionary, a thesaurus, and the "Proofreader's Guide" in the back of this book for help.

2. **Edit** on a printed copy if you use a computer. Then make your changes on the computer.

3. **Use** the editing marks shown inside the back cover of this book.

4. **Ask** someone else to check your writing for errors, too.

Editing Keys to Editing

Remind students that during the editing stage, they have a chance to find and correct errors in

- punctuation,
- capitalization,
- spelling, and
- grammar.

The Keys to Editing list lays out the process students will be guided through on PE pages 228–230.

Model the editing process using a sample persuasive essay copied onto an overhead transparency:

- Make corrections using a different colored pencil from the color used to write the essay and suggest that students do the same.
- Begin by underlining the opinion statement, topic sentences, and call to action.
- Give students the chance to point out problems and suggest how to fix them.
- Explain the purpose of each editing mark as you use it.
- Have volunteers look up misspelled words in a dictionary.

Explain that the following pages will walk students through applying this process to their own essays.

Struggling Learners

Create a scavenger hunt for students who need extra practice becoming familiar with the Proofreader's Guide. To direct the hunt, use your knowledge of students' weaknesses and invite participants to identify their own difficulties with conventions. Turn the problems into questions. For example, "If you have trouble knowing when to use a comma, where should you look?" As students hunt for answers, extend the search to specifics, such as "commas in a series" or "commas with quotations."

Editing for Conventions

Explain that there are two main ways to **use apostrophes** *(see below)*:

- to mark where letters were dropped in combining words into contractions such as *don't* (*do not*) and *he'll* (*he will*)
- to indicate ownership

Students might be confused when they need to form the possessive of a singular proper noun ending in *s*—for example, the name *Mr. Williams*. The most accepted way to create this possessive is to add the apostrophe and *s*: *Mr. Williams's house*.

* For more about apostrophes, see PE pages 490–493.

Practice Answers

1. pet's	6. gymnasium's
2. car's	7. children's
3. greyhounds'	8. judges'
4. students'	9. contest's
5. trainer's	10. women's

228

Editing for Conventions

6 My strong control of conventions makes my writing clear and persuasive.

5 I have a few errors in punctuation, spelling, or grammar.

4 I have several errors in punctuation, spelling, and grammar.

When you edit for *conventions,* you check for punctuation, capitalization, spelling, and grammar errors. The rubric strip above can guide your revision.

When do I use an apostrophe to show ownership?

Use an apostrophe after nouns to show ownership. (See page 492 for more information.)

Singular nouns: Add an apostrophe and an *s*—dog's collar.

Plural nouns ending in s: Add just the apostrophe—dogs' collars.

Plural nouns not ending in s: Add an apostrophe and an *s*—men's ties.

Practice

For each word below, write the correct possessive form.

1. pet	6. gymnasium
2. car	7. children
3. greyhounds	8. judges
4. students	9. contest
5. trainer	10. women

 Check your possessive forms. Read your essay to be sure you have used apostrophes correctly to show possession. (Also see page 229.)

Teaching Tip: Using Apostrophes

The use of the apostrophe with both possessive nouns and contractions leads to confusion with certain word pairs: *it's/its, you're/your,* and *they're/their.* Review the differences:

- *It's, you're,* and *they're* are contractions of *it is, you are,* and *they are.*
- *Its, your,* and *their* are all possessive pronouns.

Acknowledge that it can be confusing that these possessives, unlike possessive nouns, don't have apostrophes, but point out that no possessive pronoun (see PE page 229) has an apostrophe. On the other hand, *absolutely every* contraction does. If students pause to remember what part of speech they need, they can always figure out whether or not to use an apostrophe for these tricky words.

English Language Learners

Students may not yet be using possessives in their spoken English. Analyze how students signify possession. If they use a phrase such as "the book of Julie," postpone instruction until their oral language indicates they are ready. If students are using possessives in their oral language, ask teams to use the words in sentences before they write the possessive form on their papers.

Promoting an Event   **229**

3 I need to correct errors that may confuse the reader.

2 My errors make my essay difficult to read. I need to correct them.

1 I need to correct numerous errors in my writing.

How do pronouns show ownership?

Pronouns show ownership without using an apostrophe. Some possessive pronouns come before a noun, and some stand alone.

Before a noun: my   your   his   her   our   their   its

Stand alone: mine   yours   his   hers   ours   theirs

Greg left his book at school.

(The pronoun *his* comes before the noun *book*.)

Can Greg borrow yours for the assignment?

(The pronoun *yours* stands alone.)

tip When a possessive pronoun comes before a noun, the pronoun functions as an adjective. (See 578.3.)

Practice

Use each of the possessive pronouns correctly in a sentence.

1. my
2. mine
3. her
4. hers
5. their
6. theirs

Editing in Action

The writer corrects a pronoun to show ownership.

When the weather's nice, go out and ride ^your you's bike.

Discuss with students the use of pronouns in the samples.

■ It's easy to tell what *yours* refers to, because *book* is in the first sentence.

■ *Yours* could also be replaced by *your book,* but using *yours* allows the writer to avoid having to repeat *book.*

Ask students to comment on the use of *yours* in this passage: *Greg left his book at school and his hat at Louise's house. Can he borrow yours?* (It isn't clear whether *yours* refers to *book* or *hat,* so it shouldn't be used here.)

✳ For more about possessive pronouns, see PE page 413.

Practice Answers

Answers will vary.

English Language Learners

Students often confuse and misuse pronouns while becoming proficient in English. Emphasize which pronouns come before a noun and which stand alone.

- Hold an object such as a book while stating, "This is my book."
- Place the book on a desk and point to it while stating, "It's mine."
- Give the book to different students or place it on their desks, and point to it while asking volunteers to tell whose book it is.
- After each response, state the appropriate pronoun to model when pronouns should come before nouns and when they can stand alone.

Editing Using a Checklist

Give students a few moments to look over the Proofreader's Guide (PE pages 478–605). Throughout the year, they can refer to the instruction, rules, and examples to clarify any checklist items or to resolve questions about their own writing.

Have students keep a journal of common editing errors to avoid. Encourage them to update their journal each time they edit their work. After students edit their persuasive essay, ask them to share the errors that gave them trouble. List the errors on a poster, leaving space for new additions as students discover more errors.

Adding a Title

Point out that two of the sample titles are commands—this makes sense for a persuasive essay. Ask students to make up two title choices, one of which is a command.

230

Editing Using a Checklist

Edit | **Check your editing.** Number a piece of paper from 1 to 10. If you can answer "yes" to a question, put a check mark after that number. If not, continue to edit for that convention.

Conventions

PUNCTUATION

_____ **1.** Do I use end punctuation after all my sentences?

_____ **2.** Do I use commas after introductory word groups?

_____ **3.** Do I correctly use apostrophes to show ownership?

CAPITALIZATION

_____ **4.** Do I start all my sentences with capital letters?

_____ **5.** Do I capitalize all names (proper nouns)?

SPELLING

_____ **6.** Have I spelled all my words correctly?

_____ **7.** Have I checked for words my spell-checker might miss?

GRAMMAR

_____ **8.** Do my subjects and predicates agree?

_____ **9.** Have I checked my use of possessive pronouns?

_____ **10.** Do I use the right word *(to, too, two)*?

Adding a Title

Here are some suggestions for writing a title.

- Repeat a sound: **Sign Up for Summer Reading**
- Be creative: **Befford Summer Brain Workout**
- Use an expression: **Put Some Miles on Your Imagination**

Promoting an Event 231

Publishing

It's time to proofread your essay and make a neat copy to share. Present your work on a Web page, in a newsletter or newspaper, or as a morning announcement. (See the suggestions below.)

Presentation

- Use blue or black ink and write neatly.
- Write your name in the upper left corner of page 1.
- Skip a line and center your title; skip another line and start writing.
- Indent every paragraph and leave a one-inch margin on all sides.
- Write your last name and the page number in the upper right corner of every page after the first one.

Make a Web Page
Get your teacher's help to post your work on your class or school Web page.

Create an Editorial
Turn your paper into an editorial for your school newsletter or a community newspaper.

Make a Morning Announcement
Ask permission to promote your event in the school's morning announcements. Base your announcement on your opinion statement and topic sentences.

 Create a final copy. Follow your teacher's instructions or use the guidelines above to format your essay. (If you are using a computer, see pages 44–46.) Create a clean final copy of your essay and carefully proofread it.

Publishing

Have students illustrate their final papers. Then make enough photocopies for everyone and assemble a class magazine, *The Call to Action*.

Encourage students to try out their classmates' recommendations about events or activities. Set aside class time to discuss the experiences of students who do participate.

Remind students to date their original copy of the essay and store it in their writing portfolio, along with all the planning notes they made while working on it.

✳ For students who created their essays on a computer, see PE pages 43–46 for formatting guidelines.

Rubric for Persuasive Writing

Remind students that a rubric is a chart they can use to help them evaluate their writing.

- The rubrics in this book are based on a six-point scale, in which a score of 6 indicates an amazing piece of writing and a score of 1 means the writing is incomplete and not ready to be assessed.

- Explain that the purpose of the rubric is to help students break down the assessment process by evaluating each of the six traits individually—ideas, organization, voice, word choice, sentence fluency, and conventions.

- Point out that during the writing process, rubrics can also help writers decide what elements to include and how to present them.

- Explain to students that they will most likely have different ratings for the traits. For example, they may give themselves a 5 for ideas but a 4 for organization.

✳ Four- and five-point rubrics for persuasive writing can be found on TE pages 626 and 629.

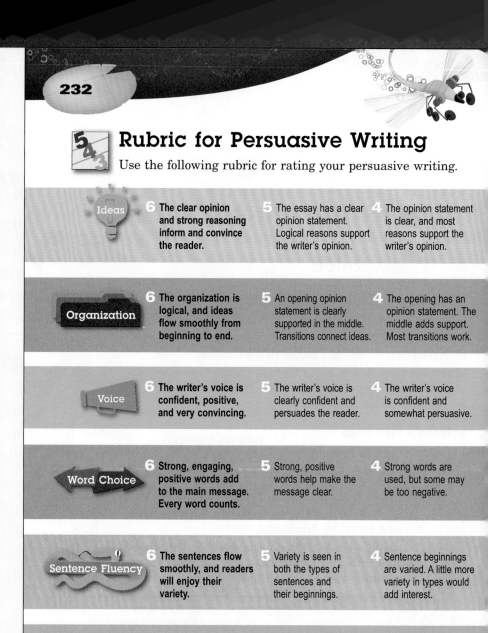

Rubric for Persuasive Writing

Use the following rubric for rating your persuasive writing.

Ideas
- **6** The clear opinion and strong reasoning inform and convince the reader.
- **5** The essay has a clear opinion statement. Logical reasons support the writer's opinion.
- **4** The opinion statement is clear, and most reasons support the writer's opinion.

Organization
- **6** The organization is logical, and ideas flow smoothly from beginning to end.
- **5** An opening opinion statement is clearly supported in the middle. Transitions connect ideas.
- **4** The opening has an opinion statement. The middle adds support. Most transitions work.

Voice
- **6** The writer's voice is confident, positive, and very convincing.
- **5** The writer's voice is clearly confident and persuades the reader.
- **4** The writer's voice is confident and somewhat persuasive.

Word Choice
- **6** Strong, engaging, positive words add to the main message. Every word counts.
- **5** Strong, positive words help make the message clear.
- **4** Strong words are used, but some may be too negative.

Sentence Fluency
- **6** The sentences flow smoothly, and readers will enjoy their variety.
- **5** Variety is seen in both the types of sentences and their beginnings.
- **4** Sentence beginnings are varied. A little more variety in types would add interest.

Conventions
- **6** Mastery of conventions adds persuasive power to the essay.
- **5** One or two grammar and punctuation errors do not distract the reader.
- **4** Grammar and punctuation errors in a few sentences may distract the reader.

Advanced Learners

Invite students to create a bulletin board highlighting the Six Traits of Writing used for the rubric. Each trait should be represented by an eye-catching design that is also informative. The rubric table provides symbols, but encourage students to invent their own. Remind them to use terms from the table and from class discussions to describe each trait.

Promoting an Event 233

3 The opinion statement is clear. Reasons and details are not as complete as they need to be.

2 The opinion statement is unclear. Reasons and details are needed.

1 An opinion statement, reasons, and details are needed.

3 There is a beginning, a middle, and an ending. Transitions are needed.

2 The beginning, middle, and ending run together.

1 The writing needs to be organized to avoid confusion.

3 The writer's voice needs to be more confident to persuade the reader.

2 The writer's voice sounds unsure.

1 The writer needs to learn more about voice.

3 Many words need to be stronger and more positive.

2 The same general words are used throughout the essay.

1 Help is needed to find better words.

3 Several sentences begin the same way. Sentence fragments need to be rewritten.

2 Too many sentences begin the same way. Fragments and rambling sentences need to be rewritten.

1 Choppy or incomplete sentences need to be rewritten.

3 There are enough errors to confuse the reader.

2 Errors make the essay difficult to read.

1 Help is needed to make corrections.

Evaluating a Persuasive Essay

Ask students if they agree with the sample self-assessment on PE page 235. If they agree with the criticisms, ask them to suggest improvements based on the comments in the self-assessment. If they disagree with any comment, ask them to explain why.

Possible suggestions:

Ideas include a quotation—*"Wow," Christina said, "this is like summer camp in the middle of the city."*

Organization & Voice ending— Reduce exclamations and eliminate bandwagon thinking: *So, if you like to stay up late and be with friends, join the Walk for a Cure. You'll have the time of your life while you help save lives. See you out there!*

Word Choice use synonyms— *Friends and families get to spend time together. It's like being at a camp . . .*

Sentence Fluency sentence errors—Fix rambling sentence: *Last year, there was . . . unicycle. People camped . . . field. They barbecued . . .* Fix fragment: *Of course, the biggest reason kids should come out is that they can help stop cancer.*

Conventions capitalization and spelling—*Walk for a Cure, hundreds, pledge, scientists*

Evaluating a Persuasive Essay

Rosa's persuasive essay appears below. Read through it, focusing on its strengths and weaknesses. (The essay contains several errors.)

Walk for a Cure!

Last year, I camped by the high school track and stayed up late and walked with friends. I also helped people with cancer. The Walk for a Cure lets people do all of these things! Kids from Rosewood School should join the Walk for a Cure.

To begin with, walk for a cure is fun. Hunderds of people come out. Some walk, some ride in wagons, and some even ride their bikes. Last year, there was a high school student on a unicycle and people camped around the track and on the football field and they barbecued food and sang songs.

Also, Walk for a Cure is like a huge sleepover outside. Friends and families get to hang out. My sister Christina and I hung out all night with our friends. It's like hanging out at a camp in the middle of the city!

Of course, the biggest reason kids should come out. They can help stop cancer. People plege money for miles or hours. Grandmas, grandpas, uncles, and aunts love to give money. All the money helps people with cancer and helps sceintists find a cure.

So, if you like to stay up late and be with friends, join the Walk for a Cure. You'll even help cure cancer! Come on out! Everybody's doing it!

Promoting an Event **235**

Student Self-Assessment

Rosa rated her writing. Under each trait, she wrote a positive comment and then something she could improve on. (She used the rubric and the number scale on pages 232–233.)

4 Ideas
1. I love my topic, and I tell three reasons.
2. I should use a quotation.

5 Organization
1. My reasons are in order.
2. My ending could be stronger.

4 Voice
1. I don't use exaggeration.
2. I guess the end has bandwagon thinking.

4 Word Choice
1. My word choice is pretty good.
2. I should find a synonym for "hang out."

3 Sentence Fluency
1. Most of my sentences read smoothly.
2. I have some sentence errors.

3 Conventions
1. I punctuated my long sentences correctly.
2. I have trouble with spelling.

Use the rubric. Rate your essay using the rubric shown on pages 232–233. On your own paper, list the six traits. Leave room after each trait to write one strength and one weakness. Then choose a number (from 1 to 6) that shows how well you used each trait.

Student Self-Assessment

To give students additional practice with evaluating a persuasive essay, use a blank assessment sheet (TE page 644) and one or both of the **benchmark papers** listed in the Benchmark Papers box below. You can use an overhead transparency while students refer to their own copies made from the copy masters. For your benefit a completed assessment sheet is provided for each benchmark paper.

Challenge students to suggest other changes Rosa could have made and tell what traits they apply to. Responses may include:

Ideas Add specific details by answering one or more of the following: How many people participated? (Not just *hundreds*.) How many miles did Rosa walk? How much money did she earn? How much was raised by the kids from Rosewood?

Organization Explain how the pledging works at the start of the essay rather than in paragraph 4.

Voice/Conventions Eliminate all but one or two of the five exclamation marks used. They weaken the voice by making the writer sound surprised or agitated.

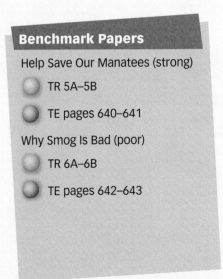

Benchmark Papers

Help Save Our Manatees (strong)

TR 5A–5B

TE pages 640–641

Why Smog Is Bad (poor)

TR 6A–6B

TE pages 642–643

Reflecting on Your Writing

Have students date their reflection sheet and keep it with the finished essay and related notes in their writing portfolio.

⁂ For more about portfolios, see PE pages 47–49.

To encourage students to make constructive use of their reflections, have them compare their answer to item 2 with the feedback you gave them for the assignment. Do the two assessments agree in any way?

Have students reread reflections they wrote for essays earlier in the year and then talk about the assessments as a group.

- Are there areas where students can see they're making progress?
- Are there certain mistakes that they keep repeating?
- Invite volunteers to share with the class what they learned about persuasive writing.
- Invite students to share what they hope to accomplish in their next persuasive essay.

Reflecting on Your Writing

Congratulations! You've finished your persuasive essay. Now take a moment to reflect on the job you have done. On your own paper, complete each sentence starter below.

Take some time to reflect on the experience of writing persuasively.

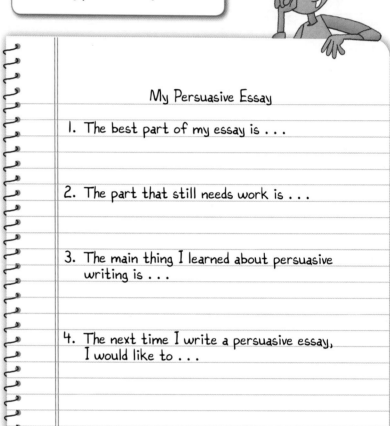

My Persuasive Essay

1. The best part of my essay is . . .

2. The part that still needs work is . . .

3. The main thing I learned about persuasive writing is . . .

4. The next time I write a persuasive essay, I would like to . . .

Persuasive Writing
Across the Curriculum

Persuasive writing is useful in all your classes as well as in extracurricular activities. In science, a problem-solution essay may convince others to work at fixing a problem in the environment. In math, a graph that tracks a fund-raising project can persuade people to contribute. And a polite letter can bring in donations for a worthy cause.

Mini Index

- **Science:** Writing a Problem-Solution Essay
- **Math:** Creating a Thermometer Graph
- **Practical Writing:** Drafting a Letter of Request
- **Assessment:** Writing for Assessment

Across the Curriculum

Objectives
- apply what has been learned about persuasive writing to other curriculum areas
- practice writing for assessment

The lessons on the following pages provide samples of persuasive writing students might do in different content areas. The first lesson guides students through the steps of the writing process in science. The second and third lessons provide models and writing tips for persuasive writing in math and in a letter of request.

Assigning these forms of writing will depend on
- the skill level of your students,
- the subject matter they are studying in different content areas, and
- the writing goals of your school, district, or state.

Encourage students to use the activities that follow to give them ideas of other ways to practice their new skills of persuading readers to agree with them—both in school and in their outside lives.

Materials

Newspaper articles about local environmental issues (TE p. 239)

Posterboard and drawing supplies (TE p. 243)

Business envelopes (TE p. 245)

Sticky notes (TE p. 251)

Copy Masters/ Transparencies

T-chart (TE p. 239)

Science: Writing a Problem-Solution Essay

Note that the problem-solution essay has a different structure than the persuasive essay on PE pages 201–202. Have students compare the two essays.

- Beginning: The opinion statement in the problem-solution essay is fairly general, because the solution paragraph (paragraph 3) that follows gives specifics about actions people should take.
- Middle: Instead of giving one reason per paragraph for taking action, in this essay all the reasons for solving the problem are given in the first middle paragraph.
- Ending: The ending urges the reader to help solve the problem. The call to action (the last sentence of the essay) does not rephrase the writer's opinion statement. It restates the solution to the problem.

Have students point out the parts of the sample essay that they find most or least effective. Ask them to explain their responses.

238

Science: Writing a Problem-Solution Essay

In the following essay, Michael names a problem and suggests how kids can help solve it.

BEGINNING

The problem is introduced, and an opinion statement (underlined) is given.

MIDDLE

One middle paragraph tells why people should care about the problem. The other paragraph describes a solution.

ENDING

The ending asks the reader to help.

Silence in the Swamp

Last week, my dad and I went to the park at night to hear the frogs sing. Their song was not as loud as it used to be. Frogs are dying out because wetlands are disappearing or being poisoned by chemicals. People should do something to save the frogs.

If frogs disappear, people will have problems. Frogs eat insects like flies and mosquitoes. Without frogs, bugs will be everywhere! Also, frogs are food for animals like cranes, herons, raccoons, opossums, and snakes. If frogs die out, other animals may die out, too. Finally, frogs sing, and their night songs would be missed.

Kids can help by joining a group called "A Thousand Friends of Frogs." Members do frog counts near their homes. The counts help scientists keep track of how the frogs are doing. Kids also help dig new ponds for frogs. The group has contests for writing essays and making posters that convince people to stop polluting wetland areas.

This problem can't be fixed by one or two people. To give frogs a fighting chance, everyone concerned about wildlife needs to get involved. Join "A Thousand Friends of Frogs," and help the frogs keep singing!

Writing in Science  **239**

Prewriting Selecting a Topic

An ideas cluster can help you find a topic.

Ideas Cluster

littering · noisy traffic · Environmental Problems · frogs disappearing * · old landfill

Prewrite

Make an ideas cluster. Write *Environmental Problems* on a piece of paper. Around this heading, list problems that you know of where you live. Put a star (✳) next to the problem you want to write about.

Gathering Details

Your problem-solution essay should show *why the problem is serious* and *how people can solve it*. A why-how chart can help.

Why-How Chart

Problem: Frogs are disappearing

Why is the problem serious?
Frogs eat bugs.
Frogs are food for other animals.
Frogs make music.

How can people solve it?
Count frogs.
Dig new ponds.
Write essays.
Make posters.

Prewrite

Create a why-how chart. Write your problem and the same underlined questions above on your own paper. Find at least three answers for each question.

Prewriting Selecting a Topic

To help students get ideas

- give students time to talk to their families and friends about environmental issues,
- provide articles from the local newspaper on various environmental topics, and
- have the class brainstorm together to create a large list of the topics they've assembled.

Prewriting Gathering Details

Distribute copies of the reproducible T-chart (TE page 645) for students to use for their why-how charts.

If possible, schedule library time so that students can research the answers to their questions in books, periodicals, and on the Internet. Encourage them to consult the librarian for extra help finding materials.

✳ For more about researching, see PE pages 321–332.

English Language Learners

Make sure students understand the term *environmental*. Invite participants to use a dictionary, thesaurus, and even their social studies or science book glossaries. While brainstorming examples for the activity, make a web that connects specific environments with problems so that students can see the direct connections.

Struggling Learners

Students may be unable to comprehend grade-level text independently. If students use the library to complete their Why-How Charts, provide a list of their topics in advance to give the librarian time to find materials at the appropriate reading levels.

Prewriting
Writing an Opinion Statement

Emphasize that students' opinion statements should express a general solution. They can provide more specific details later. This will spark readers' interest in the paragraph that follows.

Students may ask why it's okay to make a general statement here. Explain that the reason they're usually told to avoid using general words like *something* in their focus statement is that, too often, the writer forgets to add specifics to explain the general word. In this case, though, the general word will be explained.

Prewriting
Writing Topic Sentences

It's possible that some students will have enough information to write an additional paragraph, especially in answer to the question *Why is the problem serious?*

Tell students who will be writing an extra paragraph to think of a way to arrange their reasons into two groups that are related. They will need to write an additional topic sentence for their extra paragraph.

Prewriting Writing an Opinion Statement

In a problem-solution essay, your opinion statement should name the problem and the solution.

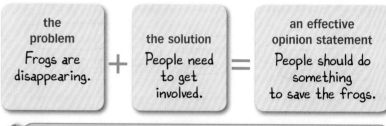

the problem	the solution	an effective opinion statement
Frogs are disappearing.	+ People need to get involved.	= People should do something to save the frogs.

  Write your opinion statement. Use the formula above to create a strong focus for your persuasive essay.

Writing Topic Sentences

Each of the middle paragraphs in your essay needs a topic sentence. Your topic sentences will sum up the answers on your why-how chart (page 239). Here are Michael's topic sentences.

Topic Sentence 1: If frogs disappear, people will have problems.

Topic Sentence 2: Kids can help by joining a group called "A Thousand Friends of Frogs."

  Write your topic sentences. Follow the instructions below.

1 Write topic sentence 1 to answer this question: Why is the problem serious?

2 Write topic sentence 2 to answer this question: How can people solve it?

Writing in Science **241**

Writing Creating Your First Draft

The beginning of your essay should introduce the problem. It must also get the reader's attention and include your opinion statement (page 240). Your middle paragraphs will begin with your topic sentences (page 240) and include details from your why-how chart (page 239). In the ending, ask the reader to do something (page 207).

 Create your first draft. Use all of the ideas you have gathered so far to write your first draft.

Revising Improving Your Writing

You can improve your essay by thinking about these questions:

- **Ideas** Have I stated the problem and shared a solution?
- **Organization** Does my beginning get the reader's interest? Does my ending ask the reader to do something?
- **Voice** Do I sound concerned about the problem?
- **Word Choice** Do I use strong nouns and action verbs?
- **Sentence Fluency** Do I use different sentence beginnings?

 Revise your essay. Use the questions above as a guide to make changes to your essay.

Editing Checking for Conventions

Before you make a final copy, you must correct any errors.

- **Conventions** Have I checked for errors in punctuation, capitalization, spelling, and grammar?

 Check your work. Correct the errors you find. Then write a clean final copy and carefully proofread it.

Writing Creating Your First Draft

Have students reread the essay on page 238 and note that the writer uses logical order.

- In middle paragraph 1, two reasons are environmental (too many bugs, and animals might die), and one is personal (he likes frogs' singing).
- In the next paragraph, the writer describes what group members do. The activities are equally important.

* For more about logical order, see PE page 57.

Revising Improving Your Writing

Guide students through the process of revision. Briefly review the goals for each trait, and then give students five minutes to read through their draft before moving on to the next trait. Circulate among students to answer questions and provide advice.

Editing Checking for Conventions

If possible, have students edit their essay as homework. Encourage them to have a parent or friend read it, too, to help spot errors in conventions. Remind them to use the Proofreader's Guide (PE pages 478–605) or their editing journal to help make corrections.

Math: Creating a Thermometer Graph

Point out that students don't have to organize their graphs by dollar amounts. For example, a Girl Scout might choose to make a graph showing her troop's goal of selling 800 boxes of Girl Scout cookies. She could divide her graph into increments of 10 or 20 boxes of cookies each.

Explain that a thermometer graph is essentially the same thing as a bar graph with a single bar. It indicates only the amounts shown on the vertical line. Even though the colored-in area at the bottom of the graph is bigger, it doesn't represent a larger amount than the smaller colored-in area just above it. (Some kinds of charts, such as pie charts, do use the size of the colored-in areas to indicate different amounts.)

✽ For more about bar graphs, see PE page 474.

Math: Creating a Thermometer Graph

Many fund-raisers use a thermometer graph. It shows how much money has been raised and how much money is still needed. Ahmad made this poster to persuade people to donate money for a new skate park. He used math calculations to divide his thermometer graph into 10 equal parts.

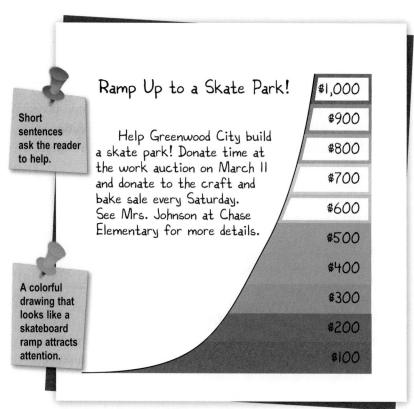

Note: The chart shows that $500 has been raised so far.

Writing in Math   243

WRITING TIPS

Before you write . . .
- **Select a topic.**
  List fund-raisers in your school or community. Choose one that could be shown with a thermometer graph.
- **Think of a fun item related to your topic.**
  Create an interesting thermometer. Use math calculations to divide the thermometer graph into equal parts.

During your writing . . .
- **Start with a sketch.**
  Plan your poster on a piece of paper. Fill the page with the art.
- **Explain your topic.**
  Write a short paragraph that tells the purpose of your poster.
- **Give suggestions.**
  Tell people how they can help.
- **Use color.**
  Use bold colors. Make your words clear and large enough to read.

After you write a first draft . . .
- **Check for errors.**
  Make sure that you have used proper punctuation, capitalization, spelling, and grammar.
- **Make a final version.**
  Make your poster on a large sheet of poster board.

Make a poster. Use these writing tips to make a thermometer graph for the topic you've chosen.

Writing Tips

Direct students' attention to the paragraph on the sample poster. How is this paragraph different from the persuasive paragraphs they've written so far? Possible responses:
- There isn't a topic sentence.
- The writer doesn't give reasons to support what he says.
- The paragraph includes three calls to action. Four, if you count the **title** (*see below*).

Explain that this different paragraph structure is fine because a poster needs to give information quickly and clearly. That way, people who are passing by can get the idea without having to stop and read a detailed paragraph.

Note, however, that the writer might have improved his sentence fluency if he hadn't used all commands.

After students have completed their posters, display them around the room. If students follow the progress of the fundraiser they promoted, encourage them to keep the graph up-to-date.

Teaching Tip: Choosing a Title

Posters need catchy, creative titles. To give students practice in coming up with titles, hold a round-robin contest:

- Have students finish their posters except for the title (leave a blank space for it).
- Hang the posters in a row. Ask students to think of titles for the two posters next to their own and for one other poster of their choice (students whose posters are at the end of the lineup will choose two).
- Have students write their ideas on slips of paper and give them to the posters' creators.
- Ask students to choose one idea—or use their own idea.

After the titles are added to the posters, invite students to share other titles they considered and explain why they chose the one they did.

Practical Writing: Drafting a Letter of Request

Have students think of additional reasons for writing a persuasive letter. Responses may include asking

- their grandparents to visit for their birthday,
- a congressperson to support a cause,
- a company to replace or repair a broken product, or
- an organization to change a policy or practice (for example, suggesting that the school lunchroom provide meals for vegetarians).

Explain that it's important for the language used in letters of request to be extra polite. Ask students to talk about how the language in the letter is different from their essays.

- Although the writer clearly thinks the reader should be a sponsor, he doesn't use the word *should*. That would sound pushy in this context.
- The call to action is phrased as a question instead of a command (*Would you be willing . . . ?*)
- The letter ends by thanking the reader for his attention.

244

Practical Writing:
Drafting a Letter of Request

A letter of request asks someone to do something. In this example, Gabriel asks for a contribution from a local organization.

8711 Snake Road
Little Rock, AR 72200
March 15, 2005

Mr. Jules Hernandez
Little Rock Rotary Club
2131 E. Main Street
Little Rock, AR 72200

Dear Mr. Hernandez:

The **opening** introduces the topic.

My elementary school is having a "Jump Rope for Fitness" program during April. The money we earn will help buy computers for the school. I am writing to ask your organization to sponsor our class for one hour during the contest.

The **body** asks the reader to act.

Would you be willing to give a penny for each time a student in my class can jump rope in that hour? Another plan is to give a dime, a quarter, or a dollar for each minute a student can each jump rope without stopping. My class has 20 students participating.

The **ending** thanks the reader.

With your help, the contest can be a big success. I hope you can help us out! Thank you.

Sincerely,

Gabriel Vasquez
Gabriel Vasquez

Advanced Learners

Challenge students to do some calculating to see if Gabriel's request for donations is reasonable. If Mr. Hernandez sponsors the entire class for one hour, how much might it cost if he gives

- a dime,
- a quarter, or
- a dollar

for each minute students can jump without stopping?

(Answers: If every student jumped for the entire hour, Mr. Hernandez would pay a maximum of $120, $300, or $1200 respectively.)

Practical Writing   245

WRITING TIPS

Before you write . . .

- **Choose a person to write to.**
  Think of a person who could help you in some way.
- **Think of what you need.**
  Write down what you want the person to do.

While you write . . .

- **Start with a first draft.**
  Write the body of your letter first. (Don't think about the letter format yet.)
- **Introduce your topic.**
  In the opening paragraph, tell why you are writing.
- **Make your request.**
  Ask the person for help.
- **Write a strong closing.**
  Explain how important the help will be and thank the person.

After you write a first draft . . .

- **Make a final version.**
  Follow the letter format shown on pages 246–247.
- **Check for errors.**
  Read over your letter to be sure you used proper punctuation, capitalization, spelling, and grammar.

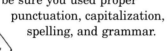

Write a letter. Follow the directions above to write a letter of request to an adult, a business, or an organization.

Writing Tips

Encourage students to write a letter they will be willing to mail. Emphasize that their requests must be reasonable. Note also that, since they are practicing business letters, they will be using that format even if they write to a friend or relative.

Have students share their drafts with partners to get feedback for revision and again during the editing stage.

After students have made final copies according to the instructions on PE pages 246–247, have them share their finished letters with the class. (At this time, make sure all requests are appropriate. Some students may need to make changes.)

In order to keep up with the letter-writing project,

- display copies of the finished letters on a bulletin board;
- discuss responses when they are received and add them to the bulletin board;
- if the letter results in action, encourage students to write a brief description of what happened and post it next to their letter.

Advanced Learners

Tell students that this is a perfect opportunity to put their problem/solution essay to work. They can make a difference in their environment. Have them convert the content of their essays to the business letter format. After reviewing your school's policy for using the Internet, provide time for students to use the Internet to research the appropriate agency or person to contact who can address their concerns. (They will learn how to address the envelope on PE page 247.)

Parts of a Business Letter

Have students review the sample on PE page 244 to see how each part appears in a finished letter. Ask them to double-check their own letter to make sure all six parts are there and in the proper order.

Provide additional hints.

- Always double-check the heading and the inside address. It is a common error to put these in the wrong order.
- Put the date on the letter. It is inserted under the heading and one space above the inside address.
- Find out the name of the person you need to contact instead of just using a title. This will make it more likely that your letter will get into the right hands.
- Always be extra careful to spell the person's name correctly.

✳ For tips on addressing envelopes, see PE page 477.

246

Parts of a Business Letter

1 The **heading** includes your address and the date. Write the heading at the left margin, at least one inch from the top.

2 The **inside address** includes the name, title, and address of the person or organization you are writing to.

- Put short titles on the same line as the name. Put longer titles on the next line.
- If you are writing to an organization, use the name of the organization.

3 The **salutation** is the greeting. Put a colon after it.

- If you know the person's name, use it.

  Dear Mr. Smith:

- Otherwise, use a salutation like one of these:

  Dear Manager:

  Dear Editor:

  Dear Salem Soccer Club:

4 The **body** is the main part of the letter. Do not indent your paragraphs; instead, skip a line between them.

5 The **closing** is placed after the body. Use **Yours truly** or **Sincerely**. Capitalize only the first word and put a comma after the closing.

6 The **signature** ends the letter. If you are using a computer, leave four spaces after the closing; then type your name. Write your signature between the closing and the typed name.

tip Turn to page 477 for more information about writing letters and about addressing envelopes properly.

Struggling Learners

Invite students to make a template of a short business letter, using the correct terms (see PE pages 244 and 246), to post in the computer lab. Remind students that they can use the margins to make captions with explanations, just like on PE page 244.

Practical Writing   **247**

Business-Letter Format

See page 477 for a model business letter.

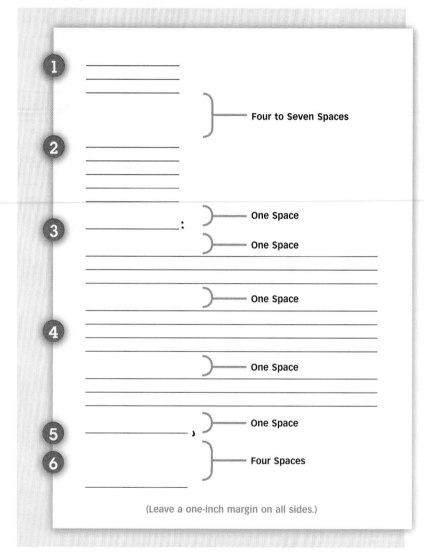

1

) Four to Seven Spaces

2

3 :)— One Space

)— One Space

)— One Space

4

)— One Space

5 ,)— One Space

6)— Four Spaces

(Leave a one-inch margin on all sides.)

Business-Letter Format

If possible, have students print out their letters on a computer.

- The letters will look more professional.
- The printed format will make the letters easier for the recipients to read.

If students do write out their letters by hand, have them take the following steps:

- Darken the lines of a regular sheet of notebook paper, using a black pen and a ruler.
- Place a sheet of blank paper over the lined paper, which will serve as a guide.
- Use a dark blue or black pen to neatly write the letter.

Writing for Assessment

If your students must take school, district, or state assessments this year, focus on the writing form on which they will be tested.

Review the goals for persuasive writing on PE page 200.

Remind students that in a testing situation they should

- bring extra pencils, an eraser, and scratch paper;
- decide how long they will spend on prewriting, writing, and revising;
- read the prompt through once before starting to work;
- decide on a specific topic that can be addressed in the time they have; and
- use organization aids such as table diagrams, time lines, or T-charts.

✳ For more about responding to writing prompts, see PE pages 404–405.

Have students read the prompt twice and then identify the key ideas to be addressed:
- Write a letter.
- Express your opinion.
- Support your opinion with reasons.

248

Writing for Assessment

Some writing tests include a persuasive prompt that asks you to convince the reader to agree with you and take some action. In the example below, Shawna responds to a proposed change at her school.

Persuasive Prompt

To save money, your principal wants to cancel all field trips for the rest of the year. Write a letter to the principal to express your opinion about canceling field trips. Support your opinion with reasons.

Table Diagram

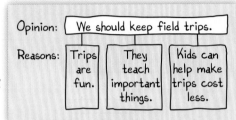

Opinion: We should keep field trips.

Reasons: Trips are fun. | They teach important things. | Kids can help make trips cost less.

> The **beginning** introduces the topic and gives an opinion statement (underlined).

Dear Principal Lane,

Do you remember being in grade school? Do you remember hayrides and visits to apple orchards? Do you remember trips to the Museum of Science and Industry? On field trips, kids get to see things they've only read about. <u>Seymore School should keep its field trips.</u>

Field trips help students learn. Some kids learn best from experiences. One day at a dairy farm could teach kids more than reading a whole unit on dairy farms would. Field trips also help kids know how

Ask students if they found the sample letter persuasive and well organized. What improvements could the writer could have made? Possible responses:

- Revise the opening to sound more friendly. Asking three questions in a row may seem pushy. (To demonstrate, have a volunteer read the paragraph aloud.)
- Consider adding details like a quotation. For example, *When my sister, Allie, got back from a trip to a farm, she told me, "I learned more today than from reading that whole unit on dairy farms."*

Respond to the reading.

Answers

Ideas **1.** Field trips should not be canceled.
2. They help students learn; kids can help pay; some places may allow students to visit at no charge.

Organization 3. Writer arranged her reasons in order of importance.

Voice & Word Choice 4. get to see, more than reading a whole unit, add to . . . learning, letting us experience, I finally understood, please, fun

---

Each middle paragraph gives reasons to support the opinion.

things work in real life. When our class went to the steel mill, I finally understood what my dad does at work all day.

Kids can help pay for the field trips. We could have craft and book sales and do chores to earn money. Also, we could ask our parents if their companies would let our class visit for free. Some field trips, like a walk to the hospital, would not cost anything.

The ending sums up the reasons and asks the reader to act.

Field trips add to our classroom learning by letting us experience what we are being taught. Please keep field trips. They make learning fun!

Sincerely,
Shawna Parks

Respond to the reading. Answer the questions below to learn more about the response you just read.

- **Ideas** (1) What is Shawna's opinion? (2) What reasons support her opinion?
- **Organization** (3) In what order does Shawna give her reasons?
- **Voice & Word Choice** (4) What key words show Shawna's enthusiasm?

Writing Tips

Point out that timed writing creates pressures and students must approach writing-on-demand assignments differently from open-ended writing assignments.

Persuasive Prompt

To teach students who must take timed assessments how to approach their writing, allow them the same amount of time to write their response essay as they will be allotted on school, district, or state assessments. Break down each part of the process into clear chunks of time. For example, you might give students

- 15 minutes for note taking and planning,
- 20 minutes for writing, and
- 10 minutes for editing and proofreading.

Tell students when time is up for each section. Start the assignment at the top of the hour or at the half-hour to make it easier for students to keep track of the time.

If your state, district, or school requires students to use and submit a graphic organizer as part of their assessment, provide a copy of one of the reproducible charts (TE pages 645–651) or refer students to PE pages 456–457.

250

WRITING TIPS

Planning your response . . .
- **Understand the prompt.**
  Read the prompt carefully and watch for key words that tell you what to write.
- **Gather your ideas.**
  Use a graphic organizer to plan your response.

Writing your response . . .
- **Include an opinion statement.**
  Write your opinion statement at the end of your first paragraph.
- **Organize your reasons.**
  List your reasons by order of importance.
- **Write a strong ending.**
  Sum up your reasons and ask the reader to act.

Checking your response . . .
- **Check for errors.**
  Be sure you have used proper punctuation, capitalization, spelling, and grammar.

Persuasive Prompt

- Your school is going to start requiring two hours of homework every night. Write a persuasive essay to let the school board know your opinion of this idea. Give reasons to support your opinion.

Respond to a persuasive prompt. Respond to the prompt above or to a prompt that your teacher gives you.

Persuasive Writing Checklist   **251**

Persuasive Writing in Review

In persuasive writing, you try to *convince* people to agree with you.

Select a topic that you feel strongly about. Be sure it will also interest your reader. (See page 204.)

Gather and organize reasons to support your opinion. You may use a graphic organizer. (See pages 205 and 208.)

Write an opinion statement that names your cause and your feeling about it. (See page 206.)

Plan a call to action that asks your reader to respond in a specific way. (See page 207.)

In the beginning, get your reader's attention and state your opinion. (See page 211.)

In the middle, each paragraph should list one reason with facts and examples to support it. (See pages 212–213.)

In the ending, repeat your opinion and give a call to action. (See pages 207 and 214.)

Review your ideas, organization, and **voice** first. Then review for **word choice** and **sentence fluency**. Make other changes to improve your first draft. (See pages 216–226.)

Check your writing for conventions. Also have a trusted classmate edit your writing. (See pages 227–230.)

Make a final copy and proofread it for errors before sharing it. (See page 231.)

Use the persuasive rubric to assess your finished writing. (See pages 232–233.)

Persuasive Writing in Review

Point out that this page serves as a quick guide to the information in the unit. Encourage students to start by consulting this review whenever they are writing a persuasive essay and need help. Distribute sticky notes so students can mark the page for easy access.

Invite students to talk about what they learned as they studied the unit. Do they have helpful hints they can pass on to classmates? Do they have questions other students might be able to answer?

Response to Literature Overview

Writing Standards

The writing standards listed below are based on a blending of state and NCTE standards.

- Develop a response that exhibits an understanding of a piece of literature and that is supported with quotations and details from the work.
- Use lists, charts, clusters, and diagrams to generate and organize ideas.
- Use a voice that demonstrates both interest in and knowledge of the work.
- Edit and revise drafts to ensure sentences flow smoothly and all punctuation, capitalization, spelling, and grammar are correct.
- Explore different modes of response and topics for response.

Writing Forms

- response paragraph
- book review
- summary

Focus on the Traits

- **Ideas** Identifying character traits to describe the main character
- **Organization** Writing a beginning that introduces the story and its author, a middle that includes important events of the story, and an ending that gives the reader something to think about
- **Voice** Creating a voice that sounds interested in the book
- **Word Choice** Choosing specific nouns and using present-tense verbs
- **Sentence Fluency** Using a variety of sentence lengths
- **Conventions** Checking for errors in punctuation, capitalization, spelling, and grammar

Unit Pacing

Response Paragraph: 1.5–3 hours

The **response paragraph** introduces the unit and lays the groundwork for more extensive writing about literature. Use this section if students need to work on crafting a paragraph. Following are some of the topics that are covered:

- Using a list to select a topic
- Creating a chart to summarize the plot
- Writing a paragraph that ends by sharing the book's message, or theme

Response Essay: 3–5.5 hours

This section asks students to write a **response to literature** in the form of a **book review.** Use this section to focus on developing an essay. Following are some of the topics that are covered:

- Making a matrix to select a topic
- Gathering and organizing details on a beginning-middle-ending map
- Creating a chart to identify character traits
- Answering the 5-W and H questions to find something interesting to tell about the book and its author
- Putting main events in time order

Other Forms of Responding: 2.5–6.5 hours

This section introduces students to some of the different forms of literature that are often included on writing assessments. Use this section if students need practice with writing for assessment.

Integrated Grammar and Writing Skills

Below are skills lessons from the resources sections of the pupil edition that are suggested at point of use (✱) throughout this unit.

Additional Grammar Skills

Below are skills lessons from other components that you can weave into your unit instruction.

Writing a Response Paragraph

SkillsBook

Commas to Set-off Interruptions, p. 11
Capitalization 2, p. 45

Interactive Writing Skills CD-ROM

Mechanics: Capitalization 2

Daily Language Workouts

Week 25: Where in the World? pp. 52–53
Week 25: Hot Spots, p. 102
Week 26: Colors and Symbols, pp. 54–55
Week 26: Don't Step on Me, p. 103

Writing a Book Review

SkillsBook

Commas Between Items in a Series 1 and 2, p. 5
Run-On Sentences 1 and 2, p. 89
Common and Proper Adjectives 1 and 2, p. 167
Demonstrative Adjectives, p. 169
Forms of Adjectives, p. 170

Interactive Writing Skills CD-ROM

Punctuation: Commas 1—Compound Sentences and in a Series
Parts of Speech 2: Adjectives—Proper, Common, and Comparative

Daily Language Workouts

Week 27: Signs and Symbols, pp. 56–57
Week 27: Safety Engineers, p. 104
Week 28: U.S. History, pp. 58–59
Week 28: Powerful Words, p. 105

Response to Literature

Other Forms of Responding

Daily Language Workouts

Week 29: The Civil War and Before, pp. 60–61
Week 29: Flags over Florida, p. 106
Week 30: Science Now and Then, pp. 62–63
Week 30: When Dinosaurs Ruled, p. 107

Response to Literature
Response Paragraph

Sam started telling Kaitlyn about a book he had read. "Don't tell me everything!" Kaitlyn said. She knew that if Sam told her everything, the book would be less fun for her to read. Kaitlyn only wanted to hear enough to decide if she would enjoy reading the book.

Writing a response to literature is much like telling someone about a good book. You want to encourage that person to read the story without giving away the most important parts, especially the ending.

Writing Guidelines

Subject: Key parts of a fiction book
Form: A paragraph
Purpose: To preview a fiction book
Audience: Classmates

Response Paragraph

Objectives
- demonstrate an understanding of the content and structure of a response paragraph
- choose a topic (key parts of a fiction book) to write about
- plan, draft, revise, and edit a response paragraph

A response paragraph briefly describes the key ideas in a story in order to encourage others to read a piece of literature. Remind students that a paragraph consists of
- a topic sentence,
- body sentences that support the topic, and
- a closing sentence that sums up the topic.

✽ For information about Paragraph Writing, see PE pages 50–61.

Ask students to talk about the difference between a response and a summary:
- A response describes important parts of the story but does not reveal how everything turns out.
- A summary attempts to give readers a complete idea of a story's important points.

Family Connection Letters

As you begin this unit, send home the Response to Literature Family Connection letter, which describes what students will be learning.

○ Letter in English (TE p. 657)

○ Letter in Spanish (TE p. 665)

Materials

Map and pictures (TE p. 254)

Copy Masters/ Transparencies

T-chart and 5 W's chart (TE p. 255)

Response Paragraph

After students read the model paragraph, ask if they are familiar with *Little House on the Prairie*. Ask those who have read the book the following questions, taking care to have them explain their responses:

- Do you agree with the writer that it's a great book?
- Do you think Laura's adventures are the best part of the story? If not, what parts do you like?
- What would *you* say is the book's theme, or main idea?
- Would you recommend this book to others?

Explain that there are no absolute right answers in a response paragraph. Students will give their own reasons for why a book is interesting, so different students might mention different things. The important thing is for readers to express their ideas convincingly.

Note also that students should use present tense verbs in their paragraph (see PE page 265).

 Respond to the reading.

Answers

Ideas 1. the closing sentence

Organization 2. the body sentences

Voice & Word Choice 3. Answers will vary.

254

Response Paragraph

A response paragraph begins with a **topic sentence** that names the book's title and author. The **body sentences** share important ideas from the story. The **closing sentence** includes the book's message, or theme.

Topic sentence

Body sentences

Closing sentence

Little House on the Prairie

Little House on the Prairie is a book by Laura Ingalls Wilder. In the story, Laura and her family move from Wisconsin to Kansas. They travel by covered wagon and have many adventures, too. For example, they cross wide rivers in their wagon. They see packs of howling wolves, and they fight a prairie fire that is coming right at their new house. You will have to read the book to find out about Laura's other adventures. *Little House on the Prairie* is a great book that tells how the Ingalls family faces many challenges in nature, works together, and has fun in the days of the pioneers.

 Respond to the reading. On your own paper, answer each of the following questions.

- **Ideas** (1) Which sentence tells about the theme of the book?
- **Organization** (2) Which part of the paragraph shares important ideas from the story?
- **Voice & Word Choice** (3) Find two sentences that make you want to read this book.

English Language Learners

Before reading the model paragraph, define the following words, using pictures if possible:

- Wisconsin and Kansas (locate on map)
- prairie (large open field) *picture recommended*
- covered wagon (a large wagon covered with fabric used for traveling long distances hundreds of years ago) *picture recommended*
- packs (groups)
- challenges (difficult situations, problems)
- pioneers (people who explore new areas)

Struggling Learners

Provide additional practice with identifying themes by analyzing familiar fairy tales, such as:

- *The Three Little Pigs* – Do the job right the first time.
- *Little Red Riding Hood* – Don't share information with strangers.
- *Cinderella* – If you're kind and responsible, things will turn out well in the end.

Writing a Response Paragraph   255

Prewriting Selecting a Topic

First, you need to choose a book to write about. Creating a list can remind you of books that you have read.

List

Fiction Book	Author
James and the Giant Peach	
Harriet the Spy	
Little House on the Prairie	Laura Ingalls Wilder✱
Grizzly	Gary Paulsen

Choose a fiction book. Make a list like the one above. List books that you have enjoyed. Include authors' names if you know them. Put a star (✱) next to the book you choose.

Remembering the Plot

The plot tells important details about the story. These details answer the questions *who, what, where,* and *when.*

Plot Chart

Who?	What?	Where?	When?
The Ingalls family	they had many adventures	from Wisconsin to Kansas	during pioneer days

Make a plot chart. Write the most important details from your book.

Prewriting Selecting a Topic

Before students make their lists, review the rules for capitalizing words in book titles.

✱ For more about capitalizing in titles, see PE page 514.

If students need ideas for their list, have them collaborate to create a list of books they have read as a class. Explain that they should feel free to choose one of these books or a book they have read on their own.

Provide photocopies of the reproducible T-chart (TE page 645) for students to use for their list.

Prewriting Remembering the Plot

Distribute photocopies of the reproducible 5 W's chart (TE page 647) for students to fill out.

Point out that, although students only have to fill out their plot chart for four of the five *W* words, they may want to add details for the question *why.* Challenge students who have read *Little House on the Prairie* to tell what they think the *why* answer is for that book (for example, to make a home and claim land in the newly settled West).

English Language Learners

Students may feel self-conscious if they are reading shorter, less complicated books than those of their English-proficient peers. If appropriate, allow students to choose books they have read in their first language if they can describe the story well. Otherwise, encourage students to work with a book that is appropriate for their level by holding a conference with them about the story.

Depending on the complexity of the story, the plot may not explicitly address all of the categories used in the chart. If this is the case, assist students in making inferences from their story, or allow them to skip the categories that are not addressed.

Writing Creating Your First Draft

Before students begin, write these sentence starters on the board:

- This book is interesting because . . .
- My favorite parts of the story were . . .

Have students complete the starters, listing at least three favorite story parts (remind them not to give away too much) that support their reason for why the book is interesting. Ask them to use this information, along with the details on their plot chart, in their drafts.

Revising

Improving Your Paragraph

Ask students to think about movie previews and how they make you want to see the movie by showing parts of the action. Have them revise their paragraphs with this idea in mind.

Editing Checking for Conventions

Remind students that the titles of books are underlined (or, if using a computer, italicized).

✱ For more about Italics and Underlining in Titles, see PE page 502.

Have students work with a partner to double-check their editing.

256

Writing Creating Your First Draft

Your paragraph should have three parts. The topic sentence names the book and its author. The body tells a few important ideas from the story. The closing sentence shares the book's theme, or message.

 Write the first draft of your paragraph. *Remember:* Your goal is to tell just enough about the book to make others want to read it.

Revising Improving Your Paragraph

Next, you'll need to make improvements in your first draft.

 Revise your paragraph. Use the following questions to guide your changes.

1. Do I name the book and its author?
2. Do I include some of the most important details?
3. Do I sound interested in my book?
4. Do my sentences read smoothly?

Editing Checking for Conventions

Finally, you'll need to correct any errors in your paragraph.

 Edit and proofread your work. Use the questions below to help you. Then make a neat copy and proofread it again.

1. Have I checked my punctuation, spelling, and grammar?
2. Are the words in the book title capitalized correctly?
3. Have I underlined the title?

Struggling Learners

To support hesitant writers, first model the paragraph process step-by-step. Do a Think-Aloud using a book you've recently read as a class and encourage student input to write a response paragraph.

Response to Literature
Writing a Book Review

Reading a new book is like making a new friend. Each time you turn a page, you learn more about the book's story. When you finish the book, you know it well enough to tell others about it. One way to do this is to write a book review.

In this chapter, you will write a review of a fiction book you have read. You will share important parts of the story without giving away the whole story. You will also tell about the main character and explain why you like the book.

Writing Guidelines

Subject: Review of a fiction book

Form: An essay

Purpose: To show your understanding of a book and its main character

Audience: Classmates

Writing a Book Review

Objectives

- demonstrate an understanding of the purpose, content, and form of a book review
- choose a topic (a fiction book) to write about
- plan, draft, revise, edit, and reflect on a book review

A book review is an essay that
■ includes important events in the story, but doesn't tell how it ends;
■ reveals the book's theme, or message (main idea); and
■ provides reasons why the writer liked the book.

Explain that students will enjoy writing the essay more and have more to say if they choose a book they really like. Talk about different ways to recognize a favorite book.
■ Has a book ever made them laugh a lot? Or cry?
■ Have they ever read a "page-turner" (a book so exciting that you want to keep reading, or turning pages)?
■ Have they ever kept thinking about a book after they've finished it?
■ Is there a book that they've read more than once?

Materials

Examples of book reviews (TE p. 258)

Paper and drawing supplies (TE p. 262)

Colored pencils or markers (TE p. 267)

Sticky notes or large paperclips (TE p. 270)

Craft supplies (TE p. 271)

Copy Masters/ Transparencies

Time line (TE p. 261)

5 W's chart (TE p. 263)

Writing a Book Review

Work through this sample essay with the class, pointing out the elements that make it a good **response** *(see below)* **to literature**.

Ideas
- The beginning tells the author's opinion, and introduces the main character and the key problem (a boy makes a bet).
- The writer describes events from the book and talks about the feelings and behavior of the main characters.

Organization
- The opening includes the book's title and the author.
- The first middle paragraph describes events in the book in time order.
- The second middle paragraph reveals details about the main character.
- The ending sums up the review by explaining why the writer likes the book.

Voice & Word Choice
- The writer's voice sounds both natural and interested in the subject.
- The writer uses a quotation from the book.
- The details given show the writer's knowledge of the story.
- The vocabulary used is appropriate to the audience.

258

Writing a Book Review

The beginning paragraph in a book review gives the book's title, names the author, and includes a sentence or two to introduce the book. The middle paragraphs tell about the story and the main character's personality. The ending paragraph tells why the writer likes the book.

BEGINNING

The writer introduces the book.

MIDDLE

The first middle paragraph tells what the book is about.

How to Eat Fried Worms

How to Eat Fried Worms by Thomas Rockwell is one of the best books I have ever read. It is a disgusting but funny story about a boy named Billy Forrester, who accepts a bet.

"I'll bet you fifty dollars you can't eat fifteen worms," says Billy's friend, Alan. Billy answers that he will do it, but he will only eat one worm a day for fifteen days. The first worm is boiled and covered with tons of ketchup, mustard, salt, pepper, and horseradish. Billy gulps it down. He is determined to win the bet. Billy tries to find different ways to eat worms so they taste better. He eats them rolled in cornmeal and fried like fish. He even eats one buried in an ice-cream cake! Of course, Alan tries everything to get Billy to lose the bet, but

---

Teaching Tip: Responding to Literature

To provide students with models of responses to literature, share a selection of book reviews. If possible, find one about a book students have read so they can compare their responses to the reviewer's. Students may also enjoy hearing a negative review. Point out how the writer phrases criticism and explains the reasons for his or her feelings.

Reviews of children's books are widely available online. For example:

- the *Horn Book* magazine Web site (www.hbook.com)
- the children's section of the *New York Times Book Review* (www.nytimes.com/pages/books)
- customer reviews at the Amazon and Barnes & Noble Web sites
- *Stone Soup* magazine reviews by kids (www.stonesoup.com/main2/brlist.html).

Writing a Book Review **259**

Billy won't give up. That is what makes this book so funny.

The best thing about Billy's personality is that he is stubborn about winning. One day, Billy almost forgets to eat his worm. When he discovers his mistake, he chomps down a raw worm just minutes before midnight. Yuck! That took courage.

I like this book because the characters are very real. It seems like everything is happening in my own backyard. Anyone who likes funny books should read How to Eat Fried Worms. I know I liked it. I will never forget Billy Forrester.

MIDDLE
The second middle paragraph tells about the main character's personality.

ENDING
The final paragraph tells what the writer likes about the book.

 Respond to the reading. Answer the following questions about the sample book review.

- **Ideas** (1) What main idea or feeling about the book does the writer share in the beginning paragraph?
- **Organization** (2) What is the purpose of each middle paragraph?
- **Voice & Word Choice** (3) What words and phrases show you that the writer liked this book?

Emphasize to students the importance of providing reasons for all their opinions. Point out how well the writer of the example explained
- why this is a favorite book (it's funny; the characters seem real), as well as
- why it's funny (the ways Billy eats the worms; his friend tries to trick him into giving up, but Billy refuses).

Respond to the reading.

Answers

Ideas **1.** Possible answers:
- It is one of the best books the writer has read.
- It is disgusting but funny.

Organization 2. The first middle paragraph tells some of the things that happen in time order; the second describes the main character.

Voice & Word Choice 3. Possible answers:
- one of the best
- disgusting but funny
- so funny
- the best thing
- I like this book

Prewriting Selecting a Topic

Remind students of the class discussion about identifying favorite books (TE page 257). Did it help them think of books they'd like to write about?

Ask volunteers to read aloud the sample sentences telling why the writer likes each book. Point out that the writer gives specific reasons. Challenge students to list overly general adjectives such as

- great,
- funny,
- sad, and
- interesting.

Warn students to avoid these words, or to pair them with the word *because,* along with a specific explanation. (For example: *How to Eat Fried Worms is funny because Billy tries so many disgusting ways to prepare worms.*)

If students don't remember their book well enough to describe its story, suggest they choose another book they're more familiar with.

An additional factor in students' choice of books is whether they can obtain a copy to refer to as they write. If a student doesn't have the book at home and can't get it from the library or another source, suggest that he or she pick another.

Prewriting Selecting a Topic

The first step in writing a book review is choosing a book. You must be able to tell about the important parts of the book and explain why you like it. One way to choose a book is to make a topic matrix.

 Make a topic matrix. Use the sample below as a guide.
- In the first column, list books that you have read and enjoyed.
- In the second column, write one sentence that tells what each book is about.
- In the last column, write one sentence that tells why you like the book.

Topic Matrix

What is the book's title?	What is the book about?	Why do you like the book?
Because of Winn-Dixie ✓	It is about a girl named India Opal Buloni and her dog Winn-Dixie.	I like reading about dogs, and I like characters that remind me of people I know.
Sarah Plain and Tall	A long-ago family gets a new mom.	My family has a new dad, so I know how the children in this story feel.

 Choose your topic. Review your completed matrix. Put a check mark next to the book you want to write about.

English Language Learners

Remind students not to worry about using correct grammar or complete sentences to write their ideas on their topic matrix. Tell them that the matrix is a personal aide for them. They can even draw sketches if it helps them to come up with ideas better than writing words does.

Writing a Book Review   **261**

Gathering and Organizing Details

When you explain what a book is about, you should put the events in time order. A beginning-middle-ending map can help you.

Beginning-Middle-Ending Map

Tell what happens first in the story.

List three important events of the story in time order.

Tell something important about how the story ends without giving away the ending.

> **BEGINNING**
> Opal finds a stray dog in the Winn-Dixie grocery store.
>
> **MIDDLE**
> 1. Opal adopts the dog and names it Winn-Dixie.
> 2. Opal feels lonely because she is new in town.
> 3. Winn-Dixie helps Opal make new friends.
>
> **ENDING**
> Opal isn't lonely anymore.

 tip Be sure that your book review doesn't give away any of the story's surprises or the ending.

 Prewrite

Create your beginning-middle-ending map. As you think about your book, write down the main events from beginning to end. Try to include at least three events from the middle part, and don't give away the ending.

Prewriting
Gathering and Organizing Details

Distribute photocopies of the reproducible time line (TE page 648) for students to use as their beginning-middle-ending map. Encourage them to consult their book if they are unsure about the order of the events they list.

✳ For information about writing details in Time Order, see PE pages 56 and 458.

Students may have difficulty identifying just a few key events to mention.

First, reassure them that there are no absolute right answers. They might pick different details from what another person would.

Next, suggest that they think of the following questions as they work (see PE page 270 for other ideas):
- What is the main character's biggest problem or desire?
- What does the character do to try to solve the problem or get what he or she wants?

Allow ten minutes for students to answer the questions. Encourage them to write down as many answers as they can. Afterward, they can go back and pick out the best ones to use.

English Language Learners

Review students' beginning-middle-ending maps or time lines before they use them to write their essay. Although there is not one correct answer, make sure that the details they have on their charts are important details from the story. Some students may have difficulty discerning important and secondary events.

Struggling Learners

If students have difficulty identifying key events, teach them the "but/so" thinking strategy. For example:
- Billy wants to win $50 . . . **but** he has to eat 15 worms . . . **so** he tries to make them tasty.
- Opal is lonely . . . **but** she finds a stray dog . . . **so** the dog helps her make friends.

- Anna and Caleb have no mother . . . **but** Papa sends for a bride . . . **so** everyone in the family must learn to adapt to the new situation.

After creating a "but/so" scenario for their book, have students use it to complete the middle section of their map.

Prewriting
Identifying Character Traits

To help students with their trait charts, have them brainstorm adjectives that can be used to describe people. Encourage them to choose adjectives that are as specific as possible, such as *ambitious, competitive, shy, generous, bold,* and *stubborn.* Write these on the board for the class to refer to as they work.

✳ For information about Describing with Adjectives, see PE pages 423–425.

Then, before students make their charts, distribute paper and drawing supplies. Ask students to think of a scene in the story that really shows the personality of the main character and then to draw it.

Remind students that details about how their character looks can be found in the book. Point out that often a character's appearance is a clue to his or her personality. (For example, Pippi Longstocking's red, funny braids and colorful clothes express her high spirits.)

After students have finished their pictures, have them make their trait chart, referring to their drawing and the adjectives on the board. Display the two items together on a class bulletin board.

262

Prewriting Identifying Character Traits

Character traits include how a character looks, acts, and behaves. A trait chart, like the one below, can help you identify the personality traits of the characters in your book.

Trait Chart

Character's name: India Opal Buloni	
How does she act and feel?	Why does she act and feel this way?
sad	Her mother left her.
lonely	She is new in town, and she doesn't know anybody.
kind	She takes care of a stray dog.
fair	She learns not to judge people.

 tip You can use adjectives (*happy, confused, nosy, angry*) to describe a character's traits.

 Prewrite **Identify character traits.** Make a trait chart for the main character in your book. List at least four personality traits and tell why you think the person acts or feels that way.

English Language Learners

In a mini lesson, discuss the placement of adjectives in a sentence. Explain that adjectives precede the predicate noun they describe, as in, *Clifford is a big, red dog.* Adjectives often follow the subject noun or pronoun when there is a *being* verb in the middle, as in, *Clifford is big and red.*

Advanced Learners

To further focus on personal traits, challenge students to create an acrostic with the name of their main character, such as the following, using the letters that spell *India* and her personality traits:

kInd
lonely
saD
faIr
cAring

Writing a Book Review 263

Writing Starting Your Book Review

The beginning paragraph of your book review should name the book's title (underlined) and the author. It should also share something interesting about the story to get the reader's attention.

> Beginning
>
> Middle
>
> Ending

Telling About the Book

Answer the 5-W and H questions to find something interesting to tell about your book.

- *Who* is the story about?
- *What* is the main character's problem?
- *Why* does the main character have this problem?
- *When* does the story happen?
- *Where* does the story happen?
- *How* does the story make you feel?

Beginning Paragraph

Review the paragraph below and the beginning paragraph in the sample review on page 258.

> **The beginning paragraph names the book and its author and introduces the story.**
>
> Sad and sweet things get mixed together in <u>Because of Winn-Dixie</u> by Kate DiCamillo. India Opal Buloni feels sad because her mama left her when she was only three. Then something sweet happens to make Opal feel better. That sweet thing is a dog named Winn-Dixie.

Write your beginning. Write the first paragraph of your book review. Include the book's title, its author, and a sentence or two that tells something interesting about the story.

Writing

Starting Your Book Review

Suggest that, when trying to think of an interesting thing to share in their opening, students think back to why they chose to review this book in the first place. Their reason for choosing the book might be just the interesting idea they can use.

Writing Telling About the Book

Distribute photocopies of the reproducible 5 W's chart (TE page 647) for students to fill out before writing their beginning paragraph. Have them add the sixth heading, *how,* to the sheet. Give general guidelines about answering the questions, such as the following:

- Every review should begin by introducing *who* the story is about and *what* the main problem is.
- If the story takes place in the past (as in historical tales) or future (as in science fiction), the beginning should tell *when* the story happens.
- If the setting is an important part of the story, the beginning should tell *where* the events happen.
- Writers should try to cover all six types of answers in the review, either in the opening paragraph or later.

Writing
Developing the Middle Part

Have students compare the sample middle paragraph to the events listed on the beginning-middle-ending map on PE page 261.

- Are all of the events from the map included in the paragraph? (Yes.)
- Did the writer make any changes to the order of events? (Yes—the writer realized that the first thing that should be mentioned is Opal's loneliness, because she was lonely before she found the stray dog.)
- Did the writer decide to add other events that aren't on the map? (Yes. The writer mentions the town librarian as an example of one of Opal's new friends, and the candy.)

Emphasize to students that it is okay if they don't follow their organizational notes exactly. Often they'll think of new things to add, or they'll change the order of details as they write.

264

Writing Developing the Middle Part

The middle paragraphs should tell the important events of the story and talk about the main character's personality. Look at your beginning-middle-ending map and trait chart from pages 261–262 to help you write these paragraphs.

Beginning
Middle
Ending

First Middle Paragraph

Share the main events of the story in the first middle paragraph. Do not tell the most surprising parts or the ending, in case your reader chooses to read the book. (Review the paragraph below and the one on page 258.)

The first middle paragraph includes important events from the story.

Opal is lonely after she moves to a new town. Soon she finds a big stray dog in a Winn–Dixie grocery store. She names him Winn–Dixie. Opal's life changes because of her new pet. Winn–Dixie helps Opal make friends. One of them is the town librarian. She gives Opal a hard candy that tastes like root beer and strawberry. It has a secret ingredient that makes whoever eats it think of sad things. Opal decides that life is like that candy. It is sweet and sad all mixed together.

 Write the first middle paragraph of your review. Use your beginning-middle-ending map to guide you. Share the main events in time order.

Writing a Book Review **265**

Second Middle Paragraph

Name the main character's strongest personality trait in the second middle paragraph. Show the character's personality by including details from the book. (Review the second middle paragraph below and the one on page 259.)

> Beginning
>
> Middle
>
> Ending

The second middle paragraph shares the character's strongest trait.

I like India Opal Buloni because she is friendly. In fact, I think I would like to be her friend. You can always count on Opal to start up a friendship. One day she is talking with the town librarian, Miss Franny. "You, me, and Winn-Dixie, we could all be friends," Opal says. By the end of the book, Opal has all kinds of friends.

Write the second middle paragraph of your review. Look over your trait chart to guide your writing. Name the character's strongest trait and support it with an example or two.

Present-tense verbs make your writing more lively.

Ask students to tell how the paragraph shows the character's personality. For example, the writer

- describes Opal as *friendly*,
- describes a time when she made a friend, and
- uses a quotation to show how she talks to a person she wants as a friend.

Focus attention on the speech balloon at the bottom of the page about using present-tense forms of verbs in reviews.

- Have students define *present tense* in their own words (a verb form used to tell what is going on now).
- Explain that it's a common practice to use the present tense when describing what happens in a book. This way, the events in the book seem to be happening in the present every time a person reads it.
- Challenge students to explain why a review in the present tense is livelier. (It seems as if the action is going on as you read.)

✱ For more information about present tense verbs, see PE page 584.

English Language Learners

Explain the conjugation of present tense regular verbs (third person singular adds -*s*) and important irregular verbs, such as *to be* and *to have*. Review the sample paragraph on PE p. 264 as well as the one on this page, and point out that both are written in the present tense.

Help students identify the different forms of the regular and irregular verbs in both middle paragraphs. Then have them go back and make any necessary revisions to write all of their verbs in the present tense.

Struggling Learners

To show the impact of present-tense reviews, rewrite the second middle paragraph in the past tense and have volunteers read aloud both versions.

I liked India Opal Buloni because she was friendly. In fact, I thought I would have liked to be her friend.

Emphasize that using the present-tense make us feel as if we are enjoying the book again.

Writing Ending Your Book Review

After reading the page, ask students to reread the ending paragraph on PE page 259 and tell what question the writer used to write the ending. (Why is this a good book?)

Note that if students choose to answer the first question (how they are like or unlike the main character), they must take care not to talk so much about themselves that they forget to make the connections to the main character.

It would be best to use this question in combination with one of the others. For example, students might say that

- they like the book because they have so much in common with the main character, or
- they learned a lot from the story because they like the main character, who learned an important lesson in life.

Note that when students write their draft, it will be easier for them to put in changes during the revising stage if they write on alternating lines of the paper. Explain that this is called *double-spacing*. Suggest that students always double-space their essays, even final copies. This will leave room for their own changes, as well as peer and teacher feedback.

Writing Ending Your Book Review

In the ending paragraph, you should tell why you like the book. The following questions will help you write this paragraph.

Beginning
Middle
Ending

- How am I like or different from the main character?
- What did I learn from the story?
- Why is this a good book?

 tip   End your story by giving the reader something to think about.

Ending Paragraph

Read the ending paragraph below. The writer shares what she learned from the story. (Also review the ending paragraph on page 259.)

> **The writer shares what she learned from the story.**
>
> I like <u>Because of Winn-Dixie</u> because it has a happy ending. In my life, just like Opal, I learned that sad things get better because of good things. Special friends and pets like Winn-Dixie can change even the saddest times.

 Write

Write your ending. Try answering one of the questions at the top of this page to help you write your ending paragraph. If that doesn't work, try another question. Keep trying until your ending sounds just right.

Form a complete first draft. Write a complete copy of your first draft. (You may want to write on every other line.)

Writing a Book Review **267**

Revising **Using a Checklist**

Revise your first draft. Number a piece of paper from 1 to 9. If you can answer "yes" to a question, put a check mark after that number. If not, work with that part of your essay.

Ideas

_____ **1.** Do I name the book and the author?

_____ **2.** Do I share three important events from the story?

_____ **3.** Do I tell about the main character's personality?

Organization

_____ **4.** Do I have a beginning, a middle, and an ending?

_____ **5.** Are events from the story in time order?

Voice

_____ **6.** Do I sound interested in the book?

Word Choice

_____ **7.** Have I used specific nouns and present-tense verbs?

Sentence Fluency

_____ **8.** Do I use a variety of sentence lengths?

_____ **9.** Are my sentences clear and easy to understand?

Make a clean copy. After revising your review, make a clean copy for editing.

Revising **Using a Checklist**

Ask students to apply the revising checklist to the sample review on PE pages 263–266. Can the writer answer yes to all questions? (Students will probably say "yes.")

Point out possible improvements that aren't on the list. For example:

- The librarian is mentioned in both middle paragraphs, but her name isn't given until the second one. It's usually best to give a name when a character is first mentioned.

- Paragraphs 3 and 4 begin with _I like _____ because._ For better variation, one of those should be changed.

- All of the sentences in the review are statements. Using an occasional question, exclamation, or command can provide interesting variation.

✳ For more about kinds of sentences, see PE page 441.

Have students begin their own revisions by **working with a partner** _(see below)_ and evaluating the essays using the checklist.

✳ Review Run-On Sentences (PE page 437) to help students check for sentence fluency.

Teaching Tip: Working with a Partner

When assigning writing partners, remind them of the basic ground rules of peer reviewing:

- Always read or listen carefully to the writer's work.
- Make all responses friendly and polite.
- Avoid using general language—make specific comments.
- Ask questions that require explanations as answers, not just "yes" or "no."

Struggling Learners

To help students make sure they've included _who, what, why, when, where,_ and _how_ details (PE page 263), assign a different color to each 5-W and H word, and have writers mark them in their manuscripts. If one or more are left out, students should confer with a partner about the best place to add these details.

Editing **Using a Checklist**

Arrange for students to take a break from their reviews (at least overnight) before editing them. Explain that this time off helps them to be more alert to errors when they read the essay again.

Before students begin editing, focus attention on question 2. Remind students that when using commas in a series, there should be a comma after the last item before the conjunction. If students need practice, write some sample sentences on the board and invite volunteers to add the commas. For example:

Micah took his helmet skateboard and a water bottle to the park.

✱ For information about using Commas in a Series, see PE page 482.

Create a Title

Students can always use the title of the book as a backup. Ask them to try both of the other strategies to see if they can come up with something they like. Have students read their titles to a partner to get feedback before choosing one.

268

Editing **Using a Checklist**

Edit your revised copy. Number a piece of paper from 1 to 9. If you can answer "yes" to a question, put a check mark after that number. If not, edit for that convention.

Conventions

PUNCTUATION

_____ **1.** Do I use end punctuation in all my sentences?

_____ **2.** Do I use commas between items in a series?

_____ **3.** Do I use commas with quotations from the story?

CAPITALIZATION

_____ **4.** Do I start all of my sentences with capital letters?

_____ **5.** Do I capitalize proper nouns and words in titles?

SPELLING

_____ **6.** Have I spelled all my words correctly?

_____ **7.** Have I double-checked the words my spell-checker may have missed?

GRAMMAR

_____ **8.** Do my subjects and verbs agree (*Ky tries,* not *Ky try*)?

_____ **9.** Do I use the right words *(to, too, two)*?

Create a Title

- Use the title of the book: ***Because of Winn-Dixie***
- Focus on the main character: **New Girl in Town**
- Be creative: **Lost and Found**

Make a clean final copy. Check your paper one last time.

English Language Learners

Allow students to edit with a cooperative, English-proficient partner or teacher to find and correct errors that the students may not have mastered. If you have asked students to keep editing notes, have them refer to them now, and add any new conventions they have learned. Remind students to refer to their notes whenever they edit.

Writing a Book Review **269**

Reflecting on Your Writing

Now that you've finished your book review, take a moment to reflect on it. Complete each sentence starter below on your own paper.

Your thoughts about your writing will help you prepare for your next review.

My Book Review

1. The prewriting activity that worked best for me was . . .

2. The best part of my review is . . .

3. The part that still needs work is . . .

4. The main thing I learned about writing a book review is . . .

5. In my next book review, I would like to . . .

Reflecting on Your Writing

Tell students to write the date on their reflections and file them in their writing portfolio, along with their final review and the notes they made as they worked on it.

Ask students to share their reflections with classmates.

- Which prewriting activity (topic matrix, beginning-middle-ending map, trait chart) worked best for most students?
- Did some students have similar difficulties?
- Have they experienced these difficulties before?
- Can others offer advice?

As students talk, encourage them to read from their reviews to help demonstrate their points (best parts, parts that need work).

Remind students to go back to their previous reflections from time to time—ideally before starting a writing project—in order to

- see how they've been progressing as writers,
- remind themselves of problem areas to focus on, and
- find ideas for their new essay.

English Language Learners

Ask students to reflect on their level of English in this review. They may want to list new vocabulary or grammar concepts they have learned during the assignment. Allow students to present their reflections in a small group. This may help reduce the anxiety of speaking English in a larger group.

Struggling Learners

Model how to complete the reflection sheet. Do a Think-Aloud as if you were the author of the *How To Eat Fried Worms* review (PE pages 258–259) or the *Because of Winn-Dixie* review (PE pages 263–266).

Additional Ideas for Book Reviews

Have students bookmark the page using a sticky note or large paper-clip. Encourage those who want to be extra prepared to complete as many of the starters as they can when they begin prewriting for a review. They may not use all the details they collect, but they'll find that thinking about the answers helps them to understand the story better and, therefore, to write a better review. On a similar note, point out that

■ students can use these starters to help them understand *any* book better, whether they need to write a review of it or not;

■ those who keep reader response journals (see PE page 271) will benefit from becoming familiar with the sentence starters and using them regularly in their journal entries.

✱ For more about reader response journals, see PE page 382.

Additional Ideas for Book Reviews

Listed below are sentence starters that will help you gather details for other book reviews.

Plot (the action of the story)

■ Several surprising events in the story are . . .
■ The most important event of the story is . . .
■ An event in the ending of the story is important because . . .
■ The ending is (surprising, believable, unbelievable) because . . .

Characters (the people—and sometimes the animals—in the story)

■ The main character changes by the end of the story because . . .
■ The main character's behavior is changed by (a person, place, or thing) . . .
■ The main character's most important personality trait is . . .

Setting (the time and place of the story)

■ The setting affects the main character because . . .
■ The setting (in a historical-fiction book) helped me to understand . . .
■ The setting (in a science-fiction book) is believable or unbelievable because . . .

Theme (the author's statement or lesson about life)

■ The theme of this book is . . . (overcoming a challenge, courage, survival, friendship)
■ The moral (in a fable) is . . . ("Look before you leap," "Haste makes waste")
■ The lesson I learned from this book is . . .

Writing a Book Review **271**

Writing in a Response Journal

One way to respond to a book is to keep a response journal. In your journal, you may write freely about the characters in the book, jot down what you think will happen next, or look for parts of the story that remind you of your own life.

How to Respond

Write in your journal several times as you read a book. For example, make an entry after you have read the first few chapters, about halfway through the book, and after you finish it. Use the following questions to help you respond as you read. (You will find more questions on page 272.)

■ First Feelings

What do you like best about the first few chapters? Do you like the characters? Why?

■ On Your Way

Are the events in the story clear? What do you think will happen next? Have your feelings changed about the characters?

■ The Second Half

Has anything surprising happened? Is the book still interesting? How do you think it will end?

■ Summing Up

How do you feel about the ending? How has the main character changed? What do you like most about the book? What do you like least? Why?

■ Reflections

How does the book relate to your own life? Does the book connect to today's world? Why or why not?

English Language Learners

In their response journals, ask students to copy short passages from stories they read that they particularly like or find meaningful. Use these passages as references for when students study new language concepts. For example, you could ask students to find examples of present tense verbs by looking back at their interesting passages.

Writing in a Response Journal

Have students dedicate a new notebook to serve as a reader-response journal.

- Provide craft supplies such as glitter glue, magazines with pictures, scissors, paste, colored markers, and stickers for students to use to decorate the cover of their journal.
- Set aside time for students to write in their journals about the books they read for class.
- Encourage them to use the journals for their pleasure reading as well.
- Suggest that students use the titles given (First Feelings, On Your Way, and so on) to indicate what kind of entry they are writing. Alternatively, they could assign a different colored pen to each type of entry.

Additional Questions for Responding

When students finish a book, start the journal-writing time with a group discussion of a Question of the Day, taken from the examples (or use a question of your own). Afterward, students can devote their journal entries to what was discussed in class, or they can write about a different issue.

Students who write insightful letters to authors should consider mailing them. Explain that many authors respond to every letter or e-mail they receive, although it might take time. (Remind students to include a stamped, self-addressed envelope—postage is expensive for someone who has hundreds of letters to answer—if they're sending their letter through the mail.) If the student receives a reply, set aside class time to share it. (For more about writing to authors, see PE pages 274–277.)

Start a Recommended Reading bulletin board and invite students to write brief reviews of their favorite books to post there—or provide a sign-up sheet, where students can list the titles of books they recommend. Have students who read a recommended book post a brief note titled *I Read It!* that tells what they thought of it.

272

Additional Questions for Responding

Whenever you need a starting point for writing in your response journal, check this page for ideas. Not every idea will work for every book you read.

Before and After

- What are your feelings after reading the first part of the book?
- What is one important thing that happens in the middle of the book? Why is it important?
- What are your overall feelings about this book?

Favorites

- What is the best part of this book? Explain.
- Which illustration in the book is your favorite? Describe it in detail.

Making Changes

- Would you like to write a new ending for this book? What would it be?
- Do you think the title of the book is a good one? Why?

Author! Author!

- What do you think the author wants you to learn from this story?
- What would you say in a short friendly letter to the author?

Cast of Characters

- What is the main character in the story like? Write about him, her, or it.
- Are you like any of the characters in the book? Write a story about how you and the character are alike.
- Do any of the characters remind you of people you know? Explain by writing a comparison.
- Would you like having one of the characters in the story as a friend? Explain why or why not.

English Language Learners

Students may also want to use their response journals to write down parts of a story that they find unclear or confusing. Volunteer to respond to students' journal questions or comments in a timely manner to help them better understand each story and to monitor their comprehension.

Advanced Learners

To help the class more easily utilize the journal response questions on PE pages 271–272, ask students to

- create posters for each category, including original samples, or
- create graphic organizers for each category that students can select, fill out, and store in a 3-ring binder.

Response to Literature

Other Forms of Responding

As you go from class to class, you'll find many different kinds of literature. Literature includes short stories, articles, reports, poems, and plays. Just think of all the things you can read.

In this section, you will learn how to respond to four different forms of literature: a biography, a poem, a nonfiction article, and a tall tale.

Mini Index

- **Responding to a Biography**
- **Responding to a Poem**
- **Responding to a Nonfiction Article**
- **Responding to a Tall Tale**

Other Forms of Responding

Objectives
- apply what has been learned about responding to books to responding to other forms of literature
- practice writing for assessment

Explain to students that a large part of education is encountering different forms of literature and then thinking about and responding to them. Learning what questions to ask when they read a work of literature will help them
- organize their thoughts,
- express their ideas to other people, and
- better remember what they've read.

Having good responding skills will also help students in other areas of life—for example, when they want to recommend a movie to a friend!

Tell students that the exercises on the following pages will
- point out other kinds of literature to respond to and
- help them practice ways of responding other than writing reviews.

Materials

Colored markers (TE pp. 278 and 280)

Chart paper (TE p. 280)

Selection of poems (TE p. 281)

Posterboard and art supplies (TE p. 284)

Children's news magazines (TE p. 287)

Nonfiction articles (TE p. 291)

Pictures (TE p. 292)

Tall tales books (TE p. 293)

Copy Masters/ Transparencies

Sensory and 5 W's charts (TE p. 285)

5 W's chart and time line (TE p. 287)

Venn diagram, T-chart, and table diagram (TE p. 293)

Responding to a Biography

Point out that although students could write a review of a biography, as they did for a fiction book, it's fun to tell their thoughts to the person who wrote the book.

Before students write a letter, discuss letter-writing etiquette. Authors receive lots of letters, and many of them try to answer every one. It's important that students

- take as much care writing the letter as they would writing an essay for their teacher to read;
- be friendly and polite and talk about something that genuinely interests them;
- evaluate questions before asking them—a question should be something the author is specially qualified to answer (about a character in the book, say), not something students could easily find out through research; and
- refrain from asking the author to send free books or other items.

Have students read the sample to see if the writer followed these rules of etiquette. (The writer did.)

274

Responding to a Biography

A **biography** is a book about a person's life. One way to respond to a book is to write to the author. In the sample below, Jeff responded to a biography he had read by sending an e-mail message to the author.

The **beginning** introduces the writer, the book, and the reason for liking the book.

The **middle** explains a favorite part of the book.

The **ending** includes something the writer wonders about and asks the author a question.

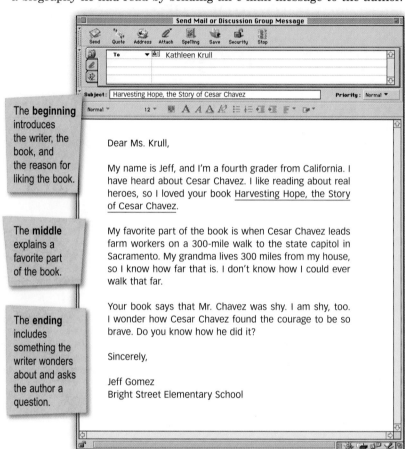

> **Send Mail or Discussion Group Message**
>
> To: Kathleen Krull
>
> Subject: Harvesting Hope, the Story of Cesar Chavez   Priority: Normal
>
> Dear Ms. Krull,
>
> My name is Jeff, and I'm a fourth grader from California. I have heard about Cesar Chavez. I like reading about real heroes, so I loved your book Harvesting Hope, the Story of Cesar Chavez.
>
> My favorite part of the book is when Cesar Chavez leads farm workers on a 300-mile walk to the state capitol in Sacramento. My grandma lives 300 miles from my house, so I know how far that is. I don't know how I could ever walk that far.
>
> Your book says that Mr. Chavez was shy. I am shy, too. I wonder how Cesar Chavez found the courage to be so brave. Do you know how he did it?
>
> Sincerely,
>
> Jeff Gomez
> Bright Street Elementary School

English Language Learners

Many cultures use a different approach for writing letters than that used for business communications in the U.S. Emphasize to students that in their opening paragraph they should introduce who they are and tell why they are writing the letter.

- Explain that introducing yourself is not too direct.

- Tell students to make the points of their letters concise, which is considered respectful.
- Refer to the example to show that each point is stated only once, and the letter as a whole is not overly flattering, but focuses on only a few parts of the story that the reader found particularly interesting.

Responding to a Biography 275

Prewriting Planning Your Response

To plan an e-mail response to a biography, follow these three steps.

1 **Select a biography.** Choose a book that you have read and enjoyed.

2 **Gather information for your message.** A gathering grid like the one below can help you plan your e-mail message. List why you like the book, your favorite part, and a question you would like to ask the author.

Gathering Grid

Title: <u>The Daring Nellie Bly</u>   Author: Bonnie Christensen

Why I like this book	My favorite part	My question for the author
I like to write. I'd like to be a reporter someday.	Nellie's trip around the world and the map that shows where she went	How can I become a great writer?

3 **Find out where to send your message.** Many authors have Web sites that include their e-mail addresses. Another way to contact an author is through the book publisher. Your teacher or school librarian can help you find the publisher's e-mail address.

Prewrite   **Plan your response.** Follow the three steps above to get ready to write your e-mail message.

Writing Developing Your Response

To prepare students for describing themselves to their chosen author, ask what they might want to mention about themselves other than their name and grade. Provide suggestions, if necessary, such as:

- special interests that apply to the book (*I'm on my school basketball team, so I loved reading about Wilt Chamberlain.*)
- ways they're like a person in the book (*Like Napoleon Bonaparte, I have red hair, too!*)

Have students write their first draft, double-spaced, on notebook paper. They can transfer the letter to the computer after they have revised and edited it.

As with other drafts, encourage them to consult their notes frequently and to get all their ideas down on paper, without worrying whether they've made things perfect. Remind them that they can make any necessary changes during the revising stage.

276

Writing Developing Your Response

In the **beginning**, you should greet the author, introduce yourself, name the book, and tell why you like the story. Be sure to use the title of the book in your subject heading.

> Dear Ms. Christensen,
>
> My name is Angie. I'm a fourth grader from Virginia. I like reading about famous women. That is why I liked your book <u>The Daring Nellie Bly.</u>

In the **middle**, you can tell about your favorite part of the book.

> My favorite part is Nellie's trip around the world. I was surprised that she did it in 80 days. There were no airplanes back then, so she had to travel by boat and t   I loved the map you drew to show where she went.

In the **ending**, you can tell what you still wonder about and ask the author a question. Sign your e-mail message with your name and the name of your school.

> I still wonder why it was so hard for women to be reporters in Nellie's time. I would like to be a famous writer someday. Can you tell me how to get started?

 Write a first draft. Write your e-mail response using the information from your gathering grid (page 275) and the guidelines above.

Struggling Learners

To support students who typically write their drafts on a computer, teach them the following two options for drafting e-mail messages:

- Compose the message using the e-mail program but save it in the "Drafts" file until it's revised and edited.

- Compose the message using the normal word-processing program and then copy and paste it into an e-mail message once it's revised and edited.

Responding to a Biography **277**

Revising and Editing Checklist

Once you finish your first draft, the following checklist can help you revise and edit your response.

Ideas

_____ **1.** Does my writing show that I understand the book?

_____ **2.** Do I include examples when I tell about my favorite part?

Organization

_____ **3.** Do I include a clear beginning, middle, and ending?

Voice

_____ **4.** Do I sound like I enjoyed reading the book?

Word Choice

_____ **5.** Do I use specific nouns and verbs?

Sentence Fluency

_____ **6.** Do my sentences read smoothly?

Conventions

_____ **7.** Do I use correct capitalization and punctuation?

_____ **8.** Do I spell all my words correctly?

Revise

Revise and edit your response. Make the necessary changes in your response. Proofread your final message and double-check the address before sending it.

Revising and Editing Checklist

When students have finished using the checklist, invite a volunteer to suggest a specific revising trouble spot. Give the group time to go through their drafts checking for this type of error, and then invite other students to suggest items to focus on, such as

- varied sentence beginnings,
- run-on or rambling sentences, and
- correct usage of *its* and *it's*.

After students finish revising, have them type their letters into an e-mail program and print out a copy to proofread. Explain that it's important to be on the lookout for errors they made while typing.

As the final proofreading step, have students look at the covers of their books to make sure they have correctly spelled the author's name and title of the book throughout their letter, and that they have properly punctuated the title. Recommend that they always recheck both items, even if they feel positive they haven't made an error—it would be impolite to get these things wrong.

Review students' final copy before they send their letter.

English Language Learners

When students are revising their own work, have them focus on the conventions of English grammar and spelling that they have already studied. Once they are done, explain that because this work will be sent out, you will edit for other conventions that they may not have studied. Try to edit directly on the computer so that they will not have their papers heavily marked if there are many errors, as this may be disheartening for beginning English students.

Struggling Learners

To help students self-evaluate their work for the *voice* trait, have them read aloud their e-mail response into a tape recorder. As they play back their recording, they can determine if their response sounds as if they truly enjoyed reading the book.

Writing for Assessment

If your students must take school, district, or state assessments this year, focus on the writing form on which they will be tested.

Remind students that they should always read the prompt all the way through once before beginning to write. This will prevent them from missing any details the prompt asks them to address. Have students point out the key ideas to be addressed for this prompt:

- Write about a biography.
- Write a letter to the author.
- Tell (1) why you liked the book, (2) a favorite part, and (3) a question you have.

Ask students to evaluate the sample letter. Does it answer all of the key points in the prompt? (Most students will agree that it does.)

Draw students' attention to the middle paragraph's topic sentence. Note that it is quite general to say that your favorite part of a biography is the *interesting facts*. It also implies that there were *un*interesting facts (something the author might be sad to hear). Suggest that students focus on a specific interesting fact or scene in their topic sentence.

278

Writing for Assessment

On a test, you may be asked to respond to a biography you have read. Study the following prompt and student response.

Prompt: *Think about a biography you have read. Write a letter to the author. Tell why you liked the book, share your favorite part, and ask the author a question.*

Notes

Title	Author	Facts	Question
On the Field with Derek Jeter	Matt Christopher	−always wanted to be a shortstop −almost got cut from his high school baseball team	Did you ever meet him?

The **beginning** introduces the writer, the book, and the reason for liking the book.

Dear Mr. Matt Christopher,

My name is Steven. I'm a fourth grader from Colorado. Baseball is my favorite sport in the world. That is why I liked your book On the Field with Derek Jeter.

The **middle** explains a favorite part of the book.

My favorite part of your book is the interesting facts about Derek Jeter. He cared a lot about his family, and he wanted to be a shortstop for the Yankees ever since he was a little boy. I was surprised to find out that when he was in high school, he almost got cut from the school baseball team.

The **ending** asks the author a question.

I wonder what it would be like to meet Derek Jeter. When you wrote your book, did you get to meet him in person?

Sincerely,

Steven Chan
Martin Luther King Elementary School

English Language Learners

To help students understand the prompt and to guide them as they write, have them copy the prompt on the top of their paper.

- Give students different colors of markers and ask them to underline the important words of the prompt.
- You might tell them to underline the genre (biography) in one color, the format (letter) in

another color, and each detail to include in other colors.

- Then circulate and ask students individually to paraphrase what they must do so that you can check for comprehension of the prompt.
- Clarify any misunderstandings or doubts that students have during the individual checks.

- Continue to monitor as they write to make sure students answer all parts of the prompt.

Responding to a Biography   **279**

WRITING TIPS

Before you write . . .

- **Choose a book that you know and enjoy.**
  Make sure you know who the author is.
- **Make a graphic organizer.**
  Jot down notes in a simple chart to organize ideas for your response.

Title	Author	Facts	Question

During your writing . . .

- **Name the book and tell why you liked it.**
  Be sure to underline the book title.
- **Develop the middle.**
  Share your favorite part. Include an example.
- **End with a question.**
  In the last paragraph, mention something that you still wonder about and ask the author a question.

After you've written your response . . .

- **Review your writing for ideas and organization.**
  Make sure your message is clear.
- **Edit and proofread.**
  Check for errors in punctuation, capitalization, spelling, and grammar.

Respond to a biography. Choose a favorite biography and write a letter or an e-mail to the author in the time your teacher allows.

Writing Tips

If students haven't read biographies, try the same exercise with a different kind of book.

Refer students to the three-column gathering grid used on PE page 275 and tell them they can use this format for their notes, if they prefer it to the four-column organizer.

Talk a little bit about the kinds of questions students might have for the author about the book:

- asking about something the author did or learned while writing the book
- asking how the author got the idea for the book
- asking for more information about something mentioned in the book
- pointing out a place where you think the author might have made a mistake

Explain that although mentioning a possible mistake can seem like criticizing a book, authors (and those who read assessments) usually appreciate thoughtful, politely phrased criticism, especially when the person giving it liked the book. It shows the reader was so interested that he or she paid extra-close attention.

Responding to a Poem

Have volunteers read the poem and response aloud. Talk about what makes the response effective. Encourage students to contribute their ideas, too (and if some disagree about the response being effective, have them tell why).

- The writer sounds interested in the poem.
- The writer uses vivid adjectives (*huge, tiny, little, awkward*) and active verbs (*trying, swat, enjoyed, wishes*).
- The writer creates variation in the kinds of sentences used by making one sentence a question.
- The writer pictures what the poem is describing and explains why it's funny.
- In addition to focusing on the funny story (the literal meaning), the writer notices that the poem describes a serious situation, too.

280

Responding to a Poem

A **poem** creates a word picture using sights, sounds, smells, tastes, and feelings. To respond to a poem, you consider its form, its sound, special words the poet uses, and the main idea of the poem. In the essay below, the writer responds to a limerick, a humorous, rhymed poem.

Toucan

There once was a toucan named Sue
Who lived in an Illinois zoo.
She dined on green peas
And swatted at bees
While she dreamed about life in Peru.

> The **beginning** names the form and the topic of the poem.

"Toucan" is a limerick. A limerick has five lines that follow a pattern. The last words of lines one, two, and five rhyme with each other. The last words of lines three and four rhyme with each other. There is a special rhythm to the sound of the poem.

> The **middle** explains how the words are used.

The poet uses rhyming words to create a funny story. The words make me laugh because the toucan has a huge bill, but it's trying to eat tiny, little peas. How could a toucan ever swat a bee with that big awkward bill? I think this poet enjoyed choosing the rhyming words for this poem.

> The **ending** explains the main idea of the poem.

Even though "Toucan" is a funny poem, I think the main idea is that Sue wishes she were in the jungles of Peru instead of in a zoo. It makes me wonder about all animals who have to live in zoos instead of in their natural habitat.

English Language Learners

Students may have difficulty understanding the rhyme of the sample poem because the rhyming words do not follow the same spelling patterns.

- Read aloud the poem several times. Copy it onto chart paper and underline each set of rhyming words in a different color.

- Ask students to explain what rhyme is (words with the same ending sounds), and ask them to brainstorm other words they know that rhyme.
- Make a chart of rhyming words and ask students if they have similar spelling patterns or not.

Advanced Learners

To promote original thinking and analysis, invite students to write their own response to the sample poem before reading the sample response. Then have students compare and contrast their ideas with one another and with the sample response.

Responding to a Poem   **281**

Prewriting **Planning Your Response**

1 **Choose a poem.** Select one that you enjoy and understand.

2 **Read the poem out loud several times.**

3 **Name the form of the poem** (*limerick, haiku, cinquain, free verse*). Ask yourself these questions: How many lines does the poem have? Do the words rhyme? Does the poem follow a pattern?

4 **List ideas for your response.** Make a graphic organizer like the one below to gather ideas.

> **State Flower**
> California
> Golden poppies, bright yellow
> Like flaming sunshine.

Gathering Chart

Form	Special Words	Main Idea
Haiku–nature poem first line–5 syllables second line–7 syllables third line–5 syllables	golden poppies– state flower of California bright yellow color like flaming sunshine	Golden poppies look like sunshine.

Plan your response. Use the guidelines above to choose a poem and gather ideas about it. If you have trouble finding a poem, you may use this one:

> **Early Evening**
> The night is blazing
> With a swarm of fireflies
> Dancing a ballet.

Prewriting
Planning Your Response

Students may worry that they won't be able to figure out a poem's theme, or message. Assure them that **interpreting poetry** (*see below*) can be very personal. The important thing is to use good reasons to support their ideas. To help students get started,

- provide example poems in the different forms students need to be able to recognize;
- for each poem, ask a student to read it aloud;
- have students identify the form and describe its characteristics;
- guide them as they interpret the poem, encouraging them to suggest different meanings if they wish;
- at least once during the discussion, ask a different volunteer to read the poem again to keep the words fresh in students' memory.

If students aren't yet comfortable interpreting poems on their own, allow them to write about one of the poems discussed as a class. Have students working on the same poem form groups to help one another during prewriting.

Teaching Tip: Interpreting Poetry

To give students more tools to use when interpreting poetry, help them to become familiar with special literary terms. Explain that two common techniques they'll find in poetry are

- Similes—comparisons that use the words *like* or *as*. In "State Flower," the phrase *like flaming sunshine* is a simile that compares the poppies to sunlight.

- Metaphors—comparisons that don't use *like* or *as*. In "Early Evening," the fireflies are described as *dancing a ballet*. They aren't really ballet dancing (only people can do that), but the writer is saying that their movement looks like ballet.

Encourage students to watch for similes and metaphors in what they read. Writers use these

techniques often because they help readers to picture what they are trying to describe.

✳ For more about special poetry techniques, see PE pages 318–319.

Writing
Developing Your Response

Point out that once students have made a gathering chart, they've done the difficult interpreting work. Now they can concentrate on expanding their notes into sentences and making each section of the chart into a paragraph.

Draw students' attention to the way quotation marks are used in the sample. What do they notice?

- The title of the poem is in quotation marks.
- Exact phrases from the poem are in quotation marks.

Note that there are a couple of reasons for putting words from the poem in quotation marks:

- Unusual phrases and entire lines (or more) should always be in quotation marks to show that they were created by the poet.
- Short, general terms like *golden poppies* (or *bright yellow*) don't need to be in quotes, unless the writer wants to emphasize that they're from the poem.

✱ For more about quotation marks, see PE page 494.

282

Writing Developing Your Response

The **beginning** paragraph names and describes the poem's form and subject.

> "State Flower" is a haiku poem about California poppies. Haiku poems are three lines long. The first and third lines have five syllables. The second line has seven syllables. Haiku poems are about nature.

The **middle** paragraph explains how the poet uses special words in the poem. Examples from the poem support your ideas.

> The first line of the poem names the state of California. The other lines describe what the golden poppy looks like. For example, golden poppies are "bright yellow." They look "like flaming sunshine." The last line reminds me that the sun is bright because it's a huge ball of fire. I think a field of poppies might look like it's on fire with sunshine!

The **ending** paragraph explains the poem's main idea.

> The poem's main idea is that golden poppies are cheerful and bright like sunshine. I think the poet loves looking at the poppies. In this poem about the Golden State's flower, I can feel that "flaming sunshine," too.

Write a first draft. Use the explanations above and your planning from page 281 to create your response. Include a beginning, a middle, and an ending.

Struggling Learners

Students might be overwhelmed trying to respond to all three requirements. In this case, narrow the focus by assigning one of the following to three different groups:

- the poem's form and subject
- how the poet uses special words
- the poem's main idea

Students can then compile their results for a group response essay.

Responding to a Poem   **283**

Revising and Editing Checklist

Once you finish your first draft, use the following checklist to revise and edit your response.

Ideas

_____ **1.** Do my ideas show that I understand the poem?

_____ **2.** Do I name the form and quote words from the poem?

Organization

_____ **3.** Do I include the beginning, middle, and ending parts?

Voice

_____ **4.** Do I sound like I understand and enjoy the poem?

Word Choice

_____ **5.** Do I use specific nouns and verbs?

Sentence Fluency

_____ **6.** Do my sentences read smoothly?

Conventions

_____ **7.** Do I use correct capitalization and punctuation?

_____ **8.** Do I spell all my words correctly?

 Revise and edit your response. Make the necessary changes to your response. Proofread your final copy before sharing it.

Revising and Editing Checklist

Have students work with partners to begin the revising process.

- Ask partners to read their essays to each other and then complete revising checklists for their own and their partner's essay.
- Ask students to suggest two specific changes for partners to try.
- Have students compare their own checklist for their essay to the one their partner made.
  - ☐ Do the two lists agree?
  - ☐ Do the writers agree with their partner's suggestions for improvements?
  - ☐ Do the partner's comments help them to see other changes they want to make?

During the editing stage, ask students to do the following:

- Double-check all quotations—are they exactly the same as in the poem?
- Look up three words in their essay using the dictionary, even if they think they've spelled everything right.

Writing for Assessment

If your students must take school, district, or state assessments this year, focus on the writing form on which they will be tested.

Ask students to read the prompt twice and then identify the key points called for (the poem's topic, its form, **description of the form** *(see below)*, special words, and main idea/message). Have them identify the part or parts of the essay that correspond to each key point.

Discuss that the writer talked about the special words' grammatical functions in the poem.

- Note that this strategy can be applied to any poem, so students can use it during a test if they can't quickly think of a way to approach the paragraph.
- Encourage them to become familiar with the parts of speech so they can use them anytime they need to respond to literature.

* Refer students to the Proofreader's Guide, PE pages 570–605, for information about the parts of speech.

Refer students to the sample responses on PE pages 280 and 282 for other ways to talk about the special words in poems.

284

Writing for Assessment

On a test, you may be asked to respond to a poem. Study the following prompt and student response.

Prompt: *Respond to the following poem. In your essay, name the topic, explain the poem's form, point out special words the poet uses, and share the poem's main idea or message.*

> **Spider**
> Smart, quick
> Weaving a web
> To trap its prey
> Arachnid.

---

*The **beginning** names the poem and explains the form.*

"Spider" is a word cinquain poem about spiders. It has five lines that follow the pattern one word, two words, three words, four words, and one word. The first line and the last line are synonyms.

*The **middle** describes special words the poet uses.*

The poet uses different kinds of words to help the reader see the spider. Smart and quick are adjectives. They describe the spider and how it moves. Weaving is a verb that shows the spider in action. The line "to trap its prey" shows the spider as a hunter. The last word, arachnid, is a synonym for spider. I like the word because it sounds scary. I think being caught in a web would be scary, especially for a bug.

*The **ending** explains the main idea of the poem.*

The poem's main idea is that spiders are very clever. This poem shows a spider setting a trap for its prey.

Teaching Tip: Describing the Forms

To help students become familiar enough with the poetic forms to be able to describe them in a testing situation, have them make posters.

- Write the forms on the board—limerick, cinquain, haiku, free verse, and others, if required.
- Divide the class into small groups and distribute poster-board and art supplies to each group.
- Assign each group one of the forms to illustrate.

Each poster should include
- the name of the form as the title,
- a poem that is an example of the form,
- text clearly describing the form, and
- additional decorations.

Display the posters in the room. Once or twice a week, read a "Poem of the Day" to the class. Have students tell its form and explain how they identified it.

Responding to a Poem 285

WRITING TIPS

Before you write . . .

- **Read the poem several times.**
  Think about its form and how the words are used.
- **Make a graphic organizer.**
  Use a gathering chart to organize ideas for your response.

Gathering Chart

Form	
Special words	
Main idea	

During your writing . . .

- **Name and describe the form of the poem.**
  Name the kind of poem *(haiku, cinquain, free verse, limerick)* and explain how it is put together.
- **Develop the middle part.**
  Tell how the poet uses special words in the poem.
- **Share the meaning of the poem.**
  In the ending, explain the poem's main idea or message.

After you've written your response . . .

- **Review your writing for ideas and organization.**
  Make sure your ideas are clear.
- **Edit and proofread.**
  Check for errors in punctuation, capitalization, spelling, and grammar.

Respond to a poem. Respond to the following poem or to a poem selected by your teacher.

> **Mid-Summer Night**
> Summer moon rising
> Turns the sleeping lake to gold
> Echoing loon calls.

Writing Tips

Focus on the term *special words*. Ask students to tell what it means. (The words that do the most to create images, describe ideas, or make the poem sound a certain way—as in rhymes or alliteration.)

Distribute photocopies of the reproducible sensory and 5 W's charts (TE pages 646 and 647). Suggest that whenever students need to find special words in a poem, they think of the following:

- The five senses—do the words apply to sight, sound, touch, taste, or smell?
- The 5 W's and H—do the words answer *who, what, when, where, why,* or *how?*

Ask students to look at the special words identified in the sample response on PE page 284. How can students apply the 5 W words?

- *smart—What* is a spider like?
- *quick—How* does it move?
- *weaving—What* does it do?
- *to trap its prey—Why* does it weave?
- *arachnid—What* is a spider?

Note also that the writer could have pointed out that the poet uses *alliteration—weaving* and *web* both begin with the *w* sound—in the second line of the poem.

English Language Learners

Make sure that when you select a poem for students to respond to, they understand all of the vocabulary and phrasing of the poem before responding. Point out that poems often do not have complete sentences, and that grammar and punctuation are often used loosely. You may want to choose different sample poems for students according to their level of fluency.

Responding to a Nonfiction Article

Remind students that a summary paragraph

- gives the key ideas from a piece of writing (unlike a review, which tries not to reveal the end of the piece);
- should use their own words, not borrow from the original; and
- should not include the opinions of the summary writer.

✱ For more about summary paragraphs, see PE pages 333–336.

Ask students to compare the sample summary carefully to the sample article and to evaluate the summary.

- The topic sentence tells the main idea of the article.
- The writer's voice sounds knowledgeable.
- The writer could have tried harder to use his or her own words: Repeated words include *to move around, by feeling the edges with its whiskers, to move around safely.*
- The writer could have tried harder to vary the sentence beginnings: Two begin with *A cat.*

Responding to a Nonfiction Article

A **nonfiction article** shares information about a real person, place, or thing. One way to respond to a nonfiction article is to write a summary of it.

Sample Article

Whiskers—A Cat's Antennae

Whiskers are an important part of a cat's body. They help a cat to move around. These long, thick hairs on a cat's face can sense even the smallest changes in air movement. As a cat gets close to an object, its whiskers sense a change in the air. This allows a cat to move about in the dark without bumping into things.

The tips of whiskers contain many nerve endings. This means that a cat can judge the width of an opening by feeling the edges with its whiskers. It can decide if it can fit through tight spaces.

You should never trim a cat's whiskers. Without them it is much harder for a cat to move around safely.

Sample Summary

The **topic sentence** names the article's main idea.

The **body** includes the most important information from the article.

The **closing sentence** includes the final important point.

A cat's whiskers help it to move around. Whiskers can sense any small movement in the air. They help a cat tell when an object is near. A cat can judge how wide a space is by feeling the edges with its whiskers. Without whiskers it would be hard for a cat to move around safely.

Prewriting Planning Your Summary

Follow these steps when you plan to write a summary of an article.

1 Select an interesting article to read, like this one:

Ah . . . Ah . . . Ah-choo!

A sneeze results from a chain of events that takes place in a matter of seconds. It may be a response to particles in the air, like dust, or to a sudden change in temperature.

First, your nose gets a tickle. The tickle tells your brain to create a sneeze. Your brain then sends a message to all the muscles that make up a sneeze. These include muscles in and near your belly, chest, lungs, vocal cords, throat, face, and eyes. All of these muscles work together, in just the right order, to build a sneeze. Ah-choo!

The sneeze sends tiny particles from your nose flying at speeds of up to 100 miles per hour. This is why you should always cover your mouth and nose when you sneeze (and wash your hands afterward). A sneeze often results in germs being spread from one person to another.

2 Make an idea cluster like the one below to name the topic. Add the most important information in your own words.

Idea Cluster

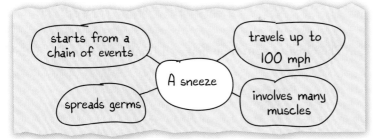

Plan your summary. Follow the steps above to get started on your summary. If you can't find an article, ask your teacher for help.

Prewriting
Planning Your Summary

To streamline the article-selection process, provide children's news magazines or bookmark news Web sites such as Kidsnewsroom.org (http://www.kidsnewsroom.org).

Alternatively, have students work in groups on longer articles, each summarizing part of the article. Consider using this approach for articles that tie in with subjects students are studying for class.

Discuss ways other than an idea cluster that students could use to organize information.

- If they have a printout or photo-copy of the article, underline or highlight directly on it.
- Use a 5 W's chart and find the answers to *who, what, when, where,* and *why.*
- Use a time line if the article describes a series of events.

Provide photocopies of the repro-ducible 5 W's chart and the time line (TE pages 647 & 648) for students to use, if they wish.

Whatever method or methods students use, remind them to read the article through once before starting to take notes.

English Language Learners

Define the following terms before reading the sample article:

- chain of events (a series of events, one after another)
- response (reaction)
- particles (bits, pieces)
- temperature (how hot or cold something is)
- germs (tiny cells that can make you to be sick)

Make sure that students choose articles that are at their indepen-dent reading level. Define new vocabulary before they begin to read so that they understand the entire article. To check for compre-hension, ask students to summa-rize the article orally before beginning to write their summary.

Struggling Learners

Point out that, although the writer puts the information in his or her own words, new details should not be added when summarizing. For exam-ple, many students know that people involuntarily close their eyes each time they sneeze or that pepper causes sneezing, but these points should not be included here. A summary states only facts from the article.

Writing
Developing Your Summary

Before students begin writing, have them practice summarizing by telling a partner about their article. Can they express the article's **main idea** (*see below*) in one sentence and then mention three or four key points?

Students may wish to mention more key points than will fit into three or four sentences. This could be a sign that they don't feel comfortable deciding what are the most important details. First have them check to see how the details are organized in the article. To help them limit the size of their paragraphs, ask them to tell you the points they want to mention. Provide feedback and guidance to help them pare down their list.

Remind students that, when writing a first draft, the main goal is to get their ideas onto paper. The draft doesn't have to be perfect because they'll go back and make improvements during the revising and editing stages.

Writing Developing Your Summary

Your summary paragraph will have three main parts: a topic sentence, the body, and a closing sentence. (See pages 333–336.)

The **topic sentence** should state the article's main idea.

> A sneeze results from a chain of events.

Tips for finding the main idea
- Look for the main idea at the beginning or end of the first paragraph in an article.
- Ask yourself, "What main message is the author communicating?"

The **body** includes *only* the most important information from the article. All of the sentences in the body should support the topic sentence. Arrange your ideas so that they are easy to follow.

> These events take only a few seconds. Many muscles work together to make a sneeze. Sneezing sends particles from your nose flying at speeds up to 100 mph.

The **closing sentence** makes a final point from the article.

> A sneeze can spread germs.

 Write a first draft. Write your summary paragraph using the information above and your idea cluster (page 287).

Teaching Tip: Identifying the Main Idea

To help students who are having trouble deciding the main idea of their article, offer additional tips.

- Always read the whole article first before worrying about what the author's message is. The end could contain important information about the main idea.
- Look for clues in the title. (See, for example, the titles on PE pages 286 and 290.)

- Ask yourself, *What single idea or thing is the author writing about?* (For example, on PE page 287, sneezing.) Then ask, *What is the writer saying about that thing or idea?* (Sneezing is caused by a series of things.)

Responding to a Nonfiction Article   289

Revising and Editing Checklist

Use the following checklist to revise and edit your summary.

Ideas

_____ **1.** Do I share the article's most important ideas?

Organization

_____ **2.** Does my topic sentence state the article's main idea?

_____ **3.** Do the body sentences include the most important ideas from the article?

_____ **4.** Does the last sentence make a final point about the topic?

Voice

_____ **5.** Do I sound confident, like I understand the article?

Word Choice

_____ **6.** Have I put the information in my own words?

Sentence Fluency

_____ **7.** Do my sentences flow smoothly?

Conventions

_____ **8.** Do I use correct capitalization and punctuation?

_____ **9.** Do I spell all my words correctly?

 Revise

Revise and edit your summary. Make the necessary changes and corrections. Proofread your final copy before sharing it.

Revising and Editing Checklist

Review the checklist and focus on the question for word choice. Note that the sample writer could have been more careful about using his or her own words in this sentence on PE page 288: *Sneezing sends particles from your nose flying at speeds up to 100 mph.* How many words in that sentence are also in the original, on PE page 287? (Twelve out of thirteen.) Remind students that using someone else's words without putting them in quotation marks and giving credit is plagiarism.

Challenge students to think of different ways the writer could have phrased the sentence. Possible answers:

■ When you sneeze, little droplets shoot out of your nose at speeds as high as 100 mph.

■ The particles that fly out of your nose during a sneeze can be traveling as fast as 100 mph.

✱ For more about plagiarism, see PE page 352.

During editing, encourage students to consult the Proofreader's Guide (PE pages 478–605) with any questions.

English Language Learners

Students may have difficulty putting the information from the article into their own words.

● Have students use a thesaurus to vary their words as they revise.

● Have students work with English-proficient peers to revise their work and to check that phrases are not copied directly from the article.

Writing for Assessment

If your students must take school, district, or state assessments this year, focus on the writing form on which they will be tested.

Have students read the prompt through twice and then tell the main thing that it asks them to do (summarize the article).

Ask students to tell what makes a good summary. List the responses on the board.

- The topic sentence tells the subject of the article.
- The body sentences tell the key ideas in the article.
- The closing sentence sums up the information.
- The writer uses his or her own words.
- The writer doesn't mention his or her own opinions.

Ask students to evaluate the sample summary. Does it meet the standards they listed? Why or why not?

- The subject given (*Roosevelt got polio*) is more limited than in the article, which emphasizes that he got polio *and* was president.
- The writer does a good job of using her own words.

290

Writing for Assessment

On a test, you may be asked to respond to a nonfiction article. Study the following prompt and student response.

Prompt: *Carefully read the following article. Then briefly summarize the article. Include the most important details.*

The Unstoppable Franklin D. Roosevelt

Franklin D. Roosevelt was the 32nd president of the United States. He was also disabled. As an adult, he had an illness called polio that left him unable to move his legs.

Roosevelt never gave up. He fought hard to walk again. Even though he regained some strength in his legs, he was never able to walk without help. He wore leg braces, and he used crutches and a wheelchair.

Polio did not stop President Roosevelt. He was elected for four terms. While in office, he created programs for disabled American citizens. Roosevelt was determined. He would not let a disability stop him from doing great things.

Sample Summary

The **topic sentence** states the subject of the article.

The **body** includes the most important details in the writer's own words.

The **closing sentence** sums up the information.

As an adult, Franklin D. Roosevelt got polio. He could not move his legs. Even with hard work, for the rest of his life, he was able to walk only with help. He was elected president of the United States four times. He also came up with programs to help other people with disabilities. Roosevelt never let his disability stop him.

Writing for Assessment

291

WRITING TIPS

Before you write . . .

- **Read the prompt and the article.**
  Be sure you understand what the prompt asks you to do.
- **Make a graphic organizer.**
  Create a cluster about the article to collect details for your summary.

Idea Cluster

main idea . . .   idea . . .
article topic
idea . . .   wrap up . . .

During your writing . . .

- **Organize your summary.**
  In the topic sentence, state the article's main idea. Use the body sentences to share other important information. End with a final important point.

After you've written your summary . . .

- **Review your writing for ideas and organization.**
  Make sure that your summary includes *only* information from the article.
- **Edit and proofread.**
  Check for errors in punctuation, capitalization, spelling, and grammar.

Respond to the following prompt.
Read a brief nonfiction article about a person. Write a summary of the article that includes the main idea and the most important information. Complete your work in the time your teacher allows.

Writing Tips

Review the tips, reminding students to choose the graphic organizer or note-taking method that best suits the article and that they like to work with (this may or may not be an idea cluster).

Remind them also to:

- Plan how long they will spend at each stage—prewriting, writing, and revising/editing.
- Read the article once before starting to take notes.
- If possible, underline and take notes directly on the copy of the article if that helps them.
- Limit paragraphs to three or four body sentences that give the most important facts or details.

To give students practice at writing a summary in a timed setting,

- distribute articles and have them follow the prompt;
- allow them the amount of time given for school, district, or state assessments; and
- decide how long students should spend on each writing stage and alert them when that amount of time has passed.

Point out that the sample summaries on PE pages 286 and 288 each include three details in the body sentences and the sample on page 290 includes four.

- Emphasize that the body sentences should contain only the most important details.
- Tell students to include no more than three or four details in their body sentences.

Limiting the number of details will help students choose only the most important details.

Responding to a Tall Tale

Discuss the term *tall tale*. Explain that *tall* isn't being used in this sense to describe a person's height (even though Paul Bunyan happens to be tall). Instead, it means "exaggerated, unlikely, or boastful." A similar phrase is *tall order,* which means something that's very difficult to achieve.

Explain to students that the sample response essay is an example of a comparison-contrast essay.

- A *comparison* tells how things are alike, and
- a *contrast* tells how things are different.

Point out that

- the first middle paragraph tells how the writer is like Paul Bunyan, and
- the second middle paragraph tells how the two of them are different.

Tell students that they'll probably write many comparison-contrast essays during their time in school. Suggest that they keep the form in mind because it can be very useful when they have to write about a topic that has two parts with similarities and differences.

292

Responding to a Tall Tale

Tall tales are filled with humor and exaggeration. They are often about superhuman characters doing amazing things. One way to respond to a tall tale is to compare yourself to one of the characters. Read this tall tale and the student response.

Paul Bunyan Grows Up and Up

Paul Bunyan was the biggest baby there ever was. Moreover, it took five giant storks to deliver him to his parents. When he arrived, his cry was like a buzz saw and a bass drum together. With just one holler, Paul emptied a whole pond of frogs. He had a giant appetite, too. He ate 40 bowls of porridge at a time, and he grew faster than bamboo. He grew so fast that before long his clothes had wagon wheels for buttons. One day, Paul's daddy gave him a blue ox named Babe. Babe grew just as fast as Paul. In fact, the two were so big that the tracks they made walking around Minnesota made 10,000 lakes.

The **beginning** names the story and tells what it's about.

The **middle** compares the responder to the tall-tale character.

The **ending** leaves the reader with something to think about.

When I read "Paul Bunyan Grows Up and Up," I discovered that Paul was a very big, strong baby. Paul and his pet ox became giants.

In some ways, I am like Paul. I can be loud like him. I have never scared frogs out of a pond, but sometimes I yell loud enough to scare my dog. I also have a big appetite. I don't eat porridge, but I can gobble up a couple bowls of cereal and three pieces of toast.

I am different from Paul because I'm not a giant. I have a pet dachshund, but she's tiny compared to Babe. Sometimes I make muddy tracks on the kitchen floor, but they turn into little brown puddles, not lakes.

When I read this tall tale, I thought about my baby brother. He is growing very fast. I guess we had better watch him. I hope he's not another Paul Bunyan!

English Language Learners

Define the following words before reading the tall tale and response:

- storks (large birds that have long legs and long beaks)
- holler (yell, cry)
- porridge (a kind of cereal, oatmeal)
- bamboo (a tropical plant)
- ox (a farm animal with horns, a bull)
- tracks (footprints)
- gobble (eat quickly)
- dachshund (a kind of small dog)

Use picture support if possible to further aid students' understanding of each word.

Advanced Learners

To further analyze "Paul Bunyan Grows Up and Up," have students read the sentences one by one and determine which might not be considered exaggerations if standing alone. For example: *Paul Bunyan was the biggest baby there ever was.* Then have students link supporting details to each statement and discuss how the details create the exaggeration.

Responding to a Tall Tale **293**

Prewriting Gathering Details

Follow these steps when you plan a response to a tall tale.

1 Read an interesting tall tale, like this one:

Pecos Bill Rides a Twister

Pecos Bill was up in Kansas one day. He wanted to ride something mean and fast, so he decided to ride a tornado. He waited for the biggest, meanest tornado to come along. When it did, it turned the sky to pea soup, and it roared so loud you could hear it clear to China. As it spun, it whipped and whirled and tied rivers into knots. Bill rode that twister all the way to California. Along the way, it made so much rain that it washed out the Grand Canyon. Finally, the tornado gave out in California, and Bill fell to the ground. He landed so hard that he sank below sea level. Today that spot is called Death Valley.

2 Use a Venn diagram to show how you are like and how you are different from the main character.

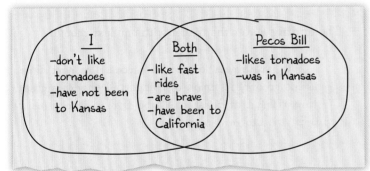

I
–don't like tornadoes
–have not been to Kansas

Both
–like fast rides
–are brave
–have been to California

Pecos Bill
–likes tornadoes
–was in Kansas

Prewrite

Plan your response. Follow the steps above to get started. If you can't find a tall tale, ask your teacher for help.

Prewriting Gathering Details

Several good books of tall tales are available (see, for example, the two books entitled *American Tall Tales,* by Mary Pope Osborne and Adrien Stoutenburg). Arrange for a class trip to the library or bring a selection of books to class for students to browse as they choose a story.

Explain that a Venn diagram is a great way to organize details for a comparison-contrast essay, but that students have other choices too.

- T-chart: List information about the tall tale character in one column and about yourself in the other column. Put asterisks next to all the similarities.
- Table chart with three legs: List things about you in the left leg, things about the character in the right leg, and things that are the same about both of you in the center leg.

Distribute photocopies of the reproducible T-chart, table diagram, and Venn diagram, (TE pages 645, 650, and 651) for students to use if they wish.

✱ For more about Venn diagrams, see PE page 457.

Writing
Developing Your Response

Encourage students to have fun with their responses. Since the tall tale is humorous, they can make jokes, too! They could even make some tall claims about themselves. Ask students to look at the sample responses on PE pages 292 and 294 and point out places where they can tell the writers had fun.

In the first response (PE page 292):

- I can gobble up . . .
- Sometimes I make muddy tracks . . . but they turn into little brown puddles, not lakes.
- I hope he's not another Paul Bunyan!

In the second response (PE page 294):

- I sure love to ride fast things . . .
- Now that's brave!

Tell students that when they write their response, they can assume that their readers have read the tall tale. This means they can refer to ideas in the tale without having to explain them fully. For example, on PE page 292, the writer says he doesn't like porridge, but he can eat two bowls of cereal. The writer refers to the part of the tale that says Paul Bunyan ate 40 bowls of porridge and assumes the reader knows this detail.

294

Writing   Developing Your Response

The **beginning** names the story and tells what it is about.

> In "Pecos Bill Rides a Twister," I found out that Pecos Bill was brave. He even went looking for danger.

The **middle** tells how you are like and how you are different from the tall-tale character.

> I think I'm a little like Pecos Bill. I sure love to ride fast things, although I prefer scooters and roller coasters. Bill liked riding tornadoes. Now that's brave! I was brave, too, when I had to get 15 stitches in my leg. We've both been to California, too.
>
> Pecos Bill and I are different because he likes tornadoes, and I don't. Twisters do way too much damage. Also, I've never been to Kansas like Pecos Bill has.

The **ending** leaves the reader with one last thought.

> My state gets lots of tornadoes. The next time the sirens go off, I'll think of Pecos Bill—having a great time riding that twister. Maybe that will keep me calm until the storm is over.

Write a first draft. Write the beginning, the middle, and the ending of your response. Use the information above and your Venn diagram (page 293.)

Responding to a Tall Tale   **295**

Revising and Editing **Checklist**

Once you finish your first draft, use the following checklist to revise and edit your response.

Ideas

_____ **1.** Do I include important details from the story?

Organization

_____ **2.** Does the beginning name the story and tell what I discovered?

_____ **3.** Does the middle make a comparison?

_____ **4.** Does the ending give the reader a final thought?

Voice

_____ **5.** Do I make a personal connection to the tall tale?

Word Choice

_____ **6.** Have I used strong nouns and vivid verbs?

Sentence Fluency

_____ **7.** Do my sentences flow smoothly?

Conventions

_____ **8.** Do I use correct capitalization and punctuation?

_____ **9.** Do I spell all my words correctly?

Revise and edit your response. Make the necessary changes and corrections. Proofread your final copy before sharing it.

Revising and Editing Checklist

Have students work in pairs to revise their drafts.

- If two students have written about the same story, pair them together. Otherwise, have them start by reading each other's tall tale.
- Have students read aloud *their partner's* response so the writer can listen to it.
- Afterward, have both take a few minutes to think about possible revisions.
- Have partners make comments and suggest ideas for improving the response.
- Repeat the process with the other response.

If possible, wait until the next class to edit the papers, so students can approach their draft with a fresh eye for finding errors. After they have gone through their response once, remind them of other editing trouble spots, and have students scan their papers for them.

- Are all proper nouns capitalized?
- Did you confuse *were* and *where*? *Its* and *it's*?
- Did you use correct end punctuation?

Struggling Learners

Point out that the trait of *voice* is particularly important in tall tales. As students revise for voice, have them check to see if

- they have used exaggerations and humor in their response (as discussed on TE page 294), and
- the response reveals amazement over the feats of the tall tale characters and excitement over the writer's personal connections.

Writing for Assessment

If your students must take school, district, or state assessments this year, focus on the writing form on which they will be tested.

Invite a volunteer to read aloud the prompt to the class, and then have students point out the key items it asks for (write a response, show how you're the same as the main character, and show how you are different).

Draw students' attention to the beginning of the sample response. Note that the writer has chosen to restate the prompt. This is one option, but it isn't a requirement for assessments. (Students are required to respond to everything the prompt asks for, but they can often do that without restating the prompt.) Another choice would be to follow the pattern of the opening paragraphs on PE pages 292 and 294, which both give the name of the story and tell what it's about.

Ask students to look at the last paragraph of the sample response. Why is it a particularly good ending? (The writer demonstrates that he recognizes the tall tale's reference to "Jack and the Beanstalk.")

296

Writing for Assessment

On a test, you may be asked to respond to a tall tale. Study the following prompt and student response.

Prompt: *Write a response to this tall tale, comparing the main character to yourself. Show how you are the same and how you are different.*

Jack and the Popcorn Stalk

One day, a farmer sent his son to see how the popcorn was growing. Jack was small, so he took a ladder with him, just in case the popcorn was taller than he was. He found the tallest stalk, and using the ladder, he climbed to the top and hung on. Before he knew it, the stalk had grown so high that Jack couldn't get back down to the ladder. He was stuck up there. Jack's father and all the other farmers tried to get him down, but the stalk was growing too fast. Poor Jack. He had to stay there till the stalk nearly reached the sun. Then the popcorn started popping. That gave Jack an idea. He jumped back down to earth—into a mountain of popcorn.

The **beginning** names the story and restates the prompt.

The **middle** compares the responder to the tall-tale character.

The **ending** gives the reader something to think about.

As I read "Jack and the Popcorn Stalk," I compared myself to Jack. He's the main character in the tall tale.

Jack and I are alike because we are both small. We also both live in the country. Jack seems to help out at home, and so do I.

We are different for two reasons. First, I am too heavy to climb up a popcorn stalk. Second, I would not be patient enough to wait for the corn to pop. I would scream and yell if I were stuck somewhere and couldn't get down.

This tall tale reminds me of the story of Jack and the beanstalk. The difference is that jumping into a mountain of popcorn is much more fun than being chased by a giant.

Responding to a Tall Tale   **297**

WRITING TIPS

Before you write . . .

- **Read the tall tale and the prompt.**
  Be sure you know what the prompt is asking you to do.
- **Make a graphic organizer.**
  Create a Venn diagram to collect details for your comparison.

Venn Diagram

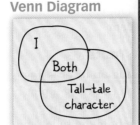

During your writing . . .

- **Organize your response.**
  In the first paragraph, name the story and tell what you discovered. In the middle part, tell how you are like and how you are different from the tall-tale character. In the ending paragraph, give the reader something to think about.

After you've written your response . . .

- **Review your writing for ideas and organization.**
  Make sure your ideas are clear.
- **Edit and proofread.**
  Check for errors in punctuation, capitalization, spelling, and grammar.

Respond to the following prompt.
Read a tall tale. Write a response comparing yourself to the tall-tale character. Show how you are the same and how you are different.

Creative Writing Overview

Writing Standards

The writing standards listed below are based on a blending of state and NCTE standards.

- Use charts and lists to generate topics and organize ideas.
- Demonstrate an understanding of story patterns and elements of fiction.
- Present a character through physical traits, actions, and dialogue.
- Present a story using different genres, such as a realistic fiction story, fantasy and play.
- Use literary devices, such as dialogue, figurative language, and poetic sounds, effectively.
- Gather sensory details and use poetry techniques to write a free-verse poem and other forms of poetry.

Writing Forms

- realistic fictional story
- free-verse poem

Focus on the Traits

- **Ideas** Creating an interesting character and a real-life problem
- **Organization** Creating a plot line that includes a beginning, rising action, a high point, and an ending
- **Voice** Using dialogue to let characters speak for themselves
- **Word Choice** Choosing action verbs to show, not tell
- **Sentence Fluency** Writing sentences that read smoothly
- **Conventions** Checking for errors in punctuation, capitalization, spelling, and grammar

Unit Pacing

Writing Stories: 3–6 hours

This section asks students to write a **realistic fictional story** and offers the opportunity to recast the story as a play. Use this section if students need to work on crafting a story. Following are some of the topics that are covered:

- Creating a character chart and a real-life problem chart to select a topic
- Making a plot chart to plan each part of the story
- Using sensory details to make the story come alive
- Building the action in the story to a high point
- Creating a title

Writing Poems: *3–4.5 hours*

This section asks students to write a **free-verse poem** and a **"Where I'm From"** poem, using special techniques. Students also explore split-couplet rhymed poems. Use this section to help students develop their ability to write poetry in various forms. Following are some of the topics that are covered:

- Making a list to select a topic
- Creating a sensory chart to gather details
- Using special poetry techniques, including repetition and line breaks

Integrated Grammar and Writing Skills

Below are skills lessons from the resources sections of the pupil edition that are suggested at point of use (✳) throughout this unit.

Writing Stories, pp. 299–310

- ✳ Commas, p. 482
- ✳ Quotation Marks, p. 494
- ✳ Capitalization, p. 514
- ✳ Improving Spelling, pp. 528–535

Writing Poems, pp. 311–319

- ✳ Sensory Details Chart, p. 456
- ✳ Writing Techniques, p. 464
- ✳ Make Comparisons, p. 411

Additional Grammar Skills

Below are skills lessons from other components that you can weave into your unit instruction.

Writing Stories

SkillsBook

Interactive Writing Skills CD ROM

Daily Language Workouts

Writing Poems

Daily Language Workouts

298

Creative Writing

Creative Writing
Writing Stories

Fictional stories let us experience life from someone else's point of view. They can make us feel strong emotions—happiness, sadness, or even fear. After reading the best stories, we may even feel changed in some important way.

In this chapter, you will learn to write a realistic fictional story. This kind of story seems real, but it is made up. You can also try writing a fantasy story or a play.

Writing Guidelines

Subject: Realistic fictional story
Form: Short story
Purpose: To entertain
Audience: Classmates

299

Writing Stories

Objectives
- demonstrate an understanding of the elements and structure of a short story
- choose a topic (realistic fiction) to write about
- plan, draft, revise, and edit a short story

A **short story** is a short piece of literature that presents a main character and a single conflict, or problem. In a realistic fiction story, the characters, setting, and events could really happen.

- The beginning introduces the main character, the setting, and problem.
- The rising action, made up of series of sequential events, shows how the character tries to solve the problem and leads toward the high point.
- At the high point, the problem is solved.
- The story ends with an explanation of how the character is changed by the events.

Family Connection Letters

As you begin this unit, send home the Creative Writing Family Connection letter, which describes what students will be learning.

 Letter in English (TE p. 658)

 Letter in Spanish (TE p. 666)

Materials

Stories (TE p. 303)

The Adventures of Tom Sawyer by Mark Twain (Sterling, 2004) (TE p. 304)

Realistic Fictional Story

Explain to students that in realistic fiction stories, writers try to create characters and situations with universal appeal. In other words, writers try to create characters that most readers will understand. This doesn't mean that readers will always like or approve of a character, but it does mean that they will find the character and the character's actions believable.

Share titles of your favorite childhood realistic fiction stories and explain why you liked these stories more than other stories you read. Point out that readers usually like stories in which the main character has qualities that make him or her seem like a real person and that the reader can connect with in some way. It may be
- a special trait (like being messy, shyness, a way of talking, or a passionate love of music),
- a problem that is similar to a problem the reader or someone the reader knows has faced, or
- goals similar to reader's goals.

Invite students to share titles of their favorite realistic stories and explain why they like these stories.

300

Realistic Fictional Story

The story below focuses on the real-life problem of being messy. The main character, Jessica, discovers why she should be more organized.

A Messy Lesson

BEGINNING

The beginning introduces the main character, the setting, and the problem.

Jessica danced into her room. She couldn't wait for tomorrow's field trip. She plopped her bulging backpack on her desk, on top of all the papers and junk. Her mother was always complaining about the messy bedroom, but Jessica didn't think it was that bad.

The phone rang, and Jessica ran to answer it. "Hello?"

Her best friend, Lacey, squealed, "Hi, Jess! I'm so excited about tomorrow!"

"Me, too!" Jessica said. "I've never been to the aquarium!"

"Did you get your permission slip signed? If you don't have it, you can't go."

"My permission slip! Sorry, Lacey, I've got to go!" Jessica hung up and rushed back to her room. "Where's that blue slip?"

RISING ACTION

The character tries to solve the problem.

Jessica started digging through stacks of books, papers, old magazines, granola-bar wrappers, broken jewelry, and piles of clothes on her desk. She started throwing away trash and sorting out important papers. Slowly, the desktop appeared, but the permission slip wasn't there.

English Language Learners

Before reading, define the following words so that students can better understand the story:
- messy (disorganized, not neat)
- plopped (dropped)
- bulging (very full to the point of swelling)
- junk (trash)
- permission slip (paper that parents sign allowing children to go on a school trip)
- wrappers (packaging)
- clothes hamper (container for dirty clothing)

To make connections to the situation, discuss with students a time that they may have had a similar experience.

Writing Stories **301**

Jessica turned to the rest of her messy room. "It could be anywhere."

She picked things up, searching for the blue slip of paper. As she looked, she filled her clothes hamper and tossed out more junk. Soon, she could see the floor, but she couldn't see that little blue paper.

Jessica's mother came to the doorway and looked around the room. "Wow, this looks great!"

"But I can't find my permission slip. If I don't have it, I can't go to the aquarium tomorrow." Jessica sat down on her newly made bed and started to cry. "I guess there is a reason to be neat."

> **HIGH POINT**
> The problem gets solved.

Her mother smiled. "There's one more messy place to check. Have you looked in your backpack?"

> **ENDING**
> The ending tells how the character changes.

Jessica lifted the pack and unzipped it. She emptied the whole mess onto her bed. Jessica started sorting through all the papers. Suddenly, she found the slip. Waving it, she said, "Here it is! Here it is! And from now on, I promise to do better! I guess neatness is important, after all."

 Respond to the reading. On your own paper, answer the following questions about the story.

- ■ Ideas **(1)** What does Jessica want? **(2)** What problem does she face?

- ■ **Organization (3)** What element of fiction does the writer use to share the characters' thoughts and feelings? (See pages 309–310.)

- ■ Voice **& Word Choice (4)** What words or phrases help create a picture of Jessica's room? List three.

Before having students do the **Respond to the reading** activity, ask them to explain in their own words what makes Jessica believable to them. (Possible responses: The dialogue between Jessica and Lacey, and between Jessica and her mom, makes her sound like a real kid. Jessica is messy and forgetful like a lot of kids are. She starts to cry when she thinks she can't go on the field trip.)

 Respond to the reading.

Answers

Ideas **1.** She wants to find her permission slip for her mother to sign so she can go on the field trip.
2. She doesn't remember where she put the permission slip, and her room is so messy she can't find it.

Organization 3. Possible choices:
- ■ action
- ■ character
- ■ dialogue

Voice & Word Choice 4. Possible choices:
- ■ papers and junk
- ■ messy bedroom
- ■ stacks of books, papers, old magazines . . . on her desk
- ■ filled her clothes hamper and tossed out more junk

Prewriting Selecting a Topic

If you think it is necessary, before asking students to create a character chart caution them against writing any vulgar or inappropriate traits in the chart. You can also circulate among students as they create their charts, quietly discourage such details, without making a major issue of it.

Prewriting Selecting a Problem

Students may find it easier to think of real, everyday problems to list in their chart. However, remind students that the story that they are writing is fiction and does not have to describe the real problem of a real person they know. Emphasize that the problem

- does not have to be a real problem that they themselves have now or had in the past,
- can be based on the problem of a character in a book they read or a movie they saw, or
- can be totally made up.

302

Prewriting Selecting a Topic

One way to create a character is to combine traits of people you know. LaToya, the writer of "A Messy Lesson," made the chart below.

Character Chart

Name	Age	Hair	Wears	Personality
Kenny	(10)	spiky blond	headphones	(messy)
Rosa	11	(long brown)	heart pin	quiet
Bette	22	short black	(lots of rings)	kooky

 Create a character chart. Make a chart like the one above. List friends and fill in each column. Circle the traits you want to use for your character. Decide on a name for your character.

Selecting a Problem

Next, you need a problem for your character to solve. To think about different everyday problems, LaToya made the following chart.

Problem Chart

School	Friends	Home	Neighborhood
−tough art class −long bus ride	−Sasha's move −Trouble on scout trip	−Billy tattles (−Mom says I'm too messy)	−Busy street −Noisy neighbors

 Create a problem chart. Make a chart like the one above. Fill it in with problems and choose one problem for your story.

English Language Learners

If students want to describe a character from their home culture, encourage them to include extra details that may be necessary for readers who are not from that culture. Explain that this will provide the background knowledge readers will need in order to understand the character and his or her reactions.

Struggling Learners

Some students could have difficulty creating both the character chart and the problem chart in the allotted time. To relieve the pressure,

- ask students to record the character traits on their own and
- then have them meet with a group to brainstorm realistic problems that their characters might solve.

Writing Stories **303**

Creating a Plot

The actions that take place during a story make up the plot line. Each part of the plot plays an important role in the story.

- The **beginning** introduces the characters and setting.
- The **rising action** gives the main character a problem to solve.
- The **high point** is the most exciting part.
- The **ending** tells how everything works out.

LaToya planned her story by making the plot chart below.

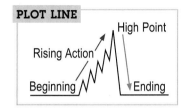

PLOT LINE

Rising Action — High Point

Beginning — Ending

Plot Chart

Beginning	Rising Action	High Point	Ending
Jessica is excited about a field trip. Lacey reminds her of the permission slip.	Jessica looks for the slip, but her room is too messy. She starts to clean up.	Jessica's room is clean, but she still can't find the slip. Her mother suggests one more place to look.	Jessica finds the slip in her backpack. She decides to be neater.

Prewrite

Create a plot chart. In each column, write what will happen in the beginning, during the rising action, at the high point, and in the ending.

Prewriting Creating a Plot

As you discuss the parts of a plot line, take the opportunity to introduce or refresh students' understanding of the element of **conflict** (*see below*) in the plot line of a fiction story.

As you review the sample plot chart, point out that the notes under the headings do not contain details. For example, under *Rising Action*, it says ". . . her room is too messy," but it does not list the specific items that make it messy. Have students look back at the Rising Action paragraph on PE page 300 to see the details in the paragraph that are not included on the plot chart. Tell students that when they create their plot chart, they should write notes like these and not include details.

Teaching Tip: Understanding Conflict

Make sure students understand the importance of conflict in the development of a story plot.

- Conflict refers to the problem, challenge, or goal that the main character faces in a story.
- Conflict is what keeps a story moving from the beginning to the ending as the main character tries to solve the problem, meet the challenge, or achieve the goal.

- There are two basic kinds of story conflicts. In an external conflict, the main character struggles with an outside force. In an internal conflict the character struggles with his or her own ideas and choices. For more specific types of conflicts, see PE page 309.
- In a short story, there is usually only one conflict. In longer stories, characters may face a series of conflicts.

Struggling Learners

To help students internalize the parts of a plot, analyze three short stories you've read together. For the first story, think aloud and model how you'd complete the chart. For the second story, have students tell you what to put on the chart and give feedback. For the third story, have students work independently and then compare notes.

Writing Creating Your First Draft

Point out that the challenge of writing a short story is telling a complete story in a limited space. Short story writers cannot devote pages and pages to the description of the setting or the development of characters and plot. As a result, they have to find creative ways to communicate as much information as possible in the fewest words. Explain that one way that writers do this is with dialogue. Good, effective dialogue allows authors to

- make the characters seem real,
- reveal the personality, thoughts, and feelings of the characters, and
- at the same time, move the plot along.

Have students look back at the use of dialogue in "A Messy Lesson," on PE page 300 and talk about how it does all of the above. Discuss also how dialogue is punctuated.

✱ For information about punctuating dialogue, see Commas, PE page 482; Quotation Marks, PE page 494, and Capitalization, PE page 514.

304

Writing Creating Your First Draft

You're ready to begin your story. Follow the tips below.

1 Set the scene by *showing* instead of *telling*.

Instead of . . . **Jessica was happy.**

Write . . . Jessica danced into her room.

2 Use action to show the reader what is happening.

Instead of . . . **She cleaned up.**

Write . . . She started throwing away trash and sorting out important papers.

3 Use dialogue to let characters speak for themselves.

Instead of . . . **Lacey was excited about the field trip.**

Write . . . Lacey squealed, "Hi, Jess! I'm so excited about tomorrow!"

4 Use sensory details to make the story come alive.

Instead of . . . **The desk was messy.**

Write . . . Jessica started digging through stacks of books, papers, old magazines, granola-bar wrappers, broken jewelry, and piles of clothes on her desk.

5 Build the tension to a high point.

Instead of . . . **Her mom told her where to look, and Jessica found it.**

Write . . . Her mother smiled. "There's one more messy place to check. Have you looked in your backpack?"

 Write your first draft. Use your prewriting and the tips above to write the first draft of your realistic story.

Advanced Learners

To emphasize the benefits of dialogue, challenge students to locate a paragraph of a fictional narrative and rewrite it as conversation. For example, read aloud the last paragraph in Chapter 1 of Mark Twain's *The Adventures of Tom Sawyer*. Suggest that it could be rewritten using dialogue like this:

"What are you doing climbing in the window in the middle of the night?" demanded Aunt Polly. "And what happened to your clothes?"

"I . . . uh . . . met this new kid . . ." stammered Tom.

"Well, whatever it is, don't make any plans for tomorrow. You'll spend the entire day whitewashing the fence, young man. Now get to bed!" Aunt Polly commanded.

Invite students to share the original paragraph and their rewrite with the class, so that all students can see the difference dialogue can make.

Revising Improving Your Writing

Once you have finished your first draft, set it aside for a while. When you are ready to revise, the following questions can help you.

- **Ideas** Have I included an interesting character and problem?
- **Organization** Have I gradually built up to the high point?
- **Voice** Have I used dialogue?
- **Word Choice** Have I used action verbs to show, not tell?
- **Sentence Fluency** Do my sentences read smoothly?

 Improve your writing. Use the questions above to guide your changes.

Editing Checking for Conventions

The following questions can help you edit your story.

- **Conventions** Have I corrected spelling and capitalization errors? Have I included end punctuation for each sentence? Have I checked for easily confused words *(its, it's)*?

 Check your story. Use the questions above to guide your editing. After correcting any errors, use the tips below to write a title. Then make a clean final copy and proofread it.

Creating a Title

- Use a repeated sound: **A Messy Lesson**
- Be playful: **Jess vs. the Mess**
- Use a line from the story: **A Reason to Be Neat**

Revising Improving Your Writing

Have students work in small groups to revise their stories.

- Have the writer read aloud the story. Tell group members to jot down notes as they listen.
- Next, have group members tell what they like about the story. Then they should give specific ideas for improvement for each of the traits.

This activity requires extra time, but short story writing can be extremely challenging for young writers. Students may find it easier to revise with the additional help.

Editing Checking for Conventions

Many people have problem words that they misspell no matter how often they write them. Have students check their story for problem words that they frequently misspell. Suggest that students keep a list of these words, spelled correctly, in their writing journal.

* Review PE pages 528–535 with students to work on Improving Spelling.

Creating a Title

Suggest that students experiment with all three kinds of titles and choose the one that they like best.

English Language Learners

Provide a checklist for students to check for each of the elements that are required in the story. For example, if they are required to use dialogue at least twice, have them check off each time they use it in their stories. Color coding each element may make it easier for students to identify all of the parts required in their stories.

Advanced Learners

Have students create an ongoing classroom chart with examples of these and other types of catchy titles, including ones from their own writing. Throughout the school year, classmates can add new titles from their assigned and independent reading and writing and use the chart as inspiration for their own stories.

Creating a Fantasy

To spark students' imaginations, have them suggest the titles of stories, books, movies, and television programs that they have read or seen that use the three ideas listed to create fantasy.

Students may enjoy working with a partner or in small groups where they can draw on each other's imagination to write a fantasy. Suggest that they use a plot chart (PE page 303) or a **story map** *(see below)* to plan their story.

Encourage students to illustrate their final draft with fun and creative drawings. Then collect all the stories in a class anthology of fantasy stories. Put the anthology in the school library or class reading center.

306

Creating a Fantasy

Another type of fictional story is a fantasy. In a fantasy, animals can talk, people can fly, and anything can happen. Here are some hints to help you write a story that is fantastic yet believable.

1 **Pretend impossible things are possible.**

Write as if your imaginary world actually exists.

Roger shook his shiny mane and stomped his hoof. "I don't like this," he snorted. His tail angrily flicked away a fly.

2 **Give the character a fantastical problem.**

Introduce your main character, set the scene, and give the character a problem that is out of this world.

One night, Luc jumped out of bed and ran to the window. Outside, a spaceship was landing. What should he do?

3 **Decide what feeling you want the story to give.**

Create the mood you want—happy, sad, funny, or so on.

Name's Snuffy. I'm a police bloodhound. I'm supposed to sniff out criminals, but I always have a cold and can't smell anything. That caused a big problem one day when . . .

 Write a fantasy. Imagine a very different world. Create an interesting character and a fantastical problem. Let your imagination run free as you write.

Teaching Tip: Using a Story Map

Most students will probably be familiar with using a story map to identify the elements of a story while reading. A story map can also be useful for planning a story.

Model how to create a story map on the board. Use the following format, along with the story notes.

- Title: *Luc's Midnight Visitor*
- Setting: *Luc's backyard*
- Characters: *Luc, the alien RX54, Luc's sister Annie*

- Story Problem: *Luc must help an alien from the planet Gorse get his spaceship fixed and launched before dawn.*
- Event 1: *Luc wakes up when a spaceship crash lands in his backyard.*
- Event 2:
- Event 3:
- Event 4:
- Ending:

Have students help complete this story map.

English Language Learners

Students may have a difficult time beginning a fantasy on their own. You may want to give a first sentence that defines the character or the setting for students struggling to come up with an original idea. Check in frequently with students as they write to ensure that they have the necessary vocabulary to make their ideas flow.

Creating a Play

A story can also be told in a play. Plays use **dialogue** (what people say) to tell the story. The **action** (what people do) is written in parentheses. Here is the start of LaToya's play.

What a Mess!

Characters: Jessica, 10 years old
Lacey, 10 years old
Mom

Setting: Jessica's room

ACT I

(Jessica and Lacey enter her room. Jessica drops her backpack on her messy desk.)

Lacey: (Moves papers off a chair and sits down.) Wow, Jess, how can you find anything in here?

Jessica: (Flops on her bed, scattering stuff.) I know where everything is. I'm just too busy to clean up.

Lacey: I can't wait for tomorrow's field trip!

Jessica: Yeah! I've never been to the aquarium.

Lacey: Well, don't forget your permission slip!

Jessica: It's right here on my desk (she looks at the messy desk) somewhere. I know I had it. . . .

 Write your story as a play. Use the sample above as a guide. List your characters, set the scene, and then write dialogue to tell your story.

Creating a Play

Ask students who have been in plays to explain how a play script works. Invite them to act out the start of LaToya's play so that students unfamiliar with scripts can see how they work.

Remind students that a play is intended to be performed by actors in front of an audience. Explain that although a play has a different written form than a short story (as shown in the sample), a play still has

- characters—listed and described briefly at the beginning of the script;
- a setting—described at the beginning of the script and, sometimes, in parentheses within the play;
- a plot with rising action and a high point—developed through the dialogue and actions of the characters; and
- an ending that wraps up the story.

Review the elements of the sample play, including the cast of characters, punctuation of name tags, and stage directions, before asking students to write their play.

Struggling Learners

To help students turn a short story into a play script, have them follow these steps:

- Make a photocopy of the story.
- Using a different color for each character, highlight the existing dialogue.
- Cross out the speaker tag lines with a pencil.
- Examine the remaining blocks of text. Re-write as much as possible as dialogue, and then color-code it as explained above.
- Assign the rest of the text to a narrator.
- Recopy the story in the new format.

Advanced Learners

Once students have written their scripts, invite them to rehearse and perform their stories either as Reader's Theater productions or as traditional plays.

Story Patterns

Students can check if a story fits a pattern by substituting details in the sample summary given for each pattern. For example, if they think a story fits The Rivalry pattern, they can reword the example summary *(two friends compete for a chance to attend the state science fair)* by substituting the story characters' names for *two friends* and the story competition for *attend the state science fair*.

If a story doesn't fit any of the patterns shown, and the student has trouble describing the pattern, ask if it fits any of the following:

- The Underdog—The main character (or group of characters) rises above all expectations to succeed.
- The Choice—The main character faces a tough decision that will prove the character's true worth.
- The Quest—The main character embarks on a journey into unknown territory, overcomes problems and obstacles, and returns victorious.
- The Discovery—The main character follows clues to solve a mystery or discover a secret.

308

Story Patterns

Stories follow different patterns. Here are five popular story patterns that you could try.

The Rivalry	Two characters face each other in competition, with a prize at stake.
	Two friends compete for the chance to attend the state science fair.
The Change	A character overcomes a challenge or a personal weakness and changes or grows in some way.
	A girl must overcome her fear of heights to save her sister stranded on a cliff.
The Obstacle	Two characters are kept apart and must find a way to be together.
	The dog is left behind by mistake when a family moves, and he must find his way to the new home.
The Rescue	A character must either be rescued or must rescue someone else who is in trouble.
	A girl searches for her grandfather, who is lost in a crocodile-filled bayou in Louisiana.
The Pursuit	A character chases another character with a goal in mind.
	A detective must hunt down a jewel thief before she can steal the world's largest diamond.

 Check the story pattern. Think of a favorite story. Does it fit one of the story patterns above? If not, how would you describe its story pattern?

English Language Learners

Make sure that students understand that their stories do not have to fit one of these story patterns in order to be a good story. Their stories may follow guidelines from their cultures, or may be like a fable or a legend, which can also make great stories. Celebrate students' cultures by praising the strong elements of their story, and decide together which story pattern it follows.

Struggling Learners

Model this analysis by working as a group to classify the read-alouds you've shared so far during the school year. Help students distill each plot down to one sentence as shown in the examples on the story pattern chart, and then use that sentence to determine which story pattern the story fits.

Writing Stories **309**

Elements of Fiction

Writers use specific terms to talk about the parts of a story. In the following list, you'll find words that will help you talk about the stories you write and read.

Action   The **action** is everything that happens in a story.

Antagonist   An **antagonist** (sometimes called a villain) is a person or thing that fights against the hero.
> The wolf is the antagonist of the three little pigs.

Character   A **character** is a person or humanlike animal in a story.

Conflict   **Conflict** is a problem or challenge for the characters. There are five basic types of conflict:

- **Person vs. Person:**
  Two characters have opposite goals.
  > A supervillain wants to sink a ship, but a superhero wants to save it.

- **Person vs. Society:**
  A character has a problem with a group of people.
  > A student has trouble fitting in at a new school.

- **Person vs. Himself or Herself:**
  A character has an inner struggle.
  > A young student wonders what to do when he discovers his best friend cheating on a test.

- **Person vs. Nature:**
  A character has to battle an element of nature.
  > A mountain climber gets caught in a blizzard.

- **Person vs. Fate:**
  A character faces something he or she can't control.
  > After falling from a horse, an injured man fights to learn to walk again.

Elements of Fiction

As you review the elements of fiction here and on PE page 310, encourage students to provide examples of each element from stories and books that they have read in class or on their own.

Take time to clarify for students any element that is not clear from a reader's point of view (which will be evident from their lack of examples) or from a writer's point of view.

- To make sure students understand the difference between antagonist and protagonist, invite them to name their favorite antagonists and protagonists from stories they have read in class.

- Invite students to describe other scenarios, from published stories or from story ideas they have, that illustrate each of the five types of conflicts.

Students may not be able to articulate the difference between the main idea of a story (what it's about) and the theme, or message of the story. Use the example given for theme to help clarify this point.

■ Main Idea—The story is about how a spider named Charlotte and a pig named Wilbur become friends.

■ Theme—The theme, or the message, of the story is the importance of friendship.

Invite students to tell the main idea and theme of other stories they have read.

310

Dialogue	**Dialogue** refers to the words characters speak to each other in a story.
Mood	**Mood** is the feeling a reader gets from a story—happy, sad, frightened, peaceful.
Moral	A **moral** is a lesson the writer wants the reader to learn from a story. The moral of "The Boy Who Cried Wolf" is that if you tell lies, no one will believe you even when you tell the truth.
Narrator	The **narrator** is the one who tells the story. Harold the dog tells the story in the book *Bunnicula*, so Harold is the narrator (even though he is a dog!).
Plot	The **plot** is the action or series of events that make up the story. Most plots have four parts: beginning, rising action, high point, and ending. (See page 303.)
Point of View	**Point of view** is the angle from which a story is told.

● A story told by the main character uses *first-person point of view*.

> I danced into my room and plopped my backpack on my desk.

● A story told by a narrator uses *third-person point of view*.

> Jessica danced into her room and plopped her backpack on her desk.

Protagonist	The **protagonist** is the hero of the story.
Setting	The **setting** is the time and place of a story.
Theme	A **theme** is a main message of a story. One theme of *Charlotte's Web* is the importance of friendship.
Tone	The **tone** is the feeling the author creates in a story. For example, the tone of a story may be serious, funny, or angry.

Advanced Learners

To help the class better understand the terms on these two pages, invite students to create skits that illustrate elements of fiction such as:

● antagonist and protagonist
● the various types of conflict
● the four parts of plot
● mood and tone
● moral and theme
● the role of a narrator

Creative Writing
Writing Poems

Some words make pictures: *shimmer* and *shine, spiky* and *sharp, yellow* and *green.* Other words make sounds: *whistle* and *toot, blare* and *bray, rumble* and *crash.* Poems use words to help the reader see, hear, feel, and experience something new.

Writing a poem can let you describe someone you know. The details you choose and the way you put them together will reveal a lot about the person. This chapter will help you write in this special way about someone interesting.

Writing Guidelines

Subject:	An interesting person
Form:	Free-verse poem
Purpose:	To entertain
Audience:	Classmates and family

Writing Poems

Objectives
- demonstrate an understanding of the content and form of a free-verse poem
- choose a topic (an interesting person the writer knows) to write about
- plan, draft, revise, and edit a free-verse poem

Most students have not acquired the same kind of familiarity with poetry as they have with other literary forms. As a result, students who ordinarily enjoy writing may show a definite lack of enthusiasm when it comes to writing poetry.

To remove the mystique surrounding poetry, inform students that every Friday, you will be appointing a poet laureate of the class for the following week. Explain that countries and states often appoint an official poet who is expected to provide poems for special occasions. The job of the class poet laureate will be to select and read a poem to begin each class day. Provide poetry anthologies as well as addresses for poetry Websites for students to look for poems (for example, www.loc.gov/poetry/180/ and www.poets.org). As they become more comfortable writing poetry, poet laureates may choose to read aloud their own poems.

Materials

Poetry anthologies, addresses of poetry Websites (TE p. 311)

Random House Book of Poetry for Children (TE pp. 312, 314)

Examples of free verse poems (TE p. 315)

Examples of rhyming poems (TE p. 317)

Three-ring binder (TE p. 319)

Copy Masters/Transparencies

Sensory Chart (TE p. 313)

Free-Verse Poem

Ask students to read "Grandpa Mac" to themselves several times. After they have had a while to study the poem, invite volunteers to read the poem aloud, using good oral expression that captures the mood or feeling of the poem. Remind readers to pause briefly at the end of each line, even if there is no punctuation. Explain that line breaks in poems indicate a brief pause.

 Respond to the reading.

Answers

Ideas 1. sawdust, peppermint

Organization 2.
- The speaker stops by Grandpa's house for a visit.
- Grandpa opens the door and grins.
- He bends down to hug the speaker.
- Then he gives the speaker a stick of gum as they go to the workshop.

Voice & Word Choice 3. sawdust in his beard, brushes his clothes but never remembers his beard and hair, grins, bends down to hug me, hands me a stick of gum

---

312

Free-Verse Poem

Free-verse poems do not follow a rhyming pattern. However, they still use language in a special way. Brant wrote the following free-verse poem about his grandfather.

Grandpa Mac

My grandpa has sawdust in his beard
whenever I visit.
He always brushes off his clothes
before he opens the door, but he never
remembers his beard and hair.
When he grins,
sawdust trembles on his chin.
When he bends down to hug me,
I smell sawdust
and peppermint gum.
He hands me a stick of gum
on the way to his workshop.

 Respond to the reading. On your own paper, answer the following questions about the traits of writing in this poem.

- **Ideas** (1) What smells are mentioned in the poem?
- **Organization** (2) The poem tells a little story. List the main events of this story in order.
- **Word Choice** (3) What words tell you something about Grandpa Mac's personality?

English Language Learners

Have students work in small groups with English-proficient students to read the poem and answer the questions. This will give them the chance to ask classmates about any phrases in the poem that they did not understand.

Advanced Learners

Focus attention on the targeted style by inviting students to locate other free-verse poems to rehearse and read to the class. Some examples from the popular *Random House Book of Poetry for Children* include:

- "Spring Is" by Bobbi Katz
- "Fog" by Carl Sandburg
- "Basketball Star" by Karama Fufuka

Writing Poems **313**

Prewriting Selecting a Topic

In order to write a poem, you need a topic. Brant brainstormed ideas by making a list of interesting people in his life.

List

> my friend Chasidy   Mr. Green, my soccer coach
> ✓Grandpa Mac   Mrs. Gill at Dobrin's Bakery
> my Spanish teacher   TJ, my youth-group leader

Make a list. Make a list of interesting people in your life. Choose one you would like to write about.

Gathering Details

Poems use sensory details to create an image. Brant gathered details about his grandfather in a sensory chart.

Sensory Chart

See	Hear	Smell	Taste	Touch
kind of short	chuckling laughter	peppermint gum	sawdust in the air	rough hands
gray whiskers				prickly beard
gray work clothes	Grandpa scratching his beard when he's thinking	sawdust from his shop	peppermint gum he gives me	tight hug
light blue eyes		machine oil on his tools		
laugh wrinkles				
sawdust shaking on his chin				

Gather sensory details. Make a chart like the one above and list details about the person you are writing about.

Prewriting Selecting a Topic

Have students work together to brainstorm a list of categories that will help students generate names for their list. Students may suggest the following categories:

- friends
- relatives
- teachers
- coaches
- instructors (music, dance, karate, and so on)
- neighborhood workers

Prewriting Gathering Details

Provide photocopies of the reproducible sensory chart (TE page 646), and have students use the chart to gather details about the person they have chosen as a topic.

Encourage students to jot down as many sensory details as they can about the person. If possible, allow students to use photographs of the person as a reference for gathering sensory details. Point out that they probably won't use all the details that they put in the chart in their poem, but the more details that they have, the easier it will be to develop ideas for their poem.

* For more information about making a Sensory Details Chart, see PE page 456.

Prewriting
Using Poetry Techniques

Take time now to review and discuss the poetry techniques here and on PE pages 318–319. As students look over their sensory charts, encourage them to look for words or details that they can use to apply a variety of poetry techniques in their poem.

Point out the repetition of sounds in the sample lines (for example, the *in* sound in *grins* and *chin*; the final *s*, in *grins*, *trembles*, and *bends*; the *r* blend in *grins* and *trembles*, and the short *e* in *when*, *trembles*, and *bends*). Explain that the repetition of sounds in poetry also contributes to the rhythmic flow, or smooth sound, of the whole poem.

Writing
Developing Your First Draft

Encourage students to let their imagination direct their writing. Tell them not to edit themselves as their write. In other words, if an idea comes into their head, they should jot it down and see where it takes them. Remind them that writing in free verse is an opportunity to play with words and images in special and unusual ways.

314

Prewriting Using Poetry Techniques

Poets use special techniques in their writing. Brant used line breaks and repetition to make his poem special.

- **Repetition** is the use of the same word, idea, or phrase. This creates rhythm or emphasis.

  When he **grins,**
  sawdust trembles on his chin.
  When he **bends down to hug me,** . . .

- **Line breaks** make the reader slow down and pay attention to certain words and phrases.

  I smell sawdust
  and peppermint gum.

 Use poetry techniques. Find important words in your sensory chart. You can emphasize them with repetition and line breaks.

Writing Developing Your First Draft

The following tips will help you write your poem.

- **Imagine being with this special person.** Review your sensory chart for details. Focus on your feelings.
- **Write whatever comes to mind.** Write descriptive words, phrases, and sentences about the person. You can organize your ideas and add line breaks later.
- **Play with words.** Have fun. Don't worry about writing a perfect poem.

 Write the first draft of your poem. Using the tips above, show the reader the special person you are writing about.

English Language Learners

To help students understand the poetry techniques, ask them to bring in examples of poetry or the lyrics of songs in their first language. Have them check to see if any of the techniques mentioned are used in their examples.

Remind students that when they are developing their first draft, they should not worry about grammar or spelling, which may slow them down and cause them to not be able to write their ideas freely. Also, tell them not to worry about finding just the right English word, but to use descriptive words or phrases from their first language that they can translate later or possibly leave in, if it gives the poem greater poignancy.

Struggling Learners

To emphasize the role of repetition in poetry, locate other poems that utilize this technique. For example, "April Rain Song" by Langston Hughes (*Random House Book of Poetry for Children*) has the phrase *the rain* in every sentence.

Writing Poems **315**

Revising Improving Your Poem

You can revise your poem by thinking about the traits of writing.

- ■ **Ideas** Do I use sensory details to *show* the person? Do I share my feelings?
- ■ **Organization** Do I arrange my ideas in an interesting way?
- ■ **Voice** Is my poem original, or fresh?
- ■ **Word Choice** Do I use repetition for emphasis?
- ■ **Sentence Fluency** Do my line breaks help make my poem interesting and easy to read?

 Revise your writing. Change your poem until you're happy with every word.

Editing Fine-Tuning Your Poem

Free-verse poems don't always follow all the capitalization and punctuation rules.

- ■ **Conventions** Are the words in my poem spelled correctly? Did I use punctuation effectively?

 Edit your work. Correct any errors in your poem.

Publishing Sharing Your Poem

There are many ways to share your poetry.

- ■ **Perform it** or read it aloud to friends and family.
- ■ **Display it** on a bulletin board or on the fridge at home.
- ■ **Send it out** to a newspaper, magazine, or Web site. Ask your teacher to help you submit it.

 Present your work. Use an idea above or one of your own.

Revising Improving Your Poem

As students check their poems for an original, or fresh, voice, suggest that they read their poem aloud to a partner or in a small group. Listeners can point out any **overused words** (*see below*) that make the poem sound flat and dull. Students can then rework those parts of the poem to make them sound more lively, original, and fresh.

✳ Discuss how students can use various Writing Techniques, shown on PE page 464, to develop an original voice.

Editing Fine-Tuning Your Poem

Provide students with several examples of free-verse poems to help them get a clearer idea of how to use capitalization and punctuation effectively.

Publishing Sharing Your Poem

Encourage students to plan a poetry appreciation program for family, friends and classmates, during which they can share their poetry in readings and as part of bulletin board displays.

Teaching Tip: Overused Words

Explain that good writers avoid overused words, such as *thing, nice, like, very, really,* and *good,* which make their writing sound boring.

- Challenge students to look for overused words in their poems.
- Help students create a class list of these overused words, along with more interesting replacement words.

- Encourage students to refer to the list and a thesaurus to replace the overused words in their writing with more colorful, interesting words.

✳ Refer students to PE page 332 as you review how to use a thesaurus to find synonyms for overused words.

English Language Learners

Encourage students to read their poems aloud as they revise and edit, since the sound of a poem is very important. Remind students that they do not always need to use complete sentences, but that they should be able to justify any variances in conventions that they use to make their poems more expressive.

Writing a "Where I'm From" Poem

Discuss the sample poem to help students see how Aleshia reveals her background and personality through the use of unique, interesting details. Use these questions to guide the discussion.

- Where does Aleshia live? What is her house near?
- How does Aleshia feel about where she lives?
- What do you know about Aleshia's family?
- How does Aleshia feel about her family?
- What words reveal Aleshia's personality?

Take time to also discuss the use of repetition and line breaks in Aleshia's poem. Encourage students to use these poetic techniques in their poem.

Writing Tips

Circulate among students as they write their poems and offer help as needed. Do not discourage them from sticking closely to the pattern or even the subject matter of the sample poem. The more opportunities students have to write poetry, the more original and creative their poems will eventually become.

Writing a "Where I'm From" Poem

A "Where I'm From" poem tells interesting details about your background. In the process, it reveals something about who you are. Aleshia wrote this poem about her own background.

Where I'm From

I'm from a house downtown,
near the library, town square, and fairgrounds,
a great place for skateboards, bikes, and squirrels.

I'm from a family with four daughters,
between one older sister and two younger,
a great place for sharing music, books, and dolls.

I'm from green parks, fresh air, giggling sisters, and happy songs.

WRITING TIPS

- **Select a topic.** This is easy. Just write about yourself.
- **Gather details.** Make a list of unusual or interesting details about at least two of the following ideas.
  - The area near your home
  - Your family and its history
  - Your friends
  - Your favorite things
- **Follow the form.** Write two stanzas (group of lines), one for each of the ideas you chose above. Use line breaks and repetition to change the rhythm and emphasis of your words. Add a final line to summarize your feelings.

 Create your "Where I'm From" poem. Follow the tips above to write your own poem. Let it show your unique personality.

English Language Learners

Encourage students to use the "Where I'm From" poetry assignment to describe their native cultures. Ask them to include details that make them unique and special. Make sure that students are comfortable with describing themselves and that they feel "at home" in the classroom or small group setting when they share their own "Where I'm From" poem.

Advanced Learners

Challenge students to research and write "Where I'm From" poems about famous biographical figures. Then invite them to read their poems aloud and have classmates guess who they're describing. The poems can then be compiled into a book with an answer key at the end.

Writing Rhymed Poetry

Rhyme can add fun and interest to a poem. It is important to find rhymes that fit your ideas naturally.

Split Couplet

A couplet is two rhyming lines of about the same length. A split couplet, however, has a long first line and a short second line. The first line has five stressed syllables; the second has two. You can put several split couplets together to make a longer poem.

Moira

Moira listens to my secret fears,
And shares her tears.
Moira stands up for me when kids say
That I can't play.
She forgot to bring a pen one time.
I lent her mine.
Now you know how this poem will end.
She's a true friend.

WRITING TIPS

- **Select a topic.** Choose an interesting person you know.
- **Gather details.** Make a list of details about that person. How does he or she look? What is his or her personality like? How does the person touch your life?
- **Follow the form.** Write sentences or phrases that use details from your list. Write the first line of a couplet; then think of a rhyming word to end the second line.

Write a split-couplet poem. Follow the tips above to write a poem containing at least two split couplets.

Writing Rhymed Poetry

Although free-verse poetry resembles students' natural speaking patterns more than rhyming poetry does, students may actually be more comfortable and enthusiastic about writing rhymed poetry. This is not surprising, since the first poems that most children are exposed to in this culture are nursery rhymes, and in their limited experience, they first believe poetry must rhyme.

Read aloud several rhymed poems with different rhyming patterns, and have students listen for the rhyming patterns in each poem.

Split Couplet

Ask students to listen carefully as you read aloud the sample split couplet, making sure to stress the end rhyme. Then have students identify the rhyming words in each split couplet.

Suggest that students look back at the list of interesting people that they generated as they selected a topic for their free-verse poem (PE page 313) and choose a different person from that list as a topic for their split couplet.

English Language Learners

Rhyming may be very difficult for students, depending on their level of English. Provide lists of rhyming words that they can use or a book that has many examples of rhymes, like a book of nursery rhymes. Monitor students closely and offer vocabulary to make sure that they do not get frustrated.

Using Special Poetry Techniques

Remind students that good writers often use figures of speech to create vivid, colorful, and memorable images in fiction and nonfiction stories, as well as in poetry.

Figures of Speech

Using the examples in the text as models, have students practice writing figures of speech.

- Have students brainstorm a list of items in the classroom or around the school, such as the big front door, the classroom clock, or a tall metal coat rack.
- Have students select a topic from the list.
- Have them work together to write a simile, metaphor, personification, and hyperbole for their topic.

✷ For more information about how to Make Comparisons using similes and metaphors, see PE page 411.

Sounds of Poetry

Encourage students to use the sound techniques on PE pages 318–319 whenever they write poetry.

Using Special Poetry Techniques

These two pages explain some special techniques that poets use.

Figures of Speech

- A **simile** (*sĭm′ə-lē*) compares two different things using *like* or *as*.

  The picket fence looked like a toothy smile.

- A **metaphor** (*mĕt′ə-fôr*) compares two different things without using *like* or *as*.

  The picket fence is a friendly guard.

- **Personification** (*pər-sŏn′ə-fĭ-kā′shən*) makes an object seem human.

  The picket fence grinned with bright white teeth.

- **Hyperbole** (*hī-pûr′bə-lē*) is an exaggeration.

  The picket fence even kept the birds out of our yard.

Sounds of Poetry

Poets use the following techniques to add interesting sounds to their work. (Also see page 314.)

- **Alliteration** (*ə-lĭt′ə-rā′shən*) is the repeating of beginning consonant sounds.

  green parks, fresh air, and giggling sisters

- **Assonance** (*ăs′ə-nəns*) is the repeating of vowel sounds in words.

  giggling sisters

- **Consonance** (*kŏn′sə-nəns*) is the repeating of consonant sounds anywhere in words.

  peppermint gum

■ **Line breaks** slow down the reader and bring attention to individual words and phrases.

> He hands me a stick of gum
>
> on the way to his workshop.

■ **Onomatopoeia** (ŏn´ə-măt´ə-pē´ə) is the use of words that sound like what they name.

> The iron hisses, sizzles, and pops as it heats.

■ **Repetition** is the use of the same word, idea, or phrase for rhythm or emphasis.

> They kept me waiting, waiting, waiting.

■ **Rhyme** (rīm) is the use of words whose endings sound alike.

> *End rhyme* happens at the ends of lines.
>
> Now you know how this poem will end.
>
> She's a true friend.

> *Internal rhyme* happens within lines.
>
> And trails of snails.

■ **Rhythm** (rĭth´əm) means the pattern of accented and unaccented syllables.

> I lent her mine.

 Write a poem. Write about a favorite person. Use one figure of speech and at least one special sound technique.

Encourage students to create a classroom Figures of Speech and Sounds of Poetry reference manual to refer to for models when writing poetry.

■ Provide a three-ring binder so that students can add an unlimited number of pages and examples to the manual.

■ Tell students to use a separate sheet of paper for each figure of speech and each sound technique, and write the figure of speech or the sound technique, followed by its definition, at the top of the page. Suggest that students organize figures of speech and sound techniques in separate sections, and alphabetically.

■ For each figure of speech or sound technique, students should copy the example in the text on PE pages 318–319.

■ Students can then look for professional examples of figures of speech and sound techniques to add to the manual.

■ When they write poems, they can look in the manual for definitions and examples.

As students become adept at using these techniques, they may be able to add original examples from their own writing to the manual.

Research Writing Overview

Writing Standards

The writing standards listed below are based on a blending of state and NCTE standards.

- Use research skills and print and electronic resources to gather ideas and information.
- Write a research report with a thesis statement, several middle paragraphs that support the thesis with facts, and a concluding paragraph.
- Create and present an interactive report.

Writing Forms

- summary paragraph
- research report
- multimedia presentation

Focus on the Traits

- **Ideas** Developing a clear thesis statement and one main idea for each paragraph's each topic sentence
- **Organization** Using a sentence outline to organize topic sentences and the details that support them
- **Voice** Using a knowledgeable and interested voice
- **Word Choice** Defining or explaining unfamiliar words
- **Sentence Fluency** Varying sentence lengths and beginnings
- **Conventions** Checking for errors in punctuation, capitalization, spelling, and grammar

Unit Pacing

Building Skills: 1.5–2.5 hours

The section on **building research skills** introduces the unit and lays the groundwork for research writing. Use this section if students need to work on building research skills. Following are some of the topics that are covered:

- Gathering information from different sources
- Locating resources on the Internet and in the library
- Using reference materials

Summary Paragraph: 45–90 minutes

The **summary paragraph** section guides students through the process of selecting and reading an article and writing a summary of it. Use this section if students need to work on crafting a paragraph. Following are some of the topics that are covered:

- Finding the main idea
- Supporting the topic sentence with information from the article
- Putting information in logical order

Research Report: *4.5–9.75 hours*

This section asks students to write a **research report** about an invention that interests them. Use this section if students need to work on using research skills to write a report. Following are some of the topics that are covered:

- Creating an ideas grid to select a topic
- Using a gathering grid and note cards to organize research
- Finding information to answer specific research questions
- Keeping track of sources
- Forming a thesis statement
- Organizing research notes in a sentence outline
- Creating a works-cited page

Multimedia Presentations: *2.25 hours*

This section provides suggestions for using a computer to create a **multimedia presentation** that incorporates multimedia effects to communicate information. Use this section to focus on developing computer skills. Following are some of the topics that are covered:

- Creating clusters to gather ideas for each slide
- Making a storyboard
- Designing slides

Integrated Grammar and Writing Skills

Below are skills lessons from the resources sections of the pupil edition that are suggested at point of use (✳) throughout this unit.

Writing a Summary Paragraph, pp. 333–336

✳ Use Different Types of Sentences, pp. 442–444

Writing a Research Report, pp. 337–362

✳ Quotation Marks in Titles, p. 494
✳ Italics and Underlining in Titles, p. 502
✳ Build an Outline, p. 459
✳ Past Tense Form, p. 420

Additional Grammar Skills

Below are skills lessons from other components that you can weave into your unit instruction.

Writing a Summary Paragraph

SkillsBook

Dashes, p. 35
Types of Sentences, p. 117

Interactive Writing Skills CD-ROM

Sentences: Types and Kinds

Daily Language Workouts

Week 33: Story Time, pp. 68–69
Week 33: A King from Camelot, p. 110

Writing a Research Report

SkillsBook

Quotation Marks 2, p. 24
Italics and Underlining, p. 32
Italics and Quotation Marks, p. 33
Parentheses, p. 36
Mixed Review 1 and 2, p. 41
Irregular Verbs 1 and 2, p. 163
Irregular-Verbs Review 1 and 2, p. 165

Interactive Writing Skills CD-ROM

Punctuation: Quotation Marks—
Set Off Dialogue
Punctuation: Punctuating Titles
Parts of Speech 1: Verbs 4—
Irregular

Daily Language Workouts

Week 34: Literature and Life, pp. 70–71
Week 34: He Let His Light Shine, p. 111

320

Research Writing

Multimedia Presentations

Daily Language Workouts

Week 35: Fictional Characters, pp. 72–73
Week 35: Mother Goose in Japan, p. 112

Research Writing
Building Skills

Research means investigating. Like a detective, when you search for information, you may find something interesting. That might give you an idea about another place you can look. Along the way, you take notes to keep track of what you learn. Finally, you pull it all together into a report.

In this chapter, you'll learn about where and how to search for information—in books, magazines, encyclopedias, and other sources. Using all these skills, you are sure to become a great research detective!

Mini Index

- **Gathering Information**
- **Researching on the Internet**
- **Using the Library**
- **Using Reference Materials**

Building Skills

Objectives

- learn about various sources for information
- understand how to do research on the Internet
- demonstrate an understanding of how to access and use library reference materials

Inspire students to become creative research detectives.

- Ask students to call out topics that they would like to learn more about. Encourage topics from a wide variety of interest areas. List the ideas on the board and, with students' help, circle the top four ideas.
- Divide students into teams of research detectives. Challenge teams to come up with two or three sources for researching each topic. Encourage your "detectives" to think creatively. For example, to learn the history of a favorite board game, they might look at the literature included with the game.
- Have teams share ideas and discuss which sources would provide the best information.

Family Connection Letters

As you begin this unit, send home the Research Writing Family Connection letter, which describes what students will be learning.

 Letter in English (TE p. 659)

 Letter in Spanish (TE p. 667)

Materials

Articles about chosen inventions (TE p. 322)

Dictionaries (TE pp. 322, 328, 330, 331)

Posterboard, paper, and drawing supplies (TE pp. 323, 331)

Samples of library resources and signs showing library locations (TE p. 324)

Library books (TE p. 327)

Thesaurus (TE p. 332)

Gathering Information

Check students' understanding of the meaning of the idiom "the big picture" in this context. Invite volunteers to explain "the big picture" in their own words. If you determine that students do not understand the meaning, have students decide which of the following definitions fits (starred).

- a large drawing or photograph of a topic,
- a lot of facts about a topic, or
- a general or full understanding of a topic.*

Guidelines for Interviewing

Explain that good interviewers research the topic ahead of time so that during the interview they
- can discuss the topic intelligently,
- will know some concepts or **special terms** (see below) they would like to have explained, and
- can ask questions that are useful and interesting to them and to the person being interviewed.

When reading the "Evaluating Your Sources" box, explain that the information here can refer to any kind of source and not only to a Web site.

Gathering Information

A good researcher uses more than one source of information. Checking different sources helps you to get "the big picture."

- **Reading** . . . Books, encyclopedias, and magazines hold many facts and details about your topic.
- **Surfing** . . . The Internet often has the latest information about a topic.
- **Viewing and Listening** . . . Television and videos can help you understand a topic.
- **Interviewing** . . . Talking to an expert is another way to learn. (See below.)

Guidelines for Interviewing

- Before the interview, prepare a list of questions. Ask questions that need more than a "yes" or "no" answer. You need information from this expert.
- During the interview, take notes on important details. Politely say, "Let me write that down," so that the person will pause.
- If the person uses any special terms, ask how to spell them.

Evaluating Your Sources

Some sources are more valuable than others. Always ask yourself these questions:
- Is the site published by an institution, an organization, or a person who knows the subject well?
- Is there background information about the authors of the site?
- Is the information on the site up to date?
- Is the point of view or purpose of the site stated? If there is more than one side of an issue, are both sides presented?
- Is the information complete and dependable?

Teaching Tip: Special Terms

Explain that in a research report, the correct use of special terms, or words that are related to the topic, gives readers confidence in the writer's knowledge of the topic.

Before students conduct an interview, encourage them to skim one or two articles about the topic they have chosen. Tell them to list any special terms related to the topic.

For example, if students are writing a report about microwave ovens, they would list
- microwave energy
- electromagnetic radiation, and
- magnetron.

If students are unsure of the meaning of any terms, they should use a dictionary. If necessary, they can ask for further clarification during the interview.

English Language Learners

Some students may not yet have the language proficiency to skim articles independently and identify special terms for their research topic. Assign considerate, cooperative partners to read and discuss the articles in order to find special terms to use in the research.

Researching on the Internet

You can use the Internet to browse the World Wide Web and send e-mail. To find the Web pages you need, use a search engine like www.Google.com or www.Yahoo.com. When you type in keywords related to your topic (see page 325), the search engine will list Web pages for you to look at. Many Web pages also give an e-mail address where you can send questions.

Check the Write Source Web site (www.thewritesource.com) for a list of search engines.

Helpful Hints

- **Be safe.** Know your school's Internet policy and follow it. Also follow any guidelines your parents may have given you.

- **Be smart.** Look for trustworthy Web sites. Sites with *.edu, .org,* or *.gov* in the address are usually the best. These are educational, nonprofit, or government Web sites. When you find a good page, watch for links to other helpful pages.

- **Be patient.** Sometimes finding the best sources takes time. If a search doesn't give the results you need, try again with different keywords.

 **Practice**

Use a search engine to find information about an invention. Write down the Internet addresses of at least two Web sites where you found details about that invention.

Researching on the Internet

If you have a classroom computer with access to the Internet, provide time for pairs of students to check the Write Source Web site (www.thewritesource.com) for a list of search engines.

Many schools have written policies for Internet use. Post this policy in the classroom computer center, or distribute copies for students to keep on hand as they do research.

Discuss specific Web sites that are reliable and trustworthy and that have links designed and written with young students in mind. Two examples are Public Broadcasting Service (PBS) and the National Geographic Society.

Practice **Answers**

Answers will vary.

Advanced Learners

Invite students to report on what information can be found on the Write Source Web site.

Ask them to design an informative poster. Topics may include the following:
- writing topics
- student models
- research links
- multimedia reports
- homework help

Each topic should be accompanied by a caption that explains how classmates can use the site.

Using the Library

Reference librarians are expert research detectives and can be the student researcher's best friend. Most reference librarians welcome a research challenge. They know where all the reference materials in the library are located, and have extensive knowledge about how to use them to the greatest advantage. They usually have additional knowledge and skill in searching the databases available on the library's computer network.

Schedule a field trip for students to meet and talk with the reference librarian at the local public library. If the school has a reference librarian, make sure students are acquainted with him or her.

Practice **Answers**

Maps will vary but should be an accurate reproduction of the layout of the library.

324

Using the Library

The library has helpful resources you can use to do research. Most libraries have books, magazines, encyclopedias, audio and video recordings, and computers, as shown on the sample map below.

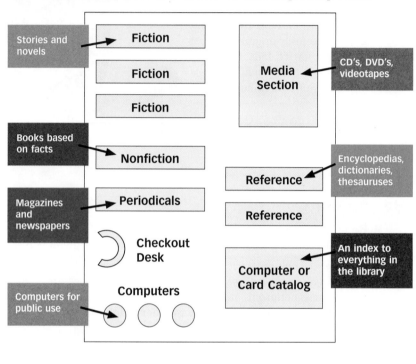

Practice

Visit your school or public library and look for each of the sections shown above. Then make a map of your library.

Struggling Learners

Gather a sampling of resources so students can practice identifying where each resource would be found in the library. Make signs designating the different parts of the library to place around the room. Give each student a resource and challenge the student to go directly to the appropriate library section. Once there, the student should describe the resource and tell why it belongs in that location.

Building Skills **325**

Searching a Computer Catalog

A **computer catalog** lets you search for library books in three different ways.

1 You can search by **title** if you know the book's title.

2 You can search by **author** if you know the author's name.

3 Or you can search by **subject** if you want to find several books on the same topic.

Using Keywords

To find a book by subject, use keywords. A keyword is a word or phrase about the subject.

If your subject is . . .	your keywords might be . . .
wool,	wool, knitting, or sheep.

Computer Catalog Screen

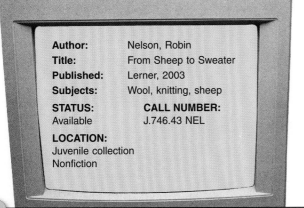

Author:	Nelson, Robin
Title:	From Sheep to Sweater
Published:	Lerner, 2003
Subjects:	Wool, knitting, sheep

STATUS:	**CALL NUMBER:**
Available	J.746.43 NEL

LOCATION:
Juvenile collection
Nonfiction

Practice

Create a computer catalog screen like the one above for a book you have read.

Searching a Computer Catalog

Many libraries belong to networks made up of a group of libraries. Library patrons who belong to a library within a network system usually have access to the computer catalog for the entire network through the Internet. In this kind of system, if students are searching for a book that is not available at the local library, they can request a book transfer with just a click of the mouse. If your local library is part of a network, encourage students to become familiar with the online services available to them through the network Web site.

Using keywords is an excellent way to search for a book. Encourage students to do some reading on their subject ahead of time and jot down keywords to use in their search.

Practice Answers

Computer screens will vary but should include the author, title, publisher, date of publication, subject(s), status, call number, and location of the book.

Searching a Card Catalog

Students who are adept at using computer catalogs and are unlikely to ever see a card catalog may not see the value in learning about card catalogs. However, since there are still some libraries that have not computerized their holdings, knowing how a card catalog is organized could prove to be an advantage to students one day.

Have students study the sample catalog cards. Then ask questions based on the information on the cards.

- Which letter would you look under to find the book by this author? (the letter *N* for *Nelson*)
- Which letter would you look under to find the book by title? *(F for From Sheep to Sweater)*
- Which card tells you when the book was published? (all three, 2003)
- What other subject headings could you look under to find this book? (wool, raising sheep)

326

Searching a Card Catalog

A **card catalog** is a cabinet of drawers that holds title, author, and subject cards in alphabetical order.

1 If you know the book's **title**, look up its first word. (If the first word is *A, An,* or *The,* look up the second word instead.)

2 If you know the book's **author**, look up the author's last name. (If the library has more than one book by that author, you will find a card for each book.)

3 If you don't know a title or an author, look up the **subject** to find books on that topic.

Sample Catalog Cards

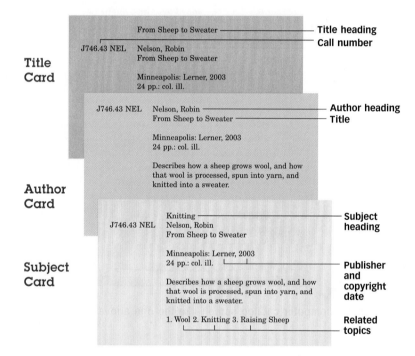

Building Skills **327**

Finding Books

Nonfiction Books ● Nonfiction books are arranged on library shelves by call number.

- **Some call numbers contain decimals.**
  The call number 520.37 is a smaller number than 520.4 (which is really 520.40). So 520.37 would appear on the shelf before 520.4.

- **Some call numbers include letters.**
  The call number 520.37F would appear on the shelf before 520.37G. In the call number J520.37, the J means that the book is shelved in the children's section.

- **Most call numbers are based on the Dewey decimal system.**

THE TEN CLASSES OF THE DEWEY DECIMAL SYSTEM			
000	General Topics	500	Pure Science
100	Philosophy	600	Technology (Applied Science)
200	Religion	700	The Arts, Recreation
300	The Social Sciences	800	Literature
400	Language	900	Geography and History

Biographies ● Biographies (books that tell the history of a person's life) are all found under the call number 921. They are arranged on the shelves alphabetically by last name of the person written about. A biography about Samuel Morse would be found at **921 MORSE**. It would come before **921 NOBEL**.

Fiction Books ● Fiction books are arranged alphabetically by the first three letters of the author's last name. A book by Judith C. Greenburg would have the letters **GRE** on the spine.

Practice

Use the computer or card catalog in your library to find a book about inventions. Write down the title and the call number of the book and see if you can find it on the shelves.

Finding Books

Read the call numbers from a variety of library books and have students identify each book as nonfiction or fiction. Point out that because biographies are about real people, they are classified as nonfiction. If students identify a book as nonfiction, ask them to tell in which of the ten classes of the Dewey decimal system the book belongs.

Tell students that the Dewey decimal system was invented in 1876 by an American librarian named Melvil Dewey.

Practice Answers

Answers will vary.

Advanced Learners

Invite students to work on their research skills by writing a brief biography of Melvil Dewey to share with the class. Students can work in small groups or with a partner. Suggest that they include a time line showing the important dates in Mr. Dewey's life (see TE pages 457 and 648).

Understanding the Parts of a Book

Before reading the page, list the terms on the board. Call on students to explain what they already know about any of these parts of a book.

As each term is discussed, ask volunteers to look up the following words and explain their meanings: *copyright, acknowledgement, contents, preface, cross-reference, appendix, bibliography.*

Practice — **Answers**

- title page—first page of book
- copyright page—ii
- acknowledgement page—ii (additional acknowledgements on page 606)
- table of contents—iv–xviii
- body—pages 1–605
- cross-reference—Answers will vary. For examples, see pages 22 and 137.
- appendix—none
- glossary—none
- bibliography—none
- index—pages 607–622

Understanding the Parts of a Book

Knowing the common parts of nonfiction books can help you to find information quickly.

- The **title page** is usually the first printed page in the book. It gives the book's title, the author's name, the publisher, and the city where the book was published.

- The **copyright page** comes next. It gives the year the book was published.

- An **acknowledgement** or **preface** (if the book has one) comes before the table of contents and explains more about the book.

- The **table of contents** shows how the book is organized. It lists the names and page numbers of chapters and other divisions.

- The **body** is the main part of the book.

- A **cross-reference** sends the reader to another page for more information. *Example:* (See page 329.)

- An **appendix** is at the back of a book and has more information such as lists, tables, or maps. (Not every book has an appendix.)

- The **glossary** (if there is one) defines special words used in the book.

- The **bibliography** (if there is one) lists sources the author used when writing the book.

- The **index** is an alphabetical list of topics covered in the book. It shows the page numbers where you can find each topic.

Practice

Look in this textbook for the parts listed above. Write down the page numbers for each part you find.

Advanced Learners

Most students are familiar with television infomercials, which often use exaggerated gestures and language to demonstrate how some new gadget works. Have partners prepare and practice an infomercial about how to use the parts of a book to find information quickly. Encourage students to be creative and to have fun. Allow time for students to present their infomercials to the class.

Using Reference Materials

The reference section of your library holds resources such as dictionaries, encyclopedias, and thesauruses.

Using Encyclopedias

An **encyclopedia** is a set of books or a CD with articles on many topics.

- The topics are listed in alphabetical order. The part of the alphabet covered in each book is listed on the spine. (Example: Q-R)
- At the end of an article, you may find a list of related topics you can look up.
- The index volume lists all the places in the encyclopedia where you can find information about your topic.

Encyclopedia Index

This is a sample index entry for the topic *wool*.

The capital letter tells which volume.

Wool W:370 *with pictures*
Clothing (Materials)
C:614
Fiber (Animal Fibers)
F:83 *with pictures*
Sheep (Raising Sheep)
S:222
See also the list of related articles in the Wool *article.*

Page number

More information is available elsewhere.

Practice

Use the index entry above to find the volume and page for the following information.

1. A picture of wool fibers
2. How wool clothing is made
3. How wool is gathered

Using Reference Materials

Point out that many libraries have dictionaries, encyclopedias, and thesauruses available on CD-ROM. Invite volunteers who have used CD-ROM encyclopedias to explain the steps for finding articles.

Using Encyclopedias

Although it is important for students to know how to use a print encyclopedia, online versions are constantly updated. They are, therefore, more reliable than out-of-date print encyclopedias. Online encyclopedias are often accessible through a library's Web site or through a link in word processing programs. Provide students with any additional information they need to access online encyclopedias.

Practice Answers

1. Volume F, page 83
2. Volume C, page 614
3. Volume S, page 222

English Language Learners

Students may not be able to comprehend grade-appropriate reference materials. Preview the school's encyclopedias with the librarian to determine what materials are available and whether materials will need to be borrowed from the public library. If appropriate reference materials cannot be located, arrange for adults to read and answer questions about the selections the students need to access.

Struggling Learners

To practice using an online encyclopedia, choose a topic that you are currently studying. Invite students to brainstorm questions about the topic. Write the questions on the board while a student volunteer copies them on paper, leaving space between the questions to insert answers later. Duplicate the list for participants. Then have students use the online encyclopedia to find the answers.

Checking a Dictionary

Have on hand a variety of student and standard dictionaries. Divide students into pairs or groups of three and give them an opportunity to page through the different dictionaries.

- Tell students to be sure to notice the dictionary overview and explanations of different features that appear at the beginning of most dictionaries.
- Remind students that some words may have more than one acceptable spelling. Most dictionaries show spelling variations, listing the preferred spelling first. For example, *acknowledgment, acknowledgement.*
- Have students point out any features of individual dictionaries that are not discussed here, such as labeled diagrams and photographs, maps, and usage notes.

Practice **Answers**

Answers will vary.

330

Checking a Dictionary

A **dictionary** defines words and provides other useful information. Dictionaries often include the following features.

- **Guide words** These words are listed at the top of each page. They tell the first and last words on that page.
- **Entry words** The entry words are defined on the dictionary page. The most commonly used meaning is usually listed first.
- **Stress marks** A stress (or accent) mark (´) shows which syllable should be stressed when you say a word.
- **Word history** Some words have stories about their origins or how their meanings have changed through the years.
- **Spelling and capital letters** If you don't know how to spell a word, try looking it up by how it sounds. If a word is capitalized in the dictionary, capitalize it in your writing.
- **Pronunciation** A dictionary respells each word phonetically (as it sounds). Special markings are found in the *pronunciation key.*
- **Synonyms** Synonyms (words with the same or similar meanings) are listed. Antonyms (words with opposite meanings) may also be listed.
- **Parts of speech** A dictionary tells how a word can be used (*noun, verb, adjective,* and so on).
- **Syllable division** A dictionary shows where to divide a word.

Practice

Open a dictionary and do the following three things:

1. Find a word you don't know. Write it with its first definition.
2. Find a word you can't pronounce. Use the pronunciation key to figure out how to say the word correctly.
3. Find an illustration that shows you something you didn't already know about a word.

English Language Learners

Because students' pronunciation of English words may be influenced by their first language, asking them to look up the spelling of a word by "how it sounds" may be frustrating. When pronunciation seems to interfere, have students tell you the word they want to find. Articulate the word clearly for them, and ask students to repeat the pronunciation. Work with them to identify initial letter-sound correspondences, and then look for the word together. Assist students in this manner whenever they are unsure of the spelling of words they do not yet pronounce properly.

Dictionary Page

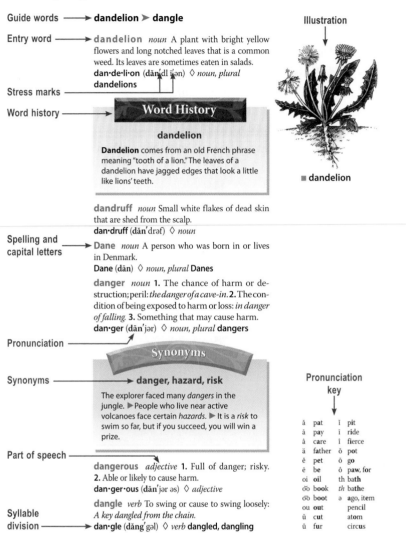

Guide words ⟶ **dandelion** ➤ **dangle**

Entry word ⟶ **dandelion** *noun* A plant with bright yellow flowers and long notched leaves that is a common weed. Its leaves are sometimes eaten in salads.
dan·de·li·on (dăn′dl ī′ən) ◊ *noun, plural* **dandelions**

Stress marks

Illustration

Word history ⟶

Word History

dandelion

Dandelion comes from an old French phrase meaning "tooth of a lion." The leaves of a dandelion have jagged edges that look a little like lions' teeth.

■ dandelion

dandruff *noun* Small white flakes of dead skin that are shed from the scalp.
dan·druff (dăn′drəf) ◊ *noun*

Spelling and capital letters ⟶ **Dane** *noun* A person who was born in or lives in Denmark.
Dane (dān) ◊ *noun, plural* **Danes**

danger *noun* **1.** The chance of harm or destruction; peril: *the danger of a cave-in.* **2.** The condition of being exposed to harm or loss: *in danger of falling.* **3.** Something that may cause harm.
dan·ger (dān′jər) ◊ *noun, plural* **dangers**

Pronunciation ⟶

Synonyms

Synonyms ⟶ **danger, hazard, risk**

The explorer faced many *dangers* in the jungle. ▶ People who live near active volcanoes face certain *hazards*. ▶ It is a *risk* to swim so far, but if you succeed, you will win a prize.

Part of speech ⟶ **dangerous** *adjective* **1.** Full of danger; risky. **2.** Able or likely to cause harm.
dan·ger·ous (dān′jər əs) ◊ *adjective*

Syllable division ⟶ **dangle** *verb* To swing or cause to swing loosely: *A key dangled from the chain.*
dan·gle (dăng′gəl) ◊ *verb* **dangled, dangling**

Pronunciation key

ă	pat	ĭ	pit
ā	pay	ī	ride
â	care	î	fierce
ä	father	ŏ	pot
ĕ	pet	ō	go
ē	be	ô	paw, for
oi	oil	th	bath
ŏŏ	book	th	bathe
ōō	boot	ə	ago, item
ou	out		pencil
ŭ	cut		atom
û	fur		circus

Copyright © 2003 by Houghton Mifflin Company. Adapted and reproduced by permission from *The American Heritage Children's Dictionary.*

To foster frequent dictionary use, create a Word of the Day (or Week) bulletin board display. Choose a challenging but useful word and display it at the top of the bulletin board. Then ask individual students to look up the word for that day in the class dictionary. Have students add the following information to the bulletin board display:

- guide words for the page on which the word appears
- part (or parts) of speech
- phonetic respelling
- syllable division
- first definition for each part of speech
- a sentence that uses the word and illustrates the meaning of the word

Encourage students to display the information in fun, creative ways, using stylized lettering, cutout letters, pictures, and so on.

English Language Learners

To expand their vocabularies, students need repeated exposure to new words in meaningful contexts. For the Word of the Day activity, make sure the assigned words come from content area discussions. Have students keep a list of new words they encounter that they would like included in the display.

Struggling Learners

To give students more practice with unfamiliar words, have them look for the Word of the Day in their reading. Guide students to use the context to discuss the appropriate meaning and identify the correct part of speech.

Advanced Learners

To heighten students' awareness of the multiple meanings of many words, have them take turns looking up each Word of the Day to check for second and third meanings. They should also identify the part of speech and write a vocabulary sentence for each use of the word. Invite students to share their work with the class.

Using a Thesaurus

A thesaurus is a wonderful tool for finding synonyms for overused words and vague, general words. However, students should keep in mind that sometimes the first word they think of may be the best word for the sentence. Point out that just because a word has more letters or several syllables, it isn't necessarily a better word. The **Practice** activity illustrates that not every word listed as a synonym for a word works in the context of the sentence.

Practice   Answer

The right synonym is *darts*.

After students complete the **Practice**, invite volunteers
■ to explain why the other two choices are not correct, and
■ to create new sentences, using *jog* and *sprint*.

To give students more practice with synonyms, create a list of words to avoid in writing, such as *really, very, good, big*, and *bad*. Have students find synonyms for the words. Encourage students to use the synonyms in context sentences.

332

Using a Thesaurus

A **thesaurus** is a book that lists words with their synonyms. (Synonyms are words with similar meanings.) It may also list antonyms (words with opposite meanings). A thesaurus can help you . . .

- find the best word for a specific sentence and
- keep from using the same word again and again.

Thesaurus Entry

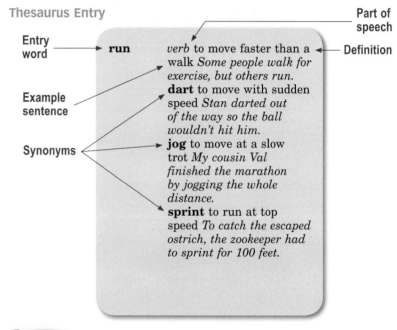

Practice

Use the thesaurus entry above to find the right synonym for the verb *runs* in the sentence below.

Our dog runs to the right and to the left because he knows we are trying to catch him for his bath.

Research Writing
Summary Paragraph

Writing a summary is like facing a big bowl of fruit salad with many kinds of fruit in it, everything from kiwi to blueberries. You only like the strawberries, bananas, watermelon, and cherries, so you carefully spoon your favorites into a bowl. In a similar way, when you write a summary, you read the whole article. Then you pick out only the main ideas and put them into a paragraph using your own words.

Summarizing is a useful research skill. It helps you to condense the information from a source so your reader gets only the main ideas.

Writing Guidelines

Subject:	A research article
Form:	Summary paragraph
Purpose:	To express the main idea
Audience:	Classmates

Objectives

- demonstrate an understanding of the purpose, content, and structure of a summary paragraph
- choose an article to summarize
- plan, draft, revise, and edit a summary paragraph

A **summary paragraph** is a shortened version of a longer piece of writing that gives only the most important ideas from the original work. Point out to students that like other paragraphs they have written, a summary paragraph has a topic sentence, body sentences, and a closing sentence.

✱ For information about paragraph writing, see PE pages 50–61.

Emphasize that a summary focuses on the most important parts or ideas of the original source, and not the reader's favorite parts, although the two may overlap.

Materials

Articles of varying difficulty (TE p. 335)

Copy Masters/ Transparencies

5 W's chart (TE p. 335)

Summary Paragraph

Read the article as a class. Then ask students to cover the sample summary with a sheet of paper. Have students work together to jot down the most important ideas in the article. Write their suggestions on the board. Then have students read the summary to see whether the details they identified in the article are included in the summary.

 Respond to the reading.

Answers

Ideas 1. Many Native American inventions are still being used.

Organization 2. Students should notice that the ideas appear in the same order as they appear in the original article, which is in logical order, or the order that made the most sense to the writer.

✻ For information about organizing writing in logical order, see PE page 56.

Word Choice 3. The summary is simpler.

Summary Paragraph

The following article is summarized in the paragraph "Native American Inventions."

The New World of Native American Inventions

People have always invented objects to improve their lives. European settlers in the New World discovered Native American inventions and took them around the globe.

Eskimo tribes made kayaks–covered, watertight canoes. People still use them for fishing and sea travel. Now, kayaks are also used for recreation on rivers, lakes, and oceans. People even ride the surf in kayaks.

People of the American Northeast invented a long sled called a toboggan. People still use toboggans to haul gear across snow and ice. Now there are toboggan races in the Olympics.

Another Native American invention is the snowshoe. At first, people strapped pine boughs to their feet so they could walk on deep snow. Later, they made wooden frames with leather webbing. Modern snowshoes are worn by winter hikers and by adventurers who explore cold places like Antarctica.

The game of lacrosse is another Native American invention. French explorers found different versions of the game being played by the Cherokee and Iroquois. Today, lacrosse leagues have spread all the way to Australia!

Topic sentence (main idea)

Body

Closing sentence

Native American Inventions

Many early Native American inventions are still being used. The Eskimo kayak is still a hunting and fishing boat, but it's also used on rivers, lakes, and oceans for recreation. The toboggan still hauls gear, but it also is used for races in the Olympics. Snowshoes still help people get through deep snow wherever they are. Finally, like other Native American inventions, the game of lacrosse is now enjoyed around the world.

 Respond to the reading. Answer the following questions.

- **Ideas** (1) What is the main idea of this summary?
- **Organization** (2) How is the paragraph organized?
- **Word Choice** (3) Compare the wording of the summary to the wording of the original. Which is simpler?

English Language Learners

Students may have difficulty restating information in their own words. Prepare them for the task by having them practice orally. After students identify the most important ideas in the sample article, and before they read the sample summary, have them retell the ideas to their partners in their own words.

Struggling Learners

Many students find it difficult to make the transition from a retelling (in which all the events are told) to a summary (in which the main ideas are told). Explain that you're going to tell them two different versions of a story they already know: one is a *retelling* and the other is a *summary*. Use a familiar tale such as *The Three Little Pigs,* and give a retelling and a summary. (Summary: Three pigs build their houses out of different materials in order to be safe from a wolf. The pig who builds his house from bricks is the only one whose house survives.) Ask students to listen and think about which is the retelling and which is the summary, and why.

Prewriting Selecting an Article

When you practice summarizing, you must first find an article. Choose one that . . .

- relates to a subject you are studying,
- discusses an interesting topic, and
- is fairly short (three to five paragraphs).

Choose an article. Look through magazines and newspapers for an article to summarize.

Reading the Article

If possible, make a photocopy of the article so that you can underline important facts, like the sample shown here. Otherwise, take brief notes.

> Eskimo tribes made kayaks—covered, watertight canoes. People still use them for fishing and sea travel. Now, kayaks are also used for recreation on rivers, lakes, and oceans. People even ride the surf in kayaks.

Read your article. Read through the article once to understand it. Then reread it to find the important ideas.

Finding the Main Idea

The topic sentence of a summary should contain the main idea of the article. By rereading the first paragraph of your article, along with the words you underlined throughout, you will find the main idea. Here's the topic sentence from the sample summary: "Many early Native American inventions are still being used."

Write the main idea. Review the first paragraph of the article and the words you underlined. What main idea do they suggest? Include this idea in a topic sentence.

Prewriting Selecting an Article

Have the whole class summarize the same article or, for variety, have groups of students select the same article to summarize. Then they can share and compare summaries and benefit from each other's efforts.

If you decide to have the whole class summarize the same article, try to select a topic from another curriculum area that interests students.

Prewriting Reading the Article

Always try to have students work from a printed copy of the article or story they are summarizing. This allows them to underline and also jot down ideas in the margin while they are reading.

Prewriting Finding the Main Idea

Remind students that the main idea tells what the article is mostly about. Tell students to make sure that their topic sentence clearly states this main idea.

✳ For more about writing strong topic sentences, see PE page 460.

English Language Learners

Students may have difficulty comprehending or recalling content area text, especially if they are not familiar with the subject. To ensure that these students find the information they need to write a topic sentence, select articles about familiar topics at the appropriate reading level. Provide photocopies of the reproducible 5 W's chart (TE page 647) for students to use to record the important ideas.

Struggling Learners

To assist students with the prewriting assignment, use these strategies:

- Provide articles of varying difficulty so students can focus on meaning without the burden of decoding unknown words.
- Pair partners of high and low reading ability. Have the more skilled reader do the first reading aloud. Then have the partner reread the article aloud.

Writing
Developing the First Draft

Remind students that a summary paragraph is supposed to be shorter than the original article. To ensure that students do not overwrite, tell them to limit the summary to their topic sentence plus one sentence for each paragraph that follows the first paragraph in the article.

Revising Reviewing Your Writing

Students may spend unnecessary time trying to reword elements of the original article. Point out that it is acceptable to use a combination of their own words and words from the article, but they should not copy entire sentences. Remind students that actual wording from the article should be placed inside quotation marks.

Encourage students to try for a variety of sentence patterns in their summary.

✱ For information about using different types of sentences, see PE pages 442–444.

Editing Checking for Conventions

Tell students to use the original article to verify the accuracy of dates, names, and facts, just in case they copied something incorrectly in their notes or draft.

336

Writing Developing the First Draft

A summary paragraph contains three basic parts. The **topic sentence** states the main idea of the article. The **body** sentences put the most important information in your own words. And, the **closing sentence** shares a final important point.

> **Write the first draft of your summary paragraph.** Write a topic sentence, support it with information from the article, and end with a closing sentence that relates to the main idea.

Revising Reviewing Your Writing

You can revise by checking your summary for the following traits.

- **Ideas** Does the topic sentence give the main idea of the article? Does the body include important supporting details?
- **Organization** Is all the information in logical order?
- **Voice** Does my voice sound interested and informative?
- **Word Choice** Do I explain things in my own words?
- **Sentence Fluency** Do I vary sentence types and lengths?

> **Revise your paragraph.** Reread the article and your summary. Using the questions above, make changes in your writing.

Editing Checking for Conventions

Editing means "correcting errors in conventions."

- **Conventions** Are dates, names, or facts correct? Do I have any punctuation, spelling, or grammar errors?

> **Edit your work.** Use the questions above as a guide to look for errors in your summary. Then make a clean final copy and proofread it again.

English Language Learners

Many students rely on copying information verbatim because of the time it takes for them to read and restate in their own words. Instead of allowing them to combine words from the article with their own words, encourage them to use the technique of covering what they read and restating the information in their own words. Modify written assignments to require fewer sentences or paragraphs, and allow students to focus on expressing ideas in their own words.

Research Report **337**

Research Report

Research Writing

Research Report

The world is full of inventions. A book is an invention. So is the chair you're sitting on, the light above your head, the door to the classroom, and so on.

In this chapter, you will write a research report about an invention that interests you. Writing a research report gives you the chance to investigate a subject on your own and share what you have learned.

Writing Guidelines

Subject:	An interesting invention
Form:	Research report
Purpose:	To find and share information about how something was invented
Audience:	Classmates and parents

Objectives

- demonstrate an understanding of the purpose, content, and form of a research report
- choose a topic (an invention) to write about
- plan, draft, revise, and edit a research report

A **research report** is a piece of expository writing on a topic that shares information collected from a variety of reliable sources and puts it together in a unified and organized way.

Writing a research report will seem daunting to many students. Lighten the mood at this stage in the process by engaging students in a friendly debate about what they think is the greatest invention of all time. Share your own ideas to get the debate started, and encourage every student to offer ideas and opinions. As an added benefit, students may be able to develop topic ideas from the inventions discussed during the debate.

Materials

Style sheet for reports (TE p. 338)

Illustrated book of inventions (TE p. 342)

Large note cards (TE p. 343)

Blank note cards (TE pp. 344, 345, 347)

Colored highlighters (TE p. 345)

Nonfiction passages (TE p. 345)

Sticky notes (TE p. 348)

Colored pencils or markers (TE p. 353)

Books, magazines, and Internet articles (TE p. 354)

Drawing supplies (TE p. 355)

Copy Masters/ Transparencies

Time line (TE p. 361)

Research Report

Have students read the entire report through twice.

- The first time, have them read for content. Tell students to pay particular attention to how the writer weaves facts and details from her research into the story of the invention of windshield wipers.
- For the second reading, have students focus on the physical features of the report, many of which are highlighted in the side notes.

Provide students with a style sheet that outlines your style requirements. If you expect students to follow the report style shown here, you will still need to provide students with margin requirements, minimum and maximum line counts, font size, and the minimum and maximum number of sources you require. This will prevent students from writing too little or too much. It will also ensure uniform submissions that will make it easier for you to evaluate the individual reports and offer helpful comments.

338

Research Report

In this report, Candra explains how the windshield wiper was invented. The side notes point out how ideas are arranged and other important features of the report.

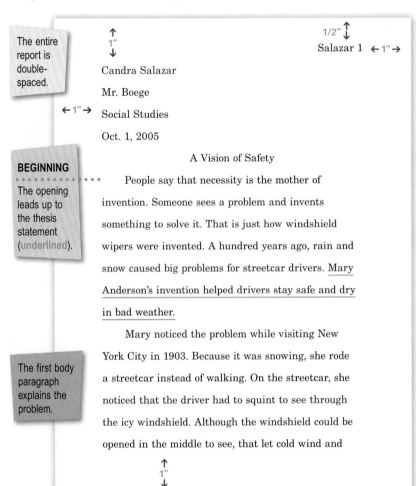

The entire report is double-spaced.

↑ 1" ↓

1/2" ↕
Salazar 1 ← 1" →

← 1" →

Candra Salazar

Mr. Boege

Social Studies

Oct. 1, 2005

A Vision of Safety

BEGINNING

The opening leads up to the thesis statement (underlined).

People say that necessity is the mother of invention. Someone sees a problem and invents something to solve it. That is just how windshield wipers were invented. A hundred years ago, rain and snow caused big problems for streetcar drivers. Mary Anderson's invention helped drivers stay safe and dry in bad weather.

The first body paragraph explains the problem.

Mary noticed the problem while visiting New York City in 1903. Because it was snowing, she rode a streetcar instead of walking. On the streetcar, she noticed that the driver had to squint to see through the icy windshield. Although the windshield could be opened in the middle to see, that let cold wind and

↑ 1" ↓

Salazar 2

An information source is shown in parentheses.

snow inside. So the driver kept stopping the streetcar and getting out to scrape off the snow (Thimmish 11).

Mary thought there should be some way to wipe the windshield from inside the streetcar. That way the driver could see clearly while staying warm and dry. She started sketching pictures of a wooden arm with rubber strips on the outside of the window. On the inside was a lever to move the arm. A weight held the arm against the glass, and a spring brought it back to its place. When Mary got back home to Atlanta, Georgia, she had a local shop make a model. Then she patented her invention (Thimmish 13).

The next body paragraph tells how the invention came about.

Mary's idea didn't catch on at first. While she was sketching plans, people told her it was no use. They said that lots of solutions had been tried before, but nothing worked. Even after her invention was patented, "Many felt the movement of the windshield wipers would distract the drivers" ("Inventor"). Mary tried to sell her patent to a manufacturer, but no one was interested (Sillery).

The next body paragraph tells how people reacted to the invention.

Ask students to point out their favorite parts of the article and to explain what they like about these parts. The following questions can help them recognize why they find a particular part appealing.

- Does it provide an interesting piece of information?
- Do you like the way the writer uses special terms to explain an idea?
- Does the writer make it easy for you to understand a difficult idea?

Have students notice that the source information in parentheses within the report corresponds to information in the Works Cited section at the end of the report. Review the Works Cited and explain that the sources are listed alphabetically by author, or by title, when the author is not known. Assure students that they will learn more about how to create a Works-Cited page later in the unit.

Have students point out the key words and ideas in the thesis statement (underlined on PE page 338) that are repeated in the ending. This will help students see exactly how the ending reminds readers of the thesis statement.

Respond to the reading.

Answers

Ideas 1. Answers will vary. Possible answers:

■ Mary Anderson invented windshield wipers in 1903.

■ Her design showed a wooden arm with rubber strips on the outside. A weight with a spring held the arm against the glass. A lever inside moved the arm.

Organization 2. Wording will vary.

■ Mary saw that snowy windshields were a problem for bus drivers.

■ Mary designed and patented her invention.

■ Mary had trouble selling her patent.

Voice 3. Answers will vary.

■ Mary Anderson's invention helped drivers stay safe and dry in bad weather.

■ Mary's invention has helped to make driving safer for everyone.

340

Salazar 3

The ending reminds the reader of the thesis statement.

In the end, Mary's idea was accepted. Thirteen years after she invented the windshield wiper, Henry Ford put it on every Model T ("Inventor"). Now every car has windshield wipers. Mary's invention has helped to make driving safer for everyone.

Salazar 4

The writer's name and page number go on every page.

Works Cited

"Inventor of the Week: Windshield Wipers." Lemelson-MIT Program. Sept. 2001. 28 Sept. 2004 <http://web.mit.edu/invent/iow/anderson.html>.

Sources are listed alphabetically.

Sillery, Bob. "FYI." Popular Science June 2002: 88.

Thimmish, Catherine. Girls Think of Everything. Boston: Houghton, 2000.

Respond to the reading. After reading Candra's research report, answer the following questions about these traits of writing.

■ **Ideas** (1) List two things you learned from the report.

■ **Organization** (2) In your own words, what is the main point of each middle paragraph?

■ **Voice** (3) Find a sentence that shows the writer's feelings about the topic.

Prewriting

Research Report 341

Prewrite ✓ Revise Publish
Write Edit

Writing a research report requires good planning. Here are five keys to help you get started.

Keys to Effective Prewriting

1. **Choose** an invention that interests you.

2. **Look** for answers to your research questions.

3. **Find** two or three details for each question.

4. **Use** a gathering grid and note cards to collect information.

5. **List** your sources so you can give them credit later.

Prewriting
Keys to Effective Prewriting

Remind students of the purpose of the prewriting stage in the writing process: It is when the writer selects a topic, gathers details, and decides how to organize those details.

The Keys to Prewriting list lays out the process students will be guided through on PE pages 342–348.

- Suggest that students consider for their topic one of the inventions that they discussed during their invention debate (TE page 337).

- Tell students that when they first begin researching their topic, they will have general questions (item 2) such as "Who was the inventor?" and "When was it invented?" As they continue their research, they will probably develop other, more specific questions related to the invention and the inventor. This is a natural step in the research process and one that usually happens when students become more interested in their topic.

Struggling Learners

To help students identify research questions (referred to in item 2), direct them back to the side notes for the three body paragraphs of the report "A Vision of Safety" (PE pp. 338–339). Ask students to change the notes into questions. For example, the note, "The first body paragraph explains the problem" becomes the question, *What was the original problem that the inventor identified?* Explain that questions such as these guided the writer's research for the report.

Prewriting Selecting a Topic

Have students ask themselves the following questions as they try to think of inventions for their chart.

- What is something I use before I leave the house in the morning?
- What is something I see on my way to school every day?
- What is something I use when I play or relax?

Students won't know if they have selected a suitable topic for their report until they have done some preliminary research to size up their topic. At this point, tell students to circle three inventions on their chart that interest them, and to number them 1, 2, and 3, with 1 being their first choice.

Prewriting Sizing Up Your Topic

Before asking students to size up their topic ideas, preview PE page 343 with them to make sure that they understand their goal is to choose a topic that is just the right size.

Then have students look up their number 1 topic choice in an encyclopedia. If their first choice seems too big or too small, tell them to follow the same process with their next two choices.

Prewriting Selecting a Topic

In order to choose a topic, Candra listed inventions she was curious about.

Ideas Chart

Inventions I'm Curious About

At home	At school	In the car
CD players	computers	gasoline
reclining chairs	pencil sharpeners	tires
microwave ovens	pencils	windshield wipers
toasters	scissors	cup holders

Make an ideas chart. List inventions that interest you in a chart like the one above. Write three or four ideas under each heading.

Sizing Up Your Topic

Some topics are too small for a research report. Other topics are too big. To decide whether your topic is the right size for a report, look it up in an encyclopedia and think about the following questions:

1. What problem did the invention solve?
2. How did the invention happen? (Who invented it? When? How?)
3. How successful was the invention?

A good research paper should include one or two paragraphs about each of these research questions.

English Language Learners

Students who do not know the English name of the invention they want to research, or who find the task of thinking of an invention daunting, may find it helpful to listen to others brainstorm ideas. Students might find it helpful to look through an illustrated book of inventions.

Advanced Learners

Explain that a patent is the legal way for inventors to keep others from making or using their inventions without their permission. Ask students why a patent would be important to an inventor. Direct students to the U.S. Patent and Trademark Office Kid's Pages (www.uspto.gov/go/kids/). To learn more about patents, trademarks, copyrights, and trade secrets, students can click on "whowhatwhenwherehowwhy". Invite students to explore the Web site for more interesting facts, including information about patented kids' inventions, and to report back to the class.

Too Big

Personal Computers

What was the problem?

- People had to take turns on expensive mainframes.
- They wanted more computer time.
- They needed cheaper computers.

How did the invention happen?

- March 1974, Scelbi Computer Consulting Company advertised a computer kit in QST.
- July 1974, Jonathan Titus advertised his Mark-8 kit in Radio Electronics.
- January 1975, the Altair kit by MITS (a calculator company) was in Popular Mechanics.
- 1977, Steven Jobs and Stephen Wozniak founded Apple Computer, Inc., and sold the first PC (Apple II).
- 1981, IBM started selling its own PC.

How successful was it?

- PC's were used in business and at home.
- The Internet made PC's useful for work and fun.

Too Small

Scissors

What was the problem?

- People wanted a better way to cut cloth.

How did the invention happen?

- Nobody knows.

How successful was it?

- All kinds of scissors exist.

Just Right

Windshield Wipers

What was the problem?

- People couldn't see through rain, ice, and snow on windshields.
- They had to get out to clear the windshield.

How did the invention happen?

- Mary Anderson felt sorry for a streetcar driver.
- She thought of a wiper with a lever inside the vehicle.
- She got her plans patented.

How successful was it?

- At first, her suggestion wasn't popular.
- Wipers became standard on Henry Ford's cars.

Review the inventions that Candra explored before settling on windshield wipers. Help students understand why Candra's choice fits her assignment: to write a four- or five-paragraph report about an invention.

- The topic *Personal Computers* has a long, complicated history. Candra thought she wouldn't be able to explain the topic in detail in four or five paragraphs.
- The topic *Scissors* has very little specific information available. Candra realized that after one or two sentences, she wouldn't have anything more to say.
- The topic *Windshield Wipers* has an interesting history with just the right amount of specific details. Candra knew she could tell the story in the space available.

Struggling Learners

When students conduct their prewriting research to find a topic, help them choose one that's just right. Review the questions they developed (TE page 341) for the side notes for "A Vision of Safety" (PE pages 338–339). Then have them write out the three research questions shown on page 343 on large note cards. Tell students that as they conduct their research, they can write the answer to each question on the back of the appropriate card. Explain that they will use the answers during their writing. Make sure students include the source information on each note card for easy reference.

Prewriting Using a Gathering Grid

Have students create their own gathering grids. Tell students to use the sample grid as a model. Offer these guidelines.

- List research questions (from PE page 342) in the left column.
- List sources (which you must find and select) across the top. Limit your sources to three or four.
- Fill in the blocks with your answers to the questions. If an answer is too long to fit in the block, jot down the number of the note card that has the answer.
- Write your notes neatly so that you will be able to read them when it is time to draft your report.
- Be sure to write dates, names, and places correctly in your notes.

Prewriting Using a Gathering Grid

A gathering grid is one way to collect information for a report. Down the side, Candra listed her research questions, and across the top, she listed her sources. In the rest of the grid, she wrote answers to her questions.

Gathering Grid

Windshield wipers	Girls Think of Everything (book)	"FYI" (magazine article)	"Inventor of the Week" (Internet article)
What problem did the invention solve?	wiping rain and snow from windshields		
How did the invention come about?	See note card #1.		Mary Anderson got the idea while watching a streetcar operator in New York City.
How successful was the invention?	She patented it in 1903.	Friends teased Mary, but by 1913, wipers were standard.	See note card #2.
Other information		In 1917, Charlotte Bridgewood patented the first automatic wiper system.	

Struggling Learners

To make it easier to cite sources later, have students include the following information on their gathering grids.

- In the source blocks, add the author's last name.
- In the information blocks and on their note cards, add the page number where the information was found.

Tell students to use quotation marks when copying word-for-word so the sentence can be used as a direct quotation later.

Research Report 345

Creating Note Cards

When answers are too long to fit on your gathering grid, you can write them on note cards. Number each card and write your research question at the top. Then write your answer on the card. At the bottom, name the source of the information. If the source has page numbers, list the pages where you found the information.

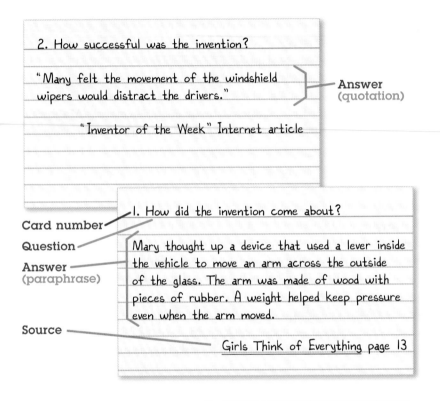

2. How successful was the invention?

"Many felt the movement of the windshield wipers would distract the drivers."
— **Answer** (quotation)

"Inventor of the Week" Internet article

Card number — 1. How did the invention come about?

Question —

Answer (paraphrase) — Mary thought up a device that used a lever inside the vehicle to move an arm across the outside of the glass. The arm was made of wood with pieces of rubber. A weight helped keep pressure even when the arm moved.

Source — Girls Think of Everything page 13

Prewrite

Create note cards. Use note cards like those above to write answers that are too long for your gathering grid.

Prewriting Creating Note Cards

Tell students to be sure to put quotation marks around any direct quotations from their sources that they include on their note cards or gathering grid. Explain that this is absolutely necessary to help them avoid plagiarism in their report. For an explanation of plagiarism, have students turn to PE page 352. Explain to students that they do not need to use quotation marks if they **paraphrase** (see below) as shown on card 1.

Make sure students understand that the number in front of the question on the sample note cards refers to the number of the card itself and not to the order in which the questions are listed in the gathering grid.

Another way to organize note cards is to color-coordinate them with the questions. Suggest that students use different colors of highlighters to mark each of the questions in the gathering grid. They can use the same color highlighter to mark the matching question on the note cards. Students can then group cards by question and easily see if a note card is in the wrong group.

Teaching Tip: Paraphrase

Students may need additional help understanding how to paraphrase. Explain that when they paraphrase they put someone else's ideas into their own words. A paraphrase of a selection is usually simpler than the original piece of writing, but unlike a summary, it doesn't always have to be shorter.

Distribute two short nonfiction passages to small groups. Have students work together to paraphrase each passage. Tell them to follow these steps.

- Read the passage through.
- Find the basic meaning of each sentence.
- Restate each sentence so that it is simpler but has the same basic meaning as the original.

English Language Learners

Students may not have the language proficiency to restate each sentence in their own words. Modify the **Paraphrase** activity to have students restate the gist of each paragraph. Have students cover the text before they restate information. For additional suggestions on helping students restate information, see TE pages 334 and 336.

Prewriting
Keeping Track of Your Sources

Take this opportunity to discuss the conventions of punctuating titles when listing sources.

✳ For information about punctuating titles, see PE pages 494 and 502.

Students often fail to record source information in its entirety during prewriting. Then if a source is misplaced, they are at a loss. Stress the importance of keeping track of sources during prewriting. For students working on a computer, recording source information can be especially helpful. When it comes time to create their works-cited page, they can simply cut and paste the information from their notes into their report.

346

Prewriting Keeping Track of Your Sources

When you give credit to your sources and make a works-cited page, you will need the following information.

Books

Author (last name first). **Title** (underlined). **City** where the book was published: **Publisher, copyright date.**

> Thimmish, Catherine. Girls Think of Everything.
> Boston: Houghton, 2000.

Magazines

Author (last name first). **Article title** (in quotation marks). **Magazine title** (underlined) **Date** (day, month, year): **Page numbers** of the article.

> Sillery, Bob. "FYI." Popular Science June 2002: 88.

Internet

Author (if available, last name first). **Page title** (if available, in quotation marks). **Site title** (underlined). **Date published** (if available). **Date visited (day, month, year) <Internet address>.**

> "Inventor of the Week: Windshield Wipers." Lemelson–MIT
> Program. Sept. 2001. 28 Sept. 2004
> <http://web.mit.edu/invent/iow/anderson.html>.

Note: If a source does not give all of the details shown above, just write down the ones it does give.

Keep track of your sources. As you read and take notes, record the publication information for each source.

Research Report 347

Organizing Ideas

When your research is finished, you will need to organize your ideas. A thesis statement and an outline will help you to put the information in a good order.

Writing Your Thesis Statement

Your thesis statement tells what your report is about. A good thesis statement starts with an interesting topic and adds a special part to emphasize.

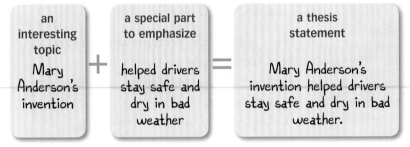

an interesting topic		a special part to emphasize		a thesis statement
Mary Anderson's invention	**+**	helped drivers stay safe and dry in bad weather	**=**	Mary Anderson's invention helped drivers stay safe and dry in bad weather.

Thesis Statements

> The typewriter (an interesting topic) did not catch on for more than 70 years after it was patented (a special part to emphasize).

> The idea for the microwave oven (an interesting topic) came when a scientist's chocolate bar melted in front of radar waves (a special part to emphasize).

Prewrite — **Create your thesis statement.** After reviewing your notes, use the formula above to write a thesis statement about your subject.

Prewriting Organizing Ideas

Tell students to make sure that they have all their prewriting notes (including their gathering grid, note cards, and source information) together and neatly organized. This will make it easier for them to locate information for their thesis statement and outline. If students will be creating their thesis statement and outline in school, try to provide them with a large flat work area so that they can keep all their prewriting notes in front of them.

Prewriting
Writing Your Thesis Statement

Have students experiment with different ideas and wording for their thesis statement. Provide students with blank note cards.

- Tell them to write *topic* at the top of one card and *special part* at the top of two or three cards.
- Have students write their topic on the *topic* card first.
- Then suggest that they write two or three different *special part* cards.

Students can then put the *topic* card together with each of the *special part* cards to form thesis statements and to decide which one works best.

Prewriting Making an Outline

Some students may have little or no experience with creating an outline for writing. Be sure to allow time to review the conventions explained in the side notes before having students create their own outline.

＊ For more information about how to build an outline, see PE page 459.

Point out that this is a sentence outline. The goal here is not necessarily for students to write the exact words that they will use in the report. Instead, the goal is to make sure that

■ the main ideas are clearly stated as topic sentences (roman numerals),
■ no important ideas are left out of the report, and
■ the ideas are arranged in the order that they will be presented in the report. Since students are telling the story of an invention, they should use **time order** *(see below)* to organize ideas in their outline.

348

Prewriting Making an Outline

A sentence outline is a plan for putting your ideas in order. Below is the first part of Candra's sentence outline.

Sentence Outline

Thesis statement	**THESIS STATEMENT:** Mary Anderson's invention helped drivers stay safe and dry in bad weather.
I. Topic sentence for first middle paragraph	I. Mary noticed the problem while visiting New York City in 1903.
A., B., and C. Supporting details	A. She rode a streetcar because it was snowy. B. She noticed the driver squinting through the icy windshield. C. Driver kept stopping to clean windshield
II. Topic sentence for second middle paragraph	II. Mary thought there should be some way to wipe the windshield from inside the streetcar. A. . . . B. . . .
Continue . . .	

Write your outline. Review your research notes (pages 344-345). Then write an outline for your report. Each topic sentence must relate to your thesis statement.

Teaching Tip: Time Order Organization

Explain that time order is a method of organization that helps readers follow the writer's ideas. Ideas and details are arranged in the order that they happened in time. Words such as *first, second, next, then,* and *finally* signal time order.

＊ For more about using time order, see PE pages 56 and 458.

English Language Learners

To help students focus on organizing their ideas, have them

● write each topic sentence on a separate page,
● record the supporting details using only words and phrases on sticky notes instead of writing complete sentences,
● attach the sticky notes to the appropriate topic sentence pages, and

● discuss their outline with you and make changes by moving and/or adding additional sticky notes to each page.

Writing

Prewrite   Write   Revise   Edit   Publish

Once your planning is finished, it's time to write! The following key points will guide your work.

Keys to Writing

1. **Write** a strong first paragraph that gives your thesis statement.

2. **Start** each middle paragraph with an effective topic sentence.

3. **Organize** the supporting details in each middle paragraph.

4. **Write** a thoughtful ending paragraph that reminds the reader of your thesis.

5. **Cite** your sources on a works-cited page.

Writing Keys to Writing

Remind students that the writing stage is when they get to write, or draft, their ideas on paper.

The Keys to Writing list lays out the process students will be guided through on PE pages 350–354.

Tell students to use their outline as a framework for their report. If students have not completed their outline, it is important that they do so now. During the writing stage, their outline will provide them with

- a thesis statement,
- topic sentences for each middle paragraph, and
- supporting details for each topic sentence.

Students should also have on hand their gathering grid, note cards, and source information so that they can add to the report

- interesting and accurate facts and details,
- direct and indirect quotations, and
- accurate source information.

Writing
Starting Your Research Report

Although it is customary to advise students to write the beginning paragraph first and the ending paragraph last, some students might be more comfortable starting with the middle paragraphs because those paragraphs have been more fully developed in the outline. If students would like to write their middle paragraphs first, tell them to write their thesis statement at the top of their draft so that they can keep the focus of their report in mind as they write.

Provide students with other ideas for beginnings.
- Begin with a surprising fact.
- Begin with an anecdote, or very short story, related to the topic.
- Use a quotation.
- Connect the topic to your everyday life.

Encourage students to experiment with two or three different beginnings. If they are not sure which one to use, they can share their beginnings with a partner and decide together which works best.

350

Writing Starting Your Research Report

Your opening paragraph should grab your reader's interest, introduce your topic, and lead to your thesis statement. Below are two possible ways to start a report about the invention of the windshield wiper.

Beginning Paragraph

> This paragraph begins with an interesting idea and ends with the thesis statement.
>
> People say that necessity is the mother of invention. Someone sees a problem and invents something to solve it. That is just how windshield wipers were invented. A hundred years ago, rain and snow caused big problems for streetcar drivers. <u>Mary Anderson's invention helped drivers stay safe and dry in bad weather.</u>

> This paragraph begins with a question and ends with the thesis statement.
>
> Have you ever thought about how important windshield wipers are? The earliest vehicles didn't have them. It was dangerous because drivers in those days had trouble seeing the road on rainy or snowy days. <u>Mary Anderson's invention helped drivers stay safe and dry in bad weather.</u>

Write your opening paragraph. Write a beginning paragraph for your report. Use one of the examples above as a guide, or try an idea of your own.

Struggling Learners

The concept of writing a paragraph that leads up to a thesis statement is new to students. This activity will help them generate information they can use for that purpose. Have partners work together to answer the following questions. Remind them to take notes.

- What surprising information did you find out about your topic?
- Why are you interested in this invention?
- How does it affect your daily life?
- What quotations did you copy? Why did you choose them?
- What would life be like without this invention?

Research Report **351**

Developing the Middle Part

The middle of your report should support your thesis statement. Each middle paragraph should have a topic sentence that relates to the thesis. Other sentences in each paragraph should support the topic sentence.

> Beginning
> **Middle**
> Ending

Middle Paragraphs

All the details support the topic sentence (underlined).

Mary noticed the problem while visiting New York City in 1903. Because it was snowing, she rode a streetcar instead of walking. On the streetcar, she noticed that the driver had to squint to see through the icy windshield. Although the windshield could be opened in the middle to see, that let cold wind and snow inside. So the driver kept stopping the streetcar and getting out to scrape off the snow (Thimmish 11).

Sentences lead naturally from one idea to the next.

Mary thought there should be some way to wipe the windshield from inside the streetcar. That way the driver could see clearly while staying warm and dry. She started sketching pictures of a wooden arm with rubber strips on the outside of the window. On the inside was a lever to move the arm. A weight held the arm against the glass, and a spring brought it back to its place. When Mary got back home to Atlanta, Georgia, she had a local shop make a model. Then she patented her invention (Thimmish 13).

Specific details are used to explain the invention.

A source is cited (in parentheses).

Writing
Developing the Middle Part

Students may still be wondering how they can turn their outline and their notes into an interesting, detailed report. Allow time for students to compare the organization and content of the sample middle paragraphs to Candra's outline on PE page 348 and to the gathering grid and note cards on PE pages 344–345. Point out the following:

- The underlined topic sentences on this page come directly from roman numerals I and II in Candra's outline.
- Candra incorporated the supporting detail sentences from the outline (I. A, B, C) into the first paragraph.
- Candra used details from her gathering grid and note cards in all the middle paragraphs.

Students should be able to conclude that the topic sentence for the final middle paragraph, on PE page 352, would be roman numeral III, and the supporting details for the second and final paragraphs would come from the A, B, and C sentences, if Candra's complete outline were shown.

English Language Learners

Allow students extra time to express their ideas in English. To help them focus on organizing and incorporating supporting details for each topic sentence in their report, require fewer middle paragraphs. Remind students that because they are writing their first draft, they may leave spaces if they cannot think of words or phrases to express their ideas.

Have students point out the topic sentence in the final middle paragraph. *(Mary's idea didn't catch on at first.)* Discuss how all the details in that paragraph support the topic sentence.

To show students how to use their outlines to construct sound middle paragraphs, have them work together to complete Candra's outline on PE page 348, using the details from her second and final middle paragraphs. Students will actually be deconstructing the paragraphs to see the basic parts.

Writing Avoiding Plagiarism and Citing Sources

It may be difficult for students to understand what constitutes plagiarism because in school they are often asked to respond to questions by quoting verbatim from their textbooks. At home, they listen to music that has been re-released by another artist or they watch "remakes" of movies.

Tell students that to avoid plagiarizing the ideas of others in their writing, they must do more than change one or two words. Instead, they should paraphrase or summarize.

352

Final Middle Paragraph

A quotation adds authority to the report.

> Mary's idea didn't catch on at first. While she was sketching plans, people told her it was no use. They said that lots of solutions had been tried before, but nothing worked. Even after her invention was patented, "Many felt the movement of the windshield wipers would distract the drivers" ("Inventor"). Mary tried to sell her patent to a manufacturer, but no one was interested (Sillery).

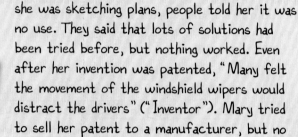

Write your middle paragraphs. Use your outline as a guide to write your middle paragraphs. A first draft doesn't need to be perfect. Just get your main ideas on paper.

Avoiding Plagiarism and Citing Sources

Plagiarism is using someone else's work without giving that person credit. Two examples of plagiarism are (1) using someone's exact words without quotation marks and (2) using ideas without giving their source. As you write your paper, do the following:

- **Use quotation marks for exact words.**
  (See final paragraph above.)

- **Show your sources in parentheses.**
  (See the author names and page numbers on page 351.)

- **List publication details on your works-cited page.**
  (See pages 340, 346, and 354.)

Writing Ending Your Report

The ending paragraph should close your report smoothly and remind your reader of the thesis. You can try one or more of the following ideas.

- **Explain what effect the invention has had on the world.**
- **Tell one last interesting fact about the invention or its inventor.**
- **Leave your reader with something to think about.**

Ending Paragraph

The ending sums up the invention's effect on the world.	In the end, Mary's idea was accepted. Thirteen years after she invented the windshield wiper, Henry Ford put it on every Model T ("Inventor"). Now every car has windshield wipers. <u>Mary's invention has helped to make driving safer for everyone.</u>
The reader is reminded of the thesis (underlined).	

Write your final paragraph. Use one of the ideas listed above to write your ending paragraph. Also remind the reader of your thesis statement.

Look over your draft. Review your notes and outline. Then read through your first draft. Did you include all the necessary details? Do they lead naturally from one to the next? Make notes about possible changes and use them when you revise.

Writing Ending Your Report

Besides reminding readers of their thesis, students can also refer back to other ideas presented in the first paragraph. For example, if students began their report with a connection to everyday life, they might refer back to that connection in their ending. Use the following to illustrate this concept.

- (Beginning paragraph) The telephone rings, and you pick it up without thinking.
- (Ending paragraph) The next time the telephone rings, think about this.

One way for students to make sure that they included all the necessary details in their draft is to use a colored pencil or marker as they review to check off each detail in their notes that they used in the draft. Then they can quickly see if there are important or interesting details that they left out.

Writing
Creating Your Works-Cited Page

Remind students that, on a works-cited page, sources are listed alphabetically by the author's last name or by the title. Point out that articles found on the Internet often do not give the author's name.

If there is time, divide students into groups. Give each group a variety of sources and have students work together to create a works-cited page that lists the different sources. Original sources can include books, magazine articles, and printouts of Internet articles. Make sure the Internet printouts show the Web address and copyright information, if available.

Writing Creating Your Works-Cited Page

Once you finish your report, you need to arrange the sources you used in alphabetical order on a works-cited page. Use the publication information you wrote down for each source (page 346). The works-cited page goes at the end of your report.

> The title "Works Cited" is centered.

> Sources are listed alphabetically.

Salazar 4

Works Cited

"Inventor of the Week: Windshield Wipers." Lemelson–MIT Program. Sept. 2001. 28 Sept. 2004 <http://web.mit.edu/invent/iow/anderson.html>.

Sillery, Bob. "FYI." Popular Science June 2002: 88.

Thimmish, Catherine. Girls Think of Everything. Boston: Houghton, 2000.

Create your works-cited page. List your sources in alphabetical order on a new page. (Put your last name and the page number in the upper right corner.) Center the title "Works Cited" and indent all lines after the first line of each entry.

Research Report **355**

Revising

Don't expect the first draft of your report to be perfect. Some ideas may be unclear or incomplete. Some sentences may be confusing or clumsy. The voice may sound dull in places. Use the keys to revising below to make changes to your report.

Keys to Revising

1. **Read** through your first draft to get an overall sense of your report.

2. **Review** each part carefully—the beginning, the middle, and the ending.

3. **Check** that your thesis statement emphasizes a special part of your topic.

4. **Be sure** the topic sentences of the middle paragraphs support your thesis.

5. **Check** that the ending reminds the reader of your thesis statement.

Revising Keys to Revising

Remind students that the revising stage is when writers have an opportunity to make improvements to their first drafts. At this stage, they can think about refinements they might not have considered when they were drafting.

The Keys to Revising list lays out the process students will be guided through on PE pages 356–358.

The task of writing a research report can be tedious and difficult for many young writers. For that reason, all students will benefit if they have an opportunity to let their report rest for a while before they move on to revising.

As a slight diversion, have students create lively, fun commercials for the invention that is the topic of their report. Although it takes them away from report writing for a while, it keeps them focused on their topic and provides practice with another form of writing.

Advanced Learners

As an alternative activity, students can create separate print ads for an invention's past, present, and future versions. For example:

Long-distance Communication
- Past: pony express or ship
- Present: U.S. postal system (including by plane) or e-mail
- Future: _____

Encourage creativity with color, texture, and form. The wording should be catchy and persuasive.

Revising Improving Your Ideas

Because the cuts and additions may be difficult for some students to follow, read aloud the sample paragraph with the revisions in place. To help students understand why the writer made these changes, provide an imaginary dialogue of questions and answers.

Candra's Question: Do my readers need to know that Mary was visiting from Atlanta? Will this fact help my readers understand anything more about Mary's invention?

Answer: Since the answer is no to both questions, you should cut this sentence.

Candra's Question: Will my readers know Mary was on the streetcar when she noticed the driver squinting?

Answer: Maybe not. You'd better make this clear.

Candra's Question: Will my readers think the last sentence is boring?

Answer: Probably. Add a sentence that tells the reader more about the problem drivers faced.

Encourage students to engage in a similar dialogue with their writing partner as they check for unnecessary details and for weak or unclear sentences in their draft.

356

Revising Improving Your Ideas

Revising means cutting, adding, and changing (or moving). You may cut details that aren't needed, add details that are missing, or change the details in some way—all to make your ideas clear to the reader.

An unneeded sentence is cut.

Helpful details are added.

A weak sentence is replaced with a more interesting one.

Mary noticed the problem while visiting
New York City in 1903. ~~She was visiting from Atlanta, Georgia.~~ Because it was snowing, She rode a streetcar instead of walking. On the streetcar, She noticed that the driver had to squint to see through the icy windshield. Although the windshield could be opened in the middle to see, So the driver kept stopping the streetcar and that let cold wind and snow inside. ~~The driver and~~ getting out to scrape off the snow ~~passengers hated that~~ (Thimmish 11).

Revise **Check your report for weak or unclear sentences.** Reread the first draft of your report. Are there details you should cut, add, or change? Make revisions to improve your paper.

Research Report 357

Improving Your Organization

When revising your first draft, you may find that your ideas are not in the best order. A sentence, or even an entire paragraph, may need to be moved. For better organization, Candra moved a sentence in the middle paragraph below.

An idea is moved for better organization.

> Mary thought there should be some way to wipe the windshield from inside the streetcar. She started sketching pictures of a wooden arm with rubber strips on the outside of the window. On the inside was a lever to move the arm. A weight held the arm against the glass, and a spring brought it back to its place. That way the driver could see clearly while staying warm and dry. When Mary got back home to Atlanta, Georgia, she had a local shop make a model. Then she patented her invention (Thimmish 13).

Revise

Check your organization. Read your report to see if any ideas or details need to be moved. Make changes to improve the organization.

Revising
Improving Your Organization

Point out that Candra's reorganization puts two sentences that show a **cause-and-effect relationship** *(see below)* together. By making this change, Candra improves the sense of the paragraph.

The sample paragraph describes the mechanics of Mary Anderson's invention. Candra presents the details in this description in order of location to help her readers form a clear mental picture of the windshield wipers. Candra does not include any unnecessary details here to distract the reader. Tell students to pay particular attention when providing a mechanical or technical description of an invention in their report. Tell them to present the details in an order that makes the most sense and to keep the description as clear and simple as possible.

✱ For more on order of location and other organizational plans, see PE pages 56–57 and 458.

Teaching Tip: Cause and Effect Relationships

Cause-and-effect relationships are an important part of any discussion of inventions. Inventions are often created because of a need or because of an event that leads to the discovery. Inventions themselves often cause things to happen.

Remind students that a **cause** is what makes something happen. An **effect** is what happens as a result of the cause. Help

students understand the cause-and-effect relationship between the first sentence of the sample paragraph (the cause) and the sentence that was moved (the effect). Point out that the words *that way* help readers recognize the cause-and-effect relationship between the sentences. Other words that show cause-and-effect relationships are *so, because, then,* and *as a result.*

Encourage students to check their reports to make sure that sentences showing cause-and-effect relationships are together.

Revising Using a Checklist

Some students may not give the checklist the attention or deliberation required to turn an acceptable report into an exceptional report. To provide students with the incentive needed to give the checklist more than a cursory reading, have them work in teams.

- Divide students into teams of four. Assign each group member a different trait (ideas, organization, voice & word choice, and sentence fluency).
- Tell each team member to listen for his or her individual trait as writers read aloud their report.
- Using the checklist questions for each trait as a guide, the team members can say whether or not the goals for an individual trait have been achieved.
- If team members decide goals have not been achieved, they should jot down suggestions for improvement to give the writer.
- Have writers and team members rotate to give each student a chance to present his or her report.

Revising Using a Checklist

Check your revising. Number a piece of paper from 1 to 8. If you can answer "yes" to a question, put a check mark after that number. If not, continue to work on that part of your report.

Ideas

_____ **1.** Have I written a clear thesis statement?

_____ **2.** Do I have one main idea in each topic sentence?

Organization

_____ **3.** Do I have an effective beginning, middle, and ending?

_____ **4.** Are my sentences in the best order?

Voice & Word Choice

_____ **5.** Does my writing show my knowledge and interest?

_____ **6.** Do I define or explain any unfamiliar words?

Sentence Fluency

_____ **7.** Do I vary my sentence lengths?

_____ **8.** Do I vary my sentence beginnings?

Make a clean copy. When you have finished revising your report, make a clean copy for editing.

Editing

Prewrite • Write • Revise • Edit ✓ • Publish

After revising, it's time to edit. Editing is checking your writing for punctuation, capitalization, spelling, and grammar errors. The keys to editing below will guide your work.

Keys to Editing

1. **Use** a dictionary and the "Proofreader's Guide" in the back of this book for help.

2. **Make** corrections on a printed copy if you use a computer. Then enter your changes on the computer.

3. **Double-check** your punctuation, capitalization, spelling, and grammar.

4. **Use** the correct format for your report. (See pages 338–340.)

Editing Keys to Editing

Remind students that during the editing stage, they have a chance to find and correct errors in

■ punctuation,
■ capitalization,
■ spelling, and
■ grammar.

Emphasize the importance of editing on a printed copy of a report that is prepared on a computer (item 2). Tell students not to rely on the computer's spell checker to catch mistakes. Point out that a spell checker will not find mistakes with misused words (*its* instead of *it's*) or typing mistakes (*form* instead of *from*). Nor will the spell checker find transposed numbers in a date (1798 instead of 1978) or most misspelled proper names.

Remind students to use the proofreading marks on the inside back cover of their book as they edit.

Editing **Using a Checklist**

Give students a few moments to look over the Proofreader's Guide (PE pages 478–605). Throughout the year, they can refer to the instruction, rules, and examples to clarify any checklist items or to resolve writing questions.

Tell students to bookmark the "Proofreader's Guide" table of contents on PE page 478. Then when they need help with a convention problem, they can quickly turn to the table of contents to find the section that deals with the problem. For practice, ask students where they would look

- to figure out which words to capitalize in a book title ("Editing for Mechanics," PE page 508), and
- to learn how to form the past tense of the irregular verb *make* (in the "Using the Parts of Speech," PE page 570).

Adding a Title

Have students experiment with all three ways of creating a title before deciding on their final title.

360

Editing **Using a Checklist**

Check your editing. Number a piece of paper from 1 to 9. If you can answer "yes" to a question below, put a check mark after that number. If not, continue to edit for that convention.

Conventions

PUNCTUATION

_____ **1.** Do I use the correct punctuation to end my sentences?

_____ **2.** Do I use quotation marks correctly?

_____ **3.** Have I correctly punctuated my works-cited page?

CAPITALIZATION

_____ **4.** Do I start all my sentences with capital letters?

_____ **5.** Do I capitalize proper nouns and titles?

SPELLING

_____ **6.** Do I spell all my words correctly?

_____ **7.** Have I double-checked the spelling of names in my report?

GRAMMAR

_____ **8.** Do I use the correct forms of verbs *(she rode,* not *she rided)*?

_____ **9.** Do my subjects and verbs agree in number *(every car has,* not *every car have)*?

Adding a Title

- Describe the topic: **Inventing Windshield Wipers**
- Be creative: **A Vision of Safety**
- Borrow words from the report: **Windshield Wipers on Every Car**

Publishing

Using a Checklist

Research Report **361**

After finishing your report, it's time to share the results of your hard work. You may decide to turn your report into a multimedia presentation, add pictures or graphs, or publish your paper online.

Focus on Presentation

- Use black or blue ink and double-space the entire paper.
- Leave a one-inch margin on all four sides of your paper.
- Write your name, your teacher's name, the class, and the date in the upper left corner of page 1.
- Skip a line and center your title. Skip another line and start your report.
- Write your last name and the page number in the upper right corner of every page.

Prepare a Multimedia Presentation
Create a computer slide show of your report. (See pages 363–367 for more information.)

Develop an Illustrated Report
Draw pictures of the invention or make a time line that shows important dates in its development.

Publish Online
Visit the Write Source Web site **www.thewritesource.com** for information about publishing your writing online.

Make a final copy. Follow your teacher's instructions or use the guidelines above to make a clean final copy of your report. (If you are using a computer, see pages 44–46.)

Publishing Using a Checklist

Have students follow the bulleted guidelines for preparing their report for presentation, or provide them with a bulleted list of your own specific guidelines and have students note how they differ from those shown.

Students have put a great deal of effort into preparing their report, so be sure to set aside sufficient time and/or space for them to present their report to the class.

If some students plan to illustrate their report with a time line, provide photocopies of the reproducible time line (TE page 648) for them to use.

Encourage students to draw and label a simple diagram to help clarify the technical or mechanical features of their invention.

Reflecting on Your Writing

To encourage reflection that will help students grow as writers, give them an opportunity to reflect in different ways. Perhaps they would like to share their responses orally with a partner or with you. Or they might like to illustrate their experience in a cartoon strip in which the writer is a character who comments about the research writing process in captions or speech balloons.

Since report writing is an example of expository writing, students may benefit from comparing reflections from earlier expository writing assignments with this reflection. Tell them to look specifically to see if they have applied to their report the information they learned earlier about expository writing.

362

Reflecting on Your Writing

Think about your research-report experience by completing the starter sentences below. This reflection will help you understand how you are growing as a writer.

My Research Report

1. The best part of my research report is . . .

2. The hardest part of writing the report was . . .

3. The main thing I learned about writing a report is . . .

4. Here is one question I still have about writing a research report:

Research Writing
Multimedia Presentations

A multimedia presentation is one special way to share your research report. Using a computer, you can prepare a slide show that presents your information—complete with moving text, illustrations, and sounds. This chapter will show you how.

Mini Index

- **Getting Started**
- **Presentation Checklist**

Multimedia Presentations

Objectives

- select a piece of writing for a multimedia presentation
- plan, draft, revise, and edit a multimedia presentation
- create a storyboard
- give a multimedia presentation

Students who wish to create a multimedia presentation will need access to a computer as well as a familiarity with the available software for creating slide presentations.

If possible, provide examples of multimedia presentations prepared by former students and faculty, as well as appropriate presentations available online. Have students watch each presentation and then tell how the presentation added to their knowledge and enjoyment of the topic.

Materials

Examples of multimedia presentations (TE p. 363)

Sticky flags (TE p. 364)

Video recording equipment (TE p. 365)

Note cards, poster board (TE p. 366)

Getting Started

Be sure students are aware that their report will be evaluated by you for its content and other pre-established criteria related to the traits of writing.

Students who wish to create a multimedia presentation may need additional assistance from you, your school's computer expert, or others with computer expertise.

Creating the Slides

Have students use colored sticky flags to mark each main idea in the final printed copy of their report. As they create a cluster for each main idea, they can remove the sticky flag. That will make it easy for them to check that they have planned a slide for each main idea.

Make sure students understand that they should create one cluster for each slide. Tell students to be sure to number their clusters according to the order in which they plan to present each slide.

364

Getting Started

Your multimedia presentation begins with an essay, a speech, or a report you've already written. You list the main ideas from that writing and then use a computer program to make slides, add graphics, and include audio (sounds).

Get organized. Choose an essay, a speech, or a report to turn into a multimedia presentation. Make sure your computer has the needed slide-show software.

Creating the Slides

1 **Find the main ideas in your report.**

Each main idea in your report should have its own slide. To plan your slides, make a storyboard, as shown on page 366.

2 **Find pictures and sounds for each slide.**

You can find pictures and sounds in your software program, on the Internet, or on special CD's. Ask your teacher where to find these multimedia files.

Gather your thoughts. Make a cluster like the one below for each slide. Write the main idea for the slide in the middle of the cluster. Then add picture and sound ideas around it.

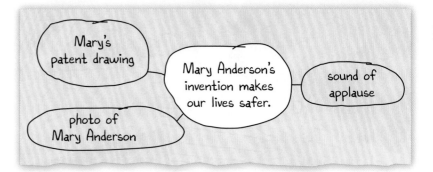

Multimedia Presentations **365**

 3 Design your slides.

Use similar colors and the same easy-to-read fonts on all your slides.

 4 Build your slides one by one.

Make your slides attractive and easy to read. Put them in order so the ideas make sense.

Improving Your Presentation

A multimedia presentation should be given smoothly. Your goal is to make the information clear and interesting. You must practice running the slide show and speaking at the same time.

 Rehearse your presentation. Practice your presentation in front of friends and family. Ask for comments and suggestions. Change any parts that are not clear.

It is also important that your slides be free of any errors. So check your slides carefully and ask a friend or an adult to check them, too.

 Make corrections. Check each slide for punctuation, capitalization, spelling, and grammar errors.

Giving a Multimedia Presentation

Giving your presentation is a lot like giving a speech. See the chapter "Giving Speeches" (pages 373–378) for help.

 Present your report. Take a deep breath, relax, and have fun giving your presentation. This is a chance to show how hard you have worked and to share some good information.

If students are creating their slides on a classroom or school computer, review the font choices that are available to them. Steer them away from fancy or decorative fonts that can be difficult to read.

Improving Your Presentation

Suggest that students use the questions on the Editing Checklist on PE page 360 to edit their slides. Remind them to pay particular attention to the capitalization of names and places and to make sure that they have copied facts from their reports accurately.

Giving a Multimedia Presentation

Stagger students' presentations over the course of a week. This will help to keep the audience's level of interest fresh.

To instill added fun and excitement into the presentation process, invite volunteers to introduce the daily presentations. These students will need to find out a little about each report being presented that day (for example, title and topic) in order to introduce them properly.

English Language Learners

Speaking in front of groups is a developmental milestone of second language acquisition. To allow students to focus on speaking, assign partners to run the slide show. Some may feel comfortable running the slide show and speaking at the same time, but they may feel uncomfortable about speaking in front of a large group. Until students have acquired the language proficiency and confidence to present to the entire class, videotape their presentations to a smaller group.

Multimedia Presentation Storyboard

Have students trace with their finger the progression of slides from beginning to end in the sample storyboard. Allow time for students to compare the ideas in the storyboard to the ideas in the report "A Vision of Safety" on PE pages 338–340. This can give students a clearer idea of how to use their own report as the basis for a multimedia presentation.

Have students create their storyboards.

- Give students blank note cards.
- Tell them to create a title card to use as the first slide on their storyboard.
- Have students create a slide for each of the clusters they created on PE page 364. Have them write the number of the cluster on the back of the note card. This will help them keep the slides in order.
- When students are satisfied with their slides, have them attach the note cards to a large piece of poster board, using the pattern shown in the sample storyboard. Students can draw arrows to show the progression of slides from beginning to end.

366

Multimedia Presentation Storyboard

This storyboard is based on the report "A Vision of Safety" on pages 338–340. Each box represents one slide in the report.

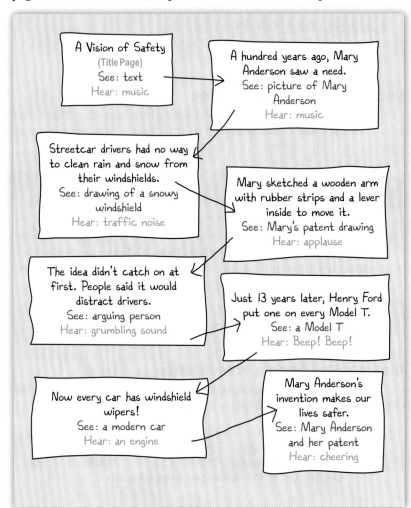

Multimedia Presentations **367**

Presentation Checklist

Use this checklist to make sure your presentation is the best you can make it. When you can answer all 10 questions with a "yes," your presentation is ready!

Ideas

_____ 1. Have I chosen an interesting speech or report for my presentation?

Organization

_____ 2. Does the beginning clearly introduce my topic?
_____ 3. Does the middle include all the main points?
_____ 4. Does the end summarize or give a final thought?

Voice

_____ 5. Do I show interest in my topic?
_____ 6. Does my voice fit my audience and topic?

Word and Multimedia Choices

_____ 7. Is the text on each slide clear and interesting?
_____ 8. Do I include interesting pictures and sounds?

Presentation Fluency

_____ 9. Do the ideas flow smoothly from one slide to the next?

Conventions

_____ 10. Have I corrected all errors in punctuation, capitalization, spelling, and grammar?

Presentation Checklist

Tell students that before producers and directors put on a play for a general audience, they often ask reviewers to watch it. Based on the reviewers' comments, changes may or may not be made to the play before it opens to the public.

After students have used the checklist to make sure their presentation is ready, suggest that they ask two student reviewers to watch a final practice presentation and to use the checklist to review the presentation. If reviewers have suggestions for improving the presentation, and if writers agree with these suggestions, then writers should make the revisions before giving the presentation to a larger audience. If the reviewers answer "yes" to all the questions, then students are ready to give their presentation to the class or to a larger assembly.

Speaking and Writing to Learn Overview

Writing Standards

The writing standards listed below are based on a blending of state and NCTE standards.

- Develop effective group listening and speaking skills.
- Prepare note cards and visual aids in order to deliver an informative speech.
- Keep journals and learning logs to explore and sort out thoughts and information.
- Use strategies such as clustering, listing, and freewriting to organize ideas.
- Take classroom and reading notes, using different graphic organizers.
- Develop critical viewing and thinking skills.
- Apply test-taking strategies to objective tests and writing test prompts.

Skills

- listening in class
- participating in a group
- speaking in class
- preparing and giving a how-to speech

Tools and Techniques

- journals
- learning logs
- writing-to-learn activities
- note taking
- graphic organizers
- viewing

Test-Taking

- test preparation
- four basic types of objective tests (multiple choice, true/false, matching, and fill-in-the-blanks)
- essay tests

Unit Pacing

Listening and Speaking: 30–60 minutes

This section instructs students on how to become better listeners and speakers, both in groups and in the whole classroom. Following are some of the topics that are covered:

- Knowing why you're listening
- Asking questions
- Cooperating in a group
- Following guidelines for speaking

Giving Speeches: 1–2 hours

In this section students are shown how to prepare and present an informative speech by adapting a previously written essay. Following are some of the topics that are covered:

- Rewriting the beginning of the essay
- Selecting and preparing visual aids
- Creating note cards
- Practicing and giving the speech

Keeping Journals and Learning Logs: 1–1.5 hours

This section offers tips on keeping journals and learning logs. Following are some of the topics that are covered:

- Understanding different kinds of journals
- Writing and drawing in learning logs
- Learning through writing activities

Taking Notes: 1–1.5 hours

This section has a dual goal: to help students recognize the value of good note taking and to help them learn how to take good notes. Following are some of the topics that are covered:

- Following guidelines for taking good notes
- Setting up and reviewing notes
- Taking reading notes
- Using different graphic organizers (time line, table organizer) to organize notes

Improving Viewing Skills: 1–1.5 hours

This section explores ways to become a better television and Web-site viewer. Following are some of the topics that are covered:

- Watching the news
- Watching television specials
- Checking what you watch
- Being aware of commercials
- Viewing Web sites

Taking Classroom Tests: 1–2 hours

This section helps students understand the test-taking process. Following are some of the topics that are covered:

- Step-by-step guidelines for preparing for a test
- Tips to use before, during, and after a test
- How to take objective tests (multiple choice, true/false, matching, fill-in-the-blanks)
- Responding to writing prompts

368

Speaking and Writing to Learn

Listening and Speaking

369

Speaking is more than talking. Parrots are famous for talking without saying anything worth hearing. When *you* talk, however, you need to deliver a clear message to listeners.

Likewise, listening is more than hearing. Sometimes people say, "I can hear you, but I'm not listening . . . la, la, la, la!" When you actually listen, you think about what you hear.

This chapter will help you improve your speaking and listening skills—and it may even open your mind!

Mini Index

- **Listening in Class**
- **Participating in a Group**
- **Speaking in Class**

Listening and Speaking

Objectives
- learn how to become a good listener
- develop skills for participating in a group
- improve skills for speaking in class

Discuss what is meant by *speaking is more than talking* and *listening is more than hearing*.

- Talking is just saying words, while speaking is thinking about what you say first.
- Speaking is talking about something important to you.
- Listening means paying attention to what you hear.

To help students understand the difference between hearing and listening, ask them to think about the music that's played at restaurants and in stores. Ask:

- Do you notice (hear) it?
- Do you pay attention (listen) to it?

Discuss how you might know that someone was listening (they might know the title and/or performer of the song; they might know the lyrics and sing along).

Materials

Paper clips and a jar (TE p. 371)

Listening in Class

Acknowledge that it can sometimes be hard to **listen carefully** *(see below)* in class. Students may be distracted by thoughts of other things, or they might not be very interested in the subject.

Suggest that following the tips for listening in class might help students to be more interested in what's going on.

- Thinking positively about why you're listening to something—rather than wishing you weren't supposed to be listening—helps keep you motivated.
- Taking notes can be interesting in itself. Challenge yourself to take clear, accurate notes without missing any facts. Think about how to express the ideas you're hearing in your own words.
- Sometimes, things seem uninteresting only because we don't understand them. Asking questions will help you to understand better—and you might discover that the topic is interesting after all.

Listening in Class

Listening in Class

When your teacher asks you to listen, you know that means thinking about what is being said. In fact, listening is one of the best ways to learn. Follow these tips to become a better listener:

1. **Know your purpose for listening.** Are you learning something new, getting directions, or reviewing for a test?

2. **Take notes.** Think about what's being said. Write the main points in your notebook. Write down questions about things you don't understand.

3. **Ask questions.** Ask specific questions about the things you don't understand. Wait until the speaker is finished and then ask your questions.

Note Taking in Action

When you take notes, write down the main ideas in your own words, as in the following example:

Sample Notes

> Electricity and Magnets   Mar. 9
>
> Magnets can be used to make electricity.
> Electricity can be used to make magnets.
>
> Electricity and magnets in our house
>   —motor in refrigerator
>   —doorbell
>
>   Question: Are there electromagnets in cars?

Teaching Tip:

To help students understand the process of careful listening, have them work with a partner.

- Ask one student to think of a brief story—a minute or two at most—to tell. It can be about an actual event or an account of a scene in a movie or book (as long as the other student isn't familiar with it).
- Advise the second student to listen carefully and take notes, if necessary, because after this, he or she will tell the story to the class.
- After the first student in each pair has told a story, return to the larger group.
- Have listeners take turns retelling the story (give them a moment to consult their notes beforehand, if they want to do so).
- After each retelling, ask the creator of the story how closely what they just heard matched the original. What details were different, if any?

Listening and Speaking **371**

Participating in a Group

Participating in a group means cooperating with others. Two important parts of cooperation are respecting yourself and respecting others.

Skills for Cooperating

In a group, you respect yourself when you . . .

- know that your own ideas are important.
- share your ideas with the group.
- ask questions when you don't understand something.

In a group, you respect others when you . . .

- listen politely.
- wait your turn before speaking or asking a question.
- make helpful comments.
- encourage everyone to participate.

Don't be afraid to ask questions.

Practice

Read the following situations. For each one, decide which of the skills listed above would help the group work together more effectively.

Situation 1

You have an idea that no one else has talked about. You're afraid to speak up because you're not sure it's a good idea.

Situation 2

One member of the group keeps interrupting while others are speaking. He has just interrupted you to ask a question.

Participating in a Group

Point out to students that they can use a lot of what they've learned about responding to a peer's writing when they participate in a group. In both situations, it's important to

- listen carefully to everything that is said,
- respond respectfully and politely,
- give positive feedback as well as asking questions,
- make specific and helpful comments, and
- ask good questions—especially questions that invite explanations rather than "yes" or "no" answers.

✱ For more about peer responding, see PE pages 40–41.

Practice Answers

Possible answers:

1. Respect yourself—give yourself credit for having an important idea and share it with the group.
2. He should respect others by listening politely and waiting his turn before asking a question.

English Language Learners

Students acquiring English go through language acquisition stages before they are ready to speak in large groups. Modify speaking activities to allow them to share in smaller groups while they are gaining language proficiency. Encourage sharing in large groups by stressing that speaking English will be easier the more they practice sharing ideas in groups.

Advanced Learners

Sometimes more confident students unintentionally monopolize group discussions. Increase awareness with the following temporary procedures:

- Give students a certain number of paperclips and have them drop one in a jar each time they speak. Once their paperclips are gone, students must wait until all others have used theirs before speaking again.

- Have a "talking token" on the table. A student must pick it up before speaking and then after speaking, pass it to a student who hasn't had a turn to speak.
- Ask the "talkative" student to record other group members' ideas and then read them aloud before adding his or her own opinions.

Speaking in Class

Focus on the second guideline (Think ahead), especially the instruction to *be sure that you have something important to say.* Explain that students shouldn't worry so much about whether what they have to say is important, that they don't speak at all. Rather, they should make sure that

- what they say applies to the topic at hand (just as a paragraph's body sentences support the topic sentence),
- they don't repeat what has already been said (although it's usually fine to briefly express agreement with someone else), and
- they've thought about how to express their idea.

When playing the **speaking skills** *(see below)* game, adjust the rules as appropriate to accommodate students who get nervous when speaking before the class. For example, allow everyone to complete the full minute, encourage them to start speaking again if they pause, or remind students to keep eye contact if they lose it.

372

Speaking in Class

Speaking in class is an important part of learning. The guidelines below will help you and your classmates become better speakers.

- **Pay attention.** Listen to what others are saying and stay on the topic being discussed.
- **Think ahead.** Think before you speak. Be sure that you have something important to say.
- **Make eye contact.** Look at your classmates as you speak to them.
- **Wait your turn.** Show respect for others by not interrupting.
- **Get to the point.** State your ideas briefly and clearly.

> Respond politely to what others say.

Work on your speaking skills. The whole class can play the following game. Everyone should take a turn being the speaker.

1. The speaker pulls a topic from a hat (prepared by your teacher).
2. He or she talks for one minute about the topic. The speaker's turn ends if he or she jumps to a different topic, stops for more than five seconds, or does not keep eye contact with the audience.
3. After everyone is finished, the class votes for the best one-minute speech.

Teaching Tip: Speaking Skills

Some students who are self-conscious about making a "speech" in front of the class may be more comfortable if the opportunity to speak seems to arise naturally. Help them build confidence by regularly engaging students in conversations in front of the others. For example, on Monday mornings, routinely ask someone to talk about a weekend experience and ask questions that require sustained answers.

English Language Learners

The behaviors associated with speaking in class (staying on topic, waiting turns, and making eye contact) are not universal across all cultures. Observe students in a variety of settings to identify those who need specific instruction and practice in these behaviors. Point out that Americans value these behaviors, and provide practice opportunities in a one-on-one setting.

Giving Speeches

Sometimes, you just can't wait to tell your friends what you're up to, like taking tae kwon do, learning to play a saxophone, or building a model submarine. Your latest hobbies or new skills are good topics for speeches.

In this chapter, you will learn to give a how-to speech. You will find tips on planning your speech, using visual aids, and helping your listeners experience what you are explaining.

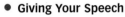

Mini Index

- **Preparing Your Speech**
- **Organizing a How-To Speech**
- **Giving Your Speech**

Giving Speeches

Objectives
- select a how-to essay to present as a speech
- prepare and organize a how-to speech
- practice and present a speech, using note cards and visual aids

To introduce the idea of public speaking, play several excerpts from speeches. Include famous speeches students already have heard and lesser-known ones. The American Rhetoric Web site (www.americanrhetoric.com) has a large collection of audio clips.

Point out that there are many opportunities to give speeches in school. Ask students to brainstorm a list of when they might be called upon to give a speech. Possible answers:

- making a show-and-tell presentation
- addressing the student body
- campaigning for office
- proposing an idea
- speaking in competitions
- accepting an award

Assure students that although giving a speech may seem scary, with careful preparation and lots of practice, they will be able to do it.

Materials

Audio clips of speeches (TE p. 373)

Preparing Your Speech

If students haven't written a how-to essay, suggest that they use one of their other expository or persuasive essays.

Ask students to use all of their planning notes and other materials they used to write the essay, as well as the essay itself. These may provide helpful information as they work on their speeches.

Have students work with partners to begin the process of converting their essays into speeches:

- Ask one student to read his or her essay to the other.
- Remind the listener to pay close attention as the essay is being read.
- Afterward, have the two students talk about the essay. Does the beginning grab attention? What might be some good ways of reworking it?
- Have the author of the essay take notes during the conversation to refer to later.
- Repeat the process so that the other student can read and get feedback.

374

Preparing Your Speech

If you want your audience to enjoy your speech, choose a topic that you find interesting. One of your completed how-to essays may be a good place to begin. Here's how to get started.

Rewriting in Action

In the opening of the original essay below ("Pinching for Fun," page 17), Fumi was excited about making a pinch pot. Notice how the rewritten speech beginning adds a new twist to grab the audience's attention.

Original Essay

Did you ever think pinching was fun? I did when I learned how to make a small bowl called a pinch pot. There are four steps to making a pinch pot: preparing, shaping, firing, and glazing.

Speech

"It's a snap. Just use your thumb and fingers to do this project." My art teacher surprised our class by telling us the tools we needed for our next project. We tried to guess what the project would be, but no one did. Then she told us the four steps: preparing, shaping, firing, and glazing. I remembered that my older sister had made a clay pinch pot, so I guessed right. I could hardly wait to start.

Rework your beginning. Choose an essay that you would like to present as a how-to speech. Rewrite your opening and add some drama to grab your audience's attention.

Giving Speeches   375

Using Visual Aids

After you write the beginning of your how-to speech, read through your essay and choose the main details for your speech. (Either list these separately or highlight them in your essay.) Next, decide what visual aids would help your listeners "see" and understand the details of your speech. Here are some possibilities:

Charts	compare ideas or explain main points.
Maps	show specific places being discussed.
Objects	allow your audience to see the real thing.
Photographs	help your audience see what you are talking about.
Posters	show words, pictures, or both.
Transparencies	highlight key words, ideas, or graphics.

The following tips will help you prepare your visual aids.

1 Make your visual aids big enough for classmates in the back of the room to see.

2 Use pictures and graphs with short, easy-to-read labels.

3 Make your visual aids colorful.

List ideas for visual aids. After you make your list, select two.

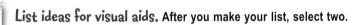

> * Clay models of each stage of the project
> Pictures of the stages from start to finish
> Chart listing the steps
> * Picture of the kiln

Using Visual Aids

Talk about the different kinds of charts students can choose to make as visual aids.

- The familiar Venn diagram or T-chart can be used to compare information.
- Bar graphs and line graphs can also show comparisons.
- Diagrams, drawings with labels, are good for explaining the parts of an object.
- A simple list is good for providing added detail, and writing just a single phrase or short sentence on a chart for a main point provides emphasis.

* For more about diagrams and graphs, see PE page 474.

Suggest that students consider drawing their charts, maps, or posters on transparencies instead of paper. Projections can always be made big enough for everyone to see.

English Language Learners

Students may find it easier to select visual aids if they understand what helps the listener "see" more clearly what they are trying to describe or tell about.

- Have students share their entire speech with the partner who helped them convert their essay into a speech (TE page 374).

- Encourage the partner to comment and/or ask questions that can be more clearly answered with the use of visual aids (for example, do you have a picture or map of ___?)

Organizing a How-To Speech

Ask students to look at the sample cards and point out the features that make them convenient for the speaker to use.

- The writing on the cards is very neat and easy to read.
- Each card is clearly numbered.
- Each one has a title at the top that tells the main point so the speaker only has to glance quickly at it to know what's on the card.
- Notes about when to use visual aids are included at the end in parentheses.

Suggest that students use a different color pencil or pen to write the instructions about visual aids on their cards. That way, they'll be able to see those notes more quickly.

Explain that the reason students don't write out word-for-word what they plan to say for the middle part of the speech is that this will help them to sound conversational and informal when they are speaking. It will also leave them free to make eye contact with the audience and to deal with visual aids, since they won't have to look down at their cards to read.

376

Organizing a How-To Speech

Next, you must organize the main details of your speech on note cards or pieces of paper. Except for the beginning and ending cards, which are written out word for word, short phrases will remind you what to say and what to do.

Sample Note Cards

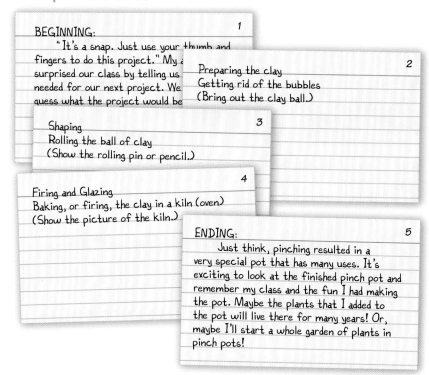

Card 1 — BEGINNING:
"It's a snap. Just use your thumb and fingers to do this project." My ... surprised our class by telling us ... needed for our next project. We ... guess what the project would be ...

Card 2 — Preparing the clay / Getting rid of the bubbles / (Bring out the clay ball.)

Card 3 — Shaping / Rolling the ball of clay / (Show the rolling pin or pencil.)

Card 4 — Firing and Glazing / Baking, or firing, the clay in a kiln (oven) / (Show the picture of the kiln.)

Card 5 — ENDING: Just think, pinching resulted in a very special pot that has many uses. It's exciting to look at the finished pinch pot and remember my class and the fun I had making the pot. Maybe the plants that I added to the pot will live there for many years! Or, maybe I'll start a whole garden of plants in pinch pots!

Create your note cards. Read the note cards on this page. Then create a note card for each step in your how-to speech. Write out your beginning and ending word for word.

Giving Your Speech

Giving Speeches **377**

After completing your note cards, you are ready to practice and present your speech.

Practicing Your Speech

Practice your speech several times. Use the following tips and the checklist at the bottom of the page.

- Practice in a quiet place, in front of a mirror, if possible.
- Practice in front of friends or parents. Listen to their suggestions.
- If possible, videotape or tape-record yourself.

Giving Your Speech

When you give your speech, remember the following guidelines.

- Look at your audience.
- Stand up straight.
- Speak loudly, clearly, and slowly.

Practicing Checklist

Number a piece of paper from 1 to 7. Practice your speech until you can answer "yes" to every question.

_____ **1.** Do I have good posture and look relaxed?

_____ **2.** Do I look at my audience as I speak?

_____ **3.** Can my voice be heard at the back of the room?

_____ **4.** Do I sound interested in my topic?

_____ **5.** Am I speaking slowly and clearly?

_____ **6.** Are my visual aids large and easy to understand?

_____ **7.** Do I point to information on my visual aids?

Giving Your Speech

Practicing Your Speech

Tell students how long their speeches should be and encourage them to time themselves as they practice. Explain that practice is one of the best ways to deal with **public speaking fears** (see below). The better they know the speech, the less likely they are to freeze up in front of an audience. Remind students to include using their visual aids in the practices.

Suggest that students write out the practicing checklist and ask the person who helps them practice to fill it out after the practice session.

Giving Your Speech

Devise hand signals to use to remind students of guidelines as they speak. Explain the signals and encourage students to glance at you occasionally to see if you are giving any signals. These might include the following:

- Look at the audience (point to eyes).
- Stand up straighter (touch shoulders and straighten up).
- Speak louder (cup hand to ear).
- Speak more slowly (hold hand up as if to say stop).

Teaching Tip: Public Speaking Fears

Many people are anxious about public speaking because

- they're nervous in front of an audience, and
- they worry that their ideas won't be well received.

To give students practice speaking in front of an audience without worrying about how their ideas are being received, have them present an*other person's* ideas instead of their own. As part of the preparation process for presenting their own speeches, hold a class event where each student recites a poem or delivers an excerpt from a historical speech.

English Language Learners

If the parents of your students do not speak English, make sure that whenever practicing before a parent is suggested, students have opportunities to practice in front of proficient English-speaking adults who can offer constructive suggestions. Develop a list of adults in the school and larger community who are willing to be trained to act as volunteer "listeners" during the school day.

Speaking Tips

Before students begin speaking, tell the class that there will be time for a question or two after each speech. Remind students to

- listen carefully to what's being said,
- jot down their questions if they want to,
- ask specific questions, and
- phrase their questions politely and clearly.

After everyone has given a speech, go through the Speaking Tips list, asking students to talk about their experiences with each of the items on the list.

Encourage students to bookmark the page and consult it anytime they need to make a speech in front of an audience.

378

SPEAKING TIPS

Before your speech . . .

- **Get everything organized.**
  Put the main points of your speech on note cards and make your visual aids.
- **Time your speech.**
  Read and talk through your note cards out loud. If your speech is too short or too long, add or remove details to adjust the length.
- **Practice.**
  The more you remember without looking at your notes, the easier it will be to give your speech.

During your speech . . .

- **Speak loudly.** Be sure that everyone can hear you.
- **Speak clearly and slowly.**
  Don't hurry through your speech.
- **Look at your audience.** Connect with your listeners.
- **Put visual aids where everyone can see them.**
  Point out the things that you are talking about.

After your speech . . .

- **Answer questions.**
  Ask if anyone has questions about your topic.
- **Collect materials.**
  Gather your visual aids and note cards and return to your seat.

Practice and present. Practice your speech one more time with a friend or family member. After you present your speech in the classroom, listen for suggestions from your teacher or classmates.

English Language Learners

Students may worry so much about how long or short their speech is, they may find it difficult to concentrate on the elements of organization and presentation. Provide support by helping them focus on one or two of the speaking tips until they are more confident with speaking in English. Organizing and delivering short speeches will help create this confidence.

Keeping Journals and Learning Logs

What is a learning log? Is it a piece of wood that goes to school? Is it a "board of education"? Of course not. A learning log is a notebook where you can write about the things you are learning . . . and become a better student.

What is a journal? A journal is a notebook where you write about your life. Can writing in a journal be a valuable experience? Well, some of the greatest people in history kept journals, so the answer is yes! The following chapter will show you how to start a journal and a learning log.

Mini Index

Keeping Journals and Learning Logs

Objectives
- understand the purpose of keeping a variety of journals
- understand the purpose of keeping learning logs in different curriculum areas
- learn strategies for writing in journals and learning logs

Talk with students about the words *journal* and *log*. Explain that both mean "an account of day-to-day events." However, they usually represent different kinds of account.

- A journal writer uses most of the traits of writing—ideas, organization, voice, word choice, and sentence fluency. A journal is like an ongoing first draft of a personal narrative.
- A log is an ongoing listing of notes about a particular subject. The focus is on ideas and organization—that is, on presenting information clearly and concisely.

Explain to students that in this section they'll try writing in a journal and in a learning log. Encourage them to consider keeping up with one or both even after they have finished working on them for class.

Materials

Sample journal and diary entries from published books (TE p. 380)

Copy Masters/ Transparencies

Sensory chart (TE p. 381)

KWL chart (TE p. 386)

Keeping a Personal Journal

Ask students if any of them keep, or have ever kept, a journal. Discuss the kinds of things one **can write in a journal** (see below). Invite those who have kept a journal to share the kinds of things they wrote in them (general topics, not specific details). Why did they start writing it? If they stopped writing, why did they stop?

Getting Started

Discuss the suggestions for starting a journal. Encourage students to share their own ideas and offer your own practical suggestions as well. These might include the following:

- People whose writing tends to be crooked should use books with lined paper.
- Fancy blank books can be intimi-dating—some writers worry that what they have to say won't be as pretty as their book. An inexpensive notebook is often best.
- Try to schedule writing time at the same time every day so it becomes a habit.

380

Keeping a Personal Journal

A personal journal is a special place to explore ideas, feelings, and experiences. You can write about people, events, ups and downs, and anything else in your life.

Getting Started

Follow these steps to begin your personal journal.

1 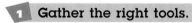 **Gather the right tools.**

All you need is a notebook and a pen or pencil. Some people buy a special book with blank pages. You could also use a computer and print or save your pages.

2 Find a special time and place to write.

Find a quiet place where you can write every day. Try to write freely for 5 to 10 minutes. As you continue to keep a journal, writing for this amount of time will become easier for you.

3 Write about what is important to you.

Here are some suggestions:

- Special events or memories
- Big things and little things
- What you see and what you hear
- Thoughts and feelings you want to capture or work through

4 Keep it organized.

Write the date at the beginning of each entry. Whenever you read your journal, underline ideas that you would like to write more about later.

 Start your journal writing. Write in a personal journal for two weeks for at least 5 to 10 minutes a day. At the end of that time, put a star next to your favorite entry.

Teaching Tip: What Can You Write in a Journal?

Read samples from published diaries, both nonfiction and fictional, to demonstrate the various things people write in journals. Possible sources of samples:

- *Anne Frank: Diary of a Young Girl* by Anne Frank (nonfiction)
- Journals related to the Lewis and Clark expedition (different books and online sources available)

- *Zlata's Diary* by Zlata Filipovic (nonfiction)
- *A Gathering of Days: A New England Girl's Journal* by Joan Blos (fiction)
- *Harriet the Spy* by Louise Fitzhugh (fiction)

Struggling Learners

Teach the following to students who can't think of what to write:

- Close your eyes. Think about what you "see."
- Open your eyes and draw a quick sketch in your journal.
- Write three sentences to describe the picture you sketched.
- Then write one or more sentences that say what you feel when you look at the picture.

Keeping Journals and Learning Logs **381**

Journal Entries

In the journal entry below, a student writes about why she especially likes one season of the year.

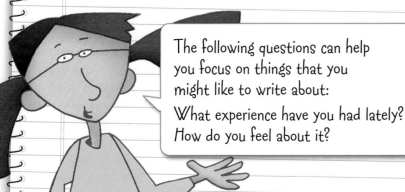

> Oct. 12
>
> The leaves crackled under my feet when I walked home from school today. I walked slower because it was warm, and I liked the crunching sounds. A blanket of yellow leaves covered the ground. The trees were yellow, too.
>
> The air smelled damp and moldy this morning. By this afternoon, it was dry and fresh.
>
> Mom taped orange, red, and yellow leaves in the front windows. Our front steps are piled with pumpkins. Cornstalks and a bale of straw guard the front door.
>
> It's getting colder outside, but I feel warm inside. For me, fall (Grandma calls it autumn) is the best time of year.

The following questions can help you focus on things that you might like to write about:

What experience have you had lately? How do you feel about it?

Journal Entries

After students have read the entry, talk about it as a class.

- Do students share the writer's feelings about fall?
- What verbs did she choose that make her description vivid? (*crackled, piled, guard*)
- What phrases show that she likes fall? (*I liked the crunching, I feel warm inside, fall is the best time of year*)
- What are students' own favorite seasons? Why?

Afterward, have students take out pencil and paper and write for five to ten minutes about their favorite season. Encourage them to

- think of this as a kind of freewriting—the main goal is to enjoy putting their ideas down on paper,
- pretend they are writing a letter to their best friend,
- use strong words, and
- focus on a specific example.

Encourage them not to

- worry about spelling or grammar mistakes,
- pause for too long, or
- try to describe too much at once—they can always write another journal entry.

English Language Learners

Some students may not be familiar with the specific seasonal changes described in the sample journal entry. Before asking them to read the entry and write about their favorite season, set the stage. Explain that the writer lives in a place where days get colder and the leaves turn many colors.

Struggling Learners

If students have trouble getting started, remind them that they can use their five senses to describe the season by asking themselves:

- What can I see?
- What can I hear?
- What can I smell?
- What can I taste?
- What can I touch?

To help students keep track of their thoughts, provide photocopies of the reproducible sensory chart (TE page 646).

Writing in Other Journals

Discuss how these kinds of journals differ from a personal journal. Remind students that in a personal journal they record their thoughts and feelings.

- A diary focuses on daily events. It is usually a simple record of what you do each day. Point out, however, that in her diary, Anne Frank not only recorded daily events but also her thoughts and feelings.

- A reader-response journal is a record of what you have read and is helpful when you have to write book reports. Suggest that students write in a reader-response journal while still reading a book, not just after finishing it, so that they'll have a record of how their feelings progress.

- Students can keep a travel journal even if they don't leave town. Suggest that they write about a trip to the mall or the park.

Point out that students can include entries about daily events, trips around town, and books they're reading, as well as their thoughts and feelings, in a personal journal.

Writing in Other Journals

Personal journals can help you keep track of your thoughts and experiences. Here are three more journals you can try.

Diary

A diary is a personal journal that focuses on day-to-day events in your life. You usually make entries in a diary every day.

Reader-Response Journal

A reader-response journal will help you better understand whatever you read. As you read a book or a story, you can write your thoughts and answer questions like these:

1 Is this book funny? Sad? Surprising?

2 Are there any connections between my life and the story?

3 Would I recommend this book to others? Why or why not?

Travel Journal

In a travel journal, you write about a trip. Whether you take a bus downtown or travel for weeks, you can write about your experience.

> July 5
> We drove up Going to the Sun Highway. Glacier Park was cool but sunny at Logan Pass. We had on shorts, but there was snow everywhere. We hiked along the wooden walkways. Suddenly, I saw a furry animal. It looked like a woodchuck. Someone yelled, "There's a marmot!" Next I heard a roar like thunder. People were shouting and pointing. A cloud of snow exploded as an avalanche roared down a nearby mountain. Wow!

 Write in a travel journal. The next time you take a long or short trip, record your thoughts and feelings in a travel journal.

Advanced Learners

To further develop the art of journaling, encourage students to write pretend entries about themselves

- in an imaginary situation or
- as a historical figure or story character in a particular set of circumstances.

When finished, invite students to share their fictional journals with the class, adding costumes and props if desired.

Keeping Journals and Learning Logs **383**

Writing in a Learning Log

In a learning log, you write about a subject you are studying. It's a place to explore how new information connects to your own experiences. Here are some tips.

1 Set up a learning log for any subject.
Learning logs can help you understand new ideas and information in all your classes.

2 Keep your logs organized.
Use a separate notebook for each subject or divide a notebook into sections. Date each entry and leave room to answer questions you jot down . . . or to ask new questions later.

3 Make drawings and charts.
Diagrams and pictures can help you understand and remember new ideas.

4 Write freely about . . .
- thoughts or feelings about a subject or an assignment.
- questions you have.
- new ideas or information.

Science Class   Oct. 18

          Sounds

Sounds are caused by vibrations.

- Put your hand on your throat.
- Say the word "sound."
- Feel the vibrations.
- The same thing happens when you play a guitar.
- The strings vibrate.

Writing in a Learning Log

Explain that writing in a learning log is different from taking notes in class. The log should be compiled outside of class and should include the notes students took in class, as well as their own ideas and thoughts about the subject.

Talk about ways students could organize their logs, such as the following:

- Use easy-to-read formats for presenting facts, like the one shown in the sample.
- To make the log easy to scan, create symbols to identify the various types of items in the log. For example,
  - write a capital *T* in the margin next to thoughts or feelings, a question mark for questions, and a large *I* next to information; or
  - use different colors of ink for each.
- Number the pages in the log so you can refer to entries by page number.
- When you answer a question, make a check in the margin beside it and note the page number where the answer is.

English Language Learners

Many students come from cultures that discourage asking questions. Do a Think-Aloud to model the types of questions they could include in learning logs. Role play being the writer of the sample entry, and ask, "What is a *guitar*?" To reinforce including questions in learning logs, do Think-Alouds and/or elicit questions from one or two students each time you ask them to write an entry.

Social Studies Log

If the schedule permits, provide time for students to practice writing in a learning log.

- Decide on a day when students will take notes during social studies (or another) class.
- Afterward, give students time to write an entry in their learning logs. Encourage them to refer to the notes they took.
- Divide the class into small groups and have students compare log entries. Did they focus on similar information? Did they have questions in common? What were the differences in their log entries?

After the groups have had time to talk, have students work on their own again to write a follow up to their first log entry. Ask them to

- add answers other students were able to provide to their questions,
- incorporate additional information that their group meeting reminded them of or brought up, and
- include their thoughts about the group conference.

384

Social Studies Log

You can use learning logs for any subject. In the sample below, a student writes about an upcoming test. She figures out a way to remember the map of her state.

> Social Studies   Oct. 1
>   Map of Wisconsin
>
>   On Friday's test I have to draw the outline of
> Wisconsin and name the capital, marked with a star.
> Then I have to label the boundaries all the way around.
>   I'll remember the state's shape by thinking of a
> left-hand mitten with the palm down. The capital's
> star goes above the middle of the wrist. Here are the
> boundaries:
> —Illinois across the bottom
> —Lake Michigan up the
>   right side
> —the state of Michigan
>   and Lake Superior on
>   the top
> —the St. Croix River and
>   the Mississippi River
>   down the left side

Log on in math or social studies. On your own paper, write about something you are studying in math or social studies. Use your own words and make a drawing.

Struggling Learners

Explain that remembering the shape of Wisconsin by picturing a left-hand, palm-down mitten is an example of a *mnemonic device*, or memory trick. Brainstorm other situations in which mnemonic devices might be helpful, such as remembering:

- the order of the planets
- certain spelling patterns
- the 9's facts in multiplication
- the line notes on a music staff
- an important telephone number

Encourage students to think of helpful mnemonic devices that can facilitate their own learning and to record them in their learning logs.

Writing-to-Learn Activities

There are many ways to write and learn in your learning logs. The next two pages cover six writing ideas.

The Basic Three

Clustering A cluster shows you a picture of how your ideas fit together. Write the subject in the middle of a page and circle it. Around the subject, write words and phrases about it. (See page 454.)

Listing This activity can give you a long list of ideas, feelings, and questions. Write words and phrases that come to mind about your subject.

Freewriting Freewriting is fast writing. Your ideas flow from your mind onto the paper until you run out of them. See the example below.

Health Class   February 18

The Skeletal System

All the systems of the body help each other. A good example is the skeletal system. I used to think that bones just help people stand up. But, they do something else. They protect us. The bones of the skull protect our brains. A soft spot on a baby's head is where the bones haven't come together yet. Bones also protect the circulatory system. The ribs make a cage for the heart and lungs. Bones sure do a lot more than I thought.

Freewriting Try freewriting about something you are learning in one of your classes. First, write the subject and the date at the top of the page. Then, write until you run out of ideas.

Writing-to-Learn Activities

Encourage students to become familiar with all six ideas for presenting information in a learning log. Each is useful in different ways.

The Basic Three

Show students how to use each of the three writing ideas.

- Model the clustering method by reminding students of a lesson that you recently taught them and creating a cluster for it on the board. Clustering is useful for representing information related to a central topic.
- Have students expand the cluster you've created into a list. As they call out their ideas, list them on the board. Point out that lists are similar to clusters, but are a better way of organizing large numbers of details that would make an overcrowded cluster.
- Invite students to base their freewriting on the cluster and the list on the board. Explain that freewriting is a good way to capture feelings and thoughts about a subject.

English Language Learners

Focusing on meaning and thinking how to express ideas in a second language require time. Some students' concerns about appearance and correctness interfere with getting their ideas on paper. If students have difficulty freewriting more than two or three sentences in the allotted time,

- emphasize that it is okay to make mistakes in spelling, grammar, and word choice when they write in their learning logs; and
- stress that they will make fewer mistakes the more they write.

More Writing-to-Learn Activities

Point out that the KWL chart provides an alternative format for arranging information in a log. Instead of listing facts learned, questions, and answers vertically on the page, in a KWL chart these items are set side by side in columns.

Provide photocopies of the reproducible KWL chart (TE page 649) for students to keep in their learning logs.

Consider placing a box in the classroom where students can leave notes with their questions to you.

- Collect and evaluate the notes every few days.
- Set aside class time to provide answers for the whole group and invite discussion.
- Tell students that they don't have to sign their name to the question—they may also request to receive their answer privately.
- Invite students to submit comments and ideas to the box, as well as questions.
- Remind students to make a note in their log when they submit a question or comment and to add more notes after it is addressed.

More Writing-to-Learn Activities

Here are three more ways to write and learn.

First Thoughts Make a list of key words that come to mind before you begin to study a new topic. In a Know-Want-Learn (KWL) chart, these words would be what you already know. Thinking about what you already know helps you begin to ask what you want or need to know. Writing down your first thoughts prepares you to learn new information.

KWL Reading Strategy		
Know	Want to know	Learned
–West Nile virus kills birds.	How is it affecting birds in my state?	

Notes to the Teacher Write down questions you have about the subject. Ask your teacher to respond to your questions in writing or in a class discussion.

Dear Mrs. Johnson,
   Would you please explain the difference between "lend" and "borrow" again?

   Thanks,
   Charlie

Drawing Add pictures and charts to your learning log to show what you have learned or thought about.

Practice

Think about a subject or topic that is hard for you. Then write a question about it. Ask your teacher to respond.

Advanced Learners

Explain that the KWL reading strategy is an ongoing process. The more we know, the more we want to know! For example, a student might set out to learn about pet care but then become interested in exotic pets, table foods that are harmful to certain animals, or how to become a veterinarian—leading to new explorations.

Encourage students who become very interested in a topic to continue adding questions and answers to their KWL chart as an ongoing activity.

Taking Notes

Musicians play beautiful notes, people write polite thank-you notes, and students take class notes. But they should never *pass* notes. How confusing! Just what should you do with notes?

The answer is simple. Always take notes to remember important ideas from class. Then read your notes when you do assignments or study for tests. Take note! This chapter will help you improve your note-taking skills.

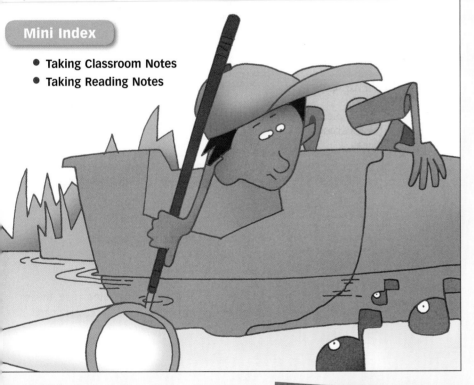

Materials

Index cards and sticky notes or scrap paper (TE p. 391)

Dollar bills and coins (TE p. 392)

Taking Notes

Objectives
- learn guidelines for taking classroom notes
- learn tips for taking reading notes
- use graphic organizers for taking notes

Invite a volunteer to look up the word *note* in a dictionary and tell the class what its roots are. (It comes from the Latin word *nota,* which means "mark.") Talk about what the different kinds of notes mentioned in this introduction have in common. Possible answers:

- Notes condense information into a brief form.
- Notes are often used for remembering things (even thank-you notes are a way of reminding yourself and the giver of a kindness).

Shopping lists, date books, and to-do lists are other common notes people use to remember things. Share a story of a mishap that occurred when you forgot to take good notes. (This could be as simple as forgetting a crucial ingredient for a recipe because you didn't make a shopping list.) Invite students to share their stories too.

Copy Masters/ Transparencies

Graphic organizers (TE p. 388)

Time line (TE p. 391)

T-chart (TE p. 392)

Taking Classroom Notes

Guidelines for Taking Good Notes

Invite students to discuss what they find hard about taking notes in class. Some may have difficulty identifying which ideas are most important.

After reviewing the guidelines for taking good notes, suggest some **other useful strategies** *(see below)*. For example, explain that listening for answers to the familiar 5 W questions—*who, what, when, where,* and *why*—will help them pick out important information.

- **Who**: Write down any names mentioned (along with a description of who they are).
- **What**: What topic is being explained at the moment? Listen carefully and try to summarize it.
- **When**: Write down any dates mentioned (and don't forget to add *what* happened then).
- **Where**: Write down place names (and *what* happened there).
- **Why**: Listen carefully as the teacher explains a reason for something, jotting down the key words. Then later, summarize the reason in your own words.

388

Taking Classroom Notes

Taking notes during class can help you remember information. Writing down important facts and ideas helps you . . .

- listen carefully,
- pay attention,
- remember what you hear, and
- review and study what you have learned.

Guidelines for Taking Good Notes

These guidelines will help you improve your note-taking skills.

> Listen carefully!
> 1. Pay close attention.
> 2. Write down information that the teacher puts on the board or on an overhead projector.

> Summarize!
> 1. Write down only the important ideas.
> 2. Draw pictures if they help you understand the ideas.

> Get organized!
> 1. Write the subject and date at the top of each page of notes.
> 2. Use numbers to organize your notes (1, 2, 3).
> 3. Check your notes and recopy anything that is hard to read.

Take class notes. The next time you take notes, use these guidelines. Also look over the sample set of notes on the next page.

Teaching Tip: Other Useful Strategies

Explain that teachers usually give many verbal hints that they're about to say something important, and students can learn to pick up on these hints. For example:

- Telling how many things they're going to talk about—*There are two reasons for this . . .* (Listen for that many important points.)
- Stating the topic directly—*I'm going to tell you about . . .*

(Expect an important subject to follow.)
- Asking questions, then immediately answering them—*Why did that happen? Well, . . .* (Expect an important explanation.)
- Repeating a word—*The process of osmosis . . . OSMOSIS . . . is . . .* (Write down the repeated word and listen for the definition.)

English Language Learners

Note-taking is difficult for students who are acquiring the skills and vocabulary needed for listening to a new language and identifying main ideas and details. Help students focus by providing graphic organizers (TE pages 645–651) for note-taking. Have them compare notes with proficient English speakers after each class and add new information/questions to their learning logs.

Taking Notes **389**

Setting Up Two-Column Notes

Two-column notes help you organize information. Fold your paper or draw a line that makes the left column narrower than the right column. Write key ideas on the left and related details on the right. You can also add drawings, questions, or comments.

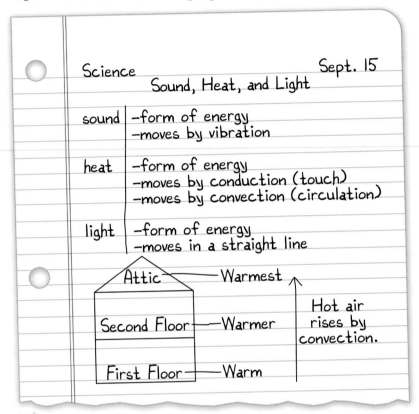

 Review your notes. After you take notes, read them over. Are they clear and complete? Add comments or drawings like the diagram shown above to help you understand the material.

Setting Up Two-Column Notes

Ask students to talk about what makes this a good example of note taking. Possible answers:

- The class name and date at the top tell when and where the notes were taken.
- The title at the top clearly tells what three key ideas will be talked about.
- Specialized words (*conduction, convection*) are defined.
- The drawing illustrates heat rising with the familiar example of a house.
- The handwriting is very neat.

Encourage students to write as neatly as they can without getting too wrapped up in forming the letters. Point out that having neat writing will help them throughout their lives, in school and out.

- Taking notes that they can easily read later will help them study more effectively.
- They won't lose credit on assignments because a word was too hard for a teacher to read—sometimes neatness can even mean extra credit.
- Family and friends will be able to read their letters and notes.

Struggling Learners

Diagrams like the one in the sample notes can help visual learners remember the information. Students can also use shapes or symbols to capture important points. For example, five ideas can be recorded on the points of a star. Other options are:

- four ideas – corners of a square
- three ideas – points of a triangle
- two ideas – tops of the lines in a letter V

Point out that the information listed next to *sound, heat,* and *light* could be recorded on a V and on a triangle. Model this on the board.

Taking Reading Notes

Explain that these instructions are designed for taking notes on nonfiction, such as a social studies textbook, but students can also adapt the idea for fiction.

- When reading a fiction assignment for the first time, don't skim. Read to enjoy the story. *Then* go back and skim so you can take notes.
- Make notes about story and character details, vocabulary words, and questions and predictions you had when you read the first time.
- Copy out quotations you like. Put quotation marks around them and note what page they're on.

If your schedule permits, extend the **Practice** exercise:

- Have students work on their own to read the chapter and take notes.
- Have partners get back together and compare notes. Did their predictions turn out to be correct? Did they highlight similar key points?
- Have students talk as a class about the assignment. Did their partner teach them something about how to take good notes?

Taking Reading Notes

Taking notes will help you understand and remember what you read. Whenever you read an assignment, keep your notebook handy to write down key ideas and details. Here are some tips to follow.

Preview the Assignment

Skim the assigned reading to see what it is about. You can get clues from . . .

- **titles,**
- **headings,** and
- **photos, illustrations, and graphs.**

Take Notes

As you read, write down . . .

- **headings** and subheadings,
- **details** about the main ideas,
- **information** shown on charts and other graphics,
- **new vocabulary words** often in bold print, and
- **questions** about things that you don't understand.

Organize Your Thoughts

Add to your notes by drawing . . .

- **diagrams,**
- **charts,** or
- **graphic organizers** (see pages 456–457).

Practice

With a partner, preview a chapter that you haven't read in science or social studies. Use the preview guidelines above and predict what the chapter will be about.

English Language Learners

Students may have learned to rely on copying sentences verbatim to help them remember how to express ideas in their new language. Explain that this is not the way to take notes. Provide note-taking practice by expanding the **Practice** activity. Pair students with proficient English speakers.

- After partners preview the chapter, have them use the note-taking guidelines to take notes together.
- Have the English speaker show their partner how they write down details and information without copying it verbatim.

Remind all students that notes do not have to be written as complete sentences. This also helps discourage copying verbatim.

Using a Time Line

Many reading assignments are about important events in history. You can organize history notes by making a **time line**, which lists events in the order in which they happened.

Read the following paragraph. Then study the time line to see how the information is listed in time order.

America's Earliest Colony Settled by Europeans

Columbus, sent by Spain, landed in the West Indies (North America) in 1492. However, many people think that America's first European colony was established more than 100 years later, in 1607. That year, England founded Jamestown, Virginia. Still, long before that, in 1513, Ponce de Leon explored Florida for Spain. By 1565, Spain had settled St. Augustine, Florida—the first permanent European colony in America.

Time Line

1492	Columbus lands in the West Indies.
1513	Ponce de Leon explores Florida.
1565	Spain settles St. Augustine, Florida.
1607	English settlers establish Jamestown, Virginia.

Practice

Create a time line for the information in the paragraph below.

By 1700, the European population of the American colonies was 250,000. The first settlers came slowly, though. The English sent 110 settlers to Jamestown in 1608 to help replace the original settlers. Of the 105 sent in 1607, only 32 were alive after the first winter. Slowly, the number of colonists grew. In 1620, 101 more English came on the *Mayflower*. Later, 30 Dutch families settled in New York in 1624.

Using a Time Line

Before students begin the **Practice** activity, suggest that they

■ read the paragraph through at least once before starting;

■ skim the paragraph, looking for dates, then write them on scrap paper;

■ number the dates from first to last and put them in order on the time line; and

■ add brief summaries of the events next to the dates.

Provide copies of the reproducible time line (TE page 648) for students to use.

Note that the verbs in time lines are usually in the present tense (so, instead of *Columbus landed,* they would write *Columbus lands*).

Practice Answers

Wording will vary.

1607—32 of the original 105 English settlers at Jamestown survive the first winter.

1608—110 new settlers come from England to Jamestown.

1620—101 English colonists arrive on the *Mayflower*.

1624—30 Dutch families settle in New York.

1700—250,000 European colonists live in America.

English Language Learners

Some students may have little or no knowledge of grade-level social studies topics and may be especially confused by the dates associated with the topics. To help them identify and order the events, have them

• write the dates on the top of individual index cards as they skim the paragraph,

• record the event in three or four words and/or pictures under the date, and then

• arrange the note cards in chronological order on a time line.

Struggling Learners

To give students more examples to study, have them use sticky notes or scrap paper to bookmark time lines in their content area textbooks. Then discuss the different ways the time lines are displayed:

• vertically or horizontally
• using dates or times
• using phrases or sentences
• with photos or drawings added

Using a T-Chart

Point out that T-charts are a good choice for notes about descriptions of two ideas, especially if they're presented in list form.

Guide students through the process used to create the sample T-chart:

- Have students read the paragraph and point out the wording that identifies the two topics. (*The euro has seven different <u>bills</u> and eight <u>coins</u>.*)
- Draw their attention to sentences in the paragraph that list details about each topic.
- Note that the sample T-chart lists the details in the exact order they appear in the paragraph.

Distribute photocopies of the reproducible T-chart (TE page 645) for students to use as they complete the **Practice** activity. Tell them to follow the above process.

Practice **Answers**

Types of Writing

Fiction	Nonfiction
tall tales	autobiographies
novels	biographies
folklore	histories
science fiction	personal diaries
	science books

392

Using a T-Chart

Writing is often organized around main ideas. Each main idea is supported by details. A **T-chart** will help you take notes when you have two types of information. The chart label names the main idea, and each column lists one type of details. (See page **204**.)

Read the following paragraph. Then look at the T-chart to see how the information is organized.

The Euro

In 2002, the currency in many European countries changed to euros. The euro has seven different bills and eight coins. The bills are available in 5, 10, 20, 50, 100, 200, and 500 euro values. There are 1 euro and 2 euros coins, also. In addition, there are coins available for 1, 2, 5, 10, 20, and 50 euro cents.

T-Chart

The Euro in European Countries	
Euro Bills	Euro Coins
5	1 euro
10	2 euros
20	1 cent
50	2 cents
100	5 cents
200	10 cents
500	20 cents
	50 cents

Create a T-chart. After you read the following paragraph, create a T-chart for the information it contains.

Writing can be divided between fiction and nonfiction. Some examples of fiction are tall tales, novels, folklore, and science fiction. Nonfiction includes autobiographies, biographies, histories, and diaries. Science books are also nonfiction.

English Language Learners

Students may not understand the vocabulary associated with currency (bills and coins), so they may find the paragraph about euros confusing. Display different American dollar bills and coins and label them *bills* and *coins*. Introduce the paragraph about euros by telling students they will be reading about bills and coins used in other countries.

Improving Viewing Skills

Do you know how to watch TV? That sounds silly, doesn't it? After all, it's simple to plop down and turn on the TV. What isn't easy, however, is to turn on your brain while you watch TV.

Always use your eyes *and* your brain when viewing TV or surfing the Internet. This is important because the information you get from those sources is sometimes incomplete or incorrect. This chapter will help you use your brain to improve your viewing skills.

Mini Index

- Watching the News
- Watching Television Specials
- Being Aware of Commercials
- Viewing Web Sites

Improving Viewing Skills

Objectives
- learn how to be aware when watching the news, television specials, and commercials
- learn how to evaluate Web sites for reliability

There may be students whose television viewing is monitored or who aren't allowed to watch at all. Send home a letter explaining what students are studying and requesting parents' cooperation. Alternatively, viewing TV programs made for kids in the classroom will take the pressure off students who don't watch TV, as well as those who have limited viewing.

Talk to students about when and why they watch television.
- Do they have rules about their TV viewing?
- What do they watch most often? Cartoons? Movies?
- Do they usually watch with somebody else or alone?
- Do they ever discuss what they see on TV with their family and friends?

Materials

Videotape of news broadcast
(TE p. 394)

Videotape of television special
(TE p. 395)

Posterboard and drawing supplies
(TE p. 396)

Selection of TV and print ads
(TE p. 397)

Copy Masters/ Transparencies

5 W's chart (TE p. 394)

Watching the News

Focus on the inclusion of *how* with the 5 W questions in item 1. Explain that journalists are taught to provide answers to all six of these questions when they write a story.

Distribute photocopies of the reproducible 5W's chart (TE p. 647) and have students add *how*. Invite them to include *how* anytime they use a 5 W's chart to organize information.

Draw students' attention to item 2—making sure facts are correct. Can they apply what they've learned about writing to the example here? (The reporter uses general wording to try to hide the fact that he doesn't have something specific to say.) Note that a good news story will contain strong words and specific details—just like a good student essay. (As news viewers, they must still be alert to the possibility that even specific details could be incorrect, though!)

Show students a videotape of a newscast and have them fill out the 5 W's and H chart. Possible sources for taping news for kids include The Weekly Reader company's *Teen Kids News* (www.weeklyreader.com), and the cable station Nickelodeon's *Nick News* (www.nick.com).

394

Watching the News

Remember that the people who put together news programs decide what you will hear and see. When you watch the news, ask yourself whether the information is complete, correct, and fair.

1 Complete: Are you getting enough information?

A news story should answer the 5 W's and H about an event.

How? *Who?* *What?*
Using climate records, scientists have been studying weather patterns
When? *Why?*
for the last 10 years to discover the cause of a serious drought
Where?
in the American Southwest.

2 Correct: Are you sure of the facts?

When reporters are unsure of their facts, they use special words like those in blue in the following sentence:

There are reports **that everyone in the United States will own an airplane by 2012,** according to sources in Washington.

3 Fair: Are both sides of the story presented fairly?

A newscast should tell the whole story, not just one side of it. Think about the facts and pictures included in the news story.

The city council says that more parking spaces are needed downtown. (The camera shows a street where all the spaces are filled.)

Think about it: Are the parking spaces filled on *all* the streets downtown? Are the spaces filled *all* the time?

 Respond to a newscast. The next time you watch a news story, answer the 5W and H questions about it to see if it is complete. (See number 1 above.)

Advanced Learners

Invite students to create skits to illustrate the three points on this page. For example:

- Demonstrate an incomplete and a complete news story.
- Present information with vague and then strong words.
- Give one side and then the other side of an issue.

Improving Viewing Skills **395**

Watching Television Specials

You may be assigned to watch a TV special, a program about one topic. Here are some tips to help you learn from this kind of program:

1 Before viewing . . .
- Write down facts you already know about the topic.
- Write down questions you have about the subject.

2 During viewing . . .
- Watch and listen for the answers to your questions.
- Take a few notes. Write down main ideas and details.
- Ask yourself whether the information is complete, correct, and fair. (See page 394.)

3 After viewing . . .
- Compare notes with someone else who saw the special.
- Write about the program in your learning log.

Notes from TV special about whales   Feb. 15

   I already knew that whales are mammals before I watched the special. Some people think that whales are fish. But I didn't know that whales are the biggest creatures that have ever lived. They're even bigger than the biggest dinosaurs!
   I also didn't know that some whales can live as long as humans. Too much hunting and pollution are killing the whales. Some kinds of whales are endangered.

Respond to a TV special. In a learning-log entry, write what you learned from a television special.

Watching Television Specials

Select a television special to screen. Ideally, the topic will be one students are learning about in class.

Have students prepare as a group for watching the program:
- Ask them to brainstorm what they know about the topic, as well as questions. Write these on the board as students call them out.
- Invite students to talk about other specials they've seen. What were they about? Did they enjoy them?
- Encourage them to predict how the special might present information. Interviews with experts? Film footage? Dramatic reenactments?

After showing the program, have students work independently to write learning log entries about it. Returning to the larger group, discuss the following:
- Were their questions answered? If so, how? What questions weren't answered?
- Did they learn anything surprising? What?
- Could the show have been improved? How?

Advanced Learners

Invite students to discuss how TV stations use previews to draw in viewers and get them to think about a certain topic or scenario so they'll be motivated to watch the program. Have students discuss how watching previews can help them brainstorm and predict in order to get more out of watching the show. Ask:

- What previews have you seen that were particularly effective?
- What previews have you seen that left you feeling let down after the program was over?

Checking What You Watch

- After reviewing the page, ask students to raise their hands if they're one of those people who wants complete quiet while watching TV. Do they shush anyone who says the slightest word? Explain that although it's distracting to have people talking during a TV show, there are times when a brief discussion could be helpful. For example, students could have a quick reality, fact, or bias check when they see something questionable. Encourage them to talk with their families about what they've learned in class so they can start discussing ideas when they watch TV. Distribute drawing supplies and posterboard.
- Have students make "Using Your Brain" posters about television watching.
- Encourage them to include information from all of the pages they've covered in the section so far.
- Display the posters in the room for a few days, and then have students take them home to show their families.

396

Checking What You Watch

It's fun to watch television, but it's also important to think about what you're watching. Do the following three checks.

Reality Check ● Some shows made for entertainment look real, but they aren't. Medical emergencies, car chases, and other scenes may be exaggerated to create excitement.

Fact-based programs (documentaries) often act out events that have actually happened, like the landing of the *Mayflower*. If the event is more recent, the program may use real movie footage along with scenes performed by actors. Try to tell the difference between what is real and what is staged.

Fact Check ● An athlete or a movie star on TV may give an opinion like "Everyone should become a vegetarian." Remember that famous people are not necessarily experts on what you should eat, wear, or do.

Prejudice Check ● A prejudice is a strong feeling held without a good reason. One type of prejudice, called a stereotype, unfairly says that all members of a group are a certain way. Here is an example of a stereotype:

> Old people live in the past. They don't want anything to change.

Some old people may not want change, but many do want it. Watch for prejudice on television. Don't judge an entire group by the actions of one member.

Log your viewing. Make entries in your learning log the next time you watch TV. Try to record one example of each of the following:

1 A program that looks like reality, but is not real
2 A reporter, an actor, or other personality who states an opinion
3 A character or statement that shows prejudice

Advanced Learners

In addition to television, periodicals provide opportunities to discern reality, facts, and biases. Have students extend their awareness of these issues by searching newspapers and magazines for examples of each of the three items in the Log your viewing activity. Invite students to create a bulletin board to provide visual examples for the class.

Improving Viewing Skills **397**

Being Aware of Commercials

Television commercials have only one purpose—to get you to buy things. Here are five common selling methods:

Selling Methods	On Television	In Real Life
1 Slice of Life looks like everyday life.	A happy family is eating Cheesy Chicken Bits for lunch.	Actors are being paid to look happy. They may never eat Cheesy Chicken Bits.
2 Famous Faces shows a celebrity using a product.	Your favorite athlete drinks Power Juice during a game.	Celebrities are paid to appear in commercials. No law says they must use the product.
3 Just the Facts focuses on a fact about the product.	Health Watch Bacon is low in carbohydrates.	All bacon is low in carbohydrates. But bacon is high in fat.
4 Problem-Solution shows a product solving a problem.	A boy is bored until his parents buy him the latest video game.	Most problems have a number of solutions, not just one.
5 Infomercial looks like a TV show.	One kitchen machine fixes a whole meal for you.	People are being paid to sell the product.

 Respond to a commercial. Watch several commercials on television. Try to find an example of each selling method listed above.

Being Aware of Commercials

Invite students to tell the class about a commercial they've seen.

- What made them remember it?
- Did it make them want to buy the product?
- Did it use any of the selling strategies described? If so, which one?

Mention other selling methods. One example is unbelievably delicious-looking food. In reality, a lot of food in ads isn't what it appears to be at all. For example, ice cream melts quickly, so a food stylist might use vegetable shortening instead. The law says ad makers have to show the actual food they're selling—but if they're selling hot fudge sauce, it doesn't have to be on a scoop of real ice cream!

Show a selection of TV ads and discuss the strategies used. (There are terrific archives of commercials available online. See www.advertisementave.com.) Display and talk about examples of print ads as well. Encourage students to be on the lookout for **commercials everywhere** *(see below)*, not just on TV.

Teaching Tip: Commercials Everywhere

Ask students to take a look at their clothes—especially T-shirts and shoes. Are any of them are wearing clothes that show

- a brand name or logo,
- a cartoon character,
- the name of a music group?

Ask them to step forward so classmates can see their clothes. Point out that while these clothes might be "cool," they are also advertisements. Begin a discussion by asking students if that makes them feel differently about the clothing they choose to wear.

Viewing Web Sites

Before having students check out the Web, review the school's policy and procedures for using the Internet and remind students that they should never give out personal information online. Discuss the following information about evaluating Web sites:

- University, government, and non-profit sites are reliable. They usually have addresses that end in *.edu, .gov,* or *.org.*
- Sites run by established companies such as Merriam-Webster (online dictionary) or Information Please (almanac) have a reputation for reliability.
- The online versions of magazines and newspapers are good sources of up-to-date information. (Refer students to PE page 394 and remind them to apply those tips to written news as well.)
- Search engines designed especially for kids, such as www.onekey.com, will return more reliable results.
- Web sites that generate a lot of pop-up advertisements or have many ads on the page should be avoided.

398

Viewing Web Sites

Like watching television, looking at Web sites on the Internet requires you to think. The following questions will help you become a smart viewer of what's on your computer screen.

Is the information fair or one-sided?

Let's say that you want to compare margarine to butter. You could get fair information from government and university Web sites. However, margarine companies or dairy organizations may present just one side of the issue.

Is the information from a reliable source?

If you're writing a report on tornadoes, the National Weather Service Web site will have information that you can trust. A personal Web site with a story about a tornado would not be as dependable.

Is the site up-to-date?

Information changes. Some Web sites are updated every day. Other sites have information that is too old to be useful. Look for sites that tell you when they were updated.

How does the information compare to other sources?

When you search the Web for information, look at several sites and at books or magazines. Do all the sources agree on the facts? Comparing sources helps you check for accuracy. Give credit to the sources you use for a report. (See page 346.)

 Check out the Web. On the Internet, look up a current topic or event. List Web sites that look like good sources of information. Also, list a few sites that do not look helpful.

English Language Learners

Some students may use home computers to access Web sites in their first language. Survey students to learn if they use the Internet to view sites in languages other than English and to learn what instruction they have had regarding evaluating those Web sites.

- If you are not bilingual and do not have access to an interpreter to evaluate the sites students mention, restrict searches on school computers to sites in English.
- Explain that searching for information in English will help improve their English.

399

Taking Classroom Tests

Have you ever helped make spaghetti sauce or chili? If you have, you know that preparing ahead of time makes the job much easier. Good cooks start with a recipe. Then they make sure they have everything else they need. The same thing is true for taking a classroom test. Having a plan is the best way to succeed.

The first step in preparing for a test is to keep up with your daily class work. Then, if you follow a few simple steps, you'll be ready for test day!

Mini Index

- **Preparing for a Test**
- **Taking Objective Tests**
- **Responding to Writing Prompts**

Pasta
Tomato
Onion
Mushroom
Olive Oil
Peppers
Spice

Taking Classroom Tests

Objectives

- understand how to prepare for tests
- learn about the different kinds of objective tests
- learn how to read and respond to writing prompts

Acknowledge that a big difference between taking tests and cooking is that a lot more people get nervous about taking tests than about cooking. Assure students that, in fact, nearly everyone worries about taking tests. For some lucky people, that butterflies-in-the-stomach feeling even helps them do better.

Explain that learning how to prepare for tests can do a lot to ease worries. Talk about other things students can do, in addition to studying, to help reduce stress before tests. These include the following:

- Get a good night's sleep.
- Eat a good breakfast or lunch before the test.
- Relax and breathe deeply for a few moments before the test starts.

Materials

Blank overhead transparencies (TE p. 400)

Drawing supplies, butcher paper (TE p. 401)

Mad Libs book (TE p. 403)

Posterboard (TE p. 404)

Preparing for a Test

Invite students to brainstorm strategies for preparing for tests. Ideas might include the following:

- Write entries in your learning log (see PE pages 383–384) during your study process—include questions, facts you want to review, and your predictions and thoughts about what will be on the test.
- Make flash cards.
- Find a quiet study area at home and keep it clean and organized.
- Use waiting times, such as in a doctor's office, to study.
- Form a study group with classmates and help each other review the material.

 **Practice**   **Answers**

Answers will vary.

Preparing for a Test

When your teacher announces a test, prepare for it by using the guidelines below:

1   **Ask questions.** Ask your teacher . . .
- What will be on the test?
- What kind of test will it be? (Multiple choice? True/false? Writing prompts?)

2   **Review.** Use your time wisely . . .
- Begin reviewing as soon as your teacher announces the test.
- Look over your notes and your textbook. List the things that you think are the most difficult.
- Be sure that you understand everything. Get help with anything that is still unclear.

3   **Study.** Use several ways to study . . .
- Write the main ideas and important vocabulary words on note cards.
- Say the information out loud and explain it to a partner in your own words.
- Study with an adult and explain the information to him or her.

 Practice

Review the information under the three headings above. List two or three suggestions that you think would help you prepare for your next test.

English Language Learners

Specific instruction in test taking and test preparation is essential for these students. Some may not be familiar with the names of the types of tests.

- Prepare transparencies with examples of questions that illustrate Multiple Choice, True/False, and Writing Prompt tests, as mentioned in Guideline 1.

- Then have students work in small groups to identify specific graphic organizers that would help them study for tests in the different content areas.

Struggling Learners

Although students must learn to study for tests on their own, you can help them learn to focus on the most important points by playing review games in the classroom. Games modeled after a sport, such as golf or baseball, or after a television game show are especially popular with students.

Taking Classroom Tests **401**

TEST-TAKING TIPS

Before you start . . .

- **Read** all of the directions. Can you use notes, a dictionary, or your textbook?
- **Have a couple of sharpened pencils** and an eraser ready.
- **Write your full name** on the test.
- **Look over the entire test** so that you can plan your time.

During the test . . .

- **Read the directions** and follow them carefully. Ask the teacher about any questions that confuse you.
- **Study each question** by looking for key words like *always, only, all,* and *never.*
- **Answer the questions** you are sure of first. Don't spend too much time on any one question.
- **Go back to any questions** that you skipped.

After the test . . .

- **Be sure** you answered all the questions.
- **Read over your answers,** if you have time, to make sure they sound correct.

Test-Taking Tips

After reviewing the tips, invite students to each draw a cartoon character who is struggling with some problem while trying to take a test.

- Tell students that they can base the cartoon character on their favorite existing cartoon character, or they can create an entirely new character.
- Ask students to consider illustrating a problem they've encountered while taking a test.
- Distribute drawing supplies and give students time to complete their cartoons.

As volunteers share their cartoons with the class, invite students to offer suggestions for ways to avoid that particular problem when taking a test.

Write the test-taking tips on a large piece of butcher paper and post it where students can refer to it when they take tests. Display the finished cartoons around the poster.

English Language Learners

Some students often have difficulty understanding written directions.

- Encourage students to read the directions and tell you what they are to do in their own words before beginning tests that permit that type of teacher assistance.
- Prepare students for high-stakes tests that do not permit teacher clarification of written directions by occasionally having students tell you what the directions asked them to do *after* they have read the directions and taken the test. Question students about the strategies they used to understand the directions.
  - Did they try to put the directions in their own words before responding?
  - Did they look for and identify key words?

Reinforce the strategies they used. Provide clear instruction on how to use other strategies that will help them understand written directions when no assistance can be offered.

Taking Objective Tests

Point out that sometimes students may find it difficult to decide which answer in a multiple-choice test is correct. Focus on the last question as an example.

- In the main sentence, the word *control* is a noun used to give the idea of restraining something (insects).
- In **a** and **b**, *control* is also a noun, but it isn't used in the sense of restraining something. In both of these sentences *control* is an object.
- In **c**, *control* is a verb—but it is used in the sense of restraining something (polio outbreaks).

If students are still unsure of the answer, they can eliminate the answers they know are wrong. In the main sentence, *control* is not an object, so **a** and **b** are wrong.

402

Taking Objective Tests

The four basic kinds of questions on objective tests are *multiple-choice, true/false, matching,* and *fill-in-the-blanks.*

Multiple-Choice Test

- **READ** all the choices before marking an answer. There may be more than one correct answer. If there is, look for a choice like "all of the above" or "both a and b."

  Question: A fish, a dog, and a bird all have_____.
  a. backbones   **b.** eyes   **c.** legs   **d.** both a and b

- **BE AWARE** that a question may ask you to find a mistake in one of the choices. Check for the choice "no mistake."

  Question: Circle the letter for the sentence that needs to be corrected.
  a. Gills and lungs are similar.
  b. Feathers and fur are similar.
  c. Arms and wings are similar.
  d. No mistake.

- **PAY ATTENTION** to negative words like *not, never, except,* and *unless.* Also notice any numbers.

  Question: Which two choices do not describe mammals?
  a. cold blooded   **b.** warm blooded   **c.** egg laying

- **FOLLOW DIRECTIONS** carefully. A question may ask you to mark the choice that matches a sample sentence.

  Question: Which sentence below uses the word control in the same way as the following sentence? Circle the correct letter.
  Some mammals keep the insect population under control.
  a. Our TV's remote control is broken.
  b. The pilot adjusted the fuel control.
  c. The Salk vaccine helped to control polio outbreaks.
  Answers: d., d., a. and c., c.

English Language Learners

Help students improve their test-taking skills by providing on-going instruction about the types of questions and wording that tend to confuse them.

- Analyze students' errors in content area tests.
- Select specific types of questions or written directions (for example, draw a line under; circle the correct answer) to emphasize prior to the next test.

- Have students work in small cooperative groups to figure out how to approach and answer questions during test-taking lessons.

Taking Classroom Tests **403**

True/False Test

- **READ** the whole question before you answer. For a statement to be true, the entire statement must be true.
- **WATCH** for words like *all, every, always, never.* Statements with these words in them are often false.

    Directions: Mark each statement "T" for true or "F" for false.

    _____ **1.** All titles should be underlined.
    _____ **2.** Never capitalize *a, an,* or *the* in a title.
    _____ **3.** Use apostrophes to show possession and to end sentences.

    Answers: All three are false. 1. Not *all* titles should be underlined. 2. *A, an,* and *the* should be capitalized if they are the first word in a title. 3. The first part of the statement is true, but the last part is false.

Matching Test

- **REVIEW** both lists before you make any matches.
- **CHECK OFF** each answer you use.

    Directions: Match the definitions on the right to the terms on the left.

    _____ nocturnal   **a.** kind of sonar sounds
    _____ roosts   **b.** active during the night
    _____ echolocation   **c.** bats' homesites

    Answers: b. nocturnal, c. roosts, a. echolocation

Fill-in-the-Blanks Test

- **READ** each sentence completely before filling in the blank.

    Directions: Fill in the blanks below with the correct answers.

    1. The prefix *anti* means _____.
    2. Words with the same or similar meanings are _____.

    Answers: 1. against 2. synonyms

To establish a fun association with the idea of fill-in-the-blanks tests, show students a page from a Mad Libs book, and explain that these use the idea of filling in blanks in a silly way. Working with the class as a whole, fill out a Mad Libs story and then have a volunteer read it to the class.

To help students get comfortable with all four types of tests, divide the class into groups of four.

- Have each group decide on a topic (either a subject they're studying in school or another topic that interests all group members).
- Have each member of the group pick a different one of the four types of test and make up a short test for the chosen topic.
- Either photocopy students' tests so that several students can take them, or have students trade tests with another person in their group to fill in the answers.

Responding to Writing Prompts

Students may find the idea of responding to writing prompts more daunting than objective tests. Remind them that they can practice the exact skills they need for writing tests throughout this book.

1 Find the key word in the writing prompt.

Make sure that students understand exactly what each of the key words requires in their response. For example, if a prompt asks them to list information, they should write a simple list during prewriting, and then use the list to write a paragraph or an essay.

Tell students they'll encounter other key words, but their knowledge of these words will help them to recognize other key words, too. To show students how to recognize other key words, read one or more of the prompts in Responding to Literature (PE pages 278, 284, 290, and 296), and ask students to describe what's being asked for. For example, on page 278 key words are:

1. *Tell why you liked the book* (*explain* why they liked it),
2. *share your favorite part* (*describe* the favorite part), and
3. *ask the author a question.*

Responding to Writing Prompts

Sometimes test questions ask you to write about topics that you've been studying. To answer this type of question, you must first understand the prompt. Here are two sample prompts:

- List the conditions needed to start a thunderstorm.
- Describe a thunderstorm.

Both prompts have the same topic: thunderstorms. But each prompt asks you to write about the topic in a different way. The first asks you to *list,* and the second asks you to *describe.*

1 Find the key word in the writing prompt.

It is important to understand the key words used in writing prompts. Here are some common ones:

Compare/Contrast ● To **compare**, tell how two things are alike. To **contrast**, tell how things are different. A prompt may ask you to compare, contrast, or both.

Example: Compare a hurricane and a tornado.

Define ● To **define** something, tell what it means, what it is, or what it does. Example: Define erosion.

Describe ● To **describe** something, tell how it looks, sounds, smells, tastes, and/or feels. Example: Describe a blizzard.

Explain ● To **explain** something, tell how it works, how it happens, or how to do it. Example: Explain how a lightbulb works.

List ● To **list**, give a number of facts, ideas, reasons, or other details about the topic.

Example: List three products that are made in your state.

Persuade ● To **persuade**, give facts and reasons that would convince someone to agree with your opinion.

Example: Do you think all bicyclists should wear helmets? Write a paragraph to persuade someone else of your opinion.

English Language Learners

Provide specific on-going instruction and practice to help students identify and determine how to respond to the key words associated with writing prompts.

- Create a poster listing key words used in writing prompts.
- After students have completed a book or unit of study, have partners write one or two prompts, using the key words.

- Do a Think-Aloud to model reading and planning a response for a student-generated prompt.

Taking Classroom Tests 405

② Plan your answer.

Here are the steps to answering a writing prompt:

1 **Listen** carefully to all directions.

2 **Find out** how much time you have for the test.

3 **Pay attention** to the key word.

4 **Think** about the prompt before you begin writing.

5 **List** your main points in a simple graphic organizer.

6 **Write** your response and check it for errors.

Sample Responses

The two answers below are different, even though they are about the same topic. The first *lists*, and the second *describes*.

List the conditions needed to start a thunderstorm.
(The answer lists three conditions.)

A thunderstorm needs at least three conditions to get started. First, there must be moisture for clouds and rain. Second, warm air must be able to rise. Finally, something (like a mountain or cold air) must lift the warm, moist air. When these three things come together, a thunderstorm forms.

Describe a thunderstorm.
(The answer tells about a thunderstorm using several senses.)

A thunderstorm begins with a huge, dark cloud. The air changes from warm to cool, and bright bolts of lightning flash in the sky. Booming thunder rumbles all around. Howling wind splatters rain against roofs and windows. After it stops, the air is fresh and clean again. The warm sun comes out, and a rainbow may appear in the sky.

Practice

For each prompt below, write the key word and tell what you need to do.

1. Explain how hail forms.

2. Persuade people to support a lake cleanup project.

3. Define *antonym*.

② Plan your answer.

Remind students that they should always read the prompt all the way through before doing any writing. Once they have done that, they can go back, take note of the key words, and begin to plan their response.

Suggest that students underline or circle the key word or key words in the prompt, so they'll know how many issues they have to address.

Practice Answers

1. Key word: *explain*. The response should tell how hail is formed.

2. Key word: *persuade*. The response should give reasons that convince people that a lake cleanup project is a good idea.

3. Key word: *define*. The response should tell the meaning of the word *antonym*.

The Basic Elements of Writing

Working with Words

The English language just keeps growing bigger and stronger. Some people estimate that there are nearly 800,000 words in our language! But only about 200,000 of those words are used regularly. How many of them you actually use depends on your level of reading and learning.

There are eight different types of words called **the parts of speech.** They are *nouns, pronouns, verbs, adjectives, adverbs, prepositions, conjunctions,* and *interjections.* You will learn about the parts of speech in this chapter.

Mini Index

Using Nouns

A **noun** is a word that names a person, a place, a thing, or an idea.

Kinds of Nouns

A **proper noun** names someone or something specific. Proper nouns are capitalized. A **common noun** does not name someone or something specific. Common nouns are not capitalized.

COMMON NOUNS	PROPER NOUNS
boy, airport, holiday	Sergio, O'Hare Field, Kwanzaa

Compound nouns are made up of two or more words: *firefighter, watermelon, Golden Gate Bridge, General Pershing.*

Number of Nouns

A **singular noun** names one person, place, thing, or idea. A **plural noun** names more than one person, place, thing, or idea.

SINGULAR NOUNS	PLURAL NOUNS
teacher, woman, basketball	teachers, women, basketballs

Practice

Number your paper from 1 to 4 and copy the nouns in each sentence. Label each noun "C" for common or "P" for proper. Also label each noun "S" for singular or "PL" for plural.

■ The Alamo was the site of a famous battle.
  Alamo-P, S   site-C, S   battle-C, S

1. Soldiers from Mexico stormed the Alamo.
2. Only 189 men defended the mission.
3. Jim Bowie and Davy Crockett were heroes.
4. None of the fighters inside the mission survived.

Gender of Nouns

Nouns can be *feminine, masculine, neuter,* or *indefinite.*

Feminine (female) nouns:	mother, woman, hen, cow
Masculine (male) nouns:	father, man, rooster, bull
Neuter (neither male nor female) nouns:	foot, closet, trampoline, park
Indefinite (either male or female) nouns:	parent, doctor, child, birds

Practice

List three feminine nouns, three masculine nouns, three neuter nouns, and three indefinite nouns.

Possessive Nouns

A **possessive** noun shows ownership. Singular nouns are usually made possessive by adding an apostrophe and the letter *s* to the end of the word. In most cases, plural nouns ending in the letter *s* just need an apostrophe to make them possessive. (See page **492**.)

SINGULAR POSSESSIVE	PLURAL POSSESSIVE
my *mother's* briefcase	two *mothers'* briefcases
the *dog's* collar	the three *dogs'* collars

Practice

Write a sentence for each of the following nouns. Have each of these nouns show possession.

Example: My friend's house is up for sale.

   friend   teachers   park   dogs   pirates   car

Answers

Practice
1. soldiers: C, PL; Mexico: P, S; Alamo: P, S
2. men: C, PL; mission: C, S
3. Jim Bowie: P, S; Davy Crockett: P, S; heroes: C, PL
4. fighters: C, PL; mission: C, S.

Answers

Practice Answers will vary.

Practice Answers will vary but should use these possessive nouns:
friend's
teachers'
park's
dogs'
pirates'
car's

How can I improve my writing with nouns?

Include Specific Nouns

Some nouns are **general nouns** and do not give the reader a clear picture. Other nouns are **specific nouns.** They name particular people, places, or things. Specific nouns make your writing more clear and interesting.

GENERAL NOUNS	fruit	building	coat	country	food
SPECIFIC NOUNS	apricot	Eiffel Tower	parka	Italy	tacos

tip How can you tell if a noun is specific enough? Ask yourself this question: Does the noun create a clear picture in my mind? A specific noun like *poodle* creates a clearer picture than the general noun *dog.*

Practice

Number your paper from 1 to 5. Rewrite the following sentences using specific nouns in place of the underlined general nouns. The questions in parentheses will help you change the nouns.

■ I turned quickly when I heard the sound. (*What sound?*)
  barking
1. Grandma is cooking vegetables. (*Which vegetables?*)
2. My mom bought me some clothes. (*What type of clothes?*)
3. Marta took a boat out on the lake. (*What kind of boat?*)
4. Teena spilled the snack on the carpet. (*What kind of snack?*)
5. Franco enjoys fixing things. (*What things?*)

Write NOW Write at least five sentences about an activity you like. Try to use specific nouns in your explanation.

Make Comparisons

Sometimes you can make an idea clearer and more colorful by creating a figure of speech. When you create a **simile** or **metaphor,** you compare two nouns.

Simile: A simile compares two nouns using the word like or as.
Those butterflies look like flying flowers.

Metaphor: A metaphor compares two nouns without using like or as.
In our city, high school football is king.

Practice

> At first, making comparisons may not be easy. But they can make your writing fun to read, so keep trying.

Number your paper from 1 to 5. Then, in each sentence below, list the two nouns being compared. Also tell if the comparison is a simile or a metaphor.

■ The racing cars hung together like fish.
  cars and fish—simile
1. This book is a door to the galaxies.
2. The dog danced around like loose litter blowing in the wind.
3. The hot soup was the best medicine for my cold.
4. The snowplow blasted through the snow like a stallion.
5. A beautiful sunrise is a gift of peace.

Write NOW Create at least one simile and one metaphor to share. Ask your classmates to identify the two nouns being compared.

Special Challenge: On your own paper, list four comparisons from books, stories, or articles that you have read. Tell these three things about each comparison: (1) where you found it, (2) what two nouns are being compared, and (3) whether the comparison is a simile or a metaphor.

Answers

Practice Possible answers:
1. Grandma is cooking potatoes.
2. My mom bought me some t-shirts.
3. Marta took a rowboat out on the lake.
4. Teena spilled the applesauce on the carpet.
5. Franco enjoys fixing clocks.

Answers

Practice
1. book and door—metaphor
2. dog and litter—simile
3. soup and medicine—metaphor
4. snowplow and stallion—simile
5. sunrise and gift—metaphor

Using Pronouns

A **pronoun** is a word used in place of a noun. An **antecedent** is the word the pronoun refers to or replaces. (See 576.1.)

Jamal **yelled that** he **was ready.**
(*Jamal* is the antecedent of the pronoun *he.*)

Hanna **went bowling.** She **had three strikes.**
(*Hanna* is the antecedent of the pronoun *she.*)

Personal Pronouns

Personal pronouns are the most common type of pronoun.

PERSONAL PRONOUNS	I	you	he	she	we	they
	me	it	him	her	us	them

Person and Number of a Pronoun

Pronouns can vary in **person** and in **number**.

PERSON	NUMBER: SINGULAR	PLURAL
First person *(the person speaking)*	I eat.	We eat.
Second person *(the person spoken to)*	You eat.	You eat.
Third person *(the person spoken about)*	He/She/It eats.	They eat.

Practice

Number your paper from 1 to 4. Write a sentence using each pronoun described below as the subject. Underline the subject in each sentence.

■ third-person plural <u>They</u> should make a snow fort.

1. first-person singular
2. first-person plural
3. second-person singular
4. third-person singular

Subject and Object Pronouns

A **subject pronoun** is used as the subject of a sentence.

She **told me funny stories.**   They **made me laugh.**

SUBJECT PRONOUNS CAN BE SINGULAR OR PLURAL.

Singular: I, you, he, she, it   *Plural:* we, you, they

An **object pronoun** is used as a direct object, as an indirect object, or as an object of preposition in a prepositional phrase.

Mr. Jacobs helped her. (*direct object*)

Todd gave me **the present.** (*indirect object*)

We planned a surprise party for him. (*object of the preposition*)

OBJECT PRONOUNS CAN BE SINGULAR OR PLURAL.

Singular: me, you, him, her, it   *Plural:* us, you, them

Some pronouns like *my, your, his, her, mine,* and *yours* show ownership. They are called **possessive pronouns.**

Practice

Number your paper from 1 to 6. Write a sentence using an example of each pronoun described below. Underline the pronoun.

■ singular subject pronoun
<u>She</u> saw the band arrive.

1. plural subject pronoun
2. singular object pronoun
3. singular subject pronoun
4. plural object pronoun
5. plural subject pronoun
6. singular object pronoun

Answers

Practice Answers will vary but should use these pronouns:
1. I
2. we
3. you
4. he, she, or it

Answers

Practice Answers will vary but should use these pronouns:
1. we, you, or they
2. me, you, him, her, or it
3. I, you, he, she, or it
4. us, you, or them
5. we, you, or they
6. me, you, him, her, or it

How can I use pronouns properly?

Check the Number of Your Pronouns

The pronouns in your sentence must agree in number with their antecedents. If the antecedent is singular, the pronoun also must be singular. If the antecedent is plural, the pronoun must be plural.

The girl took her cat to the veterinarian clinic.
(The pronoun *her* and its antecedent *girl* are both singular, so they agree in number.)

The clinic assistants said that they were surprised by the size of the cat.
(The pronoun *they* and its antecedent *assistants* are both plural, so they agree in number.)

Dr. Stephanie said she had never seen such a big cat.
(The pronoun *she* and its antecedent *Dr. Stephanie* are both singular, so they agree in number.)

> A pronoun can be either singular or plural in number.

Practice

Number your paper from 1 to 5 and write the correct pronoun for each sentence below. Then write the antecedent that each pronoun refers to.

■ Luis and Orlando brought *(his, their)* dog in for a checkup.
  their, Luis and Orlando

1. An assistant said that *(he, they)* would take the dog to the examining room.
2. Then Dr. Stephanie used *(her, their)* stethoscope to check the dog's heart.
3. The dog received *(its, their)* yearly shots, too.
4. Afterward, the doctor told the boys to give *(his, their)* dog more exercise.
5. The boys like Dr. Stephanie and really trust *(her, they)*.

Check the Gender of Your Pronouns

The singular pronouns in your sentences must also agree in gender with their antecedents. Singular pronouns can be masculine (male), feminine (female), or neuter (neither male nor female).

Pedro found his skateboard in the basement.
(The masculine pronoun *his* and its antecedent *Pedro* agree.)

Lisa said that she wrote a poem.
(The feminine pronoun *she* and its antecedent *Lisa* agree.)

My new shirt has an ink stain on it.
(The neuter pronoun *it* and its antecedent *shirt* agree.)

Practice

Number your paper from 1 to 5. Then write the correct pronoun for each sentence below and the antecedent that the pronoun refers to. (Make sure that the pronoun and its antecedent agree in gender.)

■ Mari Sandoz has written a book about Crazy Horse, and _____ got her information through interviews.
  she, Mari Sandoz

1. Crazy Horse was a member of the Sioux tribe, and _____ was born about 1840.
2. Crazy Horse gained _____ greatest fame in two battles—the Rosebud and the Little Bighorn.
3. Crazy Horse was greatly admired because _____ helped the needy people in his tribe.
4. Crazy Horse's first wife was Black Shawl, but _____ died very young. His second wife was Nellie Larrabee.
5. A monument to Crazy Horse is being carved from a mountain in South Dakota, but _____ has a long way to go.

Answers

Practice
1. he, assistant
2. her, Dr. Stephanie
3. its, dog
4. their, boys
5. her, Dr. Stephanie

Answers

Practice
1. he, Crazy Horse
2. his, Crazy Horse
3. he, Crazy Horse
4. she, Black Shawl
5. it, monument

Choosing Verbs

A **verb** shows action or links the subject to another word in the sentence. There are three types of verbs: action verbs, linking verbs, and helping verbs. (See page 582.)

Action Verbs

Action verbs tell what the subject is doing. Use specific action verbs in your sentences to make them interesting and fun to read.

General Action Verbs

A snowstorm came through. The wind made noise, and snow fell around the house. We got under quilts and drank hot cider.

Specific Action Verbs

A snowstorm roared outside. The wind howled, and snow drifted around the house. We burrowed under quilts and sipped hot cider.

Practice

Number your paper from 1 to 5. Skip two or three lines between each number. Study the pairs of actions verbs below. List the more specific one on your paper. Then write a sentence for each verb that you have listed.

- laugh   giggle
  giggle   Samantha and Josie giggled in the lunchroom.
1. whisper   talk
2. run   sprint
3. smash   hit
4. drink   gulp
5. stare   look

Write NOW Write three or four sentences about something fun that you have done with a friend. Use specific actions verbs in your sentences.

Linking and Helping Verbs

A **linking verb** connects a subject to a noun or an adjective in the predicate part of a sentence.

Linking Verbs: *is, are, was, being, been,* and *am;* also *smell, look, taste, feel,* and *seem.* (See page 582 for a complete list.)

Spaghetti is my favorite meal. (The linking verb *is* connects the subject *spaghetti* to the noun *meal.*)

The sauce tastes spicy. (The linking verb *tastes* connects the subject *sauce* to the adjective *spicy.*)

A **helping verb** comes before the main verb and gives it a more specific meaning.

Helping Verbs: *has, have, had, do, did, should, would,* and *could;* also *is, are, was, were,* and *been.* (See page 582 for a complete list.)

Lana will make the banners for the club.
(The helping verb *will* helps state a future action, *will make.*)

Thomas did help last year.
(The helping verb *did* helps state a past action, *did help.*)

> Words like *is, are, was,* and *were* can be linking verbs or helping verbs.

Practice

Number your paper from 1 to 4. Then identify the underlined verb as either a linking verb or a helping verb.

- Farley Mowat has written wildlife books. helping verb
1. *Never Cry Wolf* is his most famous book.
2. Mowat had lived among wolves before he wrote this book.
3. He saw that the wolves were eating mice.
4. So the author would eat mice, just like the wolves!

Write NOW Write a sentence for each of these helping verbs: *had, did,* and *should.*

Answers

Practice Answers will vary but should use the following verbs:
1. whisper
2. sprint
3. smash
4. gulp
5. stare

Answers

Practice
1. linking
2. helping
3. helping
4. helping

Tenses of Verbs

A verb's **tense** tells when the action takes place. **Simple** tenses include *present, past,* and *future.* (Also see page 584.)

Simple Tenses

The present tense of a verb shows action that is *happening now* or that *happens regularly.*

I collect models of cars, planes, and boats.

The past tense of a verb states an action that *happened in the past.* It is usually formed by adding *-ed* to the present tense verb.

Yesterday, I finished a model of a submarine.

The future tense of a verb states an action that *will take place in the future.* It is formed by using *will* or *shall* before the main verb.

Next week, I will start a new model.

I shall finish it in two days.

Practice

Number your paper from 1 to 6. Identify the tense of each underlined verb below.

■ My grandfather <u>grows</u> his own vegetables.
   Present

1. He <u>started</u> gardening many years ago.
2. Last year, he <u>planted</u> 12 different vegetables.
3. We <u>picked</u> tons of tomatoes and green peppers!
4. To help my grandfather, I <u>weed</u> the garden.
5. I <u>water</u> the garden, too.
6. Next year, we <u>will add</u> more corn, my favorite vegetable.

How can I use verbs correctly?

Number of a Verb

The subjects and verbs in your sentences must agree in number. If you use a singular subject, use a singular verb. If you use a plural subject, use a plural verb.

Subject-Verb Agreement

The chart below shows how subject-verb agreement works.

SINGULAR SUBJECT	SINGULAR VERBS		PLURAL SUBJECT	PLURAL VERBS
Mr. King	swims		exercisers	swim
Mr. King	runs		exercisers	run

Mr. King swims laps in the pool. (The subject *Mr. King* and the verb *swims* are both singular. They agree in number.)

The exercisers run laps on the track. (The subject *exercisers* and the verb *run* are both plural. They agree in number.)

Practice

Write a sentence for each pair of subjects and verbs below. Supply your own verbs for the last three subjects.

■ Kerry   plays

   Kerry plays volleyball on Saturday mornings.

1. brother   eats   4. girls   _____
2. firefighters practice   5. cat   _____
3. Max   asks   6. balloons   _____

Write NOW Write a paragraph (at least four sentences) about your favorite class. Make sure your verbs agree in number with their subjects.

Answers

Practice
1. past
2. past
3. past
4. present
5. present
6. future

Answers

Practice Answers will vary.

Irregular Verbs

Most verbs in the English language are **regular**. That means you add *-ed* to the verb to form the past tense. (See regular verbs on page **418**.) Other verbs are **irregular.** That means you do not add *-ed* to form the past tense.

Past Tense Form

To state the past action of an **irregular** verb, the word changes. (You do not add *-ed* to the verb.)

Sam made many of her own birthday cards.
(Made is the past tense form of the irregular verb make.)

Devon wrote an e-mail message to his aunt.
(Wrote is the past tense form of the irregular verb write.)

Past Participle Form

The form of a verb used with certain helping verbs (such as *has, had,* or *have*) is called the past participle. Regular verbs add *-ed* to make this form. Irregular verbs change to make this form.

Sam has made many of her own birthday cards.
(Made is the past participle form of the irregular verb make.)

Devon has written an e-mail message to his aunt.
(Written is the past participle form of the irregular verb write.)

Practice

Write a sentence using each verb form indicated below. Remember that the past participle needs a helping verb *(had, has,* or *have).*

■ think *(past participle)* I had thought about many things.

1. swim *(past tense)*
2. shake *(past tense)*
3. take *(past participle)*
4. break *(past tense)*
5. catch *(past participle)*
6. write *(past participle)*

Subject-Verb Agreement in Sentences with Compound Subjects

A **compound subject** has two or more simple subjects joined by a conjunction *(and, or).* Listed below are the two main rules for subject-verb agreement in sentences with compound subjects.

Rule 1: When a sentence has a compound subject connected by *and,* the verb should be plural.

Soccer **and** tennis **are my favorite sports.**
*(Soccer and tennis is a compound subject connected by and. The subject **agrees** in number with the plural verb are.)*

Alan **and** I **play tennis on the park courts.**
(Alan and I is a compound subject connected by and. The subject agrees in number with the plural verb play.)

Rule 2: When a sentence has a compound subject connected by *or,* the verb should agree with the subject closest to it.

Either the park directors **or** Alan supplies **the tennis balls.**
(The subject Alan is nearer to the verb supplies. They are both singular and agree in number.)

Josh **or my other** friends **usually** shoot **hoops in the park.**
(The subject friends is nearer to the verb shoot. They are both plural and agree in number.)

> See page **419** for more information about subject-verb agreement.

Practice

Write a sentence for each pair of subjects below.

■ Josie and I Josie and I make fruit smoothies.

1. backpack and books
2. my brothers or I
3. teachers or the PTO
4. cars and trucks
5. Mandi and Matt
6. a cat or dogs

Answers

 Practice Answers will vary but should use the following verbs:

1. swam
2. shook
3. taken
4. broke
5. caught
6. written

Answers

Practice Answers will vary but should use the following verb forms:

1. plural verb
2. singular verb
3. singular verb
4. plural verb
5. plural verb
6. plural verb

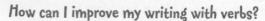

How can I improve my writing with verbs?

Avoid Too Many *Be* Verbs

Try not to use the *be* verbs *(is, are, was, were)* too often. Many times, a stronger action verb can be made from another word in the same sentence.

A *be* verb: Rosa **is** a forceful speaker.
A stronger action verb: Rosa **speaks** forcefully.

Practice

The sentences below contain *be* verbs (underlined). Rewrite each sentence by making another word in the sentence an action verb.

■ Our dog Henry <u>is</u> a loud barker.
  Our dog Henry barks loudly.

1. You <u>are</u> a wonderful singer.
2. My cousins <u>are</u> constant whiners.
3. My dad <u>is</u> a skilled cook.
4. Our car <u>was</u> a rough ride.

Share the Right Feeling

Different verbs create different feelings. Make sure that the verbs you use fit the feeling that you want to share.

Leon **tiptoed** into the room. *(moved slowly and quietly)*
Leon **strutted** into the room. *(moved proudly)*
Leon **stumbled** into the room. *(moved in a clumsy way)*

Practice

> The connotation of a word is the feeling that the word expresses.

Write a sentence using the verb *talk.* Then rewrite the sentence twice, using two different synonyms for *talk.* Each synonym should have a different connotation.

Describing with Adjectives

An **adjective** is a word that describes a noun or a pronoun. Adjectives answer four main questions: *what kind? how many? how much?* or *which one?*

EXAMPLE ADJECTIVES			
What kind?	narrow **path**	green **hat**	small **dog**
How much?	some **salt**	small **amount**	enough **rain**
How many?	several **boats**	four **miles**	no **animals**
Which one?	this **cup**	that **train**	those **people**

Placement of Adjectives

Adjectives often come right before the noun they describe.

The **golden** leaves fell.

Adjectives can also come after the word they describe, as they do when they appear after a *be* verb.

The leaves are **golden**. Soon the leaves will be **brown**.

Practice

Number your paper from 1 to 5. Write each underlined adjective and tell whether it answers *what kind? how many? how much?* or *which one?*

■ There are *many* places I would like to visit.
  many, how many

1. I would like to take a *long* trip to the Mojave Desert.
2. *Desert* sunsets are beautiful.
3. Deserts have deep *blue* skies.
4. This desert gets *little* rain but supports *gorgeous* life-forms.
5. We have an *amazing* climate, *unusual* plants, and *fantastic* animals.

Answers

Practice Possible answers:
1. You sing wonderfully.
2. My cousins whine constantly.
3. My dad cooks skillfully.
4. Our car rode roughly.

Practice Answers will vary.

Answers

Practice 1. long , what kind?
2. desert , what kind?
3. blue , what kind?
4. little , how much?
   gorgeous , what kind?
5. amazing , what kind?
   unusual , what kind?
   fantastic , what kind?

Forms of Adjectives

Adjectives have three forms: the positive, the comparative, and the superlative. For most one-syllable adjectives, add *-er* or *-est* to form the comparative and superlative. Place *more* or *most* in front of most multisyllable adjectives to form the comparative and superlative.

POSITIVE	COMPARATIVE	SUPERLATIVE
small	smaller	smallest
beautiful	more beautiful	most beautiful

The **positive** form describes a noun without comparing it to another noun.

My cat, Tasha, is a smart animal. She is a curious cat.

The **comparative** form compares a noun with another noun.

She is smarter than my dog, Rip. She is also more curious than he is.

The **superlative** form compares a noun with several other nouns.

Tasha is the smartest animal I have ever known.

She is the most curious animal in town.

Practice

Number your paper from 1 to 6. Skip one or two lines between each number. Then write a sentence using the form of the adjective given in parentheses.

■ beautiful *(superlative)*
St. Mary's Church is the most beautiful building in town.

1. large *(comparative)*
2. exciting *(positive)*
3. clean *(superlative)*
4. amazing *(comparative)*
5. surprising *(superlative)*
6. hungry *(positive)*

How can I improve my writing with adjectives?

Combine Short Sentences

Sometimes ideas included in short sentences can be combined into one longer sentence using one or more adjectives. Longer sentences can connect your ideas and make your writing flow.

Combining with One Adjective

The two short sentences below can be combined by moving the adjective *old* to the first sentence.

Short Sentences: I saw my uncle's barn yesterday. The barn was old.

Combined Sentence: I saw my uncle's old barn yesterday.

Combining with a Series of Adjectives

The string of short sentences below can be combined by using a series of adjectives. (A *series* is three items or more in a row: *red, white,* and *blue.*)

Short Sentences: The barn was smelly. It was dusty. It was creepy.

Combined Sentence: The barn was smelly, dusty, and creepy.

Practice

Combine each set of short sentences into one longer sentence. Combine the sentences using one adjective or a series of adjectives.

■ Farm machinery cluttered the yard. It was rusty.
Rusty farm machinery cluttered the yard.

1. A path led to the barnyard. The path was overgrown.
2. Once the farm was active. It was well kept. It was clean.
3. A fence circles a nearby field. The fence is useless.
4. My uncle raised cows. He raised chickens. He raised pigs.

Answers

Practice   Answers will vary but should use these adjective forms:

1. larger
2. exciting
3. cleanest
4. more amazing
5. most surprising
6. hungry

Answers

Practice
1. An overgrown path led to the barnyard.
2. Once the farm was active, well kept, and clean.
3. A useless fence circles a nearby field.
4. My uncle raised cows, chickens, and pigs.

Describing with Adverbs

An **adverb** is a word that describes a verb, an adjective, or another adverb. An adverb answers four main questions: *how? when? where?* or *how often?*

Tomorrow, we are going to make clay pots. *(when?)*
We will have to work carefully. *(how?)*
Our art class meets weekly. *(how often?)*
We meet downstairs in the old art room. *(where?)*

Forms of Adverbs

Adverbs come in three different forms: positive, comparative, and superlative. For most one-syllable adverbs, add *-er* or *-est* to form the comparative and superlative.

POSITIVE	COMPARATIVE	SUPERLATIVE
fast	faster	fastest

Comparative: **Geoff works** faster **than I do.**
Superlative: **Geoff works the** fastest **of all my friends.**

Place *more* or *most* in front of most multisyllable adverbs to form the comparative and superlative.

POSITIVE	COMPARATIVE	SUPERLATIVE
slowly	more slowly	most slowly

Comparative: **Grandpa walks** more slowly **than before.**
Superlative: **Of all the times I've seen him, Grandpa walked** most slowly **after his surgery.**

 Write NOW On your own paper, write a paragraph of at least four sentences about your typical lunch hour in school. Try to use at least one comparative form of an adverb and one superlative form.

How can I improve my writing with adverbs?

Combine Short Sentences

Sometimes ideas included in short sentences can be combined into one longer sentence by moving an adverb from one sentence to another. The two sentences that follow can be combined by moving the adverb *quickly* to the first sentence.

Short Sentences: **The deer ran through the woods. It ran** quickly.
Combined Sentence: **The deer ran** quickly **through the woods.**

Practice

Number your paper from 1 to 3. Combine each pair of sentences by moving the adverb from one to the other.

■ I followed the trail. I moved quietly.
  I quietly followed the trail. or I followed the trail quietly.
1. The breeze rustled the leaves. It rustled them softly.
2. The deer looked ahead. It looked nervously.
3. Then it stopped. It stopped suddenly.

Tell About the Verb

Using specific adverbs to modify verbs can make your writing more colorful.

The deer moved.   **The deer moved** cautiously.

Practice

Rewrite each of the following sentences two times. Each time, use a different adverb to modify the verb.

■ Kelly coughed.
  Kelly coughed loudly. Kelly coughed constantly.
1. Bev entered the room.   3. Sam waved.
2. Reggie turned around.   4. The man snored.

Answers

Practice   Possible answers:
1. The breeze softly rustled the leaves.
2. The deer nervously looked ahead.
3. Then it suddenly stopped.

Practice   Answers will vary.

Connecting with Prepositions

Prepositions are words that introduce prepositional phrases. A preposition can show direction or position.

Cory hid behind **the couch.** (The preposition *behind* introduces the prepositional phrase *behind the couch.*)

Saul tiptoed into **the kitchen.** (The preposition *into* introduces the prepositional phrase *into the kitchen.*)

Identify Prepositional Phrases

A **prepositional phrase** includes a preposition, the object of the preposition (a noun or pronoun), and any words that modify the object.

| | *object of the* | | | *object of the* |
| *preposition* | *preposition* | | *preposition* | *preposition* |

from the next room   **through the screen door**

modifiers   *modifiers*

tip See page 598 for a complete list of prepositions.

Practice

Number your paper from 1 to 5. Then identify the prepositional phrases in the sentences below. There may be more than one prepositional phrase in some of the sentences.

■ Jayden played soccer during recess.
during recess

1. I live around the corner from the grocery store.
2. The gopher burrowed underneath the front porch.
3. Ty jumped off the raft and into the water.
4. With the help of my teacher, I raised my math grade.
5. After a few days, the clay on the shelf will be dry.

Connecting with Conjunctions

Conjunctions connect individual words or groups of words.

The road is long and narrow.
We play ball after school or
on Saturday.

Kinds of Conjunctions

COORDINATING

Coordinating conjunctions (and, but, or, for, nor, so, yet) connect equal words, phrases, or clauses.

Mimi and **Leann played a saxophone duet.** *(words)*
We had a picnic after the game but **before the rain.** *(phrases)*
Jessica walked to school, and **Luis rode the bus.** *(clauses)*

CORRELATIVE

Correlative conjunctions are used in pairs (either/or, neither/nor) to connect words or groups of words.
Either **Linda** or **Ashley will take care of your dog.**

SUBORDINATING

Subordinating conjunctions (after, because, when, until) introduce the dependent clauses in complex sentences. (Dependent clauses cannot stand alone as a sentence.)
Angel likes Tuesdays because **he has photography club.**

(For a more complete list of conjunctions, see page 600.)

Write **NOW** Write four sentences about your typical Saturday morning. Use at least two different types of conjunctions in your writing.

Answers

Practice 1. around the corner; from the grocery store
2. underneath the front porch
3. off the raft; into the water
4. with the help, of my teacher
5. after a few days; on the shelf

How can I use prepositions and conjunctions?

Add Information

Prepositional phrases are useful for adding information to sentences.

Sentence without prepositional phrases:
Kelli's mom made a fruit salad.
Sentence with prepositional phrases:
In the morning, **Kelli's mom made a fruit salad** for the banquet.

Practice

Expand the following sentences by adding one or more prepositional phrases.

1. Kara brought a sleeping bag.   3. The stars twinkled.
2. Tyler saw a black bear.   4. We slept in cabins.

Connect Short Sentences

Conjunctions can connect short, choppy sentences. Combining sentences makes your writing sound smoother.

Two short sentences:
Ben's brother went to the movies. Ben stayed home.
The two sentences combined:
Ben's brother went to the movies, but **Ben stayed home.**

Practice

Combine each pair of sentences using the conjunction in parentheses.

1. We can't go swimming. The lifeguard's not on duty. *(because)*
2. Vicki read a book. Molly watched a movie. *(but)*
3. Hector plays baseball. He plays basketball. *(and)*

Building Effective Sentences

Look around. Do you see walls and windows? Do you see desks and chairs? Most things around you were built by someone. Now, look at the sentences you are reading. They were built, too! Word by word, writers and editors built every sentence in this book.

Good writing begins with strong sentences. Sentences of different types and lengths all work together to build ideas. Whether you want to create a little clubhouse of memories or a huge castle of dreams, this chapter can help you build the sentences you need.

Mini Index

Answers

Practice   Answers will vary.

Practice   Possible answers:
1. We can't go swimming because the lifeguard's not on duty.
2. Vicki read a book, but Molly watched a movie.
3. Hector plays baseball, and he plays basketball.

Writing Complete Sentences

How can I write complete sentences?

A **complete sentence** is a group of words that expresses a complete thought. A sentence needs a **subject** and a **predicate**. Without a subject and a predicate, a sentence is incomplete.

INCOMPLETE THOUGHT	COMPLETE SENTENCE
My best friend Lupe *(A predicate is missing.)*	My best friend Lupe *plays* the piano.
plays very well *(A subject is missing.)*	*She* plays very well.
in a concert *(Both the subject and predicate are missing.)*	Last week, *she played* in a concert.

Practice

Number your paper from 1 to 5. Then study each group of words below. If the words form a complete sentence, write the sentence with correct capitalization and punctuation on your paper. If the thought is incomplete, add words to make it a complete sentence.

■ after the concert *We will have pizza after the concert.*

1. the front-row seat
2. Raji asked us to sit with him
3. wore special hats for one song
4. the band director
5. the band played my favorite song

Write NOW Write five complete sentences about a time you went to a concert, a play, or a movie. Be sure each sentence has a subject and a predicate.

Simple Subjects and Predicates

A **simple subject** (shown in orange) is the subject without the words that modify or describe it. A **simple predicate** (shown in blue) is the predicate without the words that modify it.

SIMPLE SUBJECT	SIMPLE PREDICATE
My friend Amber	came to the party.
A new student	introduces herself to the class.
All the club members	welcome Mrs. Greene.
We	talked.

> The simple predicate can also be called the verb.

Practice

Number your paper from 1 to 5. List the simple subject and simple predicate for each sentence below.

■ Our fourth-grade class visited the state capitol building. *class, visited*

1. Our teacher planned a meeting with our senator.
2. Senator O'Reilly showed us the senate chamber.
3. We saw Governor Sanchez!
4. He said hello to our class.
5. Our chaperone took pictures of us with the governor.

Write NOW Write four or five sentences about an important building you have visited. In each sentence, underline the simple subject with one line and the simple predicate with two lines.

Answers

Practice Corrected fragments will vary.
1. fragment
2. Raji asked us to sit with him.
3. fragment
4. fragment
5. The band played my favorite song.

Practice
1. teacher, planned
2. Senator O'Reilly, showed
3. We, saw
4. He, said
5. chaperone, took

434

Compound Subjects and Predicates

A **compound subject** includes two or more simple subjects.

> **COMPOUND SUBJECT**
>
> Mr. Clark **and** Mrs. Stewart plan our field trips.
>
> Bubbles **and** smoke formed in the bottle.

A **compound predicate** includes two or more simple predicates.

> **COMPOUND PREDICATE**
>
> Our class wrote **and** illustrated a book about pets.
>
> The students measure **and** mix the materials.

> A simple sentence can have both a compound subject and a compound predicate.

Practice

Copy sentences 1 to 5 on your paper. For each sentence, underline the simple subject with one line and the simple predicate with two lines.

■ The teacher and students looked at the overflowing liquid.
   The <u>teacher</u> and <u>students</u> <u><u>looked</u></u> at the overflowing liquid.

1. Mr. Huan gathered paper towels and mopped up the mess.
2. Then another bottle tipped over and spilled onto the floor.
3. Marah and Paul collected more paper towels.
4. Other students and teachers entered the classroom and asked about the hubbub.
5. Mr. Huan laughed and pointed at the messy experiment.

Write NOW Write three or four sentences about a class project. Use at least one compound subject and one compound predicate in your writing.

Complete Subjects and Predicates

The **complete subject** is the simple subject with all the words that modify it. The **complete predicate** is the simple predicate with all the words that modify it.

COMPLETE SUBJECT	COMPLETE PREDICATE
Who or what is doing something?	*What is being done?*
Our teacher	brought two gerbils to school.
Grandpa's loud snoring	keeps me awake.
The giant oak tree	fell over during the storm.
Our principal and music teacher	act in the community theater.

> See pages 560 and 562 for more information about subjects and predicates.

Practice

Copy sentences 1 through 5 on your own paper. Then draw a line between the complete subject and the complete predicate in each sentence.

■ I had a funny dream.
   I | had a funny dream.

1. Jennie and I were exploring Antarctica.
2. Both of us stood on an iceberg.
3. Cute little penguins swam all around us.
4. Some laughing seals pushed us into the water.
5. My mother woke me up.

Write NOW Write four sentences about a funny dream you've had. Then draw a line between the complete subject and the complete predicate in each sentence.

 Answers

Practice 1. <u>Mr. Huan</u> <u><u>gathered</u></u> paper towels and <u><u>mopped</u></u> up the mess.
2. Then another <u>bottle</u> <u><u>tipped</u></u> over and <u><u>spilled</u></u> onto the floor.
3. <u>Marah</u> and <u>Paul</u> <u><u>collected</u></u> more paper towels.
4. Other <u>students</u> and <u>teachers</u> <u><u>entered</u></u> the classroom and <u><u>asked</u></u> about the hubbub.
5. <u>Mr. Huan</u> <u><u>laughed</u></u> and <u><u>pointed</u></u> at the messy experiment.

 Answers

Practice 1. Jennie and I | were exploring Antarctica.
2. Both of us | stood on an iceberg.
3. Cute little penguins | swam all around us.
4. Some laughing seals | pushed us into the water.
5. My mother | woke me up.

Fixing Sentence Problems

How can I make sure my sentences are correct?

Check your writing for sentence fragments. A **fragment** is an incomplete sentence that is missing a subject, a predicate, or both.

FRAGMENT	SENTENCE
Collects stuffed animals. *(Missing a subject)*	My sister collects stuffed animals.
Family members. *(Missing a predicate)*	Family members give her stuffed animals for presents.
All around her room. *(Missing a subject and a predicate)*	They are all around her room.

 Practice

Number your paper from 1 to 5. Write "C" if a group of words is a complete sentence. Write "F" if it is a fragment. Rewrite each fragment to make it a complete sentence.

■ Started many years ago.
   F | Her collection started many years ago.

1. Aunt Susan bought her the first stuffed animal.

2. A small stuffed giraffe.

3. Her favorites.

4. My father made shelves for the animals.

5. Sit on her bed.

> Reading your sentences aloud will help you check for fragments.

Write NOW Write four sentences about something you collect or would like to collect. Make sure your sentences are complete.

 Building Effective Sentences **437**

Check for Run-On Sentences

A **run-on sentence** happens when two sentences run together without punctuation or a connecting word. You can correct a run-on sentence by forming two sentences or by adding a comma and a conjunction *(and, but, or)* between the two sentences.

RUN-ON SENTENCE	CORRECTED
The sky turned dark lightning flashed in the distance.	The sky turned dark. Lightning flashed in the distance. *(Form two sentences.)*
The wind picked up a few sprinkles started to fall.	The wind picked up, and a few sprinkles started to fall. *(Add a comma and a conjunction.)*

Practice

On your own paper, correct the run-on sentences below. Correct each one according to the directions in parentheses. Use the conjunctions *and* and *but*.

■ My horse started to trot I bounced up and down. *(Add a comma and a conjunction.)*
   My horse started to trot, and I bounced up and down.

1. My friend Marti rode up next to me then my horse slowed down. *(Form two sentences.)*

2. We tried to turn our horses around they wanted to go in a different direction. *(Add a comma and a conjunction.)*

3. Finally, the horses headed back to the stable they were probably hungry and thirsty. *(Form two sentences.)*

4. A stable worker was waiting for us we were glad to see him. *(Add a comma and a conjunction.)*

Answers

 Practice Corrected fragments will vary.

1. C
2. F
3. F
4. C
5. F

Answers

Practice

1. My friend Marti rode up next to me. Then my horse slowed down.

2. We tried to turn our horses around, but they wanted to go in a different direction.

3. Finally, the horses headed back to the stable. They were probably hungry and thirsty.

4. A stable worker was waiting for us, and we were glad to see him.

Watch for Subject-Verb Agreement

Subjects and verbs should always agree in number in your sentences. That means that whenever you use a singular subject, you need to use a singular verb; and whenever you use a plural subject, you need to use a plural verb.

SINGULAR AGREEMENT	PLURAL AGREEMENT
Brad builds birdhouses.	Brad and Paul build birdhouses.
My dog barks all night.	Our dogs bark all night.
I bake bread.	Lan and I bake bread.

> Most nouns ending in "s" or "es" are plural, but most verbs ending in "s" are singular.

Practice

Number your paper from 1 to 5. For each sentence below, write the correct form of the verb in parentheses.

■ My <u>mother</u> (*decorate, decorates*) the house for every holiday.
decorates

1. <u>She</u> (*set, sets*) candles and flowers on the tables.
2. My <u>brother</u> and <u>I</u> (*hang, hangs*) strings of colorful lights around the windows.
3. My <u>father</u> (*say, says*) that it always looks like we're having a party.
4. My <u>friends</u> (*think, thinks*) that it's great.
5. <u>They</u> (*like, likes*) to see what we've done.

Write NOW   Write four sentences about your favorite celebration or holiday. Try to use some singular and some plural subjects. Make sure the verbs agree with the subjects.

Subject-Verb Agreement with Compound Subjects

Subject-verb agreement is trickier when there is a compound subject. Look carefully at the compound subject and the conjunction to decide whether to use a singular or a plural verb.

COMPOUND SUBJECT	PREDICATE
Metal and glass	form pieces of art.
Welders and artists	work with these materials.

If the conjunction *and* is used, the verb must be plural.

Glass beads or links	decorate a necklace.
Either the artists or the welder	locks the studio door.

If the conjunction *or* is used, the verb must agree with the subject closest to it.

Practice

Number your paper from 1 to 5. For each sentence below, write the correct form of the verb in parentheses.

■ Allie and Susan (*like, likes*) the artwork at Pigs and Pots.
like

1. The girls and their mothers (*visit, visits*) the shop often.
2. Statues and a row of pots (*line, lines*) the shelves.
3. That necklace or those earrings (*look, looks*) pretty.
4. Susan and her mom (*buy, buys*) it for Grandma's birthday.
5. Thursday or Friday (*is, are*) her birthday.

Answers

Practice
1. sets
2. hang
3. says
4. think
5. like

Answers

Practice
1. visit
2. line
3. look
4. buy
5. is

Improving Sentence Style

How can I add variety to my sentences?

Here are five ideas for improving your writing by adding variety to your sentences.

1 Try different kinds of sentences.

2 Use different types of sentences.

3 Combine short sentences.

4 Expand sentences with prepositional phrases.

5 Model sentences other writers have created.

SENTENCES LACKING VARIETY

I went go-kart racing for the first time. I went on Saturday. I was a little nervous when I got into my go-kart. It was bright orange. The attendant showed me how to drive my machine. Before I knew it, I was on my way. I had a blast!

SENTENCE VARIETY IMPROVED

On Saturday, I went go-kart racing for the first time. I was a little nervous when I got into my go-kart, a bright orange one. Then the attendant showed me how to drive my machine, and before I knew it, I was on my way. I had a blast!

Your stories will be fun to read if you use a variety of sentences.

Try Different Kinds of Sentences

You can add variety to your writing by using the four different kinds of sentences.

KINDS OF SENTENCES			
Declarative .	Makes a statement	My cousin is always late.	This is the most common kind of sentence.
Interrogative ?	Asks a question	Are you ready?	A question gets the reader's attention.
Imperative . or !	Gives a command	Drink your milk. Hurry up!	Commands often appear in dialogue or directions.
Exclamatory !	Shows strong emotion or feeling	Wow, we're late!	These sentences emphasize a point.

Practice

Number your paper from 1 to 5. Label each sentence as "DEC" for declarative, "INT" for interrogative, "IMP" for imperative, or "EX" for exclamatory.

■ Stop tapping your pencil. IMP

1. It's so annoying!

2. Put your pencil down.

3. Did you realize you were doing it?

4. You must be thinking very hard.

5. What is your story about?

 Write NOW Write a paragraph about going to the dentist or the doctor. Use at least three different kinds of sentences.

Answers

Practice **1.** EX

2. IMP

3. INT

4. DEC

5. INT

Use Different Types of Sentences

You can add style to your writing by using different types of sentences. There are three types of sentences: **simple**, **compound**, and **complex**.

Use Effective Simple Sentences

A **simple sentence** states one complete thought.

SIMPLE SENTENCES	
Single subject with single predicate	Lisha **wrote** a report on marsupials.
Single subject with compound predicate	Marsupials **carry** and **nurse** their young in pouches.
Compound subject with compound predicate	Kangaroos and koalas **amuse** and **astound** people.

Practice

Copy sentences 1 through 5 on your own paper. In each sentence, underline the simple subject once and the simple predicate twice.

■ Gray kangaroos and red kangaroos are taller than wallaroos.
  Gray <u>Kangaroos</u> and red <u>Kangaroos</u> <u>are</u> taller than wallaroos.

1. Some kangaroos weigh more than 150 pounds.
2. These marsupials walk and hop very quickly.
3. Most kangaroos roam the plains or live in woodlands.
4. Potoroos and wallabies are small kangaroos.
5. Australian law protects them.

Write NOW Write four simple sentences about an animal that you find interesting.

Write Compound Sentences

A **compound sentence** is made up of two or more simple sentences joined together. One way to join simple sentences is by using a comma and a coordinating conjunction. (See 482.3.)

COMPOUND SENTENCES		
My brother Joe went hiking	**, and**	he asked me to go.
Our hike was exhausting	**, but**	we learned a lot about nature.
I asked Joe about a bird	**, or**	I looked in my bird book.

Practice

On your paper, combine the pairs of sentences in numbers 1 to 5 below. Use a comma and the coordinating conjunction given in parentheses.

■ I want to be a Scout. I want to be in my brother's troop. *(and)*
  I want to be a Scout, and I want to be in my brother's troop.

1. Scouts do volunteer work. They also have fun. *(but)*
2. I could work on a cleanup project. I could volunteer at a nursing home. *(or)*
3. I like helping people. It's a good way to make friends. *(and)*
4. My brother's troop meets every Tuesday. Everybody works on projects at other times. *(but)*
5. Our troop will go on a campout. We will go to the nature center. *(or)*

Write NOW Write two compound sentences about volunteer activities you could do in your community. Punctuate your sentences correctly.

Answers

Practice
1. Some <u>kangaroos</u> <u>weigh</u> more than 150 pounds.
2. These <u>marsupials</u> <u>walk</u> and <u>hop</u> very quickly.
3. Most <u>kangaroos</u> <u>roam</u> the plains or <u>live</u> in woodlands.
4. <u>Potoroos</u> and <u>wallabies</u> <u>are</u> small kangaroos.
5. Australian <u>law</u> <u>protects</u> them.

Answers

Practice
1. Scouts do volunteer work, but they also have fun.
2. I could work on a cleanup project, or I could volunteer at a nursing home.
3. I like helping people, and it's a good way to make friends.
4. My brother's troop meets every Tuesday, but everybody works on projects at other times.
5. Our troop will go on a campout, or we will go to the nature center.

Write Complex Sentences

You can join simple sentences by forming a **complex sentence.** A complex sentence has one independent clause and one or more dependent clauses.

An **independent clause** expresses a complete thought and can stand alone as a sentence. A **dependent clause** does not express a complete thought and cannot stand alone as a sentence. It often begins with a subordinating conjunction such as **when, because,** or **as.** (See page 600 for a list of subordinating conjunctions.)

COMPLEX SENTENCE		
AN INDEPENDENT CLAUSE	+	**A DEPENDENT CLAUSE**
I take the bus to school		when my mom can't drive me.
A DEPENDENT CLAUSE	+	**AN INDEPENDENT CLAUSE**
As the marching band went by,		we cheered and yelled.

Practice

Copy each complex sentence below. Underline the dependent clause in each sentence.

■ When Abe Lincoln was a flatboat pilot, he settled in Illinois.
  <u>When Abe Lincoln was a flatboat pilot,</u> he settled in Illinois.

1. The future president liked the town of New Salem because it was built along the Sangamon River.
2. As the town developed, Lincoln became a merchant.
3. While Lincoln lived in New Salem, he also studied law.
4. Lincoln became a militia captain before he moved on.
5. After Lincoln left New Salem, he moved to Springfield.

 Write NOW Write a paragraph about a person or place from history. Use at least two complex sentences.

Combine Short Sentences
Use Key Words and Phrases

You can combine short sentences by moving a key word or phrase from one sentence to another.

SHORT SENTENCES	COMBINED SENTENCES
Karly writes letters. They are <u>crazy.</u> *(The key word is underlined.)*	Karly writes crazy letters. *(The adjective crazy has been moved to the first sentence.)*
Grant draws cartoons. He draws them <u>for the newspaper.</u> *(The prepositional phrase is underlined.)*	Grant draws cartoons for the newspaper. *(The prepositional phrase has been moved to the first sentence.)*

Practice

On your own paper, combine the pairs of short sentences below. Move a key word or phrase from one sentence to the other.

■ Stephanie wrote a play. She wrote it for her friends.
  Stephanie wrote a play for her friends.

1. Her play starts in a snowstorm. The snowstorm is blinding.
2. The girls are trapped. They are trapped in an old barn.
3. They search everywhere in the barn. They search for tools.
4. One of the girls finds a ball of twine. The ball is huge.
5. The twine gives them an idea. It gives them an idea for their escape.

 Write NOW Write a paragraph describing how the girls in the sentences above escape from the barn. Try not to use any short, choppy sentences.

Answers

 Practice

1. The future president liked the town of New Salem <u>because it was built along the Sangamon River.</u>
2. <u>As the town developed,</u> Lincoln became a merchant.
3. <u>While Lincoln lived in New Salem,</u> he also studied law.
4. Lincoln became a militia captain <u>before he moved on.</u>
5. <u>After Lincoln left new Salem,</u> he moved to Springfield.

Answers

Practice

1. Her play starts in a blinding snowstorm.
2. The girls are trapped in an old barn.
3. They search for tools everywhere in the barn.
4. One of the girls finds a huge ball of twine.
5. The twine gives them an idea for their escape.

Use a Series of Words or Phrases

Ideas in short sentences can be combined using a **series of words or phrases**. All of the words or phrases in a series should be parallel. That means they are stated in the same way. (See 482.1.)

SHORT SENTENCES	COMBINED SENTENCES
The cabin is dusty. The cabin is musty. It is also messy.	The cabin is dusty, musty, and messy.
We watch games on TV. We watch games in the park. We also watch games at the high school.	We watch games on TV, in the park, and at the high school.

Practice

Combine each group of sentences using a series of words or phrases. (Some words may need to be changed to make the sentences work.)

■ In the winter, I go sledding. I go downhill skiing. I also go ice-skating.
   In the winter, I go sledding, downhill skiing, and ice-skating.

1. While ice-skating, I can spin. I can go backward. I can stop suddenly.
2. Angie likes to do tricks. Mora likes to do tricks. Kala likes to do tricks, too.
3. I always feel the cold on my face. I feel it on my fingertips. I also feel it on my toes.
4. To get warm, I go to the skating shelter. To rest, I go to the shelter. To have a snack, I go to the shelter.

Write NOW Write three sentences for a classmate to combine. Make sure your sentences can be combined using a series of words or phrases.

Combine Sentences with Compound Subjects and Predicates

Sometimes you can combine two sentences by moving a subject or a predicate from one sentence to another. This makes a compound subject or a compound predicate. (See page 434.)

SHORT SENTENCES	COMBINED SENTENCES
Maria makes posters for the school carnival. Brandi also makes posters.	Maria and Brandi make posters for the school carnival. *(A compound subject is formed.)*
The girls finished five posters. Then they hung them up.	The girls finished five posters and hung them up. *(A compound predicate is formed.)*

Practice

Combine the following sets of short sentences using a compound subject or a compound predicate. (Some words may need to be changed.)

■ The PTO organized the carnival. The Booster Club did, too.
   The PTO and the Booster Club organized the carnival.

1. The students designed the booths. They also built them.
2. Ling sold tickets for each activity. Bette sold tickets, too.
3. Bowling was a popular activity. Shooting baskets was popular. Tossing rings was popular, too.
4. Devon fished for prizes. He threw beanbags for popcorn.
5. Mr. Harris dressed as a clown. Ms. Butler did, too.

Write NOW Write two sets of short sentences for a classmate to combine. Make sure that the sentences can be combined using a compound subject or a compound predicate.

Answers

 Practice

1. While ice, skating, I can spin, go backward, and stop suddenly.
2. Angie, Mora, and Kala like to do tricks.
3. I always feel the cold on my face, on my fingertips, and on my toes.
4. To get warm, to rest, or to have a snack, I go to the shelter. (or) I go to the shelter to get warm, to rest, or to have a snack.

Answers

Practice

1. The students designed and built the booths.
2. Ling and Bette sold tickets for each activity.
3. Bowling, shooting baskets, and tossing rings were popular activities.
4. Devon fished for prizes and threw beanbags for popcorn.
5. Mr. Harris and Ms. Butler dressed as clowns.

Expand Sentences with Prepositional Phrases

A prepositional phrase can add information to a sentence. Prepositional phrases begin with words like *on, in, to, about, at, of, with, down, through, for, until,* and *under*. (See page 598 for more prepositions.)

Prepositional phrases add details to your sentences.

PREPOSITIONAL PHRASES

Crystal flew down the waterslide.
We went to lunch with my grandma.
I found my backpack on a shelf in the library.

Practice

Number your paper from 1 to 5. Write the prepositional phrases you find in each of the following sentences.

■ Every day the sun moves across the sky.
across the sky

1. In ancient Greece, people believed it was a golden chariot.
2. Apollo drove the chariot of heat and light.
3. His son, Phaeton, tried steering the chariot through the sky.
4. Apollo warned his son about the danger.
5. Phaeton dropped the reins and fell to the earth.

Write NOW Think of one or two prepositional phrases to add information to each of the sentences below. Write the new sentences on your own paper.

1. Casey plays softball.
2. She catches and pitches.
3. Casey won the last game.
4. Her team practices.

Model Sentences

You can learn a lot about sentences by studying and modeling the work of your favorite writers. Modeling is following a writer's pattern of words and punctuation in sentences of your own.

PROFESSIONAL MODEL	STUDENT SENTENCE
In the clearing, I saw a deer, slim and silent, staring at me.	Under the steps, I noticed a kitten, small and frightened, meowing for food.

Guidelines for Modeling

• **Varying Sentence Beginnings**
Try starting sentences with a dependent clause or phrase, set apart by a comma.

No matter how hard he tries, **Walnut doesn't see as well as others do.**
—*Sees Behind Trees* by Michael Dorris

• **Moving Adjectives**
Sometimes you can vary a sentence by placing an adjective or two after the noun it modifies.

Ramona Quimby, brave and fearless, **was half running, half skipping to keep up with her big sister Beatrice on their way home from the park.**
—*Ramona the Brave* by Beverly Cleary

• **Repeating a Word**
You can repeat a word to emphasize a particular idea or feeling.

Pigs enjoy eating, **and they also** enjoy **lying around most of the day thinking about** eating **again.**
—*Babe the Gallant Pig* by Dick King-Smith

Practice

Write three of your own sentences modeled after the examples given above. Try to follow the pattern of the original sentence as closely as you can.

Answers

 Practice

1. In ancient Greece
2. of heat and light
3. through the sky
4. about the danger
5. to the earth

Answers

Practice   Answers will vary.

Preparing for Tests

How can I check my sentence knowledge?

Read the paragraph below. Then answer the questions that follow it.

1. Skijoring is an interesting winter sport. **2.** It started in Scandinavia and has spread to many other countries. **3.** The word is Norwegian and means "ski driving." **4.** To skijor, you need cross-country skis, a harness, a tow line, and a dog. **5.** Yes, I said a dog! **6.** Skijoring is a form of dogsled running. **7.** The dog doesn't tow a sled. **8.** But tows a skier. **9.** A skier can use any dog more than a year and a half old and weighing more than 35 pounds. **10.** Sometimes the skier uses just one dog, and sometimes two or three dogs make up a team. **11.** Can you imagine being towed by three dogs, yelping and racing? **12.** Skijorers even takes part in races. **13.** Some races are sprints of five miles, but distance racers can go a lot farther. **14.** Although it doesn't seem possible, some dogs often average speeds as high as 20 miles per hour!

1. Which of the sentences is a fragment?
  a. Sentence 5
  b. Sentence 8
  c. Sentence 12
  d. Sentence 14

2. Which of the sentences is an interrogatory sentence?
  a. Sentence 2
  b. Sentence 3
  c. Sentence 11
  d. Sentence 12

3. Which of the sentences contains an error in subject-verb agreement?
  a. Sentence 7
  b. Sentence 10
  c. Sentence 12
  d. Sentence 14

4. Which sentence is an exclamatory sentence?
  a. Sentence 3
  b. Sentence 5
  c. Sentence 11
  d. Sentence 13

5. Which of the sentences is a complex sentence?
  a. Sentence 9
  b. Sentence 10
  c. Sentence 13
  d. Sentence 14

6. Which of the sentences are compound sentences?
  a. Sentences 2 and 3
  b. Sentences 9 and 11
  c. Sentences 4 and 12
  d. Sentences 10 and 13

7. Which of the sentences contain adjectives or modifying phrases after the noun they modify?
  a. Sentence 1
  b. Sentence 2
  c. Sentence 7
  d. Sentence 11

Answers

1. b   **5.** d
2. c   **6.** d
3. c   **7.** a
4. b

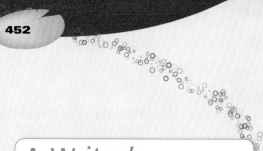

452

A Writer's Resource

453

A Writer's Resource

When a frog needs help with his writing, what can he do? He can't attend a school of fish, but he can flip to the "A Writer's Resource."

This chapter can help you find topics, organize details, create a strong voice, improve vocabulary, and write better sentences—just to name a few things. Whenever you have questions, check these pages for answers.

Mini Index

You will learn how to . . .

- find topics and get started. 454
- collect and organize details. 456
- write strong topic sentences. 460
- create an effective voice. 462
- use new techniques. 464
- increase your vocabulary. 466
- write better sentences. 470
- connect your ideas. 472
- improve your final copy. 474
- write effective letters. 476

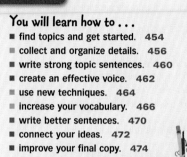

How can I find a good topic to write about?

Try a Topic-Selecting Strategy

The following strategies will help you select specific topics that you truly want to write about.

Clustering Begin a cluster by writing the topic or main idea of your assignment in the center of your paper. Then list, circle, and connect related words and ideas around it. (See the cluster on page 456.)

Freewriting With your general subject in mind, write freely for 3 to 5 minutes. Do not stop to make corrections or look up facts—just write. As you freewrite, you may find one or two specific topics you could use.

Sentence Completion Another way to find a topic is to complete a sentence starter in as many ways as you can. Make sure that your sentence starter has something to do with your assignment. Here are some samples:

I remember when . . .	I really get excited when . . .
One thing I know about . . .	I just learned . . .
I wonder how . . .	School is . . .

"Basics-of-Life" List

Look at the list below for more possible topic areas. Here's how to use the "Basics-of-Life" list: (Also see page 148.)

1. Choose a subject category. *(school)*
2. Decide what part of this subject fits your assignment. *(performing arts)*
3. List possible specific topics. *(dance and drama)*

animals	school	clothing	sports	food
friends	community	family	faith	environment
health	computers	games	rules	books
movies	science	exercise	money	television

What else can I do to get started?

Use a List of Writing Topics

The following topics are organized according to the four basic forms of writing. Look through these lists to find ideas that relate to your assignment.

Descriptive Writing

People: a clerk, a teacher, a friend, a neighbor, yourself, a family member, someone you admire, someone from history

Places: a room, a garage, a cave, a canyon, a rooftop, the alley, the gym, a store, an art gallery, a river, the jungle, a farm, a circus

Things: a pet, a painting, a video game, a junk drawer, a photograph, a special object, a Web site, a stuffed animal, a car, a tree

Narrative Writing

Tell about . . . getting in trouble, getting lost, making a memory, helping someone, being surprised, being scared, learning to do something

Expository Writing

How to . . . make a sub sandwich, care for a pet, juggle, earn money, get in shape, be a good friend, eat a balanced diet, saddle a horse

The causes of . . . pollution, rust, hurricanes, infections, success in school, happiness, accidents, tornadoes, erosion, tooth decay

Kinds of . . . music, commercials, clouds, heroes, clothes, restaurants, fun, books, games, animals, houses, vehicles, art, governments

The definition of . . . friendship, courage, a hero, geology, freedom, love, a team, family, compassion, failure, peace

Persuasive Writing

Issues: school rules, recycling, helmets (bicycle, skateboard), things that need to be changed, causes to support, pet peeves, something to avoid, a need for more or less of something

How can I collect details for my writing?

Try Graphic Organizers

You can use graphic organizers to gather details for different types of writing.

Web Organizer A web or cluster will help you gather facts and ideas for reports, narratives, and poems. Begin by writing the subject in the middle of the page. Then list, circle, and connect related words around it.

Personal Narrative: My first train trip to the city

Sensory Details Chart This organizer will help you collect descriptive details for observation reports and other types of expository writing. At the tops of the columns, write the names of the five senses. In each column, list sensory details related to your topic.

Expository Essay: Kinds of transportation

Sight	Sound	Smell	Taste	Touch
- gleaming jet	- rumbling truck	- city bus exhaust	- salty spray on an ocean-going ship	- floating in hot-air balloon
- yellow schoolbus	- squeal of train wheels			

Time Line Time lines help you organize events in chronological (time) order. Personal narratives and how-to essays are often arranged this way. Start your time line by writing the topic at the top. Then list the events or steps in order, the earliest ones first.

How-To Essay: Making a papier-mâché piñata

1. Mix two cups each of flour and water in a big bowl.
2. Dip newspaper strips in flour and water mixture.
3. Lay the coated newspaper on the form.
4. When the papier-mâché is dry, decorate it with paint.

Venn Diagram A Venn diagram can be used to organize your thoughts when you need to compare and contrast two subjects. List the specific details that only one of your subjects has in area 1. List the specific details that only the second subject has in area 2. In area 3, list the details the two things have in common.

Expository Writing: Apples versus oranges

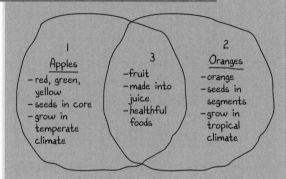

How can I organize my details effectively?

Put Ideas in Order

After you choose your topic and collect details, you should organize your information. First, decide on an order and then make an outline. Here are three ways to put your information in order.

Time Order

The details are explained in the order in which they happen (*after, before, during,* and so on). Time order works well in narrative or expository writing.

> The **first** step in planning a bug hunt is to call your friends and set up a time. **Next**, everyone should find a pencil and a notebook. If someone has a bug identification book, that would also be helpful. **Finally**, go outside and see how many bugs you can find!

Order of Location

Details are described in the order in which they are located (*above, behind, beneath,* and so on). Order of location works well in descriptive or expository writing.

> Bugs are all **around** you **in** your backyard. When you look **under** rocks or logs, bugs scurry away. **Above** the ground **on** a tree trunk, bugs run **up and down**. Flying insects buzz **over** your head. Bugs are everywhere.

Order of Importance

The most important detail comes either first or last (*most important, best, funniest,* and so on). Persuasive and expository writing can be organized in this way.

> **For one thing**, a bug hunt gets you outside. You can **also** have fun with your friends and enjoy nature. **Best of all**, you can learn something about the hundreds of interesting insects that are all around you every day.

Build a Topic Outline

After you have decided what kind of order to use, you can write an outline. Choose several main points that support your topic. Under each main point, list the details that explain it. A **topic outline** contains only words and phrases, and a **sentence outline** contains complete thoughts.

Topic Outline

> I.   Problem of icy streetcar windshields seen by Mary Anderson in New York City in 1903
>   A. Streetcar ride on snowy day
>   B. Driver squinting and stopping to clean windshield
> II. Plan to clean windshield from inside streetcar
>   A. Sketches of wooden arm with rubber strips
>   B. Arm on outside connected to lever inside
>   C. Weight to hold arm and spring to return it
> III. Idea doesn't catch on
>   A. Failure of other solutions
>   B. Distraction for drivers

Sentence Outline

> I. Mary Anderson saw a windshield problem in New York City in 1903.
>   A. She rode a streetcar on a snowy day.
>   B. She saw the driver squinting and stopping to clean off snow.
> II. Mary thought there should be some way to wipe the windshield from inside the streetcar.

How can I write strong topic sentences?

Try a Special Strategy

A good paragraph starts with a strong topic sentence. A topic sentence should (1) name the topic and (2) state a detail or feeling about it. The strategies below will help you write great topic sentences.

Use a Number

Use number words to tell what the paragraph will be about.

Four forces shape and reshape the earth's surface.

Create a List

Create a list of the things that the paragraph will include.

We didn't think our puppy would get out of its crate, chew up a shoe, and break a lamp before we got home.

Join Two Ideas

Combine two ideas by using a comma and a coordinating conjunction: *and, but, or, for, so, nor, yet.*

Jamie wanted to get up early, but we wanted to sleep late.

Explorers never found a city of gold, yet their adventures led them to new lands.

Quote an Expert

To get your paragraph off to a strong start, quote someone who knows something about your topic.

My Dad tells me that professional carpenters always say, "Measure twice, cut once."

"You have to love dolphins to be a good trainer," says dolphin expert Sue Stanson.

"If you want to be a good musician," my piano teacher, Mrs. Wright, always says, "you must practice, practice, practice."

What forms can I use for my writing?

Try These Forms of Writing

Finding the right form for your writing is very important. When you choose a form, think about *who* you're writing for (your *audience*) and *why* you're writing (your *purpose*). Listed below are a few different forms of descriptive, narrative, expository, and persuasive writing.

Anecdote	A little story used to make a point
Autobiography	The story of the writer's own life (See pages 83–124.)
Biography	The story of someone else's life
Book Review	Writing that shares your thoughts and feelings about a book (See pages 257–272.)
Cartoon	A simple drawing with a funny message
Character Sketch	A description of one character in a story
Editorial	Newspaper letter or article that gives opinions
Fable	A short story that often uses talking animals as characters to teach a lesson
News Release	An explanation of a newsworthy event using the 5 W's (*who, what, where, when,* and *why*)
Pet Peeve	A personal feeling about something that bugs someone
Proposal	Writing that asks for approval of an idea, a report, or a schedule
Tall Tale	A funny, exaggerated story about a character that does impossible things (See pages 292–297.)
Travelogue	Writing that describes a trip or travel pictures

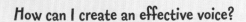

How can I create an effective voice?

Make Your Voice Fit Your Purpose

Your writing should sound like it fits your purpose. The four basic purposes of writing are to describe, to narrate, to explain, and to persuade.

Descriptive Voice

A good descriptive voice sounds *interested*. One way to improve your descriptive voice is to follow this rule: "*show,* don't *tell.*"

Telling: (The writer tells about a mouse.)

The little mouse came into the room.

Showing: (The writer shows us the mouse.)

Everyone at the table was eating and talking. In a quiet moment, I heard a scratching sound coming from across the room. No else seemed to notice. Then I saw Tasha our cat lift her head and look toward the noise. Then she got into pounce position. That's when I spotted a little mouse in the corner.

Narrative Voice

A good narrative voice sounds *natural* and *personal*. Your narrative writing should sound like you're telling a story to a friend.

Not Natural and Personal:

Uncle Ned came from Texas. He came to visit us last week. He always surprises me. He makes me laugh.

Natural and Personal:

When I came home last Wednesday, the front door was open. I called for Mom. She answered from the kitchen. Then the closet door squeaked and flew open! I jumped back before I saw a huge handlebar mustache. My uncle Ned from Texas jumped out. I couldn't stop laughing. He had surprised me again.

Expository Voice

An effective expository voice uses interesting (specific) *details*.

- **Without Interesting Details:**

The Rocky Mountains stretch through most of North America. The Rockies include many mountain ranges. The highest point is in Colorado.

- **With Interesting (Specific) Details:**

The Rocky Mountains stretch almost 2,000 miles from northern Mexico through the western part of the United States and Canada into eastern Alaska. The Rockies include more than 100 mountain ranges. At 14,433 feet, Mt. Elbert near Leadville, Colorado, is the highest point in the Rocky Mountain chain.

Persuasive Voice

A persuasive voice sounds *positive,* not negative.

- **Negative:**

Our Bloomfield Youth Club meetings are boring. We have to sit still and be quiet, and that's not fun. Somebody should do something about it.

- **Positive:**

We should have more activities at our Bloomfield Youth Club meetings. We could practice our camp and map skills to get ready for our summer outing. After that, we could play some games. Youth club meetings would be a good time to get things done and have some fun.

How can I spice up my writing style?

Use Some Writing Techniques

You can develop a lively writing style by using some special effects. For example, you can add dialogue to your stories to make them more personal and natural (see page 96). Experiment with some of the following techniques in your own writing.

Exaggeration Stating something that goes beyond the truth to make a point (works well in descriptive and narrative writing)

The giraffe peeked over the clouds **and spotted the missing balloon.**

Idiom Using a word to mean something different from its usual or dictionary meaning

Julian got up and said, "I'm cutting out."
(Here, *cutting out* means "leaving.")
Ray said he'd buy the bike sight unseen.
(Here, *sight unseen* means "without seeing it first.")

Metaphor Comparing two things without using the word *like* or *as*

Dad's temper **was** a pot boiling over.
The cruise ship **was** a floating hotel.

Personification Giving human qualities to nonhuman things

The wind whispers **through the trees.**
(The verb *whispers* describes a human activity.)

Sensory Details Details that help the reader hear, see, smell, taste, or touch what is being described

The soft black **kitten** purred quietly **as I** cuddled **her** in my arms.

Simile Comparing two things using the word *like* or *as*

A cold lemonade **refreshes me just** as a dip in the pool does.
In track meets, Sophie **runs** like a deer.

How can I learn to talk about my writing?

Study Some Writing Terms

This glossary includes terms that name important parts of the writing process.

Audience	The people who read or hear your writing
Dialogue	Written conversation between two or more people
Focus Statement	A sentence telling the specific part of a topic the writer will concentrate or "focus" on (See page 151.)
Point of View	The angle or viewpoint from which a story is told (See page 310.)
Purpose	The main reason for writing a certain piece to describe to narrate to explain to persuade
Style	The way a writer puts words, phrases, and sentences together
Supporting Details	Specific details used to develop a topic or bring a story to life
Theme	A main idea or message in a piece of writing
Topic	The specific subject of a piece of writing
Topic Sentence	The sentence that expresses the main idea of a paragraph (See page 460.)
Transition	A word or phrase that ties ideas together in essays, paragraphs, and sentences (See pages 472–473.)
Voice	The tone or feeling a writer uses to express ideas

How can I increase my vocabulary skills?

Try Vocabulary-Building Techniques

Use context.

When you are reading, you may come to a word you don't know. Check the words around it to see if you can figure out its meaning. (See the next page.)

Everyone thought that Jason was making a frivolous **comment, but he was being** serious. (The word *but* suggests that *serious* is the opposite of *frivolous*. So *frivolous* means "not serious, or of little importance.")

Look up words in the dictionary.

When you come to a word you don't know, look it up in the dictionary. (See page 331.)

My cousin Clare likes mush **for breakfast.**

> **mush**[1] (mŭsh) *n.* **1.** A porridge made of cornmeal boiled in water or milk.

Learn about word parts.

You can figure out the meanings of new words by learning about prefixes, suffixes, and roots. (See pages 468–469.) The following sentence contains three examples:

During revising, **you make sure your** para graph **flows smooth**ly. (*Re-* is a prefix meaning "again"; *graph* is a root meaning "write"; *-ly* is a suffix meaning "in some manner.")

Use Context

You can often figure out a challenging word by looking at the words around it. Here are some ways to do this:

- Study the sentence containing the word, as well as the sentences that come before and after it.

  Chuck Yeager broke the sound barrier in 1947. That year he flew the first successful supersonic **flight. No one had ever flown faster than the speed of sound before.** (*Supersonic* means "faster than the speed of sound.")

- Look for **word parts.** In the example above, *super* is a prefix that means "over and above," and *sonic* is a root word meaning "sound."

- Search for **synonyms** (words with the same meaning).

  Mom calls me an aviator **because I want to be a pilot.** (An *aviator* is a "pilot.")

- Search for **antonyms** (words with the opposite meaning).

  Sandy thought the bug was repulsive, **but I thought it was beautiful.** (The word *but* suggests that *repulsive* is the opposite of *beautiful.* So *repulsive* means "ugly.")

- Search for a **definition** of the word.

  My friend Mark has a hedgehog, **a small porcupine-like animal.** (A *hedgehog* is a porcupine-like animal.)

- Search for **familiar words in a series** with the new word.

  Is that a Lhasa apso, **a poodle, or a terrier?** (A *Lhasa apso* is a small dog.)

Learn About Word Parts

Beginning with Prefixes

Prefixes are word parts that come before the root or base word (*pre-* means "before"). Prefixes can change the meaning of a word. For example, *kind* means "gentle." When you add the prefix *un-*, meaning "not," the resulting word, *unkind*, means "not gentle." Here are some other common prefixes:

equi *(equal)*
 equinox (a day and night of equal length)

ex *(out)*
 expel (to drive out)

inter *(among, between)*
 international (between two or more nations)

mal *(bad, poor)*
 malnutrition (poor nutrition)

multi *(many, much)*
 multicultural (including many cultures)

non *(absence of, not)*
 nonfat (without fat)

pre *(before)*
 preview (to show something before the regular time)

re *(again, back)*
 rewrite (to write again)

Ending with Suffixes

Suffixes are word parts that come at the end of a word. Sometimes a suffix will tell you what part of speech a word is. For example, many adverbs end in the suffix *-ly*. Add the suffix *-able*, which means "able to," to the word *agree*, and the resulting word, *agreeable*, means "able or willing to agree." Here are some other suffixes:

ion *(state of)*
 infection (state of being infected)

less *(without)*
 careless (without care)

ly *(in some manner)*
 bashfully (in a bashful manner)

ness *(state of)*
 carelessness (state of being careless)

logy *(study, science)*
 biology (study of living things)

y *(tending to)*
 itchy (tending to itch)

Knowing Your Roots

A **root** is the main part of a word. If you know the root of a difficult word, you may be able to figure out the word's meaning.

Suppose that you hear your teacher say, "I couldn't understand what the speaker said because his voice was *inaudible*." If you know that the prefix *in-* means "not" and the root *aud* means "hear or listen," you will know that your teacher couldn't hear the speaker's voice. Here are some other roots:

alter *(other)*
 alternate (another choice)

bio *(life)*
 biography (book about a person's life)

chron *(time)*
 chronological (in time order)

cise *(cut)*
 incision (a thin, clean cut)

cycl, cyclo *(wheel, circular)*
 bicycle (a cycle with two wheels)
 cyclone (a circular wind)

dem *(people)*
 democracy (ruled by the people)

fin *(end)*
 final (the last or end of something)

flex *(bend)*
 flexible (able to bend)

fract, frag *(break)*
 fracture (to break)
 fragment (a small piece)

geo *(earth)*
 geography (the description of the earth's surface)

graph *(write)*
 autograph (writing one's name)

mit, miss *(send)*
 emit (send out, give off)
 missile (an object sent flying)

port *(carry)*
 export (to carry out)

scope *(see, watch)*
 microscope (an instrument used for viewing objects too small to be seen with the naked eye)

spir *(breath)*
 expire (breathe out, die)
 inspire (breathe in, give life to)

therm *(heat)*
 thermostat (a device for controlling heat)

voc *(call)*
 vocalize (to use the voice; sing)

How can I write better sentences?

Study Sentence Patterns

Use a variety of sentence patterns to create better sentence fluency. Some basic sentence patterns are shown below.

1 Subject + Action Verb

    S   AV
Sally walked. (Some action verbs, like *walked,* do not need a direct object to make a complete thought.)

2 Subject + Action Verb + Direct Object

    S   AV   DO
Thad collects coins. (Some action verbs, like *collects,* need a direct object, like *coins,* to make a complete thought.)

3 Subject + Action Verb + Indirect Object + Direct Object

    S   AV   IO   DO
Mom gave Allison an apple.

4 Subject + Action Verb + Direct Object + Object Complement

    S   AV   DO   OC
Miss Dyer named Alexis treasurer.

5 Subject + Linking Verb + Predicate Noun

    S   LV   PN
Palominos are horses.

6 Subject + Linking Verb + Predicate Adjective

    S   LV PA
Clydesdales are huge.

In the patterns above, the subject comes before the verb. In the patterns below, the subject (called a *delayed subject*) comes after the verb.

    LV S   PA
7 Are you sleepy? (A question)

         LV   S
8 There are five ants. (A sentence beginning with *there* or *here*)

Practice Sentence Diagramming

Diagramming a sentence can help you see the purpose of each word in the sentence. Below you can see diagrams of the sentences on page 470.

1 **Sally walked.**

Sally | walked

2 **Thad collects coins.**

Thad | collects | coins

3 **Mom gave Allison an apple.**

Mom | gave | apple / Allison

Note: Place an indirect object on a straight line that is connected to the verb by a diagonal line.

4 **Miss Dyer named Alexis treasurer.**

Miss Dyer | named | Alexis \ treasurer

Note: Place a vertical line between a verb and its direct object. Use a diagonal line before the object complement.

5 **Palominos are horses.**

Palominos | are \ horses

Note: Place a diagonal line between a linking verb and the predicate noun or adjective.

6 **Clydesdales are huge.**

Clydesdales | are \ huge

How can I connect my ideas?

Use Transitions

Transitions can be used to connect sentences and paragraphs. The lists below show different groups of transitions.

Words that show location:

above	around	between	inside	outside
across	behind	by	into	over
against	below	down	near	throughout
along	beneath	in back of	off	to the right
among	beside	in front of	on top of	under

My favorite bakery is near our apartment. Around the corner, there's a coffee shop that Mom likes.

Words that show time:

about	during	until	yesterday	finally
after	first	meanwhile	next	then
at	second	today	soon	as soon as
before	third	tomorrow	later	when

Today I saw frost on the lawn. Yesterday it was warm when I walked to school.

Words that compare (show similarities):

in the same way	likewise	as	while
similarly	like	also	

The summer clouds looked like giant balloons floating across the sky.

Words that contrast (show differences):

on the other hand	otherwise	but	although
even though	however	still	yet

Be sure to eat a balanced diet. Otherwise, you won't get enough vitamins and minerals.

Words that emphasize a point:

again	truly	especially	for this reason
to repeat	in fact	to emphasize	

In fact, of all the ways you can protect yourself while skateboarding, the most important way is wearing a helmet.

Words that add information:

again	for instance	and	as well
also	besides	next	along with
another	for example	finally	in addition

The principal could tell the tree was dead and would have to be cut down.

Words that summarize:

as a result	finally	in conclusion
therefore	lastly	because

Finally, write your name at the bottom of the page and turn in your paper.

How can I make my final copy look better?

Add Diagrams and Graphs

Diagrams are simple drawings that include labels.

Line diagrams help you see how or where someone or something fits into a situation (like in a family tree). A line diagram can also show how things are organized into groups.

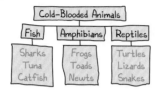

Graphs show information about how things change over time or about how things compare to each other. They show information that includes a range of numbers.

A **bar graph** compares two or more things at one point in time—like a snapshot. The bars on a graph can be shown horizontally in rows or vertically in columns.

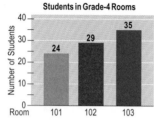

A **line graph** is plotted on a grid. The information at the bottom shows equal amounts of time. The vertical side refers to the subject of the graph. The plotted line shows how the subject increased and decreased within the time frame shown.

Add Pictures

Pictures will help make your final copy clear and interesting. Use photos from magazines or newspapers, or download pictures from the Internet (if you have permission). Consider making your own drawings or taking your own photographs for a more personal touch.

■ **To Inform** . . . Pictures can help the reader understand your topic. They add color and interesting details in the body of a report or an essay. They can also be used to decorate a report cover. The picture below is part of an essay about how to search the Internet.

If you don't know how to search the Internet, here's how you do it. Turn on your computer, grab the mouse, and open your browser. Find a search engine like Yahoo.com or Google.com, and you will have plenty of information to research.

■ **To Set the Tone** . . . Pictures can show the reader how you feel about your topic. The picture below could be included in a report on pets. The reader would see what the writer thinks about cats. Notice how the words and picture work together.

Many people think that cats make the best pets. They are clean and quiet. It's possible to leave them alone for several days with their food, water, and litter box. Cats often like to curl up in a lap or stay close to people. A soft, purring cat can make a very good pet.

How should I set up my practical writing?

Follow Guidelines for Letters

Friendly letters and **business letters** have the same basic parts—*heading, salutation, body, closing,* and *signature*. In addition, a business letter has an *inside address.*

Friendly Letter

In a friendly letter, the paragraphs are indented. The side notes below explain the parts.

Heading
Sender's address and date

Salutation
A greeting followed by a comma

Body
Paragraphs indented; no space between them

Closing
First word capitalized; a comma at the end

Signature
Written signature

> 712 Main Street
> Salina, KS 67402
> November 15, 2005
>
> Dear Aunt Min,
>
> Thank you very much for sending me the birthday gift. I am already halfway through the book. You got me interested in the author, and now I want to read all of her books.
>
> I love horse stories. Dad says that maybe we can get a pony next spring. Sarah, Danny, and I are very excited about that. We're lucky to have a small barn. Maybe we'll get more than one pony!
>
> I'm sorry that you won't be coming to our house for Thanksgiving. Your trip to Florida should be interesting, but we will miss the stories you always tell as we sit around the dinner table. Send me a postcard when you go to the Everglades.
>
> Your niece,
> Julie

Business Letter

The parts of a business letter all start at the left margin. Check the side notes below for more details.

Heading
Sender's address and date

Inside Address
Name and address of person or company

Salutation
A greeting followed by a colon

Body
No indentations and double-spaced between paragraphs

Closing
First word capitalized; a comma at the end
Signature
Written signature above the typed or printed name

> 401 Horace Street
> Burlington, CO 80807
> January 21, 2005
>
> Mr. Darjeeling, Manager
> Pets and More
> 1017 Tomike Avenue
> Burlington, CO 80807
>
> Dear Mr. Darjeeling:
>
> We are studying mammals in Mr. Leonard's fourth-grade class. The class chose me to organize the supplies for our study. I would like to order two hamsters, one male and one female. We also need a bag of sawdust and a box of hamster food.
>
> If you have a small book about raising hamsters, we need one copy. Please call Burlington Elementary School office to find out who should get the bill for our project.
>
> Sincerely,
> *Sandy Delaney*
> Sandy Delaney

Envelope

Address envelopes for business and friendly letters the same way: Use all capital letters and no punctuation.

> SANDY DELANEY
> 401 HORACE ST
> BURLINGTON CO 80807
>
>
>
> MR DARJEELING MANAGER
> PETS AND MORE
> 1017 TOMIKE AVE
> BURLINGTON CO 80807

478

Proofreader's Guide

Marking Punctuation

Periods

A **period** is used to end a sentence. It is also used after initials, after abbreviations, and as a decimal point.

479.1

At the End of a Sentence

Use a period to end a sentence that is a statement, a command, or a request.

> **Taro won the pitching contest.** (statement)
>
> **Take his picture.** (command)
>
> **Please loan me your baseball cap.** (request)

479.2

After an Initial

Use a period after an initial in a person's name. (An initial is the first letter of a name.)

> **B. B. King** (blues musician)
>
> **A. A. Milne** (writer)

479.3

As a Decimal Point

Use a period as a decimal point and to separate dollars and cents.

> **Robert is 99.9 percent sure that the bus pass costs $2.50.**

479.4

In Abbreviations

Use a period after an abbreviation. (See page **520** for more about abbreviations.)

> **Mr. Mrs. Jr. Dr. B.C.E. U.S.A.**

Use only one period when an abbreviation is the last word in a sentence.

> **A library has books, CD's, DVD's, magazines, etc.**

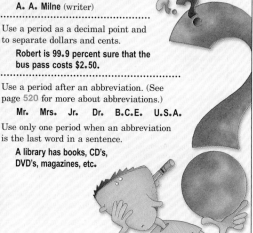

Question Marks

A **question mark** is used after a direct question (an interrogative sentence). Sometimes it is used to show doubt (uncertainty) about the correctness of a detail.

480.1 **In Direct Questions**	Place a question mark at the end of a direct question. **Do air bags make cars safer?** No question mark is used after an indirect question. (In an indirect question, you tell about the question you or someone else asked.) **I asked if air bags make cars safer.**
480.2 **In Tag Questions**	A question mark is used when you add a short question to the end of a statement. (This type of statement is called a *tag question*.) **The end of this century is the year 2099, isn't it?**
480.3 **To Show Doubt**	Place a question mark in parentheses to show that you aren't sure a fact is correct. **The ship arrived in Boston on July 23(?), 1652.**

Exclamation Points

An **exclamation point** is used to express strong feeling. It may be placed after a word, a phrase, or a sentence.

480.4 **To Show Strong Feeling**	**Surprise!** (word) **Happy birthday!** (phrase) **Wait for me!** (sentence) **TIP:** Never use extra exclamation points (Hooray!!!) in school writing assignments or in business letters.

End Punctuation

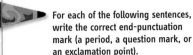

For each of the following sentences, write the correct end-punctuation mark (a period, a question mark, or an exclamation point).

Example: My gosh, look at that!

1. Is that what I think it is
2. There are many kinds of flying fish
3. Can a fish really fly
4. Some flying fish can glide more than 300 feet.
5. They spread out their large fins
6. Of course, their fins look like wings
7. Why do they jump out of the water
8. They are trying to escape other fish that want to eat them
9. How far can they go
10. Flying fish actually jump out of the water and glide through the air

Next Step: Write an exclamatory sentence about an unusual creature. Make sure you use the correct end punctuation.

---

1. Is that what I think it is?
2. There are many kinds of flying fish.
3. Can a fish really fly?
4. Some flying fish can glide more than 300 feet!
5. They spread out their large fins.
6. Of course, their fins look like wings.
7. Why do they jump out of the water?
8. They are trying to escape other fish that want to eat them.
9. How far can they go?
10. Flying fish actually jump out of the water and glide through the air.

Commas

Commas keep words and ideas from running together. They tell your reader where to pause, which makes your writing easier to read.

482.1 **Between Items in a Series**	Place commas between words, phrases, or clauses in a series. (A series is three or more items in a row.) **Hanae likes pepperoni, pineapple, and olives on her pizza.** (words) **During the summer I read mysteries, ride my bike, and play basketball.** (phrases)
482.2 **To Set Off Dialogue**	Use a comma to set off the words of the speaker from the rest of the sentence. **The stranded frog replied, "I'm just waiting for the toad truck."** If you are telling what someone has said but are not using the person's exact words, do *not* use commas or quotation marks. **The stranded frog told me that he was just waiting for the toad truck.**
482.3 **In Compound Sentences**	Use a comma between two independent clauses that are joined by the coordinating conjunction *and, but, or, nor, for, so,* or *yet.* **Aunt Carrie offered to pay my way, so I am going to the amusement park with her.** **We'll try to get on all the rides, and we'll see one of the stage shows.** **TIP:** Do not connect two independent clauses with a comma only. That is called a comma splice. (See 564.2 for more information about independent clauses.)

Commas 1

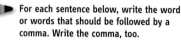
- In Compound Sentences
- To Set Off Dialogue

► For each sentence below, write the word or words that should be followed by a comma. Write the comma, too.

Example: A bunch of cows came to Chicago in 1999 and we went to see them.
1999,

1. My little sister yelled "Look at the cows, Daddy!"

2. I saw the cows, too but they weren't what I expected.

3. "They're not real cows" I said. "They're statues!"

4. Artists had decorated the cows and local businesses displayed them all around the city.

5. "People worked very hard to make these" Dad noted.

6. "They're really beautiful" my sister said.

7. We walked around the city all day but we didn't see every cow.

8. Dad told us "There are 300 cows in the exhibit."

Next Step: In two sentences, explain what the cows thought about their visit to Chicago. (Write as though the cows were alive and could talk.) Write one compound sentence and one sentence with dialogue.

Answers

1. yelled,
2. too,
3. cows,
4. cows,
5. these,
6. beautiful,
7. day,
8. us,

484

Commas . . .

484.1
To Separate Introductory Phrases and Clauses

Use a comma to separate a long phrase or clause that comes before the main part of the sentence.

> After checking my knee pads**,** I started off. (phrase)
>
> If you practice often**,** skating is easy. (clause)

You usually do not need a comma when the phrase or the clause comes after the main part of the sentence.

> **Skating is easy** if you practice often.

Also, a comma is usually unnecessary after a short opening phrase.

> In time **you'll find yourself looking forward to practice.** (No comma is needed after *In time.*)

484.2
In Dates and Addresses

Commas are used to set off the different parts in addresses and dates. (Do *not* use a comma between the state and ZIP code.)

> **My family's address is 2463 Bell Street, Atlanta, Georgia 30200.**
>
> **I will be 21 years old on January 15, 2015.**

Do not use a comma if only the month and year are written (January 2015).

484.3
To Keep Numbers Clear

Place commas between hundreds, thousands, millions, and billions.

> **Junji's car has 200,000 miles on it. He's trying to sell it for $1,000.**

When a number refers to a year, street address, or ZIP code, no comma is used. Also, write numbers in the millions and billions this way: 7.5 million, 16 billion. (See 524.2.)

> **Brazil is a country of 184 million people.**

Commas 2

- To Separate Introductory Phrases and Clauses
- To Keep Numbers Clear

 For each sentence below, write the number that needs a comma or the word that should be followed by a comma. Write the comma, too.

Example: There are lots of mountain peaks above 10000 feet in the Alps.
10,000

1. When people lived there long ago there were no phones.

2. To communicate neighbors yodeled at each other.

3. Yodeling probably began more than 1500 years ago.

4. With no words to sing a true yodeler simply calls out different notes.

5. Imagine calling out to a neighbor on 15771-foot-high Mont Blanc!

6. Echoing off the mountains a yodel makes an amazing sound.

Next Step: Write a sentence about an amazing sound you have heard. Begin with an introductory phrase or clause and use commas correctly.

Answers

1. ago,
2. communicate,
3. 1,500
4. sing,
5. 15,771
6. mountains,

486

Commas . . .

486.1
To Set Off Interruptions

Use commas to set off a word, phrase, or clause that interrupts the main thought of a sentence.

> You could, for example, take the dog for a walk instead of watching TV.

Here is a list of words and phrases that you can use to interrupt main thoughts.

for example	to be sure	moreover
however	as a matter of fact	in fact

TESTS: Try one of these tests to see if a word or phrase interrupts a main thought:

1. Take out the word or phrase. The meaning of the sentence should not change.
2. Move the word or phrase to another place in the sentence. The meaning should not change.

486.2
To Set Off Interjections

Use a comma to separate an interjection or a weak exclamation from the rest of the sentence.

> Wow, look at that sunrise!

> Hey, we're up early!

If an interjection shows strong feeling, an exclamation point (!) may be used after it.

> Whoa! Let's slow down.

The following words are often used as interjections.

Hello	Hey	Ah
Oh my	No kidding	Hmm
Really	Wow	Well

486.3
In Direct Address

Use commas to separate a noun of direct address (the person being spoken to) from the rest of the sentence.

> Yuri, some computers do not need keyboards.

> I know that, Maria. They respond to voice commands.

Commas 3

- In Direct Address
- To Set Off Interruptions

 Rewrite each sentence, inserting commas where needed.

Example: "Ken do you think we should go to a movie today?" Aunt Mabel asked.

"Ken, do you think we should go to a movie today?" Aunt Mabel asked.

1. "We could for example go see the outer-space movie," she added.

2. "Is that the one in the big museum theater Aunt Mabel?" asked Ken.

3. "I was as a matter of fact just thinking about going there," he said.

4. "Oh Ken I meant the one in the multiplex," said Aunt Mabel.

5. "Auntie do you know if they have popcorn at those theaters?" Ken asked.

6. "The last time we went if you remember they did have popcorn," she answered.

Next Step: Write two sentences about going to the movies. Use an interruption in one and direct address in the other. Use commas correctly.

Answers

1. "We could, for example, go see the outer-space movie," she added.
2. "Is that the one in the big museum theater, Aunt Mabel?" asked Ken.
3. "I was, as a matter of fact, just thinking about going there," he said.
4. "Oh, Ken, I meant the one in the multiplex," said Aunt Mabel.
5. "Auntie, do you know if they have popcorn at those theaters?" Ken asked.
6. "The last time we went, if you remember, they did have popcorn," she answered.

Commas . . .

**488.1
To Separate
Equal
Adjectives**

Use commas to separate two or more adjectives that equally modify a noun.

There are plenty of nutritious, edible plants in the world. (*Nutritious* and *edible* are separated by a comma because they modify *plants* equally.)

We may eat many unusual plants in the years to come. (*Many* and *unusual* do *not* modify *plants* equally. No comma is needed.)

TESTS: Use one of the tests below to help you decide if adjectives modify equally:

1. Switch the order of the adjectives. If the sentence is still clear, the adjectives modify equally.

2. Put the word *and* between the adjectives. If the sentence sounds clear, the adjectives modify equally.

TIP: Do not use a comma between the last adjective and the noun.

**488.2
To Set Off
Explanatory
Phrases and
Appositives**

Use a comma to set off an explanatory phrase from the rest of the sentence. (*Explanatory* means "helping to explain.")

Sonja, back from a visit to Florida, showed us some seashells.

Use commas to set off appositives. An appositive is a word or phrase that is another way of saying the noun or pronoun before it. (See 566.5.)

Mrs. Chinn, our science teacher, says that the sun is an important source of energy.

Solar power and wind power, two very clean sources of energy, should be used more.

**488.3
In Letter
Writing**

Place a comma after the salutation, or greeting, in a friendly letter and after the closing in all letters.

Dear Uncle Jim, (greeting)   **Love,** (closing)

Commas 4

- To Set Off Appositives
- In Letter Writing

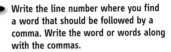

Write the line number where you find a word that should be followed by a comma. Write the word or words along with the commas.

Example: 1 I wrote to Uncle Ted
         2 my mother's brother to tell
         3 him about my new pet.

  1. Uncle Ted,
  2. my mother's brother,

                    October 11, 2005

 1 Dear Uncle Ted

 2   I got an iguana a kind of lizard as a present. Ramona
 3 a good friend of mine gave it to me. I named him Rocky. I
 4 like him very much.

 5   Rocky's dewlap the flap of skin under his throat sticks
 6 out whenever he sees me. That is normal for iguanas. He
 7 is an herbivore a plant eater. We feed him mostly greens
 8 and vegetables.

 9   I hope you can meet Rocky soon.

10   Love
11   Jolene

Next Step: Pretend you are Uncle Ted. Write a short letter back to Jolene.

 Answers

line 1.   Dear Uncle Ted,
line 2.   iguana, a kind of lizard,
          Ramona,
line 3.   a good friend of mine,
line 5.   Rocky's dewlap, the flap of skin
          under his throat,
line 7.   herbivore,
line 10. Love,

490

Apostrophes

An **apostrophe** is used to form contractions, to show possession, to form some plurals, or to show that letters have been left out of a word.

490.1 **In Contractions**	Use an apostrophe to show that one or more letters have been left out of a word, forming a contraction. The list below shows some common contractions. **Common Contractions** couldn't (could not) it's (it is; it has) didn't (did not) I've (I have) doesn't (does not) she's (she is) don't (do not) they'll (they will) hasn't (has not) they're (they are) haven't (have not) we've (we have) I'll (I will) wouldn't (would not) isn't (is not) you'd (you would)
490.2 **To Form Singular Possessives**	Form the possessive of most singular nouns by adding an apostrophe and -s. **My sister's hobby is jazz dancing.** When a singular noun ends with an s or a z sound, the possessive may be formed by adding just an apostrophe. **Carlos' weather chart is very detailed.** **(or) Carlos's chart** If the singular noun is a one-syllable word, form the possessive by adding both an apostrophe and -s. **Chris's lab report is incomplete.** **TIP:** An apostrophe is never used with a possessive pronoun (*its, hers, yours*). **The horse had its hooves trimmed.**

Apostrophes 1

- In Contractions
- To Form Singular Possessives

Find the words in the following sentences that should have apostrophes but don't. Write these words correctly.

Example: Jacks uncle brought him a gift.
Jack's

1. "Its not my birthday," Jack said.

2. "It doesnt have to be your birthday to get a little something from me," Uncle James said.

3. The packages wrapping was simply a bag tied with a bow.

4. As Jack opened it, Uncle Jamess smile got bigger.

5. Jack didnt have a clue about the bags contents.

6. Then he exclaimed, "Theyre goldfish!"

7. The fish, in a bag of water inside a fishbowl, werent very big.

8. Jack couldnt wait to pour the two goldfish and the water into the bowl.

9. "Ill take good care of them," Jack promised.

10. "Get your moms help," his uncle suggested.

Answers

1. It's
2. doesn't
3. package's
4. James's
5. didn't, bag's
6. They're
7. weren't
8. couldn't
9. I'll
10. mom's

Apostrophes . . .

492.1
To Form Plural Possessives

Add just an apostrophe to make the possessive form of plural nouns ending in *s*.

> **The visitors' ideas were helpful.**

> **The girls' washroom should be expanded.**

For plural nouns not ending in *s*, add an apostrophe and an *-s*.

> **The children's team practices today, and the men's league starts this weekend.**

Remember: The word before the apostrophe is the owner.

> **Justin's CD** (The CD belongs to Justin.)

> **the boys' shoes** (The shoes belong to the boys.)

492.2
To Form Possessives with Indefinite Pronouns

Form the possessive of an indefinite pronoun (*someone, everyone, no one, anyone*) by adding an apostrophe and *-s*.

> **everyone's idea**   **no one's fault**

> **somebody's book**   **another's suggestion**

492.3
To Form Shared Possessives

When possession is shared by more than one noun, add an apostrophe and *-s* to the last noun only.

> **Danetta, Sasha, and Olga's science project deals with electricity.**

492.4
To Form Some Plurals

An apostrophe and *s* are used to form the plural of a letter, a number, or a sign.

> **A's   B's   3's   10's   +'s   &'s**

492.5
In Place of Omitted Letters or Numbers

Use an apostrophe to show that one or more letters or numbers have been left out.

> **class of '15** (*20* is left out)

> **fixin' to go** (*g* is left out)

Apostrophes 2

■ To Form Plural Possessives
■ To Form Some Plurals

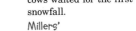

Find the words in the sentences below that should have apostrophes but don't. Write these words correctly.

Example: Every year the Millers cows waited for the first snowfall.
Millers'

1. When it came, the cows snowmobiles came out of the shed.

2. They checked both of the snowmobiles engines.

3. Carla, Bessie, and Daisy hopped onto the snowmobile with three 3s painted on it.

4. The cows hats and scarves were ready.

5. Two of the friends mittens were missing.

6. All their boots buckles had gotten rusty since last winter.

7. A stiff brush with bristles shaped like upside-down Js took care of the rust.

8. Soon the cows were zooming across the local ranchers pastures.

Next Step: Write two sentences about animals that act and speak like humans. Use two plural possessives.

Answers

1. cows'
2. snowmobiles'
3. 3's
4. cows'
5. friends'
6. boots'
7. J's
8. ranchers'

Quotation Marks

Quotation marks are used to enclose the exact words of the speaker, to show that words are used in a special way, and to punctuate some titles.

494.1
To Set Off Dialogue

Place quotation marks before and after the spoken words in dialogue.

> Martha asked, **"How long did you live in Mexico?"**

494.2
Placement of Punctuation

Put periods and commas *inside* quotation marks.

> Trev said, **"Let's make tuna sandwiches."**
> **"Sounds good,"** said Rich.

Place question marks or exclamation points *inside* the quotation marks when they punctuate the quotation.

> **"Do we have any apples?"** asked Trev.
> **"Yes!"** replied Mom.

Place them *outside* the quotation marks when they punctuate the main sentence.

> Did you hear Rich say, **"We're out of pickles"**?

494.3
To Punctuate Titles

Place quotation marks around titles of songs, poems, short stories, book chapters, and titles of articles in encyclopedias, magazines, or electronic sources. (See **502.1** for information on other kinds of titles.)

> **"Oh! Susanna"** (song)   **"Casey at the Bat"** (poem)
> **"McBroom Tells the Truth"** (short story)
> **"Local Boy Wins Competition"** (newspaper article)

(See **514.2** for information on capitalization of titles.)

494.4
For Special Words

Quotation marks may be used to set apart a word that is used in a special way.

> The queen wanted to sell the royal chairs rather than see them **"throne"** away.

Quotation Marks

- To Set Off Dialogue
- To Punctuate Titles

For each sentence below, write the words—along with any punctuation marks—that should be enclosed in quotation marks.

Example: What chapter are you reading? Lea's dad asked.
"What chapter are you reading?"

1. The title of the chapter was Castles in the Air.

2. It's a good book, Lea said.

3. She had learned about the book *Little Women* in a magazine article called Great Books for Kids.

4. Lea's favorite song, Bongo Bop, played loudly on the radio.

5. Can you read with the music on? her father asked.

6. I'm doing research for a poem I'm writing, Dad, she said.

7. He said, I'd like to see it.

8. Lea gave him her poem called Read to the Beat.

Next Step: Write two sentences. Use quotation marks to set off dialogue and to punctuate a title.

Answers

1. "Castles in the Air."
2. "It's a good book,"
3. "Great Books for Kids."
4. "Bongo Bop,"
5. "Can you read with the music on?"
6. "I'm doing research for a poem I'm writing, Dad,"
7. "I'd like to see it."
8. "Read to the Beat."

Hyphens

A **hyphen** is used to divide a word at the end of a line. Hyphens are also used to join or create new words.

496.1 **To Divide a Word**	Use a hyphen to divide a word when you run out of room at the end of a line. A word may be divided only between syllables *(ex-plor-er)*. Always refer to a dictionary if you're not sure how to divide a word. Here are some guidelines for hyphenating words: • Never divide a one-syllable word *(act, large, school)*. • Try not to divide a word of five or fewer letters *(older, habit, loyal)*. • Never divide a one-letter syllable from the rest of the word *(apart-ment, not a-partment)*. • Never divide abbreviations or contractions *(Mrs., Dr., don't, haven't)*.
496.2 **In Compound Words**	Use a hyphen in certain compound words. the two-year-old sister-in-law
496.3 **In Fractions**	Use a hyphen between the numbers in a fraction. one-half (1/2) five-tenths (5/10)

496.4
To Create New Words
	Use a hyphen to form new words beginning with the prefixes *all-, self-, ex-,* or *great-*. A hyphen is also used with suffixes such as *-elect* and *-free*.
	   all-star team self-respect president-elect
	   great-grandmother ex-hero smoke-free
	Use a hyphen to join two or more words that work together to form a single adjective *before* a noun.
	   school-age children lightning-fast skating

496.5 **To Join Letters and Words**	A hyphen is often used to join a letter to a word. T-shirt X-ray e-mail U-turn

Hyphens

■ To Divide a Word
■ To Join Letters and Words

▶ If a word at the end of a line is hyphenated incorrectly, or if a hyphen is needed to join a letter to a word, write the word correctly on your paper.

Example: Della loves trying to do tricks on her skateboard and bike.
skate—board

1. When she's riding her board, she likes to wear a special T shirt.

2. "This is my lucky shirt," Della tells almost an-yone who will listen.

3. The art on the back of her shirt is by the famo-us skateboarder Davy Downhill.

4. Della likes doing U turns and other fancy moves.

5. "Every week I try to do something more comp-lex than I did the week before," she says.

6. She knows she has to be careful if she wants to avoid an X ray.

Next Step: Pretend that the words *doctor, Thanksgiving,* and *connect* come at the end of a line in some sentences. Write each word with a hyphen in the correct place.

Answers

1. T-shirt
2. any-one
3. fa-mous
4. U-turns
5. com-plex
6. X-ray

Next Step: doc-tor
Thanks-giv-ing
con-nect

Colons

A **colon** may be used to introduce a list or a quotation. Colons are also used in business letters and between the numbers expressing time.

498.1

To Introduce a List

Use a colon to introduce a list that follows a complete sentence.

> The following materials can be used to build houses: plants, shells, sod, and sand.

When introducing a list, the colon often comes after summary words like *the following* or *these things*.

> On cleaning day, I do these things: sweep the floor, clean the bathroom mirror, and take out the garbage.

TIP: It is incorrect to use a colon after a verb or after a preposition.

498.2

As a Formal Introduction

Use a colon to introduce an important quotation in a serious report, essay, or news story.

> President Lincoln concluded the Gettysburg Address with these famous words: " . . . government of the people, by the people, for the people, shall not perish from the earth."

498.3

In Business Letters

A colon is used after the greeting in a business letter.

> Dear Ms. Kununga:
>
> Dear Sir:
>
> Dear Dr. Watts:

498.4

Between Numbers in Time

Place a colon between the parts of a number that shows time.

> 7:30 a.m.   1:00 p.m.   12:00 noon

Colons

- Between Numbers in Time
- In Business Letters

Write the line number where you find a number that needs a colon or a word that should be followed by a colon. Write the number or word along with the colon.

Example: 1 Mr. Ugh set out his
2 recycling bin at 1000 a.m.
3 on Thursday.

2. 10:00

1 Dear Sabertooth Recycling
2   I put my recycling bin out before 1000 a.m.
3 on Thursday, but you never picked it up. If the
4 pick-up time has changed, please let me know.

5 Sincerely,
6 Ig Ugh

7 Dear Mr. Ugh
8   We changed your pick-up time to 800 a.m.
9 We're sorry you missed our letter about this
10 change! We sent it at 900 a.m. last Monday.

11 Sincerely,
12 Sabertooth Recycling

Next Step: Write a short business letter setting up a time to meet someone. Correctly use colons after the greeting and in the time.

Answers

line 1. Dear Sabertooth Recycling:
line 2. 10:00 a.m.
line 7. Dear Mr. Ugh:
line 8. 8:00 a.m.
line 10. 9:00 a.m.

500

Semicolons

A **semicolon** sometimes works in the same way that a comma does. At other times, it works like a period and indicates a stronger pause.

500.1	
To Join Two Independent Clauses	You can join two independent clauses with a semicolon when there is no coordinating conjunction (like *and* or *but*) between them. (See 564.2 for more information about independent clauses.) **In the future, some cities may rest on the ocean floor; other cities may float like islands.** **Floating cities sound great; however, I get seasick.** **TIP:** Independent clauses can stand alone as separate sentences.
500.2	
To Separate Groups in a Series with Commas	Use a semicolon to separate a series of phrases that already contain commas. **We crossed the stream; unpacked our lunches, cameras, and journals; and finally took time to rest.** (The second phrase contains commas.)

Ellipses

An **ellipsis** (three periods with a space before, between, and after) is used to show omitted words or sentences and to show a pause in dialogue.

500.3	
To Show Omitted Words	Use an ellipsis to show that one or more words have been left out of a quotation. **"Give me liberty or give me death."** **"Give me liberty or . . . death."**
500.4	
To Show a Pause	Use an ellipsis to indicate a pause in dialogue. **"That's . . . incredible!" I cried.**

Semicolons

For each sentence below, write the word or words that should be followed by a semicolon. Write the semicolons, too.

Example: Our family drove from Omaha to New York City the trip was very long.
 City;

1. We locked up the house packed our luggage, toys, and extra food in the trunk and then got on the road.

2. My mom checked a map to find the best route Dad drove the car.

3. We drove through some midwestern states the middle Atlantic states of Ohio, Pennsylvania, and New Jersey and finally crossed the bridge into New York City.

4. We could see the skyscrapers of New York long before we got there the buildings were really tall!

5. We were all very tired on our first night in the city we checked into our hotel and went to bed.

6. The next day we were ready to see the sights our first stop was Central Park.

Next Step: Write a compound sentence about something that might happen on a family trip. Use a semicolon to join the independent clauses.

Answers

1. house; trunk;
2. route;
3. states; New Jersey;
4. there;
5. city;
6. sights;

502

Italics and Underlining

Italics is a style of type that is slightly slanted, like this: *girl*. It is used for some titles and special words. If you use a computer, you should use italics. In handwritten material, underline words that should be in italics.

502.1
In Titles

Use italics (or underlining) for the titles of books, plays, very long poems, magazines, and newspapers; the titles of television programs, movies (videos and DVD's), and albums of music (cassettes and CD's); and the names of ships and aircraft. (See **494.3** for information on other kinds of titles.)

The Giver . . . The Giver (book)

National Geographic . . . National Geographic (magazine)

Air Bud . . . Air Bud (movie)

Dance on a Moonbeam . . . Dance on a Moonbeam (CD)

Los Angeles Times . . . Los Angeles Times (newspaper)

Titanic . . . Titanic (ship)

Discovery . . . Discovery (spacecraft)

502.2
For Special Words

Use italics (or underlining) for scientific names and for words or letters being discussed or used in a special way.

The marigold's scientific name is *Tagetes*.

The word *friend* has different meanings to different people.

Punctuation Marks

'	Apostrophe	. . .	Ellipsis	.	Period
:	Colon	!	Exclamation point	?	Question mark
,	Comma	-	Hyphen	" "	Quotation marks
–	Dash	( )	Parentheses	;	Semicolon

Italics and Underlining

■ In Titles
■ For Special Words

For each sentence, write the words that should be italicized and underline them.

Example: First Men in the Moon, a book by H. G. Wells, was also made into a movie.
First Men in the Moon

1. The film The Ugly Duckling was based on a short story by Hans Christian Anderson.

2. The movie The Raven came from a poem by Edgar Allan Poe.

3. The magazine All the Year Round first printed some of Charles Dickens' work.

4. My dad reviews movies for our town's newspaper, the Smithville Call.

5. Jarrett liked the sound track from a movie he just saw and bought the CD Shark Tale.

6. I hope to see the book Olive's Ocean as a movie someday.

Next Step: Write a sentence that includes the title of your favorite book or movie.

Answers

1. The Ugly Duckling
2. The Raven
3. All the Year Round
4. The Smithville Call
5. Shark Tale
6. Olive's Ocean

Dashes

A **dash** is used to show a break in a sentence, to emphasize certain words, or to show that a speaker has been interrupted.

504.1

To Show a Sentence Break

A dash can show a sudden break in a sentence.

> Because of computers, our world—and the way we describe it—has changed greatly.

> With a computer—or a cell phone—people can connect to the Internet.

504.2

For Emphasis

Use a dash to emphasize a word, a series of words, a phrase, or a clause.

> You can learn about customs, careers, sports, weather—just about anything—on the Internet.

504.3

To Show Interrupted Speech

Use a dash to show that someone's speech is being interrupted by another person.

> Well, hello—yes, I—that's right—yes, I—sure, I'd love—I'll be there!

Parentheses

Parentheses are used around words that add extra information to a sentence or make an idea clearer.

504.4

To Add Information

Use parentheses when adding information or making an idea clearer.

> I accidentally left the keys to Mom's car (a blue Osprey) on the front seat.

> Five of the students provided background music (very quiet humming) for the singer.

Dashes and Parentheses

For each sentence, write whether you would use parentheses or a dash (or dashes) to set off the underlined words.

Example: A big group of fire ants <u>major pests in the South</u> went to Chicago.

parentheses

1. A big ant said, "I want to climb the Sears Tower <u>all 1,725 feet of it.</u>"

2. "But <u>let me speak, please</u> I want to see Navy Pier," a second ant spoke up.

3. The ants went to both Navy Pier <u>named in honor of Navy veterans</u> and the Sears Tower.

4. At Navy Pier, they shopped for gifts <u>very tiny ones, of course</u> and ate lunch.

5. They also saw the big Ferris wheel, which <u>imagine this</u> is 150 feet tall.

6. Later, they went to the Field Museum <u>home of the T. rex Sue.</u>

Next Step: Suppose you hear only one side of a telephone conversation. Write a sentence telling what you hear, using dashes to show interrupted speech.

Answers

1. dash
2. dashes
3. parentheses
4. parentheses or dashes
5. dashes
6. parentheses or dash

Test Prep

▶ **Number your paper from 1 to 10. For each underlined part of the paragraphs below, write the letter (from the answer choices on the next page) of the best way to punctuate it.**

Have you ever been to a natural history <u>museum</u> When I
₁
took a trip to New York City with my <u>family we</u> went to the
₂
American Museum of Natural History.

   <u>Look at those dinosaurs!</u> Mom exclaimed.
₃

   After learning about <u>dinosaurs we</u> saw the Hall of North
₄
American Forests. I liked the Butterfly Conservatory.

   "There are about <u>18000</u> species of butterflies in the world,"
₅
a guide said.

   My two <u>sisters</u> gasps were easy to hear. "I <u>cant</u> imagine
₆   ₇
that many butterflies!" Delia said.

   We visited the rock <u>collections; then</u> we gaped at a model
₈
of a huge blue whale. We ended our day at the planets exhibit.
Some of <u>Jupiters</u> moons have their own atmospheres. <u>Io</u>
₉   ₁₀
<u>Europa and Callisto</u> are three of that planet's moons. We
₁₀
learned a lot during our museum visit.

1. **A** museum.
    B museum!
    C museum?
    D correct as is

2. **A** family—we
    B family, we
    C family; we
    D correct as is

3. **A** "Look at those
        dinosaurs!
    B "Look at those
        dinosaurs!"
    C "Look at those
        dinosaurs"!
    D correct as is

4. **A** dinosaurs, we
    B dinosaurs. We
    C dinosaurs' we
    D correct as is

5. **A** 18,000
    B 18.000
    C 180,00
    D correct as is

6. **A** sister's
    B "sisters"
    C sisters'
    D correct as is

7. **A** c'ant
    B can't
    C cant'
    D correct as is

8. **A** collections then
    B collection's then
    C collections Then
    D correct as is

9. **A** Jupiters'
    B Jupiters's
    C Jupiter's
    D correct as is

10. **A** Io, Europa, and
        Callisto
    B Io, Europa and,
        Callisto
    C Io, Europa and
        Callisto
    D correct as is

Answers

1. c
2. b
3. b
4. a
5. a
6. c
7. b
8. d
9. c
10. a

508

Editing for Mechanics
Capitalization

508.1
Proper Nouns and Adjectives

Capitalize all proper nouns and proper adjectives. A proper noun names a specific person, place, thing, or idea. A proper adjective is formed from a proper noun.

Proper Nouns:

Beverly Cleary	Golden Gate Bridge
Utah Jazz	Thanksgiving Day

Proper Adjectives:

American citizen	Chicago skyline
New Jersey shore	Belgian waffle

508.2
Names of People

Capitalize the names of people as well as the initials or abbreviations that stand for those names.

John Steptoe	Harriet Tubman
C. S. Lewis	Sacagawea

508.3
Titles Used with Names

Capitalize titles used with names of persons.

President Carter   Dr. Li Tam   Mayor Rita Gonzales

TIP: Do not capitalize titles when they are used alone: *the president, the doctor, the mayor.*

508.4
Abbreviations

Capitalize abbreviations of titles and organizations.

M.D. (doctor of medicine)   **Mr. Martin Lopez**
ADA (American Dental Association)

508.5
Organizations

Capitalize the name of an organization, an association, or a team, as well as its members.

Girl Scouts	the Democratic Party
Chicago Bulls	Republicans

Capitalization 1
- Proper Nouns and Adjectives
- Organizations

▶ For each sentence below, correctly write any word or words that need to be capitalized.

Example: Our boy scout troop went on a bus trip to Washington, D.C.
Boy Scout

1. Mr. rodriguez, our troop leader, went with us.

2. We rode on a bridge over the chesapeake bay.

3. The bus driver took us right to the white house.

4. A guide from capital tour company met us there.

5. She had just finished taking a canadian group on a tour.

6. She led us through the jefferson memorial.

7. We had american cheese sandwiches for lunch.

8. The troop leader said, "I would love to come back here on independence day."

Next Step: Write a brief paragraph about a trip you've taken or would like to take. Use at least one proper noun, one proper adjective, and one name of an organization.

Answers

1. Rodriguez
2. Chesapeake Bay
3. White House
4. Capital Tour Company
5. Canadian
6. Jefferson Memorial
7. American
8. Independence Day

510

Capitalization . . .

510.1
Words Used as Names

Capitalize words such as *mother, father, aunt,* and *uncle,* when these words are used as names.

> **Ask** Mother **what we're having for lunch.**
> (*Mother* is used as a name; you could use her first name in its place.)

Words such as *dad, uncle, mother,* and *grandma* are not usually capitalized if they come after a possessive pronoun (*my, his, our*).

> **Ask my** mother **what we're having for lunch.**
> (In this sentence, *mother* refers to someone but is not used as a name.)

510.2
Days, Months, and Holidays

Capitalize the names of days of the week, months of the year, and holidays.

Wednesday	**March**	**Easter**
Arbor Day	**Passover**	**Juneteenth Day**

TIP: Do not capitalize the seasons.

> **winter** **spring** **summer** **fall** (or **autumn**)

510.3
Names of Religions, Nationalities, and Languages

Capitalize the names of religions, nationalities, and languages.

> **Christianity, Hinduism, Islam** (religions)
> **Australian, Somalian, Chinese** (nationalities)
> **English, Spanish, Hebrew** (languages)

510.4
Official Names

Capitalize the names of businesses and official product names. (These are called trade names.)

> **Budget Mart** **Crispy Crunch cereal** **Smile toothpaste**

TIP: Do not capitalize a general word like *toothpaste* when it follows the product name.

Capitalization 2

■ Days, Months, and Holidays
■ Words Used as Names

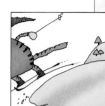

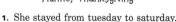

For each sentence below, correctly write any word that is not properly capitalized.

Example: Last month, auntie came over for thanksgiving.
Auntie, Thanksgiving

1. She stayed from tuesday to saturday.

2. My sister and I won't have school for the last two weeks of december.

3. We're going to spend some time with grandma.

4. We will go skiing after christmas.

5. We asked mom and dad if they wanted to join us.

6. Dad said that he has to work until new year's day.

7. Mom said that she could join us on thursday.

8. Grandma will take care of us until january 2.

Next Step: Write a sentence or two about your favorite holiday. Tell what month and day it is on.

Answers

1. Tuesday, Saturday
2. December
3. Grandma
4. Christmas
5. Mom, Dad
6. New Year's Day
7. Thursday
8. January

Capitalization . . .

512.1
Names of Places

Capitalize the names of places that are either proper nouns or proper adjectives.

Planets and heavenly bodies	**Earth, Jupiter, Milky Way**
Continents	**Europe, Asia, South America, Australia**
Countries	**Chad, Haiti, Greece, Chile, Jordan**
States	**New Mexico, West Virginia, Delaware**
Provinces	**Alberta, British Columbia, Quebec, Ontario**
Cities	**Montreal, Portland**
Counties	**Wayne County, Dade County**
Bodies of water	**Hudson Bay, North Sea, Lake Geneva, Saskatchewan River, Gulf of Mexico**
Landforms	**Appalachian Mountains, Bitterroot Range**
Public areas	**Vietnam Memorial**
Roads and highways	**New Jersey Turnpike, Interstate 80, Central Avenue**
Buildings	**Pentagon, Oriental Theater, Empire State Building**
Monuments	**Eiffel Tower, Statue of Liberty**

512.2
Sections of the Country

Capitalize words that name particular sections of the country. (Also capitalize proper adjectives formed from these words.)

A large part of the United States population lives on the East Coast. (*East Coast* is a section of the country.)

Southern cooking   out West

Do *not* capitalize words that simply show direction.

If you keep driving west, you will end up in the Pacific Ocean. (direction)

western Brazil   northeasterly wind

Capitalization 3

■ Names of Places

For each sentence, write the word or words that should be capitalized.

Example: My family took a trip around one of the great lakes.
Great Lakes

1. We started at our home in Traverse City, michigan.

2. Mom and Dad drove us south along the lakeshore all the way to chicago.

3. We saw the sears tower as we went through the city.

4. The road followed the shore of lake michigan into wisconsin.

5. If we had kept going north, we would have ended up in canada.

6. Instead, we drove east through hiawatha national forest.

7. We loved going over the mackinac bridge.

8. We took interstate 75, which intersected with the road back to our house.

Next Step: Write a few sentences about a trip you would like to take. Tell where you would start and where you would end up.

Answers

1. Michigan
2. Chicago
3. Sears Tower
4. Lake Michigan, Wisconsin
5. Canada
6. Hiawatha National Forest
7. Mackinac Bridge
8. Interstate

Capitalization . . .

514.1
Historical Events

Capitalize the names of historical events, documents, and periods of time.

> **Boston Tea Party**
>
> **Emancipation Proclamation**
>
> **Stone Age**

514.2
Titles

Capitalize the first word of a title, the last word, and every word in between except short prepositions, coordinating conjunctions, and articles *(a, an, the)*.

> *National Geographic World* (magazine)
>
> "The Star-Spangled Banner" (song)
>
> *Beauty and the Beast* (movie)
>
> *In My Pocket* (book)

514.3
First Words

Capitalize the first word of every sentence.

> **We** play our first basketball game tomorrow.

Capitalize the first word of a direct quotation.

> **Jamir shouted, "Keep that ball moving!"**

Capitalize	Do Not Capitalize
January, March . . . . .winter, spring
Grandpa (as a name) . . . . my grandpa
Mayor Sayles-Belton . . . . the mayor
President Washington . . . . our first president
Ida B. Wells Elementary School . . . . the local elementary school
Lake Ontario . . . . .the lake area
the South (section of the country) . . . . .south (a direction)
planet Earth . . . . .a mound of earth (dirt)

Capitalization 4

- Titles
- First Words

For each sentence, write the word or words that should be capitalized.

Example: Jeanne and Joe Pacific wrote a book called *Big blue planet*.
Blue Planet

1. they were famous for working under the sea.

2. They wrote articles about the ocean for *wide seas* magazine.

3. The publisher said, "our readers love their articles!"

4. Jeanne and Joe also made films about fish for the TV show *undersea Animals*.

5. People around the world saw their movie *Watching the whales.*

6. would you like to sail the seas with Joe and Jeanne Pacific?

Next Step: Have you seen a movie, a TV show, or an article about animals or nature lately? Write a sentence about it that includes its title.

Answers

1. They
2. *Wide Seas*
3. Our
4. *Undersea*
5. *Whales*
6. Would

Plurals

516.1 **Most Nouns**	Form the **plurals** of most nouns by adding *-s*. **balloon—balloons** **shoe—shoes**
516.2 **Nouns Ending in *sh, ch, x, s,* and *z***	Form the plurals of nouns ending in *sh, ch, x, s,* and *z* by adding *-es* to the singular. **brush—brushes** **bunch—bunches** **box—boxes** **dress—dresses** **buzz—buzzes**
516.3 **Nouns Ending in *o***	Form the plurals of most words that end in *o* by adding *-s*. **patio—patios** **rodeo—rodeos** For most nouns ending in *o* with a consonant letter just before the *o*, add *-es*. **echo—echoes** **hero—heroes** However, musical terms and words of Spanish origin form plurals by adding *-s*; check your dictionary for other words of this type. **piano—pianos** **solo—solos** **taco—tacos** **burrito—burritos**
516.4 **Nouns Ending in *-ful***	Form the plurals of nouns that end with *-ful* by adding an *-s* at the end of the word. **two** spoonfuls **three** tankfuls **four** bowlfuls **five** cupfuls
516.5 **Nouns Ending in *f* or *fe***	Form the plurals of nouns that end in *f* or *fe* in one of two ways. **1.** If the final *f* is still heard in the plural form of the word, simply add *-s*. **goof—goofs** **chief—chiefs** **safe—safes** **2.** If the final *f* has the sound of *v* in the plural form, change the *f* to *v* and add *-es*. **calf—calves** **loaf—loaves** **knife—knives**

Plurals 1

- Nouns Ending in *o*
- Nouns Ending in *f* or *fe*

Write the plural form of each of the following words.

Example: taco
     tacos

1. wife
2. radio
3. leaf
4. tomato
5. life
6. roof
7. banjo
8. brief
9. studio
10. half
11. reef
12. duo
13. proof
14. soprano
15. hoof
16. alto
17. wolf
18. potato
19. cafe
20. portfolio

Next Step: Select two words from the list above. Write a sentence for each, using the plural form of the word.

Answers

1. wives
2. radios
3. leaves
4. tomatoes
5. lives
6. roofs
7. banjos
8. briefs
9. studios
10. halves
11. reefs
12. duos
13. proofs
14. sopranos
15. hooves
16. altos
17. wolves
18. potatoes
19. cafes
20. portfolios

Plurals . . .

518.1

Nouns Ending in *y*

When a common noun ends in a consonant + *y*, form its plural by changing the *y* to *i* and adding *-es*.

sky—skies	bunny—bunnies
story—stories	musky—muskies

For proper nouns, do *not* change the letters—just add *-s*.

area Bargain Citys   **the Berrys**   **two Timmys**

For nouns that end in a vowel + *y*, add only *-s*.

donkey—donkeys   **monkey—monkeys**   **day—days**

518.2

Compound Nouns

Form the plurals of most compound nouns by changing the most important word in the compound to its plural form.

sisters-in-law	maids of honor
secretaries of state	life jackets

518.3

Irregular Nouns

Some nouns form plurals using an irregular spelling.

child—children	goose—geese	foot—feet
man—men	woman—women	tooth—teeth
ox—oxen	mouse—mice	
cactus—cacti or cactuses		

A few words have the same singular and plural forms.

Singular:	Plural:
That sheep wanders away.	The other sheep follow it.
I caught one trout.	Dad caught three trout.

Others: deer, moose, buffalo, fish, aircraft

518.4

Adding an 's

The plurals of symbols, letters, numerals, and words discussed as words are formed by adding an apostrophe and *-s*.

two ?'s and two !'s   **five 7's**   **x's and y's**

TIP: For more information on forming plurals and plural possessives, see page 492.

Plurals 2

- Nouns Ending in *y*
- Irregular Nouns

For each of the following sentences, write the correct plural form of the underlined word.

Example: Many <u>city</u> have youth centers.
          cities

1. My friends and I go to our city youth center on <u>Monday</u>.

2. Lots of the other <u>child</u> from my neighborhood go, too.

3. The two <u>Tommy</u> from down the street go.

4. They have some new <u>toy</u> to show us next time.

5. On one Monday field trip, some neighborhood <u>man</u> volunteered to take us out in boats.

6. A bunch of <u>fish</u> started flying into one boat!

7. They were probably <u>trout</u>.

8. Maybe they were trying to escape some <u>osprey</u>, which are fish-eating hawks.

9. Last week on a field trip, we got to ride <u>pony</u>.

10. We have some great <u>story</u> to tell about the center.

Next Step: Write one or two sentences using the correct plural forms of *woman* and *puppy*.

Answers

1. Mondays
2. children
3. Tommys
4. toys
5. men
6. fish
7. trout
8. ospreys
9. ponies
10. stories

Abbreviations

An **abbreviation** is the shortened form of a word or phrase.

520.1 **Common** **Abbreviations**	Most abbreviations begin with a capital letter and end with a period. In formal writing, do *not* abbreviate the names of states, countries, months, days, or units of measure. Also do *not* use symbols (%, &) in place of words.

TIP: The following abbreviations are always acceptable in both formal and informal writing:

Mr.	Mrs.	Ms.	Dr.	Jr., Sr.
M.D.	B.C.E.	C.E.	a.m., p.m. (A.M., P.M.)	

520.2 **Acronyms**	An **acronym** is made up of the first letter or letters of words in a phrase. An acronym is pronounced as a word, and it does not have any periods. SADD (**S**tudents **A**gainst **D**estructive **D**ecisions) PIN (**p**ersonal **i**dentification **n**umber)

520.3 **Initialisms**	An **initialism** is like an acronym except the letters that form the abbreviation are pronounced individually (not as a word). TV (**t**elevision) DA (**d**istrict **a**ttorney) CD (**c**ompact **d**isc) PO (**p**ost **o**ffice)

Common Abbreviations

a.m.	ante meridiem (before noon)	**Inc.**	incorporated	**oz.**	ounce
ATM	automatic teller machine	**kg**	kilogram	**pd.**	paid
B.C.E.	before the Common Era	**km**	kilometer	**p.**	page
C.E.	the Common Era	**lb.**	pound	**p.m.**	post meridiem
etc.	and so forth	**M.D.**	doctor of medicine		(after noon)
FYI	for your information	**mpg**	miles per gallon	**qt.**	quart
		mph	miles per hour		

Abbreviations 1

■ Common Abbreviations, Acronyms, and Initialisms

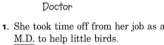

▶ **For each sentence, write the word or words that each underlined abbreviation stands for.**

Example: <u>Dr.</u> Bertha Byrd was a member of the Baby Bird Defense League.
Doctor

1. She took time off from her job as a <u>M.D.</u> to help little birds.

2. "Birds that weigh less than an <u>oz.</u> should stay out of the sun," she noted.

3. Today, just before noon, she went to the <u>ATM</u>.

4. She used her <u>PIN</u>, took out some money, and bought an umbrella.

5. She held the umbrella over the nest and played a <u>CD</u> of bird whistles to calm the babies.

6. "My husband, <u>Mr.</u> Byrd, will defend your nest tomorrow," she told them.

7. "He's one of the best bird-watchers in the <u>U.S.A.</u>"

Next Step: Make up an acronym or initialism of your own. Then write what that abbreviation stands for.

Answers

1. doctor of medicine
2. ounce
3. automatic teller machine
4. personal identification number
5. compact disc
6. Mister
7. United States of America

Abbreviations . . .

522.1
State and Address Abbreviations

You may use a state or an address abbreviation when it is part of an address at the top of a letter or on an envelope. (Also see pages 476–477.) Remember, do not use these abbreviations in sentences.

On a letter:

2323 N. Kipp St.
Cleveland, OH 52133

On an envelope:

7828 E FIRST AVE
ORONO ME 04403

In sentences:

Jasper lives at 2323 North Kipp Street, Cleveland, Ohio.

His old address was 7828 East First Avenue, Orono, Maine 04403.

State Postal Abbreviations

Alabama	AL	Idaho	ID	Missouri	MO	Pennsylvania	PA
Alaska	AK	Illinois	IL	Montana	MT	Rhode Island	RI
Arizona	AZ	Indiana	IN	Nebraska	NE	South Carolina	SC
Arkansas	AR	Iowa	IA	Nevada	NV	South Dakota	SD
California	CA	Kansas	KS	New Hampshire	NH	Tennessee	TN
Colorado	CO	Kentucky	KY	New Jersey	NJ	Texas	TX
Connecticut	CT	Louisiana	LA	New Mexico	NM	Utah	UT
Delaware	DE	Maine	ME	New York	NY	Vermont	VT
District of		Maryland	MD	North Carolina	NC	Virginia	VA
Columbia	DC	Massachusetts	MA	North Dakota	ND	Washington	WA
Florida	FL	Michigan	MI	Ohio	OH	West Virginia	WV
Georgia	GA	Minnesota	MN	Oklahoma	OK	Wisconsin	WI
Hawaii	HI	Mississippi	MS	Oregon	OR	Wyoming	WY

Address Abbreviations

Apartment	Apt.	Expressway	Expy.	Parkway	Pkwy.	Square	Sq.
Avenue	Ave.	Heights	Hts.	Place	Pl.	Station	Sta.
Boulevard	Blvd.	Highway	Hwy.	Road	Rd.	Street	St.
Court	Ct.	Lane	Ln.	Route	Rte.	Terrace	Terr.
Drive	Dr.	North	N.	Rural	R.	Turnpike	Tpke.
East	E.	Park	Pk.	South	S.	West	W.

Abbreviations 2

■ State and Address Abbreviations

▶ **Write each of the following addresses using abbreviations.**

Example: 101 Duck Pond Road
St. Ann, Missouri 63070

101 Duck Pond Rd.
St. Ann, MO 63070

1. 2001 West Lunar Highway
Houston, Texas 77001

2. 500 Sunshine Boulevard
Hollywood, California 90028

3. 1623 Pilgrim Founders Street
Plymouth, Massachusetts 02360

4. 1 South Parthenon Way
Nashville, Tennessee 37201

5. 1337 East Tundra Terrace
Juneau, Alaska 99801

6. 1963 West Route 66
Lake Havasu City, Arizona 86403

Next Step: Write your own address as if you were writing it at the top of a letter.

Answers

1. 2001 W. Lunar Hwy.
Houston, TX 77001

2. 500 Sunshine Blvd.
Hollywood, CA 90028

3. 1623 Pilgrim Founders St.
Plymouth, MA 02360

4. 1 S. Parthenon Way
Nashville, TN 37201

5. 1337 E. Tundra Terr.
Juneau, AK 99801

6. 1963 W. Rte. 66
Lake Havasu City, AZ 86403

Numbers

524.1
Numbers from 1 to 9

Numbers from one to nine are usually written as words. (Most of the time, numbers 10 and higher are written as numerals.)

one   three   nine   10   115   2,000

Keep any numbers that are being compared in the same style, either words or numerals.

Students from 8 to 11 years old are invited.

Students from eight to eleven years old are invited.

524.2
Very Large Numbers

You may use a combination of numbers and words for very large numbers.

15 million   1.2 billion

You may spell out large numbers that can be written as two words, but if you need more than two words to spell out a number, write it as a numeral.

three million   fifteen thousand   3,275,100   7,418

524.3
Sentence Beginnings

Use words, not numerals, to begin a sentence.

Fourteen new students joined the jazz band.

Fifty-two cards make up a deck.

524.4
Numerals Only

Use numerals for numbers in the following forms:

decimals **25.5**
with dollar signs **$3.97**
percentages . . . . **6 percent**
chapters . . . . **chapter 8**
pages . . . . **pages 17–20**
addresses . . . . **445 E. Acorn Dr.**
dates . . . . **June 19, 2005**
times with a.m. or p.m. . . . . **1:30 p.m.**
statistics . . . . **a vote of 5 to 2**

Numbers

■ Numbers from 1 to 9
■ Very Large Numbers

▶ **For each sentence, write the numbers correctly. If the number is already correct, write "C."**

Example: I went on a field trip with twenty-eight classmates.
28

1. We rode a school bus to an apple farm 3 miles out of town.

2. "Wow! There must be thirty-nine million apples here!" Evan said as we drove up.

3. "I've never counted them all," the farmer told us, "but we do sell thirty-four varieties."

4. He handed us each an apple and said, "We sell about three hundred sixty apples in an hour."

5. "That means you sell two thousand eight hundred eighty apples a day!" Judy exclaimed.

6. "We sell even more when we keep the store open longer than 8 hours," the farmer replied.

7. Someone said farmers in the United States sell more than one hundred fifty million apples in one year.

Next Step: Write two sentences about something you like to eat. Tell how much you might eat in a day and in a year. Use numbers in their correct forms.

Answers

1. three
2. 39 million
3. 34
4. 360
5. 2,880
6. eight
7. 150 million

Test Prep

Number your paper from 1 to 10. For each underlined part in the following paragraph, write the letter of the reason it is incorrect. Your choices are listed below and on the next page.

<u>2</u> ways to rank the states are by size and by population.
<small>1</small>

<u>for</u> example, <u>alaska</u> is the largest state in size, but it is
<small>2</small>   <small>3</small>

number <u>forty-seven</u> in population. The state with the most
<small>4</small>

people (over <u>thirty-five million</u>) is California. <u>498,703</u> people
<small>5</small>   <small>6</small>

live in <u>wyoming</u>. It has the fewest residents. Rhode <u>island</u>
<small>7</small>   <small>8</small>

has <u>one thousand forty-five</u> square miles. <u>it</u> is the tiniest state.
<small>9</small>   <small>10</small>

1. The numeral *2* should be written as a word because . . .
   A it is a large number.
   B it begins a sentence.
   C it is being compared to another number in the sentence.

2. *For* should be capitalized because . . .
   A it is part of a title.
   B it is a proper adjective.
   C it is the first word in a sentence.

3. *Alaska* should be capitalized because . . .
   A it is a geographic name that is a proper noun.
   B it is the first word in a sentence.
   C it is the name of a language.

4. The number *47* should be written as a numeral because . . .
   A it is between one and nine.
   B it is a number larger than nine.
   C it is part of an address.

5. The number *35 million* can be written as a combination of numbers and words because . . .
   A it is a very large number.
   B it is between one and nine.
   C it begins a sentence.

6. The beginning of this sentence should be rewritten using words because . . .
   A words, not numerals, begin a sentence.
   B the number is less than nine.
   C the number is a decimal.

7. *Wyoming* should be capitalized because . . .
   A it names a religion.
   B it is the first word in a sentence.
   C it is a proper noun.

8. *Island* should be capitalized because . . .
   A it names a religion.
   B it is part of a geographic name that is a proper noun.
   C it is a historical event.

9. The number *1,045* should be a numeral because . . .
   A it is between one and nine.
   B it is a large number that requires more than two words.
   C it is part of a date.

10. *It* should be capitalized because . . .
   A it is a proper noun.
   B it is an abbreviation.
   C it is the first word in a sentence.

Answers

1. b
2. c
3. a
4. b
5. a
6. a
7. c
8. b
9. b
10. c

Improving Spelling

528.1 *i* before *e*	Write *i* before *e*—except after *c* or when the word rhymes with *say* as in *neighbor* and *weigh*. **believe chief receive freight** Exceptions to the *i* before *e* rule include the following: **either neither heir leisure species** **foreign height seize weird**
528.2 Silent *e*	If a word ends with a silent *e*, drop the *e* before adding a suffix (ending) that begins with a vowel. **judge**—judging **continue**—continual **create**—creative—creation **relate**—relating—relative
528.3 Words Ending in *y*	When a word ends in a consonant + *y*, change the *y* to *i* before adding a suffix. Do not, however, change the *y* when adding the *-ing* suffix. **happy**—happiness **try**—tries—trying **lady**—ladies **cry**—cried—crying When forming the plural of a word that ends in *y* with a vowel just before it, add *-s*. **holiday**—holidays **key**—keys **boy**—boys
528.4 Words Ending in a Consonant	When a one-syllable word ends in a consonant that has a single vowel before it, double the final consonant before adding a suffix that begins with a vowel. **beg**—begging **hop**—hopped **sit**—sitting When a word with more than one syllable ends with a vowel + consonant, double the final consonant only if the accent is on the last syllable and the suffix begins with a vowel. **admit**—admitting **occur**—occurrence

Spelling 1

- *i* before *e*
- Silent *e*

For each sentence, write any misspelled words correctly. Follow the rules on page 528.

Example: Fred recieved a letter from Fran.

 received

1. Fran and Fred have been good friends since they met.

2. Aren't they a loveable pair?

3. Fran is saveing some money to buy Fred a gift.

4. They like jogging through parks and feilds.

5. They go skateing together sometimes.

6. Today they are bikeing in the state park.

7. Although Fred looks a bit tired, Fran seems tirless!

8. Fred needs a breif break.

9. Fred's dad was bakeing yesterday, so Fred brought some homemade granola bars with him.

10. In a quiet moment, Fran says, "I'd love a granola bar."

Next Step: Write a sentence describing what Fred and Fran did next. Make sure you spell all words correctly.

Answers

1. friends
2. lovable
3. saving
4. fields
5. skating
6. biking
7. tireless
8. brief
9. baking
10. quiet

530

Spelling 2

- Words Ending in *y*
- Words Ending in a Consonant

▶ **For each sentence, write the correct spelling of the underlined word or words.**

Example: Harley is the <u>hungryest</u> dog in the neighborhood.
hungriest

1. In fact, he eats more than any dog in the nearby <u>countys</u>.

2. His owner <u>grined</u> and said, "He eats people food."

3. He eats pizza with lots of <u>topings</u>.

4. He doesn't just like people food; he also likes children's <u>toyes</u>.

5. He likes human music, too. The <u>Flieing Donkies</u> seems to be his favorite group.

6. He <u>buryed</u> some of their CD's so he could listen to them later, I guess.

7. I suppose he'll be <u>diging</u> them up again.

8. He put them in the two <u>allies</u> next to his favorite bones.

Next Step: Write a list of three words that end in *y*. Then add a suffix and write the correct spelling of the word.

Improving Spelling **531**

Spelling Review

▶ **For each of the following sentences, write the correct spelling of the underlined word.**

Example: This kite is not <u>behaveing</u>!
behaving

1. I have trouble <u>geting</u> it up in the air.

2. I wonder if the kite <u>wieghs</u> too much.

3. The wind keeps <u>changeing</u> direction.

4. The kite <u>flys</u>, but then it crashes to the ground.

5. Maybe the wind is too <u>feirce</u>.

6. It keeps <u>tuging</u> at the kite.

7. Does the <u>cloudyness</u> cause a problem?

8. Does my kite need <u>batterys</u>?

9. This really <u>annoyes</u> me.

10. I am <u>leaveing</u>.

11. Next time I'll be <u>tieing</u> a long tail on my kite.

12. Then my only <u>worrys</u> will be trees and houses.

Next Step: From the spelling words list, select three words that give you trouble. Write a sentence for each.

Answers

1. getting
2. weighs
3. changing
4. flies
5. fierce
6. tugging
7. cloudiness
8. batteries
9. annoys
10. leaving
11. tying
12. worries

Proofreader's Guide to Improved Spelling

Be patient. Becoming a good speller takes time and practice. Learn the basic spelling rules.

Check your spelling by using a dictionary or a list of commonly misspelled words.

Check a dictionary for the correct pronunciation of each word you are trying to spell. Knowing how to pronounce a word will help you remember how to spell it.

Look up the meaning of each word. Knowing its meaning will help you to use it and spell it correctly.

Study the word in the dictionary. Then look away from the dictionary page and picture the word in your mind's eye. Next, write the word on a piece of paper. Finally, check its spelling in the dictionary. Repeat these steps until you can spell the word correctly.

Make a spelling dictionary. Include any words you frequently misspell in a special notebook.

A

ability	addition	almost	another	arrange
able	address	alone	answer	arrival
aboard	adjust	along	antarctic	article
about	admire	a lot	anxious	asleep
above	adventure	already	anybody	assign
absence	advise	although	anyone	assist
absent	afraid	altogether	anything	athlete
accept	afternoon	aluminum	anyway	athletic
accident	again	always	anywhere	attach
according	against	American	apartment	attack
account	agreeable	among	apologize	attention
ache	agreement	amount	appointment	attitude
achieve	aisle	ancient	April	attractive
acre	alarm	angel	architect	audience
across	alert	anger	arctic	August
action	alley	angle	aren't	aunt
actual	allow	angry	argument	author
	allowance	animal	arithmetic	automobile
	all right	announce	around	autumn

avenue	bright	choose	could	distance
average	brother	chorus	country	divide
award	brought	chose	county	division
awareness	buckle	church	courage	doctor
awful	budget	circle	cousin	does
awhile	build	citizen	cozy	doesn't
	built	city	crawl	dollar
	burglar	clear	cried	done

B

	bury	climate	crowd	doubt
baggage	business	climb	cruel	during
baking	busy	close	crumb	
balance		closet	curiosity	
balloon		clothes	curious	**E**
banana	**C**	coach	current	
bandage		cocoa	customer	eager
barber	cafeteria	cocoon	cycle	early
bargain	calendar	college		earn
basement	cancel	color		easily
beautiful	candidate	column	**D**	easy
beauty	candle	comedy		edge
because	canoe	coming	daily	eight
becoming	canyon	commercial	damage	eighth
been	captain	committee	danger	either
before	cardboard	common	dangerous	electricity
beginning	care	communicate	dare	elephant
behave	career	community	daughter	eleven
behind	carpenter	company	December	else
believe	catalog	comparison	decide	embarrass
belong	catcher	complain	decision	emergency
between	caught	complete	decorate	encourage
bicycle	ceiling	concern	definition	enormous
blizzard	celebration	concert	delicious	enough
borrow	century	concrete	describe	entertain
bother	certain	condition	description	entrance
bottom	challenge	conference	design	environment
bought	champion	confidence	develop	equal
bounce	change	confuse	dictionary	equipment
breakfast	chapter	congratulate	difference	escape
breath	character	connect	different	especially
breathe	chief	continue	disappear	every
breeze	children	convince	discover	everybody
bridge	chocolate	cooperate	discuss	exactly
brief	choice	correction	discussion	excellent
	choir	cough	disease	except

534

excited
exercise
exhausted
expensive
experience
experiment
explain
extinct
extreme
eyes

genius
gentle
geography
giant
ghost
goes
gone
government
governor
graduation
grammar
grateful
great
grocery
group
guarantee
guard
guess
guilty
gymnasium

F

face
familiar
family
famous
fashion
favorite
February
field
fierce
fifty
finally
first
foreign
forty
forward
fountain
fourth
fragile
Friday
friend
frighten
from
fuel

H

half
handsome
happen
happiness
have
headache
health
heard
heavy
height
history
holiday
honest
honor
horrible
hospital
however
hundreds
hygiene

G

gadget
general
generous

I

icicle
ideal
illustrate
imaginary
imagine
imitate
imitation
immigrant
important
impossible
incredible
independent
individual
initial
innocent
instead
intelligent
interest
interrupt
invitation
island

J

January
jealous
jewelry
join
journal
journey
judgment
July
June

K

knew
knife
knives
knowledge

L

label
language
laugh
lawyer
league
learn
least
leave
length
library
lightning
liquid
listen
loose
lovable

M

machine
magazine
many
March
marriage
material
mathematics
May
mayor
meant
measure
medicine
message
might
millions
miniature
minute
mirror
mischief
misspell
Monday
morning

mountain
multiplication
muscle
music
musician
mysterious

N

nation
national
natural
nature
necessary
neighborhood
neither
nephew
nervous
newspaper
nickel
niece
nineteen
ninth
nobody
noisy
no one
nothing
notice
November

O

obey
occasion
o'clock
October
of
off
office
often
once
only

operate
opinion
opposite
ordinary
original
over

P

package
paid
paragraph
parallel
patience
people
perfect
perhaps
personal
persuade
photo
picture
pleasant
please
point
popular
possess
possible
practical
practice
preparation
president
pretty
privilege
probably
problem
produce
protein

Q

quarter
quickly

quiet
quit
quite
quotient

R

raise
ready
really
reason
receive
recipe
recognize
recommend
relatives
relief
remember
responsibility
reply
restaurant
review
revolves
rhyme
rhythm
right
rough
route

S

safety
salary
Saturday
says
scared
scene
schedule
science
scissors
search
secretary

separate
September
serious
several
similar
simple
sign
since
sincerely
skiing
soldier
something
sometimes
spaghetti
special
south
statement
statue
stomach
stood
straight
strength
stretch
studying
subtraction
succeed
success
suddenly
sugar
Sunday
suppose
sure
surprise
surround
system

T

table
teacher
tear
temperature
terrible

Thanksgiving
theater
themselves
thief
though
thought
thousand
through
Thursday
tired
together
tomorrow
tongue
touch
toward
treasure
tried
trouble
truly
Tuesday
type

U

uncle
unique
universe
unknown
until
unusual
upon
upstairs
use
usually

V

vacation
vacuum
valuable
vegetable
vehicle

view
visitor
voice
volume
volunteer

W

wander
was
watch
weather
Wednesday
weigh
weight
weird
welcome
went
what
whenever
where
which
while
who
whole
women
wonderful
worse
world
write
written
wrong
wrote

Y

yellow
yesterday
young
yourself

Using the Right Word 1

- a, an; **accept, except;** allowed, aloud; **a lot;** ant, aunt

For each sentence, write the correct word or words from the choices in parentheses.

Example: Over the summer I received an *(ant, aunt)* farm as a gift.

ant

1. *(Ant, Aunt)* Jo gave it to me.

2. I like the ant farm *(a lot, alot)*.

3. Auntie Jo always brings my sister and me *(a, an)* present.

4. She reads *(allowed, aloud)* to us, too.

5. I like all her stories *(except, accept)* the one about the fairy princess.

6. We're *(allowed, aloud)* to stay up until nine o'clock.

7. Dad says I have to *(except, accept)* this bedtime until I get older.

8. Then I can have *(a, an)* later bedtime.

Next Step: Write two more sentences using the words *ant* and *aunt* correctly.

Answers

1. Aunt
2. a lot
3. a
4. aloud
5. except
6. allowed
7. accept
8. a

538.1 ate, eight	I ate a bowl of popcorn. He had eight pieces of candy.
538.2 bare, bear	She put her bare feet into the cool stream. She didn't see the bear fishing on the other side.
538.3 blew, blue	I blew on my cold hands. The tips of my fingers looked almost blue.
538.4 board, bored	One board in the wooden floor was loose. With nothing to do, I felt bored.
538.5 borrow, lend	It's so cold—could I borrow a sweater? (*Borrow* means "receive.") It's so cold—could you lend me a sweater? (*Lend* means "give.")
538.6 brake, break	Pump the brake to slow down. You could break a bone if you skateboard without pads and a helmet.
538.7 breath, breathe	Take a deep breath and calm down. (*Breath* is a noun.) My nose is so stuffed up that it's hard to breathe. (*Breathe* is a verb.)
538.8 bring, take	Please bring me my glasses. (*Bring* means "to move toward the speaker.") Take your dishes to the kitchen. (*Take* means "to carry away.")
538.9 by, buy	Chuck stopped by the store window. He wanted to buy a new baseball glove.

Using the Right Word 2

■ ate, eight; **bare, bear**; blew, blue; **brake, break**; breath, breathe; **by, buy**

Write the correct word from each pair in parentheses.

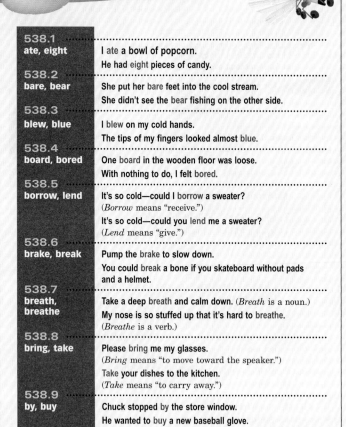

Example: A *(bare, bear)* will eat all summer long to get ready for a long winter.

bear

1. One bear *(ate, eight)* too much junk food and gained a lot of weight.

2. He couldn't *(by, buy)* his own food, so he looked for scraps all the time.

3. Once he gulped down *(ate, eight)* picnic baskets from a campground *(by, buy)* the lake.

4. A camper got so mad that she turned *(blew, blue)* in the face.

5. The bear would *(brake, break)* anything he sat on.

6. If he sat on me, I would not be able to *(breath, breathe)*!

7. To scare the bear away, the park ranger took a deep *(breath, breathe)* and *(blew, blue)* her whistle.

8. Unfortunately, that bear had no *(brake, break)* on his appetite.

Next Step: Write an ending to this story. Use two or more of the words from the list at the top of the page.

Answers

1. ate
2. buy
3. eight, by
4. blue
5. break
6. breathe
7. breath, blew
8. brake

540

540.1 can, may	Do you think I can go off the high dive? (I am asking if I have the *ability* to do it.) May I go off the high dive? (I am asking for *permission* to do something.)
540.2 capital, capitol	The capital city of Texas is Austin. Be sure to begin Austin with a capital letter. My uncle works in the capitol building. (*Capitol*, with an *ol*, refers to a government building.)
540.3 cent, scent, sent	Each rose cost one cent less than a dollar. The scent of the flowers is sweet. Dad sent Mom a dozen roses.
540.4 choose, chose	David must choose a different instrument this year. Last year he chose to take drum lessons. (*Chose* [chōz] is the past tense of the verb *choose* [cho͞oz].)
540.5 close, clothes	Please close the window. Do you have all your clothes packed for your trip?
540.6 coarse, course	A cat's tongue feels coarse, like sandpaper. I took a course called "Caring for Cats."
540.7 creak, creek	Old houses creak when the wind blows hard. The water in the nearby creek is clear and cold.
540.8 dear, deer	Amber is my dear friend. The deer enjoyed the sweet corn in her garden.

Using the Right Word 3

■ can, may; cent, scent, sent; choose, chose;
close, clothes; creak, creek; dear, deer

Look at the underlined word in each of the following sentences. Write a "C" if it is used correctly. If it is not, write the correct word.

Example: Last night, Mr. Elk and his wife <u>choose</u> a nice restaurant for dinner.
chose

1. They dressed in their best <u>close</u> and went downtown.
2. "<u>May</u> we sit here?" Ms. Elk asked the waiter.
3. "I like the view of the <u>creak</u>," she said.
4. "Yes," he agreed, as he went to <u>clothes</u> the kitchen door.
5. "We might see some <u>dear</u> there," she said.
6. When they were seated, Mr. Elk said, "There is so much to <u>choose</u> from on the menu."
7. "I don't think I <u>may</u> decide!" he continued.
8. Ms. Elk <u>cent</u> the waiter to the kitchen for a bowl of soup.
9. After his meal, Mr. Elk noticed a <u>creak</u> in his chair.
10. "Oh, <u>dear</u>," he said, "I think I ate too much."

Answers

1. clothes
2. C
3. creek
4. close
5. deer
6. C
7. can
8. sent
9. C
10. C

542

542.1 desert, dessert	Cactuses grow in the desert near our house. My favorite dessert is strawberry pie.
542.2 dew, do, due	The dew on the grass got my new shoes wet. I will do my research after school since the report is due on Wednesday.
542.3 die, dye	The plant will die if it isn't watered. The red dye in the sweatshirt turned everything in the wash pink.
542.4 doesn't, don't	She doesn't like green bananas. (*Doesn't* is the contraction of *does not*.) I don't either. (*Don't* is the contraction of *do not*.)
542.5 fewer, less	We had fewer snow days this winter than we did last year. (*Fewer* refers to something you can count.) That meant less time for ice-skating. (*Less* refers to an amount that you cannot count.)
542.6 flower, flour	A tulip is a spring flower. Flour is the main ingredient in bread.
542.7 for, four	The friends looked for a snack. They found four apples on the table.
542.8 forth, fourth	We set forth on our journey through the forest. Reggie was the fourth player to get hurt during the game.
542.9 good, well	Ling looks good in that outfit. (*Good* is an adjective. Adjectives modify nouns or pronouns.) It fits her well. (*Well* is an adverb modifying *fits*.)

Using the Right Word   **543**

Using the Right Word 4

■ desert, dessert; die, dye; doesn't, don't; flower, flour; for, four; good, well

 For each sentence, write the correct word from each pair in parentheses.

Example: I (*doesn't, don't*) like my
cowboy job very much.
don't

1. My horse (*doesn't, don't*) like it, either.

2. This sandy, old (*desert, dessert*) is very hot.

3. Sand always gets into the (*flower, flour*) I use (*for, four*) cooking.

4. A person could (*die, dye*) from thirst out here.

5. Nothing much grows here, so we hardly ever see a (*flower, flour*).

6. The (*die, dye*) from my kerchief has stained all (*for, four*) of my work shirts.

7. My horse's saddle doesn't fit very (*good, well*), either.

8. I'd rather be eating a nice (*desert, dessert*), like some (*good, well*) old-fashioned apple pie.

Next Step: Imagine that this cowboy weren't so grouchy. Write two sentences about his experiences from a happier point of view.

Answers

1. doesn't
2. desert
3. flour, for
4. die
5. flower
6. dye, four
7. well
8. dessert, good

544

544.1 **hair, hare**	Celia's hair is short and curly. A hare looks like a large rabbit.
544.2 **heal, heel**	Most scrapes and cuts heal quickly. Gracie has a blister on her heel.
544.3 **hear, here**	I couldn't hear your directions. I was over here, and you were way over there.
544.4 **heard, herd**	We heard the noise, all right! It sounded like a herd of charging elephants.
544.5 **hi, high**	Say hi to the pilot for me. How high is this plane flying?
544.6 **hole, whole**	A donut has a hole in the middle of it. Montel ate a whole donut.
544.7 **hour, our**	It takes one hour to ride to the beach. Let's pack our lunches and go.
544.8 **its, it's**	This backpack is no good; its zipper is stuck. (*Its* shows possession and never has an apostrophe.) It's also ripped. (*It's* is the contraction of *it is.*)
544.9 **knew, new**	I knew it was going to rain. I still wanted to wear my new shoes.
544.10 **knot, not**	I have a knot in my shoelaces. I am not able to untie the tangled mess.
544.11 **knows, nose**	Mr. Beck knows at least a billion historical facts. His nose is always in a book.

Using the Right Word 5

■ hair, hare; hear, here; heard, herd; hi, high; hole, whole; hour, our; its, it's; knows, nose

For each pair of words in parentheses below, write the line number and the correct choice.

Example: 1 Before their famous race,
2 the turtle and the
3 *(hare, hair)* were chatting.
3. hare

1   "(Hi, High), Turtle. (Its, It's) a nice day for the race,
2   isn't it?" Rabbit said.
3   "Yes," Turtle replied. "I (heard, herd) that everyone
4   expects you to win."
5   Rabbit said, "You (hear, here) a lot, even without big
6   ears." He stroked the fine (hare, hair) on his long ears.
7   "I like your ears," Turtle said, "but who (knows, nose)
8   how the race will turn out? I have been training for a
9   (hole, whole) month. I may win by a (knows, nose)."
10 "I'll stop by my rabbit (hole, whole) for a nap," Rabbit
11 laughed. "There's one (hour, our) before the race."
12 "Be sure you're back (hear, here) by then," said Turtle.
13 Rabbit grinned at the turtle. "I think (hour, our) little
14 race will be over almost before it begins," he said. "I can
15 already see my victory flag waving (hi, high) on (its, it's)
16 pole at the finish line."

Answers

line 1. Hi, It's
line 3. heard
line 5. hear
line 6. hair
line 7. knows
line 9. whole, nose
line 10. hole
line 11. hour
line 12. here
line 13. our
line 15. high, its

546.1
lay, lie

Just lay the sleeping bags on the floor.
(*Lay* means "to place.")

After the hike, we'll lie down and rest.
(*Lie* means "to recline.")

546.2
lead, led

Today I will lead (lēd) the ponies around the show ring.
Yesterday I led (lĕd) them, too.
(*Led* is the past tense of the verb *lead*.)

Some old paint contains the metal lead (lĕd).

546.3
learn, teach

I need to learn these facts about the moon.
(*Learn* means "to get information.")

Tomorrow I have to teach the science lesson.
(*Teach* means "to give information.")

546.4
loose, lose

Lee's pet tarantula is loose!
(*Loose* [loos] means "free or untied.")

No one but Lee could lose a big, fat spider.
(*Lose* [looz] means "to misplace" or "to fail to win.")

546.5
made, maid

Yes, I have made a big mess.

I need a maid to help me clean it up!

546.6
mail, male

Many people get more mail on their computers than in their mailboxes.

Men are male; women are female.

546.7
meat, meet

I think meat can be a part of a healthful diet.

We were so excited to finally meet the senator.

546.8
metal, medal

Gold is a precious metal.

Is the Olympic first-place medal actually made of gold?

Using the Right Word 6

■ learn, teach; **loose, lose;** made, maid; **mail, male;** meat, meet

For the following sentences, write the correct word from each pair in parentheses.

Example: A letter about a cooking contest arrived in the (*mail, male*).

mail

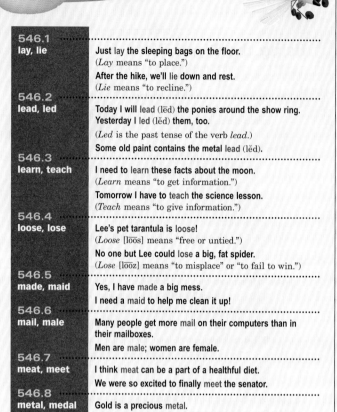

1. I asked Dad to (*learn, teach*) me how to make egg rolls.

2. When he was young, he (*made, maid*) a lot of egg rolls in my grandma's restaurant.

3. He said that he was the only (*mail, male*) baker there.

4. "I'm sure you'll (*learn, teach*) this in no time," he said, "as long as you don't (*loose, lose*) the recipe!"

5. The recipe called for (*loose, lose*) flour, so I started by sifting the flour into a fine powder.

6. We used cabbage and (*meet, meat*) to fill the egg rolls.

7. When we finished cooking, I wished we had a (*made, maid*) to clean up the mess!

8. I called Grandma to see if she could (*meat, meet*) us at the contest and taste our egg rolls.

Next Step: Write two sentences about something you'd like to cook. Use the words *learn* and *teach* correctly.

Answers

1. teach
2. made
3. male
4. learn, lose
5. loose
6. meat
7. maid
8. meet

548

548.1 miner, minor	A coal miner may one day get black lung disease. A minor is a young person who is not legally an adult. A minor problem is one of no great importance.
548.2 oar, or, ore	Row the boat with an oar in each hand. Either Kim or Mike will give a report on the iron ore mines near Lake Superior.
548.3 one, won	Markus bought one raffle ticket. He won the bike with that single ticket.
548.4 pain, pane	Injuries like cuts and scrapes cause pain. After cleaning the dirty window, we could see through the pane of glass.
548.5 pair, pare, pear	A pair (two) of pigeons roosted on our windowsill. To pare an apple means to peel it. A ripe pear is sweet and juicy.
548.6 passed, past	The school bus passed a stalled truck. In the past, most children walked to school.
548.7 peace, piece	Ms. Brown likes peace and quiet in her room. Would you like a piece of pizza, Jake?
548.8 peak, peek	The whipped topping formed a peak on my pudding. Alex stood on a footstool to peek inside the jar.
548.9 pedal, petal	Even though one pedal on the bike was broken, I was still able to pedal to school. Chantal plucked one petal after another from the daisy.

Using the Right Word 7

■ one, won; pair, pare, pear; passed, past; peace, piece; peak, peek; pedal, petal

▶ For the following sentences, write the correct word from the choices in parentheses.

Example: My egg rolls *(passed, past)* the first round of tasting in the cooking contest.

passed

1. I took a *(pair, pare, pear)* of the egg rolls to the school for judging.

2. I almost didn't make it in time because a *(pedal, petal)* on my bike jammed.

3. When I arrived, I took a *(peak, peek)* at the other entries.

4. *(One, Won)* entry was a whole cooked salmon.

5. Another looked like a *(pair, pare, pear)* cobbler, and I could smell the sweet fruit.

6. A *(peace, piece)* of cinnamon stick stood in a dish of applesauce; I'm glad I didn't have to *(pair, pare, pear)* all those apples!

7. The judges were *(passed, past)* winners.

8. The judging took time, but my egg rolls *(one, won)* first place!

Next Step: Use the words *petal, peak,* and *peace* correctly in three sentences.

Answers

▶ 1. pair
2. pedal
3. peek
4. One
5. pear
6. piece, pare
7. past
8. won

550

Using the Right Word

550.1
plain, plane

Toni wanted a plain (basic) white top.

The coyote ran across the flat plain.

A stunt plane can fly upside down.

550.2
poor, pore,
pour

The poor man had no money at all.

Every pore on my nose is clogged with oil.

Please pour the lemonade.

550.3
principal,
principle

Our principal visits the classrooms often.
(The noun *principal* is a school administrator.)

Her principal job is to be sure we are learning.
(The adjective *principal* means "most important.")

She asks students to follow this principle: Respect each
other, and I'll respect you.
(*Principle* means "idea" or "belief.")

550.4
quiet, quit,
quite

Libraries should be quiet places.

Quit talking, please.

I hear quite a bit of whispering going on.

550.5
raise, rays

Please don't raise (lift) the shades.

The sun's rays are very bright this afternoon.

550.6
read, red

Have you read any books by Betsy Byars?

Why are most barns painted red?

550.7
real, really

Mom gave me a stuffed animal, but I wanted a real dog.
(Use *real* as an adjective.)

I was really disappointed.
(*Really* is an adverb.)

550.8
right, write

Is this the right (correct) place to turn right?

I'll write the directions on a note card.

Using the Right Word 8

■ poor, pore, pour; **quiet, quit, quite**; read, red; **real, really;**
right, write

Look at each underlined word in the
following sentences. Write a "C" if it
is used correctly. If it is not, write the
correct word.

Example: The teacher asked Peter
to <u>poor</u> the juice.
pour

1. Peter was a <u>quite</u> boy.

2. Those who talked to him knew that he was <u>quiet</u> nice.

3. Peter would often <u>write</u> letters to his uncle.

4. "Our class did a <u>real</u> fun experiment," Pete wrote.

5. When Pete's uncle wrote back, Pete <u>red</u>, "I'd like to
hear about it, Peter."

6. For the experiment, Mr. Baxter asked Roberto and
Matt to wear big <u>red</u> paper bags over their heads.

7. Mr. Baxter told those <u>pore</u> kids to go left, <u>right</u>,
backward, and forward until they were all mixed up.

8. Then he asked the rest of the class, "Who is the <u>real</u>
Roberto?"

Next Step: Write two sentences about the end of the
experiment. Use two words from the list at the
top of the page.

Answers

1. quiet
2. quite
3. C
4. really
5. read
6. C
7. poor, C
8. C

552

552.1 road, rode, rowed	My house is one block from the main road. I rode my bike to the pond. Then I rowed the boat to my favorite fishing spot.
552.2 scene, seen	The movie has a great chase scene. Have you seen it yet?
552.3 sea, see	A sea is a body of salty water. I see a tall ship on the horizon.
552.4 seam, seem	The seam in my jacket is ripped. I seem to always catch my sleeve on the door handle.
552.5 sew, so, sow	Shauna loves to sew her own clothes. She saves her allowance so she can buy fabric. I'd rather sow seeds and watch my garden grow.
552.6 sit, set	May I sit on one of those folding chairs? Yes, if you help me set them up first.
552.7 some, sum	I have some math problems to do. What is the sum of 58 + 17?
552.8 son, sun	Joe Jackson is the son of Kate Jackson. The sun is the source of the earth's energy.
552.9 sore, soar	Our feet and legs were sore after the long hike. We watched hawks soar above us.
552.10 stationary, stationery	A stationary bike stays in place while you pedal it. Wu designs his own stationery (paper) on the computer.

Using the Right Word 9

■ sea, see; **seam, seem;** sew, so, sow; sit, set; some, sum; **son, sun**

Look at each underlined word in the following sentences. Write a "C" if it is used correctly. If it is not, write the correct word.

Example: It's not hard for the postal carrier to <u>sea</u> me every day.

see

1. Most often, the postal carrier will just <u>set</u> the mail by the gate.

2. I have never bitten the carrier, but once she tore a <u>seam</u> in her pants while she ran away.

3. My people offered to <u>sow</u> it for her.

4. Mostly I just <u>set</u> around my people's house by the <u>see</u> all day.

5. Their <u>son</u> plays with me, <u>sew</u> I get some exercise.

6. Sometimes I lie in the <u>son</u> to warm up.

7. <u>Some</u> days I crawl into the shade of my house to cool down.

8. I may <u>seam</u> scary, but I don't look for trouble.

Next Step: Write two sentences using the words *sow* and *sum* correctly.

Answers

1. C
2. C
3. sew
4. sit, sea
5. C, so
6. sun
7. C
8. seem

554.1 steal, steel	Our cat tries to steal our dog's food. The food bowl is made of stainless steel.
554.2 tail, tale	A snake uses its tail to move its body. "Sammy the Spotted Snake" is my favorite tall tale.
554.3 than, then	Jana's card collection is bigger than Erica's. (*Than* is used in a comparison.) When Jana is finished, then we can play. (*Then* tells when.)
554.4 their, there, they're	What should we do with their cards? (*Their* shows ownership.) Put them over there for now. They're going to pick them up later. (*They're* is the contraction of *they are*.)
554.5 threw, through	He threw the ball at the basket. It swished through the net.
554.6 to, too, two	Josie passed the ball to Maria. Lea was too tired to guard her. (*Too* means "very.") Maria made a jump shot and scored two points. The fans jumped and cheered, too. (*Too* can mean "also.")
554.7 waist, waste	My little sister's waist is tiny. Do not waste your time trying to fix that bike chain.
554.8 wait, weight	I can't wait for the field trip. Many students complain about the weight of their bookbags.
554.9 way, weigh	What is the best way to get to the park? Birds weigh very little because of their hollow bones.

Using the Right Word 10

■ tail, tale; **than, then**; their, there, they're; **threw, through**;
to, too, two; **waist, waste**; wait, weight;
way, weigh

▶ For each of the following sentences,
write the correct word from the
choices in parentheses.

Example: Herbert was listed in
Dragons of the World for
(to, too, two) years.
two

1. He was proud of getting *(threw, through)* the judging.

2. "*(Their, There, They're)* very picky about who they let
in," he told his friends.

3. He sniffed, "It would be a *(waist, waste)* of time
(to, too, two) put dragons like Nokum and Wally in
(their, there, they're)."

4. "This magnificent *(tail, tale)* surely helped me."

5. "I'm sure my *(wait, weight)* impressed the judges,
(to, too, two)," he added.

6. He fetched his mirror, sucked in his *(waist, waste),*
admired himself, and *(than, then)* smiled.

7. "I'm so much greater *(than, then)* other dragons in
every *(way, weigh),*" Herbert said.

Next Step: Write a paragraph telling what you think about
Herbert. Use words from the top of this page.

Answers

1. through
2. They're
3. waste, to, there
4. tail
5. weight, too
6. waist, then
7. than, way

556.1 **weak, week**	The opposite of strong is weak. There are seven days in a week.
556.2 **wear, where**	Finally, it's warm enough to wear shorts. Where is the sunscreen?
556.3 **weather, whether**	I like rainy weather. My dad goes golfing whether it's nice out or not.
556.4 **which, witch**	Which book should I read? You'll like *The Lion, the Witch, and the Wardrobe.*
556.5 **who, that, which**	The man who answered the phone had a loud voice. (*Who* refers to people.) The puppy that I really wanted was sold already. Its brother, which had not been sold yet, came home with me. (*That* and *which* refer to animals and things. Use commas around a clause that begins with *which.*)
556.6 **who, whom**	Who ordered this pizza? And for whom did you order it?
556.7 **who's, whose**	Who's that knocking at the door? (*Who's* is a contraction of *who is.*) Mrs. Lang, whose dog ran into our yard, came to get him.
556.8 **wood, would**	Some baseball bats are made of wood. Would you like to play baseball after school?
556.9 **your, you're**	You'll get your ice cream; be patient. You're talking to the right person! (*You're* is the contraction of *you are.*)

Using the Right Word 11

■ weak, week; **wear, where;** which, witch; who's, whose; wood, would; **your, you're**

▶ For the following sentences, write the correct word from each pair in parentheses.

Example: Just as a *(witch, which)* has a certain hat, so do I.

witch

1. You can see by the hat I *(wear, where)* that I'm a park ranger.

2. *(Who's, Whose)* job is it to manage a national park? It's mine.

3. Rangers work every *(weak, week)* of the year.

4. If *(you're, your)* wondering *(wear, where)* to pitch *(your, you're)* tent, I'll be happy to show you.

5. I know *(which, witch)* locations in the park are best.

6. I keep track of *(who's, whose)* visiting the park.

7. I might cut the *(wood, would)* of a fallen tree into logs—so this is not a job for a *(weak, week)* person!

8. *(Wood, Would)* you like to have a job like mine?

Next Step: Write a sentence or two about a job you'd like to do. Use at least one of the words from the list at the top of the page.

Answers

1. wear
2. Whose
3. week
4. you're, where, your
5. which
6. who's
7. wood, weak
8. Would

Test Prep

For each sentence below, write the letter of the line in which the underlined word is used incorrectly. If there is no mistake, choose "D."

1. A <u>Aunt</u> Josephine
    B <u>scent</u> me a bunch
    C of <u>blue</u> flowers.
    D no mistakes

2. A Down by the <u>see</u>,
    B we <u>sit</u> and smile
    C because we feel so
       <u>good</u>.
    D no mistakes

3. A If you <u>pour</u> juice
    B over <u>your</u> computer,
    C it will <u>brake</u>.
    D no mistakes

4. A We hired a <u>maid</u>
    B to clean <u>sum</u> rooms
    C and <u>two</u> hallways.
    D no mistakes

5. A The floorboards <u>creak</u>
    B in <u>our</u> family cabin;
    C they seem <u>weak</u>.
    D no mistakes

6. A I <u>through</u> the ball
    B so <u>high</u> in the sky that
    C it got lost in the <u>sun</u>.
    D no mistakes

7. A The <u>hare</u> and the turtle
    B <u>meet</u> once a year
    C down <u>buy</u> the forest.
    D no mistakes

8. A Sometimes they <u>sit</u>
    B near the rabbit's <u>whole</u>
    C and <u>learn</u> bunny songs.
    D no mistakes

9. A The silly grizzly <u>bear</u>
    B <u>threw</u> away his clock
    C just to <u>sea</u> time fly.
    D no mistakes

10. A That dragon <u>don't</u>
    B <u>breathe</u> fire and smoke
    C out of his <u>nose</u>.
    D no mistakes

11. A Try not to <u>loose</u>
    B any of my <u>mail</u> as
    C you <u>pedal</u> downtown.
    D no mistakes

12. A <u>Set</u> your boots by the
       door
    B <u>sow</u> you don't get mud
    C on our <u>wood</u> floor.
    D no mistakes

13. A One <u>peace</u> of pear
    B for <u>dessert</u> will
    C not add to my <u>waist</u>.
    D no mistakes

14. A We are not <u>aloud</u> to
    B leave the cabinets
       open <u>here</u>;
    C we must <u>close</u> them.
    D no mistakes

15. A We climbed a
       mountain <u>peak</u>
    B one day last <u>week</u>;
    C after that we were
       <u>real</u> tired.
    D no mistakes

16. A I think <u>their</u> dog
    B is meaner <u>then</u> any
       dog
    C <u>except</u> my cousin's
       dog.
    D no mistakes

17. A <u>Its</u> a perfect day
    B to <u>sit</u> by the fire
    C and <u>read</u> a book.
    D no mistakes

18. A I will <u>write</u> a
    B note to <u>except</u>
    C <u>your</u> invitation.
    D no mistakes

19. A Mom wants to <u>learn</u>
    B me how to <u>sew</u>
    C my own <u>clothes</u>.
    D no mistakes

20. A We could not <u>weight</u>
    B to taste the
    C <u>meat</u> we grilled.
    D no mistakes

Answers

1. b
2. a
3. c
4. b
5. d

6. a
7. c
8. b
9. c
10. a

Answers

11. a
12. b
13. a
14. a
15. c

16. b
17. a
18. b
19. a
20. a

Understanding Sentences

A **sentence** expresses a complete thought. Usually it has a subject and a predicate. A sentence begins with a capital letter and ends with a period, a question mark, or an exclamation point.

Parts of a Sentence

560.1 **Subjects**	A **subject** is the part of a sentence—a noun or pronoun—that names who or what is doing something. **Marisha** baked a pan of lasagna. A subject can also be the part that is talked about. **She** is a marvelous cook.
560.2 **Simple Subjects**	A simple subject is the subject without the words that describe or modify it. Marisha's little **sister** likes to help.
560.3 **Complete Subjects**	The complete subject is the simple subject along with all the words that describe it. **Marisha's little sister** likes to help.
560.4 **Compound Subjects**	A compound subject has two or more simple subjects joined by a conjunction *(and, or)*. **Marisha and her sister** worked on the puzzle.

Pasta
Tomato
Onion
Mushroom
Olive
Pepp
Spic

Parts of a Sentence 1

■ Subjects

Write the complete subject of each sentence.

Example: Mark Twain was born in Missouri in 1835.
Mark Twain

1. His real name was Samuel L. Clemens.

2. His job for about five years was Mississippi riverboat pilot.

3. Mark Twain's first story was published in 1865.

4. "The Celebrated Jumping Frog of Calaveras County" is a funny story.

5. Twain and his wife moved to Hartford, Connecticut, in 1870.

6. People enjoy Mark Twain's tall tales.

7. His most famous book is *The Adventures of Huckleberry Finn*.

8. Many pictures of Twain show him dressed in a white suit.

Next Step: Which sentence above has a compound subject? Write the two simple subjects in the compound subject.

Answers

1. His real name
2. His job for about five years
3. Mark Twain's first story
4. "The Celebrated Jumping Frog of Calaveras County"
5. Twain and his wife
6. People
7. His most famous book
8. Many pictures of Twain

Next Step: Sentence 5: Twain, wife

Parts of a Sentence . . .

562.1
Predicates

A **predicate** is the part of the sentence that contains the verb. The predicate can show action by telling what the subject is doing.

Marisha baked the cake for my birthday.

A predicate can also say something about the subject.

She is a good cook.

562.2
Simple Predicates

A simple predicate is the verb without any of the other words that modify it.

Marisha baked the cake yesterday.

562.3
Complete Predicates

The complete predicate is the verb along with all the words that modify or complete it.

Marisha baked the cake yesterday.

She had made cupcakes, too.

562.4
Compound Predicates

A compound predicate has two or more verbs.

She decorated the cake and hid it in a box in the cupboard.

562.5
Modifiers

A modifier is a word (an adjective or an adverb) or a group of words that describes another word.

My family planned a surprise party. (*My* modifies *family*; *a* and *surprise* modify *party*.)

They hid behind the door and waited quietly. (*Behind the door* modifies *hid*; *quietly* modifies *waited*.)

Parts of a Sentence 2

■ Predicates

Write the complete predicate of each sentence. Then underline the simple predicate (the verb or verbs).

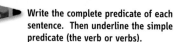

Example: A dog named Junkyard lives in the city.
lives in the city

1. Junkyard likes to eat a lot.

2. He will gulp down almost anything.

3. He looks for food scraps behind garbage cans.

4. Some people drop food on the sidewalk or in the park.

5. Junkyard can find it like a detective.

6. Some of these people chase Junkyard.

7. Junkyard escapes every time.

8. His favorite food is sub sandwiches.

9. He loves old sandwiches with stale bread and cheese.

10. Junkyard has little taste!

Next Step: Write two sentences about a dog. Underline the simple predicate in each sentence.

Answers

1. <u>likes</u> to eat a lot
2. <u>will gulp</u> down almost anything
3. <u>looks</u> for food scraps behind garbage cans
4. <u>drop</u> food on the sidewalk or in the park
5. <u>can find</u> it like a detective
6. <u>chase</u> Junkyard
7. <u>escapes</u> every time
8. <u>is</u> sub sandwiches
9. <u>loves</u> old sandwiches with stale bread and cheese
10. <u>has</u> little taste

Parts of a Sentence . . .

564.1
Clauses

A **clause** is a group of words that has a subject and a predicate. A clause can be independent or dependent.

564.2
Independent Clauses

An independent clause expresses a complete thought and can stand alone as a sentence.

> I ride my bike to school.
>
> Bryan gets a ride from his dad.

564.3
Dependent Clauses

A dependent clause does not express a complete thought, so it cannot stand alone as a sentence. Dependent clauses often begin with subordinating conjunctions like *when* or *because*. (See 600.2.)

> when the weather is nice

Some dependent clauses begin with relative pronouns like *who* or *which*. (See 580.1.)

> who works near our school

A dependent clause must be joined to an independent clause. The result is a complex sentence.

> I ride my bike to school when the weather is nice. Bryan gets a ride from his dad, who works near our school.

Parts of a Sentence 3

■ Clauses

 For each clause below, write an "I" for independent clause or a "D" for dependent clause.

Example: the tired knight didn't see the owl on his shoulder
I

1. since he was asleep

2. Sir Gordon often stayed up too late

3. when he worked on guard duty

4. which made him doze off

5. the owl didn't like to be alone

6. Sir Gordon's armor was cold

7. before the sun came up

8. because the owl kept quiet

9. the knight never noticed his new friend

Next Step: Choose a dependent clause and an independent clause from the list above. Combine them to make one complex sentence.

Answers

1. D
2. I
3. D
4. D
5. I
6. I
7. D
8. D
9. I

Parts of a Sentence . . .

566.1
Phrases

A **phrase** is a group of related words. Phrases cannot stand alone as sentences since they do *not* have both a subject and a predicate.

566.2
Noun Phrases

A noun phrase doesn't have a predicate. A noun and the adjectives that describe it make up a noun phrase.

the new student

566.3
Verb Phrases

A verb phrase doesn't have a subject. It includes a main verb and one or more helping verbs.

could have written

566.4
Prepositional Phrases

A prepositional phrase begins with a preposition. It doesn't have a subject or a predicate. However, it can add important information to a sentence. (See page 598.)

about George Washington

566.5
Appositive Phrases

An appositive phrase is another way of saying or renaming the noun or pronoun before it.

George Washington, our first president

NOTE: When you put these phrases together, they become a sentence.

The new student could have written about George Washington, our first president.

Parts of a Sentence 4

■ Phrases

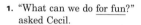

Identify the underlined phrases. Write "N" for a noun phrase, "V" for a verb phrase, "P" for a prepositional phrase, or "A" for an appositive phrase.

Example: Cecil called his two best friends, <u>Mary and Andy</u>.
    A

1. "What can we do <u>for fun</u>?" asked Cecil.

2. "We <u>could set up</u> a lemonade stand," Mary suggested.

3. "I'll get <u>the old wooden table</u> we used last year," Cecil said.

4. "I'll get the can Cecil keeps <u>under his bed</u>," Andy said.

5. The can, <u>Cecil's money bank</u>, had a big "five cent" sign on it.

6. The three friends made two big batches <u>of lemonade</u>.

7. "We <u>will need</u> to sell lots of lemonade to fill that can," Andy said.

8. Cecil said, "All we need is <u>a few good customers</u>."

Next Step: Write a sentence about two good friends. Include an appositive phrase and a prepositional phrase in your sentence.

Answers

1. P
2. V
3. N
4. P
5. A
6. P
7. V
8. N

568

Test Prep

Number your paper from 1 to 10. Read the paragraphs below. Then identify each underlined sentence part. Choose from the answers on the next page.

A grocery store in our town held a cooking contest for
    1
kids. I wanted to enter the contest. My dad and I read food
         2   **3**
magazines together. Then my two sisters got interested, too.
                                     4
We found good recipes and made them. We must have made
   5   **6**
nearly a hundred kinds of food!

My favorite recipe turned out to be the one for tamales.
    7
My sisters liked the meat loaf best. The three of us entered
          8   **9**
our creations in the contest. Our dinners didn't win the prize.
                                            10
But it was a fun family project—and we got to eat our entries!

1. **A** simple subject
    B complete subject
    C simple predicate
    D complete predicate

2. **A** simple subject
    B complete subject
    C simple predicate
    D complete predicate

3. **A** simple subject
    B complete subject
    C simple predicate
    D complete predicate

4. **A** simple subject
    B complete subject
    C simple predicate
    D complete predicate

5. **A** simple subject
    B complete subject
    C simple predicate
    D complete predicate

6. **A** verb phrase
    B noun phrase
    C prepositional phrase
    D appositive phrase

7. **A** simple subject
    B complete subject
    C simple predicate
    D complete predicate

8. **A** simple subject
    B complete subject
    C simple predicate
    D complete predicate

9. **A** simple subject
    B complete subject
    C simple predicate
    D complete predicate

10. **A** simple subject
    B complete subject
    C simple predicate
    D complete predicate

Answers

1. b   6. a
2. d   7. b
3. c   8. c
4. a   9. a
5. d   10. c

Using the Parts of Speech
Nouns

A **noun** is a word that names a person, a place, a thing, or an idea.

Kinds of Nouns

570.1 **Proper Nouns**	A proper noun names a specific person, place, thing, or idea. Proper nouns are capitalized. **Roberta Fischer Millennium Park *Shrek* Labor Day**
570.2 **Common Nouns**	A common noun does *not* name a specific person, place, thing, or idea. Common nouns are not capitalized. **woman park movie holiday**
570.3 **Concrete Nouns**	A concrete noun names a thing that you can experience through one or more of your five senses. Concrete nouns are either common or proper. **magazine rose Washington Monument chocolate**
570.4 **Abstract Nouns**	An abstract noun names a thing that you can think about but cannot see, hear, or touch. Abstract nouns are either common or proper. **love democracy Judaism Wednesday**
570.5 **Compound Nouns**	A compound noun is made up of two or more words. **busboy** (spelled as one word) **blue jeans** (spelled as two words) **two-wheeler sister-in-law** (spelled with hyphens)
570.6 **Collective Nouns**	A collective noun names a certain kind of group. Persons: **class team clan family** Animals: **herd flock litter pack** Things: **bunch batch collection**

Nouns 1
- Common and Proper Nouns
- Compound Nouns

For each sentence, write whether the underlined noun is common or proper. If the word is a compound noun, add a "C" after your answer.

Example: Kayla worked on her <u>seashell</u> collection last summer.
common, C

1. <u>Kayla</u> had a great time playing in the sand with her brother, Sam.

2. They found a <u>starfish</u> hiding behind a bunch of rocks.

3. A pair of old <u>sunglasses</u> had fallen on top of the starfish.

4. "This starfish looks like it's wearing the sunglasses!" <u>Sam</u> exclaimed.

5. Before going <u>home</u>, Sam and Kayla fed a flock of seagulls.

6. "I really love coming to <u>Swift's Beach</u>," Kayla said.

Next Step: Write down three more nouns from the sentences above. Tell whether each is proper or common. Also write a "C" if it's a compound noun.

Answers

1. proper
2. common, C
3. common, C
4. proper
5. common
6. proper, C

Next Step:
1. time, common; sand, common; brother, common; Sam, proper
2. bunch, common; rocks, common
3. pair, common; top, common; starfish, common, C
4. starfish, common, C; sunglasses, common, C
5. Sam, proper; Kayla, proper; flock, common; seagulls, common, C
6. Kayla, proper

Nouns . . .

Number of Nouns

572.1

Singular Nouns

A singular noun names just one person, place, thing, or idea.

room   paper   pen pal   hope

572.2

Plural Nouns

A plural noun names more than one person, place, thing, or idea.

rooms   papers   pen pals   hopes

Gender of Nouns

572.3

Noun Gender

The gender of a noun refers to its being *feminine* (female), *masculine* (male), *neuter* (neither male nor female), or *indefinite* (male or female).

Feminine (female): mother, sister, women, cow, hen

Masculine (male): father, brother, men, bull, rooster

Neuter (neither male nor female): tree, closet, cobweb

Indefinite (male or female): child, pilot, parent, dentist

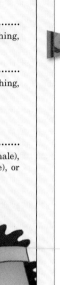

Nouns 2

■ Number of Nouns
■ Gender of Nouns

Identify the underlined noun in each sentence as "F" for feminine, "M" for masculine, "N" for neuter, or "I" for indefinite.

Example: My <u>sister</u> Kitty likes to climb a lot.
F

1. Kitty climbs on the monkey bars at the <u>playground</u>.

2. <u>Dad</u> always tells her to be careful.

3. One day, she spotted a <u>bluebird</u> in a tall tree.

4. She climbed into the tree's top <u>branches</u> to get a better look.

5. Unfortunately, <u>Kitty</u> got stuck.

6. She called out to some <u>kids</u> playing nearby.

7. Two kids told their <u>mothers</u>, who called the fire department.

8. The rescue unit came in a big red fire <u>truck</u>.

9. One <u>firefighter</u> put up a big ladder and got Kitty down.

Next Step: Look at the underlined nouns above again and add either "S" for singular or "P" for plural to your answer.

Answers

1. N
2. M
3. I
4. N
5. F
6. I
7. F
8. N
9. I

Next Step:

1. S
2. S
3. S
4. P
5. S
6. P
7. P
8. S
9. S

Nouns...
Uses of Nouns

574.1
Subject Nouns

A noun may be the subject of a sentence. (The subject is the part of the sentence that does something or is being talked about.)

> **Joe** ran away from the bee.

574.2
Predicate Nouns

A predicate noun follows a form of the verb *be* (*is, are, was, were*) and renames the subject.

> **The book is a mystery.**

574.3
Possessive Nouns

A possessive noun shows ownership. (See **490.2** and **492.1** for information on forming possessives.)

> **The book's ending is a big surprise.** (one book)
>
> **The books' bindings are torn and weak.** (more than one book)

574.4
Object Nouns

Direct Object: A direct object is the word that tells *what* or *who* receives the action of the verb. The direct object completes the meaning of the verb.

> **Nadia spent all her money.** (*What* did Nadia spend? The verb *spent* would be unclear without the direct object, *money.*)

Indirect Object: An indirect object names the person *to whom* or *for whom* something is done.

> **Joe gave Nadia the book.** (The book is given *to whom*? The book is given to *Nadia,* the indirect object.)

Object of a Preposition: An object of a preposition is part of a prepositional phrase. (See page **598.**)

> **Nadia put the book on the shelf.** (The noun *shelf* is the object of the preposition *on.*)

Nouns 3
■ Uses of Nouns

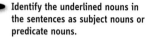

Identify the underlined nouns in the sentences as subject nouns or predicate nouns.

Example: One day, a penguin named Paulie went out for a walk all by himself.
subject noun

1. Paulie was an adventurer.

2. A snowstorm blew in while he walked, and Paulie got lost.

3. The nearby mountains disappeared into the blizzard.

4. The blowing snow was a sheet of white.

5. Paulie couldn't see his flippers in front of his face!

6. "I am a very lost bird," he moaned.

7. "My binoculars are fogging up, too."

8. Paulie's toes started to feel very cold.

9. Just then, the little penguin's mother and father appeared.

10. They were two relieved parents!

Next Step: First find the two possessive nouns in the sentences above. Then write a sentence using a possessive noun to finish Paulie's story.

Answers

1. predicate noun
2. subject noun
3. subject noun
4. predicate noun
5. subject noun
6. predicate noun
7. subject noun
8. subject noun
9. subject noun, subject noun
10. predicate noun

Next Step: Paulie's
penguin's
Sentences will vary.

Pronouns

A **pronoun** is a word used in place of a noun.

576.1 **Antecedents**	An antecedent is the noun that a pronoun refers to or replaces. All pronouns have antecedents. **Anju's brother has his own skateboard now.** (*Brother* is the antecedent of the pronoun *his*.)

Number of Pronouns

576.2 **Singular and Plural Pronouns**	Pronouns can be either singular or plural. **I grabbed my skateboard and joined LeRon.** **We were going to the skate park.**

Person of Pronouns

The *person* of a pronoun tells whether the antecedent of the pronoun is speaking, being spoken to, or being spoken about.

576.3 **First-Person Pronouns**	A first-person pronoun is used in place of the name of the speaker. **Petra said, "I like raspberry ice cream."** (*I* replaces the name *Petra*, the person who is speaking.)
576.4 **Second-Person Pronouns**	A second-person pronoun names the person spoken to. **Su, have you decided on a flavor?** (*You* replaces the name *Su*, the person being spoken to.)
576.5 **Third-Person Pronouns**	A third-person pronoun is used to name the person or thing spoken about. **Jon said that he wants pumpkin ice cream because it is so good.** (*He* refers to *Jon*, the person being spoken about, and *it* refers to *ice cream*, the thing being spoken about.)

Pronouns 1

- Antecedents
- Number of Pronouns

For each underlined pronoun in the paragraph below, write its antecedent. Then write whether the pronoun is singular or plural.

Example: The baseball park was hosting its home team.
park, singular

(1) Wendy grabbed her bat. (2) She was the best hitter on the Fairweather baseball team. (3) Carrie and Phyllis cheered when they saw her. (4) Wendy was focusing and didn't notice them. (5) Wendy thought, "I must try to get a home run so we'll win the game." (6) As Wendy's home run cleared the wall, the fans cried, "Our team wins!"

Next Step: Pretend you were at the celebration in the ballpark. Write a sentence using a pronoun with an antecedent. Then underline the pronoun and circle the antecedent.

Answers

1. Wendy, singular
2. Wendy, singular
3. Carrie and Phyllis, plural
4. Carrie and Phyllis, plural
5. Wendy, singular
6. fans, plural

Pronouns . . .

Uses of Pronouns

578.1
Subject Pronouns

A subject pronoun is used as the subject of a sentence.

I can tell jokes well.

They really make people laugh.

578.2
Object Pronouns

An object pronoun is used as a direct object, an indirect object, or the object of a preposition.

Mr. Otto encourages me. (direct object)

Mr. Otto gives us help with math. (indirect object)

I made a funny card for him. (object of the preposition)

578.3
Possessive Pronouns

A possessive pronoun shows ownership. It can be used before a noun, or it can stand alone.

Gloria finished writing her story.
(*Her* comes before the noun *story*.)

The idea for the plot was mine. (*Mine* can stand alone.)

Before a noun: *my, your, his, her, its, our, their*

Stand alone: *mine, yours, his, hers, ours, theirs*

Uses of Personal Pronouns

	Singular Pronouns			Plural Pronouns		
	Subject Pronouns	Possessive Pronouns	Object Pronouns	Subject Pronouns	Possessive Pronouns	Object Pronouns
First Person	I	my, mine	me	we	our, ours	us
Second Person	you	your, yours	you	you	your, yours	you
Third Person	he	his	him	they	their, theirs	them
	she	her, hers	her			
	it	its	it			

Pronouns 2

■ Uses of Pronouns

For each sentence, write whether the underlined pronoun is a subject pronoun, an object pronoun, or a possessive pronoun.

Example: My sister and I like going outside during the winter.
subject pronoun

1. We put on <u>our</u> coats, hats, and scarves.

2. Then <u>we</u> go outside and wait for the snow to fall.

3. When we see the first snowflakes, we try to catch <u>them</u>.

4. I always try to catch snowflakes in <u>my</u> hand.

5. My sister likes catching them on <u>her</u> tongue.

6. <u>She</u> gets one every time!

7. After a while, the cold gives <u>her</u> a red nose.

8. Sometimes Dad fixes hot orange drink for <u>us</u>.

Next Step: Write two sentences about going to the movies. Use at least one subject pronoun, one object pronoun, and one possessive pronoun.

Answers

1. possessive pronoun
2. subject pronoun
3. object pronoun
4. possessive pronoun
5. possessive pronoun
6. subject pronoun
7. object pronoun
8. object pronoun

Pronouns . . .

Types of Pronouns

580.1
Relative Pronouns

A relative pronoun connects a dependent clause to a word in another part of the sentence.

Students who want to join band should see Carlos.

Relative pronouns: *who, whose, whom, which, what, that, whoever, whomever, whichever, whatever*

580.2
Interrogative Pronouns

An interrogative pronoun asks a question.

Who is going to play the keyboard?

Interrogative pronouns: *who, whose, whom, which, what*

580.3
Demonstrative Pronouns

A demonstrative pronoun points out a noun without naming it. Demonstrative pronouns: *this, that, these, those*

That sounds like a great idea!

TIP: When *this, that, these,* and *those* are used before nouns, they are adjectives, not pronouns. *That* hat is red.

580.4
Intensive and Reflexive Pronouns

An intensive pronoun stresses the word it refers to. A reflexive pronoun refers back to the subject. These pronouns have *-self* or *-selves* added at the end.

Carlos himself taught the group. (intensive)

Carlos enjoyed himself. (reflexive)

580.5
Indefinite Pronouns

An indefinite pronoun refers to people or things that are not named or known.

Nobody is here to videotape the practice.

Singular	Plural	Singular or Plural
another, something, nobody, neither, either, everybody, everyone, anybody, anyone, no one, somebody, anything, someone, one, each, everything, nothing	both few many several	all, any most none some

Pronouns 3

- Interrogative Pronouns
- Demonstrative Pronouns

Identify the underlined pronouns in the paragraphs below. Write the line number and then write "I" for interrogative or "D" for demonstrative.

Example: 1 <u>This</u> was supposed to be
2 a lovely day.
1. D

1 <u>What</u> is going on here? The sun is out, but it's raining.
2 The rain starts, and stops, and starts again. What could
3 make <u>that</u> happen? I don't think <u>these</u> are normal rain
4 showers.
5 I'm glad I brought umbrellas. <u>Which</u> of <u>these</u> should I
6 use? <u>Whose</u> is this red one with yellow daisies, I wonder.
7 I just noticed that the island I'm perched on is
8 moving. <u>What</u> could be causing <u>this</u>? Should I ask the
9 whales I see nearby? Their spouts shoot into the sky like
10 fountains, and <u>those</u> look very much like the rain that's
11 been bothering me.
12 Hey, wait a minute . . . maybe I should be asking <u>who</u>
13 is causing the rain!

Next Step: Write another question the bird might have asked. Use an interrogative pronoun.

Answers

line 1. I
line 3. D, D
line 5. I, D
line 6. I
line 8. I, D
line 10. D
line 12. I

Verbs

A **verb** shows action or links the subject to another word in the sentence. The verb is the main word in the predicate.

Types of Verbs

582.1
Action Verbs

An action verb tells what the subject is doing.

The wind blows.   **I pull my sweater on.**

582.2
Linking Verbs

A linking verb links a subject to a noun or an adjective in the predicate part of the sentence. (See chart below.)

That car is a convertible. (The verb *is* links the subject *car* to the noun *convertible*.)

A new car looks shiny. (The verb *looks* links the subject *car* to the adjective *shiny*.)

582.3
Helping Verbs

Helping verbs (also called auxiliary verbs) come before the main verb and give it a more specific meaning.

Lee will write in his journal. (The verb *will* helps state a future action.)

Lee has been writing in his journal. (The verbs *has* and *been* help state a continuing action.)

Linking Verbs

am, is, are, was, were, being, been, smell, look, taste, remain, feel, appear, sound, seem, become, grow

Helping Verbs

shall, will, should, would, could, must, can, may, have, had, has, do, did, does

The forms of the verb *be* (*am, is, are, was, were, being, been*) may also be helping verbs.

Verbs 1

■ Action, Linking, and Helping Verbs

For each sentence, write whether the underlined verb is an action verb, a linking verb, or a helping verb.

Example: Mightyman <u>flies</u> through the air high above the city.
action verb

1. He <u>is</u> the most powerful superhero in the area.

2. To hunt down criminals, Mightyman <u>uses</u> his mega-vision.

3. "They <u>will</u> not escape!" he shouts.

4. "We <u>must</u> do everything we can to stamp out crime," Mightyman declares.

5. When criminals see Mightyman, they <u>shake</u> in their boots.

6. They <u>look</u> frightened of him.

7. They know they <u>do</u> not have a chance against him.

8. We <u>are</u> lucky Mightyman is around.

Next Step: Write a sentence about a superhero. Underline a verb in the sentence and exchange papers with a classmate. Tell whether each other's verb is an action verb, a linking verb, or a helping verb.

Answers

1. linking verb
2. action verb
3. helping verb
4. helping verb
5. action verb
6. linking verb
7. helping verb
8. linking verb

Verbs . . .

Simple Verb Tenses

The tense of a verb tells when the action takes place. The simple tenses are *present, past,* and *future.* (See page 418.)

584.1

Present Tense Verbs

The present tense of a verb states an action (or state of being) that is *happening now* or that *happens regularly.*

I like **soccer.   We** practice **every day.**

584.2

Past Tense Verbs

The past tense of a verb states an action or (state of being) that *happened at a specific time in the past.*

Anne kicked **the soccer ball.   She** was **the goalie.**

584.3

Future Tense Verbs

The future tense of a verb states an action (or state of being) that *will take place.*

I will like **soccer forever.   We** will practice **every day.**

Perfect Verb Tenses

Perfect tense is expressed with certain helping verbs.

584.4

Present Perfect Tense Verbs

The present perfect tense states an action that is *still going on.* Add *has* or *have* before the past participle form of the main verb.

Alexis has slept **for two hours so far.**

TIP: The past participle (underlined) is the same as the past tense of most verbs.

584.5

Past Perfect Tense Verbs

The past perfect tense states an action that *began and ended in the past.* Add *had* before the past participle.

Jondra had slept **for eight hours before the alarm rang.**

584.6

Future Perfect Tense Verbs

The future perfect tense states an action that *will begin in the future and end at a specific time.* Add *will have* before the past participle form of the main verb.

Riley will have slept **for 12 hours by 9:00 a.m. tomorrow.**

Verbs 2

■ Present, Past, and Future Tenses

► **Write the tense—past, present, or future—of the underlined verbs in the following sentences.**

Example: The chicken <u>wants</u> to cross the road.
present

1. She <u>crossed</u> the road this morning.

2. She <u>will cross</u> the road again soon.

3. The grass on the other side of the road always <u>looks</u> greener than it does on the side she is on.

4. She <u>stands</u> at the side of the road to think.

5. "Yesterday, I <u>came</u> over to this side," she says.

6. "If I go back to the other side today," she wonders, "<u>will</u> I <u>want</u> to come back to this side tomorrow?"

7. She <u>knows</u> she must decide before long.

8. Otherwise, she <u>will waste</u> her whole day by the side of the road!

Next Step: Write a sentence telling what the chicken decided to do. Underline your verb and tell what tense it is.

Answers

1. past
2. future
3. present
4. present
5. past
6. future
7. present
8. future

Verbs . . .

Forms of Verbs

586.1
Transitive and Intransitive Verbs

An action verb is called a transitive verb if it is followed by a direct object (noun or pronoun). The object makes the meaning of the verb complete.

> **Direct Object:** Ann Cameron writes **books** about Julian.

A transitive verb may also be followed by an indirect object. An indirect object names the person *to whom* or *for whom* something is done.

> **Indirect Object:** Books give **children** enjoyment.
> (*Children* is the indirect object. *Give* is a transitive verb, and *enjoyment* is the direct object.)

A verb that is not followed by a direct object is intransitive.

> **Ann Cameron writes about Julian in her books.** (The verb is followed by two prepositional phrases.)

586.2
Active and Passive Verbs

A verb is active if the subject is doing the action.

> **Tia threw a ball.** (The subject *Tia* is doing the action.)

A verb is passive if the subject does not do the action.

> **A ball was thrown by Tia.** (The subject *ball* is not doing the action.)

586.3
Singular and Plural Verbs

A singular verb is used with a singular subject.

> **Ben likes cream cheese and olive sandwiches.**

A plural verb is used when the subject is plural. (A plural verb usually does not have an *s* at the end, which is just the opposite of a plural subject.)

> **Black olives taste like wax.**

586.4
Irregular Verbs

Some verbs in the English language are irregular. Instead of adding *-ed*, the spelling of the word changes in different tenses. (See page 588 for a chart of irregular verbs.)

> **I speak.   Yesterday I spoke.   I have spoken.**

Verbs 3

■ Singular and Plural Verbs

For each sentence below, tell whether the underlined verb is singular or plural.

Example: The players <u>meet</u> at the field.
plural

1. They <u>pick</u> sides to make teams.

2. One player <u>volunteers</u> to be the team captain.

3. Another <u>chooses</u> a name for the team.

4. The Herd, the Grazers, and the Cheeseheads <u>are</u> some of the names.

5. I <u>think</u> these are funny names.

6. To these players, though, they <u>seem</u> normal.

7. The best hitter <u>is</u> named Babe Moooth.

8. The pitcher <u>throws</u> the first ball of the game.

9. The ball <u>zooms</u> over home plate and into the catcher's glove.

10. The fans <u>cheer</u> wildly.

Next Step: Write two sentences about this baseball game. Use a singular verb in one and a plural verb in the other.

Answers

1. plural
2. singular
3. singular
4. plural
5. singular
6. plural
7. singular
8. singular
9. singular
10. plural

Verbs . . .
Forms of Verbs

Common Irregular Verbs

The principal parts of some common irregular verbs are listed below. The past participle is used with the helping verbs *has, have,* or *had.*

Present Tense	I hide.	She hides.
Past Tense	Yesterday I hid.	Yesterday she hid.
Past Participle	I have hidden.	She has hidden.

Present Tense	Past Tense	Past Participle	Present Tense	Past Tense	Past Participle	Present Tense	Past Tense	Past Participle
am, is, are	was, were	been	give	gave	given	shrink	shrank	shrunk
begin	began	begun	go	went	gone	sing	sang, sung	sung
bite	bit	bitten	grow	grew	grown	sink	sank, sunk	sunk
blow	blew	blown	hang	hung	hung	sit	sat	sat
break	broke	broken	hide	hid	hidden, hid	sleep	slept	slept
bring	brought	brought	hold	held	held	speak	spoke	spoken
buy	bought	bought	keep	kept	kept	spring	sprang, sprung	sprung
catch	caught	caught	know	knew	known	stand	stood	stood
come	came	come	lay (place)	laid	laid	steal	stole	stolen
dive	dived, dove	dived	lead	led	led	swear	swore	sworn
do	did	done	leave	left	left	swim	swam	swum
draw	drew	drawn	lie (recline)	lay	lain	swing	swung	swung
drink	drank	drunk	make	made	made	take	took	taken
drive	drove	driven	ride	rode	ridden	teach	taught	taught
eat	ate	eaten	ring	rang	rung	tear	tore	torn
fall	fell	fallen	rise	rose	risen	throw	threw	thrown
fight	fought	fought	run	ran	run	wake	woke	woken
fly	flew	flown	see	saw	seen	wear	wore	worn
freeze	froze	frozen	shake	shook	shaken	weave	wove	woven
get	got	gotten	shine (light)	shone	shone	write	wrote	written

* The following verbs are the same in each of the principal parts: *burst, cost, cut, hurt, let, put, set,* and *spread.*

Verbs 4
■ Irregular Verbs

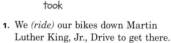

For each sentence, write the correct past tense form of the verb or verbs in parentheses.

Example: Aunt Tamika and her friend *(take)* me to the park yesterday.
took

1. We *(ride)* our bikes down Martin Luther King, Jr., Drive to get there.

2. First, I *(swing)* on the swings.

3. Then we all *(throw)* a baseball to each other until we *(get)* hungry.

4. Aunt Tamika *(bring)* bagged lunches for all of us.

5. We *(sit)* down on the grass and *(eat)* our sandwiches.

6. After lunch, we *(run)* around on the soccer field.

7. I *(give)* Aunt Tamika a daisy I found near the goalpost.

Next Step: Use the past tense of the words *spring, teach,* and *break* in sentences.

Answers

1. rode
2. swung
3. threw, got
4. brought
5. sat, ate
6. ran
7. gave

Next Step: Sentences will vary but should use the verbs *sprang, taught,* and *broke.*

Adjectives

Adjectives are words that modify (describe) nouns or pronouns. Adjectives tell *what kind, how many,* or *which one.* (Also see pages 423–425.)

590.1
Articles

The adjectives *a, an,* and *the* are called articles.

> **"Owlet"** is the name for a baby owl.

The article *a* comes before singular words that begin with consonant sounds. Also use *a* before singular words that begin with the long *u* sound.

> a **shooting star**   a **unique constellation**

The article *an* comes before singular words that begin with any vowel sounds except for long *u.*

> an **astronaut**   an **inquiring mind**   an **unusual outfit**

590.2
Proper and Common Adjectives

Proper adjectives are formed from proper nouns. They are always capitalized.

> On a cold **Minnesota** day, a **Hawaiian** trip sounds great.

Common adjectives are any that are *not* proper.

> I'll pack my **big blue** suitcase for a **weeklong** trip.

590.3
Predicate Adjectives

Predicate adjectives follow linking verbs and describe subjects. (See page 470.)

> The apples are **juicy.** They taste **sweet.**

590.4
Compound Adjectives

Compound adjectives are made up of more than one word. Some are spelled as one word; others are hyphenated.

> **evergreen** tree   **white-throated** sparrows

590.5
Demonstrative Adjectives

Demonstrative adjectives point out specific nouns.

> **This** nest has four eggs, and **that** nest has two.
> **These** eggs will hatch before **those** eggs will.

TIP: When *this, that, these,* and *those* are not used before nouns, they are pronouns, not adjectives.

Adjectives 1

- Common and Proper Adjectives
- Demonstrative Adjectives

For the sentences below, tell whether each underlined adjective is common or proper. Add a "DA" if it is a demonstrative adjective.

Example: <u>Those</u> muffins look delicious!
common, DA

1. Tami brought <u>banana</u> muffins to school.

2. They were our <u>Friday</u> treats.

3. Some of them had <u>roasted</u> nuts on top.

4. Some had <u>cream-cheese</u> frosting.

5. Tami did not use <u>Swiss</u> chocolate in them.

6. <u>This</u> muffin has raisins on top.

7. Nick is going to bring spumoni <u>next</u> week.

8. It's his <u>Italian</u> grandmother's recipe.

9. Mmmm . . . I can't wait to taste <u>that</u> treat!

Next Step: Write a sentence or two about a yummy treat. Use adjectives that help the reader see, smell, and taste the treat.

Answers

1. common
2. proper
3. common
4. common
5. proper
6. common, DA
7. common
8. proper
9. common, DA

592

Adjectives . . .

592.1 Indefinite Adjectives

Indefinite adjectives tell approximately (not exactly) *how many* or *how much*.

> **Most** students love summer.
> **Some** days are rainy, but **few** days are boring.

Forms of Adjectives

592.2 Positive Adjectives

The positive (base) form of an adjective describes a noun without comparing it to another noun. (See page 424.)

> A hummingbird is **small**.

592.3 Comparative Adjectives

The comparative form of an adjective compares two people, places, things, or ideas. The comparison is formed by adding *-er* to one-syllable adjectives or the word *more* or *less* before longer adjectives.

> A hummingbird is **smaller than** a sparrow.
> Hummingbirds are **more colorful than** sparrows.

592.4 Superlative Adjectives

The superlative form of an adjective compares three or more people, places, things, or ideas. The superlative is formed by adding *-est* to one-syllable adjectives or the word *most* or *least* before longer adjectives.

> The hummingbird is **the smallest** bird I've seen.
> The parrot is **the most colorful** bird in the zoo.

592.5 Irregular Forms of Adjectives

The comparative and superlative forms of some adjectives are different words. *More* or *most* is not needed with these words.

Positive	Comparative	Superlative
good	better	best
bad	worse	worst
many	more	most
little	less	least

Adjectives 2

■ Positive, Comparative, and Superlative Adjectives

For each sentence, write whether the underlined adjective is positive, comparative, or superlative.

Example: <u>Many</u> competitors arrived for the pond track meet.
positive

1. There was a <u>bigger</u> crowd than Franklin expected.

2. "I will show everyone that I'm the <u>best</u> jumper," he said.

3. Hilo was a <u>good</u> runner.

4. Hilo said, "Ellie is a <u>faster</u> runner than I am."

5. She added, "Frederick is the <u>fastest</u> runner of all."

6. "I just want to have a <u>better</u> finish than I did last time," Hilo said.

7. When the contest ended, Franklin had the <u>highest</u> jump of all.

8. Everyone who took part did a <u>fine</u> job.

Next Step: Write three sentences about an activity you and your friends enjoy. Use a different form of adjective in each sentence.

Answers

1. comparative
2. superlative
3. positive
4. comparative
5. superlative
6. comparative
7. superlative
8. positive

Adverbs

Adverbs are words that modify (describe) verbs, adjectives, or other adverbs. (Also see pages 426–427.)

> **The softball team practices** faithfully.
> (*Faithfully* modifies the verb *practices*.)
>
> **Yesterday's practice was** extra **long.**
> (*Extra* modifies the adjective *long*.)
>
> **Last night the players slept** quite soundly.
> (*Quite* modifies the adverb *soundly*.)

Types of Adverbs

594.1 **Adverbs of Time**	Adverbs of time tell *when*, *how often*, or *how long*. **Max batted** first. (when) **Katie's team plays** weekly. (how often) **Her team was in first place** briefly. (how long)
594.2 **Adverbs of Place**	Adverbs of place tell *where*. **When the first pitch curved** outside**, the batter leaned** forward. **"Hit it** there!**" urged the coach, pointing to right field.**
594.3 **Adverbs of Manner**	Adverbs of manner tell *how* something is done. **Max waited** eagerly **for the next pitch.** **He swung** powerfully **but missed the ball.**
594.4 **Adverbs of Degree**	Adverbs of degree tell *how much* or *how little*. **The catcher was** totally **surprised.** (how much) **He** scarcely **saw the fastball coming.** (how little) **TIP:** Adverbs often end in *-ly*, but not always. Words like *not*, *never*, *very*, and *always* are common adverbs.

Adverbs 1

■ To Modify Verbs, Adjectives, and Other Adverbs

For each sentence, write the word that the underlined adverb modifies. Tell whether the word is a verb, an adjective, or an adverb.

Example: I'll <u>always</u> remember my trip to the circus.
remember — verb

1. My Uncle Tito <u>never</u> missed the circus when it came to town.

2. He promised to take me if I was <u>extra</u> good.

3. We <u>eagerly</u> drove out to the fairgrounds to see the show.

4. The elephants performed <u>first</u>.

5. The audience cheered <u>wildly</u>.

6. Lions and tigers growled <u>fiercely</u> in their cages.

7. An acrobat walked <u>very</u> slowly on a tightrope above a big net.

8. A <u>brightly</u> painted clown smiled happily at us.

Next Step: Write a sentence about a circus. Use an adverb in your sentence. Circle the adverb and draw an arrow to the word it modifies.

Answers

1. missed—verb
2. good—adjective
3. drove—verb
4. performed—verb
5. cheered—verb
6. growled—verb
7. slowly—adverb
8. painted—adjective

Adverbs . . .

Forms of Adverbs

596.1
Positive Adverbs

The positive (base) form of an adverb does not make a comparison. (See page 426.)

Max plays **hard** from the first pitch to the last out.

596.2
Comparative Adverbs

The comparative form of an adverb compares how two things are done. The comparison is formed by adding *-er* to one-syllable adverbs or the word *more* or *less* before longer adverbs.

Max plays **harder** than his cousin plays, and he plays **more often** than his cousin does.

596.3
Superlative Adverbs

The superlative form of an adverb compares how three or more things are done. The superlative is formed by adding *-est* to one-syllable adverbs or the word *most* or *least* before longer adverbs.

Max plays **hardest** in close games. He plays **most often** in center field.

596.4
Irregular Forms of Adverbs

The comparative and superlative forms of some adverbs are different words. *More* or *most* is not needed with these words.

Positive	Comparative	Superlative
well	better	best
badly	worse	worst

TIP: Do not confuse *well* and *good*. *Good* is an adjective and *well* is usually an adverb. (See 592.5.)

Adverbs 2

■ Comparative and Superlative Adverbs

For each sentence, write the correct comparative or superlative form of the adverb from the choices given in parentheses.

Example: My dog Bosco learns the *(most quickly, quicker)* of any other dog in his class.
most quickly

1. He behaves *(better, weller)* than the other dogs do, too.

2. During Bosco's lessons, he sits *(most quiet, more quietly)* than my friend's dog sits.

3. The obedience-school teacher says that Bosco works the *(most hard, hardest)* of any pet in the school.

4. Of all his obedience-school "classmates," Bosco gets treats *(most often, oftenest)*.

5. He can run *(faster, fastest)* than any kid on our block.

6. Of all the kids who love Bosco, it is my neighbor Kendra who *(clearliest, most clearly)* adores him.

Next Step: For each answer you wrote, write a "C" for a comparative adverb or an "S" for a superlative adverb.

Answers

1. better
2. more quietly
3. hardest
4. most often
5. faster
6. most clearly

Next Step:
1. C
2. C
3. S
4. S
5. C
6. S

Using the Parts of Speech 599

Prepositions

Prepositions are words that introduce prepositional phrases. They can show position or direction, or they can show some other relationship between the words in a sentence. (Also see pages 428 and 430.)

Our cats do what they please in our house.

598.1
Prepositional Phrases

Prepositional phrases include a preposition, the object of the preposition (a noun or pronoun that comes after the preposition), and any words that modify the object.

Jo-Jo sneaks toward the gerbil cage. (*Toward* is the preposition, and *cage* is the object of the preposition. *The* and *gerbil* modify *cage*.)

Smacker watches from the desk drawer **and then ducks** inside it. (The noun *drawer* is the object of the preposition *from*, and the pronoun *it* is the object of the preposition *inside*.)

NOTE: If a word found in the list of prepositions has no object in a sentence, then it is not a preposition in that sentence. It could be an adverb or a conjunction.

Common Prepositions

aboard	around	but	into	over	until
about	at	by	like	past	up
above	before	down	near	since	up to
across	behind	during	of	through	upon
across from	below	except	off	throughout	with
after	beneath	except for	on	till	within
against	beside	for	on top of	to	without
along	besides	from	onto	toward	
along with	between	in	out	under	
among	beyond	inside	outside	underneath	

Prepositions

For the sentences below, write each prepositional phrase and underline its preposition.

Example: The Roman Empire started long ago in Italy.
<u>in</u> Italy

1. The empire soon spread across much of Europe.

2. Romans lived without modern tools.

3. Sundials and water clocks measured time for them.

4. Water clocks had a set amount of water that flowed from one part to another.

5. Most Romans did not have horses, so they walked to nearby towns.

6. Wealthy Romans with two homes rode horses between them.

7. People who lived near the sea often traveled in boats.

8. People of the Roman Empire valued art, reading, and writing.

Next Step: Write two sentences about what you think it would be like to live during the Roman Empire. Underline any prepositional phrases you use.

Answers

1. <u>across</u> much of Europe
2. <u>without</u> modern tools
3. <u>for</u> them
4. <u>of</u> water, <u>from</u> one part, <u>to</u> another
5. <u>to</u> nearby towns
6. <u>with</u> two homes, <u>between</u> them
7. <u>near</u> the sea, <u>in</u> boats
8. <u>of</u> the Roman Empire

Conjunctions

Conjunctions connect individual words or groups of words.

600.1
Coordinating Conjunctions

A coordinating conjunction connects equal parts: two or more words, phrases, or clauses.

The river is wide and **deep.** (words)

We can fish in the morning or **in the evening.** (phrases)

The river rushes down the valley, and **then it winds through the prairie.** (clauses)

600.2
Subordinating Conjunctions

A subordinating conjunction is often used to introduce the dependent clause in a complex sentence.

Our trip was delayed when **the snowstorm hit.**

Until **the snow stopped, we had to stay in town.**

TIP: Relative pronouns can also be used to connect clauses. (See 564.3.)

600.3
Correlative Conjunctions

Correlative conjunctions are used in pairs.

Either **snow** or **wind can make the trip dangerous.**

Common Conjunctions

Coordinating Conjunctions
and, but, or, nor, for, so, yet

Subordinating Conjunctions
after, although, as, as if, as long as, as though, because, before, if, in order that, since, so, so that, that, though, unless, until, when, where, whereas, while

Correlative Conjunctions
either/or, neither/nor, not only/but also, both/and, whether/or, as/so

---

Conjunctions

- Coordinating Conjunctions
- Subordinating Conjunctions

Write the conjunction or conjunctions from each sentence below.

Example: Our cat likes to run and play outside.
and

1. It doesn't matter if it's sunny or cloudy.
2. The cat sits by the door and meows until we let him out.
3. When I let him out earlier today, he quickly climbed a tree.
4. He has climbed very high, and now he can't get down.
5. He looks scared because all of his fur is standing up.
6. Should we get a ladder, or should we call someone for help?
7. We could call the fire department, but rescuing cats is really not their job.
8. While we were wondering what to do, that cat came down on his own.

Next Step: Now write "C" for coordinating conjunction or "S" for subordinating conjunction next to each conjunction you wrote.

Answers

1. if, or
2. and, until
3. When
4. and
5. because
6. or
7. but
8. While

Next Step:
1. S, C
2. C, S
3. S
4. C
5. S
6. C
7. C
8. S

Interjections

Interjections are words or phrases that express strong emotion. Commas or exclamation points are used to separate interjections from the rest of the sentence.

> Wow, look at those mountains!
>
> Hey! Keep your eyes on the road!

Quick Guide: Parts of Speech

Nouns	Words that name a person, a place, a thing, or an idea (Bill, office, billboard, confusion)
Pronouns	Words used in place of nouns (I, me, her, them, who, which, those, myself, some)
Verbs	Words that express action or state of being (run, jump, is, are)
Adjectives	Words that describe a noun or pronoun (tall, quiet, three, the, neat)
Adverbs	Words that describe a verb, an adjective, or another adverb (gently, easily, fast, very)
Prepositions	Words that show relationship and introduce prepositional phrases (on, near, from, until)
Conjunctions	Words that connect words or groups of words (and, or, because)
Interjections	Words (set off by commas or exclamation points) that show emotion or surprise (Wow, Oh, Yikes!)

Parts of Speech Review

Write down the part of speech that is underlined in each sentence below.

noun   preposition   adjective
pronoun   conjunction   adverb
verb   interjection

(1) An <u>eel</u> is not a kind of water snake; it is a fish. (2) Like all other fish, eels <u>breathe</u> with their gills and have scales and fins. (3) Unlike <u>most</u> fish, however, eels do not have fins at the rear of their bodies.

(4) Baby eels <u>are called</u> "elvers." (5) All <u>they</u> want to do is eat, eat, eat! (6) They do not see very well, <u>but</u> they have a good sense of smell. (7) They eat at night, <u>and</u> they rest during the day.

(8) The <u>largest</u> eel is the moray eel. (9) Some <u>of</u> these eels can grow to be 11 feet long! (10) They have sharp <u>teeth</u>, which they use to eat other fish. (11) A moray eel could <u>possibly</u> reach 30 years of age.

(12) Eels are <u>flavorful</u> fish with lots of protein. (13) People in Japan and Europe especially like to eat <u>them</u>. (14) American colonists used to eat them <u>often</u>. (15) People like me may say "<u>Ugh!</u>" if eel is on the menu.

Answers

1. noun
2. verb
3. adjective
4. verb
5. pronoun
6. conjunction
7. conjunction
8. adjective
9. preposition
10. noun
11. adverb
12. adjective
13. pronoun
14. adverb
15. interjection

Test Prep

Tell the part of speech for each underlined word below by writing the correct letter from the answer choices on the next page.

Late in the <u>afternoon</u>, Elgin the eel arrived at his
1

aunt's home near the city. Aunt Eeloise lived <u>in</u> a drainpipe.
2

"Hello, Elgin," Eeloise <u>said</u>. "It's nice to see you again."
3

<u>They</u> decided to visit the <u>new</u> art exhibit. "We should see
4   5

it soon," Eeloise said.

They swam <u>swiftly</u> upstream to a lagoon near a parking
6

lot. There they saw dozens <u>of</u> brightly colored street signs
7

lying in the water.

"That one is new," Elgin said. He <u>swam</u> circles around a
8

red <u>and</u> white stop sign.
9

"I like it," Eeloise said, "<u>but</u> I prefer <u>this</u> 'One Way' sign."
10   11

"It's too bad <u>we</u> cannot take these pieces of art home with
12

us," Elgin said with a sigh.

1. **A** noun
   B verb
   C pronoun
   D adjective

2. **A** preposition
   B adverb
   C adjective
   D conjunction

3. **A** noun
   B interjection
   C adverb
   D verb

4. **A** verb
   B pronoun
   C noun
   D adverb

5. **A** conjunction
   B preposition
   C adjective
   D verb

6. **A** conjunction
   B preposition
   C adverb
   D verb

7. **A** adverb
   B verb
   C adjective
   D preposition

8. **A** noun
   B verb
   C pronoun
   D adjective

9. **A** interjection
   B noun
   C adverb
   D conjunction

10. **A** conjunction
    B verb
    C preposition
    D adverb

11. **A** adjective
    B adverb
    C verb
    D noun

12. **A** verb
    B noun
    C pronoun
    D adjective

Answers

1. a	**7.** d
2. a	**8.** b
3. d	**9.** d
4. b	**10.** a
5. c	**11.** a
6. c	**12.** c

Credits

Photos:

www.jupiterimages.com: page 475

Acknowledgements

We're grateful to many people who helped bring *Write Source* to life. First, we must thank all the teachers and students from across the country who contributed writing models and ideas.

In addition, we want to thank our Write Source/Great Source team for all their help:

Steven J. Augustyn, Laura Bachman, Ron Bachman, William Baughn, Heather Bazata, Colleen Belmont, Evelyn Curley, Sandra Easton, Chris Erickson, Mark Fairweather, Jean Fischer, Hillary Gammons, Mariellen Hanrahan, Tammy Hintz, Mary Anne Hoff, Rob King, Lois Krenzke, Mark Lalumondier, Joe Lee, Joyce Becker Lee, Ellen Leitheusser, Dian Lynch, Cheryl Mendicino, Kevin Nelson, Douglas Niles, Sue Paro, Pamela Reigel, Pat Reigel, Jason C. Reynolds, Christine Rieker, Susan Rogalski, Chip Rosenthal, Janae Sebranek, Lester Smith, Richard Spencer, Julie Spicuzza, Thomas Spicuzza, Stephen D. Sullivan, Jean Varley, and Claire Ziffer.

Introducing the Traits

Write Source offers a way of teaching writing that helps students understand what good writing is and how to achieve it. The program provides instruction in the six traits of effective writing. The term *trait,* as it is used here, refers to a characteristic or quality that defines writing.

The six-trait model of writing instruction and assessment was developed in 1984 by teachers in the Beaverton, Oregon, School District. Because it has been so widely embraced by teachers at all grade levels, kindergarten through college, the model has since spread throughout the country—and much of the world. Traits themselves, of course, have been around as long as writing; writers have always needed intriguing ideas, good organization, a powerful voice, and so on. What is *new* is using consistent language with students to define writing at various levels of performance.

The six traits of writing are the following:

Ideas

Excellent writing has a clear message, purpose, or focus. The writing contains plenty of specific ideas and details.

Organization

Effective writing has a clear beginning, middle, and ending. The overall writing is well organized and easy to follow.

Voice

The best writing reveals the writer's voice—his or her special way of saying things.

Word Choice

Good writing contains strong words, including specific nouns and verbs. The words fit the audience and deliver a clear message.

Sentence Fluency

Effective writing flows smoothly from one sentence to the next. Sentences vary in length and begin in a variety of ways.

Conventions

Good writing is carefully edited to make sure it is easy to understand. The writing follows the rules for punctuation, grammar, and spelling.

Students learn to use the six traits of effective writing as a guide while they write and as a tool to assess their writing when they revise. A rubric based on the six traits is at the center of the instruction in each major genre lesson in *Write Source.* Using the traits and rubrics based on the traits, students learn to recognize a strong piece of writing and to pinpoint aspects of writing that may need improvement.

Teaching the Traits of Good Writing

Six-trait writing is based on the premise that students who become strong self-assessors become better writers and revisers. No matter where student writers are now, working with the traits will improve their skills and will also give them the confidence that comes from knowing writer's language and having options for revision.

Use the following definitions and examples from trade books to introduce the traits to students. (See *Books, Lessons, Ideas for Teaching the Six Traits* by Vicki Spandel, Great Source Education Group, 2001.) As students become comfortable with the traits, encourage them to assess many pieces of writing, including other students' work, professional writing, and your own writing.

Ideas

The first trait provides an understanding of what constitutes good, strong ideas in a piece of writing and encourages students to work with ideas to shape and improve them.

Ideas are all about information. In a strong creative piece, ideas paint a picture in the reader's mind. In an informational piece, strong ideas make difficult or complex information easy to understand. Three things make ideas work well, and they should be the focus of your instruction: a *main idea* that is easy to identify and narrow enough to be manageable, *interesting details* that bring the main idea to life, and *clarity,* which is achieved in part through the careful selection and presentation of important details. Finally, good writing always includes details about those beyond-the-obvious bits of information that thoughtful, observant writers notice.

Organization

The second trait focuses on putting information in an order that makes sense and that both entertains and enlightens a reader.

Organization is about the logical and effective presentation of key ideas and details. Good organization holds a piece of writing together and makes it easy to follow—like good instructions or a clear road map. Several things make organization work well: an organizational pattern that makes sense and matches the purpose for the writing, strong transitions that link the writer's ideas together, a compelling lead that pulls the reader in, and an appropriate conclusion that effectively wraps things up.

Voice

The third trait focuses on the skillful blending of detail, enthusiasm, topic knowledge, audience awareness, and a writer's personality.

As one teacher put it, your ideas are what you have to say; **your voice is how you say it.** Students and teachers often worry that voice cannot be taught because it is too closely linked to personality. Voice is much more than personality, however. It is the skillful use of detail that helps readers make personal connections. It is the writer's concern for the audience; voice changes as audience changes so that the voice in a business letter is not the voice in an impassioned personal narrative. Voice is also a reflection of the confidence gained from knowing a topic well.

Word Choice

The fourth trait teaches students to use sensory language to make readers part of the writer's experience, revise writing to take it from flat to lively, and cut excess language to make writing concise and readable.

Word choice is the selection of appropriate words to fit audience, topic, and purpose. Good word choice results in clear, colorful, and precise writing, and helps readers see, hear, and feel the world of the writer. The secrets to successful word choice include simplicity, sensory detail, use of powerful verbs, and, of course, variety—all of which come from an expanded vocabulary. In a business letter, writing must be brisk, clear, and to the point. A technical or research report calls for knowledge of content expressed through the skillful use of a specialized vocabulary. A poem or personal narrative allows the writer more freedom to use words in unexpected ways.

Sentence Fluency

The fifth trait helps students see, hear, and think like readers as they create text that is readable. Writers who look and listen for the flow in a piece of writing usually come up with something smooth and pleasurable to read silently or aloud.

Sentence fluency is the rhythm and flow of language. It is more than how words look on the page; it is also how they play to the ear. Reading aloud is a good way to test fluency, since fluent writing invites strong, expressive reading. Sentences that vary in both structure and length contribute significantly to fluency by snapping the reader to attention—much the way a shift in musical rhythm helps wake up a sleepy listener. In general, a strong writer avoids repetition or run-ons, although either may be used sparingly by a skilled writer for stylistic effect. The fluent writer also recognizes the difference between complete sentences and fragments but may slip in a fragment to lend punch to the writing now and then. Good dialogue is also a component of fluency.

Conventions

The sixth trait provides students with skills and tools for editing their writing. Editors' tools include not only such basics as a sharp pencil, a good dictionary, and a handbook but more personal things as well. For example, a good editor needs to develop an editor's eye and an editor's ear in order to weed out every mistake hiding within the text. Editors also need a code—a set of symbols with which to mark the text for editing—and a personal checklist to keep track of hard-to-remember conventional rules.

The trait of conventions includes anything a copy editor would deal with: spelling, punctuation, usage and grammar, capitalization, and indentation (or other indicators of paragraphing, such as spacing). Editing for the conventions shows respect for the writer, the writing, and the reader. Writers want to be recognized as skilled and considerate creators, not as people who care little about their profession and who are disinterested or lazy. By presenting error-free pieces, writers demonstrate self-respect. In addition, writers who have respect for their writing want nothing to interfere with their ability to convey their message. They want to honor their ideas by presenting them as cleanly and clearly as possible. If they don't show respect for their writing, they cannot expect their audience to respect it either. Finally, writers who attend to the conventions respect their readers. Errors in grammar, usage, and spelling put up barriers to comprehension and force readers to work harder than necessary to discern the meaning the author is trying to convey. Sloppy editing interrupts the flow of the reading and causes readers to stumble through a piece of writing.

Presentation

This characteristic is sometimes described as a separate trait, but *Write Source* addresses it as part of the publishing stage of the writing process. Presentation describes the qualities and features writers should attend to when presenting their work.

Presentation includes anything that affects how the written piece looks: general layout, headings and subheadings, citations, use of white space, formatting, use of fonts for stylistic effect, and incorporation of charts, graphs, illustrations.

The material on the six traits of effective writing was taken from *Write Traits Classroom Kits* by Vicki Spandel and Jeff Hicks (Great Source Education Group, 2002).

Using the Traits in *Write Source*

Instruction in *Write Source* integrates the six traits of effective writing into the writing process. Three traits relate to the development of the content and the form of writing. In the instruction, these traits provide a focus during the prewriting, drafting, and revising stages.

- ■ Ideas
- ■ **Organization**
- ■ Voice

The other three traits relate more to form. In the instruction, checking them is part of the revising and editing process.

- ■ **Word Choice**
- ■ Sentence Fluency
- ■ Conventions

In addition to being a vital part of the writing process, the traits also form the backbone of the evaluation process in *Write Source*. Students use rubrics based on the six traits to evaluate not only their own writing but also models and benchmark papers provided throughout the program. Discussing as a group students' evaluations of various pieces of writing allows them to gain a solid understanding of the rubric and a sense of its scale. Finally, the six traits are at the core of the Six-Trait Checklist (see TE page 623), which teachers can use as a generic evaluation form or an assessment guide.

Students develop their understanding of the traits over time. It is best to focus on one or two traits at first and help students to understand those traits thoroughly before expanding the focus to include other traits. For a more in-depth approach to the traits, we recommend *Creating Writers Through 6-Trait Writing Assessment and Instruction,* 3rd ed., by Vicki Spandel (Addison Wesley Longman, 2001) and the *Write Traits Classroom Kits* by Vicki Spandel and Jeff Hicks (Great Source Education Group, 2002).

The Writing Process and the Six Traits

In the three core units of *Write Source*—Narrative Writing, Expository Writing, and Persuasive Writing—students are taught how to develop each kind of writing using the traits that are specific to the genre *at the appropriate stages* of the writing process. The following chart shows which traits are the focus during different stages of the writing process and provides some of the questions writers can ask themselves as they develop their writing.

Prewriting

Ideas,
Voice

Writer's Questions:
- Who is my audience?
- What do they know now?
- What do they need or want to know?
- What information is new and interesting?
- How well do I know this topic?

Drafting

Ideas,
Organization

Writer's Questions:
- Do I have enough information to answer readers' questions?
- Do I have so much information it's overwhelming?
- What is an organizational pattern that makes sense?
- Where do I begin?
- Where do I go next?
- How do I know when I've covered everything?
- How do I know when to stop?

Revision

Ideas,
Organization,
Voice,
Word Choice,
Sentences

Writer's Questions:
- What are the unanswered questions?
- Does the organizational pattern work?
- Did I waste time telling readers things they know already?
- Is my opening a grabber?
- What is my MAIN message? Is it clear?
- Did I end in a good spot? Did I end with a thought, surprise, or question that will make my readers think?
- Is this the right tone and voice for this audience and topic and format?
- Does the language communicate with this audience?
- Is it formal or informal enough?
- Do the sentences show enough variety to keep a reader interested?
- Are sentences in informational or business writing concise and to the point?

Editing

Conventions,
Presentation

Writer's Questions:
- Is this text as error-free as I can make it?
- Is it readable? Can I breeze right through it?
- Did I read it both silently and aloud?
- Did I use page layout in a way that will attract the reader's eye and make main points easy to find?

Writing Across the Curriculum

What is writing across the curriculum?

Writing across the curriculum (WAC) is an instructional approach that recognizes the importance of writing as a teaching and learning tool in all curriculum areas. Research shows that writing can help students synthesize, analyze, and apply course content. Teachers who participate in WAC choose appropriate writing activities on the basis of the course content and their learning goals for students.

What types of WAC activities work best?

Two approaches that work well are writing to learn and writing in the disciplines. Writing to learn makes use of journals, logs, short essays, and other informal writing assignments. Students who use these tools to write personal reactions to information received in class or from reading often comprehend and retain the information better. Frequent writing also helps students improve and maintain their writing skills. In "Keeping Journals and Learning Logs" on PE pages 379–386, there is a discussion of specific writing to learn activities.

Writing in the disciplines makes use of reports, article reviews, research papers, and other formal writing assignments. This approach takes into consideration the terminology and conventions unique to science, geography, mathematics, and other disciplines. Students who write for a particular discipline learn to use the appropriate terms and apply logical thinking.

The *Write Source 4* pupil edition contains eleven WAC activities, several summary paragraphs, and a unit on developing a research paper, in addition to extensive lessons with step-by-step analyses of essays that are useful across the curriculum.

Why should students write in all courses?

WAC activities help students to

- think through and find meaning in their learning,
- retain what they learn, and
- develop their writing skills.

WAC gives students practice in such writing skills as gathering and organizing information, evaluating arguments, and supporting ideas. In addition, writing helps students construct meaning in a course, make connections between ideas in various courses across the curriculum, and connect learning to their daily lives.

How does writing enhance learning?

Whether a WAC activity is a 10-minute freewriting or a research paper, writing helps students learn by enabling them to

- develop and record their thoughts,
- connect and analyze their ideas,
- receive input from classmates and teachers,
- refine specific points or arguments,
- take ownership for what they say and how they say it.

Setting Up Writing Across the Curriculum (WAC)

Without being aware of it, many content area teachers already do things that support a writing curriculum. However, when faced with a formal WAC program, their first questions are often about how they can make writing across the curriculum work. With the knowledge you already have about writing, and with *Write Source* at your fingertips, you can help your colleagues work successfully with WAC. Following are some questions content area teachers ask when they are first asked to participate in a WAC program.

How will I make WAC work? For me? For my students?

When you and your colleagues begin a WAC program, the *Write Source* materials can play a critical role. The information is reassuring and the teaching methods are helpful. *Write Source* provides a wide variety of WAC activities and assignments. This teacher's edition provides information to help you help your colleagues adopt teaching strategies that will support WAC.

Why am I expected to teach writing?

When adopting WAC, writing is not added to the content, but the content is entered and learned through writing. Students will still acquire the skills and knowledge of the course's content as set forth in the course objectives. The success of WAC will depend on the professional commitment of all teachers to active learning, not on their ability to teach writing.

Am I expected to check grammar, spelling, verb agreement, and so on?

Content area teachers will correct the formal WAC activities such as research papers and essay tests as they have in the past. The informal activities such as keeping learning logs and journals are not checked for grammar. Content area teachers will use WAC to become aware of the progress each student is making in developing the following skills:

- Thinking clearly
- Expressing thoughts precisely
- Asking worthwhile questions
- Understanding and using facts and opinions appropriately
- Developing support for an argument
- Thinking beyond first impressions
- Dealing with difficult problems and concepts

How does WAC promote learning?

There are several reasons students write in the content areas. Teachers need to decide what the goal is for students before assigning writing. Once they understand the purpose they want to achieve, they can choose an appropriate activity. On the next three pages are several of the reasons for using WAC, along with suggested activities from *Write Source* that teachers can fit into the curriculum.

Writing to Show Learning

The most common reason content-area teachers have students write is to show learning. The following forms of writing are commonly used for this purpose. The numbers in parentheses below indicate page numbers in *Write Source* where guidelines and models are found.

- The (Writing) Process in Action (6–7)
- Writing Paragraphs (51–61)

- Descriptive Paragraph (63–66)
- Descriptive Essay (67–74)

- Narrative Paragraph (83–86)
- Personal Narrative (87–102)

- Expository Paragraph (139–142)
- Expository Essay (143–158)

- Persuasive Paragraph (195–198)
- Persuasive Essay (199–214)

- Response Paragraph (253–256)
- Book Review (257–266, 270)
- Response Journal (271–272)
- Response to a Biography (274–279)
- Response to a Poem (280–285)
- Response to a Nonfiction Article (286–291)
- Response to a Tall Tale (292–297)

- Summary Paragraph (60–61, 333–336)
- Research Report (337–362)
- Paraphrasing (345)

- Learning Logs (383–384)
- Clustering, Listing, Freewriting (385)
- Taking Classroom Tests (399–405)

Writing to Share Learning

Having students share their writing lets them interact with an audience and builds a healthy learning community. Writing that will be shared is revised and edited for that purpose, and the means of presenting is often graded. The numbers in parentheses below indicate page numbers in *Write Source* where guidelines and models are found.

- Listening and Speaking (369–372)
- Giving Speeches (373–378)
- Book Review (257–270)
- Multimedia Presentation (363–367)
- Publishing Ideas (43–46, 119, 175, 231, 315, 361)

Writing to Learn New Concepts and Ideas

Popular writing-to-learn activities are unrehearsed and ungraded activities like those listed below. The purpose is not to produce a finished piece of writing but rather to record one's thoughts on paper in order to organize, explore, and understand them.

- **Taking Notes** (387–392)
- **Using Graphic Organizers** (474)
- **Question-of-the-Day**

  Students respond to a "What if?" or "Why?" question that is important to a clear understanding of the lesson. These responses may be read in class to promote discussion.

- **Warm-Ups**

  Students write for the first 5 or 10 minutes of class. The writing can be a question of-the-day, a freewriting, a focused writing, or any other writing-to-learn activity that is appropriate. Warm-ups not only help students focus on the lesson at hand but also provide students with material to use for reviewing. Students find warm-ups are an opportunity to rehearse answers, opinions, and perspectives for discussion.

Writing to Reflect on Learning

Exploring personal thoughts and feelings helps students to extend a line of thought beyond the range of first impressions, to actively look for connections among subjects, and to enlarge their global perspective.

- **Keeping Journals and Writing Logs** (379–386)
- **First Thoughts**

  Students write or list their immediate impressions or what they already know about a topic they are preparing to study. The writing helps students focus on the topic, and it serves as a reference point for measuring learning.

- **KWL**

  Students use a three-column graphic organizer to list what they know (the K column), what they wonder about (the W column), and after the lesson is completed what they learned (the L column). KWL helps students connect with prior learning, find gaps in what they know, and measure their learning.

Writing to Plan and Complete Classroom Tasks

Writing to plan is a beneficial lifelong skill. When assigning writing for this purpose, teachers often choose forms of workplace writing. Workplace writing helps students (1) organize materials, develop plans, and budget time; (2) correspond with others regarding progress on course work; and (3) learn how to use writing to do work in the marketplace.

Specific WAC Activities for Content Areas

Social Studies

- **Describing a Historical Landmark** (76–77)

Math

- **Creating a Story Problem** (126–129)
- **Explaining a Math Concept** (186–187)
- **Creating a Thermometer Graph** (242–243)

Science

- **Describing a Plant** (78–79)
- **Writing an Observation Report** (130–131)
- **Writing a How-To Essay** (182–185)
- **Writing a Problem-Solution Essay** (238–241)

Practical Writing

- **Writing to an E-Pal** (132–133)
- **Taking Two-Column Notes** (188–189)
- **Drafting a Letter of Request** (244–247)

Editing and Proofreading Strategies

Editing and proofreading are difficult tasks for most students. To help them be successful, you may want to use a variety of techniques. The goal is not only to help students correct errors but also to give them opportunities to grow more independent when editing. The following techniques help meet both these goals. They employ a variety of learning styles and offer ample teaching opportunities.

Published Checklists

Editing checklists are a part of each writing unit in the pupil edition. These checklists remind students what to look for when editing and proofreading. They work well for students who understand the concepts and rules being checked. For students who need more help with grammar, usage, and mechanics, however, the checklists may need to be worked with over time, covering one rule at a time. After each skill on the checklist is taught, students can be held responsible for corrections. You can use mini-lessons for small groups and modeling on overhead transparencies to teach the rules that students don't know.

Personal Checklists

Students make personal checklists by keeping a list of errors that they frequently make in their writing. They use this list to edit their writing for all classes, and it can be shared with parents. The lists are maintained by the student. Teachers may ask students to use a listed rule correctly three to four times in their writing before students can cross it off the list.

Personal Spelling Book

A personal spelling book is a list of words that students frequently misspell. Students can use either a notebook or index cards to compile their spelling list and can refer to it when editing. When time permits, learning partners can help each other learn to spell their words correctly. This list can be shared with parents.

Buddy System

When editing and proofreading, two heads are definitely better than one! Having students look for errors in each other's writing is always a good idea because first-time readers find errors more easily. Students may edit each other's papers and then meet to compare their findings and fix the errors. The checklists at the end of each unit can help students edit one another's papers.

Brackets

Students come to class with brackets around the places in their writing where they have doubts about their correct use of conventions. Students are then given class time (10–15 minutes) to find the information they need in a resource and, if necessary, make a correction. The Proofreader's Guide (the yellow pages at the back of the pupil edition, PE pages 478–605) is most useful.

Using resources such as the Proofreader's Guide is a lifetime skill that students need to be practice. In real life, students will often need to depend on a resource to answer their editing questions. While students look for the rules they need, the teacher can help them by suggesting where to look. In this way, students learn terminology that is needed in order to look up and understand grammar rules.

Classroom Editors

Students serve as editors for specific problems. A person who knows the most about capitalization becomes the "Capital Editor." Another who knows about end punctuation becomes the editor who helps classmates with end punctuation. Being able to teach a rule to another not only helps the recipient, but it also helps the "editor" clarify and understand the rules. Sometimes the last 10 minutes of a class period is a good time to have classroom editors open for business. Other times classroom editors may hang a sign on their desk announcing they can help classmates at this time.

Ask a Question

When using this technique, a teacher sets aside a period of time—10 to 15 minutes—for students to ask questions. Students should locate and fix as many errors as possible on their own, saving their questions for something they don't understand or something that seems to conflict with a rule or concept. Teachers often request that students ask specific questions, and when first using this technique, you may want to model how to ask specific questions. For example, "Do I need a comma here because this is an introductory word group?" Ask a Question can be done as a whole group or individually. This is an excellent technique to use several times just before a paper is due.

Target List

A Target List is a checklist written by the teacher for a particular writing unit. The list contains the grammar rules and concepts that will be assessed in the unit and is given to students at the beginning of the unit. Mini-lessons, desk-side conferences, and worksheets are used throughout the unit to teach each rule on the list. Using this method provides for instruction before assessment, and it limits the types of errors that will be assessed. Students who have a lot of trouble with grammar can often gain self-confidence and score well.

Modeling the Use of Resources

The teacher becomes the editor-with-a-resource, looking up the answer to a question using any resource available. Modeling the use of a resource sets a good example for students. The teacher talks out loud while using the resource. Usually this is done as a whole class so that all students hear the questions and the answers. Students learn to ask specific questions that reveal how much the student knows. For example, "Do I capitalize *mom* in this sentence, 'Today Mom starts a new job'?" indicates the student is aware that sometimes *mom* is capitalized and other times it is not.

In this case, the teacher could say, "I'm going to look under capitalization in the yellow pages of your book. Once I find that section, I'll read the headings to find the rule. Here it is. Look on page 510 at number 1."

Teacher Editing and Proofreading

When using this technique, the teacher places brackets around the errors in a student's writing. The teacher will add a number from the Proofreader's Guide to which students can go to find the information they need to make a correction. This technique can precede the use of the technique called "Brackets." It is also an excellent technique to use for ESL students and other students who need extra support.

Practice Sentences

The teacher prints a number of incorrect sentences on a piece of paper or an overhead transparency (or the teacher can use *Daily Language Workout*). As a group, the class works to make these sentences correct. After the teacher models this technique several times, students themselves may take the place of the teacher. If a student has a particular sentence that he or she would like help correcting, the student can copy the sentence onto a transparency and present it to the class. This technique can be used with small groups or the class as a whole on a weekly basis or shortly before an assignment is due.

When students need or want a piece of information, both their attention span and their commitment to the task increase. These NOW (Needed Or Wanted) moments are teaching opportunities. Many variations of this technique are used. Sometimes students are given a number of sentences to correct on their own. The activity is often graded. Sometimes a corner of the blackboard is reserved where students can write sentences they need help with. Classmates copy these sentences, correct them, and turn them in for credit before giving them to their classmate.

Assessment and Instruction

In past decades, writing assessment was generally held to be the province of the teacher. Students turned in work—then waited to see what grades they would receive. Now it is widely recognized that learning to be a good assessor is one of the best ways to become a strong writer. In order to assess well, students must learn to recognize good writing. They must know and be able to describe the difference between writing that works and writing that does not work. Students learn to assess, generally, by going through three key steps:

■ Learning about the traits of writing by which their work—and that of others—will be assessed
■ Applying the traits to a wide variety of written texts
■ Applying the traits to their own work—first assessing it for strengths and weaknesses, then revising it as needed

Why should students be assessors?

Students who learn to be assessors also

■ learn to think like professional writers,
■ take responsibility for their own revising, and
■ make meaningful changes in their writing—instead of simply recopying a draft to make it look neater.

Role of Teachers and Students

Here is a quick summary of the kinds of activities teachers and students usually engage in while acting as assessors in the classroom.

Teachers

As assessors, teachers often engage in the following activities:

■ roving conferences: roaming the classroom, observing students' work, and offering comments or questions that will help take students to the next step
■ one-on-one conferences, in which students are asked to come prepared with a question they need answered
■ informal comments—written or oral—in which the teacher offers a personal response or poses a reader's question
■ reading student work, using a checklist such as the one in this teacher's edition (TE page 623)
■ tracking scores over time to calculate a final grade for a grading period

Students

As assessors, students often engage in the following activities:

■ using the rubrics in the student text
■ using an *assessment sheet* such as the one on page 34 in the pupil edition and page 644 in the teacher's edition
■ assessing and discussing written work that the teacher shares with the class
■ assessing their own work, using a rubric
■ compiling a portfolio and reflecting on the written work included

Effective Assessment in the Classroom

Good assessment gives students a sense of how they are growing as writers. It indicates to teachers which students are finding success, as well as the specific kinds of help other students may need. To ensure that assessment is working in your classrooms, here are some things you can do.

- Make sure ALL students know the criteria you will use to assess their writing. If you are going to use a rating sheet or rubric, provide them with copies.
- Give copies of rubrics or checklists to parents, too, so they can help their children know what is expected of them.
- Make sure your instruction and assessment match.
- Involve students regularly in assessing
  - published work from a variety of sources,
  - your work (share your writing—even if it's in unfinished draft form), and
  - their own work.
- Don't grade *everything* students write. Instead, encourage students to write *often*; then choose or have students choose a few pieces to grade.
- Respond to the content *first*. Then look at the conventions. Correctness is important, but if you comment on spelling and mechanics before content, the message to students is, "I don't care so much about what you say as I do about whether you spell everything correctly."
- Encourage students to save rough drafts and to collect pieces of work regularly in a portfolio. This type of collection gives students a broad picture of how they are progressing as writers.
- Ask students if they mind having comments written directly on their work. For some students, comments on sticky notes may seem less obtrusive.

Conducting Conferences

Conduct conferences to maintain an open line of communication with student writers at all points during the development of a piece of writing. Here are three common practices that you can employ to communicate with student writers during a writing project:

- **Desk-Side Conferences** occur when you stop at a student's desk to ask questions and make responses. Questions should be open-ended. This gives the writers "space" to talk and clarify his or her own thinking about the writing.
- **Scheduled Conferences** give you and a student a chance to meet in a more structured setting. In such a conference, a student may have a specific problem or need to discuss or simply want you to assess his or her progress on a particular piece of writing.

  Note: A typical conference should last from 3 to 5 minutes. Always try to praise one thing, ask an appropriate question, and offer one or two suggestions.
- **Small-Group Conferences** give three to five students who are at the same stage of the writing process or are experiencing the same problem a chance to meet with you. The goal of such conferences is twofold: first, to help students improve their writing, and, second, to help them develop as evaluators of writing.

Formative vs. Summative Assessment

Formative assessment is ongoing and is often not linked to a letter grade or score. It may be as simple as a brief one-on-one conference or an informal review of the beginning of a student's draft to suggest possible next steps. **Summative assessment**, on the other hand, is a summing up of a student's performance and is generally reflected in a grade. Formative assessments usually occur in the form of a comment—oral or written. Summative assessments take the form of

- a letter grade,
- total points earned,
- a percentage score, or
- some combination of these.

Responding to Nongraded Writing (Formative)

- React noncritically with positive, supportive language.
- Use marginal dialogue. Resist writing on or over the student's writing.
- Respond whenever possible in the form of questions. Nurture curiosity.
- Encourage risk taking.

Evaluating Graded Writing (Summative)

- Ask students to submit prewriting and rough drafts with their final drafts.
- Scan final drafts once, focusing on the writing as a whole.
- Reread them, evaluating their adherence to previously established criteria.
- Make marginal notations as you read the drafts a second time.
- Scan the writing a third and final time. Note the feedback you have given.
- Complete your rating sheet or rubric, and write a summary comment.

Approaches for Assessing Writing (Summative)

The most common forms of direct writing assessment are listed below.

Analytical assessment identifies the features, or traits, that characterize effective writing, and defines them along a continuum of performance from *incomplete* (the first or lowest level) through *fair* (the middle level) to *excellent* (the highest level). Many analytical scales run from a low of 1 point to a high of 5 or 6 points. This form of assessment tells students exactly where their strengths and weaknesses lie: "Your writing has strong ideas but needs work on voice," or "Your writing has powerful voice but lacks accuracy."

Holistic assessment focuses on a piece of writing as a whole. In this sense, it is like letter grading. Holistic assessors often use a checklist of traits to identify the kinds of characteristics they're looking for; this is called focused holistic assessment. The assessors do not, however, score traits separately, so student writers do not know where they were most or least successful in their work.

Mode-specific assessment is similar to analytic assessment except that the rating scales or scoring guides (rubrics) are designed specifically for particular modes of writing, such as narrative, expository, persuasive, and so on. This kind of assessment works best in a structured curriculum where students will be assigned particular forms and subjects for writing.

Portfolio assessment gives students a chance to showcase their best writing or to document their growth as writers over time. In assembling a portfolio, students generally choose which pieces of writing they will complete and which ones they will include in their portfolios. (See pages 47–49 in the pupil edition.)

Assessment in *Write Source*

Using Rubrics Assessment of writing in *Write Source* is based on mode-specific rubrics. In each core unit—narrative, expository, and persuasive—genre-specific rubrics guide both the development of written work and the evaluation of the work. The rubrics are organized around the six traits of effective writing: ideas, organization, voice, word choice, sentence fluency, and conventions. Each trait is evaluated individually as part of a total assessment. When you first start using rubrics in the classroom, either with students' own work or with published writing, it may be more manageable to have students focus on one specific trait (such as organization). Gradually, you can add other traits until you ask them to evaluate a piece of writing for all of the traits.

Benchmark Papers In addition to assessing their own writing, in each core unit of the pupil edition—narrative, expository, and persuasive—students (and teachers) have the opportunity to evaluate a student paper and review the student's self-assessment of that paper. This evaluation follows in-depth instruction on the genre. Furthermore, for each of these units there are two additional writing samples, or benchmark papers, representing different levels of expertise that teachers can use with students for further assessment practice. The writing samples are provided in transparency form so that you can discuss them together as a group, and in copy master form so that students can have a version in front of them. A blank assessment sheet, based on the traits of writing, allows students and you to rate the writing samples. Finally, a completed assessment sheet is provided for each benchmark paper to guide teachers through the assessment. Following are the benchmark papers and their level of competence.

Benchmark Papers

Narrative Writing
El Niño at Its Best (strong)
Out of Gas (good)
Las Vegas (poor)

Expository Writing
Something You Can Sink Your Teeth Into
   (strong)
Call Me "Copter Charlie" (good)
Fluffy (poor)

Persuasive Writing
Help Save Our Manatees (strong)
Walk for a Cure! (good)
Why Smog Is Bad (poor)

Assessment Book In addition to rubrics-based assessment of students' writing, teachers can assess students' writing skills through the four tests in the *Assessment Book*. These 3-part tests are designed to be taken throughout the year, with a pretest at the beginning of the year, two progress tests during the year, and a post-test at the end of the year. The first two parts of each test are aligned with two reference sections in the back of the pupil edition, the Basic Elements of Writing and the Proofreader's Guide. The third part is a writing prompt. These tests are available in the Teacher's Resource Pack.

Six-Trait Checklist

Ideas

☐ focuses on a specific topic
☐ has a clear focus statement
☐ contains specific details

Organization

☐ has a beginning, middle, and ending
☐ has a topic sentence for each paragraph
☐ has enough details to develop each topic sentence
☐ uses transitions to connect paragraphs

Voice

☐ speaks in an engaging way that keeps readers wanting to hear more
☐ shows that the writer really cares about the subject

Word Choice

☐ contains specific nouns and action verbs
☐ presents an appropriate level of language (not too formal or too informal)

Sentence Fluency

☐ flows smoothly from sentence to sentence
☐ shows variety in sentence beginnings and lengths
☐ uses transitions to connect sentences

Conventions

☐ follows the basic rules of grammar, spelling, capitalization, and punctuation

4-Point

Rubric for Narrative Writing

Use this rubric for guiding and assessing your narrative writing. Refer to it whenever you want to improve your writing using the six traits.

Ideas
4 Rich ideas and details are used in the narrative, focused on one experience.

3 The writer tells about one experience. More details are needed.

2 The writer needs to focus on one experience. Some details do not relate to the story.

1 The writer needs to focus on one experience. Details are needed.

Organization
4 Details are in order, and transitions are used well throughout.

3 The beginning, middle, and ending are clear. Some transitions are used.

2 Most details are in order. Transitions are needed.

1 The beginning, middle, or ending parts need to be organized.

Voice
4 A strong storytelling voice creates a solid narrative. Dialogue is used.

3 A natural voice creates interest in the story. Some dialogue is used.

2 Sometimes a voice can be heard. More dialogue is needed.

1 The voice needs to be stronger. Dialogue is missing.

Word Choice
4 Strong nouns and verbs create a vivid picture.

3 Some strong nouns and verbs add to the narrative.

2 Strong nouns and verbs are needed to create a clear picture.

1 Fewer general and overused words would improve the narrative.

Sentence Fluency
4 The sentences are skillfully written and make the narrative enjoyable to read.

3 The sentences show a variety of lengths and beginnings.

2 A better variety of sentence lengths and beginnings is needed.

1 Many sentences are the same length or begin the same way.

Conventions
4 Accurate use of conventions adds clarity to the writing.

3 Some errors in spelling, punctuation, or grammar exist.

2 Many errors could confuse the reader.

1 Help is needed to make corrections.

4-Point

Rubric for Expository Writing

Use this rubric for guiding and assessing your expository writing. Refer to it to help you improve your writing using the six traits.

Ideas

4 The essay is informative with a clear focus and supporting details.

3 The essay is informative, with a clear focus. More supporting details are needed.

2 The topic needs to be narrowed or expanded. Many more supporting details are needed.

1 The topic has been chosen but needs to be developed.

Organization

4 The organization makes the essay easy to read.

3 The beginning, middle, and ending work well. Some transitions are used.

2 The middle needs transitions and a paragraph for each main point.

1 The beginning, middle, and ending all run together. Paragraphs are needed.

Voice

4 The writer's voice sounds confident, knowledgeable, and enthusiastic.

3 The writer's voice sounds informative and confident most of the time.

2 The writer sometimes sounds unsure.

1 The writer needs to sound much more confident.

Word Choice

4 Specific nouns and action verbs make the essay clear and informative.

3 Some nouns and verbs could be more specific.

2 Too many general words are used. Specific nouns and verbs are needed.

1 The writer needs help finding specific words.

Sentence Fluency

4 The sentences flow smoothly and read well aloud.

3 Most of the sentences read smoothly, but some are short and choppy.

2 Many short, choppy sentences need to be rewritten to make the essay read smoothly.

1 Many sentences are choppy or incomplete and are difficult to follow.

Conventions

4 Mastery of conventions gives this essay authority.

3 The essay has a few errors in punctuation, spelling, or grammar.

2 Several errors confuse the reader.

1 Many errors make the essay confusing and hard to read.

4-Point

Rubric for Persuasive Writing

Use the following rubric for guiding and assessing your persuasive writing. Refer to it whenever you want to improve your writing using the six traits.

Ideas

4 The essay has a clear opinion statement. Logical reasons support the writer's opinion.

3 The opinion statement is clear, and most reasons support the writer's opinion.

2 The opinion statement is clear. Reasons and details are not as complete as they need to be.

1 The opinion statement is unclear. Reasons and details are needed.

Organization

4 An opening opinion statement is clearly supported in the middle. Transitions connect ideas.

3 The opening has an opinion statement. The middle adds support. Most transitions work.

2 There is a beginning, a middle, and an ending. Transitions are needed.

1 The beginning, middle, and ending run together.

Voice

4 The writer's voice is confident, positive, and persuades the reader.

3 The writer's voice is confident and somewhat persuasive.

2 The writer's voice needs to be more confident to persuade the reader.

1 The writer's voice sounds unsure.

Word Choice

4 Strong, engaging, positive words add to the main message. Every word counts.

3 Strong words are used, but some may be too negative.

2 Many words need to be stronger and more positive.

1 Help is needed to find better words.

Sentence Fluency

4 The sentences flow smoothly, and variety is seen in both types of sentences and their beginning.

3 Sentence beginnings are varied. A little more variety in types would add interest.

2 Several sentences begin the same way. Sentence fragments need to be rewritten.

1 Too many sentences begin the same way. Fragments and rambling sentences need to be rewritten.

Conventions

4 Mastery of conventions adds persuasive power to the essay.

3 Grammar and punctuation errors in a few sentences may distract the reader.

2 There are enough errors to confuse the reader.

1 Help is needed to make corrections.

5-Point

Rubric for Narrative Writing

Use this rubric for guiding and assessing your narrative writing. Refer to it whenever you want to improve your writing using the six traits.

Ideas

5 Rich ideas and details are used in the narrative, focused on one experience.
4 The writer tells about one experience. More details are needed.
3 The writer needs to focus on one experience. Some details do not relate to the story.
2 The writer needs to focus on one experience. Details are needed.
1 The writer needs to tell about an experience and use details.

Organization

5 Details are in order, and transitions are used well throughout.
4 The beginning, middle, and ending are clear. Some transitions are used.
3 Most details are in order. Transitions are needed.
2 The beginning, middle, or ending parts need to be clearer.
1 The narrative needs to be organized.

Voice

5 A strong storytelling voice creates a solid narrative. Dialogue is used.
4 A natural voice creates interest in the story. Some dialogue is used.
3 Sometimes a voice can be heard. More dialogue is needed.
2 The voice needs to be stronger. Dialogue is missing.
1 The writer's voice does not come through.

Word Choice

5 Strong nouns and verbs create a vivid picture.
4 Some strong nouns and verbs add to the narrative.
3 Strong nouns and verbs are needed to create a clear picture.
2 Fewer general and overused words would improve the narrative.
1 Some words are confusing or incorrect.

Sentence Fluency

5 The sentences are skillfully written and make the narrative enjoyable to read.
4 The sentences show a variety of lengths and beginnings.
3 A better variety of sentence lengths and beginnings is needed.
2 Many sentences are the same length or begin the same way.
1 Too many sentences sound the same.

Conventions

5 Accurate use of conventions adds clarity to the writing.
4 Some errors in spelling, punctuation, or grammar exist.
3 A number of errors could confuse the reader.
2 Many errors make the narrative hard to read.
1 Help is needed to make corrections.

5-Point
Rubric for Expository Writing

Use this rubric for guiding and assessing your expository writing. Refer to it to help you improve your writing using the six traits.

Ideas
5 The essay is informative with a clear focus and supporting details.
4 The essay is informative, with a clear focus. More supporting details are needed.
3 The focus of the essay needs to be clearer, and more supporting details are needed.
2 The topic needs to be narrowed or expanded. Many more supporting details are needed.
1 The topic has been chosen but needs to be developed.

Organization
5 The organization makes the essay easy to read.
4 The beginning, middle, and ending work well. Some transitions are used.
3 The middle needs transitions and a paragraph for each main point.
2 The beginning, middle, and ending all run together. Paragraphs are needed.
1 The essay is hard to follow.

Voice
5 The writer's voice sounds confident, knowledgeable, and enthusiastic.
4 The writer's voice sounds informative and confident most of the time.
3 The writer sometimes sounds unsure.
2 The writer sounds unsure in many parts.
1 The writer needs to sound much more confident.

Word Choice
5 Specific nouns and action verbs make the essay clear and informative.
4 Some nouns and verbs could be more specific.
3 Too many general words are used. Specific nouns and verbs are needed.
2 General or missing words make this essay hard to understand.
1 The writer needs help finding specific words.

Sentence Fluency
5 The sentences flow smoothly and read well aloud.
4 Most of the sentences read smoothly, but some are short and choppy.
3 Many short, choppy sentences need to be rewritten to make the essay read smoothly.
2 Many sentences are choppy or incomplete.
1 Many sentences are difficult to follow.

Conventions
5 Mastery of conventions gives this essay authority.
4 The essay has a few errors in punctuation, spelling, or grammar.
3 Several errors confuse the reader.
2 Many errors make the essay confusing and hard to read.
1 Help is needed to make corrections.

5-Point
Rubric for Persuasive Writing

Use the following rubric for guiding and assessing your persuasive writing. Refer to it whenever you want to improve your writing using the six traits.

Ideas

5 The essay has a clear opinion statement. Logical reasons support the writer's opinion.

4 The opinion statement is clear, and most reasons support the writer's opinion.

3 The opinion statement is clear. Reasons and details are not as complete as they need to be.

2 The opinion statement is unclear. Reasons and details are needed.

1 An opinion statement, reasons, and details are needed.

Organization

5 An opening opinion statement is clearly supported in the middle. Transitions connect ideas.

4 The opening has an opinion statement. The middle adds support. Most transitions work.

3 There is a beginning, a middle, and an ending. Transitions are needed.

2 The beginning, middle, and ending run together.

1 The writing needs to be organized to avoid confusion.

Voice

5 The writer's voice is confident, positive, and persuades the reader.

4 The writer's voice is confident and somewhat persuasive.

3 The writer's voice needs to be more confident to persuade the reader.

2 The writer's voice sounds unsure.

1 The writer needs to learn more about voice.

Word Choice

5 Strong, engaging, positive words add to the main message. Every word counts.

4 Strong words are used, but some may be too negative.

3 Many words need to be stronger and more positive.

2 The same general words are used throughout the essay.

1 Help is needed to find better words.

Sentence Fluency

5 The sentences flow smoothly, and variety is seen in both types of sentences and their beginning.

4 Sentence beginnings are varied. A little more variety in types would add interest.

3 Several sentences begin the same way. Sentence fragments need to be rewritten.

2 Too many sentences begin the same way. Fragments and rambling sentences need to be rewritten.

1 Choppy or incomplete sentences need to be rewritten.

Conventions

5 Mastery of conventions adds persuasive power to the essay.

4 Grammar and punctuation errors in a few sentences may distract the reader.

3 There are enough errors to confuse the reader.

2 Errors make the essay difficult to read.

1 Help is needed to make corrections.

Narrative Writing

El Niño at Its Best

1   My family and I had been planning a trip to see Uncle Mike in

2   Spokane for a long while. We were going to drive about 1,800 miles to

3   visit him. We decided to spend several nights camping along the way.

4   The first day we got an early start and covered the distance from

5   our home in Nashville to Kansas City. We checked into our

6   campground, set up our tent, and got a fire going to cook our dinner.

7   As we were watching the beautiful sunset, we noticed dark clouds

8   rolling in from the west.

9   Luckily, it didn't start to rain until we had already eaten. We

10   gathered in the tent and played cards. Drip, drop, drip. It rained

11   through the night. Drip, drop, drip. When we woke up, we were in a

12   foot of water! The whole campground was flooded, and our "yard" was

13   knee-high in water!

14   It was still raining, but there we were, pulling up stakes and

15   putting the wet tent into the van. Then we piled in, too, and left the

16   muddy mess behind to find a restaurant for breakfast. After we used

17   the restrooms to change into some dry clothes, we ordered hot

18   chocolate and pancakes.

19   The next time we stopped, we were in western Nebraska. It was

20   a hot, sunny afternoon. We found the Shady Nook Campground and

21   set up camp again, allowing the tent to air out before we spent

22 another night in it. And, once again, it began raining after dinner. We

23 played cards and charades into the night. We laughed about our

24 predicament.

25   The campground did not flood this time, but it did rain the

26 following night in Idaho, too. But despite the rain, we had a blast.

27 The rain just made it more memorable. In fact, it changed our lives

28 for the better. We now own a pop-up camper.

Assessment Sheet

Title *El Niño at Its Best*

__4__ Ideas

- Your narrative focuses on one experience. You include many interesting details about what happened on your family's trip. This makes your readers feel as if they were traveling along with you.
- Your essay does not answer one of the 5 W's. Why did your family take a trip to see your Uncle Mike? Your readers would likely want to know why your family traveled across the country to see your relative.

__4__ Organization

- Organizing the events in time order makes your story easy to follow.
- While your beginning clearly identifies the topic of the narrative, it could be revised to grab the readers' attention. You might start with dialogue or an interesting fact to make your readers want to keep reading.

__6__ Voice

- Your writer's voice sounds natural and is suited to your audience.
- Your strong storytelling voice creates a solid narrative.

__6__ Word Choice

- Your writing includes strong nouns and verbs that create clear, vivid pictures.
- Your use of onomatopoeia, or words for sounds such as "drip" and "drop," makes readers feels as if they were actually inside your tent during the rainstorm.

__5__ Sentence Fluency

- Your use of different types of sentences makes the narrative enjoyable to read.
- You begin many sentences with the pronoun *we* (see paragraphs 1 and 5). A greater variety of sentence beginnings could be used.

__6__ Conventions

- You have correctly spelled every word!
- Your paper is neat and ready for sharing.

Narrative Writing

Las vegas

1 My trip to Las Vegas was grate. I always wanted to go their. My

2 friend went their, too. He went with his uncle. I went with my family.

3 We got their and unpacked and went swimming. It was fun. The pool

4 had a slide. I went down many times.

5 Then we went to an arcade. I had to get change. The machines

6 don't take coins. they take tokens. I got a bunch of them. Then I

7 played. My mom played too. She got 700 tickets on a single game.

8 Then it was time to go to bed. It had been a long day. Then we

9 went to an indoor amusement park. There were lots of rides. a roller

10 coaster went threw many different rooms. It went inside and outside,

11 too. I rode it twice. it was a lot of fun.

12 We came back and played in the arcade again. The next day we

13 cashed in tickets and I got a stuffed bear. Amy got a bear too. My

14 other sister got a bunch of candy. My mom gave us her tickets. We

15 split them up. Then we got more good stuff. It was fun. On the way

16 home we played with the stuff we won in the car. And that was my

17 trip it was good!

Assessment Sheet

Title <u>*Las Vegas*</u>

__3__ Ideas

- Most of your narrative focuses on one event—your trip to Las Vegas.
- Your narrative would be stronger if you added more details about the topic. Revise your essay so that it answers the 5 W's (*who, what, when, where, and why*).

__2__ Organization

- Your narrative needs a clearer organization. Transition words, such as "then," "after," "before," and "later," will help you arrange the events in time order.
- Your narrative needs a stronger ending. You might tell readers how the trip changed you or what you learned from the experience.

__5__ Voice

- Your writer's voice shows that you were excited about the trip and the fun things you did in Las Vegas.
- Including dialogue in your story would have given it more personality.

__3__ Word Choice

- Stronger nouns, verbs, and modifiers would create clearer pictures for the reader.
- Words like "stuff," "fun," and "good" are common words. You could find other words that help readers create vivid images.

__2__ Sentence Fluency

- Many sentences in your narrative begin the same way. Starting a sentence with an introductory word or phrase will make your writing more interesting.
- Many of your sentences are short and choppy. You could expand these sentences by adding details that answer *who, what, when, where,* or *why.*

__2__ Conventions

- You used an incorrect form of various homophones in your narrative (see "grate" and "their" in paragraph 1). Using a dictionary will help you find the correct word.
- Your narrative contains capitalization errors. The first word of a sentence and proper nouns always begin with a capital letter (see the title of your essay, paragraph 2, and paragraph 3).

Expository Writing

Something You Can Sink Your Teeth Into

1 Have you ever tasted a homemade pizza? If so, you know just how

2 good it tastes. You might be surprised to discover that its really easy

3 to make this tasty treat. All you have to do is follow these totally

4 simple directions.

5 First, you need to gather the necessary materials. You will need

6 an aluminum pan. You need pizza dough. You need dark red tomato

7 sauce. You need gourmet cheese and a stainless steel spoon. You also

8 need a topping. Some people think the taste of pepperoni is really

9 good. But, you could top off your pizza with mushrooms, meatballs, or

10 onions. Some people even use fruit, such as pineapple, as a topping!

11 Once your materials are together, you're ready to start cooking.

12 First, preheat your oven to 425 degrees. Then carefully peel off the

13 paper wrapper from the container holding the pizza dough. Unroll the

14 sticky dough and place it in the pan. Press the soft dough with your

15 fingertips and palm of your hand to spread it out evenly throughout

16 the pan.

17 Now its time for the sauce. Open the jar or can and pour it on the

18 center of the dough. Next, use the bottom part of a spoon to spread the

19 tomato sauce across the dough. Be sure to move the sauce to all the

20 edges of the dough so that every spot is covered.

21   After that, tear open the plastic bag of shredded cheese. Sprinkle

22 it all over the sauce. Then drop spoonfuls of you're favorite topping

23 all over the cheese. Be sure to cover the entire top of you're pizza

24 with a generous amount of topping.

25   Finally, put the uncooked pizza in the hot oven for six to eight

26 minutes. When the cheese is bubbling, remove it from the oven. Then

27 you can enjoy your delicious homemade food with your family or

28 friends.

Assessment Sheet

Title   *Something You Can Sink Your Teeth Into*

_6_ Ideas
- Your essay is informative with a clear focus.
- Your supporting details help readers understand each step of the process.

_5_ Organization
- Your introductory question captures the reader's attention.
- Your transition words connect the details given in the middle paragraphs.
- The ending of your essay is weak. It would be stronger if you left your readers with a final thought or connected the end to the beginning.

_6_ Voice
- Your writer's voice shows that you are knowledgeable about the pizza-making process.
- Your writer's voice fits your topic and audience.

_4_ Word Choice
- Your essay includes empty modifiers such as "really" and "totally." Since these words do not make your ideas clearer, they should be removed.
- You could add descriptive words and phrases that make your writing even more interesting to read. You could describe what the pizza smells like as it bakes in the oven. You could describe what the dough feels like as you press it into the pan.

_4_ Sentence Fluency
- Using different sentence beginnings makes your essay easy to read.
- Some sections of your essay are made up of short, choppy sentence (see paragraph 2). You should combine these to make your writing flow smoothly.

_5_ Conventions
- Your writing contains the wrong form of "your" and "you're." A dictionary will help you select the correct form of these homophones.
- Your paper is neat and ready for sharing.

Expository Writing

Fluffy

1   I am going to tell you about my pet cat Fluffy. The four things

2   are what he eats, what he looks like, wats interesting about him and

3   where he lives. Fluffy is three. We got him when I was six. I want a

4   dog. My brother wants a cat. he won. So we got Fluffy.

5   Fluffy eats cat food, chips and other people food. When I spill

6   milk I go get a towl Fluffy has alredy cleaned it up. Somtimes he

7   sneaks food. it happened at my birthday party. We played a game

8   after having ice cream and cake. My friend Barb one the game. We

9   came back to the table. Fluffy was walking on it. he went from plate

10   to plate. he licked up melted ice cream. he ate cake two.

11   Fluffy looks like a lion but with no main he roars like a lion

12   two. But he has a loud myou. His myou sounds like a roar two.

13   When Fluffy lies down he looks like a person. But he doesnt look

14   like me. He looks more like my brother. He has light brown hair two.

15   He needs a toy at night to keep him happy.

16   Fluffy lives in san diego california. But he also lives with us. He

17   mostly lives with me. And my brother in our house.

Assessment Sheet

Title *Fluffy*

__4__ Ideas

- Your opening lets readers know that you are writing about your pet Fluffy. You stayed on this topic throughout your essay.
- You did include examples to give the reader a clearer picture of what it is like to be around Fluffy.
- Your writing contains some unnecessary information about Fluffy. For example, you tell his age and describe how old you were when you got your pet. You should eliminate some of these extra details to give your essay a clearer focus.

__3__ Organization

- You separated the main points of your essay into different paragraphs.
- Your essay lacks a clear ending. Add a paragraph that connects the end to the beginning, gives the reader a final thought, or connects with the reader.

__5__ Voice

- Your writer's voice shows that you care about your pet.
- Your writer's voice fits your topic and audience.

__3__ Word Choice

- Your writing contains many general nouns. Replacing these with more specific nouns will make your writing easier to follow.
- You could add descriptive words to make your writing more interesting to read.

__2__ Sentence Fluency

- Many of your sentences are quite short. This makes the essay choppy and difficult to read. You need to combine your short sentences.
- Try to vary your sentence beginnings to make your writing more interesting to readers.

__1__ Conventions

- Many punctuation, grammar, and usage errors make your essay confusing and hard to read.
- Check your essay for spelling errors.

Persuasive Writing

Help Save Our Manatees

1   Manatees are giant marine mammals that live in the water
2   around Florida. They are worth saving because only about 1,900 of
3   these lovable animals remain.

4   By eating lots of water plants, manatees help clear rivers for
5   boaters and fishers. A 1,000-pound manatee eats 150 pounds of
6   weeds in one day! That's more than 1,000 pounds of weeds each
7   week! Just think how clogged the rivers would be without hungry
8   manatees. Their huge appetites help many people enjoy their favorite
9   hobbies. Many people just like watching these graceful creatures
10   swim peacefully along in Florida's coastal waterways.

11   Unfortunately, people are not so kind to manatees. More than
12   two-thirds of manatee deaths are caused by people. People have shot
13   manatees. That is illegal. Often manatees are badly injured or killed
14   when boats run over them. People who throw trash in the water cause
15   other manatee deaths. The creatures die from swallowing fishhooks
16   and old fishing lines and choke on garbage that litters the waterways.

17   There are things people can do to help save the manatee. They
18   can throw their trash in garbage bins. They can obey boating speed
19   limits. They move their boats slowly through areas where manatees
20   live. They can write letters. They can send e-mails and make phone
21   calls. They can ask lawmakers to make laws to help save the manatee.

Assessment Sheet

Title *Help Save Our Manatees*

_5_ Ideas

- Your essay includes many details that help convince readers that they should take action to save the manatee.
- Your beginning could be a bit longer. You might want to explain that the number of manatees is decreasing. Perhaps you could find out how many manatees lived in Florida waters ten years ago?

_5_ Organization

- Your opinion statement is clear and you give various reasons for saving manatees.
- You should return to your call to action at the end of the essay.

_6_ Voice

- Your writer's voice shows that you are serious about this issue and determined to persuade readers to help manatees.
- Your writer's voice shows that you know a lot about these unusual creatures.

_4_ Word Choice

- Your essay is persuasive, but more synonyms or modifiers would help.
- You should revise your essay to include a few more persuasive words that make strong statements.

_4_ Sentence Fluency

- You write clear and complete sentences.
- You should revise your essay to include a greater variety of sentence beginnings. Many sentence in the last paragraph begin with the pronoun "They."

_6_ Conventions

- You have correctly spelled every word!
- Your paper is neat and ready for sharing.

Persuasive Writing

Why Smog Is Bad

1   I have allergies. If it gets too dusty my chest hurts. If our planet

2   gets any dirtier, then I can't breath. I'll have to go to the hospital. I

3   already went there once. It was last year. It was a very hot day. I was

4   riding my bike. All of a sudden. My throat was tight. My chest hurt

5   bad. I had truble breathing. I walked home. My mom took me to the

6   hospitle. It was scarey. I don't want it to happen again.

7   When people drive cars it makes the air dirty. The cars let off

8   gases. They get into the air. They eat away earths atmosfere. People

9   also toss garbage in lakes and oceans. It kills the animals in them.

10   They choke on the trash. We should buy electric cars. They don't run

11   on gas. We would save money. We also should walk more places.

12   Walking is healthy. It keeps the body strong. We can share rides with

13   others. Then we use less cars. Then less gas is put into air. Then I can

14   breath.

Assessment Sheet

Title _Why Smog Is Bad_

__2__ Ideas

- Your essay lacks a clear opinion statement. Without it, the reader is unsure what topic you are promoting.
- Your essay describes many reasons why people should protect Earth. Your anecdote about your own trip to the hospital captures the reader's interest.

__2__ Organization

- Your essay lacks middle paragraphs that begin with a topic sentence and contain supporting reasons.
- Your closing lacks a call to action.

__6__ Voice

- Your writer's voice shows that you feel strongly about the need to keep the air free from pollution.
- Your writer's voice shows that you are serious about the issue.

__2__ Word Choice

- Your essay contains overused words. You should replace words like "bad" and "scary" with synonyms. A thesaurus will help you find stronger synonyms.
- You should revise your essay to include stronger words that persuade the reader.

__2__ Sentence Fluency

- Your essay contains short choppy sentences. Revise these sentences by asking the 5 W questions and adding details to answer them.
- Many of your sentences begin with a pronoun. Revise your essay to include different kinds of sentence beginnings.

__2__ Conventions

- Your essay is free of any capitalization or punctuation errors.
- Your essay contains many spelling errors (see "hospitle" and "truble"). Ask a classmate to check your writing for spelling errors before making your final draft.

Assessment Sheet

 **Directions** Use one of the rubrics listed below to rate a piece of writing. Circle the rubric your teacher tells you to use. If you need information about assessing with a rubric, see pages 34–35 in your *Write Source* book.

Narrative Rubric (pages 120–121)   **Expository Rubric (pages 176–177)**
Persuasive Rubric (pages 232–233)

Title _____

____ **Ideas**

____ **Organization**

____ **Voice**

____ **Word Choice**

____ **Sentence Fluency**

____ **Conventions**

Evaluator_____

T-Chart

Topic:

Sensory Chart

Topic: _____

See	Hear	Smell	Taste	Touch

5 W's Chart

Topic: _____

Who?

What?

When?

Where?

Why?

Time Line

Topic:

_____

K-W-L Chart

Topic: _____

K What do I know?	W What do I wonder about?	L What did I learn?

Table Diagram

Venn Diagram

Subject A

Differences

Similarities

Subject B

Dear Families,

Your child already knows how to carry out many step-by-step processes, such as making a bed, setting up a board game, or bathing a dog. Now we're getting ready to learn the steps in the writing process. To **prewrite** is to select a topic, plan, and gather details. To **write** is to get all the ideas down on paper. To **revise** is to reread, get feedback from others, and make needed changes. To **edit** is to fix mistakes in spelling, punctuation, capital letters, and grammar. To **publish** is to share the writing. We'll also learn about six different qualities, or traits, of good writing. One is **ideas.** Others are **organization, voice, word choice, sentence fluency,** and **conventions.** We'll define each trait in a future letter, but first let's look at how they're scored:

6 Amazing   **5** Strong   **4** Good   **3** Okay   **2** Poor   **1** Incomplete

To help your child start thinking about the writing process:

• Cook together and talk about why the recipe steps are in a certain order.

• Read and discuss a book, magazine, or newspaper for at least 15 minutes each evening. *What did you both like? What questions would you like to ask the authors?*

• Play "Stump the Family" by asking each person to share a new word and three definitions, only one of which is correct.

Thank you!

Dear Families,

It's often hard to find time to simply visit as a family. So, when we share a meal or travel, it's fun to tell each other about the things we've seen and done. As we move into the study of descriptive writing, we'll learn to use our five senses to create "word pictures" of people, places, objects, and activities. To focus on the writing trait called *voice,* we'll choose words and details that express our own unique ideas and feelings. We'll also learn to arrange our descriptions into three connected parts. The **beginning** tells what or who is being described and gets the reader's attention. The **middle** presents the details in a logical order. The **end** revisits the topic by sharing a final thought.

To help your child start thinking descriptively:

- Take turns describing a "mystery person" and letting the other person guess who it is. For example: *He's wearing a black-and-white striped shirt. He's running. He's blowing a whistle and pointing.* Guess: A basketball referee.

- Read some travel articles together and discuss how the authors share their feelings about the scenery, landmarks, and culture.

- Have your child secretly draw a picture or design and then describe it to you. Based on the description, try to duplicate the drawing. Compare pictures. Then switch roles.

Thank you!

Dear Families,

We all enjoy "I remember when . . ." stories. People's real lives are often better than a novel! As we move into the study of narrative writing, we'll share experiences from our lives using the "5 W's"—**who, what, where, when,** and **why**. A trait especially important to this style of writing is *organization*. Using a time line, we'll put the events in the right order with transition words such as *first, then, next, after,* and *finally*. We'll also arrange our narratives into three parts. The **beginning** sets the stage and grabs the reader's attention. The **middle** describes what happened, what we saw, how we felt, and what people said. The **end** tells what we learned or how the experience changed us.

To help your child start thinking about narration:

• Read a magazine story together and highlight the transition words.

• Pretending to be news reporters, use the 5 W's to take notes about an event you attend. When you get home, write an article.

• Invite family members to share letters and e-mails that describe funny or exciting experiences.

• Help your child create a book with one page for each year of his or her age. Together, write your favorite memories.

• Write topics, such as *school, games, clothing, movies, holidays,* or *vacations,* on slips of paper. At dinner, choose a topic and invite everyone to share a memory.

Thank you!

Dear Families,

How many times have we asked (or been asked), "Can you explain that?" Learning to explain, tell why, and give examples is the focus as we move into the study of expository writing. We'll choose an interesting topic and share what we know about it in such a way that our readers will become excited about it, too. This information is organized into three parts. The **beginning** tells the purpose of the essay and captures the reader's interest. The **middle** explains the concept or skill in a logical order. The **end** gives additional support to the topic and summarizes the writer's thoughts. An important trait in the expository genre is *ideas*, which includes facts, details, data, and instructions.

To help your child start thinking about expository text:

- Discuss special terms that are related to your occupation or hobby. For example, restaurant managers use the word *patrons* and knitters use the word *purl*.

- Play the "Why? Because!" game with your child. Make a statement, such as "I wish cars could fly." Then have your child ask you *why* at least three times while you give answers beginning with the word *because*. Then switch roles.

- Together, explore some "how-to" reading materials, such as a cookbook, craft article, and safety manual. Talk about tricks the authors use to help make the meaning clear. Do you see a numbered list? A glossary? Photos? A diagram?

Thank you!

Dear Families,

When was the last time you tried to persuade your child to do something—or vice versa? Probably today! As we move into the study of persuasive writing, we'll learn that the formula for success includes **an opinion + reasons why + a call to action**. A writing trait that helps achieve this goal is *word choice*. Persuasion requires strong, specific nouns and verbs. To sound convincing, we must be positive. However, we must avoid exaggeration or bandwagon phrases such as "everyone is doing it." We must also choose powerful, accurate facts and examples to back our opinions and arrange them in order of importance.

To help your child start thinking about persuasion:

- Talk about some current problems or needs in your community (for example, lowering the speed limit on your street). Take turns "arguing" both sides of the issues.
- As you watch TV together, keep a running list of exaggerations you hear during commercials.
- Read some "junk mail" together. In the columns, label the opinions stated, reasons given, and calls to action.
- The next time your child has an important request to make, ask him or her to put it in writing, listing at least three reasons.
- Next chore day, allow family members to make one-minute speeches about the tasks they'd most (or least) like to do.

Thank you!

Dear Families,

Do your family and friends sometimes suggest books for you to read? As we move into responding to literature, we'll learn to share "just enough" about a story. We want to intrigue our audience, but we don't want to spoil the important parts. We'll discuss the **characters** (who), **setting** (where and when), and **plot** (what), especially the story problem. We'll describe how we feel about the outcome, how the story relates to our own lives, and what we wish we could ask the author. We'll use the writing process (**prewriting, writing, revising, editing,** and **publishing**). We'll also consider the six traits of writing (**ideas, organization, voice, word choice, sentence fluency,** and **conventions**). Finally, we'll learn how to respond to a biography, a poem, a nonfiction article, and a tall tale.

To help your child start thinking about literature response:

- Discuss the following quote from our writing textbook: *Reading a new book is like making a new friend.*

- Discuss the "theme" in a story you read together. Did you learn how to overcome a challenge? How to make a friend?

- Read a short newspaper article aloud. Challenge your child to summarize it in three sentences and then switch roles.

- Make a list of describing words, such as *strong, kind, brave, mean, creative,* and *funny.* Beside each one, write the name of a book, TV, or movie character who exhibits that trait.

Thank you!

Dear Families,

Some people love fantasies where anything is possible. Others prefer realistic fiction in which characters solve everyday problems. As we move into the study of creative writing, we'll have a chance to try both. An important writing trait for this genre is *sentence fluency*. We'll work to make sentences flow smoothly from one to the next, begin in different ways, and vary in length. We'll learn to plot our stories with a beginning, rising action, high point, and ending. We'll learn to change our stories into plays by changing thoughts and actions into dialogue. Finally, we'll learn techniques for writing different types of poems. In all our creative writing, we'll choose titles that make our readers eager to see where our imaginations have taken us.

To help your child start thinking creatively:

- After reading a story together, take turns making up a new ending.

- Ask your child to retell a familiar fairy tale from a different point of view. For example, how did the giant feel about Jack climbing his beanstalk? How did Little Red Riding Hood's grandmother feel about being locked in the closet?

- Cut out catchy words from newspaper headlines and put them facedown on the table. Have your child select five words and use them in an oral story or poem.

Thank you!

Dear Families,

Research! For some, this word brings back memories of note cards, outlines, and late nights writing school reports. Others light up at the word, relishing the chance to study fascinating topics. As we move into the study of research writing, we'll learn to use many types of sources, such as books, magazines, the Internet, interviews, encyclopedias, videos, dictionaries, and maps. We'll learn about nonfiction text features, such as the table of contents, glossary, and index. We'll also learn how to take notes and credit authors in such a way that we avoid plagiarism. Because research reports are accepted as fact, a vital writing trait is *conventions*. Published copies must be accurate and free of errors in punctuation, capital letters, grammar, and spelling.

To help your child start thinking about research:

- Together, explore interesting topics on the Internet. You'll find quality, safe links from our writing program Web site at www.thewritesource.com. Also look for sites that end with *.edu* (education), *.org* (organizations), or *.gov* (government).

- Call your local library and arrange for a guided tour. You'll likely find resources you never knew were available.

- Help your child conduct e-mail interviews with friends and relatives about how they use research in their careers.

- Collect and share "fun facts" that you learn from reading, watching TV, and talking with others.

Thank you!

Queridas familias,

Su hijo ya sabe cómo hacer procesos por etapas: arreglar la cama, organizar un juego de mesa o bañar al perro. Ahora nos preparamos a aprender las etapas del proceso de escritura. **Preescribir** es seleccionar un tema, planear y acumular datos. **Escribir** es poner todas las ideas en papel. **Revisar** es volver a leer, recibir comentarios y hacer los cambios que sean necesarios. **Editar** es verificar la ortografía, las mayúsculas, la puntuación y la gramática. **Publicar** es compartir el escrito con los demás. También aprenderemos seis cualidades o rasgos de la buena escritura. Una son las **ideas. Otras son organización, voz, escogencia de palabras, fluidez de oraciones** y **convenciones.** Más adelante, definiremos cada rasgo en otra carta. Por el momento, veamos cómo los calificamos:

6	5	4	3	2	1
Asombroso	Sólido	Bueno	Está bien	Malo	Incompleto

Ayúdele a su hijo a pensar en el proceso de escritura:

- Cocinen juntos. Comenten por qué los pasos de la receta se siguen en cierto orden.

- Lean y comenten un libro, revista o periódico todas las noches durante 15 minutos. *¿Qué les gustó a los dos? ¿Qué preguntas les gustaría hacerles a los autores?*

- Jueguen a "Adivina la respuesta". Pídale a cada persona que diga una nueva palabra y tres definiciones, de las cuales sólo una es correcta.

¡Gracias!

Queridas familias,

A menudo resulta difícil hallar tiempo para estar reunidos en familia. Por eso, cuando compartimos la mesa de la cena o cuando viajamos, es divertido contarnos las cosas que hemos visto y hecho. A medida que avanzamos en el estudio de la escritura descriptiva, aprenderemos a usar los cinco sentidos para crear "imágenes en palabras" de gente, lugares, objetos y actividades. Para concentrarnos en el rasgo de la escritura llamado *voz,* escogeremos palabras y detalles que expresen nuestras propias ideas y sentimientos. También aprenderemos a organizar nuestras descripciones en tres partes conectadas. El **principio** nos dice qué o quién será descrito y atrae la atención del lector. El **desarrollo** presenta los detalles en orden lógico. Por último, la idea **final** es una compilación del tema.

Ayúdele a su hijo a pensar descriptivamente:

- Por turnos, describan a una "persona misteriosa" y pídanles a los demás que traten de adivinar quién es. Por ejemplo: *Tiene camisa de rayas negras y blancas. Está corriendo. Tiene un pito y hace señas con la mano.* Adivinanza: Un árbitro de básquetbol.

- Lean juntos algunos artículos acerca de viajes y discutan cómo los autores expresan sus sentimientos sobre los paisajes, los lugares históricos y la cultura.

- Dígale a su hijo que haga un dibujo o un diseño y que luego se lo describa. Trate de duplicar el dibujo con base en la descripción. Compare los dibujos. Luego inviertan los papeles.

¡Gracias!

Queridas familias,

Todos disfrutamos aquellas historias que dicen: "Yo recuerdo cuando. . .". ¡A menudo, la vida de la gente es mejor que una novela! A medida que avanzamos en el estudio de la escritura narrativa, compartiremos experiencias de nuestra vida usando las cinco preguntas básicas: *quién, qué, dónde, cuándo* y *por qué*. Un rasgo importante en este estilo de escritura es la *organización*. Pondremos sucesos en el orden correcto usando una línea cronológica con palabras de transición, como *primero, luego, siguiente, después* y *finalmente*. También organizaremos nuestras narraciones en tres partes. El **principio** establece la escena y atrapa la atención del lector. El **desarrollo** describe qué pasa, qué vimos, cómo nos sentimos y qué dijo la gente. El **final** dice qué aprendimos y cómo esa experiencia nos hizo cambiar.

Ayúdele a su hijo a pensar en narración.

- Lean juntos alguna historia en una revista y resalten las palabras de transición.

- Imaginen que ustedes son reporteros de un noticiero. Usen las cinco preguntas básicas para tomar notas en algún evento al que asisten. Escriban un artículo cuando lleguen a casa.

- Pídale a los miembros de la familia que compartan cartas y correos electrónicos que describen experiencias emocionantes o graciosas.

- Ayúdele a su hijo a hacer un libro. Cada página representa un año de edad. Escriban juntos sus recuerdos favoritos.

- Escriba algunos temas en tiras de papel. Por ejemplo escuela, juegos, ropa, cine, días feriados o vacaciones. A la hora de la cena, escoja un tema y pídales a todos que compartan alguno de sus recuerdos.

¡Gracias!

Queridas familias,

¿Cuántas veces hemos preguntado (o nos han preguntado): "¿Puedes explicar eso?" A medida que avanzamos en el estudio de la escritura explicativa, aprenderemos a explicar, decir por qué y dar ejemplos. Elegiremos un tema interesante y compartiremos lo que sabemos de él de tal forma que nuestros lectores también se emocionen por conocerlo. Esta información se divide en tres partes: el **principio** presenta el propósito del ensayo y atrapa el interés del lector. El **desarrollo** explica el concepto o la destreza en orden lógico. El **final** le suministra apoyo adicional al tema y resume las ideas del autor. Un rasgo importante del género explicativo son las *ideas,* que comprenden hechos, detalles, datos e instrucciones.

Ayúdele a su hijo a pensar en textos explicativos.

- Hablen de palabras especiales que se relacionen con su ocupación o su pasatiempo. Por ejemplo, los administradores de restaurantes usan la palabra *clientes* y los tejedores dicen *tejer del revés* .

- Juegue con su hijo el juego de "¿Por qué? Porque". Diga una afirmación. Por ejemplo: "Quisiera que los carros volaran." Luego, pídale que le pregunte *por qué* por lo menos tres veces. Usted le debe responder comenzando sus respuestas con la palabra *porque.* Luego inviertan los papeles.

- Lean juntos cómo hacer cosas. Por ejemplo, lean un libro de cocina, un artículo sobre artesanías o un manual de seguridad. Hablen de las ayudas que usan los autores para explicar sus ideas con claridad. ¿Encontraron listas numeradas? ¿Un glosario? ¿Fotos? ¿Diagramas?

¡Gracias!

Queridas familias,

¿Cuándo fue la última vez que trató de persuadir a su hijo de hacer algo—o viceversa? ¡Tal vez hoy! A medida que avanzamos en el estudio de la escritura persuasiva, aprenderemos que la fórmula para tener éxito consiste de ***una opinión + las razones de por qué + un llamado a actuar.*** Un rasgo de la escritura que ayuda a alcanzar esta meta es la *escogencia de palabras*. La persuasión requiere sustantivos y verbos fuertes y específicos. Para sonar convincentes, debemos ser positivos. Sin embargo, debemos evitar la exageración o los argumentos tontos, como por ejemplo "es que todos lo hacen". También tenemos que escoger hechos y ejemplos sólidos y exactos que sustenten nuestras opiniones y ponerlos en orden de importancia.

Ayúdele a su hijo a ser persuasivo:

- Hablen de los problemas y necesidades actuales de su comunidad (por ejemplo, bajar el límite de velocidad en su calle). Por turnos, discutan dos puntos de vista sobre un tema.

- Juntos, hagan una lista de las exageraciones que dicen los comerciales de la televisión.

- Lean juntos un poco de correo publicitario. Marquen en las columnas las opiniones emitidas, las razones dadas y los llamados a actuar.

- La próxima vez que su hijo tenga que hacer una solicitud importante, pídale que la escriba y que suministre por lo menos tres razones.

- La próxima vez que realicen las labores del hogar, pídale a cada miembro de la familia que de un discurso de un minuto acerca de la labor que más le gusta (o la que menos le gusta) hacer.

¡Gracias!

Queridas familias,

¿A veces sus familiares y amigos les sugieren libros para leer? A medida que avanzamos en reacciones frente a la literatura, aprenderemos a contar "apenas lo necesario" de una historia. Queremos intrigar a nuestros lectores, pero no vamos a echar a perder las partes importantes. Hablaremos de los **personajes** (quién), la **escena** (dónde y cuándo) y la **trama** (qué), es decir, el problema que trata la historia. Describiremos lo que sentimos por el resultado, cómo la historia se relaciona con nuestra vida, y qué nos gustaría preguntarle al autor. Usaremos el proceso de escritura (**preescribir, escribir, revisar, editar** y **publicar**). También tendremos en cuenta los seis rasgos de la escritura (**ideas, organización, voz, escogencia de palabras, fluidez de oraciones** y **convenciones**). Finalmente, aprenderemos a reaccionar ante una biografía, un poema, un artículo de no ficción y un cuento.

Ayúdele a su hijo a reaccionar frente a la literatura:

- Comenten la siguiente cita tomada de nuestro libro de escritura: *Leer un nuevo libro es como tener un nuevo amigo.*

- Discutan el "tema" de una historia que lean juntos. ¿Aprendiste a sobreponerte a un desafío? ¿Aprendiste a hacer amigos?

- Lean un artículo corto de periódico en voz alta. Pregúntele a su hijo si puede resumirlo en tres oraciones. Luego inviertan los papeles.

- Hagan una lista de palabras descriptivas, por ejemplo *fuerte, amable, valiente, odioso, creativo* y *chistoso.* Junto a cada palabra escriban el nombre de un personaje de libro, televisión o cine que posea esa característica.

¡Gracias!

Queridas familias,

A algunas personas les encanta la fantasía, donde cualquier cosa es posible. Otras prefieren la ficción realista, donde los personajes solucionan los problemas de diario. A medida que avanzamos en el estudio de la escritura creativa, tendremos la oportunidad de ensayar las dos. Un rasgo importante de este género es la *fluidez de oraciones*. Haremos que las oraciones fluyan fácilmente de una a otra, que empiecen diferente y varíen de tamaño. Aprenderemos a planear nuestras historias con principio, desarrollo, punto culminante y final. Aprenderemos a convertir nuestras historias en obras, expresando las ideas y las acciones mediante diálogos. Finalmente, aprenderemos técnicas para escribir diferentes tipos de poemas. En nuestra escritura creativa pensaremos en títulos interesantes que les muestren a nuestros lectores hasta dónde puede llegar nuestra imaginación.

Ayúdele a su hijo a pensar creativamente.

- Después de leer una historia juntos, tomen turnos para inventar un nuevo final.
- Pídale a su hijo que le cuente un cuento de hadas conocido, pero desde otro punto de vista. Por ejemplo: ¿Qué pensó el gigante cuando Jack se trepó a la col? ¿Qué sintió la abuelita de Caperucita Roja encerrada en el armario?
- Recorte palabras sonoras de los titulares de periódico y póngalos boca abajo sobre la mesa. Luego, pídale a su hijo que escoja cinco y que las use para crear una historia oral o un poema.

¡Gracias!

Queridas familias,

¡Investigar! Para algunos, esta palabra les trae recuerdos de tarjetas de notas, resúmenes y noches largas escribiendo informes para la escuela. A otros les gusta la palabra porque les entusiasma la posibilidad de estudiar temas fascinantes. A medida que avanzamos en el estudio de la escritura investigativa, aprenderemos a usar muchas fuentes como libros, revistas, Internet, entrevistas, enciclopedias, vídeos, diccionarios y mapas. Aprenderemos algunas características de la no ficción, por ejemplo la tabla de contenido, el glosario y el índice. También aprenderemos a tomar notas y dar crédito a los autores para evitar el plagio. Dado que los informes de investigación se consideran hechos, uno de sus rasgos fundamentales son las *convenciones.* Las publicaciones deben ser precisas y sin errores de puntuación, mayúsculas, gramática y ortografía.

Ayúdele a su hijo a pensar en la investigación:

- Examinen juntos algunos enlaces seguros y buenos en Internet de nuestro programa de escritura en www.thewritesource.com. También busquen sitios que terminen en *.edu* (educación), *.org* (organizaciones), o *.gov* (gobierno).

- Llamen a la biblioteca de su localidad y organicen una visita guiada. Encontrarán recursos que jamás imaginaron que existían.

- Ayúdele a su hijo a hacerles entrevistas por correo electrónico a sus amigos y familiares sobre cómo usan ellos la investigación en su profesión.

- Reúnan y compartan "hechos graciosos" que hayan aprendido leyendo, mirando televisión o hablando con la gente.

¡Gracias!

Scavenger Hunt 1: Find the Threes

Directions Find the following "threes" in your book by turning to the pages listed in parentheses.

1. **Three** ways to review your reasons in the ending of a persuasive essay (page 214)

   _____

2. **Three** things you can add to make your final copy look better (pages 474–475)

   _____

3. **Three** guidelines for preparing for a test (page 400)

   _____

4. **Three** tips for becoming a good writer (page 4)

   _____

   _____

5. **Three** things dialogue can do to make your writing come alive (page 96)

   _____

   _____

6. **Three** kinds of conjunctions (page 600)

   _____

7. **Three** tips for becoming a better listener (page 370)

   _____

   _____

8. **Three** ways to catch the reader's attention in the beginning paragraph of an expository essay about a career (page 155)

   _____

   _____

Scavenger Hunt 2: What Is It?

 **Directions** Find the answers to the following questions using the index in the back of the book. The underlined words below tell you where to look in the index.

1. What is a <u>beginning-middle-ending map</u>?

   _____

2. What is <u>time order</u>?

   _____

   _____

3. What is a <u>free-verse poem</u>?

   _____

   _____

4. What is a <u>fragment sentence</u>?

   _____

   _____

5. What are the <u>traits of writing</u>?

   _____

   _____

6. What is a <u>simile</u>?

   _____

7. What is an <u>antecedent</u>?

   _____

8. What are <u>entry words</u>?

   _____

Getting to Know *Write Source*

© Great Source. Permission is granted to copy this page.

> **Directions**   Locate the pages in *Write Source* where answers to the following learning tasks can be found. Both the index and the table of contents can help you.

_____   **1.**   Your teacher has asked you to explain the difference between assonance and consonance. You need to look up the definition of each.

_____   **2.**   You are writing a paragraph and are not sure of what to include. You need to know the parts of a paragraph.

_____   **3.**   The sentences in your paragraph are all declarative sentences. You need to try different kinds of sentences.

_____   **4.**   Your teacher suggests you turn your short story into a play. You need to know how to create a play.

_____   **5.**   You are writing a descriptive essay about a place and your teacher reminds you to use transitions. You need to know words that show location.

_____   **6.**   Your teacher asks you to rate your persuasive essay. You need a rubric for persusasive writing.

_____   **7.**   Your teacher assigns a response to literature and tells you to choose whatever genre you wish from your text. You need to review the different kind of responses.

_____   **8.**   There are several sets of words like *knew* and *new* that confuse you. You need to know which is the right word to use.

_____   **9.**   A classmate tells you the Writer's Resource section has helpful information. You decide to check it out.

_____   **10.**   Your teacher suggests using a Venn diagram to gather details. You need to know how to make a Venn diagram.

Unit Planning

Writing Form

PARAGRAPH ___ days

- **FOCUS**

- **SKILLS**

ESSAY ___ days

Prewriting

- **FOCUS**

- **SKILLS**

Writing ___ days

- **FOCUS**

- **SKILLS**

Revising ___ days

- **IDEAS**

- **ORGANIZATION**

- **VOICE**

- **WORD CHOICE**

- **SENTENCE FLUENCY**

See Lesson Planning Guidelines on pp. xxvii–xviii.

Unit Planning (continued)

Editing

___ days

- **PUNCTUATION**

- **CAPITALIZATION**

- **SPELLING**

- **GRAMMAR**

Publishing

___ days

- **OPTIONS**

Evaluating

___ days

- **SELF-ASSESSMENT**

- **BENCHMARK PAPERS**

ACROSS THE CURRICULUM

___ days

- **SOCIAL STUDIES**

- **SCIENCE**

- **MATH**

- **PRACTICAL**

Index

A

A / an, 536.1
A lot, 536.4
Abbreviations, 520–523
  Acronyms, 520.2
  Address, 522.1
  Capitalization of, 508.4
  Initialisms, 520.3
  Punctuation of, 479.4, 520.1
Abstract noun, 570.4
Academic writing, see *Writing, academic*
Accept / except, 536.2
Acknowledgement, 328
Acronyms, 520.2

Across the curriculum writing,
    612–616
  Math, 126–129, 186–187,
    242–243
  Practical, 132–133, 188–189,
    244–247, 476, 477
  Science, 78–79, 130–131,
    182–185, 238–241
  Social studies, 76–77

Action, in a story, 307, 309
Action verbs, 28, 416, 421, 582.1
Active verbs, 110, 586.2
Address,
  Abbreviations, 522.1
  Envelope, 477, 522.1
  Inside, 246–247, 477
  Punctuation of, 484.2
Address, direct, 486.3
Adjectives, 423–425, 428,
    590–593
  Articles, 423, 590.1
  Colorful, 28
  Combining sentences with,
    425, 445
  Common, 590.2
  Comparative, 424, 592.3
  Compound, 590.4
  Demonstrative, 590.5
  Equal, 488.1
  Forms of, 424, 592.2–592.5
  Indefinite, 592.1

  Irregular, 592.5
  Positive, 424, 592.2
  Predicate, 590.3
  Proper, 508.1, 590.2
  Punctuation of, 488.1, 508.1
  Superlative, 424, 592.4
Advanced Learners, 4, 7, 12, 13,
    18, 22, 23, 26, 29, 32, 44, 47,
    53, 57, 70, 71, 72, 79, 94, 99,
    108, 111, 123, 124, 132, 144,
    151, 156, 160, 166, 167, 191,
    202, 211, 212, 217, 231, 232,
    244, 245, 259, 262, 272, 280,
    292, 304, 305, 307, 310, 312,
    316, 323, 327, 328, 332, 342,
    355, 371, 382, 386, 394, 395,
    396
Adverbs, 426–427, 594–597
  Combining sentences with,
    427
  Comparative, 426, 596.2
  Irregular, 596.4
  Positive, 426, 596.1
  Superlative, 426, 596.3
  Types of, 594
Agreement,
  Antecedent-pronoun, 414
  Subject-verb, 172, 173, 419,
    421, 438–439
Alliteration, 318
Allowed / aloud, 536.3
Already / all ready, 536.5
Anecdote, 216, 461
  Response to an, 292–297
Ant / aunt, 536.6
Antagonist, 309
Antecedent, 576.1
Antonym, 330, 467
Apostrophes, 490–493
Appendix, 328
Appositives,
  Phrase, 566.5
  Punctuating, 488.2
Article,
  Nonfiction, response to an,
    286–291
  Summarizing an, 286–291,
    333–336
Articles, 590.1

Assessment, 619–622, 644
  Final copy, 19
  Grammar tests,
    Capitalization, 526–527
    Parts of speech, 422, 430,
      604–605
    Punctuation, 506–507
    Sentences, 450–451,
      568–569
    Using the right word,
      558–559
  <u>MODELS</u>, 36, 37, 60–61, 122,
    134–135, 178, 190–191, 234,
    248–249, 296
  Response sheet, 42
  Rubrics, 19, 31–38
    Expository, 176–177
    Narrative, 34, 35, 120–121
    Persuasive, 232–233
  Self, 36–37, 123, 179, 235
  Writing prompts,
    Descriptive, 80–81
    Expository, 190–192
    Narrative, 134–136
    Persuasive, 248–250
    Response to literature,
      278–279, 284–285,
      290–291, 296–297

Assonance, 318
Ate / eight, 538.1
Audience, 465
Aunt / ant, 536.6
Author card / entries, 325, 326
Autobiography, 461, also see
    Personal narrative

Bandwagon thinking, 220
Bar graph, 474
Bare / bear, 538.2
Basics-of-life list, 454
"Be" verbs, 422
Beginning, 25, 53, 72, 78, 80, 84,
    98, 99, 126, 130, 132, 134,
    145, 155, 182, 190, 211, 263,
    274, 276, 282, 288, 294, 350